Anna Del Conte's definitive work, *Gastronomy of Italy*, defines the country's regions, ingredients, dishes and techniques for a new generation and leaves no stone unturned in its exploration of Italian cuisine. Recipes include the great dishes from every major region of Italy. Variations on the classics – pasta, polenta, gnocchi, risotto and pizzas – sit alongside Anna's recipes for versions of Italian favourites such as peperonata, lamb fricassée and osso buco.

Gastronomy of Italy

Anna Del Conte

Gastronomy of Italy

PAVILION

First published by Bantam Press in the United Kingdom in 1987.
First published by Pavilion Books in the United Kingdom in 2001.
Revised and expanded in the United Kingdom in 2013 by
Pavilion
43 Great Ormond Street
London
WC1N 3HZ

An imprint of Pavilion Books Company Ltd

ISBN: 978-1-86205-958-0

A CIP catalogue record for this book is available from the
British Library.

10 9 8 7 6 5

Repro by Mission Productions Ltd, Hong Kong
Printed and bound by 1010 Printing International Ltd, China

www.pavilionbooks.com

CONTENTS

A–Z of dishes, ingredients, cooking techniques and regions 13–471

Introduction

The 20th-century Chinese scholar Lin Yu Tang said, 'We are, in the end, loyal to the food of our youth: perhaps this is what patriotism means.' If that is so I am certainly patriotic, even to the extent of hoping that this book will breed many traitors among non-Italians, who may come to love Italian food for all the fascinations it offers, as well as for the eating of it. Although the food itself is in the foreground of this book, it is my hope that reading it will light up the background, to give a clear picture of the whole scene of Italian gastronomy, so much of which has never before been described in English.

I have included recipes in order to give a fuller understanding of particular entries. Some are classics, and others are little known, but all are for dishes I love and feel to be representative of the huge variety of Italian cuisine.

One cannot understand a cuisine and its development without seeing it in relation to the history of the country in question. The cooking of Italy is based on two civilizations that first flourished there: the Greek and the Etruscan. They established the foundations of Italian cooking in two different fields. The Greeks brought the cuisine of the sea, with their unerring knowledge of all sea creatures, while the Etruscans turned towards the land and its produce. These characteristics still, to some degree, divide the cooking of the South, which was Magna Graecia, and of Sicily, from that of the more northerly regions whither the Etruscans went from their original settlements between Siena and Rome.

The chief role of the Romans was to develop and improve, rather than to create something new. They were extremely knowledgeable about agriculture, about the raising of animals and birds, about fishes and about food. All these subjects were exhaustively studied and written about. There followed the Dark Ages, when almost all that had been known was lost, the flame of culture and civilization being kept alive only in the monasteries. When the Saracens occupied Sicily and southern Italy in the late 8th century, they brought civilization back in all its forms, from medicine to philosophy, music and cooking. They came with foods that are now an intrinsic part of the Italian cuisine and, as well as new foods and flavourings, they also brought new techniques and ideas. These the Italians made their own.

With such a rich background, it is not surprising that in the 14th century the Italian cuisine emerged as the one that influenced the whole of Europe. This was the Renaissance, the most extraordinary chapter in the history of Italy. For some 250 years this divided country gave the rest of Europe most of what we still regard as among the supreme achievements of western civilization. One element of this rebirth was the foundation of European cooking as we know it, with a flourish of cookery books published between the 15th and 17th centuries.

The first cookery books to be printed in Italy are slightly later than *Le Viandier* by the French cook Taillevent (c.1310–95), and while a great deal is known about Taillevent's life, nothing is known of the early Italian authors, not even their names. They are simply referred to as Anonimo Veneziano and Anonimo Toscano, and their *ricettari* – recipe books – are thought to have been written at the end of the 14th century. It is thanks to the humanist philosopher Platina that we can study the food of the period, a time when the important Arab influence was grafted onto the medieval cuisine, and the foundations laid for most of the developments that have since taken place.

Our ancestors preferred birds, game and small animals to the larger breeds; these meats were usually parboiled with flavourings before being roasted or grilled, or they were used for making the fashionable pies, tarts and *pasticci*. Spices, being a symbol of wealth, were used in abundance – often to create an impression – and sugar was a constant flavouring in savoury dishes, since the tastes of sweet and salty were not kept apart as they are today. The greatest contributor to the gastronomic renaissance was the 16th-century writer Bartolomeo Scappi who, in his *Opera*, covered a vast range of subjects in the greatest detail. At that time the heavy spicing began to give way to lighter flavourings in a balanced harmony characteristic of the High Renaissance, thus heralding the changes that took place during the next century, when the leadership of European gastronomy moved over the Alps into France.

The swansong of the great period of Italian gastronomy took the form of a book of great merit, *L'Arte di Ben Cucinare* by Bartolomeo Stefani. This was published in Mantua in 1662, 11 years after *Le Cuisinier François* by the French chef La Varenne. Yet Stefani totally liberated himself from the flavourings used by his contemporaries, which were vestigial relics of the late Middle Ages. His tastes are fresh, his hand light and his recipes simple. He was also the first cookery writer to write recipes and menus for ordinary people, and to take into consideration the cost of food and its value.

During the 17th and 18th centuries, two important foods, the potato and the tomato, were becoming established in European cuisines. While the potato was adopted by the French, the tomato found two great exponents in the next important cookery writers to appear on the Italian scene. Vincenzo Corrado and Francesco Leonardi, both Neapolitan, established tomatoes as a vital ingredient in the haute cuisine of Europe just at the time when dried pasta began to be produced on a large scale, and the union of these two foods formed a pillar of southern Italian cooking that remains in place to this day.

In northern Italy, however, the acceptance of the 'golden apple' was much slower, no doubt due to the fact that it could not be grown there with the same success as in the south. Rice, butter, polenta, veal and beef are the mainstays of traditional northern Italian cooking, and their virtues were never sung to greater effect than by Artusi, who wrote his bestselling cookbook in the late 19th century, after the political unification of Italy.

However profound the effects of that political event, which occurred a century and a half ago, it has not yet resulted in the gastronomic unification of Italy. I cannot emphasize too strongly the degree to which, with regard to its cooking, Italy is still a collection of regions with their different traditions, their different cuisines and even – a problem that haunts this encyclopedia – their different terminologies.

The other source that sustains the variety, the appeal and above all the quality of Italian cooking must surely be the intense concern the Italians have, from early childhood, with what they eat and how it should be cooked. I certainly have a passionate interest in the subject, and it is my hope that in this book I may share the fruits of this passion with my readers. It is not – and was never intended to be – the 'ultimate bible' of Italian food; it is a distillation of my personal reflections on the many recipes I have cooked, foods I have tasted, books I have read and regions I have visited.

The first edition of this book was published in 1987, as a gastronomic dictionary, set out entirely from A to Z; it included recipes to allow readers to experience the *Gastronomy of Italy* for themselves. A second edition appeared in 2001, in which the emphasis was on the recipes, many of them photographed in colour. This new edition, which has been thoroughly – I can truly say exhaustively – revised, combines the best elements of both books: an easy-to-use A–Z format and inspiring colour photography.

Anna Del Conte

How to use Gastronomy of Italy

Cross-references are used to make information easily accessible. Within the body of the text certain words have been **CAPITALIZED**, for example Italian words or dishes that you may not recognize. This is to indicate that they have entries of their own, where you will find an explanation of their meaning and additional details about their background or uses. However, terms or ingredients with their own entries are *not* capitalized where their meaning is self-evident or their usage is so frequent that you will quickly become familiar with them (for example, Parmesan, mozzarella, pasta, prosciutto, risotto, spaghetti). There are full details of these items within their entries, but as they are so essential to Italian cooking their presence in the *Gastronomy of Italy* is taken as read. Only the less usual items have been capitalized, to ensure that you are able to find out more about them.

The capitalized word is often in the plural, with the full entry in the singular. It should be explained that feminine words end in either A (singular) or E (plural) and masculine ones end in either O (singular) or I (plural). Singular words ending in E take I in the plural and words finishing in CO, CA, GO or GA in the singular become CHI, CHE, GHI or GHE in the plural. *Italics* are used for foreign words that do not have their own entry.

Recipe names often vary according to the dialect in different parts of the country. Also, ingredients frequently have more than one name. To help you find the full entry for such items, therefore, alternative names may be included to point you in the right direction – for example: muggine see **CEFALO**.

Entries are listed alphabetically by their Italian name. The index beginning on page 477 includes both English and Italian ingredients and recipes.

The spoon symbol ●━━━ indicates that there is a recipe linked to the entry.

a

abbacchio
baby lamb

The meat of a baby lamb, which traditionally would have been slaughtered when still milk-fed. Nowadays, however, some baby lambs are killed when they begin to eat grass. If properly butchered, abbacchio is a very pale meat, tender and delicate, closer in taste to free-range chicken than to lamb.

Abbacchio is one of the great specialities of Rome, where it is cooked in several different ways. It is roasted in the oven or on the spit, served BRODETTATO or alla CACCIATORA.

abbrustolire
to grill

A method mainly related to rustic cooking on charcoal, such as the grilling of bread (BRUSCHETTA) and POLENTA. It can also refer to the grilling of peppers or aubergines over a live flame, although this method is more correctly called *fiammeggiare*.

abruzzese, all'
Abruzzo style

In the style of Abruzzo, which implies a considerable use of chilli, the favourite local spice, combined with tomatoes.

 [see recipe on page 14]

Abruzzo

The region of Abruzzo is situated in the southern part of central Italy. Abruzzese cooking belongs to the south and consists of two distinct cuisines: the coastal one based on fish and that of the hinterland, based on pork and lamb. But all the dishes have one thing in common: they are highly spiced with chilli – such as *maccheroni alla* CHITARRA (see recipe on page 106) and the succulent stew *'ndocca 'ndocca*, made with every bit of the pig from the snout to the tail.

Pasta-making was once a craft but is now a large-scale industry, with local brands in strong competition with those from Naples. The craft tradition is what has made the modern product so

ABRUZZO

ADRIATIC SEA

•Teramo

•Pescara

•L'Aquila

Pescara

•Chieti

•Sulmona

Apennines

successful, as well as the high-quality durum wheat grown locally.

Vegetables abound in this region and many local specialities have been created around them; there is one soup that contains them all. It is an ancient recipe with a strange name, le VIRTÙ, the virtues. It is made at the beginning of May when there are still some dried pulses in the larder and the new vegetables are just ready for picking.

The Abruzzesi love feasts and celebrations. They have even managed to create a special occasion for eating POLENTA as an accompaniment to hare

during the shooting season. The hare is boned, cut up in small pieces and stewed in wine. The cooked polenta is placed directly onto the table in a huge yellow mound alongside the cooked hare, and a contest ensues to see who can eat the most.

However, this is a minor affair compared with a *panarda*, a dinner served in Aquila on special occasions and consisting of at least 35 courses, from a formidable series of ANTIPASTI to an even more formidable series of puddings, all served at a single sitting. There is a story about a journalist in the early 20th century who, after the 28th course,

brodetto abruzzese
fish soup from Abruzzo

Serves 4–5

1.5kg/3¼lb assorted fish, such as monkfish, rascasse (scorpion fish), red and grey mullet, John Dory or hake, but not salmon or blue fish such as mackerel or sardines, gutted

1 onion, sliced

4 tbsp red wine vinegar

1 bay leaf

500g/1lb 2oz small cuttlefish or squid

100ml/3½fl oz/7 tbsp extra virgin olive oil

3 garlic cloves, finely sliced

1 dried red chilli (or more depending on strength), crumbled

400g/14oz canned plum tomatoes, with their juice, chopped

1½ tsp tomato puree

salt

1kg/2¼lb mussels, well scrubbed (discard any broken shells and any open shells that do not close when sharply tapped)

150ml/5fl oz/⅔ cup dry white wine

slices of toasted ciabatta or Pugliese bread, rubbed with garlic

BRODETTO is the fish soup of the Adriatic, and there are as many versions as there are ports. Of all the *brodetti*, this is one of the very best.

Remove the heads and tails from the fish and put them in a saucepan with the onion, vinegar and bay leaf. Cover with cold water, bring slowly to the boil, then simmer for 30 minutes. Strain the stock and discard the heads and tails.

Meanwhile, cut the fish into bite-sized pieces. Clean the cuttlefish or squid and cut into strips. Put the oil, garlic and chilli in a heavy pan and sauté over a low heat until the garlic is just coloured. Add the tomatoes and juice and the tomato puree and cook for 5 minutes, stirring frequently. Add the cuttlefish or squid and some salt and cook until they are tender – about 40 minutes to 1 hour, depending on their size.

Choose an earthenware pot that can be put directly on the heat and is large enough to hold all the ingredients. Put some of the cuttlefish and tomato sauce into the pot, cover with a layer of raw fish and a few mussels and then add some more cuttlefish and tomato sauce. Repeat the layers until all the ingredients are used. Pour over the wine and enough fish stock to come to about 2.5cm/1in above the level of the fish. If necessary, top up with hot water. Cook over a medium heat for 15 minutes or so, shaking the pot occasionally, but without stirring, which would break the fish. Discard any mussels that remain closed. Serve very hot, with the toasted garlic-rubbed bread.

got up and told his host, '*Grazie, ma ho mangiato abbastanza*' – 'Thank you, but I have eaten enough.' The host simply got his gun and said, 'Either you go on or I'll shoot you.'

PORCHETTA, piglet roasted on the spit, is a speciality shared with the other regions of central Italy. Some of the many other pork products include *prosciutto d'Aquila* and *ventricina*, a sausage made with the stomach of the pig flavoured with chilli, wild fennel and orange zest.

As in other mountainous regions, lamb is prepared by the shepherds just as it was hundreds of years ago. It might be cooked *a catturo* – in a large copper pan in the open air, with basil, onion, sage and chilli, a method which, sadly, is dying out. *Agnello, cacio e uova* (see recipe on page 159) is still very popular, as is *agnello all'*ARRABIATA, 'in the angry way', so called because the sauce is doused with chilli. Part of the sauce is often used to dress pasta, which is served as a first course.

Cheeses are of great importance in the regional diet, PECORINO being the favourite. The local CACIOCAVALLO is made from buffalo's milk and is, as might be expected in the region, highly spiced with chilli. The mozzarella is made from cow's rather than buffalo's milk, as is SCAMORZA, another delicious soft cheese, which is sometimes grilled on the spit.

The Abruzzesi have a sweet tooth, too. Although the sweets are only made on special occasions, the variety is remarkable. Some are simple, others are elaborate, like the delicious *nocci attorrati*, a version of almond praline. See CASSATA DI SULMONA recipe on page 93.

The most remarkable contribution of this region to the culinary scenario is that a large number of Abruzzese chefs achieved international fame. This might be due to the excellence of the local cooking as well as to professional traditions. In the 19th century a local chef emigrated to Nagasaki in Japan, where he became so famous that he was awarded an honour by the Emperor. In the 20th century another Abruzzese became head chef at the White House under President Eisenhower.

Accademia Italiana della Cucina
Italian academy of cooking

This learned society was founded in Milan in 1953 by Orio Vergani, a well-known writer, journalist and a great gourmet, together with a group of illustrious people from various walks of life. The purpose of the Accademia is to rediscover and safeguard the most genuine traditions of Italian regional cooking. The *Accademici* meet every year in a different region for a symposium. The subject of the meeting is always connected with the particular region and has a strong historical flavour. Local specialities are also sampled, discussed and criticized. The Accademia has branches all over the world and the members meet to taste and discuss the merits or demerits of local Italian restaurants.

acciuga
anchovy

A small sea fish, also known as *alice*, common around the coasts of Italy. It is smaller than the sardine, its distinguishing feature being a projecting upper jaw. The anchovy has a delicate and tasty flesh, but it should be eaten very fresh because, like all small fish, it deteriorates very quickly. When fresh, its back is a lovely blue-green colour and its sides silvery grey, but when the fish is not so fresh its back turns deep blue or black. When really fresh it is eaten raw, after being filleted and marinated in olive oil and lemon juice. Otherwise, anchovies are boiled whole for 2–3 minutes or grilled (after the head and entrails have been removed with a single pull) and dressed with olive oil and lemon juice.

 [see recipe on page 18]

acciughe, pasta d'
anchovy paste

A mixture of preserved anchovies and olive oil or vegetable oil, sold in a jar or tube.

acciughe conservate
preserved anchovies

Anchovies are preserved in salt (*acciughe sotto sale*) or in oil. The former are fresh whole anchovies preserved in small barrels and layered with rock salt, a practice that has changed little since Roman times. Before being used they are washed under cold water and boned. Anchovies are also filleted and preserved in olive oil, in cans and jars.

Both kinds are used extensively in cooking, imparting their characteristic pungent flavour to many sauces and dishes. Pasta sauces are made from mashed anchovies, the best known of these being the one used in Venice to dress BIGOLI. The sauce is a thick puree of onions strongly flavoured with preserved anchovies. Anchovies go into stuffings for baked vegetables, they are mashed into oil-based sauces for boiled vegetables, especially potato, spinach and cauliflower, and they decorate the toppings of many pizzas, from the traditional to the modern. In a dish called *manzo alla certosina*, anchovies are added to the oil in which a joint of beef has been browned, before slow cooking in a casserole

A final word of warning: when cooking anchovies, take care not to burn them or they will become unpleasantly bitter.

aceto
vinegar

In Italy this is usually wine vinegar. It is produced by oxidation of the alcohol in wine, which gives rise to acetic acid. Both red and white wine vinegar are used, the red being made from black grapes and the white from white grapes. Good white vinegar should be clear, transparent and of a pale pinkish yellow colour; good red vinegar should also be clear, and the colour varies from pale pink to dark ruby. The colour has no bearing on the quality of the vinegar. Traditionally, vinegar is coloured by enocyanin, a natural colouring found in wine. The use of flavourings is not allowed except in aromatic vinegars.

The main use of vinegar is in salad dressings. Vinegar is also used in sweet-and-sour sauces for vegetables and fish, for pickling vegetables, for marinating meat, game or fish and for adding to the cooking juices of meat and fish.

aceto balsamico
balsamic vinegar

This vinegar is not made from wine, but from the cooked and concentrated must of white Trebbiano grapes. Aceto balsamico is aged in a series of casks, called a *batteria*, made of different woods: oak, cherry, chestnut, mulberry and ash, a different wood being used each year. When the new grapes arrive in the autumn, some must from the previous year's barrel is siphoned off into the next barrel, some of this into the third-year barrel, and so on. The result of this complicated process is a nectar with a well-balanced flavour and a rich velvety-brown colour.

By law, vinegar that is labelled *aceto balsamico tradizionale* must be at least 12 years old and, in fact, is sometimes 50 years old or more. It is a full-bodied vinegar with a dark brown colour glinting with gold, and is very aromatic, with a peculiarly delicious flavour all of its own.

There is also a commercial version, called simply aceto balsamico, which cannot be sold as *tradizionale*. It has a similar flavour, but it has not been aged for as long: the flavour is obtained by adding a little caramel to a good-quality white wine vinegar.

Balsamic vinegar is produced in the province of Modena in Emilia-Romagna, and also, by a slightly different method, in the province of Reggio Emilia. Up to the 1980s it was almost unknown outside the region, but now it is a popular ingredient in many dishes throughout Italy.

Balsamic vinegar is used to dress strawberries, to sharpen vanilla ice cream, to flavour consommé and for special marinades. Aceto balsamico tradizionale also makes a thirst-quenching drink diluted with ice and sweetened with a little sugar.

acquacotta
vegetable soup

A traditional soup, made in the countryside all over Tuscany. It varies from one place to another, but consists basically of onion, tomato and celery sautéed in the best Tuscan olive oil and then cooked in water, as its name – 'cooked water' – implies. It is thickened with eggs.

affettato
sliced meats

A dish of sliced pork meats, a feast to the eye and a joy to the palate. Affettato must include PROSCIUTTO – crudo and cotto – at least two kinds of SALAMI, COPPA and MORTADELLA, all spread out on a large dish and often scattered with small curls of butter; it is the only Italian dish with which butter is sometimes served. Of course, there will also be lots of crusty white bread.

Traditionally, affettato is served as an ANTIPASTO, but only at lunch, and not with salad. Nowadays it is often served as a first course or a main course. A well-arranged platter of affettato is nearly always one of the most attractive dishes at a buffet lunch.

acciughe alla moda di Reggio Calabria
baked fresh anchovies

Serves 4

700g/1lb 9oz fresh anchovies (see introduction)
4 tbsp olive oil, plus extra for oiling the dish
5 tbsp fresh breadcrumbs
1 tbsp capers, preferably in salt, rinsed
2 garlic cloves, crushed
½ dried red chilli, chopped
1 tbsp chopped fresh marjoram
salt

You can use sardines or sprats in this recipe instead of anchovies. They are less delicate in flavour than fresh anchovies, but they are more readily available. This applies particularly to sprats, a good fish and always sold very fresh.

Preheat the oven to 200°C/400°F/Gas Mark 6.

Take the head off each anchovy with a sharp pull. This should also remove the central bone and the inside. Otherwise, gently free the bone from the flesh. Open the fish like a book and then wash them under cold water and pat them dry.

Mix together all the other ingredients. Grease a shallow ovenproof dish with a little oil and cover the bottom with a layer of anchovies. Spread half the breadcrumb mixture over the fish, cover with another layer of anchovies and then with the rest of the crumbs. Bake for 20 minutes. Serve hot, but not straight from the oven, or at room temperature.

RIGHT: Acciughe alla moda di Reggio Calabria

affettatrice
a meat slicer

A rotary meat slicer, usually electric. As well as the familiar machine seen in every Italian deli, there is a small version for family use. It is gaining popularity owing to the number of people choosing to buy whole PROSCIUTTI, CULATELLI and SALAMI. It is also useful for slicing roast meat.

affogato
poached

Food cooked in water, usually applied only to eggs. There is a long list of recipes using poached eggs, the principle being that they can lie on many delicious beds or be served with many different sauces. Among the most famous recipes are *uova affogate con pomodori e mozzarella*, poached eggs with tomatoes and mozzarella; *uova affogate alla parmigiana*, covered with melted butter and grated Parmesan; and *uova affogate all'acciuga*, served with a sauce of butter, anchovy paste and finely chopped parsley, and sometimes a touch of garlic.

The other food which is affogato is ice cream. A ball or two of vanilla or chocolate ice cream is served covered with hot coffee. Called *affogato al caffè*, this is a delicious modern concoction.

affumicato
smoked

Smoked food does not play an important part in traditional Italian dishes. However, a few pork products are cured by smoking, the most common being PANCETTA *affumicata* and SPECK. Most smoked fish is of foreign origin, although around the lakes of northern Italy there is a tradition of smoking trout. Smoked swordfish is a fairly recent product; it is excellent when properly smoked.

Mozzarella, PROVOLONE and SCAMORZA cheeses are also often smoked.

africano
a small cake

A cupcake, always professionally made, of almond sponge stuffed with ZABAIONE and covered with chocolate. It is one of the most popular small cakes, always on display in any PASTICCERIA, or cake shop.

agliata
breadcrumb or herb sauce

There are two sauces with this name. The Ligurian agliata is of Provençal origin: breadcrumbs that have been soaked in vinegar are pounded with lots of garlic, then a good quantity of olive oil is slowly added. It is served with boiled fish. The agliata from Piedmont consists of chopped parsley, celery, basil and garlic mixed with the soft local cheese and dressed with olive oil and lemon juice. It is served with hot toast dripping with olive oil, and a bottle of the local white wine, cool, young and fresh.

Agliata has a long history and features in the *Libro per cuoco* ('Book for cook'), written by an anonymous Venetian cookery writer in the 14th century. In his recipe, the garlic is grilled and pounded with breadcrumbs and spices, and the mixture diluted with capon broth.

aglio
garlic

An important ingredient in Italian cooking, although never a principal component except in such sauces as AGLIATA and BAGNA CAÓDA, and with olive oil and chilli in a sauce for LINGUINE and other long, narrow pasta. Garlic is widely used as a flavouring in many dishes, either as a basic element or as an ingredient in larding or in marinating. However, Italian cooking is not as garlicky as foreigners think. Often, and especially in northern Italian cooking, the garlic clove is used whole and discarded before the dish is served. In Piedmont garlic is often steeped in milk for some hours – *aglio dolce* – so that it imparts a mellow flavour. Fresh garlic, available in late spring and in summer, is sweeter than dried garlic.

When garlic is no longer young, many cooks, myself included, remove the germ (the tiny pale green shoot) inside the clove. This makes the garlic far less pungent and more digestible.

agnello
lamb

Lamb is the traditional Easter fare everywhere in Italy. The best recipes come from central Italy where, when young, the lamb is roasted whole on a spit with rosemary, garlic and other herbs. If the lamb is a little older, the leg or shoulder is oven-roasted with a little wine and/or vinegar, or cut into pieces and stewed with various sauces, usually containing tomatoes. Vinegar, lemon juice and anchovy fillets are often used in lamb dishes. In Venezia Giulia, in the north-east, a lamb stew is finished with horseradish (RAFANO), a flavouring hardly ever found in Italian cooking.

[see recipe on page 22]

agnolotti
stuffed pasta

A kind of stuffed pasta made in Piedmont, agnolotti are square-shaped with ruffled edges. There is not a standard recipe for them; they are stuffed with leftover cooked meat to which spinach or chicory is often added. They used to be made on Monday, to use the leftover meat from Sunday. They are dressed with melted butter. During the white truffle season a grating of truffle is sometimes added – a delicate garnish for these glorified leftovers.

agone
a freshwater fish

A fish found in the Alpine lakes, from Lake Maggiore to Lake Garda. It is a rather coarse fish, both in taste and in texture, usually fried when small, or grilled when larger. On Lake Como it is transformed into a delicacy by being dried in the sun, when it is known as *missoltit*.

agresto
verjuice

A condiment made from the juice of unripe grapes. Agresto has a strong, sour taste and should be added with great discretion. It can be replaced by lemon juice or vinegar.

agretti

The name given in central Italy to BARBA DI FRATE.

agro, all'
in the sharp style

This flavouring is achieved by pouring a little lemon juice over steamed or blanched vegetables, such as spinach, beet leaves or broccoli, while they are sautéed in olive oil.

agrodolce
sweet and sour sauce

A sauce made with wine vinegar and sugar, to which onion, garlic, herbs and spices may be added. Agrodolce, using honey and not sugar, dates back to Roman times and was reintroduced in Sicily by the Saracens. Versions of agrodolce were favourites of the Renaissance chefs. It is served with fish, game and vegetables, especially onions and aubergines.

[see recipe on page 22]

agnello alla cacciatora con le patate
lamb and potato stew

Serves 6
20g/³⁄₄oz/³⁄₄ cup dried porcini
4 tbsp olive oil
1kg/2¼lb boned shoulder of lamb, cut
*   into 5cm/2in cubes*
1 small onion, finely chopped
250g/9oz fresh porcini, sliced
2 tbsp tomato puree
750g/1lb 10oz waxy potatoes, cut
*   into chunks*
1 bay leaf
salt and freshly ground black pepper
6–8 tbsp meat stock (page 61) or
*   chicken stock*
2 tbsp chopped fresh flat-leaf parsley

The term alla CACCIATORA is applied to a number of different dishes, which are usually rustic and made with seasonal ingredients. In this recipe from Liguria, potatoes and porcini are cooked with lamb. When fresh porcini are not in season, you can use cultivated brown mushrooms instead. If you prefer you can cook this dish in the oven preheated to 160°C/325°F/Gas Mark 3.

Soak the dried porcini in a cupful of hot water for at least 10 minutes and then drain, reserving the liquid.

Heat the olive oil in a flameproof casserole and brown the meat well on all sides. Lift out the meat and set aside. Add the onion and the dried and fresh porcini to the casserole and cook for 10 minutes, until tender, stirring frequently. Return the meat to the pot and add the tomato puree, potatoes and bay leaf. Strain the porcini liquid through a sieve lined with cheesecloth and add to the pot. Season with salt and pepper to taste.

Cover and simmer very gently for about 1½ hours. If necessary, add a few tablespoons of warm stock or water to the sauce during cooking. Sprinkle with the parsley before serving.

cipolline in agrodolce
onions in a sweet and sour sauce

Serves 4
700g/1lb 9oz small white onions
50g/1³⁄₄oz/4 tbsp unsalted butter
1 tbsp tomato puree diluted with 2 tbsp
*   warm water*
1 tbsp sugar
2 tbsp wine vinegar
salt and freshly ground black pepper

There are many versions of this dish. This one, made with butter and flavoured with tomato puree, is characteristic of Emilia.

To peel the onions, plunge them into boiling water for a few seconds. It will then be quite easy to remove the skins. Do not remove the roots or the onions will fall apart during cooking.

Put the onions and butter in a large sauté pan with the diluted tomato puree and about 300ml/10fl oz/1¼ cups warm water. Cook, uncovered, over a medium heat for about 30 minutes, stirring frequently but very gently.

Add the sugar, vinegar, salt and pepper. Mix well, turn the heat down to low and continue cooking for about 1 hour. Add more water if necessary during cooking. At the end of cooking, the onions should be a rich brown colour and soft but still whole.

Serve at room temperature.

RIGHT: Agnello alla cacciatora con le patate

agrumi
citrus fruits

No fruits are so redolent of southern Italy as lemons, oranges, citrons, mandarins, bergamots.

Apart from the sweet orange, most citrus fruits were brought to Sicily by the Arabs, but it was not until the beginning of the 19th century, when their commercial value was fully appreciated, that extensive production started. Nowadays they are the most important produce of Sicily and Calabria, where they all grow very well, from lemons and sweet oranges to the more exotic bergamot and citron.

There are a few traditional recipes that combine citrus fruits with meat, poultry and fish. The best known is *paparo all'arancia* – duck with orange, which must be the forefather of the French recipe. References to this dish were found in Florentine documents of the 13th and 14th centuries.

Alberini, Massimo
1909–2000

The greatest historian of Italian gastronomy of the 20th century. Alberini wrote many books on cooking traditions and on great chefs of the past, but he never wrote a single recipe. He was a rigorous researcher into the roots of Italian culinary traditions and he always upheld the regional cuisine. I met Alberini when I began to write about Italian food and his help and advice were invaluable, especially when I started this encyclopedia, which was first published in 1987. I still remember the agony I went through when I asked him to dinner. What could I possibly cook for this eminent man, used to dining in Michelin three-starred restaurants? Well, I decided to cook a traditional English dinner: a soup of dried split peas followed by fish pie and finishing with apple crumble. And he loved it all. On another occasion my husband and I decided to take him out to dinner. After days of confabulation and research we booked a table at Alastair Little's, whose restaurant in Soho was all the rave at the time. We went in and Alberini looked around in a rather surprised way at the polished nakedness of the place. We sat at a grey plastic table and that's when Alberini's look changed to horrified. He exclaimed: 'Mah, there aren't even tablecloths here!' We decided to cut our losses, got up, called a taxi and went to Rules, and that was a great success. Tradition coupled with excellent food was what he truly valued.

albicocca
apricot

Although the botanical name of this plant is *Prunus armeniaca*, it appears that the apricot tree was first grown in China and Turkestan, and spread from there to the Middle East. Alexander the Great tasted this incomparable fruit in Armenia and brought the plant to Greece. The Saracens, to whom early European gastronomes and gourmets owed so much, brought the plant to Spain and Sicily.

The apricot is cultivated in all the temperate areas of Italy, in the same climatic conditions as the almond. It flowers early, just after the almond, and the fruit is ready in June. Like figs, apricots should ideally be picked off the tree, warm from the sun, and popped straight into one's mouth.

Italians usually prefer to eat apricots raw, but they are also used to make jam, this in its turn being used in ZUPPA INGLESE, CROSTATA and other puddings; they are also stewed in a white wine and cinnamon syrup.

In her book *Tutti gli usi della frutta*, Ilaria Rattazzi has an interesting recipe called *albicocchine*. The apricots are stoned, pureed and then mixed with icing sugar until thick. The paste is formed into small balls which are rolled in granulated sugar and left in a warm place to dry. Albicocchine keep for up to two months in an airtight container.

An excellent tip from the same writer is to add three or four of the kernels when making apricot jam. A few apricot kernels are sometimes added to AMARETTI, AMARETTO and other preparations instead of bitter almonds.

Apricots are also dried and eaten in a compote or poached in cinnamon-flavoured syrup, and are baked with rice boiled in sugared milk.

alborella
a freshwater fish

A very small freshwater fish found in the lakes of northern Italy, particularly Lake Como. Alborelle are fried in olive oil and served with lemon wedges.

alchermes
a liqueur

As its name implies, alchermes was brought to Europe by the Arabs. It arrived in Tuscany via Spain, and has been made there by the monks of S. Maria Novella in Florence for many centuries. Alchermes has a beautiful crimson colour, derived from a small insect. It is flavoured with spices, and sometimes scented with rose, jasmine and iris. Its principal use is in ZUPPA INGLESE and in other puddings.

alice
see ACCIUGA

allodola
skylark

The sweet bird loved equally by poets and gourmets. In some regions of Italy skylarks are hailed as the best small game and arguments flare concerning their preparation. One recipe from Piedmont suggests splitting each skylark in half, flattening it out and cooking it in butter. Covered by a grating of white truffles, skylarks are served

with polenta and butter. Whatever you do, you must be prepared to eat them daintily with your hands, sucking the juicy meat off the tiny bones.

alloro
Another name for LAURO.

Alto Adige
see TRENTINO-ALTO ADIGE

amarena
morello cherry

Very dark red in colour and softer than other cherries, morello cherries have a slightly sour taste. Although sometimes eaten as fresh fruit, they are more often used for jam or jelly making, preserved in alcohol – a practice common in Naples – or made into water-ice or ice cream. The marasca cherry, a variety of morello, gives its name to maraschino, a liqueur originally from Dalmatia in Croatia, which is made from the pulp and crushed stones of the cherries and sweetened with honey.

amaretti
macaroons

Amaretti are made with sweet and bitter almonds; these latter give the characteristic flavour which distinguishes amaretti from other macaroons. Originally from Lombardy and Piedmont, they are now made all over northern Italy and sold in bakeries, or PASTICCERIA. They vary in size, but are never more than about 3cm/1¼in across. The most famous are the *amaretti di Saronno,* those little things wrapped in white paper with blue print, named after a town in Lombardy.

There are a few savoury dishes that contain amaretti, including pumpkin ravioli, stuffed courgettes with ricotta and Parmesan, and some spinach TORTE.

25

amaretto
a liqueur

A fascinating legend relates the origin of this sweet, almond-flavoured liqueur. In the early 16th century, Bernardino Luini, a great Lombard painter and Leonardo da Vinci's favourite pupil, was commissioned to paint a picture of the Madonna for a church in the town of Saronno. He asked his innkeeper's lovely wife to be the model and in return for this honour she gave him a jug of a beautiful amber-coloured drink that she had made by macerating apricot kernels in *acquavite*. Thus she created the liqueur called 'amaretto di Saronno', which the firm of Domenico Reina began to produce commercially at the beginning of the 20th century.

Amaretto used to be drunk exclusively by bourgeoise ladies after a meal. Recently, however, it has become well known everywhere. I have had it in a sauce with poached apricots and also in a sauce with stuffed peaches.

amatriciana, all'
pasta dish

Pasta, traditionally BUCATINI, dressed with a sauce made with GUANCIALE (cured pig's jowl), tomatoes, onions and chilli. The sauce is a speciality of the town of Amatrice in Lazio, where it is prepared for the local fair on the first Sunday after the bank holiday on 15 August.

[see recipe below]

bucatini all'amatriciana
pancetta and tomato sauce

Enough for 4–5 helpings of pasta
450ml/16fl oz/2 cups tomato sauce
   (see method)
350g/12oz unsmoked pancetta, cut into
   1cm/½in cubes
1 tbsp olive oil
1 small onion, very finely chopped
salt and freshly ground black pepper
1 garlic clove, finely chopped
1 dried red chilli, finely chopped
125ml/4fl oz/½ cup dry white wine

BUCATINI is the traditional pasta to serve with this sauce, but spaghetti is a good alternative. In Italy this sauce is made with GUANCIALE (cured pig's jowl), but pancetta may be used instead. Grated PECORINO cheese is handed round separately, to counterbalance the fattiness of the meat.

First prepare the tomato sauce, either your favourite or using the recipe for salsa di pomodoro 2 (page 331).

Put the pancetta cubes and olive oil in a non-stick frying pan and sauté, stirring frequently, until the fat has run out of the pancetta and it is crisp and brown.

Add the onion and a pinch of salt to the pan and sauté for about 10 minutes. Mix in the garlic and chilli. Cook for a further minute or so and then add the wine. Turn up the heat and let the wine bubble away to reduce it by half.

Pour in the tomato sauce and simmer for 15 minutes for the flavours to combine. Taste and adjust the seasoning.

When the pasta is cooked, drain and transfer to the pan. Stir for a minute or two and then serve.

anatra/anitra domestica
domestic duck

This bird, which was not very popular in Italy until the late 20th century, is now widely bred in northern Italy. The most common breeds are the *anatra comune* and the *muschiata*, so called because of its musky smell and known in English as the Muscovy duck.

A rather special recipe from Venice is called (in Venetian dialect) *bigoli co'l'anara*: the duck is boiled with carrot, onion and celery, then removed and a kind of spaghetti called BIGOLI is cooked in the strained stock. The bigoli are dressed with a RAGÙ made with the duck's liver and heart, and served as a first course. The duck itself follows, accompanied by the piquant PEVERADA sauce. Another splendid Venetian recipe is *anara col pien*, a traditional dish served on the day of the Festa del Redentore, on the third Sunday in July. The boned duck is stuffed with minced veal or chicken, the bird's liver, some SOPPRESSA (a soft Venetian sausage) and bread soaked in MARSALA. And then, of course, there is the *anitra all'arancia*, duck with orange, or rather *paparo all'arancia* as it is called in Tuscany, where it originated. Although the French contest the Tuscan origin of this dish, the Tuscans say that it arrived in France with Caterina de'Medici and her courtiers. What is certain is that the first ever recipe for *anitra all'arancia* was written by an anonymous Tuscan cookery writer in the 14th century. In it the duck is stuffed with herbs, garlic and vinegar and roasted on the spit. It was served with bitter orange juice.

anatra/anitra selvatica
wild duck

The many species of wild duck vary in size, plumage and colour. The best species for the table are the *germano* (mallard) and *mestolone* (shoveler).

Wild duck is drawn immediately after it has been shot, plucked after one day and then hung for up to two days. It is roasted on the spit, in the oven, pan-roasted or braised in the same way as the domestic duck, but for longer.

anguilla
common eel

Eels vary in length from a few centimetres to 1.5m/around 5ft. The very small eels are called CIECHE, *capillari*, *sementare* or *cirioli*, depending on the region of Italy. Eels from the Comacchio lagoon at the mouth of the Po in Emilia-Romagna are the best in the country.

They may be grilled, gently sautéed with bay leaves, roasted on the spit or marinated in wine vinegar and then stored in earthenware jars. But the best recipe is a stew, with plenty of onion and tomato sauce, to which ACETO BALSAMICO (balsamic vinegar) is added halfway through the cooking.

anguria
watermelon

Watermelon is also called *cocomero* in central and southern Italy. In July and August pyramids of fruit can be seen piled up by the roadside, much as cannon balls used to be piled on the ramparts of medieval castles.

Watermelon is eaten chilled. Half a small watermelon can be an attractive container for a fruit salad. A popular dessert is small balls of watermelon mixed with similar sized balls of deep yellow melon, sweetened and flavoured with a dash of kirsch, served in scooped-out melon halves.

anice
anise

A tall herb, native to the Middle East, with pretty white flowers. The aromatic fruit contains the oil-bearing seeds – *semi di anice*, aniseeds – for which the plant is cultivated. Aniseed is used in biscuits, cakes and puddings, and in Tuscany it is used in salads and to flavour grilled fish. It should not be confused with dill, whose flavour is weaker and more subtle.

animelle
sweetbreads

The thymus gland of a calf or lamb, which disappears in the adult animal. In Italy animelle are usually blanched, coated in egg and breadcrumbs and fried, or they are sautéed in butter and sprinkled with lemon juice. Because they lack a pronounced taste, animelle are ideal for stuffings or for thickening sauces.

The Romans, who are the best offal cooks, use sweetbreads and peas to stuff very young artichokes, which are then coated in a light batter and fried.

The 19th-century chef Giovanni Felice LURASCHI included many recipes for sweetbreads in his *Nuovo Cuoco Milanese*.

[see recipe below]

anitra

see ANATRA

animelle fritte
fried sweetbreads

Serves 3–4
600g/1lb 5oz sweetbreads
½ organic or unwaxed lemon
1 large egg
salt and freshly ground black pepper
3 tbsp plain (all-purpose) flour
6 tbsp dried breadcrumbs
40g/1½oz/3 tbsp unsalted butter
3 tbsp olive or vegetable oil
lemon wedges, to serve

Brains and sweetbreads are well suited to this method of cooking, where their delicate texture and flavour is enveloped in a golden buttery crust. Calf's sweetbreads are considered superior, but I find lamb's are good too.

Rinse the sweetbreads under cold water and put them in a saucepan of cold water, with the lemon. Bring to the boil and then simmer for 8–10 minutes. Drain, then cool them, pressed between two plates. When they are cold, cut off any pieces of fat and skin and cut the sweetbreads into neat pieces.

Lightly beat the egg with salt and pepper. Spread the flour on a plate and toss the sweetbreads very lightly in the flour. Coat them in the egg and then the breadcrumbs, pressing the crumbs firmly into the meat.

Heat the butter and oil in a large frying pan and when the fat is beginning to turn golden, slide in the pieces of sweetbread. Cook on both sides until a deep golden crust has formed, then turn down the heat and cook for a further 5 minutes. Transfer the sweetbreads to a heated dish, pour over the sizzling butter and serve immediately, with lemon wedges.

anolini
stuffed pasta

Small stuffed pasta, half-moon shaped with ruffled edges, anolini originate from Emilia-Romagna, where they are usually cooked in stock and eaten 'in brodo', as a soup. The stuffing can vary, but always contains braised meat. *Timballo di anolini* is a rich dish, in which the cooked anolini are dressed with the meat juices, some butter and grated Parmesan and put in a pie dish lined with sweet pastry.

[see recipe below]

---

anolini alla piacentina
anolini stuffed with braised beef

Serves 4–6
85g/3oz/6 tbsp unsalted butter
2 tbsp olive oil
350g/12oz braising steak in one piece
1 onion, finely chopped
1 celery stalk, finely chopped
1 small carrot, finely chopped
150ml/5fl oz/²⁄₃ cup dry white wine
1 tbsp tomato puree
200ml/7fl oz/generous ¾ cup meat stock (page 61) or chicken stock
salt and freshly ground black pepper
50g/1¾oz/1 cup fresh breadcrumbs
50g/1¾oz Parmesan cheese, grated
a grating of nutmeg
2 large eggs
egg pasta (page 282) made with 300g/10½oz/scant 2½ cups Italian 00 flour and 3 large eggs
a dozen sage leaves, to serve

In this recipe from Piacenza the ANOLINI are drained and dressed with butter and Parmesan.

Heat 25g/1oz/2 tbsp of the butter with the oil in a small saucepan. Add the meat and brown very well on all sides. Lift out of the pan and set aside.

Add the onion, celery and carrot to the pan and sauté until soft, stirring frequently. Return the meat to the pan and then pour over the wine. Boil briskly until reduced by three-quarters.

Dissolve the tomato puree in the stock and add to the pan, with salt and pepper to taste. Cover with the lid and cook over a very low heat for about 3 hours, turning the meat over from time to time and adding a little warm water if necessary. The juices should be quite thick.

In a bowl, mix together the breadcrumbs with half the Parmesan. Spoon over about half the cooking juices of the meat.

Cut the meat into pieces and then chop finely or process to a coarse mixture. Add to the cheese and breadcrumbs together with the nutmeg and the eggs. Taste and adjust the seasoning.

Prepare the pasta. Working with about one-third at a time and keeping the rest covered with a cloth, roll it out and cut into rounds using a fluted cutter about 5cm/2in in diameter. Place a small spoonful of the meat mixture in the middle of each round, lightly moisten the edge of the pasta with cold water and fold it over the stuffing in a half-moon shape. Press firmly around the edges.

Drop the anolini into a large saucepan of boiling salted water and cook until ready: from 5 to 15 minutes depending on how dry they are. Using a slotted spoon, lift them out of the water into a colander and then transfer to a heated bowl. Melt the remaining butter, add the sage leaves and, when lightly fried, spoon over the anolini with the remaining cheese.

antipasto
hors d'oeuvre

Literally, 'before the meal', and not 'before the pasta' as it is sometimes taken to mean. The sight of an antipasto counter, which greets you as you enter a restaurant, is both a joy to the eye and a promise of the delights to come. The counter is loaded with appetizing dishes, some traditional, some the creation of the chef.

Antipasti can be cold, as they mostly are, or hot. Among the cold you can choose between an *antipasto misto* (mixed), an AFFETTATO or an *antipasto di pesce* (fish). The antipasto misto will usually include tuna fish and beans, hard-boiled eggs with various fillings, anchovy fillets preserved in olive oil, olives from Gaeta (round and blackish), grilled peppers, stuffed vegetables and various vegetables stewed in tomato sauce or in a sweet and sour sauce.

The affettato consists of sliced pork products such as PROSCIUTTO and SALAME. The antipasto di pesce may include stuffed mussels, raw anchovies marinated in olive oil and lemon juice, fish marinated in a sweet and sour sauce, or a seafood salad.

The hot antipasto could be a slice or two of COTECHINO or ZAMPONE, a dish of snails, a few croquettes or small meatballs, or a slice of vegetable TORTE.

Nowadays, antipasti usually take the place of a first course.

Apicius
Roman gastronome

Apicius is the name linked with the first-ever cookery book, *De Re Coquinaria*, a collection of about 470 recipes from the Roman Empire. Marcus Gavius Apicius was not the author of the book, although he was most probably the collector of the recipes. He was a gourmet who lived in the 1st century AD and took a great interest in the scientific aspects of food and cooking. The recipes,

nearly half of which are for sauces and garnishes, probably came from many different sources. They include a huge number of spices and herbs, plus honey, that would totally hide the intrinsic flavour of any ingredient. They do, however, give a fairly good idea of what was eaten in a patrician household at the time.

Marcus Gavius Apicius was immensely rich, but managed to consume his fortune, literally, by spending it on his belly. The story, as related by both Seneca and Martial, is that when he saw his fortune coming to an end, he killed himself by taking poison at a banquet specially arranged for the occasion.

A translation of Apicius' book by Joseph Dommers Vehling gives a fascinating account of the period. The recipe that follows is my interpretation of one of the recipes in this book.

 [see recipe on facing page]

Apulia
see PUGLIA

aragosta
spiny/rock lobster

This crustacean differs from the true lobster in being smaller and having no claws. Although it is found around the coasts of Sardinia and the Tremiti Islands in the Adriatic Sea, the aragosta has become rare in the seas around Italy. This is partly because its inflated price has encouraged over-fishing. In Italy aragosta is usually eaten cold with olive oil and lemon juice or split in half and grilled.

arancia
orange

The pride of the citrus family. The *Arancia amara* – bitter orange – was brought to Sicily by the Saracens

CONTINUES OVERLEAF

anatra all'Apicio
a duck recipe from Apicius

Serves 3

1 sprig of fresh dill

1 bay leaf

salt

1 duck, preferably a Barbary or
    Gressingham, with giblets

150ml/5fl oz/²⁄₃ cup strong red wine

1 sprig of fresh rue (optional)

5 garlic cloves, bruised

1 onion stuck with 2 cloves

1 celery stalk, roughly chopped

1 carrot, roughly chopped

3–4 parsley stalks

1 tbsp olive oil

Sauce

a bunch of fresh coriander

1 sprig of fresh lovage or celery leaves

1 tsp cumin seeds

6 black peppercorns

1 tbsp dried oregano

1 tbsp golden unrefined sugar

1 tsp sea salt

1 tbsp wine vinegar

15g/¹⁄₂oz/1 tbsp unsalted butter

1 tbsp plain (all-purpose) flour

The Romans loved duck, judging by the number of recipes in APICIUS'
book *De Re Coquinaria*. As with the cooking of most meats in Roman
times, the duck is plunged into boiling water before it is roasted. This
rids the bird of some of its fat.

Bring a saucepan of water to the boil. Add the dill, bay leaf, a little salt
and the duck (setting aside the giblets) and bring slowly back to the boil.
Simmer for 15 minutes and then lift the duck out of the stock.

Remove the legs and the breast from the carcass and remove and discard
the skin. Cut the breast into diagonal slices. Marinate the legs and
breast slices in the wine with the rue, if using, the garlic and a little salt
for 2–3 hours at room temperature.

Put the carcass, with the neck and gizzard, into the stock in which the
duck has cooked. Add the onion, celery, carrot and parsley stalks and
simmer for about 1 hour. Using a metal spoon, remove as much as you
can of the fat which has risen to the surface. Strain the stock.

To prepare the sauce, first chop the duck liver. In a mortar, pound together
the coriander, lovage, cumin seeds, peppercorns, oregano, sugar, sea
salt and the duck liver, moistening with the vinegar. (You can use a food
processor, of course.) In a saucepan, make a roux with the butter and flour
and add 300ml/10fl oz/1¼ cups of the duck stock. Stir in the pounded
ingredients and cook very gently for 10 minutes, stirring frequently. Taste
and adjust the seasoning. Remove from the heat and keep warm.

Lift the duck legs and breast slices out of the marinade and dry
thoroughly. Strain the marinade. Heat the olive oil in a non-stick frying
pan and, when it is really hot, fry the duck legs for about 8 minutes. Add
the breast slices and fry for 2 minutes. Remove from the pan and keep
warm. Pour the marinade into the frying pan and reduce over a high heat
until about 3 tablespoons remain. Pour this over the duck and then serve,
with the sauce.

33

in the tenth century and was cultivated there with great success. It was grown as a flavouring, rather than for eating. The orange soon became the symbol of riches and opulence, so much so that the Medici incorporated it in their coat of arms: the five golden balls are oranges. Nowadays the *Arancia amara* is not cultivated for culinary use but as a decorative tree or for the extraction of oil.

The *Arancia dolce* – sweet orange – was introduced to Europe from China, via India, by the Portuguese at the end of the 15th century. At first it was mainly served as a luxury drink, but by the end of the 18th century the fruit had become quite popular. It is widely cultivated in Sicily and southern Italy, especially in the fertile area of Calabria around Reggio Calabria, at the tip of the Boot.

A traditional dish that is still very popular in Sicily is a salad made with orange slices, finely sliced sweet onion, olive oil, salt and pepper. It is served either before the dessert or, in more important meals, between one course and the next, to help the digestion and refresh the palate. Such combinations of oranges with savoury foods were more common in the past than they are today.

[see recipe below]

arancini
stuffed rice croquettes

The literal translation of arancini is 'little oranges' but these are, in fact, little rice croquettes stuffed with various ingredients. They are made with risotto or boiled rice dressed with butter and grated cheese. Coated in egg and breadcrumbs, they are fried in butter, STRUTTO or oil. The four traditional stuffings are meat and tomatoes, chicken livers and tomatoes, mozzarella and tomatoes, or a RAGÙ of ham and peas.

34

arance caramellate
caramelized oranges

Serves 4

6 blood oranges, organic or unwaxed

175g/6oz/generous ¾ cup caster (superfine) sugar

2 tbsp lemon juice, from an organic or unwaxed fruit

2–3 tbsp Grand Marnier

The usual practice is to serve these oranges whole, but I find it easier to serve them sliced. It is a classic, and perfect, end to a meal.

Scrub 2 of the oranges very thoroughly and remove the peel with a swivel-action potato peeler, trying not to remove any pith. Cut this peel into thin batons. Plunge the batons of peel into boiling water and boil them for 6–7 minutes to rid them of their bitterness. Drain and set aside.

Peel all the oranges completely (don't leave any pith on them), then slice them and put the slices in a bowl.

Put the sugar, lemon juice and 2 tablespoons water in a small saucepan. Heat gently until the sugar has dissolved, then boil to make a pale caramel; do not stir the syrup, just let it become golden. Mix in 150ml/ 5fl oz/⅔ cup boiling water, then add the sliced peel. Simmer for 5 minutes or so, then add the Grand Marnier.

Pour the caramel over the oranges, leave until cold, then cover the bowl and chill until ready to serve.

Arancini are originally from Sicily, and are the best known of the very few traditional rice dishes from that island. In the Sicilian recipe arancini are made with boiled rice dressed with eggs and PECORINO cheese and stuffed with meat juice and young pecorino. In Rome, arancini are made with a plain risotto and stuffed with a Bolognese sauce or a mushroom *ragù*. Arancini have now been adopted by Italians up and down the country, who love to eat them in bars with aperitifs.

arista
Tuscan roast loin of pork

Arista is an ancient dish; one account of the origin of its name dates back to the 15th century. It is said that the dish was served at a meal during the Ecumenical Council of 1450 in Florence. Present were some Greek bishops who, having tasted the dish, gave their approval, exclaiming, '*Aristos, aristos*!' – 'The best!'. The name stuck, as well it might, since this roast is certainly one of the best. The boneless joint is larded with garlic and rosemary (or wild fennel), brushed with olive oil and roasted.

[see recipe on page 36]

aromi
herbs

The general name used to describe herbs such as rosemary, sage and thyme. The term is used when no specific herbs are mentioned, their choice being left to the discretion of the cook: *un po' di aromi*, 'a few aromatic herbs'.

arrabbiata, all'
cooking style

Literally meaning 'in the angry way', it implies a lot of chilli in a tomato sauce. It applies only to meat and to pasta, *penne all'arrabbiata* being a well known dish.

arrostire
to roast

Three basic methods of cooking come within the scope of this term. They are *arrosto alla griglia* (on the spit), *arrosto al forno* (in the oven) and *arrosto in tegame* or *arrosto morto* (pot roast). Meat can be roasted by any of these three methods, but most fish is only roasted by the last two; large and oily fish, however, can be roasted on the spit. Vegetables are roasted in the oven or in the pot.

Arrosto alla griglia is the oldest method of cooking, and still the best for a large piece of meat (PORCHETTA or ABBACCHIO) and most game, both furred and feathered. The meat is regularly moistened with its own fat which is collected in a container (*leccarda*) placed underneath. A sprig of fresh rosemary is often used to moisten the meat using this fat.

The meat roasted in the oven is usually a joint of beef, pork or lamb, but seldom veal, poultry or game, which are considered too lean for cooking that way. The meat may be flavoured with herbs, onion or celery and moistened with wine during cooking. This method was the favourite of the great ARTUSI, who, in his book *La Scienza in Cucina e l'Arte di Mangiar Bene,* wrote, 'If I knew who invented the oven I would build a monument to him.' Artusi also cooks veal in the oven, but a milk-fed breast of veal or a leg, which are fattier cuts.

The most common method of roasting veal and poultry is on the hob. The *arrosto morto* (see recipe on page 38) illustrates the most popular method. The meat is cooked in a pan or in a casserole. It is first browned over a high heat and then cooked over a lower heat, with the addition of wine, stock, balsamic vinegar and water, or a combination of these. These additions must be small – just enough to prevent the meat from burning. The meat must never braise, let alone stew. In another recipe the meat begins its cooking in liquid; the liquid is poured off and the meat returned to the pan over a medium

35

heat. The liquid is then added to the pan very gradually, while the meat browns, which takes 7–10 minutes.

A large, delicate fish, such as sea bass or daurade, is best roasted in the oven (*pesce al forno*), while a smaller one is more suited to being cooked in the pan. The fish is usually marinated in oil, lemon, herbs and other flavourings.

Vegetables are cut into chunks and roasted in the oven. Often, three or four different vegetables are placed together, as in a dish from Umbria called *la bandiera*, 'the flag'.

arrosto
roast(ed)

The word can be a noun, as in *arrosto morto* (pot roast) or *arrosto di manzo* (roast beef), or it can be an adjective, as in *pollo arrosto* (roast chicken). For preparation methods see ARROSTIRE.

 [see recipes overleaf]

arsella

A Genoese name for clam. See VONGOLA.

arista alla fiorentina
Florentine roast pork

Serves 6
2 garlic cloves, finely sliced
2 sprigs of fresh rosemary, about
  10cm/4in long
salt and freshly ground black pepper
1kg/2¼lb boned loin of pork, without
  rind
2 cloves
3 tbsp olive oil

This is one of the most popular Tuscan roasts, usually served cold, accompanied by cannellini beans. Ask your butcher for the bones from the pork and put them around the meat in the roasting pan. They make the juices much tastier.

Chop the garlic and rosemary needles together, add salt and pepper and mix well. Make small incisions in the pork and push a little of the rosemary mixture into the meat. Pat the rest of the mixture all over the meat, stud the meat with the cloves and then rub with half the olive oil. Leave to stand in a cool place for a few hours to absorb the flavourings.

Preheat the oven to 180°C/350°F/Gas Mark 4.

Put the remaining oil and the meat in a roasting pan and roast for about 2 hours, basting and turning the meat every 20 minutes or so. Turn the oven up to 220°C/425°F/Gas Mark 7 for the last 10 minutes to brown the meat.

When the meat is tender, transfer it to a wooden board and leave it to rest for 10 minutes or so.

Remove as much fat from the cooking liquid as you can. Add 4 tablespoons hot water to the roasting pan and boil briskly, stirring vigorously to loosen the residue.

Carve the meat and spoon over the cooking juices. The pork is equally succulent and delicious served hot or cold.

RIGHT: Arista alla fiorentina

arrosto morto
pot-roast veal

Serves 6

1kg/2¼lb boned joint of veal or beef,
  securely tied
25g/1oz/2 tbsp unsalted butter
2 tbsp olive oil
1 garlic clove, bruised
1 sprig of fresh rosemary
150ml/5fl oz/²⁄₃ cup dry white wine
salt and freshly ground black pepper

The odd name of this recipe — *morto* means dead — is apparently due to the fact that the meat is 'killed' by some liquid after being browned over a high heat. It is a very common method of cooking a joint of meat or a bird.

Dry the meat thoroughly. Heat half the butter and the oil with the garlic and rosemary in a heavy casserole in which the joint will just fit. When the butter foam begins to subside, remove and discard the garlic and add the meat. Brown well on all sides over a medium heat.

Add the wine and bring to a lively bubble. Turn the heat down to low, add salt and cook slowly, with the lid slightly askew so that the steam can escape. Turn the meat over every 20 minutes or so, and keep a watch that there is always some liquid in the pan. Add a little hot water if needed. When the meat is tender — which will take about 1½ hours for veal and about 2 hours for beef — remove it to a warm dish and keep warm while you make the sauce.

If there is too much liquid in the pan, boil rapidly to reduce. If there is not enough liquid, add a couple of tablespoons of hot water. Add the remaining butter a little at a time, while whisking or stirring with a fork. Sprinkle with a generous grinding of pepper. Taste and adjust the seasoning.

Arrosto morto should be sliced to a thickness of about 1cm/½in.

pollo arrosto
roast chicken

Serves 4–6

50g/1¾oz/4 tbsp unsalted butter

1 sprig of fresh rosemary

4–6 fresh sage leaves

1 garlic clove

salt and freshly ground black pepper

*1 organic or free-range chicken, about
    1.5kg/3¼lb*

1 organic or unwaxed lemon, cut in half

2 tbsp olive oil

150ml/5fl oz/²⁄₃ cup dry white wine

When it comes to cooking a whole chicken, pot roasting is more common than oven roasting in Italy.

Put a knob of butter, the herbs, garlic, 1 teaspoon salt and a generous grinding of pepper into the cavity of the bird, then rub it all over with one of the lemon halves and sprinkle with salt and pepper.

Heat half the remaining butter and the olive oil in an oval casserole and brown the chicken on all sides. Pour over the wine, boil briskly for 1 minute and then cook slowly, with the lid slightly askew so that the steam can escape. Turn the chicken over halfway through cooking and add a little boiling water if there is no liquid left at the bottom of the casserole. The chicken should be cooked in about 1¼–1½ hours. Test to see whether it is ready by pricking the thickest part of a thigh: the juice that runs out should be clear.

When cooked, transfer the chicken to a board and cover with foil. Squeeze the juice from the remaining lemon half into the casserole and add 4–5 tablespoons hot water. Boil for 2–3 minutes, stirring constantly and scraping up the cooking residue at the bottom of the pan. Carve the chicken and serve with the cooking juices.

39

arsumà
custard

Ancestor of the more famous ZABAIONE, arsumà
has its origins in Biella, a town in north Piedmont,
where it is still made. Whole eggs are whipped
with sugar and dry white wine and eaten without
any cooking.

Artusi, Pellegrino 1820–1911

The greatest cookery writer of the 19th century.
Artusi was born in Forlimpopoli in Romagna, but
lived in Florence and Viareggio in Tuscany. Apart
from his cookery masterpiece *La Scienza in Cucina
e l'Arte di Mangiar Bene* (Science in the Kitchen
and the Art of Eating Well), he wrote books on
the poets Ugo Foscolo and Giuseppe Giusti.
He was also a keen anthropologist. His cookery
book, which has been the most popular cookery
book in Italy for decades, was first published by
Artusi himself, because no publisher wanted it.
Artusi assumed his readers to have a sound basic
knowledge of cooking, andå his excellent recipes
are full of anecdotes, pertinent hints, regional
folklore and useful information on diet and
nourishment. It is a fascinating book, to be enjoyed
as general reading as much as a cookery book.

asciutto
drained

In a culinary context this word is only used in
connection with pasta, RAVIOLI, GNOCCHI and rice
that is drained of the water or stock in which
it was cooked. Thus what is generally known
as 'pasta' is more properly called *pastasciutta*, to
distinguish it from *pasta in brodo* ('in stock').

Asiago
a cheese

A DOP semi-fat cheese made from cow's milk,
named after the area near Vicenza, in Veneto,
where it originates. The large meadowlands of
this plateau enjoy a mild, dry climate suitable for
the production of a cheese that cannot be made
industrially, as the process requires continuous
care. There are two kinds of asiago. *Asiago da
allevo* is a very hard table cheese which is also
suitable for grating. It is ready for the table after
two months and for grating after 12 to 18 months.
Asiago pressato is a young hard cheese, tangy
but delicate, excellent for the table. It is made
between June and September and matures in about
a month. Both types of cheese are excellent for
cooking. Asiago has been made since the Middle
Ages, but has only been known outside Veneto
since the beginning of the 20th century.

asparago
asparagus

A plant belonging to the lily family, asparagus has
been highly regarded in Italy since Roman times.
Cultivation declined during the Middle Ages, but
flourished again in the early Renaissance. The
first known recipe was written by an anonymous
Tuscan writer in the 14th century: 'Take the
asparagus and boil them. And when they are
cooked put them in a pan with oil, onion, salt,
saffron and with ground spices, or without.'

Asparagus can be boiled or steamed; the
Italian method of cooking them is a combination
of the two. The trimmed spears, tied in bundles,
are put in a special saucepan that has a perforated
liner holding them upright. The butt of the spears
is under water, while the tips are cooked by the
steam rising from the boiling water. Asparagus are
usually eaten cold with olive oil and lemon juice,
or hot with butter. The recipe given here is for

asparagi alla parmigiana, which is the traditional way of serving asparagus in Italy. Asparagus can also be part of a FRITTO MISTO, with the raw asparagus tips coated in batter and deep-fried in oil. They are often used in risotto.

Asparagi di campo – wild asparagus – are still found along sandy roads in central Italy. They are thin and green and very tasty. Contemporary Romans sauté the spears in butter and oil with just a few anchovy fillets. The dish is finished with a handful of chopped parsley and a sprinkling of lemon juice, and served with fried bread. In Umbria wild asparagus are stewed in oil with two or three fresh tomatoes to make a delicate pasta sauce.

[see recipe below]

attorta
a cake

A cake from Umbria, made in the shape of a coiled snake, hence another name for it, *serpe* ('snake'). Most of the sweets and cakes of Umbria are made from simple ingredients, in this case flour, ground almonds, sugar and lemon zest. The same cake is also found in the mountainous regions of Le Marche and Abruzzo.

avanzi
leftovers

Italians are masters at making the best of leftovers. They hardly ever serve the remains of a roast just as it comes from the larder. They add other flavours and make POLPETTE, a RAGÙ for pasta, or a stuffing for RAVIOLI. A POLPETTONE is often made with leftovers from different meats, prosciutto and other ingredients. Cooked in a tomato sauce, it becomes an excellent dish in its own right. Another such is the *bollito rifatto alla genovese*. The leftover boiled beef is cut into pieces and placed on a bed of crumbled crackers moistened with white wine; it is served with a vinaigrette and with capers and garlic. Many vegetables are stuffed with leftover meat that is minced and mixed with béchamel sauce and other ingredients. Courgettes and onions are particularly good stuffed in this way.

FRITTATE and TORTINI are made with leftover pasta, rice or vegetables simply by adding eggs and, usually, Parmesan. Even leftover fish is used up. If fried it is prepared 'in CARPIONE' (a sweet and sour sauce). If it has been cooked in tomato sauce it can be used to dress a dish of pasta, and if it was poached or grilled it can be covered with a thin SALSA VERDE.

asparagi alla parmigiana
asparagus with melted butter and cheese

Serves 4
900g/2lb asparagus
50g/1 ¾oz Parmesan cheese, grated
70g/2½oz/5 tbsp unsalted butter
salt

No pepper is added in this simple traditional recipe from Parma.

Trim the asparagus spears and wash under cold water. Tie them in bundles and steam or boil them until they are thoroughly cooked, not crunchy. Transfer the bundles to an oval dish, remove the string and sprinkle with some of the Parmesan. Keep warm in a low oven. Preheat the grill.

Melt the butter and pour over the asparagus. Sprinkle with the rest of the Parmesan and a little salt. Place under the grill for a few minutes until a light golden crust forms. Serve immediately.

b

babà
a pudding

This sweet is said to have been christened by Stanislas Leczinsky, the deposed king of Poland, who dedicated it to Ali Baba, the hero of one of his favourite stories. In Italy, it was first made in Naples, probably by French chefs employed by the aristocracy.

Babà is made with a sweet yeast dough studded with sultanas, baked in a tall mould with a central hole until a rich golden colour. Removed from the mould, it is then soaked in a syrup strongly laced with rum, thin icing is poured on and shredded almonds sprinkled over. Babà is served with a hot sauce made with sweet wine.

baccalà
salt cod

The repertoire of Italian specialities would be greatly diminished without baccalà, a name that in Venice refers to STOCCAFISSO (stockfish), thus causing endless confusion. The difference between baccalà and stoccafisso is in the curing process, not in the type of fish. Baccalà is cod that has been salted on the ship, then dried on land, and it consists of large chunks or a side of fish only lightly dried. It needs soaking in milk or water for no less than 24 hours. In Italy it is also sold ready-prepared for cooking.

Several regions of Italy offer excellent recipes for baccalà. In Liguria it is cooked with spinach – *baccalà in zimino* – or fried and served with a sauce made from fresh breadcrumbs and chopped garlic. In Tuscany *baccalà alla fiorentina* is pan-fried and stewed in tomato sauce, while in Rome the baccalà is coated in a light batter to which whipped egg white has been added, and then deep-fried. A recipe from Abruzzo combines baccalà with celery, pine nuts, sultanas, black olives and tomatoes. A similar dish is made in Naples, while another Neapolitan recipe adds grilled peppers to the fried fish.

In fact every region has its special recipes for baccalà, and probably every cook has a favourite version. In my home in Milan baccalà was always served on Friday with POLENTA – Friday was a *giorno di magro* (meatless day) then – either 'in UMIDO', stewed in tomato sauce, or 'in BIANCO', a good recipe in which the floured pieces of baccalà are sautéed in butter with lots of onion and then cooked in milk laced with MARSALA. Nowadays baccalà is cooked far less at home because of its very high price, but it still appears in the menus of traditional trattorie.

baci
chocolates

Literally, 'kisses'. These very popular chocolates, made by the firm of Perugina, were launched after World War II and have been an outstanding success. They are more or less spherical, about two-thirds of the size of a golf ball, and coated with dark chocolate. Inside, they are filled with chopped hazelnut and chocolate paste, with a whole hazelnut protruding at the top. Baci are individually wrapped in silver foil printed in blue, and inside the wrapping, on tissue paper, is an epigram, always on the theme of love.

42

baci di dama
lady's kisses

Makes about 35–40

140g/5oz/1 cup blanched almonds

140g/5oz/scant ¾ cup caster (superfine) sugar

140g/5oz/generous ½ cup unsalted butter, at room temperature, plus extra for greasing

1 tsp pure vanilla extract

a pinch of salt

140g/5oz/generous 1 cup Italian 00 flour

175g/6oz dark chocolate (minimum 70% cocoa solids)

The name of these almond and chocolate biscuits comes from their shape, which suggests the pouting of a lady's lips. They are a speciality of Tortona, a town in southern Piedmont, but they are now made commercially throughout Italy.

Preheat the oven to 180°C/350°F/Gas Mark 4. Butter a baking sheet.

Put the almonds on a small baking sheet and place in the oven for 5 minutes to toast them lightly, which will bring out the flavour.

Put the almonds in a food processor. Add 1–2 tablespoons of the sugar and process to a powder. Add the remaining sugar, butter, vanilla and salt and process until the mixture is very creamy. Transfer to a bowl.

Sift the flour over the almond mixture. Mix in the flour very thoroughly – hands are the best tools here. Break off pieces of the dough the size of cherries, and roll them into balls. Place them on the buttered baking sheet, about 2cm/¾in apart. Bake for 15 minutes, or until golden brown. Leave to cool and firm up on the baking sheet and then transfer to a wire rack to cool completely.

Melt the chocolate in a bain-marie or microwave oven. When the biscuits are cold, spread a little melted chocolate over the flat side of one biscuit then stick the flat side of another similar-sized biscuit to it – like a sandwich. Repeat with the remaining almond biscuits.

43

bagna caôda
hot garlic and anchovy dip

Serves 6–8

50g/1¾oz/4 tbsp unsalted butter

4 garlic cloves, very finely sliced

5 salted anchovies, boned and rinsed,
    or 10 canned or bottled anchovy
    fillets, drained

200ml/7fl oz/generous ¾ cup extra
    virgin olive oil, preferably Ligurian or
    another mild variety

Bagna caôda is one of the most popular of Piedmontese ANTIPASTI. The name means 'hot bath', since this sauce is kept hot when it's at the table, usually in an earthenware pot over a spirit flame. The vegetables to dip into it can be anything seasonal. Traditional choices include raw peppers, cardoons, cabbage, celery and fennel. In some localities boiled vegetables such as onions, carrots, potatoes and turnips are used, when cold. Then, when there is only a little of the sauce left, eggs are broken into it and scrambled. It is a very old sauce, already popular in the 16th century and then, as now, a convivial dish for festive occasions, shared by everyone at the table.

Melt the butter in a small deep earthenware pot or a very heavy-bottomed saucepan over the lowest possible heat. As soon as the butter has melted, add the garlic and sauté for a few seconds. The garlic should not colour.

Add the anchovies to the pot and pour in the olive oil very gradually, stirring the whole time. Cook for about 10 minutes, always on the lowest possible heat and stirring constantly. The dip is ready to serve when all the ingredients are well blended and smooth.

bagnet rosso
Piedmontese tomato sauce

Enough for 6 servings

700g/1lb 9oz ripe fresh tomatoes, peeled
    and chopped

1 small onion, 1 carrot and 1 celery
    stalk, thickly sliced

2 garlic cloves

2 fresh sage leaves, torn, and a few fresh
    marjoram leaves

1 small sprig of fresh rosemary

a small bunch of fresh flat-leaf parsley

1 small dried red chilli

1 tsp tomato puree

salt

7 tbsp wine vinegar

1 tbsp sugar

a pinch of ground cinnamon

This is one of the two sauces always served in Piedmont BOLLITO MISTO (boiled meats). The other sauce is the *bagnet verd* or SALSA VERDE (green sauce).

Put the tomatoes, onion, carrot, celery, garlic, herbs, chilli, tomato puree and salt in a saucepan and cook over a very low heat for 30 minutes. Puree through a food mill or sieve and return to the pan.

Mix in the vinegar, sugar and cinnamon and cook over a low heat for about 20 minutes, until the sauce is thick. Taste and adjust the seasoning. Serve warm or cold.

bagoss
a cheese

In Lombardy many cheeses, such as this one, are still farm-produced. Bagoss is made in the Valle del Caffaro, an Alpine valley, from partially skimmed cow's milk. It is a hard cheese, similar to GRANA, but with a stronger and slightly bitter taste due to the aromatic herbs that grow in the pastures where the cattle feed. It is grated and used in cooking, or, when young, it is cut in slices and grilled.

baicoli
biscuits

The most popular of Venetian biscuits, baicoli are made with flour, butter, sugar, egg white and fresh yeast. The dough is baked in a roll about 30cm/12in long and then set aside for 48 hours. The roll is cut into thin slices and the slices are baked again.

Baicoli are sold in tins of a traditional design, which include wording in praise of the biscuits in Venetian dialect. The Venetians like to dip them in sweet white wine, in hot chocolate or in ZABAIONE.

barba di frate
a green vegetable

The name of this small plant, meaning 'friar's beard', derives from its appearance – like a long and very thick bunch of chives. It grows wild wherever the soil is damp and sandy. It is cultivated in central Italy, where it is also called *agretti*. Barba di frate tastes like samphire and, when it is very young, is eaten raw in salad. When older it is boiled, like spinach, and either dressed with olive oil and lemon juice or sautéed in olive oil with garlic. It is excellent with fish and good in a FRITTATA, having been first sautéed in butter and/or oil with a little garlic.

Basilicata

This small region, also known by its Latin name of Lucania, is the poorest in Italy. Its food reflects its poverty. The pig is the king of the table in all poor homes and a pig is raised by nearly every family. On the day it is killed, a great feast takes place. The pig, lovingly cared for over the previous year, is now enjoyed in all its different forms: SALSICCE, SALAMI, CAPOCOLLO, prosciutto and lard, which, with olive oil, is the basic fat of the local cooking.

The Lucani are famous for their pig products, including a sausage known as *pezzenta*. Pezzenta means 'miserably poor' in Italian and this sausage is so called because it is made from all the cheapest parts of the pig, sometimes even mixed with odd bits of sheep and goat. It is highly flavoured with chilli. I tasted it once when I was in Matera with a group of American journalists,

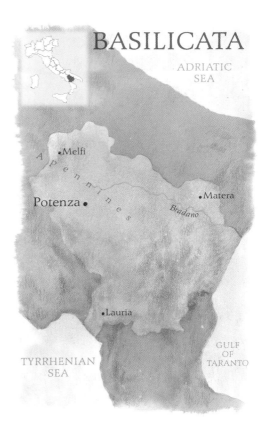

BASILICATA

ADRIATIC SEA

Melfi

Potenza

Matera

Bradano

Apennines

Lauria

TYRRHENIAN SEA

GULF OF TARANTO

some of whom were rather horrified by my daring. I loved it, although I had to chew bread for some 5 minutes afterwards to try to extinguish the fire in my mouth. But of all these, the sausage that gave fame to the region is the LUGANEGA, whose name implies its origin, Lucania, and which dates from Roman times: it is mentioned in APICIUS' *De Re Coquinaria*.

Lamb, as in all southern Italy, is the other popular meat, usually cooked long and slow, cut into small pieces, either with potatoes or with *cardoncelli*, the local mushrooms, and always highly flavoured with chilli, the most popular spice in the region's cuisine. Suffice to say that chilli has five names in the local dialect, the most frequently used being *il forte* – 'the strong one' – and that's that.

Bread is made with durum wheat flour and the traditional shape, called *panella*, can be as large as a cartwheel. The women used to make it once a week and bring it to the baker to cook, since very few households had even the most primitive outdoor oven. Even today bread is seldom made at home, although pasta is, in all its many different shapes. LASAGNE, STRASCINARI, *fusilli* and CAVATIEDDI are all made with durum wheat flour and water, a very difficult dough to knead and stretch. Some of these shapes are achieved by using special wooden boards, called *cavarole*. The traditional dressing for pasta is the local RAGÙ, which contains small bits of pork or sheep meat called *'ntruppic*, meaning 'obstacles'. The final touch is given by chilli fried in olive oil and a very generous grating of salted hard RICOTTA, the local speciality.

Vegetables make handsome dishes in their own right, such as *ciammotta*, a mixed dish of fried vegetables, and the interesting *mandorlata di peperoni*,

peperoni in agrodolce
sweet and sour fried peppers

Serves 3–4
vegetable oil, for frying
4 large peppers (2 yellow, 2 red),
   deseeded and cut into vertical strips
   about 2–3cm/1in wide
salt and freshly ground black pepper
3 tbsp red wine vinegar
1½ tbsp soft brown sugar

The original recipe for this dish from Basilicata comes from the book *I Sapori del Sud* by Mariano and Rita Pane. The vinegar must be top quality. The peppers are best left for at least 24 hours before serving.

Pour enough vegetable oil into a wok or deep frying pan to come about 2.5cm/1in up the side of the pan. (I use a wok because it is more economical, since I never reuse oil.) Heat the oil over a high heat until it is very hot, but not smoking, then slide in as many strips of peppers as will fit loosely in the pan and fry them on both sides until tinged a light golden brown. Fry the peppers in two or three batches, adding a little more oil if necessary.

Transfer the peppers to a board or a plate lined with kitchen paper. I use tongs for this job, because I find them the best tool to let the oil drip back into the pan. Pat the peppers with kitchen paper to absorb excess oil and then lay them on a serving dish. Sprinkle with salt and pepper.

Put the vinegar and sugar in a small pan over a gentle heat. When the sugar has dissolved, pour the mixture over the peppers and let the dish cool completely. Serve at room temperature.

combining peppers with almonds. Pulses (legumes) are also important, and they are prepared in many imaginative ways, of which *lagane e lenticchie* (wide TAGLIATELLE and lentils) is the oldest.

The fish dishes from the two stretches of coast, the Ionian and the Tyrrhenian, are the same as in Puglia and Calabria respectively. But the Lucani created their own special recipe for BACCALÀ, baked salt cod layered with potatoes, dressed with olive oil, oregano, garlic and the ubiquitous chilli. *Scapice*, fried anchovies or sardines flavoured with mint, is one of many regional variants of SCAPECE.

BURRATA, BURRINI and mozzarella are the local cow's milk cheeses.

Many of the puddings are rich with almonds. Particularly interesting are PANZAROTTI – sweet ravioli filled with pureed chickpeas flavoured with chocolate, sugar and cinnamon.

[see recipe on facing page]

basilico
basil

A native of India, basil was known to the ancient Greeks and the Romans and flourished wherever it could find warmth, sun and sea breezes. In Boccaccio's *Decameron*, basil is the symbol of love when the noble Lisabetta, whose brothers have murdered her plebeian lover, buries the lover's head in a pot of basil, a story that is taken up some 400 years later by Keats in his poem 'Isabella, or the Pot of Basil'. During the Renaissance basil is mentioned by PLATINA, who suggested using it in moderation. It was popular all over Italy, often kept in pots on window sills, as it appears in some Renaissance paintings.

For hundreds of years, basil had been used around the Italian coast in salads, with fish and in tomato sauces. In the 18th century, CORRADO is the first cookery writer to mention the use of basil to dress stewed meat and to flavour vegetable soups. ARTUSI adds basil to his tomato sauce which, he writes, is 'good with boiled beef and it is excellent to make very pleasant a dish of pasta dressed with butter and cheese, or a risotto'.

Basil gained a wider fame when PESTO crossed the borders of Liguria to become one of the favourite pasta sauces of the world. But that didn't happen until well after World War II. Apart from pesto and in tomato sauces, basil also gives an extra dimension to a MINESTRONE or a vegetable soup and it makes a delicious salad with tomatoes and mozzarella, insalata CAPRESE.

There are many varieties of basil, including: the Genovese, with a very strong yet sweet flavour; the Napoletano, with rather crinkly leaves and a minty aroma; the Fine Verde Compatto, with very small leaves and a more delicate scent; and the Mammoth, with very big leaves, the best for drying. However, basil does not dry well and its flavour changes considerably. The best way to preserve basil is to layer the leaves with olive oil in a sterilized jar, or to freeze the leaves.

batteria di cucina
kitchen equipment

An old country kitchen is the best place to see the variety of utensils that come under this heading. What you would see, however, is nothing compared to what was considered necessary in a grand Renaissance house. Bartolomeo SCAPPI's list of implements needed in a well-equipped kitchen included 120 items, from the largest cauldron to the various types of copper saucepan, strainers, knives etc. Seven different sizes of skewer are listed, seven ladles and slotted spoons of various shapes for different uses. This does not include the moulds needed by chefs and confectioners.

Today's batteria di cucina, modest by comparison, might consist of the following items. Two or three earthenware pots of the kind you can also put directly on a flame, which are certainly the best pots for cooking RAGÙ, stew and pulses.

Another receptacle that we consider essential is a sauté pan with a well-fitting lid in two different sizes, plus the usual frying pans and saucepans and casseroles for pot-roasting and stews. A pot that I find invaluable in any kitchen is the *bollitore del latte*, a tall and narrow saucepan in which we heat milk. Being tall, it stops, or at least delays, the boiling milk from overflowing, thus saving you from that most boring job of cleaning all around the hob. The other essentials are a tall and narrow pot, just like a metal top hat, for cooking pasta, and a wide, deep, round, heavy-bottomed saucepan for risotto.

An Italian kitchen is often embellished by an array of copper receptacles: pans, moulds, rings and a large PAIOLO for making POLENTA. The usual selection of knives includes a heavy, flat-bladed one for cutting TAGLIATELLE and a MEZZALUNA for chopping vegetables and meats. A long MATTARELLO for rolling out the pasta dough will be hanging in the corner. Also considered necessary are a food mill, a deep slotted spoon for retrieving GNOCCHI and RAVIOLI, a large grater for Parmesan and a small one for lemon rind and nutmeg, plus a large colander with two handles, and feet, to stand in the sink when draining pasta. Most kitchens will have a pair or two of tongs, one with a comb-like end for lifting spaghetti. Another implement to be found in most kitchens is the BATTICARNE to pound the veal for SCALOPPINE. A MORTAIO with its pestle is a utensil few Italian cooks would be without. A food processor would never be regarded as an adequate alternative.

Ovenproof dishes, oven pans and baking sheets are not as numerous, since Italian cooking is not particularly strong in this area. The batteria di cucina also includes all the crockery, glasses and bowls for the presentation of food.

batticarne
meat pounder

This utensil, which is found in most Italian kitchens, is necessary for pounding veal slices or other meat cuts in the preparation of escalopes, COTOLETTE and other special dishes. A batticarne consists of a thick, heavy metal disc of about 7.5cm/3in diameter, with a handle fixed to the centre.

battuto
finely chopped vegetables and herbs

This is the first step in the making of a great number of Italian dishes. Battuto, which means beaten, is a mixture of PANCETTA or LARDO (pork back fat), onion and/or garlic. Celery, carrots and parsley are optional extras in some recipes. These ingredients are very finely chopped, so as to appear nearly pounded, and they are then gently sautéed in a little olive oil. This transforms a battuto into a SOFFRITTO. Battuto is sometimes used *a crudo*, which means it is added to the dish without being previously sautéed.

bavette
a pasta

Another name for LINGUINE.

beccaccia
woodcock

This migratory bird is shot in the winter in the woods of central and southern Italy and in Sicily. Woodcock are hung unplucked for three or four days, and when plucked they may be cooked undrawn, as with all small birds, or drawn, as is more customary nowadays.

Being such rare game, there are not many Italian recipes for woodcock. In Arezzo they

RIGHT: Using a *mezzaluna* to prepare *battuto*

are drawn and stuffed with their chopped entrails mixed with stewed and boned thrushes, PANCETTA, black truffle and VIN SANTO. The bird is then roasted in the oven or on the spit. In Basilicata the drawn woodcock is cooked in a pot with a little white wine. The finely chopped entrails are sautéed with capers and salted anchovies in olive oil, moistened with MARSALA and spread on grilled bread. The simpler method, and perhaps the most successful, is to roast a drawn bird wrapped in pancetta or prosciutto. The liver and heart are mashed in the cooking juices with some anchovy fillets.

beccaccino
snipe

The snipe is one of the most difficult birds to shoot because of the sudden start of its flight. In Italy it appears between September and November, and February and April. There is disagreement as to whether snipe should be cooked drawn or undrawn. If the weather is warm and damp, they must be drawn. Snipe are roasted in the oven or on the spit, or pot-roasted, and always served on a crouton of white bread.

Bel Paese
a cheese

This cheese was christened by its creator, Egidio Galbani. Bel Paese, meaning 'beautiful country', was the title of a children's geography book written by Antonio Stoppani, a close friend of the Galbani family. It is Stoppani's portrait, as well as a map of part of Italy, that appears on the familiar wrapper. Galbani began to manufacture Bel Paese in 1906 on his return from a voyage through France, where he learnt the secret of making Port Salut, a not dissimilar cheese. Bel Paese is a mild, soft and creamy table cheese and, as it melts easily, it is also good for cooking.

bergamotto
bergamot

This citrus fruit, similar to a large lemon, is cultivated for its essence, which is the basis of eau-de-Cologne. It was a Lombard, Giovanni Farina, who took the formula of the scent to Cologne, which then gave it its name. Bergamots grow only in Calabria, thus giving that poor southern region its biggest income. The Calabresi make a delicious marmalade with bergamots; unfortunately it is impossible to find on the market. When I went to Calabria some years ago I was given two jars of this marmalade. I ate one jar spoonful by spoonful but when I went to start the second, to my great dismay, I found it empty. My daughter Julia had decided she liked it too.

besciamella
béchamel sauce

A classic French sauce, although some food historians say it has been made in Italy for centuries, and by a simpler method than the French béchamel. Besciamella is an integral part of most oven-baked pasta dishes. It is also used with vegetables for gratin dishes or for stuffing, as well as for binding ingredients in POLPETTE and CROCCHETTE.

bianchetti
anchovy or sardine larvae

Bianchetti are also called *gianchetti* in Liguria, and many other names in the various dialects. They look like a whitish grey mass and can be bought boiled and dressed with olive oil and lemon juice from delicatessens. They are also available uncooked in good fishmongers, in which case they must not have been out of the sea any longer than a day, and should be boiled in sea water.

bianco, in
'in the white state'

'In bianco' is a phrase used to describe food that has been prepared simply by boiling and then dressing with butter or oil, such as *riso in bianco*, where the boiled rice is dressed with butter and grated Parmesan. The expression is also applied to dishes that are more usually served 'coloured', for example with a tomato sauce. Thus, *spaghetti alle vongole*, when served without a tomato sauce, is called *spaghetti alle vongole in bianco*. Food prepared in bianco is particularly light and digestible and is therefore usually associated with people who are convalescing or on a diet.

bietola
leaf beet, Swiss chard

This green vegetable, *Beta vulgaris*, is similar to the beetroot but it is grown for its leaves. Some varieties have a slender green stem, others a broad silvery white, orange or purple stalk; the latter are also called COSTE (Swiss chard). The green beets are cooked in the same way as spinach. A recipe from Rome suggests cooking the raw *bietole* in a tomato sauce. A recipe from Liguria uses beet for one of the delicious local pies: the fried beet and onion are mixed with cream cheese and baked within two sheet of pastry.

bignè
profiteroles

The word is the Italianization of the French *beignet*, but in Italy these pastries are not fried. Bignè are made with choux pastry, baked and filled with CREMA PASTICCERA, chocolate custard or Chantilly cream – similar to profiteroles. They are seldom made at home but are bought in PASTICCERIE.

There are a few savoury bignè, the most common being those filled with cheeses.

bigoli
a pasta

The Venetian name for thick spaghetti made (sometimes by hand) by pressing pasta dough through a small tool called a *bigolaro*. The dough is made with flour (traditionally wholewheat), butter and eggs – which may be duck eggs. Bigoli are dressed with an anchovy and onion sauce, *bigoli in salsa*, or a sauce made with onion and mashed-up duck giblets, *bigoli all'anatra*.

biova
bread

Large loaf of bread, round in the centre but coming to a point at the ends. It is a typical Piedmontese loaf, highly leavened so that the inside is almost hollow.

biovetta
bread roll

A small version of the *biova*, this roll is a favourite in northern Italy. It has a crusty outside and near-hollow inside.

biroldo
a sausage

A fresh blood sausage from Tuscany, which must be eaten within a week of being made. In Pistoia two kinds of biroldo are made, a sweet one with pig's blood, flavoured with sultanas and pine nuts, and a savoury one made with calf's blood, cheese and pork meat.

bisato
eel

The name in Venetian dialect for the eel (otherwise ANGUILLA), which is very popular in

51

Venice. Many recipes for eel are of Venetian origin, such as the *Bisato in tecia*, where the cut-up eel, first marinated in vinegar for a few hours, is fried and then stewed in tomato sauce and served with polenta.

biscotto
biscuit, cookie

Biscotto (literally, 'cooked twice') is a biscuit, but the word is also occasionally used to describe an unleavened cake or bread, *pan biscotto*. Biscotti are sweet unless otherwise specified. Many towns and regions have their own particular biscuits, often made for feast days or other special occasions.

Biscotti began to appear at the table in various forms during the 16th century, usually served with fruit, jellies and other sweet things at the beginning of a meal. It was only in the 19th century that they began to be produced commercially and therefore became widely popular at the time when drinking coffee and chocolate also became fashionable. Biscotti are still served with these drinks, as well as with the less common tea. Hard biscuits are also eaten, as in the past, with sweet wines into which they are dunked. Some biscuits are also served as an accompaniment to ice creams, mousses or custards.

bistecca
steak

A phonetic Italian rendition of 'beefsteak'. A bisteccca is a thick slice of beef cut from the fillet or rump, but it can also mean a chop (as in *bistecca alla fiorentina*), a thin slice of beef, a slice or chop of veal, or a pork steak. In these cases, however, the kind of steak would be specified, for example, *bistecca di vitello* or *di maiale*. A classic recipe is *bistecca all'*ARRABBIATA, a thin slice of beef sautéed in oil and flavoured with plenty of chilli.

Bitto
a cheese

One of the best Italian cow's milk cheeses, Bitto is a DOP cheese, made in Valtellina, a valley between Lake Como and St Moritz in Switzerland, whose majestic beauty has captured the imagination of many people, from Leonardo da Vinci to me, if I dare to put myself in such company. I was there, as a guest of the region, some time in the 1990s, and had a most interesting and enjoyable week discovering local food and tasting the best local products, such as this cheese. I was taken up into the mountains where Bitto is made from the strongly aromatic milk of the wiry and agile cows that graze there during the summer months. We went to visit a shepherd in his hut. There on the earth floor were three or four large shallow vessels full of milk, ready to be transformed into Bitto. I looked down and saw a little shrew quietly lapping at the milk, its two front paws delicately poised on the brim of the vessel. I bought a packet of Bitto, had it at the hotel for supper, thought of the little shrew and never enjoyed a cheese so much.

Bitto is usually eaten fresh, but it is also aged in situ and used for grating on the local pasta dish called PIZZOCHERI, in *polenta taragna* (the local POLENTA made with half maize and half buckwheat), and in *sciatt*, fritters made with buckwheat and flavoured with GRAPPA.

bocconcini
'little mouthful'

Bocconcini means 'little mouthful' and refers to various dishes, of which the most popular are: *bocconcini di vitello*, small chunks of veal sautéed in butter and finished off in white wine and tomato sauce; *bocconcini di ricotta*, small fried balls of egg-coated and breaded flavoured ricotta; and *bocconcini modenesi*, consisting of two small rounds of crustless white bread made into sandwiches containing prosciutto, sliced cheese and slivers of white truffle, which are then coated in flour and egg, and fried.

Bocconcini are also small balls of mozzarella, sold in bags.

boeri
chocolates

Literally, Boers. Round chocolates containing a cherry surrounded by some of the spirit in which it has been preserved. When you bite into the hard chocolate shell, your mouth is suddenly filled with the taste of the liqueur, which combines deliciously with the flavour of the chocolate.

bollito misto
boiled meats

The particular mixture of meats in this well-known dish varies with the locality. In Piedmont and Lombardy beef is the main ingredient, while in Emilia-Romagna pork products – COTECHINO and ZAMPONE – take first place. A classic bollito misto should include beef, veal, chicken, tongue, a cotechino and half a calf's head. The meats are lowered into boiling water at different times, according to how long they take to cook.

Bollito misto is made in large quantities for at least eight people. Restaurants that offer bollito misto (and only the best still do) serve it on special trolleys with the meats in different compartments full of piping hot stock. The meat is removed from the stock and carved especially for each customer, so that it never gets dry.

It is accompanied by different sauces, depending on the locality. The two most common are SALSA VERDE and BAGNET ROSS, or salsa rossa (a tomato sauce, sometimes sweet and sour). The best-known bollito, the Piedmontese gran bui, is served with at least three sauces, the green and red, as above, plus saussa d'avie (a delicious sauce made with honey, walnuts and enough mustard

to give the sauce the kick it needs to be served with meat). In Veneto bollito is accompanied by PEVERADA, while in Lombardy a bowl brimming with MOSTARDA di Cremona is put on the table together with salsa verde.

bolognese, alla

This definition nowadays refers to many dishes from Emilia-Romagna, rather than only Bologna. The best known are CIAMBELLA, FRITTO MISTO, LASAGNE, RAGÙ, TAGLIATELLE, TORTELLINI.

bomba
savoury or dessert

Literally, 'bomb'. In the kitchen there are two sorts of bombe, savoury and sweet. The savoury is the bomba di riso, a speciality of Piacenza in Emilia, made with half-cooked risotto dressed with the juices of two braised pigeons. The risotto is pressed around the side of a dome-shaped mould, the centre is filled with the boned pigeons and other ingredients such as sweetbread, truffles, peas and mushrooms, and then the whole thing is baked. Similar dishes are made in Naples, called SARTÙ, and in Piedmont, goffa.

The sweet bombe are the bomba gelata and the bomba di mascarpone. The first consists of different ice creams lining the mould in concentric layers. The centre is filled with whipped cream studded with almond praline, bits of chocolate and candied fruits. The bomba di mascarpone looks like a dome-shaped cake. The cake, a shell of sweet yeast dough, is filled with MASCARPONE enriched by toasted hazelnuts, chocolate and candied fruit.

bomboloni
doughnut

Bomboloni, a Tuscan speciality, are ring-shaped doughnuts without jam. They are made with a yeast and egg dough, fried and sprinkled with sugar, similar to KRAPFEN. There was nothing we loved more, as children, than to sink our teeth into a soft, light bombolone after a swim. The bombolone seller used to walk down the beach carrying a huge tray strapped round his shoulders with a mountain of bomboloni on top. We all ran around him and queued patiently for our turn. I have been told that Mr Bombolone is still walking along the beaches of Tuscany and his bomboloni are still the children's delights. Bomboloni are now popular in many regions.

bônet
a pudding

The name of this Piedmontese pudding comes from the bonnet-shaped copper mould in which it is cooked. Bônet is made with crushed AMARETTI, eggs, sugar, milk, cocoa and rum, and is cooked in a bain-marie in the oven.

Boni, Ada
1881–1973

The most important cookery writer of the 20th century, Ada Boni was more than a writer of recipes, she was also a real teacher and this is the strength of her books. *Il Talismano della Felicità*, her most famous book, contains over 1,000 recipes and is the most comprehensive Italian cookery book; it examines all methods of preparation, from the most basic to the very elaborate. Ada Boni leads the cook step by step through her method in a very informative and clear prose. Most, if not all, Italian cooks value this book above all others.

boraggine
borage

A sturdy annual, native to the Mediterranean, which grows wild on the hillsides close to the sea.

Ligurian women can still be seen in the spring climbing the hills to collect the PREBOGGION, a mixture of different herbs, which is used to make PANSÔTI. Borage is necessary in the pansôti, because of its distinctive taste, somewhat reminiscent of cucumber. I often add some borage flowers to a bowl of salad, not only as a decoration but also for their flavour.

borlotti

see FAGIOLI

boscaiola, alla
cooking style

The term means 'in the woodland style'. It does not refer to any specific preparation, but is used, especially on restaurant menus, for dishes that contain mushrooms, either wild or cultivated, and tomato sauce.

bottarga
dried roe of grey mullet or tuna

Bottarga is an artisanal product, mostly made in Sardinia, which is sold all over Italy and abroad in the best delicatessens. The roe of the grey mullet, removed immediately after the fish is caught, is pressed hard and then salted and dried in the sun. It resembles a square sausage of a lovely brown colour. This delicate preparation is served as an ANTIPASTO, cut into thin slices and marinated in olive oil and lemon juice. It is also grated to make an excellent pasta sauce. A recipe from Oristano, where the fattest grey mullet are caught, suggests sautéeing bottarga in olive oil and then mixing cooked spaghetti into it.

Bottarga can also be made from tuna roe; this has a grey colour and a stronger, saltier flavour and is made mainly in Sicily.

bovolo
snail

The Venetian dialect word for snails is *bovoli*. The small snails served in Venice as an ANTIPASTO are known as *bovoletti*.

Bovolo is also the name of a bread made in Venice in the shape of a snail.

Bra
a cheese

A highly valued cheese of DOP status made in the province of Cuneo in Piedmont, Bra is made from cow's milk, sometimes with the addition of ewe's or goat's milk. There are two kinds of Bra: a fresh semi-soft cheese, aged for 45 days, and a hard cheese aged for at least 6 months. It has a very full but delicate flavour when young and is quite strong and pungent when mature.

brace, alla
barbecue

This oldest method of cooking, and also the most modern, is used for sausages, meats, fish, peppers, aubergines, and all other things that can be cooked on embers. It is also the method for making the popular BRUSCHETTA.

braciola
a cut of meat

As so often with Italian culinary terms, this word is used in different regions to describe different kinds, or cuts, of meat. In most regions a braciola is a chop or a steak of various animals, usually cooked *alla* BRACE (grilled), hence its name.

However, in southern Italy a braciola is a dish in which a slice of meat is covered with various ingredients, then rolled up, tied and cooked. In *braciola Napoletana* the stuffing consists of chopped prosciutto, sultanas and pine nuts, and the rolled pork is cooked for a long time in white wine. In Puglia some of the cooking juices, made with tomato puree and red wine, are used to dress pasta as a first course, while the braciole are served as a second course – traditionally never together.

Braciola can also refer to a steak of a large fish, such as swordfish.

branzino or spigola
sea bass

This fish is one of the most highly prized, with firm white flesh and no lateral bones. Sea bass are now extensively farmed in Puglia and in the Po delta. The farmed fish is recognizable not only by its price but also by its colour, which does not show the shimmering shades of the wild species – from grey-black on the back to pale silver at the sides. All farmed fish come more or less in the same size, 250–350g/9–12oz, which is what most restaurants want per portion. As with farmed salmon, it is inferior in taste and texture to the wild fish.

As with all good fish, the simplest method of cooking is the best. Small bass are grilled, while the bigger fish are boiled in a court bouillon and served with lemon juice and olive oil. Although this is the best dressing, more elaborate sauces are sometimes offered. Branzino is also good boned and stuffed, wrapped in foil and gently baked. The usual stuffing is seafood, but I have come across a very interesting recipe in which the sea bass, boned from the back, is stuffed with calf sweetbreads and kidneys, prosciutto, Swiss chard, truffles and spices. It is cooked in meat juices and served with veal juices. Sea bass is often roasted in the oven, as in the following recipe.

[see recipe overleaf]

55

spigola al forno
baked sea bass

Serves 6

1 garlic clove, chopped

lots of fresh herbs (rosemary, thyme and
    marjoram are all suitable), chopped

lots of fresh flat-leaf parsley, chopped

1 sea bass, about 1.5kg/3¼lb, scaled
    and cleaned

salt

1 tbsp dried breadcrumbs

1 tsp lemon juice

about 150ml/5fl oz/⅔ cup olive oil

This recipe comes from *Mediterranean Seafood* by Alan Davidson. In his introduction he writes, 'Success depends on having in the first place a really fresh fish.'

Preheat the oven to 200°C/400°F/Gas Mark 6. Oil a shallow ovenproof dish.

Put the garlic, herbs and parsley into the cavity and gills of the fish. Place the fish in the oiled dish, salt it lightly and sprinkle with breadcrumbs. Beat the lemon juice into the olive oil and and pour over the fish. Cook for 25–30 minutes and serve hot.

brasato alla lombarda
beef braised with vegetables and spices

Serves 6

2 tbsp vegetable oil

1kg/2¼lb boneless braising beef in one
    piece, such as silverside or chuck
    steak, neatly tied

1 large onion, quartered

2 carrots, cut into big chunks

2 celery stalks, cut into pieces

2 bay leaves

2 cloves

a generous grating of nutmeg

½ tsp ground cinnamon

50g/1¾oz/4 tbsp unsalted butter

1 tbsp olive oil

200ml/7fl oz/generous ¾ cup red wine

7 tbsp strong meat stock (page 61),
    chicken stock or ¼ bouillon cube
    dissolved in 7 tbsp water

salt and freshly ground black pepper

This BRASATO is spiced with what used to be called the four Lombard spices: cloves, cinnamon, pepper and nutmeg.

Preheat the oven to 150°C/300°F/Gas Mark 2.

Heat the vegetable oil in a frying pan. When it is hot, brown the meat very well on all sides. Transfer the meat to a plate.

In a casserole with a tight-fitting lid, put the onion, carrots, celery, bay leaves, cloves, nutmeg, cinnamon, butter and olive oil. Place the meat on top.

Put the frying pan back on the heat, pour in the wine and boil briskly for 20 seconds, scraping the bottom of the pan with a spoon. Pour the contents of the pan over the meat and vegetables and add the stock and salt and pepper. Cover the casserole with foil and place the lid on tightly.

Cook in the oven for about 3 hours, turning the meat over every 30 minutes. The meat is cooked when it can be pricked easily with a fork. Transfer to a board and leave it to cool a little.

Skim the fat from the cooking liquid and discard the bay leaves. Puree the sauce using a food processor or food mill, then taste and adjust the seasoning and keep warm. Cut and pull off the string. Carve the meat into 1cm/½in slices and arrange them on a heated dish. Cover with some of the sauce and serve the rest separately.

RIGHT: Brasato alla lombarda

brasato
braised beef

A boneless joint of beef cooked very slowly in wine and stock, brasato is a classic dish from the northern regions of Italy, which can be prepared in many ways. What characterizes a brasato is that the piece of beef is first browned in hot fat, and then cooked very slowly for a long time. In some recipes, the joint is first larded and marinated in wine, to which onions, carrots, celery, herbs and spices may be added. Brasato used to be served on Sundays and important occasions in northern Italian homes.

The best-known recipes for brasato are from Piedmont, the joint of local beef being cooked in Barolo or Dolcetto wine. Another Piedmontese recipe uses mustard powder, vinegar, anchovy fillets and garlic, but no wine.

Brasato is also used as an adjective: a fish can be brasato, as can a joint of pork, either directly over the heat or in the oven, very slowly and tightly covered. The recipe given here is from Lombardy and it is a dish often made in my home in Milan.

[see recipe on page 56]

bresaola
cured beef

Raw fillet of beef that has been cured in salt and then air-dried for 2 to 3 months. It is a speciality of Valtellina, an Alpine valley in Lombardy, where bresaola is always served, thinly sliced, as an ANTIPASTO at important dinners. Its taste is similar to prosciutto but a little sharper. If young, bresaola is eaten as it is; if mature it is dressed at the very last minute with a little olive oil, a few drops of lemon juice and freshly ground black pepper. It should be eaten within a few hours of being sliced, otherwise it will become leathery.

brigidini
biscuits

Many orders of nuns in Italy have added to the repertoire of delicious confectionery. Brigidini were first made in the convent of St Brigida in Pistoia, Tuscany. They are very thin biscuits made with flour, sugar and eggs, flavoured with aniseed and cooked in waffle irons, usually in the open air.

broccoli
broccoli

There are three common varieties of broccoli: *precocissima di Napoli* – very early broccoli from Naples; *precoce calabrese* – early broccoli from Calabria; and *tardiva d'inverno* – the winter latecomer. Also from Calabria is a dark purple variety, *broccoli neri*.

All the recipes for broccoli come from the south. It is usually blanched very briefly and then sautéed in olive oil, garlic and chilli. Fried breadcrumbs and pecorino cheese are often added.

A recipe from Calabria puts all these ingredients in layers in an ovenproof dish, and this is baked for 30 minutes in a hot oven. Another dish from Calabria is *vruoccolata*, made with half a pig's head, previously boiled and boned, purple broccoli, grated pecorino, olive oil and lots of pepper, baked in layers in an earthenware dish. Broccoli is also delicious with pasta.

It should be noted that broccoli is often called *cavolfiore* in southern Italy, a word that elsewhere means cauliflower. Such a confusion of names between one region and another is frequent in Italy. See also CIME DI RAPA.

[see recipe on page 60]

brodettato
cooking style

A joint of lamb or kid – or sometimes rabbit – first cooked in white wine, to which egg yolks, lemon juice and pecorino cheese are added at the end. It is a dish of central Italy.

brodetto
fish soup

A fish soup made all down the coast of the Adriatic, from Venice to Puglia. There are as many variations as there are ports, but the common theme is the large assortment of fish that go into the making of it. These include red and grey mullet, squid, mackerel, sole, rascasse, sea bass, dogfish, monkfish and cuttlefish. The fish, usually with their heads on, are cut into large chunks and cooked in winey stock flavoured with vegetables.

The traditional brodetto of Venice does not contain tomatoes; the brodetto in Romagna is flavoured with vinegar; the *brodetto marchigiano* – from Le Marche – has saffron added halfway through the cooking, while in Abruzzo this is replaced by a good amount of chilli (see recipe on page 14). Ada BONI, in *Il Talismano della Felicità*, gives a recipe in which the fish are cooked in meat broth with plenty of garlic and celery; the brodetto is sharpened with a glug of white wine vinegar.

---

orecchiette con i broccoli
orecchiette with broccoli

Serves 4

3 tbsp sultanas

500g/1lb 2oz broccoli

salt and freshly ground black pepper

1 onion, sliced

6 tbsp extra virgin olive oil

2 salted anchovies, boned, rinsed and chopped, or 4 canned or bottled anchovy fillets, drained and chopped

25g/1oz/3 tbsp pine nuts

350g/12oz orecchiette, shells or any medium-sized pasta shapes

50g/1¾oz pecorino cheese, grated

The use of anchovies, sultanas and pine nuts is a feature of the cooking of southern Italy, in this case Puglia. Here the sauce is used to dress the local pasta, ORECCHIETTE.

Soak the sultanas in a cup of warm water. Wash the broccoli. Remove the outer layer and cut the thicker stalks into rounds; divide the heads into small florets. Cook the florets and the stalks in boiling salted water for 3 minutes after the water has come back to the boil. Drain and set aside.

Sauté the onion in 4 tablespoons of the oil in a fairly large frying pan until soft. Meanwhile, heat the rest of the oil in a small saucepan, mix in the anchovies and cook over a really low heat for 1 minute, pressing the anchovies down to reduce to a pulp. Set aside.

Drain the sultanas and mix into the onion together with the broccoli and pine nuts. Stir very gently, taking care not to break up the florets, and cook over a low heat for 10 minutes or so. Add the anchovy sauce and salt and pepper to taste.

Cook the pasta in plenty of boiling salted water until al dente. Drain and turn into the frying pan, then gently toss over the heat for a minute or two. Add the pecorino, toss well and serve immediately, preferably straight from the pan.

brodo
stock

The two traditional stocks are meat stock, *brodo di carne*, and vegetable stock, *brodo di verdure* – chicken being less common in Italy.

Meat stock is a standby in most kitchens, a vital ingredient for making many soups, risotti, braised meats and sauces. It is a light, freshly flavoured stock, unlike the concentrated, full-bodied stock of France or Britain. A good meat stock must be made with a fair assortment of bones from beef, veal and chicken (never pork or lamb, as these would give the stock too strong a taste), with scraps of meat and chicken, and some vegetables and herbs to give flavour.

Vegetable stock is made with carrots, onions, leeks, turnips, potatoes, parsley and dried or cultivated mushrooms or a good selection of these. The vegetables, cut into small pieces, are covered with cold water and cooked over a very low heat for at least 3 hours. The strained liquid is used for vegetable or fish soups, risotti and sauces. For a richer stock, the vegetables are first sautéed in butter and then cooked at length in water.

Nowadays many cooks use stock cubes, DADO, or powder, which are of excellent quality.

[see recipe below]

---

brodo di carne
meat stock

Makes 1.5–2 litres/3–3½ pints/ 1½–2 quarts

1.5kg/3¼lb assorted beef, veal and chicken, cut into large pieces

1 onion, halved and stuck with 3 cloves

1 or 2 carrots, cut into pieces

2 celery stalks, cut into pieces

1 fennel stalk or a few feathery fennel tops

1 leek, cut into pieces

a handful of mushroom peelings or stalks

6 parsley stalks

1 bay leaf

1 garlic clove

1 ripe fresh tomato, quartered

6 peppercorns

1 tsp salt

Italian brodo di carne is much more delicate than English or French meat stock. This is the meat stock I have used in testing the recipes in this book, but if you don't have the time or inclination to make it then use a good-quality bouillon cube or powder dissolved in boiling water.

Put all the ingredients in a stockpot. Add about 3 litres/5 pints/3 quarts cold water, or enough to cover everything, and bring to the boil. The water must be cold to start with, so that the meat and vegetables can slowly release their juices. Set the lid very slightly askew so that the steam can escape and turn the heat down to the minimum for the stock to simmer. The best stock is made from liquid that cooks at 80°/175°F, rather than 100°C/210°F (boiling point). Using a slotted spoon, skim off the scum that comes to the surface during the first 15 minutes of cooking. Cook for about 3 hours.

Strain the stock through a large sieve into a large bowl, leave to cool and then put in the refrigerator.

Remove any fat that has solidified on the surface. Heat the stock and drag a piece of kitchen paper gently across the surface; any remaining fat will stick to the paper. Taste the stock. If it is too mild, reduce over a high heat to intensify the flavour. Cover with clingfilm and keep in the refrigerator for up to 3 days, or in the freezer for up to 3 months.

bros
a cheese

You have to be an aficionado to appreciate this cheese from Piedmont. Its making, always a family affair, is very complicated, not to say ritualistic. A fresh cheese, usually a ROBIOLA, is cut up and placed in an earthenware pot. A glass of GRAPPA and a glass of white wine are poured over it. The cheese is put aside for a week, then it is stirred clockwise twelve times, at the same time adding more cheese – often bits of leftovers – and more wine and spirit, olive oil and vinegar, and even chilli. The variations are endless, since they depend on the whim of the maker. This process is repeated once a week for seven weeks, after which the bros is ready. It is spread over grilled bread or grilled polenta. The first mouthful is like fire, but after a time you may get used to it.

bruschetta
grilled bread

Bruschetta originates from Rome, where it consists of slices of rustic bread grilled on charcoal, rubbed with garlic and dressed with extra virgin olive oil.

The traditional Tuscan bruschetta adds tomatoes, cut into small bits. Nowadays bruschetta is covered in various different ingredients. It is the classic ANTIPASTO to start a meal in the summer. The recipe below is for the popular tomato version.

[see recipe below]

brüscitt
beef dish

A Milanese dish. Stewing beef, cut into very small cubes, is cooked for a long time in an earthenware pot with butter, pancetta, red wine and fennel seeds. It is always accompanied by polenta.

brutti ma buoni
biscuits, cookies

Biscuits from Piedmont whose name, 'ugly but good', refers to their rather knobbly appearance. They are made with eggs, chopped almonds and sugar, flavoured with cinnamon and vanilla. As with most Italian biscuits, they are not often made at home but bought in PASTICCERIE in northern Italy.

bruschetta col pomodoro

Serves 4
6 ripe tomatoes
sea salt
1 ciabatta
2 garlic cloves, cut in half
6 tbsp extra virgin olive oil
a dozen fresh basil leaves, torn

This BRUSCHETTA is worth making only with very good tomatoes with thin skins, since they should not be peeled.

Cut the tomatoes in half and then cut away and discard the cores. Cut the tomatoes into small cubes and season with salt. Leave them for about 30 minutes.

Cut the ciabatta diagonally into 1cm/½in thick slices. Score each slice lightly with the point of a small knife, rub with the garlic on both sides, moisten with some olive oil and place them on a grill or barbecue rack. Grill until charred on both sides.

Place a few pieces of tomatoes on each slice, dress with the remaining oil and scatter a few pieces of basil over them.

bucatini
a pasta

Similar to thick spaghetti but with hollow strands, bucatini is a versatile pasta shape which can be used instead of spaghetti in many sauces. It is a favourite pasta in central Italy and should be used for AMATRICIANA and CARBONARA.

buccellato
a bread

There are two kinds of buccellato: one from Lucca, the other from Sicily; both are simple sweet bread containing candied peel, made in the shape of a ring, which can be up to 1m/3ft in diameter. The buccellato from Lucca is traditionally given to a child by its godparents on the day of Confirmation.

budino
a pudding

Though hard to define, the word budino suggests a dish usually of a round shape, a soft texture and a trembling consistency, often cooked in a bain-marie.

A budino is most likely to be sweet, though *budino alla Genovese* is made with veal, chicken, prosciutto, béchamel and eggs. In Friuli there are three recipes for budino. In the *budino di avena*, oats are cooked in milk and then mixed with eggs and sugar and poured into a mould which is chilled before serving. The *budino alle uova* is a sweet béchamel held together by eggs and strongly laced with MARSALA. Finally there is an interesting *budino di patate*, potato pudding. The mashed potatoes are mixed with butter, sugar, cream and eggs, some sultanas and pine nuts are added, and the pudding is baked and served hot. In Tuscany the *budino di riso*, rice pudding, is studded with candied fruits, pistachios and walnuts and sprinkled with cocoa before receiving a final baking. My favourite

budino is this one of ricotta from Rome, which I make in a cake tin – far easier to unmould.

[see recipe on page 64]

buongustaio
gourmet

A buongustaio is a person of any class or creed who appreciates and loves eating good food: a gourmet, not a gourmand.

buridda
fish stew

A fish stew from Liguria made with monkfish, rascasse, cuttlefish or squid, and sometimes some pieces of STOCCAFISSO, previously soaked. All the ingredients are stewed in an earthenware pot in layers with onions, tomatoes, dried wild fungi, pine nuts and salted anchovies, covered with olive oil and dry white wine.

63

burrata
a cheese

This soft cheese, made from full-fat cow's milk, is one of the most delicious specialities of Puglia, so delicious that the Shah of Persia used to have it flown to Tehran once a week, or so they say.

The making of burrata is a difficult and interesting craft. The milk of the previous evening is heated to a low temperature and rennet is added. When the milk has coagulated, it is broken up very thoroughly to release the whey. The small curdled bits are then plunged into boiling water and, through a laborious mixing process, they take the shape of long square strings, called *lucini*. Now the dairy man has to master the same art as his northern compatriot in Murano does with glass. He blows inside one *lucino*, which swells up, forming a little balloon-shaped casing into which some flaked lucini are pushed, together with some cream. The neck of the blown lucino is tied up and the burrata is made.

It is highly perishable and it used to be available only in Puglia. It is now made on a semi-industrial scale and can be found more or less everywhere, although to the detriment of its flavour and consistency. The proper artisanal burrata should be eaten just as it is, and not messed about in salads with other, fiercer, ingredients.

burrida
fish dish

This fish dish from Sardinia is different from the Ligurian BURIDDA. Although the Genovese sailors brought their fish soup to Sardinia, the Sardinians made a new dish out of it. The burrida is made with only one fish, usually dogfish or skate, which is fried and then covered with a sweet and sour sauce containing a lot of garlic and pine nuts.

budino di ricotta alla romana
ricotta pudding

Serves 6–8
50g/1¾oz/⅓ cup sultanas
(golden raisins)
4 tbsp white rum
unsalted butter and dried breadcrumbs,
for the tin
250g/9oz/1 cup fresh ricotta
2 heaped tbsp crème fraîche
3 large eggs, separated
200g/7oz/1 cup caster (superfine) sugar
3 tbsp Italian 00 flour
½ tsp ground cinnamon
25g/1oz mixed candied peel, chopped
grated rind of 1 organic or unwaxed
lemon
1 tsp lemon juice
icing (confectioners') sugar, to decorate

This is one of the many RICOTTA dishes from central Italy. It is far better made with fresh ricotta, rather than the heat-treated kind sold in tubs.

Put the sultanas in a bowl. Pour over the rum and leave until the sultanas are plump.

Preheat the oven to 180°C/350°F/Gas Mark 4. Grease a 20cm/8in diameter cake tin or 1 litre/1¾ pint/4 cup metal mould very generously with butter and then cover the buttered surface with breadcrumbs. Shake out excess crumbs.

Pass the ricotta through a food mill or sieve into a bowl to aerate it (a food processor cannot be used for this) and then mix in the crème fraîche lightly but thoroughly. Mix in the egg yolks one at a time, then the sugar, flour, cinnamon, candied peel, sultanas and rum and the lemon rind. Mix thoroughly.

Whisk the egg whites with the lemon juice until stiff and fold lightly into the mixture. Spoon the mixture into the prepared tin. Bake for 40–50 minutes, until a skewer inserted in the middle comes out dry. Turn out immediately onto a round dish and sprinkle lavishly with icing sugar before serving.

This pudding should be eaten warm or cool, but not straight from the oven or chilled.

RIGHT: Budino di ricotta alla romana

burrino or butirro
a cheese

A hard cheese from southern Italy, shaped like a small balloon tied up at one end, with a soft centre of pure butter. Apparently it was first made to preserve butter in Calabria – hence its name, deriving from BURRO (butter) – where the tradition of making burrino is still very strong. Burrini are made from the milk of a cow which has produced a calf the previous year, thus the milk is richer than normal. Found only in farms in southern Italy, it is usually eaten very fresh, about a week after being made.

burro
butter

In the early days of ancient Rome, butter was largely unknown in Italy. The story goes that Julius Caesar first tasted butter in Lombardy on his return from the Gallic wars and was much taken by its delicate flavour.

It was not until the Renaissance that butter first appeared in the kitchens of the wealthy and the nobility; at that time it was occasionally used to make centrepiece decorations for the table.

Butter, always unsalted, is primarily used in northern Italy, to the extent that up to World War II there was a so-called 'butter-line' dividing the country in two. This is because the Po Valley and lower Alps, being rich in pasture, are excellent cattle-breeding areas, unlike the more arid south.

Because of health concerns, butter is used far less now in cooking, even in Lombardy, which used to be its supreme territory. However, it remains an integral part of many hot sauces, since it gives a lovely shine and delicate taste to the finished dish, and it is essential to the flavour of many cakes, biscuits and sweet pastry. A risotto made without any butter is for any northern Italian a non-risotto.

In Italy butter is never put on the table, even with cheese. But it is occasionally served with a plate of AFFETTATO, mixed cured meats.

büsecca

A Milanese tripe dish. See TRIPPA.

büsecca matta
an egg dish

A Milanese dish that looks like the tripe dish known as BÜSECCA. It consists of a FRITTATA cut into thin strips, which are mixed into a tomato sauce and to which borlotti beans are added. A similar dish – without the beans – is made in Rome, where it is called *finte trippe*.

C

cacciatora, alla
cooking style

Literally, this means cooked 'the hunter's way', but what the hunter's way is cannot be pinned down precisely. Dishes cooked alla cacciatora, most of which are from central Italy, are based on meat, game or poultry; typically, this is first sautéed and then cooked slowly with mushrooms, onions, celery, carrots and herbs or a selection of all these. Tomatoes and wine are frequently added. In other recipes from central Italy olives and/or anchovy fillets are added, while in Basilicata sweet peppers and chilli are often important ingredients. A recipe from Liguria for *agnello alla cacciatora con le patate* (lamb and potato stew) is given on page 22.

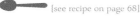 [see recipe on page 68]

cacciatore
a salame

A very popular small hard SALAME, originally from Piedmont and Lombardy. Its name – 'hunter' – refers to the fact it was the salame taken by hunters on a day's shooting. It is made of very thickly ground pure pork. A good cacciatore and a piece of fresh bread is the best snack you could possibly wish to have.

cacciucco
Tuscan fish soup

The Livornesi claim that theirs is the oldest Italian recipe for fish soup. It is, in fact, a stew rather than soup, rich, black and thick. Its particular feature is that it contains chilli and must be made with at least five fish – one for each of the c's in cacciucco. It is served ladled onto slices of bread that have been dried in the oven and rubbed with garlic.

cacio
cheese

A less common word for cheese than FORMAGGIO, still in use in central and southern Italy.

caciocavallo
a cheese

The name, literally 'horse-cheese', derives from the fact that, when drying, the cheeses used to be hung in pairs astride a pole. Caciocavallo is one of the cheeses of southern Italy and Sicily. It originated in Campania, but is now produced all over southern Italy, from cow's milk and sometimes from buffalo's milk.

Caciocavallo can be eaten fresh, when its crust is pale yellow and its flavour mellow, or it can be aged up to 6 months. By then it will be piquant and suitable for grating. Fresh caciocavallo is used in cooking, as it melts beautifully, and as a table cheese. When aged, it is grated and used as Parmesan. In Sicily it is sliced and fried quickly in olive oil, then lightly sprinkled with wine vinegar, oregano and a generous grinding of black pepper.

pollo alla cacciatora
chicken with vinegar

Serves 4

1 organic or free-range chicken, about
1.25–1.5kg/2¾–3¼lb, cut into
6–8 pieces

1 organic or unwaxed lemon, rind pared,
then cut in half

salt and freshly ground black pepper

4 tbsp red wine vinegar

2 garlic cloves

1 small dried red chilli

3 sprigs of fresh rosemary, about
10cm/4in long

4 tbsp extra virgin olive oil

There is an endless number of recipes for pollo alla CACCIATORA, most of which contain tomatoes and mushrooms. This one, from Le Marche, is typical of central Italy. Without tomatoes or mushrooms, it is a fresh dish, full of flavour. If you prefer, you can just use chicken leg portions.

Wash and thoroughly dry the chicken pieces and rub them with the lemon halves. Rub a little salt and pepper over each piece.

Put the vinegar, 1 garlic clove, the chilli, 1 rosemary sprig, ½ teaspoon salt and a little pepper in a dish. Add the lemon rind and lay the chicken in the dish, turning the pieces over to coat them. Leave to marinate for 2 hours or longer.

In a large sauté pan. heat the oil with the remaining garlic and rosemary and sauté for 1 minute. Remove and discard the garlic. Add the chicken pieces, laying them down in a single layer, and brown them very well on all sides. Turn the heat down and, after about 7 minutes, add a couple of tablespoons of the marinade and a couple of tablespoons of hot water. Continue cooking and pouring over small amounts of marinade and hot water until the thighs feel tender when pricked with a fork. If you finish the marinade, just add hot water. When the breast pieces are cooked, remove and keep them warm while the legs finish cooking. The chicken will be cooked in about 20–25 minutes.

Transfer the chicken pieces to a heated dish and keep warm. Turn the heat up to high, add a couple of tablespoons of water and bring to the boil while stirring to loosen the cooking residue from the bottom of the pan. Pour the pan juices over the chicken and serve immediately.

RIGHT: Pollo alla cacciatora

cacciatora, alla

caciofiore
a cheese

This is made in Lazio and Umbria from ewe's milk during the first three months of the year. It is made only locally, in small round shapes and aged for 10–15 days. Sometimes saffron is added to the milk, giving the cheese a lovely golden colour. It has a taste similar to a very delicate fresh PECORINO.

caciotta
a cheese

A word for different cheeses of the same shape: small and flat, no more than 20cm/8in in diameter and 7.5cm/3in thick. Caciotta can be made with cow's, goat's or ewe's milk, or a mixture of the three, and varies from white and sweet to buff yellow and piquant. A typical farm cheese of central Italy, caciotta is now made industrially.

caffè
coffee

Coffee arrived in Europe via Venice and the first coffee shop, La Bottega del Caffè, opened in Venice in 1640. Today, American-style coffee shops with their supersize milky drinks are a global phenomenon, but espresso remains quintessentially Italian. Nowhere else have I drunk an espresso that can beat any espresso in a bar in Italy, especially in Naples, which boasts the best espressi.

Caffè espresso, black and strong, has become one of the hallmarks of Italy, but there are many variations, all made in a machine that forces steam through the finely ground coffee. *Caffè macchiato* is espresso with a dash of cold milk; *caffè corretto* is espresso with a shot of GRAPPA or brandy. *Caffè ristretto* is an even stronger espresso, while *caffè lungo* is the opposite, a less strong and a bigger cup of coffee, the steam being pushed through for longer. Then there is *caffè e latte*, fifty-fifty coffee and hot milk, and *caffè con latte*, which is usually understood as a caffè lungo with more than a dash of cold milk. Cappuccino, so called because its colour resembles that of the habit of the Capuchin friars, is caffè lungo with hot milk whisked in, often topped with grated chocolate. In the last ten years or so a new variation has appeared on the scene, the *marocchino*, which is an espresso topped with a little cream and a dusting of cocoa powder. Served in small glasses, it is similar to the 19th-century Turinese *bicerin*, the favourite drink of Cavour, the first prime minister of Italy. Its name relates to its colour, similar to that of a Moroccan leather. Marocchino is very popular in northern Italy.

Cappuccino senza spuma is similar but the hot milk is added without whisking. The delicious *caffè con panna* is caffè lungo topped with sweetened whipped cream. In the summer a very popular drink is *caffè freddo* (cold coffee), a long and sugared drink, and GRANITA al caffè, which is more a water ice than a drink.

Caffè e latte is drunk only for breakfast, while cappuccino is acceptable until 11, but certainly not with or after a meal. Years ago, in Ischia, I remember my amazement – or should I say disgust – when I saw the American couple next to us in the restaurant sipping cappuccino while eating fish soup. After mid-morning most Italians drink only espresso – though rarely after dinner. 'It keeps me awake,' being the explanation.

One very special coffee is drunk in Valle d'Aosta. *Caffè valdostano* is a ceremony rather than a drink. The piping hot coffee, flavoured with lemon peel, is served in a large shallow wooden bowl with a central opening and four to ten small beaks around its edge. At the table a generous amount of grappa is poured into the coffee and a match is put to it. While the coffee is on fire, sugar is added slowly through the central opening. The bowl is handed round the table and, as soon as the flames die down, each diner drinks through his own beak. It is fiery, hot and powerful.

Calabria

Nothing now remains of the wealth that Calabria knew in Grecian times, when the town of Sybaris was the most opulent centre of all Magna Graecia. Twentieth-century Calabria is poor, still suffering from the greed of landowners and the power of the local mafia, called 'ndangreda. This spectacularly beautiful region has very high mountains where, although so far south, the snow often stays until May, while along the sea and especially in the plain around Reggio Calabria, the capital, the climate is extremely mild. Citrus fruit of every kind is widely cultivated. There is a variety of orange that grows only in Calabria. Sweet chestnuts grow on the high mountains of the Sila. Another important contribution of the Sila to the gastronomy of Calabria lies in the rich harvest of many species of fungi that grow there.

The other important crop is vegetables, of which the aubergine, MELANZANA, is the king. The Calabresi have created dozens of recipes around it. These include: *al funghetto*, diced and sautéed in olive oil with garlic and parsley; *fritte*, sliced, coated in egg and breadcrumbs and fried; *alla parmigiana*, layered with tomatoes, mozzarella, Parmesan and hard-boiled eggs and then baked (see recipe on page 277); *in agrodolce*, in a sweet and sour sauce; *alla cariatese*, stuffed with salted anchovies, breadcrumbs, capers, black olives and garlic; *alla finitese*, PROVOLONE cheese and peppery sausage sandwiched between two slices of aubergine, coated in egg and flour and then fried. Tomatoes also grow sweet and abundant.

Pasta-making is still a rite in Calabria and, up to World War II, a girl had to master fifteen different shapes if she wanted to marry. Pasta is dressed with a vegetable sauce or a pork RAGÙ, both strongly flavoured with chilli which, as in neighbouring Basilicata, is the favourite spice. And, as in that region, pork, together with all its products, is the most popular meat. CAPOCOLLO and SALAMI such as *soppressata* and the soft *'ndugghia*, or *'nduja*, are – predictably – flavoured with chilli.

Offal is used to make MORSEDDU, generally eaten at breakfast-time.

The most popular cheese is PECORINO, made by every family that owns a sheep.

The sea around Calabria is rich in fish, especially tuna fish, swordfish, sardines and anchovies, all of which are cooked simply, either pan-fried or baked, as in the recipe on page 18 – or are exported fresh, frozen or preserved. A local speciality is *mustica*, sometimes called *rosamarina*, and known as the caviar of the poor. It is made from BIANCHETTI (newly hatched anchovies) which are salted, dried and then preserved in oil, with lots of chilli.

Sweets are prepared for special occasions and most of them have strong connections with those of Sicily, with which they share the exotic Middle Eastern flavours.

[see recipes overleaf]

CALABRIA

Cosenza
La Sila
Crotone
Catanzaro
TYRRHENIAN SEA
Vibo Valentia
IONIAN SEA
Reggio di Calabria

71

minestra di pomodori alla calabrese
tomato soup with pasta

Serves 4–5

6 tbsp extra virgin olive oil

2 garlic cloves, finely chopped

5 ripe fresh tomatoes, peeled and
coarsely chopped

1 onion, thinly sliced

2 tbsp chopped fresh flat-leaf parsley

salt and freshly ground black pepper

140g/5oz/1 1/3 cups ditalini or other
small tubular pasta

freshly grated mature pecorino cheese,
to serve

A recipe from Calabria in southern Italy, where excellent tomatoes grow. Make it only when you can get hold of really good tomatoes.

Heat the olive oil in a pan, preferably earthenware, and add the garlic, tomatoes, onion and half the chopped parsley. Sauté for about 10 minutes, stirring frequently.

Add 1.5 litres/3 pints/6½ cups water, salt and plenty of pepper. Bring to the boil and cook, uncovered, over a very low heat for about 20 minutes.

Raise the heat, drop in the pasta and cook until al dente. Add the remaining parsley before serving. Serve the pecorino in a bowl for sprinkling over the soup.

peperoni e patate in padella
sautéed peppers and potatoes

Serves 4

500g/1lb 2oz waxy potatoes

225ml/8fl oz/scant 1 cup extra virgin olive oil

4 garlic cloves, finely chopped

1 or 2 dried chillies, depending on strength and taste

a bunch of flat-leaf parsley, chopped

salt and freshly ground black pepper

500g/1lb 2oz red and yellow peppers, deseeded and cut into thin strips

I had this dish at a country feast, high in the middle of the Calabrian mountains. My host, who was a very good cook, told me that this is one of the many ways she likes to prepare peppers and I had to agree that it is indeed a very good way.

Peel the potatoes, cut into thin wedges and wash them thoroughly to get rid of some of the starch. Dry thoroughly.

Heat half the olive oil in a heavy frying pan and add half the garlic, half the chillies and half the parsley. Cook gently for no more than a minute and then throw in the potatoes. Cook for about 5 minutes, turning the potatoes over frequently so that they brown on all sides. Turn the heat down a little, season with salt and cook until the potatoes are tender, adding a couple of tablespoons of hot water whenever they stick to the bottom of the pan.

While the potatoes are cooking, put the remaining oil, garlic, chillies and parsley in another frying pan. Sauté for about 30 seconds, then add the peppers and a little salt and sauté, stirring frequently, until the peppers are cooked but still crunchy, about 20 minutes.

73

Scoop the potatoes and the peppers with all the juices into a warmed serving bowl, mix gently but thoroughly – two forks are less likely to break the potatoes – check the seasoning and serve. This dish is equally good at room temperature.

calamari
squid

Squid are a favourite food everywhere in Italy, and there are many ways to prepare them. They are mostly fried, either by themselves or in a FRITTO MISTO DI MARE.

Medium-size squid are stuffed with soft or dried breadcrumbs, parsley, garlic and pepper plus the chopped tentacles, everything lightly sautéed in olive oil. Boiled rice replaces the breadcrumbs in some recipes. When stuffed, the squid are sewn up and cooked in white wine, tomato sauce, or both, either in the oven or on top of the cooker. In a mouthwatering recipe from Abruzzo, *calamari agli scampi*, the stuffing is made from raw shrimps plus breadcrumbs, garlic, parsley and a touch of chilli;

the squid are cooked in white wine. In the same region, and in Puglia, small squid, straight out of the sea, are eaten raw, thinly sliced and dressed with olive oil, lemon juice, a few paper-thin rings of the local sweet onions and salt. When very small, about 3–5cm/1–2in, *calamaretti* are fried, often without being cleaned, and they are utterly delicious. In Naples, these tiny squid are stewed in a tomato sauce with sultanas, pine nuts and olives.

Large squid are generally stewed. Although they have a less rich flavour and a more chewy consistency than cuttlefish, they share the same recipes. Cleaned and cut into strips or pieces, they are cooked in tomato sauce and wine to which onions, garlic and other flavourings are added.

[see recipe below]

---

calamari ripieni
stuffed squid

Serves 4

4 squid, about 20cm/8in long
2 tbsp chopped fresh flat-leaf parsley
1 tbsp chopped fresh marjoram
1 small mild dried chilli, crumbled
3 garlic cloves, chopped
100ml/3½fl oz/7 tbsp extra virgin
  olive oil
2 salted anchovies, boned, rinsed and
  chopped, or 4 canned or bottled
  anchovy fillets, drained and chopped
50g/1¾oz/1 cup fresh breadcrumbs
salt and freshly ground black pepper
1 small onion, finely chopped
4 tbsp dry white wine
400g/14oz canned plum tomatoes,
  drained and chopped

Preheat the oven to 200°C/400°F/Gas Mark 6.

Clean the squid, leaving the body sacs whole. Wash them very well. Detach the wings and the tentacles and chop them.

Sauté the parsley, marjoram, chilli and garlic in a frying pan with 3 tablespoons of the olive oil for 1 minute, then add the squid wings and tentacles and cook for 5 minutes. Add the anchovies and after 30 seconds or so, stir in the breadcrumbs. Cook until the crumbs begin to get crisp and golden. Season to taste and then put the mixture into the squid sacs. The sacs should only be two-thirds full or they will burst during cooking. Close each top by threading with a wooden toothpick.

Pour the remaining oil into a flameproof roasting pan over a medium heat. When hot, add the onion and sauté until soft. Add the squid and cook for 5 minutes over a gentle heat, turning them over carefully. Pour over the wine and tomatoes, season to taste and bring slowly to the boil. Boil for 5 minutes. Cover the pan with foil, place in the oven and cook for 1 hour.

To serve the squid you can either cut each one in half and give each person two halves, or you can slice the squid into 2cm/¾in slices and spoon them and the tomato sauce on to a bed of boiled rice.

calzone
a stuffed pizza

To make calzone, pizza dough (see recipe on page 314) is rolled out to an oval and one half of it is covered with various ingredients – which differ according to the regional recipe, the whim of the cook or the food in the larder. The other half is folded over to form a large half-moon shape and sealed. It is then baked.

There are a few calzoni in the regional cuisine of southern Italy, of which the best known is the *calzone napoletano*, stuffed with SALAME or prosciutto, mozzarella, RICOTTA and Parmesan. *Calzone pugliese* is also called *calzone di* MAGRO, because it contains no meat. The stuffing consists of onions, tomatoes, salted anchovies and capers. The third calzone of note comes from Basilicata and is again 'di magro', with a filling that includes BIETOLA (leaf

beet) or INDIVIA (batavia), flavoured with chilli. In Puglia the same stuffing is used for small calzoni, *calzuneddi*, which are deep-fried in olive oil and make a superb snack.

Campania

The fertile volcanic soil of Campania combined with a perfect climate produces some of the best fruit and vegetables in Italy. The Romans were quick to appreciate the richness of the soil, the beauty of the landscape, the dry, soft climate and the warmth of the inhabitants. Campania became their vast vegetable garden and their orchard, as well as the playground of the wealthy.

Naples, the region's capital, returned to the height of fashion during the first half of the 19th century, when the upper classes of Europe gathered there to enjoy a life of pleasure. The expeditions they arranged to Pompeii, Herculaneum, Paestum and Pozzuoli were dedicated as much to the mind as to the palate.

The ordinary Neapolitans, meanwhile, were deriving their pleasure from the spaghetti stalls, where the *maccheronaro* (macaroni-seller) dished out hot spaghetti, covering it with tomato sauce and Parmesan. From another stall they could buy *fritture* (tiny savoury fritters) or raw seafood. They finished their ambulatory meal with a GELATO (ice cream) from the *gelatiere*, who wheeled his goods around the streets.

To this day, the Neapolitans love to eat out-of-doors. Pizza is munched in the street after the cinema or during a walk along the seafront on a balmy night. It is in fact hardly ever made or eaten at home, where other vegetable pies, rarely served in restaurants, are prepared. Called **TORTE** *di verdura*, these are made with spinach, artichokes, broccoli or batavia sautéed in olive oil, bound with ricotta and eggs, then flavoured with cheese, pine nuts and anchovy fillets. The mixture is then encased in pastry, which is sometimes made with ricotta for a lighter, shorter result.

Vegetables play such an important role in the local cooking that the Neapolitans were called *mangiafoglie* (leaf eaters) before they became the great spaghetti eaters they are now. The region's classic pasta sauces are based on the sweet and flavoursome plum tomatoes called San Marzano, although on Sunday much richer RAGÙ are prepared. The pasta is dressed with the cooking juices, while the meat is served as a second course. A recipe for one such ragù is given overleaf. The best-known version is made with small slices of veal, rolled and stuffed with cheese, garlic, sultanas and pine nuts, simmered gently in wine and homemade tomato puree. This ragù was made famous in a play by the Neapolitan playwright Eduardo De Filippo. I remember years ago seeing the play – *Filumena Marturano* – in London, where there on stage Joan Plowright, all dressed in black, hair in a scarf knotted up on the forehead, was cooking the ragù. When you entered the auditorium it was like entering a Neapolitan kitchen on Sunday morning, when the cook – whoever he/she may be – is in the kitchen at six to prepare the ragù for lunch. It needs constant supervision and it must cook very slowly so that only a few bubbles break occasionally on the surface of the thick liquid, which is kept at the same density by regular additions of a few drops of hot water. Neapolitan cuisine is so rich that it has also created the grandest dish for rice, SARTÙ.

However, on the whole the local cooking is quick and simple. This is exemplified in the FRITTO MISTO, a dish aptly described in Neapolitan dialect by the expression *frienno magnanno* –'frying and eating'. The food is fried for only a few minutes and must be eaten straight after it comes out of the frying pan.

The cheese that immediately comes to mind when speaking of Naples is mozzarella, which, in union with the tomato, has found its apotheosis in the pizza. But many other excellent cheeses are produced in Campania, from both cow's and sheep's milk: SCAMORZA, PROVOLONE, CACIOCAVALLO and PECORINO, all of which can be fresh or aged. They are an everyday component of a Neapolitan meal, as is the sublime local fruit.

It is only on special occasions that sweets arrive at the table, usually rich and elaborate, reminiscent of Arab cooking. PASTIERA, a sweet ricotta tart, is as typical of Naples as PANFORTE is of Siena and PANETTONE of Milan. STRUFFOLI are generally served at Christmas, while the deliciously light SFOGLIATELLE are eaten all the year round. *Gelati* (ice creams) are also an integral part of Neapolitan culinary traditions.

[see recipe overleaf]

canederli
dumplings

The GNOCCHI of the Trentino region, similar to the Austrian KNOEDEL, from which their name derives. Canederli are made with stale bread soaked in milk, eggs and a little flour. To this mixture, SPECK, onion, parsley and marjoram, all finely chopped, are added. Pieces of the mixture are shaped like golf balls and cooked in boiling meat or chicken stock. Canederli are served in stock as a soup or drained and dressed with melted butter and sage leaves, or with the juices of a roast.

canestrato
a cheese

Several cheeses from central and southern Italy, usually from ewe's or goat's milk, are called canestrato. The name refers to the baskets in which the curd matures and the resulting cheeses are cylindrical, with rounded sides.

canestrello
a shellfish

Canestrelli are small scallops, called queen scallops, or 'queens', in English. They are usually sold without their shells; if still in the shells they can be opened by placing them in a pan over a high heat for a few minutes. Canestrelli are usually fried in olive oil and served by themselves, or as part of a FRITTO MISTO DI MARE. They are also excellent in a risotto or in a pasta sauce with fried breadcrumbs, garlic and a touch of chilli.

cannella
cinnamon

Cinnamon is the dried bark of a tree of the laurel family, native to South-East Asia and known around the Mediterranean since ancient times. Pieces of the bark are rolled to form cinnamon sticks, or ground to a powder. It is widely used in sweet preparations, as well as in some stews and braised meat dishes. It is one of the four so-called Lombard spices — the other three being nutmeg, cloves and pepper — which are often referred to in old cookery books simply as SPEZIE, 'spices'.

ragù alla napoletana
Neapolitan meat sauce

Enough for 6–8 helpings of pasta
1kg/2¼lb lean boneless pork or beef
*   rump, in one piece*
50g/1¾oz unsmoked pancetta, diced
6 tbsp olive oil
salt
½ garlic clove, finely chopped
3 onions, finely chopped
2 carrots, finely chopped
1 celery stalk, finely chopped
150ml/5fl oz/⅔ cup red wine
1 tbsp tomato puree
300ml/10fl oz/1¼ cups hot meat stock
*   (page 61) or chicken stock*
300ml/10fl oz/1¼ cups tomato sauce
*   (Salsa di pomodoro 1, page 331)*

This recipe, typical of Campania, is quite different from the better-known Bolognese RAGÙ. The sauce is used to dress pasta (ZITI or MACCHERONI) as a first course and then the meat is eaten as a second course, served with a little of the sauce. You should cook this dish at the lowest possible simmer for a very long time.

Wipe the meat with a damp cloth and make a few incisions in it with the point of a sharp knife. Push a small piece of pancetta into each incision. Heat the oil in a flameproof casserole, add the meat and brown it all over. Sprinkle with salt and add the garlic, onions, carrots and celery. Cook slowly until the vegetables are lightly browned. Add the wine, bring to the boil and let it evaporate.

Dilute the tomato puree with 150ml/5fl oz/⅔ cup of the stock. Add to the pan and simmer for 30 minutes.

Add the remaining hot stock and the tomato sauce and continue cooking over a very low heat for at least 3 hours, until the meat is very tender. Turn the meat over every 30 minutes or so and add a few tablespoons of hot water if the liquid is getting low.

cannelloni
stuffed pasta tubes

There are various recipes for cannelloni, of which those of Campania and of Piedmont are the most famous. The *cannelloni alla Piemontese* are made with pancakes stuffed with veal, prosciutto and Parmesan. They are covered with béchamel sauce and baked in the oven. The other kind of cannelloni are made with pasta dough. These include the *cannelloni alla napoletana*, traditionally filled with tomato sauce and mozzarella and covered with tomato sauce and Parmesan before being baked, and the most common cannelloni, those stuffed with a rich RAGÙ and covered with béchamel, just like baked LASAGNE.

Other cannelloni are made with pasta dough in Le Marche and in Abruzzo; they are called *fregnacce* and are stuffed with minced meat, which, in Abruzzo, is highly flavoured with chilli; melted butter is poured over them before baking. There are also *cannelloni di pesce*, which are stuffed with minced fish and/or seafood and covered with béchamel, and cannelloni di MAGRO, stuffed with spinach and cheeses.

Cannelloni are sold dry, already shaped as tubes, ready to be stuffed, and are baked without being pre-boiled.

cannocchia or canocchia
a crustacean

Also called *spanocchia*, mantis shrimp in English, cannocchie are generally about 10cm/4in long. They are seen mostly on the Adriatic coast, from Venice down to Le Marche, the best being found on flat sandy beaches.

Cannocchie are blanched for 3 minutes in a court bouillon and left in the liquid until cool. They are either served as they are so that people can peel off the shells at the table, or they are shelled and used in other preparations. Shelled cannocchie can be coated with flour, dipped in egg and breadcrumbs and fried. They can also be sautéed in olive oil, garlic and white wine, with some breadcrumbs mixed in at the end. *Risotto di cannocchie* is made with the strained stock in which the shells and claws have cooked for a further 15 minutes. The shelled cannocchie are mixed in with a knob of butter when the rice is nearly done.

cannoli
filled pastry tubes

This is one of two sweets that have been described as 'the two unshakeable rocks of Sicilian desserts', the other being CASSATA. They were once the Sicilian sweets made for Carnival, but they are now sold all over Italy at any time of the year. Cannoli are cylinders of a brittle pastry that is made with melted pork fat and flavoured with cocoa and MARSALA. Shaped around a special tube, originally made of bamboo, but now made of tin, cannoli are fried in oil and, when cold, stuffed with sweetened RICOTTA flavoured with orange water and studded with candied peel, pistachios and pieces of chocolate. Nowadays, cannoli are also filled with CREMA PASTICCERA or chocolate cream.

cannoncino
a small cake

This is one of the most popular PASTE, sold in any PASTICCERIA. It consists of puff pastry rolled in a spiral around a metal tube, baked and then stuffed with CREMA PASTICCERA, Chantilly cream or chocolate custard.

cantarello

see GALLINACCIO

cantucci di Prato
almond biscuits

Makes about 40
a pinch of saffron strands
100g/3½oz/¾ cup almonds in their
  skins
40g/1½oz/generous ¼ cup pine nuts
250g/9oz/2 cups Italian 00 flour
225g/8oz/generous 1 cup caster
  (superfine) sugar
generous ¼ tsp baking powder
2 large eggs
½ tsp fennel seeds, bruised
unsalted butter, for greasing

These biscuits originate in Prato, near Florence. Many cooks have their own way of making cantucci. I find this recipe a very good one, the cantucci having just the right biscuity hardness.

Preheat the oven to 200°C/400°F/Gas Mark 6. Grease and flour a large baking sheet.

Reduce the saffron strands to a powder by crushing them between 2 metal spoons, pour on 1 teaspoon boiling water and leave to infuse. Put the almonds and pine nuts on a baking sheet and lightly toast in the oven for 5 minutes. Remove from the oven (leaving the oven on at the same temperature), then chop each almond in half if large.

Sift the flour, sugar and baking powder onto the work surface. Stir to mix and make a well in the middle. Beat the eggs lightly with the fennel and saffron. Pour the mixture into the well and work it gradually into the dry ingredients, adding the nuts at the end. When everything is well mixed, divide in half and, using well-floured hands, pat and roll each piece to a 30cm/12in long sausage. Lay them well apart on the baking sheet and bake for 15–18 minutes.

Take the baking sheet out of the oven and reduce the temperature to 150°C/300°F/Gas Mark 2 or a little less. Cool the cantucci for 10 minutes, then cut them diagonally into 1cm/½in thick slices. Lay the slices side by side on the baking sheet and return to the oven for the second baking – 45 minutes or so, until well dried out.

Cool completely before storing in an airtight container. They will keep for up to 2–3 months.

capelli d'angelo
a pasta

Literally, 'angel's hair'. Extremely fine strands of dried pasta, usually cooked in a light broth and served as a soup.

capillari

see CIECHE

capitone
large eel

The capitone is a very long (sometimes reaching 1.5m/around 5ft) and fat female eel. It is cooked in the same way as other eel (ANGUILLA), and it is also preserved in oil. Capitone is traditionally eaten on Christmas Eve in Rome, Milan and other parts of Italy.

capocollo
a cured cut of pork

The boned and rolled shoulder and neck of a pig, capocollo is aged for 4 to 6 months, and eaten thinly sliced. It is a SALUME characteristic of central and southern Italy, and may be flavoured with wine, garlic and/or different herbs or spices according to the region where it is made. In Puglia capocollo is also lightly smoked.

caponata
aubergines in a sweet and sour sauce

Serves 4
vegetable oil, for frying
750g/1lb 10oz aubergines, cut into
*   1cm/½in cubes*
salt and freshly ground black pepper
the inner stalks of 1 head of celery,
*   coarse strings removed, cut into*
*   1cm/½in cubes*
100ml/3½fl oz/7 tbsp olive oil
1 onion, very finely sliced
225g/8oz canned plum tomatoes,
*   drained and chopped*
1 tbsp granulated sugar
6 tbsp white wine vinegar
1 tbsp grated dark chocolate (minimum
*   70% cocoa solids)*
4 tbsp capers, preferably in salt, rinsed
50g/1¾oz large green olives, pitted and
*   quartered*
2 hard-boiled eggs, to serve

A Sicilian dish, which appears in many different versions throughout the island. It is based on a mixture of fried aubergine, celery, onion and tomato, to which artichokes or wild asparagus may be added. The mixture is sometimes garnished with small octopus, prawns or shrimps, small pieces of lobster or BOTTARGA (dried mullet or tuna roe). The recipe I give here includes a small amount of chocolate. For an even richer caponata, a special sauce, called *salsa di San Bernardo*, is poured over it. This is made with sugar, vinegar, toasted almonds and dark chocolate: a sweet and sour sauce very much in the medieval style.

Heat 2.5cm/1in vegetable oil in a frying pan. When the oil is hot, add a layer of aubergines and fry until golden brown on all sides. Drain on kitchen paper, sprinkling each batch lightly with salt. Repeat until all the aubergines are cooked.

Fry the celery in the oil in which the aubergines were cooked, until golden and crisp. Drain on kitchen paper.

Pour the olive oil into a clean frying pan and add the onion. Sauté gently for about 10 minutes, until soft. Add the tomatoes and cook, stirring frequently, over a moderate heat for about 15 minutes. Season with salt and pepper to taste.

While the sauce is cooking, heat the sugar and vinegar in a small saucepan. Add the chocolate, capers and olives and simmer the mixture gently until the chocolate has melted. Add to the tomato sauce and cook for a further 5 minutes.

Mix the aubergines and celery into the tomato sauce. Stir and cook for 20 minutes, so that the flavours of the ingredients can blend together. Pour the caponata into a serving dish and leave to cool.

Before serving, pass the eggs through the smallest holes of a food mill or push through a metal sieve over the caponata.

cappa santa

The Venetian name for CONCHIGLIA DI SAN GIACOMO.

cappellacci
stuffed pasta

One of the most delicious kinds of stuffed pasta, cappellacci, from Ferrara, are a large version of CAPPELLETTI. The pejorative suffix -acci refers to their shape, as cappellacci are not as attractive as cappelletti. Cappellacci are filled with a mixture of pureed pumpkin, Parmesan, breadcrumbs, nutmeg and eggs. The best way to serve them is to pour golden melted butter over, and a generous grating of Parmesan. This dressing enhances the very delicate flavour of the filling.

cappelletti
stuffed pasta

Cappelletti ('little hats') vary according to the region. The prettiest are those from Emilia-Romagna, with turned-up peaks, while the cappelletti from Umbria and Le Marche are half-moon shaped, and similar to a traditional *carabiniere*'s hat.

The stuffings differ as well as the shapes. The cappelletti from Gubbio in Umbria, the richest of them all, are stuffed with a mixture of capon, pigeon, pork, brains and sausage, plus the usual eggs and Parmesan. Served in hot capon broth, they are traditional Christmas fare. The cappelletti from Reggio in Emilia, which are very small, have a succulent stuffing of different kinds of meat, prosciutto and grated Parmesan. The *cappelletti di grasso* of Romagna are stuffed with capon breast, ricotta and Parmesan, while cappelletti di MAGRO contain no meat but only fresh ricotta and eggs.

By tradition, cappelletti are served in a BRODO (stock) made with capon, or drained and dressed with butter and Parmesan.

Industrially produced cappelletti are stuffed with meat or with spinach and ricotta.

cappello da prete
a sausage

This sausage, as its name suggests, is in the shape of a priest's triangular hat. The meat is the same as that for ZAMPONE (originally the meat remaining on a pig's hind leg after the CULATELLO was cut off). But while the latter is encased in a pig's trotter, cappello da prete is wrapped in a very thin rind from the intestine of the pig. It is a very expensive sausage to make, because it requires a lengthy and difficult manipulation. Before cooking, cappello da prete is lightly punctured with a needle; it is served with potato puree, boiled beans or stewed lentils. It is also industrially produced and sold pre-cooked.

cappero
caper

A wild bush that grows on walls and rocks along the coasts of southern Italy and the islands. Italian capers are supposedly the best in the world, and those grown on the island of Pantelleria are particularly acclaimed – the volcanic soil and hot, dry climate provide ideal conditions. The best capers are the smallest ones.

It is the buds of the flowers, not the fruit, that are eaten. They are preserved layered with rock salt, in wine vinegar or in brine, the best being those preserved in salt. Capers are one of the hallmarks of Mediterranean dishes, added to a pasta sauce, a pizza topping or a fish dish, but always at the last minute, since capers should not be cooked.

cappon magro
a Genoese salad

Made with various kinds of boiled fish and vegetables dressed with SALSA VERDE. Cappon magro is like many other Genoese dishes in being extremely elaborate, and the explanation of this dates from the time when Genoa was an all-powerful maritime republic. Her menfolk were at sea for months at a time, perhaps waging war against other republics or bringing spices and other products from the East. When the men eventually returned, their women used to prepare extravagant feasts of welcome, and on these occasions cappon magro was the pièce de résistance.

cappone
capon

Capon is a cock neutered at around 60 days and killed at 6 or 7 months. It has a delicious flavour, stronger than a chicken and yet more delicate. Its production is limited and is concentrated around Christmas, when this bird is traditional fare, especially in northern Italy, where the farms are.

The usual method of cooking capon is to boil it. This is probably a legacy from the past, when this bird was always boiled for the stock. In Renaissance recipes, MACCHERONI and TORTELLI were cooked in capon stock and the flesh was used for the stuffing. This is still the case today with CAPPELLETTI and ANOLINI. Capon is also pot-roasted, sometimes stuffed with the same stuffing as a turkey. At a friend's house in Milan, I had one of the most delicious birds imaginable. It was a capon cooked on the spit, stuffed with the liver and heart sautéed in butter and finished off with a generous grating of white truffles.

cappone
gurnard

There are several slightly different species of this fish, which has white meaty flesh, not many bones and a delicious flavour. The best species can be grilled or roasted in the oven, while other gurnards are used in fish soups or are stewed in a tomato sauce.

cappuccino
see CAFFÈ

capra
goat

Goat seldom features in present-day Italian cooking, although it is sometimes eaten in an oniony stew in the lost villages in the mountains of Sardinia or of Molise.

caprese
salad from Capri

A salad of tomatoes, mozzarella and basil dressed with olive oil, salt and pepper.

There is also a sauce called caprese for dressing GNOCCHI or RAVIOLI. It is made with the same ingredients as the salad, briefly cooked.

capretto
kid

Kid is eaten mainly in central and southern Italy, where it is a traditional dish. It is cooked in many different ways, similar to those used for lamb. Its meat resembles that of lamb, although more tasty and more chewy.

In one recipe, kid is boned then stuffed with VERMICELLI dressed with a tomato sauce containing the offal of the kid and the giblets of a chicken. The kid is roasted in the oven and then brought to the table whole, surrounded by new potatoes and small onions.

caprino
a cheese

A cheese that, judging by its name (capra means 'goat'), should be made with goat's milk. In fact, only a few farm-made caprini are still made entirely with goat's milk. Most of the caprini on the market are made industrially with a mixture of goat's and cow's milk, or just cow's milk. The best are made in Lombardy, using cow's milk that has been processed to obtain a high fat content. The small cylindrical cheeses are kept in olive oil and eaten dressed with best olive oil and plenty of pepper.

capriolo
roebuck

Capriolo used to be found throughout Italy, except on the islands. However, it is now very rare and is a protected animal. For this reason, capriole are now farmed. The flavour is similar to kid (CAPRETTO) but more gamey, and it can be cooked in the same way. A young roebuck is excellent roasted on the spit, the best part being the saddle. If the capriolo is older, it is marinated in wine with onion, celery, carrot, parsley, juniper berries, pepper and salt. It is then roasted on the spit or in a large oven, basted frequently with wine to keep the meat moist, or it is stewed.

[see recipe on page 86]

caraxiu
cooking method

A Sardinian word meaning buried, it refers to the ancient method of cooking used by the island's shepherds. A fire is made in a deep pit using aromatic woods; when these have burnt through, branches of myrtle, rosemary and thyme are laid on the hot embers. A piglet or a suckling boar is placed on top and covered with more scented branches, after which earth is piled on to close the pit. Further heat is applied by lighting a bonfire on top. After several hours the meat is ready.

carbonade or carbonata
meat dish

A speciality of Valle d'Aosta, carbonade was made in the past with preserved meat, as were all the meat dishes eaten by the locals. Finely sliced meat was preserved by storing it in barrels, layered with salt, sage and rosemary. Nowadays carbonade is usually made with fresh meat, as in the recipe given here.

 [see recipe on page 87]

carbonara
pasta sauce

This now renowned pasta sauce was unknown outside Rome and its region until World War II. It apparently was the common fare of the *carbonari* (hence its name) who went up the mountains east of Rome to make charcoal. They used pig fat instead of butter or olive oil, and cured pig jowl, and the latter is still used in Rome instead of PANCETTA. Whatever its origins, it gained international fame thanks to the Allied armies, who took it back from Rome to their native countries after the war. They found in the sauce the familiar foods of their homelands, eggs and bacon, successfully combined with their new love, spaghetti.

The sauce has endless variations. Some cooks add a little onion, garlic or herbs to the pancetta, others like to cut the fattiness of the pancetta by adding a little white wine, others use only egg yolks. I give a classic recipe here.

[see recipe on page 87]

capriolo alla Alto Atesina
stewed venison

Serves 6

1.5kg/3¼lb boneless venison
4 tbsp olive oil
2 tbsp flour
50g/1¾oz smoked pancetta, diced
50g/1¾oz/⅓ cup salted pork fat, diced,
*   or 4 tbsp olive oil*
1 or 2 Spanish onions, about 225g/8oz,
*   very thinly sliced*
salt and freshly ground black pepper
¼ tsp ground cinnamon
¼ tsp ground cloves
300ml/10fl oz/1¼ cups sour cream

Marinade

1 carrot, cut into pieces
1½ onions, coarsely sliced
1 celery stalk, cut into pieces
1 tbsp coarse sea salt
12 juniper berries, bruised
8 black peppercorns, crushed
3 cloves
1 sprig of fresh rosemary
2 or 3 sprigs of fresh thyme
1 sprig of fresh sage
3 tbsp olive oil
3 bay leaves
3 garlic cloves
1 bottle of good full-bodied red wine

In the Tyrol the meat used is roebuck, which is often from farmed animals — their meat has less flavour, but needs to be hung for a shorter period. You can use venison, which in the UK may be from any species of deer, usually red, fallow or roe deer.

Put all the ingredients for the marinade into a pot and heat until boiling. Leave until cold.

Cut the venison into pieces about 5cm/2in thick. Put them in a bowl and add the marinade. Cover the bowl and leave for 2 days, preferably in a cool place other than the refrigerator.

Lift the meat from the marinade and pat dry with kitchen paper. Strain the marinade, saving the liquid.

Preheat the oven to 160°C/325°F/Gas Mark 3.

Heat 2 tablespoons of the olive oil in a large cast-iron frying pan. Add half the meat and brown very thoroughly on all sides. Fry in two batches so that it browns properly. Transfer to a plate.

Add the flour to the pan and cook until brown, stirring and scraping the bottom of the pan with a spoon. Add about half the marinade liquid and bring to the boil, stirring constantly and breaking down any lumps of flour with the back of the spoon.

Put the rest of the oil, the pancetta and pork fat in a flameproof casserole and cook for 5 minutes. Add the onions and a pinch of salt and continue cooking until the onion is really soft. Add a couple of tablespoons of hot water to prevent the onion from burning.

Now add the meat with all the juice that has leaked out, the thickened marinade from the frying pan and about 150ml/5fl oz/⅔ cup of the remaining marinade. Season with salt, pepper and the spices and bring slowly to the boil. Cover the casserole and cook in the oven for about 1 hour, adding a little marinade twice during cooking.

Heat the cream in a small pan and add to the casserole. Cook for a further 30 minutes, or until the meat is very tender. The cooking time depends on the quality and age of the animal.

carbonade
beef casserole

87

Serves 4

800g/1 ¾lb beef in a single piece, from
the shoulder (chuck steak) if possible
50g/1 ¾oz/4 tbsp unsalted butter
1 tbsp vegetable or olive oil
700g/1lb 9oz onions, finely sliced
salt and freshly ground black pepper
1 tbsp flour
500ml/18fl oz/2 ¼ cups strong red wine
½ tsp grated nutmeg

A traditional recipe from Valle d'Aosta, the region just to the east of the Alps from France, where the food has strong French and Swiss influences. CARBONADE is always served with polenta.

Cut the meat into thin slices. Heat the butter and oil in a heavy flame–proof casserole, add the meat – in batches so that it cooks in a single layer – and brown on all sides, transferring each batch to a plate after frying.

Add the onions to the casserole and season with a little salt, which will help them soften without browning. When the onions are soft, return the meat to the pan and add the flour. Cook for a minute or so, stirring constantly, then pour in about a ladleful of the wine. Bring to the boil and then reduce the heat and cook over a very low heat for a couple of hours, adding half a ladleful of wine whenever the meat becomes too dry.

When the meat is tender, add a good grinding of pepper and the nutmeg and continue cooking for a further 10 minutes or so.

carbonara
egg and pancetta sauce

Enough for 4 helpings of pasta

2 tbsp olive oil
1 garlic clove, chopped
150g/5 ½oz unsmoked pancetta, cut
into small cubes
3 large eggs
40g/1 ½oz Parmesan cheese, grated
20g/¾oz mature pecorino cheese, grated
1 tbsp chopped fresh flat-leaf parsley
3 tbsp double (heavy) cream
salt and freshly ground black pepper

The pasta used for CARBONARA can be spaghetti or BUCATINI; it could also be LINGUINE – as long as it's a long strand pasta. In Rome, where this sauce comes from, cured pork jowl (GUANCIALE) is used, but as this is not available outside Italy, pancetta is a good substitute.

Put the olive oil and garlic in a frying pan and sauté until the garlic begins to turn golden. Add the pancetta and cook for about 10 minutes, until all the fat has run out and the pancetta begins to crisp up.

Meanwhile, cook your pasta in plenty of boiling salted water.

Lightly beat the eggs in a large bowl and then beat in the cheeses, parsley and cream. Add a little salt – the pancetta and Parmesan are quite salty – and a generous grinding of pepper. Place the bowl in the oven, at 120°C/250°F/Gas Mark ½. Leave the oven door slightly ajar.

When the pasta is cooked, reserve a cupful of the water and drain. Turn the pasta into the warm bowl with the sauce and mix well. Add the pancetta and its fat and mix well. Pour in 2–3 tablespoons of the reserved pasta water and mix again. Serve immediately, on warmed plates.

carciofo
globe artichoke

Artichokes grow in fields called *carciofaie* all over the peninsula and the islands. There are many varieties of artichoke, some with thorns, some without. Very small carciofi are usually preserved in oil and served as part of a mixed ANTIPASTO. Young artichokes with thorns – called *spinosi* – are eaten raw, dipped in olive oil. With older specimens the tough outer leaves and the 'beard' or 'choke' near the heart have to be removed before they are cooked in various ways.

In Sardinia, the excellent local artichoke, the *spinoso sardo*, is cut into segments and baked with oil, water and a fair amount of mint. Young specimens are sliced very thin and mixed with BOTTARGA in one of the best salads ever. The similar *spinoso di Liguria* is the main ingredient in the TORTA PASQUALINA. However, the best recipes are from Rome. Here the local variety is the thornless *romanesco*. *Carciofi alla giudea* is a recipe from the city's Jewish quarter. The artichokes, opened up like a rose, are gently fried whole in olive oil. In *carciofi alla romana* the artichokes are stuffed with parsley, mint, breadcrumbs and garlic and cooked in the oven in oil and water. In Venice there are the excellent yellow *canarino* and the early *castraure* varieties, which are simply cooked with oil, parsley, garlic and water.

Artichoke hearts or bottoms, *fondi di carciofo*, are sold in cans, preserved in brine, and during the spring they are sold ready prepared, from buckets of acidulated water, in greengrocer's shops. Artichoke bottoms are stewed in olive oil with garlic and herbs. They can be eaten raw, finely sliced, or blanched and stuffed with chicken, tuna or prosciutto and then baked.

[see recipe below]

carciofi coi piselli
artichokes with peas

Serves 4

4 tender young artichokes
lemon juice
2 shallots or 1 small onion, finely chopped
50g/1¾oz prosciutto, finely chopped
3 tbsp olive oil
15g/½oz/1 tbsp unsalted butter
150ml/5fl oz/⅔ cup meat stock (page 61) or chicken stock
300g/10½oz/2 cups shelled fresh garden peas, or frozen petits pois, thawed
salt and freshly ground black pepper

This is one of the traditional recipes from Rome, prepared in the spring with the first peas and the first romanesco artichokes.

Prepare the artichokes by discarding the tough outer leaves, cutting off about 2cm/¾in from the tops and removing the stalks. Plunge the artichokes into cold water, to which 1 tablespoon of lemon juice has been added, to prevent them from turning black.

Put the shallots and prosciutto in a heavy saucepan or flameproof earthenware pot with the olive oil and butter. Sauté gently while you cut the artichokes in half (removing the furry chokes) and then – unless they are really small – into quarters. Dry them and add to the pan. Cook over a medium heat for about 5 minutes, turning them over in the fat.

Pour the stock over the artichokes, add the fresh peas and season with a little salt and plenty of pepper. Cook until the artichokes and peas are tender – you might have to add a couple of tablespoons of water during cooking if the dish seems too dry. If you are using frozen peas, add them about halfway through cooking the artichokes.

RIGHT: Carciofi coi piselli

cardo
cardoon

In central Italy also called *gobbo* (hunchback) because of the way the plant curves during blanching, this vegetable, cultivated for its leaf-stalks, is a spectacular Mediterranean thistle, like the globe artichoke. But in cardoons it is the stem that is eaten, not the flower bud. In its method of cultivation it is more akin to celery than to artichoke, but its flavour is reminiscent of the artichoke, though slightly sweeter.

When young, cardoons are eaten raw, as they are with the Piedmontese BAGNA CAÒDA, to which they are the principal accompaniment. They can also be cooked in very little water, flavoured with oil, garlic and parsley and finished off with a light sauce of egg yolk and lemon. Only the inner stalks and the heart of older cardoons are eaten. When cut they should be rubbed with lemon to prevent discoloration and then simmered for between 30 and 45 minutes, after which they may be dressed with anchovy butter, or baked in the oven with butter and grated Parmesan, or with béchamel sauce.

Carnacina, Luigi
1888–1981

A great chef and cookery writer, Carnacina started his career at the age of 12 in a trattoria belonging to his godfather. He progressed through various hotels in Europe and worked with the legendary Auguste Escoffier at the Savoy in London; in 1920 he became manager of Escoffier's restaurant in Ostend, Belgium; later he worked in famous establishments in Europe and the USA. He retired in 1956 and dedicated himself to writing cookery books. His greatest work, *La Grande Cucina*, is an encyclopedia of the culinary art of Europe. *Il Carnacina* is a collection of his famous recipes and *La Buona Vera Cucina Italiana* gathers 1,547 recipes from all regions of Italy, which Carnacina wrote in collaboration with Luigi Veronelli, a journalist, wine writer and gastronome.

carne
meat

The Italians generally eat less meat than the northern Europeans, pork being the most popular meat all over the peninsula, both fresh and cured. In the north, where a lot of the land is pasture, beef and veal are the favourites. In Tuscany, the best beef in Italy comes from the Chianina breed of cattle. Lamb and, to a lesser degree, kid are the meats of the mountainous central and southern Italy. Every part of the animal is eaten, although offal (FRATTAGLIE) is considered distinct from the meat (*carne*) from the muscles. Chicken is popular everywhere, but the stronghold of chicken dishes is Tuscany, famous for the free-ranging birds of the Valdarno. Other meats eaten in Italy are rabbit, hare, horse, donkey, game (including almost anything that flies), frogs and snails. These last two are considered great delicacies.

Meat is cooked by many different methods, either as a joint, cut into pieces or sliced. A joint or bird can be roasted (ARROSTO) in various ways. The whole animal, which could be a piglet (PORCHETTA), a wild boar or a young deer, is roasted on the spit, and this is the central dish in many country feasts. Joints from tougher cuts are stewed in stock, wine or both, with flavouring vegetables, herbs and spices – BRASATO, STUFATO or STRACOTTO. The tougher cuts are also cut into pieces and stewed – SPEZZATINO. Sliced meat or chops of any kind are often stuffed or finished off with a sauce, as in PIZZAIOLA. Minced meat is used to make RAGÙ and also in the various POLPETTE and POLPETTONI that are standard fare everywhere, partly because the actual meat content is relatively small. Beef is eaten raw in CARPACCIO and *carne all'albese*, a delicious dish from Piedmont where the local beef, raw and very thinly sliced, is dressed with olive oil and lemon juice and then covered by a heavenly shower of shredded white truffles.

Quick methods of cooking meat include grilling and frying, often coated in egg and breadcrumbs, or sautéed in butter or other fat, for example the Roman speciality SALTIMBOCCA.

carota
carrot

Carrots grow all over Italy and are widely cultivated in the north and in Le Marche. There are many different varieties and colours of carrot, from white to purplish red, but the most common are the orange-coloured ones, which are either short and fat, or long and thin. They are harvested all year round.

Carrots are used primarily as a flavouring for soups, stocks, marinades and SOFFRITTO – the basis of so many dishes. When young they are also eaten raw in salads, simply dressed with olive oil and lemon juice. When not so young, carrots are cut into sticks or rounds and braised in stock, or sautéed slowly in butter and/or oil. They are often flavoured with Parmesan, with oregano or parsley, and in one of the very few recipes from southern Italy, a couple of tablespoons of MARSALA are added at the end.

Boiled carrots are one of the classic accompaniments to BOLLITO MISTO. They can also be coated in flour and fried in olive oil. Grated carrots make a good sauce for roast or boiled meat: they are first sautéed with grated onions in olive oil and butter, and then cooked in stock and vinegar with some tomato puree and a little sugar.

carpa
carp

The male carp with its soft roe makes better eating than the female. The best variety of carp is the *carpa a specchi*, with large scales and a golden-green colour with shimmering reflections. Unfortunately, a lot of these are now farmed, and have a muddy flavour, one of the reasons why carp is no longer appreciated in Italy as it was in past centuries. The best wild carp are caught in Lake Trasimeno in Umbria. The traditional way of cooking carp is to bake it in the oven with PANCETTA and tomatoes.

carpaccio
raw beef

A dish which, within a few decades, has become a favourite the world over. Carpaccio was created in 1961 by Giuseppe Cipriani of Harry's Bar in Venice for an aristocratic Venetian lady who was on a strict diet. He named the dish after the famous painter Vittore Carpaccio (c.1460–1525), because there was an exhibition of his paintings in Venice at the time, and 'because the colours of the dish remind me of the reds that Carpaccio used'.

Carpaccio, or *filetto al Carpaccio* to give it its proper name, is very thinly sliced fillet of beef, dressed with a small amount of mayonnaise to which is added a touch of mustard, a drop of brandy and of Tabasco sauce, plus enough cream to make the sauce of a fluid consistency. Sometimes a teaspoonful of thick tomato sauce is added.

Many cooks mistakenly use the name carpaccio to describe what is in fact CARNE *all'albese*. And I have recently seen recipes named carpaccio that share nothing with the original. They are called carpaccio simply because they are made with any thinly sliced raw meat or fish or vegetable, dressed with any sort of dressing. Unfortunately, there is no copyright on the names of recipes.

carpione
marinated fish

This ancient method of preparing fish, in which the fish is marinated in a sweet and sour sauce for

91

2 days, dates from the time when fish was plentiful but refrigeration non-existent. It goes by different names in different regions. Carpione is the Lombard name, while in Veneto it is *in saor* (see recipe on page 391) and in Le Marche and Sicily it is called SCAPECE. In the original Lombard recipe, freshwater fish such as tench or perch is used, but sardines or sole can be treated in the same way. Carpione makes an excellent ANTIPASTO.

carrettiera, alla
pasta sauce

The name given to pasta sauces with strong hearty flavour. *Carrettiere* means 'cart driver' and supposedly these men liked meaty sauces made with wine and tomatoes. There are many variations of pasta alla carrettiera, mostly from central Italy, where the most popular pasta shape used in conjunction with this sauce is FUSILLI.

carta da musica
a bread

Carta da musica is a Sardinian bread made with unleavened dough rolled into thin rounds, similar to the parchment paper on which music was written. Because it keeps well for long periods, it is the staple bread of the shepherds, who take it with them while tending their flocks away from home.

cartoccio
cooking method

A method of baking, principally used for fish. It is an old method but one that is now used also for meat escalopes, vegetables and even rice and pasta. The fish, usually whole, is sprinkled with olive oil, lemon juice, salt and pepper and wrapped in foil or greaseproof paper. It is baked and brought to the table still in the wrapping, which has captured all the aromatic juices. The most exuberant of all food 'al cartoccio' is a large fish – a sea bass or a daurade – wrapped in foil together with delicate shellfish such as clams, oysters, prawns, shrimp, scallops. My favourite dish cooked this way is *spaghetti al cartoccio*, in which the cooked spaghetti are mixed with seafood, slightly sautéed in oil, garlic and chilli, wrapped in foil, and finished in a very hot oven for about 5 minutes.

casalinga or casareccia
homely

These two adjectives derive from *casa*, meaning house or home, here with an overtone of family. The best Italian cooking is casalinga, the cooking one hardly ever meets in restaurants, the cooking that is passed down from mother to daughter. The terms are now often used to describe rustic dishes.

casonsei
stuffed pasta

An ancient speciality of Bergamo and Brescia in Lombardy, first mentioned in a local booklet at the end of the 14th century.

Casonsei are of an unusual shape, like a short, fat sleeve, tucked in at both ends. They are stuffed with AMARETTI, sultanas, SALAME, spinach, egg and Parmesan and, when cooked, lavishly dressed with butter and sage.

cassata
dessert

Three desserts share the name cassata. The oldest is the *cassata siciliana*, a concoction consisting of an outer layer of Madeira cake containing a mixture of sweetened RICOTTA flavoured with vanilla, chocolate or cinnamon, sometimes studded with candied peel or pumpkin and/or pieces of chocolate. The cake is covered with almond paste, traditionally green from the inclusion of powdered pistachio nuts, and decorated with candied fruit or fruits made of marzipan.

A second cassata is the layered cake from Sulmona in Abruzzo for which the recipe is given here. The third cassata is the popular iced cassata, *cassata gelata*, a modern concoction comprising layers of ice cream.

[see recipe below]

cassata di Sulmona
praline and chocolate cassata

Serves 6–8

75g/2¾oz/⅓ cup caster (superfine) sugar

100g/3½oz/7 tbsp unsalted butter, at room temperature

3 large egg yolks

25g/1oz/¼ cup hazelnuts, toasted, skinned and coarsely chopped

25g/1oz dark chocolate (minimum 70% cocoa solids), chopped

1 tbsp unsweetened cocoa powder, sifted

350g/12oz Madeira cake, sliced about 1cm/½in thick

75ml/2½fl oz/5 tbsp Centerbe, Strega, Chartreuse or any other herb liqueur

icing sugar, chocolate flakes and/or ground hazelnuts, to decorate

Praline

2 tbsp granulated sugar

1 tsp lemon juice

25g/1oz/3 tbsp blanched almonds

Less famous than the Sicilian ricotta-filled CASSATA, but arguably even better, this cassata comes from Abruzzo.

First, prepare the praline. Heat the sugar and lemon juice with ½ tablespoon water over a low heat until the sugar has completely dissolved. Turn up the heat and boil rapidly until the syrup is golden, not brown. Remove from the heat and mix in the almonds. Pour onto an oiled baking sheet and leave to set.

When the praline is cold, put it between two sheets of greaseproof paper and crush with a rolling pin. Alternatively, crush the praline in a food processor. Set aside.

Prepare the cassata. Put the sugar and butter in a bowl and beat until creamy, then beat in the egg yolks, one at a time. Divide the mixture into three parts and add the praline to one part, the hazelnuts and chocolate to the second and the cocoa to the third.

Line a 900g/2lb loaf tin with clingfilm. Cover the bottom with a layer of cake, moisten with some liqueur and spread over the praline mixture. Cover with more cake, moisten with liqueur and spread over the chocolate and hazelnut mixture. Add the final layer of cake, moisten with liqueur and spread over the cocoa mixture. Cover with clingfilm and place in the refrigerator for at least 6 hours or overnight.

To serve, turn out the cassata onto an oval dish and decorate with icing sugar, chocolate flakes and/or ground hazelnuts.

93

cassoeula
pork casserole with cabbage

Serves 8

2 pig's trotters, cut into 4 pieces

1 pig's tail, cut into pieces (optional)

1 pig's ear (optional)

250g/9oz pork rind

1 tbsp vegetable oil

50g/1¾oz/4 tbsp pure pork lard

1 large onion, coarsely chopped

2 carrots, sliced

2–3 celery stalks, diced

500g/1lb 2oz boneless pork belly, cut
    into cubes

salt and freshly ground black pepper

500g/1lb 2oz mild pure pork sausage,
    diced

2kg/4½lb Savoy cabbage, shredded

94

An ancient Lombard dish, also called *bottaggio*, which is similar to the French cassoulet and the Spanish *pote gallego*. It is made with several different cuts of the pig, such as ribs, ears, tail, rind and trotters, and in some places goose is added. The recipe given here is for a slightly simplified version. It is an adaptation of my mother's recipe, which is one of the best cassoeula I have ever tasted. Like all traditional dishes it is the subject of passionate controversy. Should it be eaten the day after it is made? Should it contain tomato puree? Should the Savoy cabbage be al dente or mushy? Whatever it is, a genuine cassoeula should contain different cuts of pork. I always make it one or two days in advance and chill it, then reheat it before serving. Cassoeula is always served with POLENTA.

Put the trotters, tail and ear, if using, in a large pan, cover with cold water, bring to the boil and simmer for 30 minutes. Add the pork rind and cook for a further 5 minutes. Remove the meat from the pan and cut the tail and ear into chunks; cut the rind into 5cm/2in squares. Leave the pork stock to cool and then refrigerate. When the fat has solidified on the surface, remove and discard it.

Put the oil, lard and onion in a large, heavy, flameproof casserole and sauté until soft. Add the carrots and celery and cook gently for 5 minutes, stirring frequently.

Increase the heat, add the trotters, tail, ear and rind and fry for 2 minutes. Add the pork belly and fry for 5 minutes, stirring frequently. The meat must not stick to the bottom of the pan or it will give a slightly bitter taste to the whole dish.

Add the reserved stock, and more water if needed, to cover the meat. Sprinkle with salt and pepper, cover with a lid and cook over the gentlest possible heat for 2 hours.

Add the sausage and the cabbage, mix well and cook for 30 minutes, turning the ingredients over once or twice. Taste and adjust the seasoning.

castagna
chestnut

This beautiful, shiny nut has for centuries been one of the staple foods of the mountain regions, especially of the Apennines. Chestnuts come in many varieties, of which *marroni* is the best, usually with a single large nut in each prickly shell. Marroni are a light brown colour, sometimes striped with white, and the thin inner skin is easily peeled. Other varieties have two or even three nuts per shell.

There are many savoury and sweet recipes for chestnuts, all from northern Italy. The exception is one from Le Marche called *castagne dei morti* (because it is made on All Souls' Day, 2 November), in which the cooked and peeled chestnuts are sprinkled with sugar and GRAPPA, which is then flamed.

Chestnuts are roasted, boiled in milk or stock and then eaten or used in other preparations. Apart from the now universal chestnut stuffing for turkey, a similar stuffing is used in Lombardy for rabbit. A recipe from Piedmont suggests roasted chestnuts and baked onions as an accompaniment to pot-roast beef, in the juice of which they receive a final cooking. And there is also a good rustic soup made with chestnuts and rice, flavoured with a glass of red wine.

The prize for all chestnut preparations must go to MONTEBIANCO, the pudding from Valle d'Aosta. But the best-known sweet made with chestnuts is *marrons glacés*, extensively made both commercially and artisanally in Piedmont and Lombardy.

Chestnuts are also dried – *castagne secche* – and can then be eaten all the year round. To reconstitute them the dried chestnuts are soaked in warm water for several hours and then boiled in milk, to which a bay leaf is usually added. They can be used in savoury or sweet dishes. However, when dried, chestnuts lose their richness and are definitely inferior in flavour to the fresh variety. In Lombardy, there is a very old recipe for a kind of thick soup called *busecchina*, which is served at the end of the meal. The soaked dried chestnuts are cooked in milk and white wine and served with cream. No sugar is usually added, because the chestnuts release a sweet fragrance in the milky broth.

There is also a flour, *farina di castagne*, made with ground dried chestnuts. It is used to make CASTAGNACCIO, NECCI and fritters. It is also mixed with white wheat flour to make TAGLIATELLE *di farina di castagne*, an excellent pasta when dressed with a game sauce.

castagnaccio
chestnut bread

A flat bread made with chestnut flour. Originally from Tuscany, it is now found all over Italy. The basic ingredients of castagnaccio are chestnut flour and oil, to which are added sultanas, pine nuts, walnuts and fennel seeds. The mixture, bound together with water, is baked in large, flat copper pans.

Castelmagno
a cheese

One of the greatest Piedmontese cheeses, and definitely one of my favourites, Castelmagno has the DOP stamp. It is made from cow's milk and is quite sweet when young, but it becomes stronger in flavour, with blue veins, after being aged for from 2 to 5 months in natural caves.

Castelvetro, Giacomo
1546–1616

The author of a classic book on vegetarian food published in 1614. Castelvetro spent much of his life in England, where he wrote his *Brief account of all the roots, herbs and fruits which, raw or cooked, are eaten in Italy*. His recipes could figure proudly in the most modern vegetarian cookery book.

castrato
young sheep

In gastronomic terms this is a castrated young ram.
Castrato is still popular in central Italy, though
less so than it used to be, since many people now
prefer the sweeter taste of lamb to the stronger,
fuller meat of a castrato. Castrato is roasted in the
oven or on a spit when young. When it is older it
is marinated for at least 24 hours in wine with lots
of herbs and then cooked for some 6 hours in the
marinade with the usual flavouring vegetables.

catalogna

see CICORIA

Cavalcanti, Ippolito, Duke of Buonvicino
1787–1859

A Neapolitan aristocrat who wrote *La Cucina
Teorico-Pratica* (*Theoretical and Practical Cooking*). To
the second edition he added an appendix called
Cucina Casareccia, in Dialetto Napoletano (*Family
Cooking, in Neapolitan Dialect*), which is full of
anecdotes and wise advice. This book is the most
reliable source on Neapolitan cooking.

[see recipe below]

filetto di maiale alla Cavalcanti
pork fillet with elderberries, almonds and balsamic vinegar

Serves 4
600g/1lb 5oz pork fillet (tenderloin)
40g/1 1/2oz/3 tbsp unsalted butter
2 tbsp olive oil
125ml/4fl oz/1/2 cup good red wine
salt and freshly ground black pepper
4 tsp sugar
a pinch of ground cinnamon
2 tbsp balsamic vinegar
1 tbsp very finely ground almonds
2 tbsp elderberries
1 tbsp capers, preferably in salt, rinsed

The Neapolitan haute cuisine of the 18th and 19th centuries was very
sophisticated, often using sweet ingredients in savoury dishes.

Trim the fat off the pork and cut in half, if necessary, so it will fit in a
large sauté pan.

Heat half the butter and the olive oil in the pan, then add the pork and
brown on all sides.

Bring the wine to the boil in a separate pan and pour over the meat,
together with 2 tablespoons hot water. When the liquid comes back to
the boil, add salt and pepper. Turn the heat down so that the liquid is just
simmering, cover the pan tightly and cook for 10 minutes, until the pork
is done. Remove the meat from the pan and keep warm.

Add the sugar and cinnamon, balsamic vinegar, almonds and elderberries
to the pan and cook, stirring constantly, for 2 minutes. Break the
remaining butter into small pieces and add gradually to the sauce while
gently stirring and swirling the pan. Mix in the capers.

Slice the meat (not too thinly) and return to the pan for 2 minutes to
absorb the flavour of the sauce. Serve immediately.

cavallo
horse

Horse meat is still eaten in Italy, although less than it used to be prior to, and during, World War II. It is tougher than beef, though more nourishing and digestible, and has a sweetish taste that some people find objectionable. In the past, horse meat was cheaper than other meats, and was often bought to save money; nowadays prices are much the same and horse meat is bought by those who prefer it. Horse meat butchers make sausages and salami from horse, donkey or mule meat, all slightly different and all very good.

cavatieddi
a pasta

A kind of homemade pasta from Puglia, made with durum wheat semolina and plain flour, kneaded with warm water. Cavatieddi are similar in shape to small mussel shells. They are dressed with the local RAGÙ made with lamb or horse meat, or with a delicious sauce made with rocket.

cavolfiore
cauliflower

A very popular vegetable, particularly in the north. In southern Italy, broccoli is often known as cavolfiore, which can be confusing.

Boiled cauliflower florets are often dressed with olive oil and vinegar or lemon juice. Salted anchovies, previously pounded, are sometimes added. Another popular way to serve cauliflower is to sauté the blanched florets gently in butter and cover them with Parmesan before bringing to the table. The SFORMATO di cavolfiore is an elegant dish which can be served as a first course. As with many other vegetables, cauliflower can also be breaded and fried and served as an accompaniment to meat, or as part of a FRITTO MISTO. It is also the main ingredient of a Neapolitan dish called *insalata di rinforzo*, in which the boiled florets are dressed with anchovy fillets, green and black olives, olive oil, vinegar, capers, garlic and salt – traditionally it is served in a dome-shaped mound.

[see recipe on page 98]

cavolini di Bruxelles
Brussels sprouts

There are no traditional recipes for Brussels sprouts, which are grown in northern Italy, where they have recently become more popular. They are always blanched and then sautéed in butter, covered with Parmesan-flavoured béchamel sauce and baked, or gently fried with PANCETTA. A modern pasta sauce combines shredded Brussels sprouts sautéed in oil with smoked pancetta and chilli, to which a few tablespoons of cream and grated Parmesan are added at the end with the pasta.

cavolo
cabbage

There are two main species of cabbage: the compact, firm *cavolo cappuccio*, which includes the types known as primo, white/Dutch and red cabbage, and *cavolo verza* – Savoy cabbage. Cavolo verza is also called *cavolo di Milano* because of its use in traditional Milanese cooking.

Delicious as cabbage undoubtedly is, it is now less popular than it used to be. My ancestors were fond of cabbage both for its culinary uses and for its therapeutic properties, and they cooked it in many ways. The earliest known recipe is found in the 15th-century book by MARTINO da Como, who writes: 'Break up the cabbage with your hands according to the old custom, and put in boiling water. And when it is about half cooked, throw away the water and take some good pork fat, chopped fine, in the right quantity. Cook the cabbage in the lard, turning it over with a spoon. Then add some good fatty stock and boil for a little.'

Savoy cabbage is a fundamental part of CASSOEULA, for which the recipe is given on page 94. In another dish, an ancestor of FAGOTTINI di verza (see recipe on page 140), its leaves are stuffed with meat, nutmeg and a little brain or bone marrow and stewed in stock. Savoy cabbage is also used in soups, particularly MINESTRONE, and as a vegetable. One of my favourite recipes is *verze sofegae* ('smothered Savoy cabbage'), in which the cabbage is 'smothered' in white wine.

cavolo nero
'black cabbage'

The leaves, deep green rather than black, do not form a head and are slightly more bitter and less 'cabbagey' tasting than ordinary varieties. Cavolo nero appears in many Tuscan soups, of which la RIBOLLITA is the most famous, and it is cooked with pork in nourishing and rich stews. It is best after the first frost, when its texture becomes softer.

ceci
chickpeas

Chickpeas are always sold dried. They are soaked for at least 8 hours and then cooked at length. They were appreciated in Roman times and are popular all over Italy, although the best recipes come from the south. There are a number of chickpea and pasta dishes (see recipe overleaf), usually containing tomatoes and garlic and always dressed with olive oil; the pasta varies from region to region, from LAGANE to DITALI and long strands. A salad of chickpeas and rocket is popular in Puglia, and in Rome chickpeas are sautéed in garlic-flavoured oil with rosemary and anchovies, to which a pinch of chilli may be added. There are two traditional dishes from the north: *ceci in zimino*, from Liguria, is a thick soup of chickpeas with spinach and anchovy fillets; *ceci con la tempia*, from Lombardy, is a rich stew of chickpeas, pork ribs and the pig's temple — it is traditional fare in Milan on All Souls' Day.

Chickpeas are also sold in cans, but they lose some of their delicious mealiness.

[see recipe on page 100]

cavolfiore in umido
cauliflower with tomato sauce

Serves 4

3 tbsp olive oil

2 tbsp chopped fresh flat-leaf parsley

1 garlic clove, chopped

1 tbsp tomato puree

1 cauliflower, about 500g/1lb 2oz, divided into florets

200ml/7fl oz/generous ¾ cup meat stock (page 61) or vegetable stock

salt and freshly ground black pepper

Various vegetables, most commonly potatoes and green beans, are cooked in this way. At the end, the cauliflower must be very tender, not crunchy.

Put the olive oil, parsley and garlic in a heavy saucepan over a low heat and cook gently for 1 minute. Add the tomato puree and cook, stirring, for a few seconds, then add the cauliflower florets. Sauté for 5–7 minutes, turning the florets gently to coat them in the oil and tomato mixture.

Pour in the stock, season with a little salt and pepper and cook, covered, over a very low heat for 10–15 minutes, until the cauliflower is tender.

Lift the florets onto a serving dish and, if necessary, reduce the liquid until rich and full of flavour. Pour over the florets and serve.

RIGHT: Cavolfiore in umido

cavolo nero

pasta e ceci
pasta and chickpeas

Serves 4

200g/7oz/1 cup dried chickpeas, soaked
*   for about 12 hours*
1.5 litres/3 pints/6½ cups vegetable
*   stock*
2 sprigs of fresh rosemary
4 garlic cloves, chopped
75ml/2½fl oz/5 tbsp extra virgin
*   olive oil*
225g/8oz ripe fresh tomatoes, peeled
*   and chopped, or canned tomatoes,*
*   chopped*
salt and freshly ground black pepper
150g/5½oz/1⅓ cups small tubular
*   pasta, such as ditalini*
freshly grated Parmesan cheese, to serve
*   (optional)*

Chickpeas are best eaten within a year of being harvested, so try to buy them from a store that has a rapid turnover. I don't recommend using canned chickpeas to make this soup, as it needs the flavour of the liquid in which the chickpeas have cooked.

Drain and rinse the chickpeas and put them in a stockpot, preferably earthenware. Add the stock. Tie the rosemary sprigs in a cheesecloth bag and add to the pot. Add the garlic and half the olive oil. Bring to the boil, cover the pot tightly and cook at the lowest simmer until the chickpeas are tender, which can take from 2 to 4 hours. Do not add salt, or it will harden the skins.

When the chickpeas are nearly done, puree the tomatoes and add to the soup. Remove and discard the rosemary bundle. Stir well, add salt and pepper to taste and cook for a further 10 minutes or so.

Check that there is enough liquid in the pan: there must be at least 5cm/2in above the level of the chickpeas; if necessary add some boiling water. Add the pasta and cook until al dente. Ladle the soup into individual bowls and drizzle a little of the remaining oil into each bowl. Parmesan can be handed separately.

cefalo con le zucchine
grey mullet with courgettes

Serves 4

500g/1lb 2oz courgettes
salt and freshly ground black pepper
1 garlic clove, chopped
2 tbsp chopped fresh flat-leaf parsley
1 fresh grey mullet, at least 1kg/2¼lb,
*   scaled and gutted, but with head and*
*   tail on*
150ml/5fl oz/⅔ cup extra virgin olive oil

The sweetness of the courgettes is a good foil for the grey mullet.

Cut the courgettes into rounds, put them in a colander and sprinkle lightly with salt. Leave for about 30 minutes. This will draw out the excess water. Drain and dry them and then mix in the garlic, parsley and pepper.

Preheat the oven to 190°C/375°F/Gas Mark 5.

Season the fish inside and out with salt and pepper and sprinkle 1 tablespoon of the oil inside. Lay the fish in a large ovenproof dish or a roasting pan and spoon the courgettes around it. Pour over the rest of the oil and mix with the courgettes.

Cover the dish with foil and bake for 20 minutes. Remove the foil, stir the courgettes and spoon some of the cooking liquid over the fish. Cook for a further 15 minutes or so, until the fish is ready.

cedro
citron

A fruit in the citrus family that grows plentifully in Calabria and Sicily. It resembles a large lemon in colour, a quince in shape, and has a very thick skin. It is seldom eaten fresh, but is cultivated mainly for its thick rind, which is candied and used in confectionery. A drink called *cedrata*, made with the juice of this fruit, was quite popular in the 1970s and 80s and may be experiencing a revival.

cefalo
grey mullet

Also called *muggine*. There are many species of this fish, the best being the golden grey mullet. When caught in clean water, grey mullet is an excellent fish with rather fatty white flesh of a firm texture and very few bones. But the fish's flavour can be changed for the worse if it has lived in muddy water or waters close to industrial waste. Any species must be eaten very fresh and be cleaned thoroughly to wash away any muddy flavours.

Grey mullet is grilled, boiled, cooked in CARTOCCIO with herbs and olive oil, or baked as in the dish from Le Marche for which the recipe is given here. Like sea bass and red mullet, it is also good baked on a bed of fennel or, better still, of wild fennel leaves.

A great delicacy, called BOTTARGA, is made from the dried roe of the female fish.

[see recipe on facing page]

cena
dinner

Dinner takes place between 7.30 and 8 o'clock in northern Italy, and later in the south. In Rome dinner may start as late as 10. It often starts with a soup, sometimes followed by a dish of meat, fish or some vegetables and then cheese and fruit. It is the meal usually eaten with all the family. Cena can also refer to a grand meal, when it is also called *cenone*.

cenci
fritters

The Tuscan Carnival fritters, made as CHIACCHIERE but flavoured with vin santo instead of MARSALA.

centerbe
liqueur

One of the best-known Italian herb-based liqueurs, of which there are as many as there are monks and monasteries. Centerbe is made with 'a hundred herbs' – *cento* means 'hundred' – gathered on and around the massive peaks of the Maiella in Abruzzo. Centerbe has a high alcohol content – up to 70% alcohol. It is drunk as a digestive or is used to moisten PAN DI SPAGNA for some soft puddings, and to soak sultanas and candied fruits for fruit cakes or sweet stuffings.

cernia
grouper

This Mediterranean fish, of which there are many species, can be as long as 1m/3ft. In spite of its rather ugly appearance, grouper has an excellent flavour, is free from lateral bones and lends itself to many different methods of cooking. The whole fish is delicious roasted with various herbs, or boiled and served with a thin SALSA VERDE. The steaks can be grilled or stewed in tomato sauce. Alan Davidson, in *Mediterranean Seafood*, gives an interesting recipe for *cernia ripiena*, in which the grouper is stuffed with prawns, dried porcini and grated Parmesan, all bound with eggs, and then baked with butter and white wine.

certosino
spiced fruit cake

Serves 8–10

75g/2³⁄₄oz/¹⁄₂ cup seedless raisins

2 tbsp sweet Marsala or sweet sherry

150g/5¹⁄₂oz/scant ¹⁄₂ cup clear honey

150g/5¹⁄₂oz/³⁄₄ cup caster (superfine) sugar

40g/1¹⁄₂oz/3 tbsp unsalted butter, plus extra for greasing

1 tbsp aniseed

1 tsp ground cinnamon

350g/12oz/scant 3 cups Italian 00 flour

150g/5¹⁄₂oz/²⁄₃ cup apple puree, slightly sweetened

150g/5¹⁄₂oz/generous 1 cup blanched almonds, coarsely chopped

50g/1³⁄₄oz/6 tbsp pine nuts

75g/2³⁄₄oz dark chocolate (minimum 70% cocoa solids), chopped

140g/5oz/scant 1 cup candied orange and lemon peel, chopped

¹⁄₂ tbsp bicarbonate of soda

4 tbsp apricot jam

crystallized fruits and/or blanched almonds, to decorate

Also called *pan speziale*. This is the traditional Christmas cake of Bologna. Its name derives from the fact that it was created by the monks of the Certosa – Charterhouse – of Bologna for Cardinal Lambertini, who later became Pope Benedetto XIV. Knowing he was very fond of their special cake, the monks used to send the Pope a certosino every Christmas. Certosino is similar to an English fruit cake in that it contains dried fruits and nuts, but it is lighter and it becomes more mellow and rich on keeping.

Soak the raisins in the Marsala for 20 minutes.

Meanwhile, preheat the oven to 180°C/350°F/Gas Mark 4. Butter a shallow loose-bottomed 25cm/10in diameter cake tin.

Gently heat together the honey, sugar, butter and 3 tablespoons water until the sugar has dissolved. Add the aniseed and cinnamon. Slowly pour this over the flour, mixing thoroughly. Mix in the soaked raisins, apple puree, almonds, pine nuts, chocolate and chopped peel.

Dissolve the bicarbonate of soda in a little warm water and add to the cake mixture. Mix the ingredients very gently but thoroughly and spoon into the prepared tin. Bake for about 1¹⁄₄–1¹⁄₂ hours. Turn out onto a wire rack and leave to cool.

Gently warm the apricot jam and brush over the top of the cooled cake. Stud with crystallized fruit and/or blanched almonds. Brush more jam over the fruit and leave to dry, then wrap in clingfilm. Store in an airtight container for 2–3 months.

cervellata
a sausage

A kind of fresh pork sausage made in Milan, Naples and Puglia, where chilli is also added. It has been suggested that its odd name derives from one of the very early ingredients, CERVELLO – brain. The first documented recipe for cervellata appears in *Il Cuoco Milanese*, published in 1791: the sausage was flavoured with the four Lombard spices – pepper, cinnamon, nutmeg and cloves – and it contained beef bone marrow.

cervello
brain

Because of their creamy texture, melting consistency and delicate flavour, brains are one of the most highly appreciated foods in Italy, as indeed in all continental Europe. Calves' brains are eaten in Lombardy and Tuscany, while lambs' brains are a favourite of the Romans and Neapolitans. *Cervello alla napoletana* are baked lambs' brains scattered with black olives, capers, dried breadcrumbs and olive oil. The other traditional recipe, from the north, is *cervello fritto alla Milanese*, in which the brains are coated with egg and breadcrumbs and fried in butter and oil until golden.

cervo
red deer

Nowadays red deer is no longer wild but farmed in huge fenced-off reserves, especially in Sardinia, and its meat has lost some of the deep, gamey flavour. Most recipes for CAPRIOLO (roebuck) and DAINO (roe deer) are also suitable for red deer. The loin is roasted, while the leg should be pot-roasted in the same way as a leg of wild boar. The meat is marinated, and cooked, in wine.

checca, spaghetti alla
a pasta sauce

A Roman sauce made with raw tomatoes. The ripe tomatoes are cut into pieces, put in a bowl with torn basil leaves, sliced garlic, salt and pepper. The cooked spaghetti are added about 1 hour later and eaten hot or at room temperature. In Naples the dish is called *vermicelli in insalata*.

chiacchiere
fritters

No food is more reminiscent of carnival week in Milan than chiacchiere. Big trays full of them are displayed in every bakery and PASTICCERIA. Children in costumes wander around the city blowing trumpets and munching chiacchiere in a harmonious euphoria.

Chiacchiere are a kind of fried sweet pastry, flavoured with MARSALA and rolled out very thin, as for fresh pasta. The dough is cut into rectangles and two cuts are made in each piece to make the chiacchiere lighter when cooked. Nowadays chiacchiere are baked rather than fried – not as good. They are then sprinkled with icing sugar.

chifel
a bread roll

A small curved bread stick which is covered with cumin seeds and has a very thin, crisp crust. Of Austrian origin and found mostly in the South Tyrol, chifel are eaten with frankfurters, washed down by large mugs of beer.

chiodi di garofano
cloves

One of the most popular spices, cloves are added to braised and stewed meat, vegetables preserved in vinegar, and stewed fruits. One or two cloves are always stuck in an onion for flavouring stocks. Cloves are also available ground.

chiodini
wild fungi

This is the name given to two varieties of wild fungi. Correctly, chiodino is the *Armillaria mellea*, a small fungus growing in clusters on the trunks of deciduous and evergreen trees during autumn. However, a similar fungus, the *Clitocybe tabescens*, is also often known as a chiodino. The latter can be identified by the fact that it does not have a ring around the stem and its habitat is different: it grows in the ground in deciduous woods during late summer and autumn. The chiodini that grow on trees are one of the most common of the fungi that people gather in the woods and are easily recognizable. Chiodini are also sold in shops and markets during autumn.

Both these species of chiodini are good, but the *Clitocybe tabescens* has firmer flesh and a sweeter flavour. Chiodini are usually cooked in olive oil, garlic and parsley. They also make good pasta sauces and are excellent in a FRITTATA.

chitarra
cooking utensil

A tool used to make *maccheroni alla chitarra*, a speciality of Abruzzo. The chitarra is a wooden frame with steel wires stretched across it, through which the rolled-out sheet of fresh pasta is pressed with a rolling pin. The resulting pasta, known as TONNARELLI, looks like square spaghetti. The traditional recipes for this pasta are the lamb RAGÙ given here or a piquant tomato sauce made with PANCETTA.

 [see recipe on page 106]

chizze
savoury snacks

Little pillows of bread dough, usually stuffed with prosciutto, Swiss chard and young Parmesan, or sometimes with other stuffings; they are then fried in STRUTTO. They are the traditional snack food of Reggio Emilia, always there at country festivities or with an aperitif.

ciabatta
a bread

A relatively modern shape of bread, so called because, being oval, stunted and rather flat, it resembles a *ciabatta*, a down-at-heel house shoe. The homely associations of the name are appropriate for this friendly bread, but the name does not do justice to its feathery light texture or its delicious taste.

The dough, which contains a great deal of water, is subjected to a prolonged rising period, thus producing a light bread with a thin crust.

cialzons
stuffed pasta

These are the RAVIOLI of Carnia, a very mountainous area of Friuli. There are many variations of these ravioli, but what distinguishes them from other kinds of ravioli is that the stuffing, based on spinach, always contains sweet ingredients such as cocoa powder, sultanas, candied citron and sugar, and bread, usually the local rye bread, along with Parmesan and eggs.

ciambella
a cake

Originally from Le Marche and Emilia-Romagna, this cake, in the shape of a large ring, is now made in most regions. It is a very homely confection, and one for which every housewife has her own 'authentic' version. The dough is made from flour, butter, eggs and sugar, with various flavourings. Ciambella, served with CREMA PASTICCERA, can be eaten at the end of a meal. It is also eaten at breakfast dipped in coffee and milk, or at any time of the day with a glass of sweet wine.

Ciambella plays its part in a strange custom that takes place only in the town of Bobbio, in the province of Piacenza, Emilia-Romagna. On Ascension Day, all the children of the town, dressed in their Sunday best, put multi-coloured ciambelle round their necks and join a procession, headed by the clergy, through the village up to the castle. There the bishop blesses the people, adults and children alike, and the children can now rest and eat their ciambelle. They do not eat them all, a few being kept until the next Ascension Day as hostages to fortune (and perhaps as a treat for the chickens, as by then they must be rather stale).

maccheroni alla chitarra
macaroni with lamb ragù

Serves 3–4

50g/1¾oz salted pork back fat (LARDO) or unsmoked fatty pancetta, chopped

300g/10½oz lamb fillet (boneless neck of lamb), trimmed and diced

½–1 tsp crushed dried chillies, depending on strength

1½ tsp dried oregano

1 garlic clove, chopped

salt

4 tbsp olive oil

100g/3½oz mushrooms, chopped

1 small onion, finely chopped

4 tbsp red wine

3 tbsp red wine vinegar

1½ tbsp tomato puree diluted with 4 tbsp warm water

1 tbsp flour

TONNARELLI made with 300g/10½oz/ scant 2½ cups Italian 00 flour and 3 large eggs (page 282), or 500g/1lb 2oz fresh tagliatelle or 350g/12oz dried egg spaghetti

2 tbsp chopped fresh flat-leaf parsley

The odd name of this recipe from Abruzzo – 'guitar-style maccheroni' – comes from the CHITARRA, which is the name of the instrument traditionally used to cut the homemade pasta. However, the best pasta to use for this dish is dried egg spaghetti, which is very similar to the 'maccheroni' of the original recipe.

Put the pork back fat or pancetta in a sauté pan and heat until hot. Add the lamb, chillies, oregano and garlic and brown well on all sides. Sprinkle with salt, cook for about 30 seconds and then lift the meat out with a slotted spoon and set aside.

Add the oil to the pan and heat. Add the mushrooms and sauté for 5 minutes. Lift out the mushrooms and set aside with the lamb. Put the onion into the pan and sauté gently until soft. Pour in the wine and vinegar and boil briskly until the liquid has nearly all evaporated.

Add the diluted tomato puree and the flour to the pan. Cook, stirring constantly, for 2 minutes or so. Sprinkle with some salt. Return the lamb and the mushrooms to the pan and cook, covered, over a very low heat, until the lamb is very tender, about 45 minutes. Taste and adjust the salt.

Cook the pasta in plenty of boiling salted water. Drain as soon as it is al dente, which will only take about 1 minute if you are using homemade tonnarelli. Do not overdrain the pasta. Turn the pasta into a warmed bowl, toss with the sauce and sprinkle with the parsley. Serve immediately.

ciauscolo
a salame

Ciauscolo is a soft SALAME from Le Marche, made with minced pork meat and fat and flavoured with garlic. Like the peppery 'nduja of Calabria, ciauscolo is often spread on bread instead of sliced.

cibreo
giblets with egg and lemon

This delicious mixture of chicken livers, cockscombs and other giblets and embryo eggs is gently sautéed and then enriched by egg yolk and lemon juice; this sauce was far more common in the 19th century than it is now. ARTUSI starts his recipe for cibreo with one of his typically amusing openings: 'Cibreo is a simple ragù, delicate, suitable to ladies with little appetite and to people who are convalescing.' Actually, my humble opinion is that cibreo is suitable for anybody interested in good food.

cicala
a crustacean

Cicala grande, or *magnosa*, which looks like a flattened lobster, is quite rare in Italian seas. Because of its rarity there are no specific recipes. It is cooked in the same ways as a spiny lobster. In Tuscany and Liguria, cicala means CANNOCCHIA and it is mostly used in fish soups.

ciccioli
crackling

These succulent tiny morsels of crackling are formed when the fat parts of the pig are melted to obtain fresh lard. Ciccioli are best eaten as soon as the liquefied fat is poured away, when they are still light and hot. Ciccioli are eaten as an ANTIPASTO.

In Emilia-Romagna they are also mixed with the dough of the local flat bread, or spread over a leavened bread.

They are now industrially prepared and sold in delicatessens and supermarkets, but the flavour of these ciccioli is certainly not as good.

ciceri e tria
a soup

These two words, one of Latin origin and the other Arab, describe a soup made in Puglia. The ciceri (chickpeas) are cooked with olive oil, onion, garlic and bay leaves; the tria, short TAGLIATELLE made with durum wheat semolina and water, are added at the end when the chickpeas are done. It is one of the great soups of Puglia.

cicoria or radicchio
chicory

Many plants, wild and cultivated, make up this large family, which includes the very popular red RADICCHIO, the long bunchy *catalogna* and the Roman PUNTARELLE. All these cultivated varieties are best in autumn and winter, their proper season. They have a pleasingly bitter flavour and can be eaten raw or cooked. Raw chicory is usually cut into thin strips and dressed with olive oil and vinegar. In the provinces of Modena and Reggio Emilia this is usually balsamic vinegar, whose sweetness counteracts the bitterness of the plant. It is also dressed with PANCETTA sautéed with garlic in oil, with a little vinegar added at the end. Young chicories are excellent grilled, and all chicories can be boiled and then dressed, or finished off in other ways.

The wild variety is usually referred to as *cicorino*. It is more bitter than the cultivated variety and, when eaten raw, should be very young. In Puglia it accompanies INCAPRIATA.

cieche
baby eels

Called *cee* in Tuscany, these elvers are caught at the river's mouth as they start to swim upriver from the open sea by fishermen who use glaring lights to attract them into huge sieves. Cieche are now found only in the Tuscan provinces of Pisa and Livorno. They must be still alive when they are thrown in a pan of smoking oil. A lid is immediately put on the pan, to prevent the elvers from jumping out of the hot oil. Cieche are also known as *capillari*, *sementare* and *cirioli*.

ciliegia
cherry

This cheerful fruit, whose rich shades of red replace the delicate whiteness of its blossom, is in season in late spring and early summer. Ciliegia is a member of the large genus of *Prunus*, and it is a hybrid derived from two species, *Prunus cerasus*, the morello cherry, and *Prunus avium*, the sweet cherry. There are two main types of cherries, *tenerine* (ones with soft pulp) and *duracine* (those with hard pulp), the latter being paler in colour and larger. The best Italian cherries come from Campania, Puglia, Veneto and, notably, Emilia-Romagna, where, in the orchards around Modena, the famous dark cherries called *nero di Vignola* are grown.

In present-day Italy cherries are normally eaten fresh. They are also candied or preserved in alcohol after being dried in the sun for at least a day. They are often used in cakes and sweet-making.

cima alla genovese

see PUNTA DI PETTO

cime di rapa
a green vegetable

Also called *broccoletti*, these are the green tops of a variety of turnip, which are harvested in the spring or summer before the florets appear. They are very similar to sprouting broccoli and are usually boiled and served all'AGRO or stewed in oil with garlic and chilli. Cime di rapa are widely grown in southern Italy, where they are also used for a pasta sauce, as in the recipe for *orecchiette con i broccoli* on page 60. In Naples cime di rapa are called *friarielli*. (Confusingly, in some regions of southern Italy, friarielli refers to small mild green peppers.)

cinghiale
wild boar

Wild boars, which some 20 years ago had almost disappeared in Italy, have come back with a vengeance in the Apennines of central and southern Italy, where they can gobble up the juicy grapes of a vineyard or destroy a vegetable garden in a night or two. They are legally hunted but the quota is pretty low and, because of their large litters, wild boars have become the scourge of the local farmers.

Wild boar, which is also farmed in fenced-off reserves, is a favourite meat in Lazio and Tuscany, where it is sometimes found fresh in the markets. The most appetizing recipe, *cinghiale in* AGRODOLCE (in a sweet and sour sauce) comes from the borders of Tuscany and Lazio. The boar, previously marinated in wine and various flavourings for 48 hours, is cooked slowly in the strained marinade. Towards the end of cooking, onion, grated chocolate, prunes, pine nuts, raisins, candied citron and orange peel are added to the cinghiale. The dish is served with toasted bread. One of my favourite recipes from Chianti is SPEZZATINO *di cinghiale*, in which the boar is flavoured with rosemary, sage, garlic, chilli and fennel seeds and cooked slowly with tomatoes and red wine. A young boar is good grilled, either whole or in steaks, and the meat should be slightly underdone; it can also be cooked as in any recipe for pork.

Wild boar is used to make SALAMI, prosciutto and COPPA. In Tuscany and Umbria there are a number of food shops that sell these products, which are made on nearby farms. Some coppe and prosciutti have a distinct taste of truffle because the boars eat truffles whenever they can find them. Most of these products are in fact made with the meat of a *meticcio*, a hybrid between a pig and a wild boar. *Meticci* are reared in farms but retain their wild characteristics.

cioccolata
hot chocolate

Cocoa powder is dissolved in hot milk, or water, with sugar added to make this drink, which became very popular in Italy in the 18th century, somewhat later than in the rest of Europe. Like coffee, it was at first the drink of the aristocracy, usually accompanied by dry biscuits. Today, cioccolata has lost popularity. However, when you are in Venice in winter, a cup of hot chocolate at Florian's on the Piazza is still the most pleasurable drink to sip while listening to the orchestra playing Léhar or Strauss.

cioccolatini
chocolates

Cioccolatini are small chocolates made with dark or milk chocolate containing nuts, candied fruit, marzipan, hazelnut paste, fruits in alcohol, mint or various liqueurs. The most popular cioccolatini are BOERI, GIANDUIOTTI and truffles. *Cornetti* and SCORZETTE *al cioccolato* are also popular; they are pieces of candied orange peel dipped in dark chocolate. Other favourites are *cioccolatini alla menta*, leaf-shaped chocolates flavoured with mint, and *alpini*, dark chocolates filled with herb liqueurs.

cioccolato
chocolate

This is the solid chocolate that Caffarel started producing commercially in Turin, using new technology, in the early 19th century. Chocolate is not used a great deal in Italian cooking. It is sometimes used to decorate or flavour cakes and desserts, and occasionally used in savoury dishes. In Milan, jugged hare is flavoured with grated chocolate, which adds colour and depth to the sauce. A recipe for pasta from Florence uses tagliatelle flavoured with cocoa powder or grated chocolate and dressed with a sweet and sour sauce. And in Sicily, CAPONATA (aubergines in sweet and sour sauce) is often flavoured with grated chocolate.

ciopa
a bread

A loaf made in Veneto and Trentino. The bread, compact and firm with a thick crust, is the same in both regions but the shape and size of the loaves are different. The *ciopa veneta* is very large and needs to be cut into slices, while the *ciopa trentina* is much smaller, more like a roll.

cipolla
onion

Throughout history, onions have been an indispensable ingredient in every country's cooking. Many of APICIUS' recipes use onions mixed with different herbs, sultanas and honey. The Arabs considered onions to be an invigorating food in lovemaking: one writer prescribed a diet of onions and eggs, adhered to for three days, as the best preparation for an 'amorous ordeal'. Many recipes from the Renaissance use onions, at times in combinations that seem odd to our palates. Bartolomeo SCAPPI gives instructions for a sauce of pounded onions, egg yolks, apples and soft breadcrumbs soaked in wine and vinegar. The mixture is then cooked with bitter orange juice, grape juice, sugar and cinnamon, but sadly he does not say which food it should go with.

There are many varieties of onions, from the tiny white ones to the large specimens of a beautiful purple colour. The onions of Brianza in Lombardy have been appreciated for centuries for their delicate flavour, and for the way they keep their pretty shape all through the cooking. They are often stewed whole in butter and meat stock. The tastiest and mildest onions are grown in Piedmont, where the high mineral content of the soil provides very favourable conditions.

Some recipes call for a particular variety. The red onions of Tropea in Calabria are used in a salad because they are sweet, while the little white ones are ideal in a sweet and sour sauce (see recipe on page 22). Onions are often stuffed, the best-known recipes being from Piedmont. An unusual recipe from the borders of Piedmont and Lombardy mixes AMARETTI and MOSTARDA di Cremona in the stuffing, while another from Liguria contains preserved tuna, and it is excellent. Finely chopped, onions are nearly always one of the basic elements of SOFFRITTO, the starting point for many recipes.

A sight that has been typical of market towns in northern Italy for many centuries is that of people keeping warm on freezing winter mornings by standing near large braziers in which onions are being roasted, with their skins on. The onions are taken home, peeled and sliced, and eaten with olive oil and salt.

ciriola
a bread roll

This is a very popular kind of bread in Rome. It is a small elongated roll with a golden crunchy crust and a soft inside, perfect for a PANINO.

ciriole

see CIECHE

ciuppin
traditional fish soup

Ciuppin differs from other Italian fish soups in that the fish, after being stewed, is usually pureed. It is a lengthy performance but the result is worthwhile, especially for those who are troubled by the skin and bones when eating fish. However, in the old days, ciuppin was a soup made by Ligurian fishermen using all the fish and seafood they didn't manage to sell. And this was certainly not pureed.

cocomero

see ANGURIA

coda
tail

Part of the offal – see FRATTAGLIE – the tails eaten in Italy are oxtail (*coda di bue*), veal and pig's tail (*codino*). They are stewed at length, usually with wine and often with tomatoes, until the meat falls off the bone. Pig's tail is usually added to the CASSOEULA of Lombardy and oxtail is mostly cooked *alla vaccinara*, for which the recipe is given here.

[see recipe on facing page]

coda di rospo
monkfish

Also called *rana pescatrice*, this is a large fish with a grotesque head. It lives at the bottom of the sea and is quite common in the Adriatic. Although ugly to look at monkfish is good to eat, with firm and elastic flesh, similar to lobster. It is usually sold without the head, but the head is worth buying, when available, because it makes excellent fish stock.

Monkfish is highly prized, especially in Venice, where it is split in half and grilled – possibly the best way. In a recipe from Romagna the monkfish is cut into steaks, fried and then baked, covered with a mixture of chopped hard-boiled egg yolks, dried breadcrumbs, parsley and garlic, all moistened by the oil in which the fish has been cooked. Another recipe from the coast further south finishes off the fried fish in a tomato sauce flavoured with oregano, anchovy fillets and garlic.

coda alla vaccinara
braised oxtail

Serves 4

1.25kg/2 ¾lb oxtail, cut into pieces

225g/8oz pork rind

50g/1 ¾oz pancetta or unsmoked streaky bacon, cut in one thick slice, chopped

3 tbsp olive oil

25g/1oz pork fat or lard

1 tbsp chopped fresh flat-leaf parsley

1 or 2 garlic cloves, chopped

1 onion, finely chopped

1 carrot, finely chopped

200ml/7fl oz/generous ¾ cup dry white wine

2 tbsp tomato puree diluted with 225ml/8fl oz/scant 1 cup meat stock (page 61) or chicken stock

salt and freshly ground black pepper

225g/8oz celery, thickly sliced

Vaccinaro is the old name for a butcher in Roman dialect and this recipe comes from the part of Rome that is near to the slaughterhouse. The freshness of the celery counteracts the rich heaviness of the oxtail. Some recipes omit the blanching of the oxtail. Coda alla vaccinara is best made one or two days in advance to allow the flavours to develop.

Preheat the oven to 160°C/325°F/Gas Mark 3.

Blanch the oxtail and pork rind in boiling water for 5 minutes. Drain and refresh under cold water. Cut the rind into strips.

Put the pancetta, olive oil, pork fat, parsley, garlic, onion and carrot into a heavy flameproof casserole and sauté until soft. Add the oxtail and pork rind and cook gently for a further few minutes. Add the wine and boil rapidly to reduce, turning the meat over a few times. Add the diluted tomato puree and salt to taste. Cover the pan and place in the oven. Cook for at least 2 hours, or until the meat is tender, turning it over two or three times. Remove from the oven and leave to cool, then put it in the fridge until required.

On the day you are serving the dish, remove and discard the solidified fat from the surface. Put the casserole over a medium heat and bring to the boil, then add the celery and cook, covered, for 30 minutes. Add a generous grinding of pepper, taste and check salt before serving.

NOTE: If you prefer, you can reheat the dish in the oven, preheated to 200°C/400°F/Gas Mark 6. Bring the casserole to the boil over a medium heat, add the celery and then cover the pan and place in the oven for 30 minutes to heat through.

colapasta
colander

No Italian kitchen is without a colander, which is invaluable for draining pasta. It has two handles and a solid base that enables it to stand in the sink.

colazione
breakfast

Nowadays colazione means breakfast, although the word can cause confusion among some northern Italians, for whom colazione might mean lunch, as it was in the old days. In hotels breakfast is referred to as *prima colazione* (prima meaning first) and it often is as rich and nutritious as a Scottish breakfast. But in most Italian homes colazione is a cup of *caffè e latte*, an espresso or, more rarely, a cup of tea – maybe with some biscuits, a brioche or a slice of bread and some honey or jam. Yogurt, cereals and fruit are now relatively popular.

colomba
a cake

If you walk past a PASTICCERIA or a bakery in any town in Lombardy during Holy Week you will be tempted by a most delicious smell. It is the smell of the *colomba pasquale* ('Easter dove'), a cake made in the shape of a dove. The colomba is made with a light and very buttery dough similar to that used for the Milanese PANETTONE, and it is covered with sugar crystals and almonds. It contains a lot of candied peel but no sultanas. A modern colomba may be covered with chocolate or with marzipan. Colomba is now popular all over northern Italy and has begun to cross the Alps.

companatico
food eaten with bread

A word derived from *con pane*, referring to food that is eaten with bread, which, for the Italians, is any food, apart from pasta, risotto and some soups. I still remember how much I suffered when I first came to England and the bread was removed after the soup. Bread is indeed the food that no Italian can do without.

concentrato di pomodoro
concentrated tomato or tomato puree

There are three varieties of concentrato, sold in tubes or cans: a light variety, which is the most common, and two stronger varieties – *doppio concentrato*, 100g of which equals 500g of fresh tomato; and *triplo concentrato*, 100g of which equals 600g of fresh tomato. All varieties should be used sparingly and allowed to cook in the sauce for some time to reduce the acidity. A small amount of sugar helps the process.

In southern Italy and Sicily, tomato paste is often made at home and is called *strattù*. It is made only in the summer, when the tomatoes and the sun are at their best. The tomatoes, cut in half and with coarse salt added, are spread out in large baskets in the sun. After four or five days they are pureed, and again placed in the sun until the liquid evaporates and takes on a reddish brown colour. Oil is added and the puree is spooned into jars and sealed. It then keeps very well through the winter.

conchiglia di San Giacomo
scallop

Also called *pettine*, *ventaglio* and, in Venice, *cappa santa*. The best scallops are found in the northern Adriatic and are one of the delights of the Rialto fish market in Venice. The Venetians like to eat them just blanched and dressed with a touch of olive oil and lemon juice, or *in tegame* – cooked in a pot for 5 minutes with oil, garlic, parsley and lemon juice. In Trieste, a favourite recipe is to cover the blanched scallops in their open shell with a mixture of butter, soft breadcrumbs, parsley and watercress and then heat them for a few minutes under the grill. But my favourite end to a few fresh scallops is in a sauce for spaghetti with fried breadcrumbs, parsley and garlic.

conchiglie or conchigliette
a pasta

This pasta shape, whose name means 'shell', can be used in recipes that recommend DITALI or ORECCHIETTE. They are good with a meat RAGÙ, with some vegetable sauces such as those made with broccoli or courgettes, or with RICOTTA or various cheeses.

condimento
condiment

An ingredient, or a mixture of ingredients, that enhances the flavour of the food to which it is added. A few examples provide the best explanation of the way the word is used. Melted butter and grated Parmesan is the best condimento for a plate of spring asparagus. Ripe plum tomatoes, cut in half, can have no better condimento than a few spoonfuls of the best olive oil and some fresh basil leaves. Different salads can have different condimenti, of which the simplest and most common is olive oil, wine vinegar and salt. Herbs, garlic, onions, anchovy fillets, capers or mustard can all be part of the condimento for salads.

In other dishes, such as a risotto, condimento usually refers to the basic fat in which the main ingredient is cooked.

confetti
almond sweets

There are two different kinds of confetti, the soft and the hard. The soft, made by hand on a small scale, consist of a paste, usually almond, covered with a layer of sugar. Hard confetti are made with a whole almond which is then coated in sugar. Hard white confetti are given by the newlyweds to their family and friends; they are also part of a buffet at first Communion and at christening parties – coloured blue for a boy and pink for a girl.

confettura
jam

After years of confusion regarding the usage of the two words, confettura and MARMELLATA, a recent official decree stated that confettura is jam and marmellata is marmalade – simple! All sorts of jam are made in the country: pumpkin, tomato and even rose petal, but the most popular are apricot, plum and peach. Jams are the most common topping for CROSTATE (tarts).

coniglio
rabbit

On most Italian tables, in a restaurant or at home, you will find domestic rather than wild rabbit. The wild rabbit generally appears only on the table of the person who shot it. In Anna Gosetti della Salda's book *Le Ricette Regionali Italiane* there are 18 recipes for rabbit, of which only two are for the wild animal: one from Sicily – jointed and cooked with aubergine, peppers and potatoes and flavoured with basil and mint; and the other from Sardinia, where the rabbit is jointed and cooked in vinegar with onion, garlic and capers. During my long life of eating, I have only once eaten wild rabbit in Italy and that was in Tuscany at the table

113

of the man who shot it. It was roasted, wrapped in caul fat. I remember my host saying that it was a young animal and it was as tender and delicious as another rabbit I ate in Le Marche – a domestic one which the day before was scampering around in the cage of Mafalda, our neighbour. She cooked it in POTACCHIO, just as she cooks her chicken. In fact domestic rabbit can be cooked just as a chicken and I find the result better because of the stronger flavour of the meat.

[see recipe below]

conserva
preserve

The conserva par excellence is that of tomato, so much so that tomato preserve is simply called conserva in southern Italy. The most popular way of making tomato preserve is to bottle the puree and boil it in the bottle. A *macchina per i pomodori* (tomato machine) still goes around from village to village in August to prepare the puree for all the locals. The conserva di pomodoro that is most commonly used these days is made commercially

coniglio ai peperoni
rabbit with peppers

Serves 4

1 rabbit, about 1kg/2¼lb, cut into
    pieces
50g/1¾oz suet or 3 tbsp olive oil
50g/1¾oz/4 tbsp unsalted butter
1 tbsp rosemary needles
1 bay leaf
100ml/3½fl oz/7 tbsp meat stock (page
    61) or chicken stock
2 tbsp extra virgin olive oil
3 salted anchovies, boned, rinsed and
    chopped, or 6 canned or bottled
    anchovy fillets, drained and chopped
2 garlic cloves, chopped
3 yellow peppers, deseeded and cut into
    thin strips
salt and freshly ground black pepper
1 tbsp wine vinegar

This is my version of a recipe published in *La Cucina d'Oro*, a book of nearly 1,500 recipes edited by Count Giovanni Nuvoletti in cooperation with the ACCADEMIA ITALIANA DELLA CUCINA. The recipe suggests the use of suet, which indicates its ancient origin. Nowadays, oil is more commonly used. If you want to use a wild, rather than a domestic, rabbit, cook it for longer, at least 10 minutes, although it is difficult to state the exact time, since it depends on the age of the animal. Just test it with a fork, and cook until tender.

Wash and dry the rabbit pieces.

Chop the suet and heat it (or the oil) in a casserole with half the butter and the rosemary. Add the rabbit and the bay leaf and brown on all sides. Pour over half the stock and cook the rabbit over a low heat, uncovered, for about 20 minutes, adding a little more stock when necessary.

In another pan, heat the remaining butter with the extra virgin olive oil and the anchovies. Cook slowly until the anchovies become a mush and then add the garlic and the peppers. Season with salt and plenty of pepper. Cook for 5 minutes and then mix in the vinegar. Continue cooking for a further 10 minutes, stirring frequently.

Add the pepper mixture to the casserole with the rabbit and finish cooking the whole thing together, about a further 20 minutes, turning the pieces of rabbit over two or three times.

and preserved in cans. The first such conserva was made by Francesco Cirio in 1875 in Parma, and not, as is often stated, in Naples.

Many other vegetables are preserved in oil, wine vinegar or *al naturale*, which means that the vegetable is parboiled and bottled with water. Some fruit is preserved in alcohol, the most common being apricots, cherries, mandarins, grapes and peaches.

Traditionally, fish and meat were also preserved in many parts of Italy, but the traditions are dying out due to the availability of frozen products. In Calabria meat is preserved in salt with chilli and fennel seeds and aged for a few months. When ready for use, it is soaked overnight and then cooked with broad beans in soup or with tomatoes to serve with pasta. In some farms in northern Italy, goose is still preserved in oil and salt and flavoured with spices, to be enjoyed during the long winter months.

contorno
accompaniment

Vegetables and/or other ingredients that accompany a main dish, be it meat, poultry or fish. The contorno may be served on the same plate or on a separate plate. The contorno is never an integral part of the main dish. Thus a roast will often be surrounded by small roasted or sautéed potatoes; braised peas or green beans are an accepted contorno to COSTOLETTA alla milanese or FRICANDÒ. Spinach sautéed in olive oil is frequently the contorno to SALTIMBOCCA alla romana, while the contorno de rigueur to a roast, but only to a roast, is a fresh green salad, especially in the spring when many different leaves are available in the market.

It is rare for more than one vegetable to be served as a contorno; more than two never are. Pasta and risotti are never referred to as contorni, nor are they served with contorni, with the exception of risotto with OSSOBUCO or with COSTOLETTA.

coppa
a cured pork product

In northern Italy, coppa is made from the pig's boned shoulder, rolled and cured in saltpetre, salt, pepper and nutmeg. Put into a natural casing, it is aged for about 3 months. A perfect coppa should be made of equal parts of lean and fat meat. When well prepared, coppa has a taste similar to prosciutto, though more earthy and vigorous. Coppa should be sliced thin, but not so thin as to be transparent.

In central Italy coppa is a kind of brawn made from a pig's head. It is called *coppa di testa* or, occasionally, *coppa d'inverno* (winter coppa) because pigs are slaughtered in the winter and it must be eaten soon after it is made.

coratella
offal

The Roman name for all the offal of a lamb or kid, which is a much-loved ingredient in Lazio and in other southern regions. There are two classic recipes from Rome: coratella with artichokes and coratella with onions.

In Sardinia, at a local food festival some years ago, I ate the most delicious small sausages, called *gnumerieddi*, barbecued on huge braziers. The little sausages were made of chopped kid or lamb offal mixed with garlic and parsley and moistened with the local red wine, and then stuffed into the cleaned intestine of the animal.

Corrado, Vincenzo
1738–1836

Few cookery books, even today, enjoy the success achieved by *Il Cuoco Galante*, written in the second half of the 18th century by Vincenzo Corrado from Naples. He wrote two other books, of which the one titled *Del Cibo Pitagorico* is a fascinating collection of vegetarian recipes, or to be more precise recipes for vegetables which sometimes also contain non-vegetarian ingredients. *Il Cuoco Galante* is divided into chapters, each dedicated to one type of food – eggs, fish, vegetables, sweets etc. Each chapter includes a few recipes which, although they contain no quantities or detailed methods, are very clear. He Italianized some French dishes, such as GATTÒ and BIGNÈ, and exalted the local cuisine with its *fritti misti* and *parmigiane*. The book is particularly strong on vegetarian food, including fresh herbs, roots, flowers, fruits, seeds and everything else the earth produces for our nourishment. Corrado is my favourite cookery writer of the past.

[see recipe below]

costa
Swiss chard

The long white – or less commonly orange or purple – ribs or stems of this plant are the part that is most valued as a vegetable. Once stripped of their outer skin and strings, the stems are boiled either in salted water or in water to which 2 tablespoons of flour and a little butter have been added. They are then sautéed in butter and sprinkled with grated Parmesan, *alla Milanese*, or covered with béchamel sauce and Parmesan and baked – *coste gratinate*. The dark green leaves can be cooked like spinach.

costata
a steak

An entrecôte or T-bone steak. A costata is usually 4–6cm/about 2in thick and weighs about 450g/1lb – enough for 2 carnivorous people. However, in some regions costata means a boneless steak, always of beef. The best way to cook a costata is to grill it, as in the famous *bistecca alla fiorentina*. Costata is usually served with roast or fried potatoes, but it goes very well with a spring salad or a salad of young and tender green beans.

sedano alla moda del '700
celery with cream

Serves 4

2 large heads of celery, about 500g/ 1lb 2oz in total, trimmed and washed, with outer hard stalks and strings removed

100ml/3½fl oz/7 tbsp full-fat (whole) milk

salt and freshly ground pepper, preferably white

unsalted butter, for greasing

150ml/5fl oz/⅔ cup double (heavy) cream

5 tbsp freshly grated Parmesan cheese

½ tsp grated nutmeg

2 large egg yolks

The Neapolitan chef Vincenzo CORRADO wrote some of the best recipes for vegetables; I have adapted this one from his book *Il Cuoco Galante*, first published in 1773. '700 means 18th century.

Preheat the oven to 190°C/375°F/Gas Mark 5.

Cut the celery into 5–6cm/2–2½in pieces and put them in a sauté pan. Pour over the milk and add a pinch of salt. Cover and cook over a low heat until the celery is tender but still al dente, about 10 minutes.

Butter an ovenproof dish and transfer the celery to it. Heat the cream to boiling point in a small saucepan. Remove from the heat and add the Parmesan, nutmeg, pepper, a pinch of salt and the egg yolks. Beat well and spoon over the celery. Cook in the oven for 15 minutes. Serve immediately.

Costata alla PIZZAIOLA, a recipe from Naples, is first fried and then finished off in a tasty tomato sauce flavoured with anchovy fillets and capers, reminiscent of a pizza topping.

costoletta
chop

Chop of veal, lamb or pork – but not beef. Of all these the best known is the *costoletta alla milanese*, for which the recipe is given on page 210. Costoletta alla milanese must have a bone, and should be 1–1.5cm/about ½in thick. Some cooks marinate the chops in milk to produce a more delicate flavour and a whiter colour. They are sometimes referred to as *cotolette alla milanese*.

The *costolette alla valdostana* are veal chops with a slice of fontina cheese, coated in breadcrumbs and fried in butter. When in season, and budget permitting, a few slices of white truffle are added to the fontina.

Lamb costolette are used mainly in central and southern Italy where, when sautéed, they are served with a thick tomato and pepper sauce. In Tuscany, lamb costolette are breaded and fried like the milanese, but – of course – in oil, not in butter. A Roman recipe for grilled lamb chops, *scottadito*, is on page 384.

The most lavish recipe for both veal and lamb costolette is from ARTUSI, who suggests that the fried costolette should be covered with slices of white truffle and Parmesan or Gruyère – 'but both must be sliced as thin as possible' – and then baked in the oven with a little stock or meat juice and finished with a sprinkling of lemon juice.

cotechino
a sausage

A large sausage sold all over the peninsula, although it is less popular in the south. It is made with pork rind mixed with lean pork meat and back fat; the coarsely chopped mixture is then flavoured with salt, pepper, cloves and cinnamon and pushed into pig casing. Although it is easy to make this sausage, it is difficult to make it well: cotechini are often too dry or too salty, or the mixture is chopped too coarsely or too finely. Cotechino is ready to eat 2 or 3 weeks after being made, and it should be eaten within 3 months. Nowadays cotechini are usually produced commercially, on a large scale, although some are also made in small quantities by pork butchers. These artisanal cotechini should be soaked in cold water for about 3 hours, pierced all over with a thick needle and then wrapped in a cloth and simmered for a long time. But most of the cotechini sold in Italy and abroad are precooked, requiring only some 30 minutes to cook. If made by a first-class manufacturer, they are very good and more reliable than some artisanal versions.

Cotechino is traditional food in northern Italy, where the usual way to serve it is either with lentils, polenta, stewed Savoy cabbage or as part of a BOLLITO MISTO. Another way of preparing it is known as *cotechino in camicia* (in a nightshirt), or *in galera* (in prison). In the recipe from Modena the cotechino is parboiled and then, with its skin removed, wrapped first in prosciutto and then in a slice of beef. It is cooked with onion in a generous amount of Lambrusco, the local sparkling red wine. In Cremona, reconstituted dried PORCINI are used instead of prosciutto, and the cotechino is sautéed with onion and then cooked in stock, which I find a more interesting recipe – although as cotechino is so rich it is far better just by itself and not '*in camicia*'. In Bergamo, sliced cooked cotechino is further cooked in a rich tomato sauce for extra flavour, and it is then baked in the oven in layers with polenta and grated Parmesan; the dish is called *polenta e codeghin*.

cotenna di maiale
pork rind

Pork rind is used to make many SALAMI, COTECHINI and other pork sausages. It is also used by itself, previously blanched, to give flavour to soups, as in a bean soup from Abruzzo to which a trotter is also added. The other cotenna used in soups, or in pork sauces for pasta, is that of prosciutto, which must be previously blanched or soaked.

cotogna
quince

This is the golden apple of classical Greece, which Paris gave to Aphrodite. Quinces, originally from Iran, were already popular in Roman times, and APICIUS gives a recipe for preserving them: 'Pick perfect quinces with stems and leaves. Place them in a vessel, pour over honey and new wine and you will preserve them for a long time.' In modern Italy quinces are used to make jams, jellies and COTOGNATA.

cotognata
quince cheese

A popular sweet all over Italy, although its birthplace is Sicily, where it is still made according to family tradition. The recipe and the attractive pottery moulds in which the cotognata is dried are handed down from one generation to the next. Cotognata is preserved, covered with sugar and cut into squares. But the best cotognata is said to be made in Genoa, famous for its candied fruits and fruit jellies. A preparation containing quinces, must and walnuts is made in Emilia-Romagna and Piedmont, where it is served with a soft polenta.

cotoletta
cooking method

Fried food that has been coated in egg and dried breadcrumbs before frying. The ingredient can be a slice of meat (though never beef), an escalope of poultry, a fish steak or a slice of vegetable such as aubergine or cep caps. The cooking style can be described as 'a cotoletta' – for example *melanzane a cotoletta* instead of *cotolette di melanzane*. The best-known meat cotolette are the Bolognese – covered with a slice of prosciutto, flakes of Parmesan and a dollop of tomato sauce – the Valdostana and the Milanese, both of which are similar to the COSTOLETTA but use an escalope instead of a chop. The latter is similar to Austria's famous Wienerschnitzel, the difference being that the Viennese escalope is first coated in flour and thus the crust formed by the egg and breadcrumbs does not adhere to the meat as it does in the Milanese version. The most lavish cotolette alla milanese is covered by a few flakes of white truffles when they are in season.

cozze or mitili
mussels

Although these are the correct Italian names, these molluscs are called PEOCI in Venice, *muscioli* in Le Marche and *muscoli* in some other regions. As this variety of regional names suggests, they are the most popular molluscs. Nowadays mussels are nearly always farmed. They are used in fish soups and in pasta sauces, sometimes with tomatoes. In many regions mussels are stuffed with breadcrumbs, parsley, garlic, tomatoes, grated **PECORINO** and eggs – or any combination of these ingredients. Doused with the best olive oil, they are baked for about 10 minutes; a recipe is given here. In Taranto in Puglia, where the mussels grow large and fat in the Mare Piccolo, a salt-water lagoon, a dish called *teglia di cozze* combines potatoes, courgettes and tomatoes with mussels in one of the most delicious dishes of that region. In a traditional dish from Chioggia, the port at the south end of the Venetian lagoon, the shelled mussels are added to diced boiled potatoes and gently stewed in fish stock, the whole dish being finished with a drizzle of the best olive oil.

[see recipe below]

crema
a smooth preparation

The word is used to describe several different preparations, most of them of foreign origin: smooth soups, butter creams and custard sauces. This word does not mean dairy cream, which is PANNA.

cozze ripiene
stuffed mussels

Serves 6
1.25–1.5kg/2¾–3¼lb mussels in
  their shells
10 tbsp dried breadcrumbs
10 tbsp chopped fresh flat-leaf parsley
2 garlic cloves, finely chopped
salt and freshly ground black pepper
100ml/3½fl oz/7 tbsp olive oil
2 tbsp freshly grated mature pecorino or
  Parmesan cheese

The Italian love of stuffed food is well demonstrated in this excellent recipe.

To clean the mussels, put them in a sink and scrub them thoroughly with a hard brush, scraping off any barnacles with a knife and tugging off the beards. Discard any broken shells, and any that remain open after you tap them on a hard surface. Put the mussels in cold water and rinse until the water is clear, changing the water as many times as necessary. Nowadays most mussels are farmed and do not need quite so much cleaning.

Preheat the oven to 230°C/450°F/Gas Mark 8.

Put the cleaned mussels in a large saucepan. Cover and cook over a high heat for about 4 minutes, until the mussels are open, shaking the pan occasionally. Shell the mussels, reserving one half of each empty shell. Discard any shells that remain closed.

If full of sand, strain the mussel liquid through a sieve lined with cheesecloth or muslin. Otherwise, simply pour the liquid very gently into a bowl, leaving any sand at the bottom of the pan. Set the liquid aside. Mix together the breadcrumbs, parsley, garlic and plenty of pepper, then add the olive oil and 4 tablespoons of the mussel liquid. Combine well together. Taste and adjust the seasoning.

Place the mussels in their half shells on 2 baking sheets. With your fingers, pick up a good pinch of the breadcrumb mixture and press it down on each mussel, covering it well and filling the shell. Sprinkle with the grated cheese. Bake for 10 minutes, swapping the baking sheets from top to bottom halfway through the cooking time if necessary. Delicious hot, warm, or at room temperature.

119

crema fritta
fried egg custard

CREMA PASTICCERA cut into pieces when cold, then coated in egg and breadcrumbs and fried. This is a very popular dish in northern Italy. In Veneto and Liguria it is served as a dessert, while in Emilia-Romagna it is an indispensable part of a grand FRITTO MISTO.

crema inglese
egg custard

A sweet sauce made with egg yolks, sugar and milk, it is served with stewed fruits and sponge cakes, as well as with other cakes such as PANETTONE or COLOMBA. It is also the basis of most ice creams, making them lighter than when made only with cream.

crema pasticcera
custard filling, crème pâtissière

Of all the various types of custard, this is the one that is used most often in Italian patisserie. It is a mixture of eggs, sugar and milk, thickened by flour. Crema pasticcera is the basis of ZUPPA INGLESE, it forms the filling of many desserts and is served by itself with MARSALA, chocolate and other flavourings.

crescentina
a bread

Also called crescenta, this bread from Emilia-Romagna is made with flour and water plus lard or crackling. It is usually cut into diamond shapes and fried, and eaten with SALUMI or cheese. In Bologna, crescentina is cut into rounds and pieces of prosciutto are often kneaded into the dough before frying. In Romagna it is known as PIADINA. There is also a crescentina from Tuscany, which, after being fried, is dusted with salt or – oddly – with sugar. In a more elaborate version, pieces of Tuscan SALAME are mixed into the dough before frying, and this is truly delicious.

crescenza
a cheese

A traditional cow's milk cheese of the STRACCHINO family, which has been made in Lombardy for centuries. It must be eaten very fresh, within one week of making. Crescenza has a creamy, spreadable consistency, a delicate, though rich, flavour and is a beautiful pure white colour. It is made industrially, on a large scale, being one of the most popular soft cheeses of northern Italy.

crespelle
pancakes

Crespelle are particularly popular in Tuscany, with the well-known recipe crespelle alla fiorentina, stuffed with spinach and ricotta, rolled up and covered with béchamel. An alternative method is to fold the crespelle like a little bag, rather than rolling them up. They are filled with a meat stuffing, and are known as fazzoletti (handkerchiefs). In some regions crespelle are known as CANNELLONI.

In scrippelle 'mbusse, a soup from Abruzzo, the batter contains parsley and the pancakes are stuffed with PECORINO cheese and covered with chicken stock.

creta, alla
cooking method

Literally 'in clay', this is an ancient method used for whole birds. The clay is moulded around the seasoned bird and baked, and the clay is broken with a hammer. Several restaurants in northern Italy cook birds, especially guinea fowl, in this way, and it is quite spectacular to break the clay open at the table. But nowadays the name also refers to the cooking of a bird in a bird-shaped clay container.

croccante
nut and sugar confectionery

Croccante, meaning 'crunchy', is a sweet preparation made in most regions with almonds or hazelnuts, caramelized sugar and flavourings. In Piedmont and Veneto it is made with roasted hazelnuts. In southern Italy the almond or hazelnut mixture is flavoured with orange rind, in Lazio with vanilla and in Liguria usually with lemon. Croccante, roughly chopped, is used in various sweets and also in many ice creams.

crocchette
croquettes

Crocchette are a northern Italian dish made with mashed potatoes, minced meat or poultry bound with béchamel sauce or risotto. Crocchette made with BACCALÀ to which the same amount of mashed potatoes is added are also popular. A frequent occasion for making crocchette is with leftover meat: minced and mixed with egg, Parmesan and other flavourings it becomes a pleasant dish in its own right. Crocchette, which are oval in shape, are always coated in egg and breadcrumbs and fried in butter.

crostacei
crustaceans

Although difficult to classify because of their diversity, the characteristic they have in common is that their bodies are protected by a horny outer layer. The most common crustaceans are GAMBERI, SCAMPI, GRANCHI, MAZZANCOLLE and CANNOCCHIE. All crostacei should be bought live and killed by plunging them into boiling water. Their freshness is detected, as with any other sea creature, by their smell, which should be sweet, and by their quick reaction when touched. The taste is utterly different from ready-cooked or frozen products.

crostata
tart

Crostate are always sweet. Although there are only three traditional tarts (of ricotta from Rome, of jam from Emilia and of marzipan from Sicily), a look in the window of any PASTICCERIA will show that today there are many different fillings. Most crostate have strips of pastry laid over the filling before baking, to make a lattice top.

crostini
toasted bread

The word covers two different preparations. Crostini can be croutons, served with soups, or slices of country bread, toasted or baked and then lightly oiled or buttered or moistened with VIN SANTO or stock. Like bruschetta, they are served as ANTIPASTI or as a snack with drinks. *In crostini alla napoletana*, the bread is covered with a slice of mozzarella, a small piece of anchovy fillet and a morsel of tomato, and then baked. *Crostini di mare* consist of thick slices of bread hollowed out, buttered and toasted in the oven, and then filled with seafood mixed with breadcrumbs, parsley, garlic and olive oil. The best known crostini are those from Tuscany, topped with chicken or game livers, for which the recipe is given here.

[see recipe on page 122]

crudo
cooking method

The expression *'a crudo'* ('raw') refers to various raw ingredients placed together in the pan and then cooked. It is a very healthy method of cooking, because it avoids the usual preliminary sautéing.

crumiri or krumiri
biscuits

Created in 1878 by a confectioner of Casale Monferrato, these biscuits, sold in Piedmont in their traditional metal boxes, are still extremely popular. They are made of maize and white flour and shaped like handlebars, apparently in honour of Victor Emmanuel II, the first king of Italy, who was very proud of his handlebar moustache.

Il Cucchiaio d'Argento
cookery book

Il Cucchiaio d'Argento (*The Silver Spoon*) is a well-known cookbook, more appreciated abroad than in Italy. It contains around 2,000 recipes from all over Italy. First published in 1950, it has gone through several editions and has been translated into English, Dutch, French and German.

---

crostini alla chiantigiana
chicken liver pâté on crostini

Serves 8

225g/8oz chicken livers
4 tbsp extra virgin olive oil
25g/1oz/2 tbsp unsalted butter
½ celery stalk, very finely chopped
½ carrot, very finely chopped
1 small onion, very finely chopped
3 tbsp dry white wine
1½ tsp tomato puree diluted with 4 tbsp
  warm water
salt and freshly ground black pepper
1 tbsp capers, preferably in salt, rinsed
  and chopped
1 small garlic clove, chopped
1 salted anchovy, boned, rinsed and
  chopped, or 2 canned or bottled
  anchovy fillets, drained and chopped
slices of toasted bread
a little vin santo

These, the most traditional of all CROSTINI, are made throughout Tuscany. In this version from Chianti a little tomato puree is added to the pâté mixture to help counteract the sweetness of the livers. Use good country bread.

Clean the chicken livers and cut them into very small pieces. Put the olive oil and half the butter in a saucepan over a medium heat. When the butter has melted, add the celery, carrot and onion. Cook for 10 minutes, stirring frequently.

Turn down the heat, add the chicken livers and cook until they have lost their raw colour. Increase the heat, pour over the wine and boil briskly until the wine has almost evaporated. Now add the diluted tomato puree and a little salt. Cover the pan and continue to cook over a low heat for 5 minutes.

Take the pan off the heat and mix in some pepper, the capers, garlic, anchovies and the remaining butter. When the butter has melted, chop the mixture or work it in a food processor for a few seconds until smooth. Return the mixture to the pan and cook for a further 3 minutes or so, stirring constantly.

The pâté is now ready for spreading over toasted bread, lightly moistened with vin santo. The crostini are excellent served warm or cold.

---

cucina
the kitchen, cooking

The word refers both to the kitchen and to the result of the activity that takes place there.

Cucina, the room, has undergone drastic changes through the centuries. A description of a 16th-century kitchen in a grand household appears in *Opera* by Bartolomeo SCAPPI. This kitchen has two water tanks, a grinder, a dough-chest, six trestle tables plus other occasional tables, built-in cupboards around the walls, an open fireplace, a large oven and a small brick construction alongside for cooking directly over the flame. It was dominated by a table 'fifteen hand-spans long and three-and-a-half hand-spans wide' on which the pasta was made. The kitchen, Scappi described, should open onto a small yard where birds can be plucked and animals can be killed, skinned and cleaned, after having hung in the winds coming from the north-facing yard. In the middle of this yard there should be a well and a large basin and many large buckets for washing fish and meat. Next to the kitchen there should be another room, much bigger than the yard, for storage.

A contemporary kitchen is a totally different affair. It may be small in a town house, while in the country it is still the main room of the house and the centre of family life – as indeed it should be. The style will vary, but the BATTERIA will include many similar utensils, pots and pans and gadgets. The ideal cooker is large, with plenty of space between the rings to allow large pans to sit one next to the other, since traditional Italian cooking is mostly done on the hob; the oven is used mainly for baking.

Cucina is also the term for cooking, which is divided into regions, sub-divided into provinces and then sub-divided again into smaller units until finally it becomes the family cooking handed down from mother to daughter. 'Italian cooking' only exists abroad, where a pot-pourri of different regional dishes is served. They are, however, a poor representation of what cooking is really like in Italy, which is in fact extremely varied because of the strong individualism and creativity of the people. There are some factors that unite all these local styles. First and foremost is the consistent use of high-quality fresh ingredients. Italians are seldom, if ever, willing to substitute one ingredient for another. Another unifying factor is that Italian cooking is always home cooking, informal, human, alive, the direct expression of its maker. Creativity and spontaneity, within certain traditional techniques, are the foundations of the cooking, which seems to spring from an instinctive enjoyment of life.

culatello
a cured pork product

The most valued pork product, culatello is made from the fillet of a pig's thigh, salted and aged for about 12 months in the humid atmosphere of the area between Parma and the river Po in Emilia-Romagna. It shares its birthplace with Verdi. Culatello looks like an oversized egg, weighs about 3kg/6½lb, has a soft, melt-in-the-mouth texture and a flavour similar to prosciutto but more well defined. It is eaten cold, as an ANTIPASTO, thinly sliced, with bread and possibly a little butter. Culatello is a very perishable product. It is now also made industrially during the Christmas season, when it is traditional fare in northern Italy.

culurzones
Sardinian ravioli

Sardinians prefer bread to pasta, but they have two or three original pasta dishes, of which this is one. Culurzones are large RAVIOLI, stuffed with very fresh PECORINO, spinach, egg and saffron. It is this last which imparts to the culurzones their particular flavour. When cooked, they are dressed with roast meat juice or tomato sauce.

cuore
heart

The most popular is the heart of a calf, which is usually sliced and marinated in olive oil, garlic, chilli and lemon and then grilled or pan-fried. It is also baked whole, wrapped in pork caul, stuffed with PANCETTA, soft breadcrumbs and the usual flavourings. Lamb's heart is eaten with all the other offal in the CORATELLA. Chicken and other birds' hearts are part of the giblets and, with the liver, make excellent sauces for pasta or risotto, or to accompany SFORMATI.

cuscusu
couscous dish

There are two dishes with this name: one is from Trapani in western Sicily, made from couscous with various fish, octopus and other seafood. The other cuscusu is made in Livorno in Tuscany and is a couscous mixed with stewed cabbage and tiny meatballs cooked in a tomato sauce. Both these ports had a thriving trade with North Africa, hence the use of couscous.

d

dado
bouillon or stock cube

Not in the least despised, even by the best cooks, dadi are an important standby in any Italian kitchen. This may be because the stock cubes sold in Italy have a genuine taste; they are full of flavour and yet delicate. They are used in many soups, added in small quantities to sauces and savoury dishes, and used to prepare some risotti. Dadi would not be used, however, in very delicate risotti such as RISOTTO ALLA MILANESE or the Venetian RISI E BISI. Some cubes are flavoured with PORCINI and these, with the addition of fresh mushrooms, make a good mushroom risotto.

daino
roe deer

This small deer is now found only in reserves in the Apennines and in Sardinia. It is cooked in the same ways as other deer. In a recipe by Ada BONI in her book *Il Talismano della Felicità*, the leg of a young roe deer is stuffed with prosciutto and herbs and cooked in a casserole with red wine. ARTUSI suggests pan-frying escalopes of roe deer in butter and sage with a finishing glug of MARSALA.

dattero di mare
date-shell

The extraordinary property of this mollusc, which looks like a date (*dattero* in Italian), is that it erodes the rock to make a lodging place for itself – its scientific name is *lithophaga* (stone-eater). It achieves this feat by emitting a kind of acid which corrodes the rock, making a hole in which it nests. Datteri di mare are now rare and it is illegal to catch them. Occasionally you may see some in the fish market in Lerici in the Gulf of La Spezia, or in Pozzuoli in the Gulf of Naples – nobody asks how they arrived there. The good news is that there are now experiments in farming them, so we might see them on the market again in the future.

Datteri di mare are highly prized for their delicate flavour. They are best eaten simply cooked, such as in a SOFFRITTO of oil, garlic and parsley into which they are thrown until the shells open up. Like most other molluscs, they are also divine raw, as I used to have them quite often at Lerici, in the old days.

DOP

This stands for *Denominazione di Origine Protetta* ('protected designation of origin'), which is granted to some products that fulfil strict definitions, laid down by law, based on the land where they grow and the methods used to produce them. The first Denominazione di Origine Controllata (DOC), modelled on the French Appellation d'Origine Contrôlée system, was granted in 1963 to wines; later it was also granted to cheeses, pork products, breeds of cattle and horticultural produce. The system has since been overhauled at European level, and the term DOP was introduced in the 1990s and it is now granted to all products except wine. There are some drawbacks to these regulations, as some excellent products, artisanally made or even made on just one farm, cannot comply. But the Italians are masters of avoiding being straitjacketed without actually breaking the law and everybody is happy.

dente, al
'to the tooth'

This expression is used primarily in connection with pasta and rice. It means that the pasta or rice, though cooked through, still offers a little resistance to the tooth, this being an essential sign of being perfectly and properly cooked.

It is impossible to determine the perfect 'al dente' point of cooking, as it depends on the different types and qualities of the pasta or rice being cooked. To some extent it is also a question of personal taste. A dish of spaghetti, for instance, considered al dente outside Italy might be considered to be *stracotto* (overcooked) in Lombardy, and inedible in Naples.

Nowadays al dente is also used to describe a point of cooking of vegetables, particularly boiled or steamed vegetables such as green beans, cauliflower and broccoli, which are often subjected to a second cooking, and so have to be kept al dente.

dente di leone
dandelion

Also called *radichella* or *insalatina di campo*. It must be picked when very young and the leaves still small and soft – before it flowers. Once thoroughly washed the leaves are ready to eat. However, to rid them of some of the bitterness, they can be cut very thinly and soaked in salted water for 2–3 hours. Dandelions are dressed like other salads, with olive oil and salt, but more vinegar or lemon juice should be used than with cultivated salads, so as to counterbalance the slightly bitter taste. Unlike other green salads, dandelions are best dressed at least 15 minutes in advance. In Emilia they are often dressed with bits of PANCETTA sautéed in STRUTTO and poured hot onto the salad. Dandelions are also good braised, although I find that this makes them more bitter.

dentice
Mediterranean dentex

This is an excellent specimen of the extensive sea bream family, the *Sparidae*. It can be as long as 1m/3ft but the average length is about 30–40cm/12–16in. Dentice are found all round the coasts of Italy. They are usually cooked by grilling or roasting/baking in the oven, and are often accompanied by a sauce made with olive oil, lemon juice and mashed salted anchovies. The larger specimens are cut into steaks and then grilled, or pan-fried in olive oil. Dentice, like sea bass, can be cooked in a crust of salt (see recipe on page 367), an ideal method for sealing in its flavour.

[see recipe on page 128]

desinare
dinner

Originally a verb meaning 'to dine', it is now used as a noun to signify the most important meal of the day. It is seldom heard in cities, but in the country, especially in central Italy, it is still used to refer to the midday meal.

diavolicchio
chilli

This diminutive of *diavolo* ('devil') is one of the names given to chilli in Abruzzo and Basilicata, where it is the most frequent flavouring and is used lavishly. It is put in SALAMI and SALSICCE, in fish soup (the BRODETTO of Abruzzo is characterized by it, see recipe on page 14), in pasta sauces and in combination with sweet peppers. Diavolicchio is used fresh and dried. It is dried in the sun, and in the country in the summer you can see doorways and balconies festooned with chains of scarlet diavolicchio.

diavolilli
almond sweets

Tiny almond sweets coated with multi-coloured icing. Said to have been invented by monks in Naples who cleverly spread the rumour that the sweets were powerful stimulants. This added to their sales, making them treats for elderly men as well as for little children. It also explains their name, diavolilli meaning 'little devil'. Diavolilli are used in Naples to decorate cakes.

diplomatico
a pudding

A very grand cake, as its name implies, rarely made at home. It consists of two layers of puff pastry containing layers of Madeira cake, CREMA PASTICCERA or butter cream, or chocolate custard and other delicacies.

ditali
a pasta

Ditali, ditalini and ditaloni are all dried pasta in a tube shape. They differ only in size, the ditali being about 1cm/½in long, the ditaloni, fatter and longer and the ditalini thinner and shorter. The two larger sizes are used mainly with vegetable sauces and the ditalini in soups and MINESTRONE.

dolce
sweet

This word covers the whole range of sweet preparations, from cakes and biscuits to small sweets and chocolates, although strictly speaking dolce is the course served at the end of a meal. When dolce is part of a dessert it always follows cheese and precedes fruit, although nowadays fruit might be omitted after a dolce. A dolce is not part of an everyday meal; it is reserved for special occasions or public feasts. As they are eaten on feast days, dolci are even more regional than other types of cooking. Every patron saint, every feast day of the year, has its own special dolce, in every town in Italy.

The dolci of the north are often little more than sweet breads, the PANETTONE of Milan being the prime example. The dolci of central Italy are richer, with lots of spices, nuts, candied peel and honey, as in the PANFORTE from Siena or the CERTOSINO from Bologna. Here also we see the birth of the *dolce al cucchiaio* – a sweet that can be eaten with a spoon, such as ZUPPA INGLESE. In southern Italy the main ingredients of dolci are almonds and candied fruits, a heritage from Arab cooking. There are many exceptions to this rule. After all, the birthplace of ZABAIONE, the dolce al cucchiaio par excellence, is Piedmont, while a CIAMBELLA (ring-shaped sweet bread) is a traditional dolce of Puglia.

In the south, the making of some dolci was a prerogative of the nuns. The 20th-century writer and gastronome Alberto Denti di Pirajno, in his *I Siciliani a Tavola*, suggests that the reason for this is that when the Arab harems were dismantled by the Normans, some of the inhabitants – all passionate sweet-eaters and makers – took refuge in convents. There they continued to occupy themselves with making sweets, and it was from them that the nuns learned the craft, which they carried on and perfected. Unfortunately, the patisseries and the large manufacturers are killing this vestige of history.

127

dolcelatte
a cheese

Dolcelatte is a mild, creamy, blue-veined cheese, created by the firm Galbani for the British market as an alternative to GORGONZOLA. It is sweeter than Gorgonzola and has a higher fat content. In Italy it is called Gorgonzola dolce.

dorare
to gild

In a culinary context the word means to turn food to a golden colour by deep or shallow frying, or baking with an egg yolk glaze. A COSTOLETTA alla Milanese or a good FRITTO must be properly *dorato*: cooked until golden outside but with the inside still moist and not overcooked.

Food that was dorato was very fashionable in the 15th century, a trend that began because doctors believed that gold (*oro*) was good for the heart. Chefs of the rich were instructed to cover various foods with gold leaf, while the not-so-rich sought a similar result by frying the food or using saffron. The story goes that RISOTTO ALLA MILANESE — risotto with saffron — was created to impress the guests at the wedding of a glassmaker of the Duomo of Milan. Whatever the truth of that story, in the past the colour of gold signified sumptuousness.

dosaggio or dose
quantity

When specifying quantities in recipes, Italian cookery writers used to be, and sometimes still are, rather vague. They presume that their readers know the right proportions of the basic ingredients: butter, oil, onion, flour, etc. So the quantities of these ingredients are often not given. When you ask an Italian cook how much stock he or she has added to that delicious sauce, the answer is 'two fingers' or 'half a glass' or 'a *bicchierino*' (small glass). The size of the glass, or the fingers, is not specified! 'A little chopped onion' can be ½ tablespoon, or as much as 2 tablespoons. It is all a question of experience, of 'just knowing'. This can be difficult for the foreign or inexperienced cook, but you should always ask. Italians love to talk about food and are flattered by the appreciation and interest shown in what they have prepared.

dentice in salsa
sea bream in tomato sauce

Serves 4

1 sea bream, about 1kg/2¼lb, cleaned but with the head left on

100ml/3½fl oz/7 tbsp extra virgin olive oil

1 small onion, finely chopped

1 small celery stalk, finely chopped

1 garlic clove, finely chopped

1 tbsp chopped fresh parsley

1 small dried chilli, crumbled

4 ripe fresh tomatoes, peeled, or 400g/14oz canned plum tomatoes, drained and coarsely chopped

125ml/4fl oz/½ cup dry white wine

salt and freshly ground black pepper

about 3 tbsp flour

This is a classic recipe for a large fish cooked in a tomato sauce. You can use sea bass, sea bream, grey mullet or any other firm white fish, but not blue, oily fish such as mackerel or salmon.

Preheat the oven to 200°C/400°F/Gas Mark 6. Pat the fish dry, inside and out.

Heat the olive oil in a saucepan, add the onion, celery, garlic, parsley and chilli and sauté until the vegetables are soft. Add the tomatoes and cook for 10 minutes or so over a lively heat, then pour in the wine and bring to the boil. Season with salt and pepper. Remove from the heat.

Mix a little salt into the flour. Coat the fish lightly with the seasoned flour. Spoon the sauce into an oiled roasting pan and add the fish. Baste with some sauce and cover with foil. Bake for about 30 minutes, or until the fish is cooked.

RIGHT: Dentice in salsa

dragoncello
tarragon

Also called *serpentaria*, *targoncello* or *estragone*, this
herb has a very distinctive aroma, strong yet at
the same time subtle. It is used very little in Italy;
only in Tuscany, especially in Siena, does tarragon
make an appearance in some dishes. It is, in fact,
also called *erba di Siena*. *Salsa al dragoncello*, made
of fresh breadcrumbs, tarragon, vinegar, garlic,
salt and pepper, all pounded to a paste with olive
oil, often accompanies boiled meats – just like
SALSA VERDE.

droghe
see SPEZIE

drogheria
grocer's shop

For me this conjures up an atmosphere redolent
of exotic smells mixed with the scent of soaps
and toiletries, as well as visions of large glass jars
full of sweets, nuts, spices, liquorice sticks and
candied fruits. These were the grocers' shops of
my childhood; nowadays they have largely been
replaced by supermarkets. There are still a few
drogheria, mainly in provincial towns, but so many
of their products are pre-packed that half the
pleasure in shopping in them has gone.

e

Emilia-Romagna

This region, whose capital is Bologna, stretches from a point only some 30km/20 miles from Genoa in the west right across to the Adriatic coast in the east. The soil is extremely fertile both in the Po Valley and in the foothills of the Apennines. The region embraces two different areas, Emilia, the western part, and Romagna, along the Adriatic. The cooking of these two sub-regions is different, yet many general characteristics are shared. It is always a richly flavoured cooking created by and for people who are deeply involved in what they eat. The three basic cooking fats, butter, lard and oil, are all used, though butter and lard predominate in the traditional local cooking because they are produced locally.

Olive trees used to be cultivated in Emilia but have been mostly replaced by crops that need the richness of the Emilian land.

Prime examples of the region's agricultural skills, combined with highly developed techniques for processing the farm products, are PROSCIUTTO di Parma and PARMIGIANO REGGIANO (Parmesan cheese). Both these products, already famous in the Renaissance, are made now exactly as they were then.

Up until World War II the popular cuisine was poor, based on soup and bread, with variations such as FOCACCE, PIADINE, CRESCENTINE. For the wealthier people meals often included meat, especially stewed or boiled, and even puddings. The cooking of the region is varied, but it is identifiable by a common factor, being robust, richly flavoured and succulent.

Emilia-Romagna is the motherland of homemade pasta. The varieties are numerous. In Piacenza and Parma, ANOLINI are the speciality. Modena offers TORTELLI, as does Ferrara; in

131

Bologna TAGLIATELLE, LASAGNE and TORTELLINI are the favourites. Ferrara also has CAPPELLETTI and CAPPELLACCI. The Emiliani housewives are without rivals when it comes to pasta-making. They can prepare tagliatelle for the whole family in 20 minutes flat. They mix, knead and roll out at fantastic speed. For the pasta in broth, they stop rolling out while the SFOGLIA is still quite thick, but for tagliatelle, lasagne or stuffed shapes they keep rolling until the dough is nearly transparent. The triumph of all homemade pasta dishes is to be found in the elaborate pies. The crust is made of PASTA FROLLA (sweet pastry) from which, when it is cut, there falls a cascade of small tortellini or anolini dressed with a luscious RAGÙ, enriched with mushrooms and chicken livers. My version of the classic ragù alla bolognese is on page 346.

As well as making great pasta dishes, the Emiliani have always been able to create masterpieces out of a pig and a bucket of milk. From the pig come as many kinds of SALAME and prosciutto as there are towns in the region. Piacenza excels in its COPPA and PANCETTA, Parma in its world-famous prosciutto, equally excellent CULATELLO and the most highly valued salame, the *felino*. Reggio Emilia is stronger in large sausages, such as COTECHINO and CAPPELLO DA PRETE. The MORTADELLA of Bologna is so well known that in Lombardy it is simply called Bologna. ZAMPONE is the trotter-shaped sausage of Modena, where prosciutto, similar to that of Parma but less delicate, is also produced, and at Ferrara there is the SALAMA DA SUGO. This is the delicious pork product that the dukes of Este, lords of Ferrara, used to serve as an aphrodisiac and which, suitably enough, now appears at every wedding feast.

The bucket of milk produces the third important product of the region, GRANA, of which Parmigiano Reggiano is the best. Grana is used with all local pasta dishes and with some meat and even fish dishes.

Romagna, being a coastal area, has a tradition of fish dishes. Sole from the coast are small and very tasty, as are all Adriatic fish. Particular mention must be made of the eels of the Comacchio lagoon, which are famous all over Italy because of their delicate taste. The Romagnoli's love for fish finds its apotheosis in the BRODETTO, the most flavoursome of all fish soups.

Many of the region's sweets are associated with particular feasts, of which the most famous is the Festa degli Addobbi of Bologna. *Addobbi* means 'decorations' and in this case refers to decorations on balconies along the route of a religious procession. On the day of the *festa*, the *torta degli addobbi* is baked – it is the same rice cake, full of candied citron and almonds, that was made during the Renaissance. The TORTA DI RISO, for which the recipe is given overleaf, is very similar and is made all year round. The SPONGATA, a speciality of the provinces of Parma and Reggio, is another traditional sweet, made at Christmas. Bologna also claims to be the birthplace of the ubiquitous ZUPPA INGLESE.

The diversity of this rich cuisine has always been the cause of great rivalry among the nine provinces, which compete in offering some of the finest dishes within the vast repertoire of Italian cooking. And a final word for yet another outstanding product of the region, ACETO BALSAMICO (balsamic vinegar), which is becoming increasingly popular all over Europe and beyond.

 [see recipe on page 134]

erbazzone
a savoury pie

Also called *scarpazzone*. A savoury pie made in Emilia and typical of the country cooking of that region. The filling is made with cooked spinach sautéed in a finely chopped mixture of PANCETTA, garlic and parsley. This is then mixed with Parmesan and eggs. The pastry is made with flour and melted lard, water and salt and the pie is baked in a hot oven for about 30 minutes.

erbe aromatiche
herbs

Herbs are used a lot, but always with discretion and discernment. Parsley is the most commonly used herb, followed by rosemary, bay leaf, marjoram, sage, oregano and basil, with mint, tarragon, thyme, borage, chives and wild fennel used less frequently.

There are always one or two particular herbs that enhance the basic characteristics of any given food or dish, while at the same time complementing its flavour with their own. For instance a rabbit should always be cooked with thyme; the herbs to go with veal escalopes are sage or parsley; an ARROSTO (roast meat or poultry) would never be cooked without a sprig or two of fresh rosemary. Wild fennel goes in the PORCHETTA (roasted pig) of central Italy, in the Tuscan ARISTA and in the famous Sicilian pasta with fresh sardines. Nor would the Tuscan bean dish FAGIOLI ALL'UCCELLETTO be what it is without the sage leaves gently sautéed in rich olive oil, while a few leaves of fresh mint on some grilled courgettes are just perfection.

erbe selvatiche
wild herbs and plants

The term covers a wide range of herbs and plants that are eaten in salads, soups or other dishes. In the past such plants were among the principal foods of the poor who, out of sheer need, had learnt how to recognize and cook them. It was by no means only the poor, however, who ate wild herbs and plants. In the early 17th century Giacomo CASTELVETRO enthuses about a salad containing 'the first leaves of the apple mint, of the nasturtium, the top of spearmint, of tarragon, the leaves and flowers of borage, the flowers of the new fennel, the leaves of the gentle rocket and of the lemony sorrel, the sweet flowers of rosemary and the petals of violets' all gently washed and generously dressed with olive oil.

Nowadays chefs have again come to recognize the culinary value of these simple plants.

estragone

see DRAGONCELLO

estratto
extract

A concentrated flavouring. The two estratti are *di carne* and *di pomodoro*. Meat extracts are industrially produced and sold in jars and tubes, while tomato extract is homemade and is a speciality of Sicily and southern Italy. It is called *strattù* in Sicilian and CONCENTRATO DI POMODORO in other parts of Italy.

133

torta di riso
rice cake

Serves 6–8

750ml/1¼ pints/3 cups full-fat (whole)
 milk
150g/5½oz/¾ cup caster (superfine)
 sugar
a strip of lemon rind, yellow part only,
 plus the grated rind of ½ organic or
 unwaxed lemon
2.5cm/1in piece of vanilla pod, split
 in half
5cm/2in piece of cinnamon stick
a pinch of salt
150g/5½oz/¾ cup arborio rice
unsalted butter and dried breadcrumbs,
 for the tin
125g/4½oz/scant 1 cup blanched
 almonds
50g/1¾oz/6 tbsp pine nuts
4 large eggs, separated
25g/1oz candied orange, lemon and
 citron peel, chopped
3 tbsp rum
icing (confectioners') sugar, to decorate

A cake not a pudding. Originally from Emilia-Romagna and Tuscany, torta di riso is always eaten cold, in slices, and should be made one or two days in advance. The many recipes for it fall into two categories — with or without a pastry shell. My recipe here is without.

Put the milk, 25g/1oz/2 tbsp of the sugar, the strip of lemon rind, vanilla, cinnamon and salt in a saucepan and bring to the boil.

Add the rice and stir well with a wooden spoon. Cook, uncovered, over a very low heat for about 40 minutes, stirring frequently, until the rice has absorbed the milk and is soft and creamy. Set aside to cool.

While the rice is cooling, preheat the oven to 180°C/350°F/Gas Mark 4. Butter a 25cm/10in springform cake tin, line the bottom with baking parchment and butter the paper. Sprinkle all over with breadcrumbs and shake off the excess.

Spread the almonds and pine nuts on a baking sheet and toast them in the oven for about 10 minutes, shaking the baking sheet once or twice to prevent them from burning. Remove them from the oven (leaving the oven on at the same temperature) and let them cool a little before chopping them coarsely by hand or in a food processor. Do not reduce them to powder.

Remove the lemon rind, vanilla pod and cinnamon stick from the rice and spoon the rice into a mixing bowl. Incorporate one egg yolk at a time into the rice, mixing well after each addition. Add the remaining caster sugar, the nuts, candied peel, grated lemon rind and rum to the rice and egg mixture and combine everything together thoroughly.

Whisk the egg whites stiffly and fold into the rice mixture.

Spoon the rice mixture into the prepared tin and bake for about 45 minutes, until the cake has shrunk away from the side of the tin. Insert a thin skewer or toothpick into the middle of the cake — it should come out moist, but clean.

Leave the cake to cool in the tin and then unclip and turn the cake over onto a dish. Remove the base of the tin and the paper, place a round serving dish over the cake and turn it over again. Sprinkle lavishly with icing sugar before serving.

f

fagiano
pheasant

In the past, the pheasant was a common bird, living in the wild; today it is found only in shooting reserves. Pheasant must be hung before it is drawn and plucked. The duration of this process was, and still is, the subject of endless controversy.

The meat of the female bird is superior in taste and tenderness to that of the male. A young hen is roasted in the oven; a male bird, dutifully covered with PANCETTA, is usually pot-roasted. Older birds are braised in wine.

In Tuscany, game of all kinds is popular, due to the passion for hunting in the region. There, the pheasant is usually roasted with pancetta and flavoured with sage and/or rosemary. In one Tuscan recipe the preparation of the pheasant combines typical elements of the French cuisine, such as brandy and cream, with the very Italian prosciutto and white truffles to give the whole dish a markedly Italian flavour. An interesting old Venetian recipe suggests a rich stuffing made with hard cheese, egg yolks, garlic, fennel, sultanas, spices, herbs, sugar and fresh morello cherries.

[see recipe below]

fagiano alla milanese
Milanese pheasant

Serves 2–3

1 hen pheasant, trussed
salt and freshly ground black pepper
50g/1¾oz/4 tbsp unsalted butter
25g/1oz unsmoked pancetta, cut into
*   cubes or strips*
100g/3½oz lean pork, coarsely minced
*   (ground)*
1 shallot, stuck with 2 cloves
¼ tsp ground cinnamon
½ tsp grated nutmeg
150ml/5fl oz/⅔ cup meat stock (page
*   61) or chicken stock*
150ml/5fl oz/⅔ cup dry white wine
100ml/3½fl oz/7 tbsp double (heavy)
*   cream*

Pheasant is popular in Lombardy, as it is in Tuscany. Lombard recipes, such as this one, are often more elaborate, influenced by French cuisine.

Season the pheasant inside and out with salt and pepper. Heat the butter and the pancetta in a heavy oval flameproof casserole, add the pheasant and brown on all sides for about 10 minutes. Add the liver from the pheasant, the pork, shallot, spices and salt and pepper. Pour over the stock and wine and bring to the boil. Cover the pan and cook at a low simmer for about 1 hour or until the bird is tender.

Remove the pheasant from the pan and keep warm.

Puree the sauce and transfer it to a clean pan. Bring to the boil and, if it is too thin, reduce over a high heat. Turn the heat down, add the cream and cook for a further 5 minutes, stirring constantly.

Cut up the pheasant into neat portions and lay it on a warmed serving dish. Coat with a little of the sauce and serve the remaining sauce separately.

fagiolino
green bean, French bean

Green beans arrived in Italy in the 17th century from the New World and soon became established, with many different species being propagated. Among the most common varieties are the green Bobis, the marbled Anellino di Trento, the yellow Meraviglia di Venezia and Corona d'Oro and the pretty purplish Trionfo Violetto. There is also a variety called Stringa or Un Metro or, in Tuscany, *fagiolino di Sant'Anna*, because it is ready for the Saint's name day on 26 July. These are very long thin beans, sometimes measuring up to 50cm/20in.

Green beans are cooked in boiling water and then, unless served cool as a salad, they undergo a second cooking, sautéed in butter or oil, possibly with garlic and anchovies (*alla genovese*), with butter and Parmesan (*alla milanese*) or stewed in a tomato sauce flavoured with fennel seeds (*alla fiorentina*). If young and of the best quality, they are not pre-boiled, but are cooked directly in a tomato sauce.

[see recipe below]

polpettone di fagiolini
green bean and potato pie

Serves 6
20g/³⁄₄oz dried porcini
250g/9oz floury (starchy) potatoes, scrubbed
500g/1lb 2oz green beans, topped and tailed
2 large eggs
75g/2³⁄₄oz Parmesan cheese, grated
salt and freshly ground black pepper
1 tsp chopped fresh marjoram
3 tbsp extra virgin olive oil
2–3 tbsp dried breadcrumbs

As with all other Ligurian vegetable pies, this one is equally good hot or cold, but it should not be eaten straight from the oven or chilled.

Soak the dried porcini in a cupful of hot water for about 30 minutes. Lift them out, rinse them if they are still gritty and pat dry with kitchen paper. Chop them coarsely and put in a large bowl.

Boil the potatoes in their skins in boiling water until tender. Drain and peel, then puree them in a food mill or potato ricer and add to the porcini.

Preheat the oven to 180°C/350°F/Gas Mark 4.

Cook the beans in boiling water until soft, not crunchy. This may take 5–10 minutes, depending on how fresh the beans are. Drain, dry with kitchen paper and chop. Add to the porcini and potatoes.

Lightly beat the eggs with the Parmesan, salt, pepper and marjoram. Fold into the porcini, potato and bean mixture. Mix in 1 tablespoon of the olive oil and then taste and adjust the seasoning.

Grease a 20cm/8in ovenproof dish with 1 tablespoon of the remaining oil and sprinkle some of the breadcrumbs all over the inside of the dish. Shake off the excess crumbs. Spoon the vegetable mixture into the dish, smooth the top with a spatula and then sprinkle lightly with breadcrumbs. Drizzle the rest of the oil evenly all over the top and bake for about 1 hour, until a light golden brown crust has formed. Remove the pie from the oven and allow to stand for at least 5 minutes before serving.

fagiolo
bean

Phaseolus vulgaris – to give it its botanical name – arrived in Italy from the New World at the beginning of the 16th century, while the *Vigna unguiculata*, FAGIOLO DALL'OCCHIO (black-eyed bean), had been cultivated since Etruscan times. The New World beans were first cultivated in Veneto, where the borlotti variety was produced, and from there their cultivation spread all over northern and central Italy, where different varieties were developed. Borlotti are perhaps the most popular variety: pale pink with red speckles, they are best in soups and stews because of their very creamy consistency. *Borlottini* are a small variety of borlotti and are used for the same dishes. Another borlotti variety, the *fagioli di Lamon* – named for a town in

Veneto – are reputed to be the ideal beans for a soup because of their creaminess and rich flavour, but they are difficult to find outside Veneto.

In Tuscany the variety developed was the cannellini, a small white bean, less mealy than the borlotti and therefore ideal for salads or simply fried. The Tuscans have a vast repertoire of bean recipes, especially for soups, and they are mostly for the white cannellini. The most interesting recipe is *fagioli al fiasco*. Cannellini beans are dropped into a wine flask with best olive oil, sage leaves, pepper and water. No salt is ever added to beans until they are cooked because it will harden the skin. The flask is corked with a wad of muslin, leaving it loose enough for the steam to escape. It is then put into smouldering embers and left for about 3 hours. A simpler, yet equally good recipe is *fagioli all'uccelletto* (below). In Umbria the same

fagioli all'uccelletto
cannellini beans with garlic, sage and oil

Serves 4
300g/10½oz/1½ cups dried cannellini beans, soaked for about 12 hours in cold water
½ onion
1 bay leaf
3 garlic cloves, unpeeled and bruised
2 sprigs of fresh sage
5 tbsp extra virgin olive oil
250g/9oz ripe fresh tomatoes, peeled and chopped, or 400g/14oz canned chopped tomatoes, drained
salt and freshly ground black pepper

The name of this popular Tuscan recipe, meaning 'beans in the bird's style', has always been a cause of dissension. ARTUSI holds that they are called this because they are cooked with sage, the essential flavouring for small birds. Other writers maintain it is because these beans are the traditional accompaniment to birds.

The beans can be stewed with or without the tomatoes. If you prefer them '*in* BIANCO', simply omit the tomatoes and add a little vegetable stock instead.

Drain and rinse the beans, then boil them in a pan with water to cover, with the onion, bay leaf, 1 garlic clove and 2 or 3 fresh sage leaves for 1–1½ hours or until tender.

Heat the olive oil in a flameproof earthenware pot. Throw in a sprig of sage and 2 garlic cloves and sauté for 1 minute. Add the tomatoes and cook for 20–25 minutes, until the oil separates from the tomato juices.

Drain the cannellini beans and add to the tomatoes. Season with salt and pepper to taste and cook for about 15 minutes.

These beans are good served hot, warm or cold, but never chilled.

dish is made without tomatoes. In contrast to the Venetian *pasta e fagioli* (below), the Tuscan *zuppa di fagioli* is a less rich soup made with cannellini beans and cooked 'a CRUDO' (without a SOFFRITTO). At the end the soup is ladled over slices of stale Tuscan bread generously rubbed with garlic, and a glug of extra virgin olive oil is poured in.

There is an interesting recipe from Calabria called *fagioli con cucchiai di cipolla*. A bowl of beans, cooked with celery and fennel seeds, is placed in the middle of the table and everyone scoops out the beans using the layers of onion as a spoon. The onion is eaten too and the dish is accompanied by bread made with maize flour.

When they are in season, fresh beans are used rather than dried.

[see recipes below and overleaf]

fagiolo dall'occhio
black-eyed bean

This bean did not come from the New World but from Asia and Africa; it was well known to the ancient Greeks and Romans. Black-eyed beans have a slightly herby flavour and are used mostly in salads, but they are suitable for any recipe that calls for dried beans. In the spring, when still small and young, they are eaten in their pods like green beans. In a recipe from Trentino the cooked beans are added to veal shanks, previously sautéed with SPECK, and everything is cooked in red wine. Another recipe is for a risotto in which the cooked beans are added with the rice to the SOFFRITTO; the risotto is finished with lots of Parmesan and a generous shower of cubed smoked pancetta, separately fried until crisp.

139

pasta e fagioli alla veneta
Venetian pasta with beans

Serves 4

200g/7oz/1 cup dried borlotti beans, soaked for about 12 hours in cold water

50g/1¾oz unsmoked pancetta, chopped

4 tbsp olive oil

1 garlic clove, chopped

1 small carrot, chopped

1 small onion, chopped

1 small celery stalk, chopped

a few needles of fresh rosemary, chopped

1 knuckle (fresh hock) of unsmoked bacon or ham

1.5 litres/3 pints/6½ cups meat stock (page 61) or chicken stock

175g/6oz small pasta, such as ditalini or conchigliette

salt and freshly ground black pepper

freshly grated Parmesan cheese, to serve

Pasta and bean soup is popular in most regions; the Venetian version is the best known.

Drain and rinse the beans. Put the pancetta and olive oil in a stockpot and sauté for 1 minute. Mix in the garlic, carrot, onion, celery and rosemary and sauté gently until soft. Add the beans and the bacon or ham knuckle, cover with stock and simmer, covered, until the beans are tender. This usually takes about 2 hours.

Lift out the knuckle. Remove the meat from the bone, cut it into strips and set aside. Using a slotted spoon, lift out half the beans from the soup and puree them in a food mill or food processor. Return the puree and meat to the soup and bring back to the boil, then add the pasta, salt and pepper. You may need to add some water before you add the pasta. Mix well and simmer until the pasta is cooked.

Serve the grated cheese separately.

fagottini di verza
stuffed cabbage parcels

Serves 4

400–500g/14oz–1lb 2oz Savoy
    cabbage, outside leaves discarded

salt and freshly ground black pepper

250g/9oz lean minced (ground) beef

100g/3½oz luganega sausage, skinned
    and crumbled

3 tbsp freshly grated Parmesan cheese

1 large egg

a grating of nutmeg

25g/1oz good-quality white bread, with
    the crust removed

5 tbsp milk

1 clove

1 garlic clove, halved and crushed

olive oil, for the dish

1 tbsp tomato puree diluted with 4 tbsp
    hot meat stock (page 61) or
    chicken stock

25g/1oz/2 tbsp unsalted butter

In older versions of this Milanese recipe the parcels are finished off in stock, the tomato puree being a 19th-century addition.

Peel off the inner leaves of the cabbage. This is easily done by cutting them off at the core end and unfolding them gently. Wash the leaves. Bring a large pan of salted water to the boil. Add the cabbage leaves and blanch for 3 minutes after the water has come back to the boil. Lift them out with a slotted spoon and place on a double thickness of kitchen paper.

Put the beef, sausage, Parmesan and egg into a mixing bowl and combine everything together. Add salt, pepper and nutmeg. Mix well.

Put the bread, milk and clove in a small pan over a low heat. Cook, stirring, until the milk has been absorbed and the bread is mushy. Remove the clove, add the bread to the meat mixture and mix well. Add salt and pepper.

Preheat the oven to 190°C/375°F/Gas Mark 5.

Pat the cabbage leaves dry. Divide the large leaves in two and remove the central stalk. Remove the core end of the stalk from the smaller leaves. Place a heaped tablespoon of the stuffing in the middle of each leaf and roll up into little bundles, tucking under the ends of the leaves. Or, if you prefer, tie with narrow strips of leek, as in the photograph.

Choose a shallow ovenproof dish that will hold the bundles in a single layer. Rub the dish with the garlic and a little olive oil. Place the cabbage bundles close to each other in the dish, pour over the hot tomato liquid and dot with butter. Cover with foil and bake for 25 minutes. Serve hot.

fagottini
small bundles

The name refers to the shape and not to the contents. Fagottini are small bundles, or parcels, usually of pasta or pizza dough, but also of thin slices of meat or of vegetables, with various fillings, which are baked or fried. The recipe given here is from Milan, where many traditional meat dishes contain Savoy cabbage,.

 [see recipe on page 140]

faraona
guinea fowl

An attractive bird, smaller than today's domestic hens, the guinea fowl comes originally from West Africa. The Romans were fond of these speckled birds, which they called Numidian hens. APICIUS' recipe suggests boiling the guinea fowl and then sautéing it with pepper, cumin, coriander, laser root (a now-extinct plant that was popular in antiquity), rue, dates and pine nuts to which broth, honey, oil and vinegar are added to make a sauce. Modern recipes are simpler.

In Tuscany guinea fowl are usually roasted, while in Veneto they are stuffed with onions and cloves and cooked in an earthenware pot, or pot-roasted and served with PEVERADA, a peppery sauce. But possibly the most succulent result is from an old Lombard recipe. The bird was wrapped in parchment with butter, herbs, salt and pepper and covered with clay. The clay parcel was cooked in the oven and when the bird inside was presumed to be ready, the clay was broken open with a hammer. The recipe that follows – which does not need clay – gives a similarly succulent result.

[see recipe below]

faraona al mascarpone
guinea fowl with mascarpone stuffing

Serves 3
1 guinea fowl, about 1.6kg/3½lb
100g/3½oz/scant ½ cup mascarpone
salt and freshly ground black pepper
2 tbsp vegetable or olive oil
100g/3½oz/7 tbsp unsalted butter
1 small celery stalk, chopped
1 small carrot, chopped
2 shallots, chopped
150ml/5fl oz/²/₃ cup dry white wine
5–6 tbsp hot milk

A recipe from southern Lombardy, the birthplace of mascarpone. This dish is best served with mashed potatoes.

Wipe the guinea fowl inside and out. Put the mascarpone inside the bird, together with some salt and pepper.

Put the oil, butter, celery, carrot and shallots in a pot into which the guinea fowl will fit snugly. Place the bird on the vegetables, add the chopped giblets (if you have them) and put the pot over a medium heat. Pour over the wine and season with salt and pepper. Cover the pot, turn down the heat and simmer gently for 1¼–1½ hours or until the bird is cooked. Keep an eye on the pot and add a couple of tablespoons of hot milk if it starts to look dry. Test to see whether it is ready by pricking the thickest part of a thigh: the juice that runs out should be clear.

Remove the bird from the pot and keep warm. Puree the cooking liquid, then reheat and serve separately.

farfalle
a pasta

A butterfly-shaped pasta that goes well with delicate creamy sauces. *Farfalline*, a small version of farfalle, are excellent in clear soup. Farfalle can be made from homemade pasta by cutting 5cm/2in squares and pinching them in the middle.

farina
flour

Finely ground dried produce, which could be cereal, legume or vegetable. But when the word is used by itself it means wheat flour, from which bread and cakes are made. In Italy flour is divided into five grades according to the proportion of husk and whole grain it contains. The grades go from 00, the whitest and silkiest, to *integrale*, which is produced from the whole grain. Bakers nowadays most commonly use grade 00 for cakes and biscuits and grade 0 for bread. Although these are the least healthy grades, most mills have now been adapted to produce the highly refined grade 00 or the less refined grade 0. As a result, flour that contains a higher proportion of bran and husk, and which should therefore be cheaper, is in fact more expensive because of the scarcity of producers.

farina gialla or farina di granturco
maize flour

Dried and ground maize (GRANOTURCO) is also known as farina gialla ('yellow flour'), and as POLENTA flour outside Italy. It can be ground fine, medium or coarse; the three grades are used for different dishes, the choice depending also on the locality. It is most commonly used to make polenta, for which it is coarsely ground in Piedmont and Lombardy and finely ground in Veneto. Biscuits

and cakes are made with finely ground farina gialla, especially in northern Italy, and the fine flour is used to coat fish in some recipes.

farinata
a pancake

A kind of thick pancake – similar to the Provençal *socca* – made with chickpea flour, a speciality of Liguria. To make farinata, chickpea flour is mixed with water to a thinnish paste and then poured into a flat round copper pan. A good amount of oil is mixed in and the farinata is baked in a brick oven, fired by burning twigs. The farinata is ready when it is golden and crusty.

Farinata is hardly ever made, or eaten, at home: its place is in the street, where it is bought from perambulating barrows while shopping at the market, or in a bar, to accompany a glass of chilled white wine.

ABOVE: Farfalle

farinata

farro
emmer wheat

This grain is the ancestor of durum wheat. It was the most popular food of the Romans, who used it to make *puls* – a sort of porridge – the staple on which the Roman legionnaires conquered Europe. With the fall of the Roman Empire farro disappeared from the culinary repertoire. There is no mention of farro in books of the Renaissance, nor in ARTUSI, and only one recipe from Umbria in Anna Gossetti della Salda's *Le Ricette Regionali Italiane* (first published in 1967), in which the farro is cooked with a prosciutto bone. But it has recently had a revival and it is now sold either whole, or polished and cracked. Soups are made in Tuscany – especially in Lunigiana – and in Umbria, often in combination with legumes. There are some good modern recipes for salads of farro mixed with vegetables or pulses and even with pasta.

[see recipe below]

---

zuppa di farro e fagioli
farro and bean soup

Serves 6

200g/7oz/1 cup dried borlotti beans, soaked for about 12 hours in cold water

vegetable stock, as necessary

1 celery stalk

2 garlic cloves

½ onion

100g/3½oz unsmoked pancetta, cut into cubes

about 6 fresh sage leaves

1 sprig of fresh rosemary, needles only

a handful of fresh marjoram

1 tbsp olive oil

1 tbsp tomato puree

salt and freshly ground black pepper

a pinch of ground cloves

2 pinches of ground cinnamon

¼ tsp grated nutmeg

150g/5½oz/¾ cup pearl farro

extra virgin olive oil, to serve

There are many different zuppe di FARRO, but they all work on the same principle: the farro cooks in a liquid bean puree. In its original version this recipe contains the fat of a prosciutto knuckle or hock instead of pancetta.

Drain and rinse the beans, then put them in a stockpot, preferably earthenware. Pour over enough water to cover the beans by about 5cm/2in. Bring to the boil, then cook at a very low simmer for 2–3 hours, until very tender.

Using a slotted spoon, lift the beans out of the cooking liquid and puree them in a food mill or food processor until smooth. Measure the bean liquid and add enough vegetable stock to make up to 1 litre/1¾ pints/ 4 cups. Set aside.

Chop or process the celery, garlic, onion, pancetta and herbs to a pounded mixture. Put into the pot in which the beans were cooked, together with the olive oil. Sauté for 5 minutes, stirring occasionally, then mix in the tomato puree and sauté for 1 minute. Add the bean puree and turn it over and over in the vegetable mixture for 5 minutes or so. Add the bean cooking liquid, stirring constantly, and bring to the boil. Season with salt and pepper and add the spices.

Rinse the farro and add to the pot. Cook until it is tender, which will take about 40 minutes.

Serve the soup in individual bowls, with a generous drizzle of extra virgin olive oil.

farsumagru or farsumauru
stuffed beef or veal

Serves 6

700g/1lb 9oz best steak, in a single slice

3 large eggs

175g/6oz minced (ground) pork

85g/3oz luganega sausage, skinned

2 tbsp freshly grated Parmesan cheese

1 tbsp chopped fresh parsley

1 tbsp dried breadcrumbs

1 garlic clove, very finely chopped

salt and freshly ground black pepper

85g/3oz prosciutto, thinly sliced

50g/1¾oz fresh provolone cheese, very finely sliced

4 tbsp olive oil

1 small onion, very finely chopped

75ml/2½fl oz/5 tbsp red wine

1 tbsp tomato puree dissolved in 3 tbsp warm water

25g/1oz/2 tbsp unsalted butter

25g/1oz/3 tbsp flour

A celebrated Sicilian dish, consisting of a lean piece of beef or veal, stuffed with many rich ingredients. It is an ancient dish which allegedly has its origins in the 13th century, when Sicily was under French dominion. It is one of the few Sicilian dishes made with a whole piece of meat, although the outer layer is thin. This is because beef in Sicily has always been both expensive and tough; eaten seldom, it is usually chopped or minced. Farsumagru is served on special occasions.

Pound the meat until it is 1cm/½in thick. Try to make a rectangular shape. Hard-boil two of the eggs and, when cold, slice them.

In a bowl, mix together the pork, sausage, Parmesan, parsley, breadcrumbs and garlic and add the remaining egg. Season with a little salt and a lot of pepper and mix thoroughly with your hands.

Spread the mixture evenly over the meat, leaving a border of about 2cm/¾in all round. Lay the prosciutto on the mixture and cover with the sliced eggs and provolone. Roll up the meat along the longest side and sew it up all the way round.

Heat the olive oil in an oval casserole in which the meat will fit snugly and sauté the onion until soft. Add the meat roll and brown all over. Add the wine and reduce by half.

Pour the dissolved tomato puree over the meat. Bring to the boil, taste and adjust the seasoning. Cover the casserole and simmer for 1½ hours. Check occasionally – you may need to add a little hot water if the pan looks dry. The meat is ready when it can easily be pierced by a fork or skewer. Remove the meat from the casserole and keep warm.

Mash together the butter and flour and whisk into the sauce a little at a time, then boil for 1 minute.

Cut the meat into 1cm/½in slices and lay them, slightly overlapping, on a warmed serving dish. Spoon a little of the sauce over it and serve the rest of the sauce separately.

145

fava
broad bean

This familiar legume grows easily everywhere in Italy. Being very nutritious it was a staple food for poorer people in central and southern Italy. In Tuscany and Lazio broad beans, when young, are eaten raw at the end of the meal, still in their pods, together with a piece of PECORINO cheese.

Southern Italian cooking is rich in recipes for broad beans, which are used fresh in the spring and dried all year round. The oldest of these recipes is for a puree of broad beans that is made in much the same way today as it was in ancient Egypt, where it originated. The dish is called *incapriata* in Puglia and MACCO in Sicily, and it consists of dried broad beans, soaked, peeled and boiled until soft enough to be mashed. This delicate puree is served dressed with olive oil, in Sicily with wild fennel mixed in and in Puglia with boiled chicory or CIME DI RAPA.

Unless very young, broad beans, both fresh and dried, should be peeled. It is a lengthy job, but a necessary one. Dried broad beans can often be found already peeled in health food shops, and they are delicious. They must be soaked for at least 8 hours.

 [see recipe below]

favata
broad beans with pork

A Sardinian stew made with dried broad beans and pork; it is eaten with CARTA DA MUSICA, the local bread.

fave dei morti
biscuits

Literally, 'broad beans of the dead'. These little biscuits, made in Lombardy and Lazio, are so called because they are about the size of broad beans, and they are prepared on All Souls' Day, 2 November. They are made with flour, sugar, almonds and pine nuts, bound together with egg white.

fecola di patate
potato flour

This has a very delicate, yet distinctive, flavour, and is used to replace some or all of the flour in certain cakes. A little potato flour is often used in sauces as a thickening agent, dissolved in a little cold water. An important attribute of this flour is that it is gluten-free.

fave col guanciale
broad beans with pancetta

Serves 4
4 tbsp olive oil
1 small onion, chopped
200g/7oz unsmoked pancetta, cut into small cubes
1kg/2¼lb young broad beans, shelled
about 150ml/5fl oz/⅔ cup vegetable stock or water
salt and freshly ground black pepper

GUANCIALE, traditional in this recipe, is the cured jowl of a pig. Outside Italy, you can use pancetta.

Heat the olive oil in a saucepan, add the onion and pancetta and cook for a good 10 minutes, stirring very frequently.

Add the broad beans and stir to coat them in the fat for 2–3 minutes. Add a couple of tablespoons of stock or water and salt and pepper to taste and cook until the beans are tender but still whole, about 10 minutes. You may need to add a little more stock during cooking.

fegatelli di maiale
pig's liver

This is a preparation of pig's liver, wrapped in caul fat and grilled or fried. It is one of the great specialities of Tuscany and Lazio. *Fegatelli alla fiorentina* are coated with a mixture of wild fennel, garlic, breadcrumbs and pepper or chilli, then wrapped in caul fat and threaded on skewers. They are grilled on charcoal or cooked in the oven. In a recipe from Arezzo the fegatelli, dressed with wild fennel, salt and pepper, are threaded on skewers alternately with pieces of lamb and then grilled. In Lazio fegatelli are flavoured with bay leaves.

fegatini
chicken livers

Chicken livers, sold fresh in *pollerie* – poultry shops – and in some butchers' shops. Tuscany is the best region for them – Tuscan chickens grow very quickly, so that large livers can be obtained from young birds, thus avoiding the unpleasant flavour that arises in livers from older birds.

The Tuscans produce the dish that makes the best use of chicken liver, CROSTINI alla Toscana; my version, from Chianti, is given on page 122. Fegatini are also used in a risotto from Padova, *risotto con i rovinassi* (which is the dialect word for chicken livers), and in a Venetian spaghetti sauce, *bigoli coi rovinassi*. In this dish the chicken livers are sautéed in butter and oil, flavoured with sage and then splashed with dry white wine. Another use of chicken livers is in sauces to accompany SFORMATI and risotti, often in combination with sweetbreads, brains or prosciutto.

fegato
liver

Liver is widely eaten all over the peninsula. The best known of all liver dishes is *fegato alla veneziana*, for which the recipe is given here. Another good way to prepare fegato is *alla milanese* (calf's liver coated in egg and breadcrumbs and fried in butter). Nearly all other recipes for calf's liver are from northern Italy, while in central and southern Italy pig's liver is more commonly used. However, one of the best recipes for pig's liver comes from Lodi in Lombardy: *fegato alla lodigiana*, in which the liver, cut into chunks and highly flavoured with wild fennel, wrapped in prosciutto and in caul fat, is fried in butter. But the main use of pig's liver is in the production of all kinds of SALUMI, mostly uncooked, such as the *mortadella di fegato* made around Lake Orta in Piedmont.

Lamb's liver is mainly eaten in combination with other lamb's offal, as in the Roman CORATELLA *di abbacchio*.

 [see recipe on page 148]

ferri, ai
cooking method

Ai ferri means grilled over embers or cooked in an iron pan. The fuel used to be wood or charcoal, and this is obviously the oldest method of cooking.

The food is brushed with olive oil before or during the cooking, using a sprig of rosemary. Most steak, cutlets or fish can be prepared ai ferri, and served with a light mixture of olive oil and lemon juice.

fesa
a cut of meat

A cut from the thigh of a calf, or of an older animal, more or less equivalent to the end of the rump. Animals are butchered differently on the Continent, so there is no British or American equivalent. Fesa is used for SCALOPPINE (escalopes) of veal or beef. Fesa of beef is the best cut for CARPACCIO. Fesa of veal is the best cut for an ARROSTO MORTO or a VITELLO TONNATO.

fettine
a cut of meat

Meaning 'small slices', fettine are thinly cut slices of beef, veal or pork. They are bought pre-sliced and are then cooked in many different ways. Very often they are simply pan-fried in butter and/or olive oil. Veal fettine are used for FRITTURA PICCATA, for SALTIMBOCCA, MESSICANI, UCCELLINI SCAPPATI, INVOLTINI, or with PIZZAIOLA sauce.

When simply sautéed, fettine are the modern food for busy (or lazy) cooks, some of whom even serve them every day! They are the Italian answer to the French steak or the American hamburger.

fettuccine
a pasta

The Roman TAGLIATELLE, traditionally a little narrower than tagliatelle, a little less than 1cm/½in wide, and a little thicker.

fettunta
bread with olive oil

Similar to BRUSCHETTA but consisting only of a grilled thick slice of bread. While still hot, the bread is rubbed on one side with a garlic clove, sprinkled with salt and pepper and lavishly doused with Tuscan olive oil.

fichi secchi
dried figs

Dried figs are part of the traditional display of desserts that appear at Christmas on any table throughout the peninsula, and especially in Calabria, where they are often minced and put in cakes, or stuffed as in the recipe given here.

 [see recipe on facing page]

fegato alla veneziana
calf's liver with onions

Serves 4
50g/1¾oz/4 tbsp unsalted butter
4 tbsp vegetable oil
700g/1lb 9oz onions, very finely sliced
salt and freshly ground black pepper
700g/1lb 9oz calf's liver, very finely sliced
1 tbsp chopped fresh flat-leaf parsley

The liver can either be sliced thin or cut into strips for this recipe. Some versions add the liver to the onions, but I prefer to remove the onions so that the liver can spread out better, and the cooking is easier to control.

Heat half the butter and the oil in a frying pan large enough to hold the liver in a single layer. When the foam subsides, add the onions and a pinch of salt to the pan, mix well and cook very gently for 30 minutes. The onion should be very soft and just coloured. Stir occasionally during cooking, pressing the onions against the sides of the pan to release the juices.

When the onions are cooked, lift them out of the pan with a slotted spoon and keep warm. Add the remaining butter to the pan and turn up the heat. When the foam begins to subside, add the liver and fry for 2 minutes on each side. Do not overcook: the liver should be pink inside.

Return the onions to the pan, season with salt and pepper and give a good stir. Sprinkle with the parsley and serve at once.

fico
fig

If you haven't eaten a fig straight from the tree, you don't know what a really good fig tastes like. When we were children, during our holidays on the Riviera, we were taken for walks up the hills in the afternoon. In the high summer we resented these walks, which took us away from our beloved sea, but come September it was a different story. We could eat as many figs as we liked as long as we ate them then and there, and so we popped them into our mouths, skin and all. Shop-bought figs are picked before they are ripe, and thus have very little flavour. There are many varieties, some of which produce fruit once a year, and others that have two fruitings, one in late summer, called *fioroni*, and the other in the autumn. Unlike the luscious second crop, fioroni are large and rather tasteless. The figs that are dried are from the second crop.

Figs are usually eaten just as they are, or as an ANTIPASTO with prosciutto or SALAME. They are also baked in a fruit tart or occasionally they are served with egg custard or sprinkled with lemon juice and sugar.

fico d'india
prickly pear

The Italian name means Indian fig, but these fruits are neither figs nor pears, being the fruit of an opuntia, a cactus. Prickly pears grow wild in Sicily and southern Italy, but the best species, the *bastardona*, is achieved with the intervention of man. The farmer removes the first fruits as soon as they begin to take shape. The next growth then

fichi alla sibarita
stuffed figs

Serves 12

3–4 tbsp candied peel, chopped

½ tsp ground cinnamon

½ tbsp Marsala or brandy

12 large fat dried figs

12 blanched almonds, lightly toasted

oil, for greasing

4 heaped tbsp icing (confectioners')
*   sugar, sifted*

2 heaped tbsp unsweetened cocoa
*   powder, sifted*

The name of this dish points immediately to its lusciousness. The word Sibarita derives from Sybaris, a town in the Gulf of Taranto in Calabria, which in the 6th and 5th centuries BC became a byword for extreme luxury and loose living. These delicacies are now sold in boxes in the best grocery shops in southern Italy.

Preheat the oven to 150°C/300°F/Gas Mark 2.

Put the candied peel in a bowl and mix in the cinnamon and the Marsala.

Slit each fig vertically down from the stalk, being careful to leave the bottom attached. Gently open the figs and put inside each of them one almond and a pinch of the candied peel mixture. Place the figs on a lightly oiled baking sheet and bake for 15 minutes.

In a bowl, mix together the sugar and cocoa powder. As soon as the figs are cool enough to handle, close them gently and roll each one in the sugar mixture.

These figs are better after 2 or 3 days.

produces fruits that are firmer and tastier. Prickly pears are best eaten raw with a squeeze of lemon juice, but it is not a fruit that I rate very highly.

finanziera
an offal dish

An elaborate creation of Piedmontese origin, made with a selection of white meat and offal, cooked in butter and flavoured with dried PORCINI or MARSALA. There are quite a few recipes for finanziera, which can be served by itself, as an accompaniment to a plain risotto, as a rich sauce for a SFORMATO or as a vol-au-vent filling.

finocchietto
herb fennel

A perennial herb with tall, feathery foliage that grows wild in Italy. It is to be distinguished from FINOCCHIO, whose bulbous stalk is used as a vegetable. Finely chopped and mixed with other herbs and breadcrumbs, finocchietto is used as a stuffing for fish. It is an important ingredient of the well-known Sicilian dish PASTA CON LE SARDE (see recipe on page 288).

finocchio
florence fennel

The bulbous part at the base of this plant's stalk is a very popular vegetable all over Italy. It is in season all the year round, depending on the region where it is cultivated. There are many varieties, which bear the name of the locality, such as Gigante di Napoli, Grosso di Sicilia, Dolce di Firenze etc.

This vegetable has a peculiar characteristic: it is said that the taste of any wine is improved after having eaten raw fennel. Personally I have not been able to verify this – but I am not a wine expert.

The old habit of eating fennel at the end of the meal has more or less disappeared except in some parts of Tuscany, where segments of fennel are still placed on the table with the fruit. However, it is often eaten raw as a salad – thinly sliced, with lemon juice and olive oil – and as a light ANTIPASTO mixed with flakes of a good GRANA. A Sicilian salad combines fennel with oranges, chicory and black olives.

There are many recipes for cooked fennel, including *finocchi fritti*, blanched, coated in egg and breadcrumbs and fried; *finocchi al burro e formaggio*, stewed in butter and stock and then sprinkled with Parmesan; *finocchi in tegame*, sautéed in oil flavoured with garlic and then stewed in a little stock; *finocchi gratinati*, boiled until al dente, sautéed in butter and then covered with a thin béchamel flavoured with nutmeg and baked. Fennel is also used in soups, and to make SFORMATI.

Fennel must have been a favourite vegetable of the 18th-century writer Vincenzo CORRADO, who offers no less than 11 recipes, many of which contain sugar, cinnamon and candied peel. One such recipe, *finocchi alla fiorentina*, suggests cooking the fennel in capon stock, dressing them with cinnamon and nutmeg, and serving them with egg custard, sugar and powdered fennel seeds. Another, simpler, recipe is given here. More to our taste is a recipe for fennel sautéed in oil with anchovies, aromatic herbs and spices and finished in a prawn coulis, flavoured with herbs and more spices.

 [see recipe on facing page]

finocchiona
pork sausage

A large, coarse-grained sausage made in Tuscany with pure pork meat plus some fat from the belly of the pig, flavoured with pepper, garlic and wild fennel (hence its name), and aged for between 7 and 12 months. In Chianti, finocchiona is coarser-grained and softer; it is called *sbriciolona*. Finocchiona is one of the best kinds of SALAME.

finocchi al latte
fennel braised in milk

Serves 4
900g/2lb fennel bulbs
salt and freshly ground black pepper
¼ tsp ground cinnamon
¼ tsp grated nutmeg
200ml/7fl oz/generous ¾ cup full-fat
*   (whole) milk*
125ml/4fl oz/½ cup double (heavy)
*   cream*
1 tsp sugar

A recipe from Vincenzo CORRADO's book *Il Cuoco Galante*, first published in 1773. I have added the quantities for the ingredients, which are not specified in the book. It is an ideal accompaniment to a roast chicken and it also makes a good first course or a vegetarian dish.

Clean the fennel by removing any bruised parts and the stalks. Blanch for 3 minutes in boiling salted water. Drain and cut into segments about 2.5cm/1in thick.

Put the spices, pepper and 150ml/5fl oz/⅔ cup of the milk in a large sauté pan and add the fennel. Cover and cook over a gentle heat until tender, about 15–20 minutes. Turn the fennel over every now and then and add a little more milk whenever the fennel looks dry. At the end of cooking there should be no liquid left.

Pour over the cream and sprinkle with the sugar. Stir gently and cook for a further 5 minutes.

salsa di fiori di zucca
courgette flower sauce

Enough for 4 helpings of pasta
12 courgette (zucchini) flowers
1 small onion, chopped
a bunch of fresh flat-leaf parsley
4 tbsp olive oil
a pinch of powdered saffron or a few
*   saffron strands*
4 tbsp hot light vegetable stock
salt and freshly ground black pepper
1 large egg yolk
70g/2½oz pecorino cheese, grated

I have dressed a bowl of pasta, such as TAGLIATELLE or FARFALLE, with this delicate sauce, and I have also used it to accompany a roast fish such as a daurade. It is just perfect. If you grow courgettes or other summer squash, you will have your own flowers to use. If not, you can sometimes buy bunches of courgette flowers (FIORI DI ZUCCA) during the season in specialist Italian shops and greengrocers.

Wash the flowers, dry them and chop them very finely, together with the onion and parsley. Put half the olive oil and the chopped ingredients in a saucepan and sauté very gently for about 10 minutes, stirring frequently.

Meanwhile, stir the saffron with the hot stock. Add to the pan, stir well and cook for a further 10 minutes. Add salt and pepper to taste and then puree the sauce using a food mill, food processor or blender.

When your pasta is cooked, drain, turn into a warmed bowl and toss at once with the remaining oil. Mix the egg yolk and pecorino into the sauce, pour the sauce over the pasta and serve.

finte trippe

see BÜSECCA MATTA

fiore sardo
a cheese

A Sardinian DOP cheese originally made only with ewe's milk. It is still made in this way by shepherds, but commercial versions are made with cow's milk, sometimes mixed with ewe's milk. It is a soft, compact cheese of a lovely creamy colour and a taste similar to PECORINO, but sweeter. It is eaten as table cheese when young, while the older cheese is used for grating, instead of Parmesan.

fiore di zucca
courgette flower

The yellow flower sprouting from the long, thin, undeveloped stem of the male courgette is a delicacy. The pistil inside the flower, and the stalk, must be removed before cooking. The classic way to cook courgette flowers is to fry them, coated in a light batter. In Lazio they are first stuffed with grated Parmesan, breadcrumbs, a piece of anchovy fillet and parsley, or with mozzarella and anchovy fillets. The recipe given here is for a sauce for pasta, a speciality of Umbria.

[see recipe on page 151]

focaccia
a bread

A kind of bread, either savoury or sweet, that can be flavoured with a number of different ingredients. It is like a thick pizza, but with a texture more like bread. The basic recipe for focaccia is simply flour, salt and yeast, kneaded with water. After being set aside to rise, focaccia is baked in a hot oven.

There are many different kinds of focaccia from all over Italy. Liguria and the southern regions offer the greatest variety of them. *Focaccia alla genovese* is the basic dough, dripping with the local olive oil. *Focaccia con le cipolle* (with onions), also known as *sardenaria*, is another Ligurian speciality, shared with Tuscany, the sliced onions being scattered on the top and liberally doused with oil. Recco, a village between Genoa and Santa Margherita, has its own focaccia, which is two layers of dough, the top one rolled out so thin as to be transparent, containing sliced *formaggetta*, a local soft cow's milk cheese. This melts during baking and its flavour permeates the focaccia.

The focacce of Puglia and Calabria are like thick pizzas stuffed with different ingredients, such as batavia, salt cod, tomatoes and mozzarella. In Naples the local focaccia is called *tortano* and it is baked in the shape of a ring. Another rich Neapolitan focaccia is *casatiello* – eggs in their shells are gently pushed into the ring-shaped dough before it is baked. In a more modern version, the eggs are broken into a hollow in the dough and then covered with more dough.

There are also some sweet focacce, such as the ancient Venetian FUGAZZA. The *focaccia vicentina* from Vicenza is made with a dough similar to its Venetian cousin and is baked in small shapes, often like doves, enveloping hard-boiled eggs. The *focaccia di Castelnuovo*, a town near La Spezia in Liguria, is made at Easter with polenta flour, pine nuts and olive oil.

[see recipe on page 154]

fondo
cookery term

The word has two meanings. It can be the French roux – also called *base di cucina* – or it can refer to the residue left at the bottom of the pan after cooking a piece of meat or fish, which becomes the basis of the sauce or the sauce itself,

152

accompanying the main ingredient, when it is correctly called *fondo di cottura*.

fonduta
a sauce

This is one of the greatest Piemontese sauces. It includes two of the best local products, FONTINA and white truffles. The fontina cheese, grated and soaked in milk, is cooked in a bain-marie with a considerable amount of butter. When it becomes creamy, three or four egg yolks are added and the mixture is beaten hard until it reaches a thick, smooth consistency. It is a very difficult sauce to make, because it must be cooked up to the point when the cheese has melted but no further, otherwise the cheese will separate. White truffles are shredded over the top. Traditionally, fonduta is served with CROSTINI or grilled polenta, but nowadays it is also used as a sauce for TAGLIATELLE or boiled rice.

Giovanni VIALARDI, chef to Vittorio Emanuele II, the first king of Italy, recommends using 60g/about 2oz of truffles in the fonduta. At the present cost of white truffles, around £1000 per 100g, very few people would be able to afford the dish.

fongadina
a stew

Made with the lungs, heart, liver, spleen and sweetbreads of a calf, lamb or kid. A mixture of garlic, PANCETTA and herbs is sautéed in oil. The offal is then added and splashed with wine. When the wine has evaporated, the offal is slowly stewed in stock flavoured with tomato puree, lemon rind, cloves and bay leaves. Fongadina, a dish from Veneto, is traditionally served with POLENTA.

fontal
a cheese

A relatively new cheese, born after World War II, fontal is an industrially produced semi-soft cheese which cooks beautifully. It is made from pasteurized cow's milk and aged for about 3 months. Although not in the same league, it can be substituted for the more expensive FONTINA in making FONDUTA. It is also used in toasted cheese and ham sandwiches, hamburgers and in savoury pies

fontina
a cheese

Possibly dating from Roman times, fontina appears in a list of cheeses from Valle d'Aosta written in 1477. Later documents, accounts and recipe books testify that it has been a cheese of great repute through the centuries as it still is now. It has DOP status.

Fontina is a semi-soft cheese, with 45% fat content, made from cow's milk as soon as it is drawn. It is made in squat round shapes of about 45cm/18in diameter and 8–10cm/about 3½in high, weighing from 8 to 12kg/18–26lb. Fontina is aged for 3 or 4 months. It is a buff-coloured cheese with a few small eyes and a thin crust. The taste is sweet with a nutty tinge. If there is a cheese that really melts in your mouth, it is fontina.

Fontina is, with Parmesan, the best cooking cheese, and its characteristic taste combines beautifully with many dishes. It is the cheese used in FONDUTA and in *gnocchi alla Bava*, in which the cooked potato gnocchi are lavishly covered with the cheese and then baked for 5 minutes.

forma
shape

In a gastronomic context, forma refers to the shape of bread or cheese.

focaccia

Serves 6–8

500g/1lb 2oz/4 cups Italian 00 flour,
    plus extra for dusting

1 ½ tsp easy-blend dried yeast

1 heaped tsp fine salt

6 tbsp extra virgin olive oil

1 tsp coarse sea salt

FOCACCIA is a pre-prandial snack eaten at home, in the street, in bars, anywhere. This recipe makes a soft focaccia – the traditional *focaccia alla genovese* from Genoa. This is the classic recipe, which can be topped with rosemary or thin slices of sweet onion before cooking.

Put the flour in a bowl. Sprinkle with the yeast and the fine salt and pour in about 4 tablespoons of the olive oil. Mix very quickly and then gradually add about 300–350ml/10–12fl oz/1¼–1½ cups warm water (it should be blood temperature). Mix quickly and stop as soon as the dough is blended.

Put the dough on a floured work surface and knead quickly for 1–2 minutes. The dough will be very damp. Wash the bowl and dry it, then oil it lightly. Return the dough to the bowl, cover the bowl with a folded damp cloth, and leave in a warm corner of the kitchen (out of any draughts) until doubled in size – about 2 hours.

Punch the dough down, turning it over and over. Put it into a 30 x 23cm/12 x 9in baking sheet and press out to an even layer. Cover and leave in a warm place for a further hour or so, until the dough is soft and light.

Preheat the oven to 240°C/475°F/Gas Mark 9.

Mix the remaining oil with a little water. Dip your fingers into this mixture and press down into the focaccia to form hollows. Sprinkle with the coarse sea salt and brush the top with the rest of the oil and water mixture. (This keeps the surface soft during baking.)

Turn the oven down to 220°C/425°F/Gas Mark 7 (you only need a blast of heat at first) and bake the focaccia until golden brown, about 20 minutes. Turn the focaccia out onto a wire rack and eat while still warm. Otherwise, reheat it in a low oven before eating.

formaggio
cheese

The history of cheese is almost as old as the history of man. Certainly ewe's milk cheeses have been made in Sicily since prehistoric times, as Homer mentions PECORINO in the *Odyssey*. The Etruscans learnt from the Greeks how to make cheese, and the Romans made great use of it, as Pliny, Cato and Virgil tell us. They wrote about the properties they believed it to have, notably that it was capable of stimulating sensuality and of fostering lovemaking.

Cheese was served at banquets as an ANTIPASTO in order to prepare the palate for the meal to follow and to enhance appreciation of the wines. Cheese was also used with honey to make cakes. The present-day Roman *budino di ricotta*, for which I give a recipe on page 64, is derived from an ancient Roman cake made with ricotta and honey, flavoured with spices and containing chopped walnuts. The soldiers and the plebs ate meals consisting mainly of bread, cheese (smoked or aged), and large quantities of garlic, which was thought to ward off all sorts of diseases.

In Roman times it was the shepherds who attended to the making of cheese; they were the first to use animal and vegetable rennet, partly replacing the method of curdling by the natural souring of the milk. Sicilian shepherds in particular became expert in the craft and their products were in great demand.

During the barbarian invasions, the craft was developed by monks, who kept it alive in their monasteries. In the 13th century the first dairy farm appeared near Parma, where surely the first GRANA was made. Other cheeses of which there are early records include GORGONZOLA, whose documentation goes back to the 9th century, and CACIOCAVALLO, mentioned in a short story by Franco Sacchetti in 1350. It is thought that cheese began to be used in cooking in the 13th or 14th century. The appreciation of cheese both in its own right

and as a condiment to be added to vegetables, meat and omelettes also began to develop.

During the 19th century cheese production saw a great change. Dairy farms became bigger and began to produce different cheeses of the region, a system of manufacture that was the precursor of the industrialization of cheese-making in the 20th century.

There are said to be about 450 Italian cheeses, the majority of them made in northern Italy. Nobody has been able to classify all these cheeses, but they are divided into groups according to the milk used in their making: cow, ewe, goat, buffalo, or a mixture of two or more of these. The cheeses are classed as fresh when they must be eaten as soon as they are made (these include MOZZARELLA and MASCARPONE); semi-soft, which must be eaten within 2 months (such as BEL PAESE and GORGONZOLA); semi-hard, to be eaten within 6 months of curing; and hard, such as Parmesan, which are only sold after at least 6 months of curing.

Most of the cheeses made in southern Italy are *'a pasta filata'* ('plastic curd' cheeses). This means that the soured curd is cut up, then covered with boiling water and worked with a wooden stick until it begins to form a thread. The cheese is then kneaded by hand until it holds its shape. The best known formaggi a pasta filata are mozzarella, PROVOLONE and CACIOCAVALLO.

From the point of view of their use, cheeses can be divided into table, grating and cooking cheeses. Some grating cheeses and cooking cheeses are interchangeable, and quite a few table cheeses can be used in cooking. Gorgonzola, for example, a typical table cheese, is used in some sauces for pasta, gnocchi and polenta, and in a risotto. FONTINA is a cooking cheese, but it is equally good as a table cheese, as is buffalo mozzarella. PARMIGIANO REGGIANO is the grating cheese par excellence, but it is a superb table cheese as well.

Cheese is always eaten before fruit, and also before puddings, if served, the order being cheese, sweet and fruit. While some people have endorsed the English habit of eating cheese with only a knife, in most families a knife and fork are used. Cheese is eaten with bread, but never with butter. In the country, Parmesan and pecorino are often eaten with pears or with young broad beans, the favourite beginning or end of a spring meal in Tuscany and Lazio.

formato
pasta shape

The various shapes of pasta are referred to as formati.

forno
oven

By extension the word also means the shop attached to the oven, the baker's shop, and it is used for a baker's shop in a small country town or village; in a large town or city a bakery is a PANETTERIA. Unlike the city *panetterie*, which sell bread of all shapes and sizes, the choice of bread in a country forno is limited. In addition to the local bread, which varies from region to region, there will be a few more types and, on certain days, there will also be pizza and/or FOCACCIA. In the past the forno was, in effect, the village oven, since the local women, few of whom had an oven of their own, took their cakes, pies, stews, jams etc to the forno to be cooked. Although many more women now have an oven at home, the practice continues, partly for reasons of economy (the baker's oven is always hot, and it's large) and partly because a wood oven cooks so much better than a domestic one.

As a method of cooking, baking is far less common in Italy than in northern Europe, and not many traditional recipes (apart from bread, cakes and biscuits) use this method. A joint, for instance, is usually roasted in a pot on top of the cooker.

fragola
strawberry

Known since antiquity, strawberries have been widely cultivated both in the open air and in greenhouses. There are many varieties of strawberry, of which the Gorella is the most popular in northern Italy, while in the south it is the Aliso. There is also a very small strawberry called *fragola di bosco*, which is the cultivated variety of the wild strawberry. It is a highly scented fruit and is used mostly in a mixed fruit salad of berries, called SOTTOBOSCO.

Strawberries are dressed with lemon and/or orange juice, or with wine. In Lazio they are also dressed with red wine vinegar, and in Emilia-Romagna with balsamic vinegar, which has been used to dress strawberries since the Renaissance. A sprinkling of sugar is always added.

Strawberries are also used to decorate tarts and tartlets, and to make sorbets and ice creams. They are sometimes added to a ZUPPA INGLESE.

157

francesina
bread stick

A bread stick made in Lombardy, similar to a small baguette, a francesina weighs about 100g/3½oz; it has a hardish crust and the inside is compact, the dough being only partly leavened.

frantoiana
Tuscan soup

Zuppa frantoiana is a Tuscan soup whose name derives from FRANTOIO, oil press. The oil used should be extra virgin oil from the first pressing. The soup is made with borlotti beans and, at the right time of year, a few leaves of CAVOLO NERO are added, along with other seasonal vegetables and herbs, depending on what is fresh in the market, or indeed depending on the whim of the cook.

frantoio
olive press

The place where olives are pressed and olive oil is made. There are two kinds of frantoio: one is called a *molazze*, in which the olives are pressed between granite stones; the other, called a *martelli*, breaks the olives with hammers. The first method is the oldest and the best method, but it is more time-consuming and costly.

frattaglie
giblets

The offal of an animal or the giblets of a bird, consisting of all the edible parts that are not muscle. All these meats – including brains, tongue, sweetbreads, liver, kidneys and tripe – are popular and cooked in many delicious ways.

fricandò
veal dish

A dish from northern Italy, of French origin, it consists of a joint of veal, larded with strips of prosciutto and thin sticks of celery and carrots. The meat is sautéed in butter and then cooked in the oven with a little MARSALA for 2–2½ hours. When sliced, fricandó is very attractive, showing a surface speckled with the pink of the prosciutto, orange of the carrots and white of the celery.

fricassea
casserole with egg and lemon

The name of this dish, and possibly also the basis of the dish itself, comes from the French. However, fricassea became Italian by leaving out the cream and increasing the quantity of lemon juice. Lamb (as in the recipe given here) and poultry are the meats cooked in fricassea. In Liguria the egg yolk and lemon juice mixture is often added when the meat is still on the heat so that the mixture will scramble, while in Tuscany they are mixed into the chicken or lamb off the heat, so that the yolks will just thicken but not scramble.

In Liguria there is a delicious fish dish called *fricassea di pesce*, made with two or three different kinds of white fish plus a few langoustines or prawns, cooked in butter and wine, with the egg yolks and lemon juice mixed in at the end, off the heat.

[see recipe on facing page]

frico
a cheese fritter

A dish made in Friuli consisting of very thin slices of MONTASIO, the local cheese, fried in butter and oil, sometimes containing sliced onion, potato and even apple. It is a dish that is as difficult to cook properly as it is delicious to eat. The cheese must cook up to the right point at the right temperature or it can melt too fast and burn. Frico is served as an ANTIPASTO or with fried eggs. When I eat a well-made frico I always think that I would choose it as part of my last meal.

friggere
to fry

A very common method of cooking: there are many kinds of fried food, or FRITTO. Friggere always implies fast cooking in hot oil, butter or another fat, or a combination of these. The amount of fat used can vary, from about 0.5–1cm/¼–½in deep for shallow frying to 5cm/2in for deep frying..

The frying pan is usually of iron with a long handle, called *la* PADELLA *dei fritti*. The fat used varies according to the region and the type of food. In Lombardy and Piedmont oil and/or butter are

CONTINUES OVERLEAF

agnello, cacio e uova
lamb fricassée

Serves 4

3 tbsp olive oil

1.3kg/3lb leg of lamb, boned and cut
into 2.5cm/1in cubes

1 onion, very finely sliced

1 tsp chopped fresh thyme

150ml/5fl oz/²/₃ cup dry white wine

salt and freshly ground black pepper

3 large egg yolks

3 tbsp freshly grated mature pecorino
cheese

15g/¹/₂oz/¹/₃ cup fresh white
breadcrumbs

juice of 1 organic or unwaxed lemon

Lamb is the most popular meat in central Italy. In this recipe for a FRICASSEA from Abruzzo it is finished off with a sauce of egg and PECORINO cheese, sharpened with lemon juice.

Heat 1 tablespoon of the olive oil in a large non-stick frying pan. When hot, add the meat and brown well on all sides. Remove the meat to a plate.

Put the remaining olive oil and the onion in a flameproof casserole and sauté until soft. Add the meat and the thyme, mix well and then pour in the wine. Bring to the boil and season with salt and pepper. Cover and cook until the meat is tender, about 45 minutes.

Beat the egg yolks with the cheese, breadcrumbs and lemon juice, add a good grinding of pepper and mix into the casserole. Cook for a further 5 minutes, until the egg sauce has thickened. Taste and adjust the seasoning before serving.

frittata al formaggio
cheese frittata

Serves 4

7 large eggs

salt and freshly ground black pepper

50g/1³/₄oz Parmesan cheese, grated

25g/1oz Gruyère cheese, grated

40g/1¹/₂oz/3 tbsp unsalted butter

This is probably the most commonly made FRITTATA in an Italian kitchen (there is always some Parmesan around). Perfect as a starter, it is also good as a light main course after a soup, or to take on a picnic.

Beat the eggs lightly in a bowl, just to blend the yolks and the whites. Season with salt and pepper and add the cheeses, beating well.

Melt the butter in a 25cm/10in diameter non-stick frying pan. When the butter begins to foam, pour in the egg mixture and turn the heat down as low as possible. Cook for about 10 minutes, until the eggs have set and only the top surface is still runny. While the frittata is cooking, heat the grill.

Place the frittata under the grill and cook until the top is set but not brown. The frittata should be set, but still soft.

Loosen the frittata with a spatula and slide it onto a round serving dish. Serve hot, warm or at room temperature.

used, while in Rome and Emilia-Romagna STRUTTO (rendered pork fat) is the favourite fat. Oil is also used in Liguria, as it is in Naples, where they also use SUGNA (melted fat from a pig's back). Modern health concerns mean that strutto and sugna, and also butter, are being replaced by vegetable oils, of which olive oil (not necessarily extra virgin) and groundnut (peanut) oil are the most popular.

friggitoria
fried food shop

This is the equivalent of a British fish and chip shop, with the difference that a friggitoria also sells other fried foods, such as TORTELLI, vegetables and meatballs in addition to fish and chips. In Piedmont, squares of semolina previously cooked in milk, fried and covered with sugar are very popular *fritti*, while Rome's speciality is fried salt cod – BACCALÀ. In Genoa, vegetables such as courgettes, cauliflower, artichokes or tomatoes are available in most friggitorie. Naples and Sicily have more friggitorie than any other region, partly due to the local tradition of eating in the street, FRITTO being a typical street food.

In the past, the food used to be fried in cauldrons at busy street corners in the markets. The American traveller William Wetmore Story, in his book *Roba di Roma,* describes huge cauldrons in the Piazza Navona in the 19th century: '...these cauldrons bubble with hissing oil into which chopped vegetables and fritters are dropped and ladled out all golden and garnished with fried pumpkin flowers, upon shining platters.'

frisedda
a roll

A crusty, ring-shaped roll of wholewheat or white durum wheat flour made in Puglia. After its first baking the roll is cut in two horizontally and baked again, so that it becomes very biscuity. Before

eating, frisedda is put in water to soften, and then dressed with oil, salt and pepper, and sometimes with tomatoes or/and onions. It is one of the staples of the farm labourer's midday meal.

frittata
omelette

Closer to a Spanish tortilla or a Middle Eastern *eggah* than to a French omelette, frittata is flat and round and should be completely set, although still moist. Other ingredients are often added to the eggs: grated cheese, sweated onions or chopped raw or cooked prosciutto, for example. Leftover pasta or PEPERONATA make an excellent frittata.

In Sicily a delicious frittata is prepared with salted and dried RICOTTA, while in Liguria courgettes, artichokes or BIANCHETTI are frequently added. Ligurian frittate are always highly seasoned with herbs, particularly marjoram, and garlic.

To make a good frittata the eggs must be very lightly beaten and mixed so that no air bubbles form. A good heavy-bottomed frying pan is essential, in which butter, or a mixture of oil and butter, is heated. When the fat is beginning to foam, the egg mixture is poured into the pan and cooked over a very low heat. A frittata must cook very slowly. When it has set and only the surface is still runny, the pan is put under the grill until the top is firm but not brown.

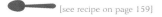 [see recipe on page 159]

frittatine
small omelettes

Frittatine are made like pancakes, but entirely with eggs. They can be stuffed like CANNELLONI or piled one on top of the other in layers with tomato sauce and mozzarella, or béchamel, mushroom and ham sauce, or spinach and ricotta, to make a sort of layered savoury cake.

frittedda
vegetable puree

A vegetable dish from Sicily consisting of a coarse puree of peas, artichokes and broad beans cooked in oil and onion. It is dressed with mint leaves and served cold. Frittedda is usually made in the spring, when the first vegetables appear.

frittelle
fritters

This term is applied to small pieces of sweet or savoury food coated in batter and deep-fried. Some frittelle are common to the whole of Italy: apple fritters, anchovy fritters, rice fritters. Others are regional specialities.

In Alto Adige they make frittelle of buckwheat flour and milk, fried in melted lard. The Sicilian frittelle are made with cut-up fruit, coated in MARSALA-flavoured batter and sprinkled with sugar. In Sardinia the frittelle are made with wild fennel: the mountain fennel, so aromatic and sweet, is boiled, chopped and mixed into an egg batter and the mixture is spooned into hot oil. These are only three examples, but frittelle are made in all the 20 regions with many different ingredients and variations. They are popular food, always enjoyed at country feasts.

The batter also varies, according to the region or the main ingredient. The batter can be made with egg, water and flour; with egg, milk and flour; or with egg whites and flour. It may contain yeast, Marsala or other wines. The *frittelle di patate* of Puglia are thick slices of potato coated in egg, flour and grated pecorino.

Sweet frittelle, such as the Venetian FRITTOLE, are a Carnival treat. Another time for frittelle is the feast of San Giuseppe, 19 March. The frittelle made for this occasion are similar to the Venetian frittole but are a speciality of Tuscany and southern Lombardy.

fritto
fried food

As well as meaning fried, fritto is also used as a noun, so that one speaks of a fritto of vegetables, of fish etc. Anyone who has been to Italy will know how many foods are served fried.

Vegetables are often shallow-fried in butter and/or oil, coated with flour, breadcrumbs or egg and crumbs. Alternatively they are coated in batter then deep-fried, in oil or STRUTTO. The batter is prepared differently according to the region and the food. Some vegetables are first stuffed, then coated in egg and breadcrumbs and fried, such as in an 18th-century recipe by Vincenzo CORRADO, in which rice – first cooked in milk and butter and flavoured with cinnamon and sugar – is bound with egg yolk and then used to stuff tomatoes. The tomatoes are then fried and served with custard.

Courgette flowers coated in batter and deep-fried, sometimes stuffed with mozzarella and anchovy fillets or with ricotta, make one of the best fried foods. In Tuscany one of the simplest and most delicious snacks is fried sage in batter.

Lombard cooking offers the lightest of all fritti, with recipes for brains, sweetbreads and calf's liver, all lightly coated in egg and breadcrumbs and fried in butter, which should be clarified. There is a Lombard fritto, which brings back memories of my childhood's Tuesday lunches. LESSO was usually served on Monday so that there was stock for the whole week; on Tuesday the joint of boiled beef was sliced, coated in egg and breadcrumbs and fried in butter. This was not a dish that one would connect with leftovers and was delicious in its own right.

161

fritto misto
fried morsels

There are many different versions of fritto misto but the best known are the Piedmontese, the Bolognese and the Neapolitan, as well as the FRITTO MISTO DI MARE.

The Piedmontese fritto, also called *fritto all'italiana*, contains slivers of calf's liver, sweetbreads, brains, bone marrow, frogs (when in season) and chicken croquettes, plus seasonal vegetables, such as courgette and aubergine slices, cauliflower florets, artichoke wedges, celery chunks, mushroom caps. The fritto misto is crowned with fried AMARETTI, apple rings and sweet semolina croquettes. The food is coated with flour, egg and breadcrumbs and fried in oil and butter.

The *fritto misto alla bolognese* is the grandest, known as *il grande fritto misto*, and is a meal in itself. More or less the same ingredients as in the Piedmontese fritto, plus STECCHI BOLOGNESI, vol-au-vents, sweet custard and apple fritters are all coated in a rich batter made with egg yolk, flour, Parmesan, oil and whipped egg white and fried in oil – although traditionally the fritto alla bolognese is fried in STRUTTO, melted pork fat.

The Neapolitan fritto misto has the amusing name of *frienno magnanno*, meaning 'frying and eating'. It is so called because of the manner in which it is served: the cook fries while the family eats, since fried food loses its crispness if kept hot. At least, that is the theory, and is how it should be. Apart from the usual small slices of liver, sweetbreads and sausages, courgettes, peppers, wedges of tomatoes, a proper *fritto misto alla napoletana* must contain PANZAROTTI, potato croquettes, slices of buffalo mozzarella and hard-boiled egg coated in béchamel. Some of the ingredients are coated in a batter of flour and water, while others are coated only in flour; everything is fried in hot olive oil.

All fritti, whether of fish, meat or vegetables, are sprinkled with salt (no pepper) and served only with lemon wedges.

fritto misto di mare
fried fish and shellfish

Also called *fritto misto di pesce* or *misto mare*, this is a dish of small fried fish, small crustaceans and molluscs – both shelled – all coated in flour and fried in sizzling olive oil for a few minutes. The difficulty of making the perfect fritto misto di mare lies in judging the cooking time of the ingredients and having the temperature of the oil high enough to make a golden crust while cooking the fish inside to the right point. The oil should never be recycled. Once the frying is over, it is thrown away.

The Neapolitans are masters of this fritto, which is sold in FRIGGITORIE, often selling only fish. The same shops are common in Venice, where the Venetians rush down at one o'clock on Fridays to buy their lunch, as they also do near the port in Genoa. The reason these shops are so popular is that not only is a good fritto misto di mare difficult to make, but its scent – or I should say its smell – permeates everywhere and stays for a long time.

All fritti are served only with lemon wedges and never with any sauce.

frittole
fritters

Venetian dialect for FRITTELLE. Frittole are always eaten at Carnival in Venice, so much so that *'fare le frittole'* is synonymous with enjoying oneself. The frittole made at carnival time used to be sold in the narrow streets or in shops called *malvasie*, so called because the frittole were served with sweet malvasia wine.

frittura
fried food

A word used colloquially in Lombardy, Lazio and other regions for FRITTO MISTO DI MARE or other fried food.

frittura piccata
milanese veal dish

Thin slices of veal are floured, sautéed in butter, splashed with lemon juice and lavishly sprinkled with chopped parsley. At the end, a little more butter is swirled into the sauce to give it a lovely shine.

Friuli–Venezia Giulia

A small region in north-eastern Italy, on the borders with Austria and Slovenia. While the basic ingredients used are those of the Po Valley and the Alps, the spices, scents and flavourings are Austrian, Hungarian Slav and Middle Eastern.

The juxtaposition of cuisines is mainly evident in Venezia Giulia, while the cooking of the mountainous area of Friuli is deeply rooted to the land and its products. This is a poor cuisine based on beans, polenta and soup. Maize is the main crop, followed by beans, other vegetables and fruit. Notable among the vegetables are the white turnips with which the Friulani make *broade, or brovade*, an odd dish of macerated turnips, which are served with MUSETTO and other kinds of sausage or pork meat. The pig, as in all poor cuisines, is an important provider.

By way of contrast, a local pork product that is a rich man's food is PROSCIUTTO di San Daniele. Venison from roebuck is reserved for grand occasions, cooked in wine and served with polenta. Kid is another festive dish. It is roasted on the spit with plenty of LARDO to moisten the meat.

BIGOLI, a Venetian pasta, is served with GULASCH or with fresh sardines. Another traditional pasta is CIALZONS, half-moon shaped ravioli, the various stuffings for which may contain herbs, sultanas, candied citron, spices, brown breadcrumbs, spinach and grated chocolate, but never meat. Cialzons are dressed either with ricotta and local aged cheese, in the ancient tradition, or with melted butter and Parmesan, according to the modern fashion.

The cooks of this region excel more in the making of soup than of pasta or risotto dishes. They make bean soup fortified with ham bones, or with milk, to which melted butter is added shortly before serving. The bean and barley soups show their Austrian origin, as does *iota, or jota*, which is more a pork and cabbage stew than a soup. A recipe for this is given overleaf.

Among the vegetables grown in this region, the asparagus of Aquilea and of Sant'Andrea near Gorizia are famous, as is the dwarf chicory, with its delicate and pleasantly bitter taste.

The local seafood and fish are excellent. From Grado, east of Venice, to Trieste the sea is dotted with strange contraptions that are part of the apparatus of mussel and oyster farms. All kinds of seafood risotti are a speciality along the coast, while bigger fish are served grilled or fried.

The most renowned cheese is MONTASIO, which is a table cheese when fresh and a grating cheese when aged. It is the cheese used for the delicious FRICO.

The foreign influences become more evident in the cakes and puddings, which include *koch*, a sort of baked orange custard, PRESNITZ, the traditional Easter sweet in the shape of a spiral, and STRUCOLO, the local strudel, all of Austrian-Hungarian origin.

Fruit is an important produce of the region. Cherries, apples, peaches and other traditional fruits have been joined by kiwi fruit, which have found ideal growing conditions here.

[see recipe below]

frullato
whisked

The term is used as a noun, as in *frullato di frutta* or *frullato di caffè*. These are drinks made with iced milk, sugar and fruit juices or coffee, whisked until very frothy – in other words, milk shakes.

frumento
wheat

Two types of wheat are cultivated in Italy: soft wheat in the north and durum (hard) wheat in the south. The common flour – FARINA – is made from soft wheat and is used for making bread, cakes and pastries, while the durum wheat flour, SEMOLINO, is used for the production of pasta, although in southern Italy it is also used to make bread.

frutta
fruit

As a child, the worst punishment I could be given was '*Stassera vai a letto senza frutta*' – 'Tonight you go to bed without fruit.' The fact that it is a punishment to deprive a child of fruit instead of sweets shows how good Italian fruit is.

iota
bean and barley soup

Serves 4

100g/3½oz/½ cup dried borlotti beans, soaked for 12 hours in cold water

25g/1oz/2 tbsp unsalted butter

2 tbsp olive oil

150g/5½oz smoked pancetta, cubed

1 garlic clove, chopped

1 small onion, chopped

2 tbsp chopped fresh flat-leaf parsley

1 tbsp chopped fresh sage

1 litre/1¾ pints/4 cups meat stock (page 61) or chicken stock, or good-quality bouillon cubes dissolved in water

100g/3½oz/½ cup pearl barley, rinsed

2 tbsp extra virgin olive oil

150g/5½oz sauerkraut

salt

This version of the soup is from Venezia Giulia, where sauerkraut is used instead of *brovade* (macerated turnips), which are traditional in Friuli.

Drain and rinse the beans.

Melt the butter with the olive oil in a stockpot and add the pancetta, garlic, onion and herbs. Sauté for 10 minutes, then add the beans and stir them around to coat them in the fat. Pour in the stock, cover the pot and simmer for about 1 hour.

Add the barley and simmer for a further hour, until the barley and beans are tender.

Heat the extra virgin olive oil in a saucepan and sauté the sauerkraut for about 10 minutes, then add it to the soup. Add some hot water if the soup is very thick, but don't add too much water, because this type of soup is meant to be thick. Add salt to taste; no pepper is added in the traditional recipe. Cook for a further 15 minutes and then serve.

A bowl of fruit is always put on the table at the end of a meal, since it is rare in Italy to finish a meal without fruit. Until recently it was never done, but now fruit is occasionally omitted when a pudding is served.

All but tropical fruit grows well in Italy. Each region has its own special fruit: we speak of the pears and apples of Valle d'Aosta, and of its SOTTOBOSCO, of the raspberries of Lombardy, the cherries of Romagna, the figs of Liguria and Tuscany, the peaches and plums of Le Marche, and the oranges and lemons of Sicily and Calabria. And last but certainly not least, UVA – grapes both black and white – everywhere.

Fruit is also used to make puddings, the most popular being the fruit salad, MACEDONIA DI FRUTTA. Apples and pears are sometimes stewed in red or white wine, peaches are steeped in wine, strawberries with peaches or oranges dressed with sugar and lemon juice, all make simple, delicious desserts. All kinds of fruit are used to produce GELATI, SORBETTI and GRANITE.

Up to the Cinquecento, fruit was eaten at the beginning of a meal rather than at the end. However, by the late Renaissance the Florentines were serving quinces, medlars and nuts after the meal.

Fruit, especially citrus fruits, are also used in savoury dishes. In Sicily oranges are used in salads with onions or fennel, while in northern Italy apples, pears, grapes and cherries are used in stuffings for chicken, turkey and game birds.

frutta candita
candied fruit

The fruits most commonly candied are mandarins, figs, plums, pears and apricots. Candied fruits, particularly the candied peel of lemon, orange and citron, add colour, texture and flavour to many sweet preparations, from PANETTONE to CASSATA *siciliana*. They are also used for decoration, chopped or cut into squares. Some flowers are also candied for decoration, the best known being Parma violets, small violets specially grown at the edges of woods around Parma.

The Sicilians claim to make the best candied fruits, strongly preserving the flavour of the fresh fruits. Elsewhere in Italy one of the best-known firms making candied fruits is Romanengo of Genoa, who have been manufacturers of candied fruits since 1780 and have served most European royal families.

frutta di Marturana
a sweet

A speciality originally made by the nuns of the convent of the same name in Palermo, who had learned how to make them from the Arab prostitutes when they took refuge in the convent to flee the Normans in the 12th century – it's a charming story. Whatever the origins, these delicious sweets are made of almond paste and are shaped and coloured like fruits. To make them, ground almonds and sugar are pounded with a little cinnamon and flavoured with a liqueur. The mixture is heated in a copper pan to make it more pliable. Nuggets of paste are then broken off, shaped and painted with natural colourings and the frutti are baked in the oven, as if they were pieces of pottery. Nowadays, frutta di Marturana is also made commercially.

frutta secca
dried fruit

Frutta secca includes all dried fruit and nuts. However, the most common frutta secca consists mostly of dried figs, dates, prunes, apricots, walnuts, hazelnuts and almonds. This is the frutta secca that is always set on the table at Christmas and New Year and is eaten with oranges, clementines and mandarins. Mixed dried fruits are also stewed in red wine and lemon juice.

frutti di mare
seafood

Many marine creatures come under this name, which means 'fruits of the sea'. In fish markets, stall after stall displays these fascinating creatures, crawling sleepily around or keeping their shiny or craggy shells firmly closed in a final attempt to survive.

For almost all seafood, the best 'recipe' of all is to eat them raw, straight from the sea, with a squeeze of lemon juice. Unfortunately this method is not altogether advisable nowadays because of the pollution of the sea.

There are many recipes for seafood and many ways of presenting it. A salad called *insalata di frutti di mare* appears on practically every restaurant's menu. To be good, it must have the right balance of the various seafood and a lemon dressing that is strong enough to enhance the flavour of the different ingredients without killing it. A good insalata contains prawns, a few mussels, some small clams, a langoustine or two, some MOSCARDINI (tiny octopus) and small squid, all cooked for the minimum time. No vegetable is added, just a sprinkle of parsley, a touch of garlic, if liked, and perhaps a little French mustard or chilli. The salad should be dressed with the best extra virgin olive oil, lemon juice and a little salt and pepper. In Versilia, the Tuscan coast north of Livorno, a few boiled potatoes are often added. Frutti di mare are also fried, grilled, sautéed or cooked in a plain and delicate tomato sauce. However they are cooked, it must be quick.

CONTINUES OVERLEAF

fugazza or fugassa
sweet focaccia

Serves 6

300g/10½oz/scant 2½ cups strong white (bread) flour

1 tsp bicarbonate of soda (baking soda)

2 tsp cream of tartar

a pinch of salt

3 large eggs, separated

100g/3½oz/½ cup caster (superfine) sugar

100g/3½oz/7 tbsp unsalted butter, at room temperature

4 tbsp milk, preferably full-fat (whole)

2 tbsp dark rum

grated rind of 1 organic or unwaxed lemon

unsalted butter and 2–3 tbsp dried breadcrumbs, for the tin

For the topping

1 egg yolk mixed with 2 tbsp milk

sugar crystals, for sprinkling

Fugazza is the Venetian dialect word for FOCACCIA, although the word now refers to a characteristic sweet bread from northern Italy. This is my adaptation of a recipe from the late Giuseppe Maffioli, an authority on the cooking of Veneto. It looks like a cake but it has a similar texture to country bread, with a most delicate and well-balanced flavour of rum and lemon. I find it a perfect accompaniment to stewed fruit, a glass of VIN SANTO, a cup of tea, coffee or even hot chocolate. A great all-rounder.

Preheat the oven to 180°C/350°F/Gas Mark 4. Grease an 18cm/7in diameter cake tin generously with butter and sprinkle the inside with dried breadcrumbs. Shake off the excess crumbs.

Sift the flour, bicarbonate of soda, cream of tartar and salt into a large bowl. Add the egg yolks, incorporating them one by one, and then the sugar, butter, milk, rum and lemon rind. Mix very hard and thoroughly.

Whisk the egg whites until stiff and then fold them into the mixture with a light upward movement. Spoon the mixture into the prepared tin. Brush the top with the egg yolk and milk mixture and then scatter sugar crystals all over.

Bake for about 1 hour, or until a thin skewer or toothpick inserted in the middle of the cake comes out dry. Turn out onto a wire rack and leave to cool.

RIGHT: Fugazza

Seafood is often used in pasta sauces and in risotti. For a *risotto alla pescatora*, four or five different kinds of seafood are added to the rice at different stages, according to the length of cooking each requires. This risotto is usually served with grated Parmesan, an addition not made to other fish risotti.

In recent years many seafood farms have been established. The biggest of these are along the coast from Trieste to Grado, east of Venice. Mussels, which are exported all over Europe, and oysters are farmed most successfully. The larvae are attached to ribbons of nylon net, which are tied around buoys. Once they have reached a good size they are placed in large pools of filtered sea water to rid them of any impurities.

funghetto, al

A method of cooking identical to TRIFOLATO.

funghi
wild mushrooms

When the wild mushroom season begins in August or September, the Italian passion for the hunt is unleashed. At dawn men, women and children start for the woods, armed with baskets and small knives. The baskets allow the spores of the picked mushrooms to fall to the ground and produce a new crop the following year. Nobody will ever tell you where his hunting ground is. People hide behind trees or pretend to have found absolutely nothing on the very spot where they have just picked a basketful of PORCINI or GALLINACCI (chanterelles). It is a sport truly in keeping with Italian tradition: individual, free and rewarded with the most welcome prize, delicious food.

Wild mushrooms are plentiful all over Italy, although the Dolomites, the Ligurian Apennines and the Sila in Calabria are the richest fungi grounds and many different species are sold in the local markets. The species for sale vary according to the area, and the local health authority usually specifies which are permitted. The fungi on sale are likely to include the most common species, such as porcini (ceps), chanterelles, some species of russula and the parasol. In the market at Trento, the richest in Italy, some 250 species have been counted on the stalls in the autumn.

There are many recipes for wild mushrooms in contemporary cooking, all relatively simple so as not to drown the taste of the mushrooms. The most common involves cooking the mushrooms in oil with garlic and parsley, sometimes sprinkled with lemon juice (funghi TRIFOLATI or *al funghetto*). In Friuli the local dry white wine is used instead of lemon juice. In Tuscany wild mushrooms and chicken livers are sautéed in olive oil flavoured with sage. The caps of the larger species are coated in egg and breadcrumbs and fried in butter and oil, or mushrooms are simply deep-fried after being coated in flour and beaten egg.

Recipes for stuffed mushrooms abound. The most popular is from Liguria, where the caps are filled with chopped mushroom stems, salted anchovies, marjoram and breadcrumbs and then baked.

Risotti of wild mushrooms and TAGLIOLINI or TAGLIATELLE dressed with a wild mushroom sauce are two outstanding classic dishes. They might vary slightly from region to region or from cook to cook, but the combination of the two basic ingredients remains the same. The mushrooms are sautéed in olive oil and butter, usually with garlic and parsley.

Which species are used in recipes depends on what one has gathered in the early morning or bought in the local market. Porcini are the most common, but several varieties can be mixed for a stew to go with polenta or a rich BRASATO. *Amanita caesarea*, *Boletus* and *Coprinus comatus* are delicious raw, dressed with lemon juice and olive oil. They can also be served in a salad with slivers of roasted chicken, finely shredded Parmesan or raw fillet of beef, very thinly sliced. The dressing is always based on olive oil and lemon juice.

Wild mushrooms can be preserved in various ways, the best known of which is by drying (see FUNGHI SECCHI). Salting is another method suitable for all except the most fragile species with a delicate taste. The mushrooms are first boiled, dried and allowed to cool, then put in jars, covered with salted water and hermetically sealed. Chanterelles, ceps, russulas and field mushrooms can be preserved under oil when they are very young. There are many ways to prepare them, but basically they are sautéed in oil, sometimes with some flavourings, splashed with wine vinegar and then pressed into jars and hermetically sealed.

Mushrooms can also be boiled in vinegar and salted water and then preserved in jars with herbs and spices. Raw mushrooms can be frozen, although this process is only suitable for a few species. Any mushrooms that have been half-cooked in oil can be satisfactorily frozen, but they should be eaten within a month.

Finally, it must be said that the most delicious fungi of all are the TARTUFI, truffles.

funghi coltivati
cultivated mushrooms

As there are not enough wild mushrooms to satisfy the Italian passion for them, mushrooms are cultivated industrially on a large scale. However, cultivated mushrooms are not very popular, probably because of the popularity of the wild species. They are used mainly in sauces and often with the addition of dried PORCINI for a stronger flavour.

funghi secchi
dried fungi

This is the most successful way to preserve some species of mushrooms, because their flavour is concentrated by the drying process. PORCINI are the best. It only takes 15g/½oz of the dried mushrooms to give a risotto or a sauce a distinctive

CONTINUES OVERLEAF

salsa di funghi secchi
dried porcini sauce

Enough for 2–3 helpings of pasta
25g/1oz dried porcini
50g/1¾oz/4 tbsp unsalted butter
2 tbsp chopped fresh flat-leaf parsley
1 garlic clove, very finely chopped
salt and freshly ground black pepper
150ml/5fl oz/²/₃ cup double (heavy)
  cream

This sauce is for spaghetti or TAGLIATELLE, but I also love it with a bowl of boiled rice.

Soak the porcini in a cupful of hot water for about 30 minutes. Lift out the porcini and strain the soaking liquid, if necessary, through a sieve lined with cheesecloth. If they appear gritty, rinse the porcini under cold water, then pat dry. Chop coarsely.

In a frying pan large enough to hold the pasta later, heat the butter with the parsley and garlic. Add the porcini and cook for about 10 minutes, adding 3–4 tablespoons of the soaking liquid. Sprinkle with salt and pepper.

When the pasta is nearly done, add the cream to the sauce and stir well. Transfer the drained pasta to the frying pan and stir-fry for 1 minute, adding more of the porcini liquid if the dish seems too dry.

flavour. Before using them the dried mushrooms must be soaked in hot water for about half an hour and then lifted out gently so as not to disturb any sand or grit at the bottom of the bowl. They are then rinsed and dried. The strained liquid has a strong mushroom flavour and can be added to make the dish tastier. I like to add a small amount of dried mushrooms to cultivated ones to enhance the flavour.

[see recipe on page 169]

fusilli
a pasta

Originally from southern Italy, this pasta is now popular all over the peninsula. The industrially made fusilli are similar to corkscrews, cut in various lengths. However, the fusilli made at home are always long. Made with durum wheat semolina, flour and water, the rolled-out dough is cut into strips of about 20cm/8in and 1cm/½in wide, wrapped around a thick knitting needle and left to dry. The sauces used with fusilli are always tomato based.

fuso
melted

Referring principally to butter. Pasta, ravioli, rice and vegetables are served *al burro fuso* – with melted butter, always unsalted and just golden – which may contain two or three sage leaves and a bruised garlic clove. It is a favourite dressing in Milanese cooking.

g

galani
sweet fritters

Sweet fritters made from ribbons of pasta dough tied together in a bow and fried (*galani* means 'bow' in Venetian dialect); they are eaten in Venice at carnival time. The dough, made with butter, egg, sugar and flour, is flavoured with GRAPPA, sweet wine from Cyprus or MARSALA. It is of the same consistency as that for pasta, rolled out thin and cut into 5cm/2in strips. The knots are fried in hot oil or STRUTTO and sprinkled with icing sugar.

gallette
unsweetened dry biscuits

In the past, gallette were the substitute for bread that soldiers and sailors took on their long voyages and campaigns. They are mostly savoury and are sometimes used as the base for various spreads. They are traditionally used in the Genoese CAPPON MAGRO and in other rustic salads. There are also some sweet gallette made with PASTA FROLLA, sweet pastry.

galletto
small chicken

Young rooster of no more than 400g/14oz in weight and no older than 6 months. It is cut in half down its back and cooked in a pan or roasted on a spit. Galletto is the ideal chicken for the recipe POLLO ALLA DIAVOLA.

gallina
hen

A hen has an important place in any Italian kitchen, thanks to its very tasty meat. It is also considered essential for making stock.

A good eating hen should be between one and two years old, a bird that is still laying eggs but whose output has slightly diminished. This is the time to put the hen in the pot. An older bird makes the best stock, but will take much longer to cook, up to 4 hours, and will be leathery to eat. The stock, however, will make the most delicate yet flavoursome soups and sauces.

Gallina, or more often half a gallina, is always part of a BOLLITO MISTO; it is also served by itself, accompanied by SALSA VERDE, MOSTARDA di Cremona and/or any of the sauces for bollito misto. A recipe from Lombardy is *gallina ripiena lessata*, the hen being stuffed with a mixture of breadcrumbs, Parmesan, eggs, chopped Savoy cabbage, garlic and sage and then boiled. But the most interesting recipe comes from Sardinia. The hen is boiled with vegetables in the usual way. It is then boned and wrapped first in myrtle leaves and then in foil and pressed between two plates for 2–3 days to allow the aromatic flavour of the herb to penetrate the meat. It is eaten cold.

gallinaccio
chanterelle mushroom

This is one of the most delicious of all wild fungi, also called *giallino*, *cantarello* or *finferlo*. It grows in deciduous woods from spring to autumn, looks like a small apricot-coloured trumpet and smells of apricot, properties that make it easy to recognize. Gallinacci are not a very common species and are rarely found on the market – it's a matter of hunting for them yourself. Gallinacci are more readily found in the Dolomites, where the inhabitants often dry them for use in the following year.

Gallinacci are best simply sautéed in butter; a flavouring of thyme is ideal. They should be cooked for only a short time, because prolonged cooking makes them tough. In the Dolomites, the chain of mountains of northern Veneto and Trentino-Alto Adige, they are stewed with other fungi to accompany the traditional polenta. They are also used in risotto: the gallinacci are sautéed in butter and onion and then added to the saffron-flavoured rice when it is almost cooked. The risotto is finished in the oven as for a pilaf.

gamberetto
shrimp

Gamberetti are small, no more than 10cm/4in, and pink or grey. The grey shrimp is also called *gambero della sabbia* ('sand shrimp') because it burrows in muddy sand. It is a favourite in Venice, where it is boiled in salted water containing a slice of lemon, drained and served with a sauce of olive oil and lemon juice, handed separately. Another favourite Venetian way to prepare gamberetti is, after blanching and shelling them, to sauté them in plenty of olive oil, parsley and garlic. They are served with the white Venetian polenta.

Both pink and grey shrimps are fried in their shells as part of a FRITTO MISTO DI MARE. They are also used in a classic Venetian risotto.

zuppa di gamberi
prawn soup

Serves 4

1kg/2¼lb raw prawns in their shells
salt
100g/3½oz/7 tbsp unsalted butter
2 tbsp Italian 00 flour
2–3 tbsp cognac
500ml/18fl oz/2¼ cups good fish stock
1 tsp paprika

This recipe is from the restaurant La Conchiglia in Lerici, a small town on the border of Liguria and Tuscany, where I have always enjoyed the food.

Cook the prawns by boiling them in salted water. Drain and peel them, reserving the heads. Pound the heads in a mortar.

Melt the butter in a saucepan over a low heat and blend in the flour, stirring vigorously over the heat for 2–3 minutes. Add the pounded prawn heads. Warm the cognac and ignite then pour into the pan. Stir in the fish stock. Sprinkle in the paprika, then pass the mixture through a fine sieve into another pan.

Add the prawn tails, bring back to simmering point and serve.

NOTE: The recipe can be used for small or large prawns. If using large prawns, cut up the tails before adding to the soup.

gambero
Mediterranean prawn

The term includes many different species, which range in size from only 6cm/2½in up to 22cm/8½in for the large MAZZANCOLLE and GAMBERONE, and vary in colour from grey to pinky red. The best are caught in deep waters, but they are also successfully farmed.

The Venetians, creators of the best seafood risotti, have a splendid *risotto coi gamberi* in which prawn heads and shells are boiled in court bouillon and gently crushed to extract the juices, which are added to rice. This gives the risotto a delicate pinkish tinge and the sweet taste of the sea. Unusually for a fish risotto, a few tablespoons of Parmesan are added at the end of cooking, not at the table.

Apart from being grilled or simply boiled and eaten as they are with olive oil and a touch of lemon juice, prawns are often cooked for a few minutes in a tomato sauce. They are also pan-fried in olive oil with garlic and parsley and finished off with capers and lemon juice. One or two chopped fresh tomatoes are sometimes thrown in as well.

[see recipe on facing page]

gamberone
large prawn

Gamberoni are large red prawns, measuring up to 30cm/12in, with quite a strong flavour. They are used in fish soups or they are grilled, often three or four threaded onto a skewer. They are also pan-fried in oil with garlic, chilli and parsley or cooked for some 5 minutes in a tomato sauce (*in salsa*). See also MAZZANCOLLA.

garganelli
a pasta

A speciality of Romagna, the dough can be flavoured with nutmeg and/or grated Parmesan. It is rolled out thinly and cut into fairly small squares; the squares are then rolled around a smooth stick which is pressed over a special comb-like device that produces deep grooves to hold the rich sauce with which they are traditionally dressed. Nowadays this shape is also made commercially.

garum
a sauce

Garum was the sauce of the Romans; it seems to have been poured on most food. It was made from fermented fish entrails. APICIUS mentioned garum in many recipes. Gastronomic historians see a similarity between garum and Worcestershire sauce, others between garum and a piquant anchovy sauce.

gattò alla napoletana
potato pie

In the 18th century French cuisine was acknowledged as the greatest in Europe and Italian chefs began to absorb French ideas and influences. A typical example is this gattò. The name is an Italianization of gateau, and the Neapolitans have added local ingredients to the non-Neapolitan potato. There are a number of gattò, all savoury rather than sweet, in the most representative book on Neapolitan cooking, *Il Cuoco Galante*, by Vincenzo CORRADO. Only the one for which the recipe is given here is still made nowadays; it is served mostly on feast days.

 [see recipe on page 174]

gelatina
gelatine, jelly or aspic jelly

Gelatina means gelatine, and also jelly or aspic, when it is followed by an attribute, for example *gelatina di pollo* (chicken aspic), *gelatina di frutta* (fruit jelly). All the aspics, or savoury jellies, are of French origin, while there are many fruit jellies from southern Italy, the best-known of which is made in Sicily, from local oranges, white rum and orange flower water.

Gelatine are also the small fruit jelly sweets, favourites of children and old people alike.

The gelatine used in Italy is always leaf gelatine.

gelato
ice cream or water ice

The word gelato – which means 'frozen' – is used generally for both ice cream and water ice, although strictly speaking a gelato is a mixture of egg custard, sugar and other flavourings, while a water ice is a SORBETTO.

Ice cream came originally from China. From there it reached India and the Middle East, and it was introduced to Italy via Sicily thanks to the Arabs in the 11th century. The early versions were frozen drinks based on milk and honey. In the 16th century some rudimentary

gattò di patate
potato cake filled with mozzarella and prosciutto

Serves 4
850g/1lb 14oz floury (starchy) potatoes
100ml/3½fl oz/scant ½ cup full-fat (whole) milk
75g/2¾oz/5 tbsp unsalted butter
salt and freshly ground black pepper
a small grating of nutmeg
50g/1¾oz Parmesan cheese, grated
2 large eggs
1 large egg yolk
200g/7oz mozzarella cheese, cut into slices
75g/2¾oz prosciutto, not too thinly sliced
75g/2¾oz mortadella or salami, sliced

For the tin and topping
20g/¾oz/1½ tbsp unsalted butter
4–5 tbsp dried breadcrumbs

You can serve this GATTÒ hot or warm as a first course, or as a second course after a soup.

Scrub the potatoes and cook them in their skins in plenty of water until you can easily pierce through to their middles with the blade of a small knife.

Meanwhile, preheat the oven to 200°C/400°F/Gas Mark 6. Butter a 20cm/8in diameter springform cake tin and coat the surface with breadcrumbs. Shake out any excess crumbs.

Drain the potatoes and peel them as soon as they are cool enough to handle. Pass them through a food mill or potato ricer to make a puree, letting it fall into the pan in which the potatoes were cooked.

Heat the milk and add to the puree with the butter. Beat well and then add ½ teaspoon salt, pepper, nutmeg and the Parmesan. Mix well, add the eggs and egg yolk and mix again very thoroughly.

Spoon half the potato mixture into the prepared tin, cover with the mozzarella, prosciutto and mortadella, then spoon the rest of the puree over the top. Dot with butter and sprinkle very lightly with breadcrumbs.

Bake for 20–30 minutes, until the gattò is brown on top and hot in the middle (test by inserting a small knife into the middle and then bringing it to your lip – it should feel hot). If it is still a bit pale, flash it under the grill. Allow the gattò to stand for 10 minutes before serving.

freezing techniques were developed by Bernardo Buontalenti, sculptor, poet, painter and – evidently – inventor. He created the first sorbets more or less as we know them today. Caterina de'Medici, wife of Henry II of France, is reputed to have made this new delicacy known throughout Europe and, allegedly, it was at the court of Charles I of England that the first ice cream, enriched with egg and cream, was made. In the 17th century the Sicilian Francesco Procopio de'Coltelli invented a machine that homogenized the mixture of egg custard, fruit juices, sugar and ice. The resulting ice cream was introduced in his newly opened café in Paris, which still exists: Le Procope. A few years later, a Neapolitan, Tortoni, opened his café in Paris, Le Café Napolitainse [sic], where he developed softer ice creams such as parfaits and SPUMONE, which he served between two slices of cake. The popularity of gelati grew so much that by the middle of the 18th century there were some 250 ice-cream shops in Paris alone.

In 1770 another Sicilian, Giovanni Bosio, opened the first ice-cream parlour in the United States. And it was in the States in 1852, in Baltimore, that the prototype of industrial ice cream was created by a dairyman, a certain Jacob Fussell, who decided to freeze his surplus of cream and milk.

In Italy gelati were relatively well known at the end of the 19th century and became quite popular thanks to *il carretto dei gelati* or *il gelataio ambulante*, the man and his tricycle, the precursor of Mr Smiley in his van.

In contemporary Italy the manufacture of ice cream is controlled by stringent regulations which do not permit more than 2% of additives. Also, the sweetness must be provided by natural rather than synthetic sugars. Many *gelaterie*, bars and PASTICCERIE show a sign saying *produzione propria*, meaning that the ice cream is made on the premises: these are the ones with the best gelati. The range of flavours, from *tiramisù* and *malaga* to *limone* or *pesca*, covers the whole gamut from thick rich ice creams laced with liqueur to ices made only with pure fresh fruit juices.

Every time I go to Italy I notice more and more ice creams, all displayed in their containers in the open window of the shop, the queue of people getting longer and longer as they wait for a *cono*, a *coppa*, a *coppetta*.

The best ice creams are still those of Naples and Palermo, or so they say. A particular Sicilian ice cream is the *brioscia di Palermo*, which looks like a sort of hamburger, made with a brioche containing two or three different kinds of ice cream.

[see recipe on page 176]

genovese
cooking style and dish

In a culinary context, this word has two meanings: alla genovese – in the style of Genoa – implies a dish flavoured with olive oil, mushrooms, both fresh and dried, herbs and garlic.

The other meaning relates to a Neapolitan dish of braised beef called *carne alla genovese*, introduced by a group of Genoese merchants, or so some gastronomic historians say. The meat is cooked for hours with flavouring vegetables, porcini mushrooms and white wine. The resulting juices, of a beautiful mahogany colour, are used to dress short pasta, which is sometimes served together with the meat.

Genovese also refers to a sponge cake – genoise, which appears to have its origins in France – and to a sauce, similar to a SALSA VERDE, but more fluid.

175

gelato di crema
custard ice cream

Serves 8–10

1 litre/1¾ pints/4 cups full-fat (whole)
  milk, or 500ml/18fl oz/2¼ cups
  milk and 500ml/18fl oz/2¼ cups
  double (heavy) cream
300g/10½oz/1½ cups caster
  (superfine) sugar
the rind of 1 organic or unwaxed lemon
8 large egg yolks

Italian ice cream is always made with an egg custard, rather than with just cream. The custard makes the ice cream lighter and easier to blend with other flavourings such as fruit juices. This is the standard recipe, which serves as a base for a vast array of flavours.

Put the milk (or milk and cream) in a saucepan with half the sugar and the lemon rind and bring to the boil. Take off the heat and leave to cool.

Whisk the egg yolks with the remaining sugar until frothy and pale. Remove the lemon rind from the milk and slowly add the milk to the egg mixture, beating continuously with a wooden spoon. Heat the mixture either over a very low heat or in a bain-marie, until the custard is thick and coats the back of a spoon. Immediately put the pan in a bowl of cold water and stir continuously for the first minute, and then leave it to cool.

Pour the mixture into the bowl of an ice-cream machine and follow the manufacturer's instructions. If you don't have an ice-cream machine, transfer the mixture to a bowl, preferably a metal one, and place it in the freezer. Stir it with a fork every 20 minutes during the first 2 hours to prevent crystals forming. After that you can leave it alone. It will be ready in about 6 hours.

ghiotta
a sauce

Originally the dripping pan in which the cooking juices collected, the word is now applied to a sauce made from those juices. A traditional Sicilian ghiotta is made with swordfish. The fish is fried in oil and then tomatoes, pine nuts, sultanas, olives, onions, celery and capers are added to make a sauce. The fish finishes cooking in the oven, covered with the sauce. The ghiotta from Abruzzo consists of sliced potatoes, tomatoes, peppers, courgettes, all layered with olive oil, salt and pepper in an earthenware pot and then baked.

In Umbria roast game is always accompanied by salsa ghiotta, made with local red wine, chopped prosciutto, sage, rosemary, garlic, juniper berries, lemon juice, vinegar and olive oil. When this mixture is well reduced, chopped chicken livers are added.

ghiozzo
goby

A fish highly prized by the Venetians and known as gô in Venetian dialect. All the recipes come from around Venice and Chioggia. Because goby is very bony it is used in fish soups, sometimes with eel, sometimes alone, often accompanied by a soft polenta. There are also risotti of goby and a rich rice dish containing goby and borlotti beans, a speciality of Murano.

gianchetti

see BIANCHETTI

gianduia or torta gianduia
a cake

A cake from Turin, which takes its name from GIANDUIOTTI because its flavour is similar. The elaborate cake consists of a fatless sponge, made with eggs and flour, moistened with cognac and Maraschino, filled with a chocolate and hazelnut cream and covered with chocolate glaze. It is one of the cakes sold in most good PASTICCERIE, and few people ever make it at home.

gianduiotti
chocolates

A speciality of Piedmont, gianduiotti were created in 1865 by Caffarel & Prochet of Turin, who gave them their name because they were originally shaped like the hat of Gianduia, the Turinese character in traditional pantomime. The chocolates, a mixture of best chocolate, toasted hazelnuts from the Langhe, vanilla and sugar, are wrapped in gold foil. Although they are now made in factories, there are still a handful of craftsmen who produce them by hand, when they are one of the very best chocolates in the world.

giardiniera
vegetable sauce

A garnish made with preserved vegetables. Those most commonly used are button mushrooms, celery, onions, cornichons, Tuscan peppers (the long, thin kind), cauliflower florets and carrots. The vegetables are blanched for 5 minutes in acidulated water and then placed in sealed jars covered with a mixture of wine vinegar, olive oil, salt and sugar. Most people buy giardiniera ready-made; it is served with brawn or cold meat.

ginepro
juniper

A bushy plant, with very prickly leaves, of which only the berries are used. The berries are small, with a scent reminiscent of pine. The principal use of juniper berries is for making gin. Lower-quality berries are pressed to extract the oil, which is used in cosmetics and perfumery. The fattest and most handsome blue berries are kept for culinary use. They are used to flavour game, stews, pork and pâté. They are also added, lightly squashed, to wine vinegar that is used for AGRODOLCE (sweet and sour) dishes.

girarrosto
a rotating device for roasting

A device attached to a spit rotating over a fire, for roasting an animal or bird. In the old days, the girarrosto was worked by clockwork or was turned by a mechanism driven by a blindfolded animal walking round and round. Some girarrosti in old country kitchens were set over a large fireplace and operated by the rising heat. Modern girarrosti are set in the oven and work by electricity.

gnocchetti sardi

see MALLOREDDUS

gnocchi
dumplings

Small dumplings, made with potatoes, SEMOLINO, maize, RICOTTA and flour, bread or other ingredients. Gnocchi are nourishing and unpretentious, but they can be harder to make than many more sophisticated dishes. The difficulty lies in making the mixture light, yet tough enough not to disintegrate in boiling water.

All northern regions have their special gnocchi. Many of these are made with pureed potatoes, with or without egg, and dressed with FONTINA cheese and butter or with melted butter and sage. One of the great dishes from Piedmont is *gnocchi alla bava*, in which the cooked gnocchi are placed in layers with fontina and butter and then baked in a hot oven for 5–10 minutes, until the cheese melts. *Gnocchi alla cadorina* from Veneto, made with potatoes, are succulent with butter and smoked ricotta or with melted butter and ground cinnamon. *Gnocchi all'ossolana* are from northern Lombardy; they are made with flour, eggs, Parmesan and nutmeg and served with plenty of melted butter and fresh sage. *Gnocchi di* ZUCCA (pumpkin gnocchi) are made in the provinces of Brescia and Mantua, in Lombardy. The cooked pumpkin is pureed and mixed with flour, eggs and some spices. Some cooks add two or three AMARETTI to the dough. The yellow dumplings are boiled in water and dressed with butter flavoured with garlic and rosemary. My favourite dressing for pumpkin gnocchi is that used in Venice, of melted butter, Parmesan, sugar and cinnamon.

Although *gnocchi di polenta*, cut into shapes rather than rolled, are less popular than potato gnocchi, they make a very appetizing dish, dressed with plenty of cheese and butter or a thin béchamel. They are also an excellent way to use leftover polenta. Another kind of gnocchi to make use of leftovers is *gnocchi di riso*, a speciality of Reggio Emilia. The cooked rice is mixed with eggs and breadcrumbs and rolled into balls the size of a walnut, which are then simmered in hot stock and dressed with butter and Parmesan.

For *gnocchi alla parigina* (à la Parisienne), choux pastry, usually made with half milk and half water, is piped through a forcing bag and cut as it drops into simmering water or stock. When cooked, the gnocchi are either dressed with plenty of butter and Parmesan, or covered with a thin creamy cheese sauce. In either case the gnocchi are placed in the oven until a golden crust has formed.

A speciality of Emilia-Romagna are the green gnocchi called MALFATTI (see recipe on page 217), made with spinach and ricotta. In Tuscany the *gnocchetti di ricotta* are made with ewe's milk ricotta, eggs, flour and herbs, dressed with melted butter,

CONTINUES ON PAGE 182

179

gnocchi di patate
potato gnocchi

Serves 4

1kg/2¼lb waxy potatoes, scrubbed

1 tsp salt

300g/10½oz/scant 2½ cups Italian 00
 flour, plus extra for dusting

1 large egg, beaten

Sage dressing

75g/2¾oz/5 tbsp unsalted butter

2 garlic cloves, lightly crushed

3–4 fresh sage leaves, torn

75g/2¾oz Parmesan cheese, grated

or

amatriciana sauce (page 27)

The recipe here is from Lazio, where the GNOCCHI are made with yellow (waxy) potatoes and egg, often dressed with an AMATRICIANA sauce. In Piedmont and Lombardy the gnocchi are made with floury (starchy) potatoes and no eggs and are usually dressed with melted butter, sage and Parmesan. Potato gnocchi are also excellent with PESTO. I have made potato gnocchi with both waxy and floury potatoes, with and without eggs: the result depends partly on the exact nature of the potatoes and partly on the amount of flour added – where experience certainly helps.

You can prepare and shape the gnocchi a day ahead. The ridges, made by flipping the dumplings against the prongs of a fork or the back of a cheese grater, are not for decoration. They serve to thin out the gnocco and to provide grooves or holes to hold the sauce.

Boil the potatoes in their skins in plenty of water until tender. Drain and peel while still hot. Sieve the potatoes in a food mill or a potato ricer, directly onto the work surface.

Sprinkle the salt onto the flour in a bowl and mix well. Add the egg and half the flour to the potatoes. Knead, gradually adding more flour, until the mixture is soft, smooth and slightly sticky. If you have time, put the mixture in the refrigerator for 30 minutes or so; it is easier to shape when it is cold. Shape the mixture into long rolls, about 2.5cm/1in in diameter, and then cut into 2cm/¾in lengths.

Take a fork and hold it with the prongs resting on the work surface at an angle of about 45 degrees. Take each piece of dough and dust it with flour, then press it lightly with the thumb of your other hand against the inner curve of the prongs and, with a quick downwards movement, flip it towards the end of the prongs. The gnocchi should be concave on the thumb side, and convex with ridges on the fork side.

For the sage dressing, put the butter, garlic and sage in a small saucepan over a low heat until the butter is light golden. Discard the garlic.

Bring 5 litres/9 pints/5 quarts water to the boil in a large saucepan. Do not put salt in the water as this tends to make the gnocchi stick together. Drop the gnocchi into the boiling water, about 30 at a time. Cook for 20 seconds after they rise to the surface, then lift out and transfer to a warmed dish. Pour over a little of your chosen sauce, sprinkle with some Parmesan and keep warm. Repeat until all the gnocchi are cooked. Serve immediately.

RIGHT: Gnocchi di patate

sage and Parmesan, or with a plain tomato sauce. And finally there are the semolina gnocchi from Rome (see recipe on page 388).

In Venezia Giulia there are sweet gnocchi: potato gnocchi containing a plum or an apricot, dressed with butter, spices and sugar. Although they are sweet they are served as a first course. The other sweet gnocchi, from Le Marche, are made with the odd-sounding combination of PECORINO cheese and sugar. Egg yolks are mixed with milk and potato flour. The mixture is brought to the boil and then spread on a marble slab. When cold it is cut into squares, which are then piled in a dish, in layers, and sprinkled with sugar, cinnamon, butter and the local fresh pecorino. Baked in the oven, these gnocchi are something quite special.

[see recipe on page 180]

gnocco fritto
bread fritter

This gnocco is made with bread dough containing about 50g/2oz of STRUTTO (pork fat). When the dough has risen, it is cut into lozenges and deep-fried in oil or in strutto. The pieces of dough become very light and airy in the frying. Eaten hot, in place of bread, with SALAME, other pork products and soft cheeses, gnocco fritto is one of the tastiest and most satisfying foods of the Emilian cuisine.

Gnocco fritto is so called in Modena and Reggio Emilia, while in Bologna the same type of fritters are called CRESCENTINE and in Romagna PIADINE.

goccia
measure

Goccia means 'a drop', used as a measure. Italians love to give recipes in which quantities are measured in terms of glasses, handfuls, fingers and drops. *Una o due gocce* means a very little, just enough to give the dish a suspicion of another flavour, not necessarily identifiable. It does not mean you must measure the liquid with a drop counter. However, when dealing with essences, *una goccia* means literally one drop.

goregone
salmon-type fish

A freshwater fish found in Lake Como in Lombardy, where it is also called *lavarello*, and in Lake Bolsena in Lazio. The goregone lives in very deep waters. It has a very delicate meat, similar to wild trout, and is usually grilled and served with lemon wedges.

Gorgonzola
a cheese

A blue-veined cheese named after its place of origin, a locality which is now part of the eastern suburbs of Milan. Its birth is connected with at least two legends. The first tells of a herdsman who, having milked his cows in the fields around Gorgonzola, left for other pastures but forgot to take the bucket of milk. When he returned he added the new, fresher milk to the forgotten milk, which by then had coagulated. From this mixture, Gorgonzola was born. The other story relates how an innkeeper in Gorgonzola used to be paid in cheeses by shepherds who came to stay at his inn. The cheese was the soft, mild CRESCENZA. One day some of the cheeses went bad and the innkeeper decided to destroy them. Just then some customers walked in, tasted the cheese and thought it very good. This crescenza that had gone bad became a new cheese – Gorgonzola.

Gorgonzola is made with pasteurized cow's milk, in cylinders about 25–30cm/10–12in in diameter, weighing from 5 to 12kg/11–26lb. It is aged for 2–3 months. In the old days it was made by mixing cold curd with hot curd. Nowadays the blue veins are produced by pricking the cheese with long copper, steel or brass needles which expose the cheese to the air in different points, helping to form the mould. The more holes that are made, the more piquant the cheese will be. In the case of farm-made Gorgonzola, the ageing of the cheese still takes place, as it has done for centuries, in natural caves in the Alpine valleys of Valsassina and Val Brembana. Industrially produced Gorgonzola is aged in store-rooms in which the climatic characteristics of the caves are reproduced. When ready, the cheese is stamped with its place of origin (DOP), cut across in half and wrapped in special foil.

Gorgonzola is a very nutritious cheese and it is sometimes eaten in place of meat. Gorgonzola is often spread on grilled polenta. It also makes an excellent risotto. And mixed with cream it makes a delicious sauce for GNOCCHI or any kind of pasta, but not spaghetti or BUCATINI.

gran bui
see BOLLITO MISTO

grana
grating cheese

The generic name for a family of cheeses that are very hard and grainy in texture, hence its name. Grana is considered the ideal partner to the great majority of traditional pasta dishes and most risotti. The most famous grana is PARMIGIANO REGGIANO, the authentic Parmesan.

Grana Padano is a very popular DOP cheese, made in many provinces of Piedmont and Lombardy, Veneto and Emilia-Romagna. It is also made in Trento. Aged Grana Padano is the cheese most commonly used for cooking and grating. It has the same good melting properties as its more famous cousin, Parmesan, but is cheaper. The young grana is also an excellent table cheese. Grana Padano is light buff in colour and grainy with tiny eyes. Its pleasing taste varies from mellow to piquant according to its age. Some cheeses are sold after 9 or 10 months' ageing and

some are aged for up to 2 years. The name is stamped all over the crust of the cheeses, which are large and heavy, weighing around 30kg/66lb.

Granone Lodigiano is a very rare cheese, made around Lodi, a town in southern Lombardy. It is very similar to other granas, but has a faint greenish tinge and when cut 'it sheds a tear' (*la goccia*) from the tiny eyes in the cheese. It is at its very best during the winter months, and is so good that it is usually eaten at table rather than grated. I recently had some perfect Granone Lodigiano at the Petersham Nurseries Teahouse in south-west London, where one of the chefs had just brought back from his native Lodi a piece of this cheese, with its small *goccia*; it was indeed superb.

granceola, granseola or grancevola
spider crab

The granceola is a large crab with hairy legs and a knobbly shell. The flavour of the meat is sweet and delicate, especially that of the granceole of the Venetian lagoon. And it is indeed in Venice that one can enjoy the best granceole. The female granceola is regarded as the better specimen, particularly during the winter months when she carries the eggs.

Spider crabs are boiled, in order to open them. The meat and coral are then extracted from the shell, chopped and served, back in the shell, dressed with olive oil and lemon juice. In Venice, granceola, as any other shellfish, is also cooked in risotto.

The 17th-century chef Giulio Cesare Tirelli wrote two recipes for spider crab. In the first, the boiled crab is dressed with olive oil, lemon juice and bruised pepper, then placed on the grill and heated very slowly. In the second and more interesting recipe a clove of garlic and some herbs are first sautéed and then pushed into the shell of the crab where the coral is, together with some 'Venetian spices', moistened with vinegar. It is then steamed.

183

granchio comune
shore crab

These smallish crabs, about 7.5cm/3in long, are found on many sandy beaches, especially in the northern Adriatic. On Sunday mornings you can see Venetian families armed with buckets bent double on the beaches of the islands in the lagoon, digging out crabs for the sauce for the spaghetti for lunch. It is hard and lengthy work because there is little meat left once the shell is removed.

In a recipe for risotto, the lower shells are pounded in a mortar and added to the rice with the bits of meat.

granciporro
edible crab, brown crab

A large crab (it can measure up to 30cm/12in) found, albeit rarely, close to the shore of the Venetian lagoon. It is boiled and served with melted butter flavoured with parsley and plenty of garlic, with garlicky CROSTINI, or dressed with a mild extra virgin olive oil and lemon juice or vinegar.

granelli
calf testicles

Unfortunately, this kind of offal is disappearing from the market. Granelli are delicious, with a taste halfway between sweetbreads and brain. They can be cooked as ANIMELLE (sweetbreads), for which there is a simple recipe on page 28. A recipe from Tuscany is used when various animals, such as calves, lambs or horses, are castrated. The blanched granelli, coated in flour and egg, are fried in olive oil.

granita
frozen drink

This iced drink should consist only of fruit juice or coffee and sugar, these being frozen and then

CONTINUES OVERLEAF

184

granita al caffè
coffee granita

Serves 4
600ml/20fl oz/2½ cups freshly brewed
espresso coffee
about 4 tbsp caster (superfine) sugar
125ml/4fl oz/½ cup whipping cream
1 tbsp icing (confectioners') sugar

The Italian ice concoction par excellence. It is usually eaten sitting at a pavement café, just watching the world go by.

Heat the coffee, add 4 tablespoons sugar and stir to dissolve. Taste, and add a little more sugar if you prefer. Pour the coffee into a freezer tray and leave until cold, then freeze until solid.

Plunge the bottom of the tray into a bowl of hot water for a few seconds, break up the coffee ice into chunks and then process in a food processor until it forms small crystals. Return to the tray and place back in the freezer.

Before serving, place 4 long-stemmed wine glasses in the refrigerator to chill. Whip the cream and stir in the icing sugar to sweeten slightly. Remove the granita from the freezer. If too solid, process for a few seconds just before serving. Spoon into the chilled glasses and top with the whipped cream.

RIGHT: Granita al caffè

granchio comune

crushed so as to obtain an icy, finely ground mush. Granite made with good-quality fruit juices and excellent coffee are regaining the popularity they once enjoyed. The most popular are *granita al caffè*, which is often served with a dollop of whipped cream on top, and *granita al limone*, the most refreshing of all drinks.

[see recipe on page 184]

grano
grain

Another word for FRUMENTO (wheat). Strictly speaking, grano is a grain of any cereal.

grano saraceno
buckwheat

Buckwheat grows at high altitudes, and all the dishes based on it come from the Alpine regions. In Lombardy a kind of pasta (PIZZOCCHERI) is made with its flour, as well as a dark polenta, called *polenta taragna*, and the fritters called *sciatt*, which contain a good deal of grated BITTO – the local cheese – and some GRAPPA. In Friuli buckwheat flour is used in a soup, dressed with milk and melted butter, while the cooking of Alto Adige, rich in superb sweet preparations, offers a cake made with buckwheat flour and filled with blackcurrant jelly, a very interesting combination of flavours.

There are two theories on the origins of the name saraceno: one is that it resembles the colour of the skin of the Saracens; the other because the grain was introduced to Italy by the Saracens.

granoturco or granturco
maize

Maize arrived in Italy from the New World in the 16th century. This yellow grain was christened granoturco (Turkish grain) because at the time

so many things of foreign origin came (or were thought to come) from Turkey that 'turco' became synonymous with foreign.

Maize established itself very well in northern Italy. It was ground into FARINA GIALLA (yellow flour), and POLENTA began to be made, soon to become the staple diet of much of northern Italy. Nutritionally, however, maize is not as good as wheat, barley or oats, as it is lacking in B vitamins, the deficiency of which caused pellagra, the disease that killed a horrendous number of country people in Lombardy and Veneto during the 19th century.

Maize is mainly eaten in its ground form. Corn cobs were – and still are – sometimes roasted and eaten by farm labourers in the countryside of Veneto. Nowadays they are also eaten by foodies keen to enjoy American-style corn on the cob.

grappa
a spirit

Also called *acquavite*, this alcoholic drink is made from the distillation of the skins, pulp, seeds and stems (called pomace) of the grapes, the best grappas being those made from the pomace of a single variety of grape.

It is drunk as a digestive after a meal. It is also added to an espresso to create a *caffè corretto* ('corrected coffee') or drunk after the espresso, when it is called *ammazzacaffè* ('kill the coffee'). While it used to be a rough drink of peasants, nowadays grappa is favoured by the most fastidious connoisseurs thanks to single-variety grappa and its ageing in special barrels.

grasso
fat

In a culinary context grasso refers to vegetable oils as well as animal fats. Nowadays the fat most commonly used in cooking is olive oil, not necessarily extra virgin, because it is regarded as healthier, but in the past the particular fat used was a defining characteristic of the regional cuisine. Thus the cooking of northern Italy was based on butter and pork fat, olive oil being used only occasionally, to dress salads. In the other regions, from Liguria and Tuscany southwards, the cooking was, and still is, based on olive oil, plus lard (STRUTTO) or other pork fats.

Unfortunately, replacing animal fats with olive oil can alter the flavour of the dish.

grasso
feast day

Un giorno di grasso is a day when meat is eaten, as opposed to un giorno di MAGRO, a fast day. It is connected with religious festivities. La settimana grassa – literally 'the week with meat' – is the week before the beginning of Lent; being the last week of Carnival, it is a week of fun and festivities when many rich dishes are served.

graticola
a grill or a cast–iron pan

Graticola means two things: it is another word for GRIGLIA (grill), and it is a ridged cast-iron pan. This latter, however, can also be called a griglia. A typical Italian confusion of names!

grattugia
a grater

One of the indispensable tools in any Italian kitchen, the grater is used almost daily. Parmesan cheese is sprinkled on most soups, pasta and risotto, and since it is very seldom bought grated, the grattugia must always be to hand. Graters come in a variety of shapes and sizes, although the most common is that made purely for grating cheese, with only one size of hole. Nowadays you can buy electric cheese graters and beautifully designed graters that are put on the table next to a big wedge of Parmesan cheese. Most cooks also have a small grattugia for grating nutmeg and lemon and orange rind.

The grattugia is an ancient utensil. In the Etruscan museum at Chiusi in Tuscany there is a bas-relief from a tomb which shows a strainer, a ladle and a grater. What, alas, is not revealed is what the Etruscans grated.

gremolada

The dressing added to OSSOBUCHI when they are cooked. (See recipe on page 256.)

griglia, alla
cooking method

When food is cooked alla griglia, it is directly exposed to the embers, flames or other source of heat. It is one of the oldest ways of cooking, and it used to be considered a primitive method that did nothing to enhance the flavour of the food. For this reason, grilling remained unfashionable all through the great cookery periods of the Renaissance up to the 20th century. Throughout that period it was deemed suitable only for peasants. Now the pendulum has swung the other way, and all the best restaurants will offer almost anything alla griglia. These restaurants are making the point that to be cooked alla griglia the food must be of prime quality, in keeping with the high standards of their establishment. Grilling is now also popular at home, where this method of cooking is appreciated for the flavour it conveys to the ingredients as well as for its speed.

Meat, fish and vegetables are all grilled, the most popular grilled vegetables being radicchio and peppers.

The best-known grilled dishes originate from Tuscany, where the prime ingredients of the food are superb, while the cooking traditions are not so

187

elaborate. Grilled dishes from this region include *bistecca alla fiorentina*, made with a steak from a special breed of cattle, or POLLO ALLA DIAVOLA, from the Valdarno, where the best chickens are raised.

grigliata mista
mixed grill

A platter of different kinds of meat or fish, grilled over direct heat. Grigliate are restaurant dishes par excellence because they need many components. A fish grigliata in Venice, for instance, will have one or two small sole, a few small cuttlefish, one or two scampi and maybe a piece of monkfish – the best local fish. A good *grigliata di carne* will contain a baby lamb chop, a slice of liver, a few kidneys, a sausage or two and a slice of PANCETTA.

grissini
breadsticks

These little breadsticks appear, usually wrapped in cellophane, on every table in every Italian restaurant inside or outside Italy. These, however, are not the same as the artisanal grissino, made by many bakeries in Piedmont, where every stick is made by hand, to produce a fatter and irregular stick, which is then lightly dusted with flour. It might not be so pretty, but it is certainly far better, with its soft crustiness.

Grissini are the most famous culinary product of Turin, so much so that Napoleon called them '*les petits batons de Turin*'. The original recipe is attributed to a Turinese baker who created them in 1679 for one of his clients, the court doctor, who wanted some light bread for the ailing son of the Duke of Savoy. There is an old Piedmontese cartoon showing a family who, during the siege of Turin in the 18th century, are sitting around a table on which stands a basket full of bread. The family looks haggard and starving, with their arms raised in an imploring gesture to the heavens. The caption reads: 'Lord, do not let us die of hunger. Please give us our daily grissini.'

My mother used to make a snack to serve with drinks, which I make too. Good grissini are cut into lengths of about 12cm/4½in. Half a slice of prosciutto, cut lengthways, is wrapped around one end of the grissino. You pick up the bare end and bite into the prosciutto end. They are good and attractive.

grongo or gronco
conger eel

A sea fish that can be as long as 3m/10ft, varying in colour from pale purple to nearly black. It is caught all year round, often close to the mouth of a river, which – unlike its cousin, the common eel (ANGUILLA) – it never enters.

Its firm meat has a strong flavour, greatly appreciated by some people (I love it), while others find it too fatty. Grongo must be skinned and cut into chunks before cooking. It is stewed for about 20 minutes in tomato sauce and/or wine. It is considered indispensable in a good Tuscan CACCIUCCO. It also makes a delicious sauce for spaghetti, in which case it is cooked in a wine and tomato sauce for about 30 minutes; the bones are removed and the pieces put back into the sauce and then spooned over the cooked pasta.

guanciale
pig's jowl

In culinary parlance (guanciale otherwise means 'pillow'), the jowl of a pig. Guanciale is salted and cured for about 3 months in the same way as PANCETTA, which it resembles in appearance and taste, although guanciale is always coated with coarsely ground black pepper. It is a speciality of central Italy, especially Lazio, where it is the main ingredient in spaghetti all'AMATRICIANA. Salt pork or pancetta are adequate substitutes for guanciale. Good guanciale is also eaten raw, thinly sliced.

guazzetto
cooking method

'In guazzetto' means cooked in a light sauce based on a good deal of chopped onions and white wine and sometimes a touch of tomato. Frogs, seafood and BACCALÀ are cooked in guazzetto. The original recipe is for frogs and comes from the area around Pavia, south Lombardy, where they abound. The frogs are sautéed in a SOFFRITTO of oil, onion, celery and garlic. Splashed with white wine, the sauce is bound with a little flour and flavoured at the end with parsley.

gubana
a sweet bread

A sweet bread from Friuli, traditionally eaten at Easter. The sweetened bread dough is rolled out thinly and filled with raisins, pine nuts, walnuts, sultanas, chocolate, prunes and candied peel, then rolled up like a Swiss roll and baked; it is served with GRAPPA. Gubana is clearly derived from Austrian strudel.

gulasch
a stew

From Hungary, gulasch spread to neighbouring regions, and it soon became a traditional dish of Venezia Giulia. It has now been adopted by *birrerie* (pubs) all over Italy. The gulasch from Venezia Giulia is less spicy than the Hungarian original, and it is sometimes Italianized by the addition of tomatoes. Gulasch is served with polenta, potatoes or with tagliatelle, in the Austrian style.

 [see recipe below]

gulasch alla triestina
goulash from Trieste

Serves 4

750g/about 1½lb boned pork shoulder
50g/1¾oz smoked pancetta or smoked streaky bacon, cut into cubes
50g/1¾oz/4 tbsp unsalted butter
2 large sweet onions, finely sliced
2–3 tsp paprika, depending on strength
1 tbsp flour
1 tbsp tomato puree
1 tsp grated lemon rind
salt and freshly ground black pepper
125ml/4fl oz/½ cup red wine
2 large yellow or red peppers, deseeded and chopped
2 large ripe tomatoes, peeled and roughly chopped
300ml/10fl oz/1¼ cups meat stock (page 61) or chicken stock

This is the type of goulash made in Venezia Giulia, the region around Trieste, where pork is the favourite meat.

Cut the pork into 2.5cm/1in pieces. Heat the pancetta and half the butter in a large saucepan. Add the onions and sauté until soft, but not brown. Add the meat and brown well on all sides.

Mix in the paprika, flour and tomato puree and cook for 1–2 minutes, stirring constantly. Add the lemon rind, salt and pepper.

Pour the wine over the meat and reduce by boiling rapidly for 2 minutes. Add the peppers and tomatoes and mix well. Cover with the stock and simmer, tightly covered, for about 1½ hours.

Just before serving, remove the lid and reduce the liquid over a high heat. The sauce should thicken and become velvety. Taste and add more paprika if necessary.

h, i, j, k

There are only four Italian words beginning with H and they are all forms of the verb *avere* – to have. The letter J does not feature in the Italian language. The letter K is used only in the parts of northern Italy where German is still spoken: Valle d'Aosta, Trentino-Alto Adige (also known as Südtirol, or South Tyrol) and Friuli-Venezia Giulia.

imbottire
to stuff or fill

This term is used mainly in connection with bread rolls. A *panino imbottito* is a large filled roll, mostly sold and eaten in bars. The bread is white and soft and is either round or oval. The filling depends on the creativity of the chef or the demand of the consumer.

impanare
to coat with dried breadcrumbs

The word comes from PANE (bread). It is the method for making COTOLETTA, which can be meat, fish or vegetable. The slice of food is first coated in beaten egg and then in breadcrumbs, when it becomes *impanato* (breaded). The food is then fried or, less frequently, grilled or cooked in the oven. The breadcrumbs protect the food, keeping it moist, and form a crust. The 'impanatura' often contains a little grated Parmesan cheese in the proportion of one part of Parmesan to four of breadcrumbs.

impastare
to knead

A verb incorporating the word 'pasta', which is the key to the action. As well as the meaning of the word pasta that has become part of the English language, PASTA in Italian means any kind of dough, from bread dough to puff pastry.

incapriata
broad bean purée

A purée of broad beans made in Puglia. See FAVA.

indivia
endive

There are two main varieties of indivia, *riccia* (curly endive or frisée) and SCAROLA (batavia). Ricciolina and scarola are both used raw and in cooking. A recipe from Sicily combines indivia with oranges and fennel in a salad. In an interesting recipe from the cuisine of the Roman ghetto the blanched leaves of the curly endive are sautéed and then baked in the oven covered with fresh anchovies, garlic, parsley and dried breadcrumbs. In another recipe from Rome batavia is braised for 15 minutes in an oil-based tomato sauce, flavoured with salted anchovies and garlic.

The *indivia belga* (Belgian endive or chicory), a close cousin, is far less popular and, being a recent import, does not have any place in traditional cooking.

inglese, all'
in the English style

Food dressed simply with butter. It applies mainly to boiled rice, pasta and some vegetables. However, being an Italian adaptation of a foreign style, a generous amount of grated Parmesan is added for good measure!

insaccato
salami and sausages

A name for all kinds of SALAMI and sausages. The word comes from *sacco* – bag – and means, literally, 'pushed into a bag', the bag in this instance being the casing.

insalata
salad

When thinking of Italian food the first thing that springs to my mind is salads. They somehow symbolize what is best in Italian cooking: first-class ingredients served in the most natural manner. And so many ingredients become insalate.

The dressing is usually simplicity itself: olive oil, wine vinegar or lemon juice and salt. The proportion of vinegar to oil is impossible to state definitively since the right combination depends on the fruitiness of the oil and the acidity of the vinegar. The olive oil must be extra virgin. The vinegar used in Italy is natural wine vinegar, usually red, and is added with great discretion. As a guideline, the dressing for 4 servings should be 4 tablespoons of oil and 1–2 tablespoons of vinegar. In Italy we say that you need four people to dress a bowl of salad: a generous person to pour the oil, a wise person to sprinkle the salt, a miser to add the vinegar and a patient soul to toss it.

Pepper is optional. Garlic is an even rarer addition, present only in particular salads. Some salads, such as lettuce, require more olive oil; others, such as beetroot and cabbage, need more vinegar. Artichokes, fennel and plum tomatoes are often dressed only with olive oil and salt. A little fresh basil or parsley, a few rings of red onion or a sprinkling of oregano are all optional additions.

Green salad is rarely served with mayonnaise or any other dressing and is never eaten without dressing. Strictly speaking, insalata is a green salad – insalata verde – made of LATTUGA, CICORIA or INDIVIA. These three species include numerous varieties. However, any vegetable, raw or cooked, can go into the salad bowl, either on its own or with other vegetables and sometimes with meat, fish, rice (*riso in insalata*), pasta (*pasta in insalata*) or even bread, as in the Tuscan PANZANELLA.

insaporire
to make more tasty

The word means to enhance the flavour of an ingredient during the preparation of a dish. It is used when the main ingredient is sautéed in an aromatic SOFFRITTO. It is a stage in the cooking that should never be skimped, since it is the only way to give the right flavour to the finished dish.

integrale
wholewheat

This refers to wholewheat flour, and to products made with wholewheat flour. Thus, GRISSINI integrali, PANE integrale, PASTA integrale (which is usually spaghetti).

intingolo
a meat sauce or fish sauce

In the old days intingolo was a rich sauce of meat or, in southern Italy, fish, into which bread was dipped. The meat, usually lamb, kid or hare, was cut into small pieces and likewise the fish, swordfish in Calabria and tuna fish in Sicily. These were cooked slowly in wine and stock, with prosciutto, onion, celery and other flavourings.

Nowadays the word intingolo is used rarely; it means a thick RAGÙ used to dress pasta, rice or even pulses.

involtini
stuffed meat or fish rolls

Rolls of meat (usually veal), prosciutto or fish containing various stuffings. The stuffing is often chopped ham and/or chicken bound with béchamel sauce and/or egg, Parmesan and other flavourings. The involtini are sautéed in butter and splashed with white wine or MARSALA. A stuffing from Naples is made with tomato sauce and mozzarella, while *involtini alla modenese* contain prosciutto, LUGANEGA and sage.

Involtini di prosciutto usually contain ricotta and béchamel. *Involtini di pesce* can be made with fillets of sole or whiting stuffed with spinach and Parmesan and braised in the oven in a little stock and wine.

Modern involtini can also be made with thin slices of pink roast beef containing blanched vegetables dressed with a sauce tartare or mayonnaise. Alternatively they may contain chopped eggs mixed with olive puree and dressed with a light vinaigrette. Involtini can also be made with cabbage leaves, when they may be known as FAGOTTINI.

iota or jota
a soup

A traditional soup of barley and other ingredients from Venezia Giulia and Friuli. The Friuli version is made with barley, beans, milk and *broade*, the local macerated turnips, while the recipe from Venezia Giulia (see page 164) includes sauerkraut.

Italico
a cheese

A mild cheese with a sweet taste, a soft creamy texture and good melting properties, similar to the better-known BEL PAESE.

knoedel
a dumpling

A kind of bread gnocchi made in Alto Adige, similar to the CANEDERLI from Trentino. A version of knoedel made only in Alto Adige are the *schwarzplentene knoedel*. These are made with rye and buckwheat bread mixed with smoked PANCETTA. They are boiled and served with sauerkraut and tomato sauce.

krapfen or crafen doughnut

These doughnuts are a speciality of Alto Adige, Venezia Giulia and Friuli, the regions that were Austrian up to 1918. Krapfen have now become quite popular all over Italy, where they are also called BOMBOLONI.

lacciada
pancakes

This festive food is traditionally served in
Lombardy at village fairs in the autumn. It consists
of pancakes stacked one on top of the other,
layered with jam and a few black grapes. Lacciada
is a favourite with children, probably because of its
connection with festive days.

lagane and laganelle
pasta strips

Homemade with durum wheat semolina flour and
water, these are one of the traditional pasta shapes
of southern Italy, usually about 3cm/1¼in wide
– or 1–2cm/½–¾in for *laganette* – and as long as
spaghetti. Commercially made lagane often have
fluted edges.

The most popular dish is *lagane e ciceri*, a
soup consisting of pasta and chickpeas, cooked
separately and then mixed together and dressed
with olive oil and plenty of garlic and chilli. This is
the traditional dish for All Souls' Day in Puglia.

Other traditional ways to dress this pasta are
simply with grated dried RICOTTA and plenty of
black pepper, or with a sauce of grilled peppers
and tomatoes.

lampascioni
muscari bulbs

The bulb of a species of *Muscari* (grape hyacinth),
lampascioni grow wild everywhere in southern
Italy and, to meet the demand, are now cultivated
in Puglia. Lampascioni are similar to small onions,

which they also resemble in taste. Although they
are bitter, their bitterness can be removed before
cooking by soaking them for up to 48 hours in cold
water or by blanching. The most common way to
prepare lampascioni is to bake or boil them and
then eat them cut in half and simply dressed with
oil and vinegar. They are also stewed with wine
and tomatoes or made into a puree which is spread
on thick slices of local bread. Lampascioni are also
sold in jars, roasted and preserved in oil.

lampone
raspberry

This berry is not a typical Italian fruit. It grows
mostly in Piedmont and Lombardy, where the
climate is suitable, and is also found wild in
Alpine woods. These wild lamponi are deliciously
fragrant, and are used as part of a SOTTOBOSCO.
Raspberries are mostly eaten raw with lemon and/
or orange juice and sugar, or, more rarely, with
cream and sugar. Sorbets and ice creams are also
made from raspberries, although they are less
popular than other fruit.

lardellare
to lard

Joints of meat are often larded in Italian cooking.
Some joints are larded with a mixture of chopped
PANCETTA or chopped LARDO, plus garlic, herbs, salt
and pepper, pushed into deep incisions in the
meat, others with long pieces of carrot and celery,
as well as strips of prosciutto or lardo. Larding not
only gives moisture and flavour to the meat, it also
makes it look attractive when sliced.

lardelli
strips of fat

Long strips of LARDO or PANCETTA used to lard a joint.

lardo
cured back fat

This is the layer of hard fat nearest to the skin of a pig's back, which is cured by salting or, more rarely, smoking. Lardo is not the same as the English lard (melted pork fat). In the old days lardo was one of the basic cooking fats in many regions, especially those where no olive trees grow. Nowadays lardo has almost disappeared from everyday cooking because of worries about health. However, a BATTUTO of lardo, with onion and/or garlic, celery and carrot, remains indispensable for giving a traditional dish its authentic taste.

The best lardo is also eaten raw, thinly sliced, by itself or with other pork products. Two lardi have been granted DOP status: *lardo di Colonnata* from Tuscany and *lardo di Arnad* from Valle d'Aosta. Both are cured with aromatic herbs and spices and aged in special containers – marble in Colonnata and glass in Arnad. They are delicious products, comparable, I think, to the best PROSCIUTTI or SALAMI. There is also another lardo that I like very much. It is the *lardo di Montefeltro*, made in Le Marche and not well known outside the region. At the time of writing it has not been granted a DOP mark. Don't ask me why, but maybe it is because its production is too small.

lasagne
a pasta

Together with spaghetti and penne, lasagne is the best known shape of pasta outside Italy, mainly used for baked dishes. The best lasagne is homemade, using flour and eggs only, this being the traditional dough of Emilia-Romagna. The dough is rolled out thin and cut into rectangles measuring about 20 x 10cm/8 x 4in. Lasagne can also be bought dried, when they are made with semolina, eggs and water. Many brands are excellent, and better than most of the fresh lasagne sold in shops outside Italy.

Lasagne is traditional in many regions, but each area makes a slightly different dough, cut in different lengths and widths, sometimes served straight away and sometimes baked and dressed with different sauces. One regional speciality is *lasagne al sangue* – literally 'bloody lasagne', which hardly sounds very appetizing. It is, in fact, a delicious and very old dish from Le Langhe, a beautiful hilly area in Piedmont. The dough is made with flour, eggs and water. The pasta is cut into strips about 2cm/¾in wide. They are first parboiled and then sautéed for 2–3 minutes in a pan containing – in addition to onion, local sausage, sweetbreads, rosemary and parsley – the blood of a newly slaughtered pig, hence their name.

In the eastern corner of Veneto, *lasagne da fornel* is a dish that tastes more central European than Italian since it is made with a buttery sauce containing sultanas, dried figs, walnuts, grated apples and poppy seeds. It is not a sweet dish, nor is it served as a pudding.

Further south, Emilia-Romagna is the real kingdom of lasagne. *Lasagne al forno* (baked lasagne) originated here. A few ounces of cooked and chopped spinach are often added to colour the dough for *lasagne verdi*, which is the original pasta for lasagne al forno. The lasagne sheets are layered with a rich and succulent meat RAGÙ and a velvety and delicate béchamel. The recipe is given here.

The traditional lasagne from the Le Marche is VINCISGRASSI, a particularly rich dish, the recipe for which is on page 459.

In southern Italy there is only one traditional dish, *lasagne di Carnevale*, eaten at carnival time. The square lasagne is lavishly layered with local sausage, tiny fried meatballs, mozzarella, ricotta and hard-boiled eggs, all generously sauced with a classic Neapolitan ragù – only the juice, not the meat (see recipe on page 78).

In modern cooking, lasagne dishes have multiplied. So we now have *lasagne ai frutti di mare* (with seafood), *lasagne al radicchio trevisano* (lasagne layered with red radicchio, béchamel and Parmesan) and *lasagne alla boscaiola*, with eggs, mushrooms, FONTINA and Parmesan.

[see recipe below]

lasagnette
pasta ribbons

A form of dried long pasta, about 2cm/¾in wide, with fluted edges. They are excellent with PESTO, and also with many southern Italian sauces. Some manufacturers call this shape of pasta *mafalde* or *reginette*.

---

lasagne al forno
baked lasagne

Serves 6

ragù alla bolognese (page 346)

egg pasta (page 282) made with
300g/10½oz/scant 2½ cups
Italian 00 flour and 3 large eggs

1 tbsp coarse sea salt

75g/2¾oz Parmesan cheese, grated

15g/½oz/1 tbsp unsalted butter, plus extra for the dish

Béchamel sauce

1 litre/1¾ pints/4 cups full-fat (whole) milk

100g/3½oz/7 tbsp unsalted butter

85g/3oz/scant ¾ cup Italian 00 flour flavoured with a grating of nutmeg

This is one of many recipes for the classic LASAGNE al forno: it's the version I usually cook. The original Bolognese lasagne are green, but this is the only corner I cut and I make them with the usual pasta dough.

While the ragù is cooking, make your pasta dough, roll it out and cut into lasagne sheets.

Cook the lasagne in plenty of boiling water to which you have added 1 tablespoon of salt. Plunge 5 or 6 sheets of lasagne into the boiling water, move them around with a fork so that they do not stick together and cook them for 1 minute. Retrieve the sheets from the water using a fish slice and lay them out on clean tea towels.

When all the lasagne sheets are cooked, make the béchamel sauce. Bring the milk to simmering point. Melt the butter in a saucepan and add the flour, beating continuously. When all the flour has been incorporated, gradually add the hot milk, stirring the whole time. Cook the béchamel over a very low heat for about 5 minutes, stirring very frequently.

Now you can begin to assemble the dish. Preheat the oven to 220°C/425°F/Gas Mark 7.

Generously butter a 30 x 20cm/12 x 8in lasagne dish and then spread 2 tablespoons of ragù over the bottom of the dish. Cover with a layer of lasagne and then spread 2 tablespoons or so of ragù over the pasta, followed by the same amount of béchamel sauce. Sprinkle with a little of the Parmesan and repeat to build the dish up with these ingredients until you have used them all. The top layer must be of béchamel. Dot with the butter and bake for about 20 minutes. Leave to rest for at least 5 minutes before serving.

lasca
roach

This rare freshwater fish is caught in Lake Trasimeno in Umbria and in some lakes and rivers of Lombardy and Piedmont. Lasca has many bones and no particular recipes have been created around it. It is not a highly prized fish, although, oddly enough, during the Renaissance it was considered a great delicacy, so much so that a large roach was sent to the Vatican every year for the Pope's Easter dinner. PLATINA grills roach and dresses them with SALSA VERDE.

Latini, Antonio
1641–97

Born in Le Marche in a very humble family, Latini educated himself and climbed up the social scale, working in the kitchens of various prelates, including that of Cardinal Barberini in Rome, and finishing his career in Naples as the steward (*scalco*) to the Minister Don Stefano Carillo y Salcedo. There he wrote *Lo Scalco alla Moderna*: the first volume, published in 1692, was about all the food and the meat dishes for *i giorni di grasso* – festive days – and the second volume, published in 1694, covered all the food for *i giorni di magro* – 'lean' days, when fish but no meat was eaten. Latini was the first cookery writer to write a recipe for tomato sauce – but not with pasta – and for SORBETTI and GELATI. His tomato sauce also contains chilli, a combination of ingredients that he must have learned in Naples, which was under Spanish rule at the time. *Lo Scalco alla Moderna* is the last book to exemplify the hegemony of Italian cooking; after that the sceptre passed to France, beginning with the publication of La Varenne's *Le Cuisinier François* in 1651.

latte
milk

Italians are not great milk-drinkers, nor are there many Italian dishes based on milk. The most common use of milk is in peasant soups, mostly from Lombardy and Piedmont. The most unusual of the recipes using milk is *maiale al latte* (pork cooked in milk), for which the recipe is given here.

Rice is cooked in milk and butter is added at the end, sometimes with a flavouring of cinnamon and/or nutmeg, and it can be savoury or sweet. Milk is also used for a number of puddings, although nowadays it is often replaced partly or wholly by cream.

[see recipe on page 198]

lattemiele
whipped sweet cream

Lattemiele is a very old preparation; it is described by PLATINA and mentioned in a wedding menu of the 16th century. The milk in the southern part of Lombardy used to be so thick that when shaken it was like whipped cream. In the old days honey and cinnamon were added, although now sugar has replaced the honey. Nowadays the word is hardly used. It sometimes refers to whipped cream in Lombardy or Emilia.

lattuga
lettuce

The most common varieties grown in Italy today are: *romana* (cos), *lattuga a cappuccio* (round) and *ricciolina* (salad bowl or curly lettuce). This last variety is also known as *la lollo*, short for Lollobrigida – after the actress Gina Lollobrigida – because of the attractive curves of its leaves. Romana, which is the most popular, is the crispest of all traditional lettuces and the best for

salads. Nowadays crisp varieties of cabbage shape
are also cultivated.

Lettuce is also used in cooking. Soups are
made with it, the oldest surviving recipe going
back to PLATINA, who suggests cooking it with
eggs and AGRESTO. This recipe has an interesting
similarity to a Greek recipe in which cos lettuce is
added to stewing lamb together with beaten eggs
and lemon juice. Vincenzo CORRADO preferred his
lettuces blanched and dressed with a pounded
mixture of tarragon, anchovies and capers diluted
in oil and vinegar. He lists six recipes for stuffed
lettuce, of which my favourite is the one in
prosciutto sauce. The lettuce is stuffed with a
'salpicon of sweetbreads, mushrooms, truffles,
onions and herbs, bound with eggs and sautéed
in veal fat and chopped prosciutto. Stuffed, they
are cooked in a *colì* of prosciutto.' Another recipe,
lattughe alla certosina, suggests a stuffing made with
fish, anchovies, herbs and spices, mixed with a
puree of peas.

Lattughe ripiene is a traditional dish still made
in Liguria. The inner leaves of a round lettuce
are stuffed with a mixture of brain, sweetbread,
mushroom, garlic, parsley and breadcrumbs. The
little bunches are tied at the top with string and
braised in meat stock, with which they are served.
A simpler stuffing can also be made with chopped
herbs, eggs and grated PECORINO and Parmesan.

A recipe from Rome combines lettuce with
beans. The dried beans, previously soaked and
boiled, are sautéed in olive oil with the lettuce and
then tomatoes are added.

lauro or alloro
bay

The leaves of the sweet lauro, a native of the
Mediterranean, are used to flavour meat dishes,
broths, fish soups, fish and meat stews and many
other dishes. The leaves are usually removed
before serving.

In Sicily a dish is made with mild sausages
lying on a bed of branches of lauro. It is baked
in the oven for 10 minutes or so, then a layer of
sliced oranges is placed on top and baked for a
further 15 minutes. In Umbria a traditional tomato
sauce for pasta contains a dozen bay leaves and a
good pinch of cinnamon.

lavarello
see GOREGONE

Lazio

The cooking of Lazio could simply be called the
cooking of Rome which is, in every sense, the centre
of the region today as it was 2,000 years ago.

Roman banquets were both a gastronomic
and theatrical experience. The same was true
during the Renaissance, when many popes were
happy to enjoy the pleasures of the world – and
among these good food ranked high. Architects

CONTINUES ON PAGE 200

197

LAZIO

L.Bolsena

Viterbo•

Rieti•

•Civitavecchia

Rome•

•Frosinone

•Latina

TYRRHENIAN
SEA

maiale al latte
loin of pork braised in milk

Serves 6

1kg/2¼lb boned loin of pork, rindless but with a thin layer of fat, tied in several places

4 tbsp vegetable oil

3 cloves

a pinch of ground cinnamon

1 sprig of fresh rosemary

2 garlic cloves, bruised

1 tsp coarse sea salt

4 or 5 black peppercorns, crushed

1 bay leaf

25g/1oz/2 tbsp unsalted butter

300ml/10fl oz/1¼ cups full-fat (whole) milk

salt and freshly ground black pepper

Many regions claim to have invented this excellent dish. This version is particularly suitable for today's less flavoursome pork.

Put the pork in a dish and add half the oil, the cloves, cinnamon, rosemary, garlic, sea salt, peppercorns and bay leaf. Coat the pork all over in the marinade and leave for about 8 hours in a cool place (not in the refrigerator unless it is hot). Turn occasionally.

Pat the meat dry. Heat the butter and the remaining oil in a heavy casserole into which the pork will fit snugly. When the foam begins to subside, add the meat and brown well on all sides.

Heat the milk to boiling point, then pour it slowly over the meat. Sprinkle with salt and pepper, place the lid slightly askew on the pan and cook for about 2 hours at a steady, low simmer. Turn the meat over and baste every 20 minutes or so. By the end of cooking the milk should be a rich dark golden colour, and quite thick. If it is too pale by the time the meat is done, boil briskly without the lid until it darkens and thickens.

Transfer the meat to a wooden board, cover with foil and leave to rest for 10 minutes or so.

Skim as much fat as you can from the surface of the sauce, add 2 tablespoons hot water and boil over a high heat for about 2 minutes, scraping the bottom of the pan with a metal spoon to loosen the cooking residue. Taste and adjust the seasoning.

Remove the string, carve the pork into 1cm/½in slices and arrange on a warmed serving dish. Spoon the sauce over the pork, or spoon over a little of the sauce and serve the rest separately in a warmed sauceboat.

were employed to make *trionfi della tavola*, table decorations made of sugar and marzipan depicting deities, fountains, flowers etc. Great chefs, some of whom wrote about their work, were in charge of the meals, which certainly often recalled the banquets of Imperial Rome in their lavishness, if not their licentiousness.

A dish that is still prepared at carnival time, and which better than most others illustrates the richness of the baroque cuisine of papal Rome, is the PASTICCIO *di maccheroni*. This is a sweet and savoury macaroni pie, eaten as a first course. Its filling consists of macaroni, cut into short lengths, dressed with meat juices, Parmesan and a RAGÙ of chicken livers, tiny rissoles and pieces of sausage. A layer of CREMA PASTICCERA is spread on top of the macaroni before it is sealed with a lid of sweet pastry.

Throughout history, the cooking of Rome seems to have been either grand and opulent or simple and down to earth. The best-loved foods were bread, cheese, olives, fresh vegetables and wild salads, all locally produced. Pasta features prominently in the popular cooking of Rome, which includes some of the best pasta recipes, such as CARBONARA, AMATRICIANA and PUTTANESCA.

The Roman countryside, with its volcanic soil, is ideal for the cultivation of vegetables. A passage in *Roba di Roma* (*Things of Rome*), written in 1863 by William Wetmore Story, an American Italophile, illustrates the wealth of a Roman vegetable market: 'Heaps of delicate, crisp lettuces and celery, enormous cabbages and pumpkins big enough to make Cinderella's carriage, creamy cauliflowers, bristling artichokes, clusters of garlic and onions, red tomatoes, and monstrous red and yellow fingers of beets and carrots, are tumbled on to the pavement. Huge baskets run over with potatoes, yellow cocuzzi, and infant pumpkins or zucchette. In some of these baskets may be seen dried mushrooms, of which the Italians make great use in the winter, and excellent truffles to cause the epicure's mouth to water.' The stalls in Campo dei Fiori, and other local markets, are still today as those described by Wetmore Story.

Artichokes are the Roman vegetable par excellence; they are used in many preparations, of which *carciofi alla giudia* is the best known.

A great variety of raw vegetables is set on the table in a large dish for PINZIMONIO, a dip of olive oil, salt and pepper. MISTICANZA, wild asparagus and LUPPOLI appear on Roman tables in great abundance as soon as spring arrives.

The Romans are adept at making succulent dishes from simple ingredients. *Gnocchi alla romana* (see recipe on page 388), for instance, are made from semolina, milk and eggs. In the hands of the Romans, however, they become 'a dream of succulent lightness', as Waverley Root describes them in *The Food of Italy*. The same combination of utter simplicity and exquisite delicacy is found in STRACCIATELLA, the best-known Roman soup. Roman FRITTATE are usually enriched with all sorts of vegetables or cheeses such as ricotta, mozzarella or pecorino. Another well-known Roman dish made from simple ingredients is SALTIMBOCCA.

The Romans also have a talent for creating appetizing dishes out of offal, for instance, CORATELLA *di abbacchio* and the delicate PAGLIATA.

Along the coast there are red mullet, large and small octopus, as well as crustaceans, including the highly prized MAZZANCOLLE. The volcanic lake of Bolsena is famous for its eels. When, years ago, I lunched at an unpretentious trattoria in Marta, on the shore of the lake, I could choose among five different ways my eel could be cooked: roasted, alla CACCIATORA, in sweet and sour sauce, on the spit or sautéed with bay leaves. I wondered then which method the French pope, Martin IV, would have chosen, his fondness for eels from Lake Bolsena having been mentioned by the poet Dante. To make their flesh more tasty, his eels, just out of the lake, were drowned in Vernaccia wine before being cooked. The Romans are also great lovers of BACCALÀ and STOCCAFISSO, which are sold ready for cooking in most *salumerie* (delicatessens).

Even down to puddings, the cuisine has not changed much through the centuries. In local trattorie they still serve the MARITOZZI and the BUDINO *di ricotta* that appeared in the inns of the 15th century. Other favourites are stuffed pastries and fritters, usually containing ricotta. And at carnival time, Rome has its *frappe* just as Milan has its CHIACCHIERE and Venice its GALANI.

legumi
legumes or pulses

The most common legumes are peas, beans, lentils, broad beans, chickpeas and vetches, all eaten widely and in abundance.

Legumes have long been a staple peasant food but they have now been elevated to the tables of the greatest restaurants, whose chefs have discovered their excellence, their nutritious and health-giving properties and their versatility.

A basically peasant recipe has been adapted by the great Milanese chef Gualtiero Marchesi to create a dish in which a puree of beans, cooked with the usual herbs and flavourings, forms the basis of a dish of tubular pasta dressed with olive oil. The mixture of pasta and legumes is traditional in southern cooking, just as rice with beans or lentils have featured in northern cooking all through the centuries. Bread often replaces pasta and rice, as in the INCAPRIATA from Puglia, made from a puree of broad beans and chunks of local bread, dressed with the rich local olive oil.

Legumes were of great importance during the Middle Ages. Taxes were paid with chickpeas and beans were accepted as alimony for wives and children. Food historian Giovanni Goria considers that there was 'a gradation of nobility among the legumi: vetches, beans and chickpeas were present mostly in peasant cooking, broad beans stood in the middle, while peas and lentils were the favourites on the tables of the rich.

lenticchia
lentil

This very popular pulse is enjoyed throughout Italy. The kind eaten are the continental lentils, which keep their shape when cooked. They grow in many regions of Italy, although the best come from Abruzzo and Umbria. The lentils from Castelluccio, a small hill town east of Spoleto in Umbria, are the most highly regarded. They are tiny, beige-green lentils that have a sweeter yet fuller flavour than others. Unlike other pulses, lenticchie do not need soaking unless they have been stored for too long.

There are many different ways to cook lentils, in soups or as vegetables. One soup from Abruzzo mixes boiled lentils with chestnuts. The cooked chestnuts are first sautéed in an earthenware pot in olive oil, together with all the herbs available, plus chilli to taste and some tomato sauce. The cooked lentils and their water are then added to this mixture, and the soup is served with slices of fried bread. In contrast, the lentil soup from Bologna is delicacy itself: the lentils are pureed with boiled chicken and then diluted with chicken stock. In Campania, in a dish simply called *pasta e lenticchie*, 2 tablespoons of olive oil, 2 garlic cloves and a few chopped tomatoes are added to the nearly cooked lentils, together with some water. When the water boils, some smallish pasta is added and the result is a delicious thick soup over which a splash of best olive oil is poured just before serving.

The recipe given here is for *lenticchie in* UMIDO, which is the way we always cooked them in my family. We ate them with ZAMPONE – and what a meal that is. In many regions lentils are eaten at midnight on New Year's Eve, or on New Year's Day, because there is a superstition that they bring wealth in the year to come.

Lentils have been eaten for thousands of years – although both PLATINA and Pisanelli, a Bolognese doctor, condemned them as unhealthy and liable to cause all sorts of diseases. However, these

201

condemnations of pulses, and of other peasant food, might well have derived from the fact that food was categorized as either light and delicate, and therefore suited to the refined palates of the upper classes, or coarse and heavy – like pulses – for the plebs. Such was the food snobbery of the 16th century.

 [see recipe below]

Leonardi, Francesco
18th-century chef

Francesco Leonardi and Vincenzo CORRADO were the two great chefs who, in the second half of the 18th century, gave a much-needed new impulse to the art of cooking in Italy. Leonardi and Corrado were both Neapolitan, and this was a time when Naples was at its apogee, the court of the Bourbons of Naples being even more extravagant than that of the Bourbons of Versailles.

After a time as chef to the Neapolitan aristocracy, Leonardi became steward of the imperial household of Catherine II, Empress of All the Russias – also known as Catherine the Great. Over his 40-year career he learnt a great deal about the cooking techniques and ingredients of other European cuisines. When back in his beloved Naples, for whose climate he had pined all through his years on the Neva, he settled down to write his masterpiece, *L'Apicio Moderno ossia l'Arte di Apprestare Ogni Sorta di Vivanda* (*The Modern Apicius, that is to say the Art of Preparing Every Kind of Food*). This title tells exactly what the book is: a gastronomic encyclopedia, divided into six volumes, beginning with a preface tracing the history of Italian cooking and ending with a glossary of French terms.

In the preface, Leonardi calls cooking 'this seducer of taste, this wantonness of good eating', and all through his recipes are testimony to this description. Although quite a few of the recipes are from other countries, Leonardi is keen to point out

lenticchie in umido
stewed lentils

Serves 4

3 tbsp olive oil
50g/1¾oz unsmoked pancetta, diced
1 small onion, very finely chopped
4–5 fresh sage leaves
350g/12oz/generous 1¾ cups Castelluccio or Puy lentils, rinsed and drained
about 1 litre/1¾ pints/4 cups meat stock (page 61), chicken stock or vegetable stock
2 tbsp wine vinegar
salt and freshly ground black pepper

This is one of the many classic recipes for LENTICCHIE in umido, the traditional accompaniment to COTECHINO sausage. Some cooks add a tablespoon of tomato puree to the lentils while they are sautéing, and then cook the lentils in water.

Put the olive oil and pancetta in a heavy saucepan and heat for 5 minutes, stirring frequently. Add the onion and sage and sauté for another 5 minutes.

Throw in the lentils and stir to coat them in the fat, then pour in about 600ml/20fl oz/2½ cups of the stock. Partially cover with a lid and simmer for about 10 minutes. Mix in the vinegar and continue simmering until the lentils are tender and nearly all the liquid has been absorbed. You may need to add more stock as the lentils cook. Add salt and pepper to taste.

the merits of Italian regional cooking. Along with Corrado he was the first writer to give the recently accepted tomato a place in the *grande cucina*.

Leonardi's recipes and methods are clear and well set out, although quantities are not always given. This one, for prawns à l'italienne, could have been written yesterday:

'Remove the small claws and beards from some live prawns and put them in a pot with a little oil, 1 or 2 glasses of white wine, the juice of 1 or ½ lemon, parsley, spring onion, shalot [sic], a touch of garlic, a little tarragon and basil, everything chopped, salt and ground pepper; boil at a lively heat and reduce until only a little sauce is left. Place them nicely on a dish and sprinkle them everywhere with the sauce and serve.'

lepre
hare

The Romans, great lovers of good food, appreciated hare which, together with pork, was their favourite meat. APICIUS lists 12 recipes for hare, more than for any other single food. In Roman times hare was first marinated and then often boiled before being braised with spices, herbs, dried fruits and nuts. A delicious-sounding recipe calls for a hare to be boned and stuffed with oregano, chicken livers, brains, minced beef and eggs to bind. The hare is wrapped in caul fat and slowly roasted. It is served with a sauce of crushed pepper and lovage moistened with stock. Hare was also smoked in Roman times.

Hare was not often included in grand Renaissance banquets and there are not many recipes from that period. In the 16th century, Domenico Romoli wrote the first recipe for the famous Tuscan dish PAPPARDELLE *con la lepre*, which sounds somewhat unappetizing, the hare being boiled with pork in the blood of both animals – quite different from the modern version of this delicious dish.

In the 18th and 19th centuries hare appears again in the recipes of grand households, as we can see in *Il Cuoco Galante* by Vincenzo CORRADO and *Nuovo Cuoco Milanese* by Giovanni LURASCHI. One of the recipes in Luraschi's book, *lepre all'imperiale di roccoco*, is, as its name implies, a very elaborate affair. The boned hare is stuffed with a boned partridge, the cooked udder of a young heifer and a piece of pig's back fat – both minced – a piece of cured tongue cut into strips and three or four truffles. The hare is larded and then braised in wine in the oven. The deglazed and strained juices are reduced and poured over the hare, accompanied by large croutons. In nearly all of his recipes Luraschi calls for the hare to be marinated. He also gives details on how to choose a good hare, which, he says, must be young and fat. Its teeth must be short and white and its snout soft and tender.

Hare is still very popular in northern and central Italy. In the north it is usually stewed in wine – *lepre in salmì* (see recipe on page 368) – following the local tradition of slow cooking, and served with polenta. Many recipes for braised hare call for the addition of the animal's blood, this giving the stronger taste that is often required. In central Italy a young hare is roasted on the spit or in the oven. The Tuscans, mad hunters of everything that runs or flies, have a delicious recipe, *lepre in dolce e forte*. The hare is stewed in wine with onion, celery, carrot, herbs, garlic and tomatoes. At the end, a sweet and sour sauce is poured over it. The sauce is made with biscuits from Siena, called *cavallucci*, containing walnuts and spices. These are crumbled and mixed with sultanas, orange and citron peel, pine nuts and cocoa powder, all moistened with vinegar and water.

lesso
boiled

As an adjective, lesso describes how the food is cooked. *Pesce lesso* is boiled fish, *verdure lesse* are boiled vegetables, *patate lesse* are boiled potatoes.

203

As a noun, it has a similar meaning to BOLLITO, but it usually refers to a dish made with only one piece of meat. The Lombard lesso is possibly the best-known: it is a joint of beef, usually boned, cooked in simmering water containing an onion stuck with one or two cloves, a celery stalk, a carrot and some parsley stalks. The carved meat is moistened with its own stock and accompanied by boiled potatoes and carrots. SALSA VERDE and MOSTARDA di frutta are the most common accompanying sauces.

lievito naturale or casalingo
sour dough

This is a piece of bread dough kept moistened with water and used as a starter for the next batch of bread. Sour dough has now been largely replaced by *lievito di birra* (bakers' yeast). However, it is still used in the country when its particular flavour is needed for the making of many kinds of local bread.

Liguria

This region is set like a narrow arch over the northern part of the Mediterranean, spanning 270km/170 miles from the Pont St Louis on the French frontier to the River Magra, its border with Tuscany. The Ligurians live between the sea and the mountains that rise steeply a few kilometres inland, and in this narrow strip they have created one of the most luscious vegetable gardens in Europe. They have been helped by a temperate climate and

the beneficial effect of the sea air on the plants. The result is to be seen in the abundance of wild salads and aromatic herbs of every species that is native to the Mediterranean.

The fruits of the Ligurian soil have always taken pride of place in the local cooking. Meat and cereals were imported from Piedmont and Provence; on the peasant's table the only meat that appeared was rabbit.

Olive trees are abundant and very productive on the western riviera, the oil being delicate, sweet, pale in colour and of a taste that blends with every dish. Olive oil is the only fat used in the local cooking: it dresses the many vegetable dishes for which the region is so well known.

FOCACCIA provides a good example of the qualities to be found in the local cuisine. It is bread dough covered with sliced onions, stuffed with soft local cheese or sprinkled with olive pulp from the first pressing. Simple it may be, but in Liguria focaccia reaches perfection. This quality of 'just rightness' is achieved by finding the perfect balance between one flavour and another, and the precise use of ingredients. The end result is to transform a basic cuisine into a sophisticated demonstration of how to combine harmonizing elements. The supreme example of this is PESTO, a simple sauce, yet one that is really delicious only

LIGURIA

Genoa
Savona
La Spezia
Magra
LIGURIAN SEA
San Remo

when made with the local basil, and when the ingredients pounded in the mortar are precisely balanced. Other examples of this perfect balance are found in the PREBOGGION, and in all the stuffings for vegetables.

Oddly enough, the cooking of a region with such a long coastline is not geared towards fish. The Ligurian sea yields a poor harvest, but the Genoese, who are thrifty and hard-working people, have learnt to make the best of what there is. They have created delicious dishes, such as mackerel with onions (see recipe on page 393), out of second-quality fish. Their CIUPPIN, a fish soup, is often pureed so as to eliminate the mass of bones from the poorer fish – and how delicious it is! There are many molluscs; the best are gathered in the Gulf of La Spezia, where there are large mussel farms as well as wild specimens. Also found there are the much sought-after TARTUFI DI MARE. The most sumptuous preparation based on fish is CAPPON MAGRO and the most humble recipes

CONTINUES OVERLEAF

branzino alla rivierasca coi carciofi
sea bass with artichokes

Serves 4

4–6 globe artichokes

½ lemon

3 tbsp lemon juice

4 tbsp olive oil

salt and freshly ground black pepper

1 sea bass, about 900g/2lb, scaled and cleaned, but with head and tail on, rinsed in cold water

1 tsp rosemary needles

An easy and excellent recipe from the Ligurian Riviera, which combines two of the favourite local foods. This version comes from Marcella Hazan's *The Second Classic Italian Cookbook*.

Preheat the oven to 220°C/425°F/Gas Mark 7.

Trim the artichokes, keeping only the tender leaves and the heart. Rub each artichoke with the lemon half each time you cut it, to prevent it turning black. Cut each artichoke in four lengthways, remove the soft purple curling leaves with prickly tips and cut away the fuzzy 'choke' beneath them. Slice the artichoke quarters lengthways into the thinnest possible slices and sprinkle a few drops of lemon juice over them.

Mix the olive oil, lemon juice, salt and pepper in a small bowl and set aside.

Pat the fish dry with kitchen paper and place it in a rectangular baking dish just large enough to contain it. Add the artichokes and three-quarters of the oil and lemon juice mixture. Sprinkle the rosemary over the fish. Turn the artichoke slices so they are all coated with juice and stuff some of the artichokes into the fish's cavity. Coat the fish with the remaining oil and lemon mixture and place it in the upper third of the oven. After 20 minutes, baste the fish and stir the artichokes. Bake for another 15–20 minutes, then transfer the fish to a warmed serving dish. This has to be done very carefully, otherwise the fish will break. Probably the best way is to lift it with two spatulas, one in each hand.

Spread the artichokes around the fish, pour over it all the juices from the baking dish and serve immediately.

205

are those for BACCALÀ and STOCCAFISSO, of which the Genoese are particularly fond.

In Liguria even the puddings are based on local ingredients. The spices that the Genoese brought from the East to Europe on their ships never touched their food. When at home, they made use of fresh, locally grown fruits and learnt from the Arabs how to crystallize them. They became such experts that during the 19th century European royal houses kept a purveyor of candied fruits in Genoa. Candied fruit, sultanas and pine nuts, all local products, appear in most of their sweets, from the rich dome-shaped PANDOLCE to the delicate fried ravioli stuffed with bone marrow, candied pumpkin and orange and citron peel.

[see recipe on page 205]

limone
lemon

For me the lemon tree is the most beautiful tree there is, magical in the way that it can produce both flowers and fruit three times a year. The flowers, known as *zagara*, have a pungent yet delicate fragrance; they contain essential oils used in the production of eau de Cologne.

The fruit was used for its aromatic properties in Roman times and the Middle Ages as well as during the Renaissance. Lemons have also been used in medicine since ancient times. The Egyptians prescribed the juice of lemons to fight fever, the Arabs to cure cardiac diseases, and during the Renaissance it was used to prepare syrups to ward off the plague. Lemon juice still

206

tagliatelle al limone e erbe odorose
tagliatelle with a lemon and herb dressing

Serves 4

40g/1 ½oz/3 tbsp unsalted butter

grated rind and juice of 1 organic or unwaxed lemon

3 tbsp chopped mixed fresh herbs, such as parsley, sage, rosemary and chives

150ml/5fl oz/²/³ cup double (heavy) cream

salt and freshly ground black pepper

egg pasta (page 282) made with 300g/10½oz/scant 2½ cups Italian 00 flour and 3 large eggs and cut into TAGLIATELLE, or 500g/1lb 2oz fresh tagliatelle or 350g/12oz dried egg tagliatelle

50g/1¾oz Parmesan cheese, grated

This is based on an old Piedmontese recipe. The herbs can be any you have to hand, as long as there is a good selection.

Melt the butter in a small heavy saucepan. Add the lemon rind, the herbs, cream and salt and pepper. Bring slowly to the boil and simmer, stirring constantly, for a couple of minutes. Add the lemon juice and bring back to the boil, then take the pan off the heat and keep warm.

Cook the tagliatelle in plenty of boiling salted water until al dente. Reserve a cupful of the pasta water. Drain, but do not overdrain, and then transfer to a warmed bowl.

Dress the pasta with the sauce and a sprinkling of Parmesan. Add a little of the reserved water if necessary. Toss very well and serve immediately, with the remaining cheese handed round at the table.

has a place in medicine, being used, among other things, as an antacid, an anti-emetic, an anti-arthritic and against scurvy.

It is, of course, in the culinary world that the lemon plays its most important role, being an essential ingredient in many dishes. Among these are *pollo al limone* (chicken with a lemon stuck inside), VITELLO TONNATO, OSSOBUCO and FRITTURA PICCATA. Fish dishes cry out for lemon juice. Can you imagine fresh raw anchovies that are not first marinated in lemon juice, or a fish baked with herbs without those few drops squeezed from a lemon? And FRITTO MISTO DI MARE is always served with lemon.

A favourite dish of mine is *tagliatelle al limone*: the pasta is dressed with melted butter flavoured with lemon juice, cream and Parmesan. The recipe is given here.

Sweets, cakes and pastries all benefit from a hint of grated lemon rind. On a hot summer's day, a GELATO *al limone* is the best gelato there is, and a SPREMUTA *di limone* – freshly squeezed lemon juice – the most thirst-quenching drink. A GRANITA *al limone* combines gelato and spremuta in a most satisfying way.

Buy only organic or unwaxed lemons and choose thin-skinned ones, not too hard and with a smooth skin. Before using, warm the lemon for no more than 20 seconds in the microwave oven on Low: this way you will get more juice out of it.

[see recipe on facing page]

lingua
tongue

Tongue is eaten fresh or pickled (cured). If fresh, it is that of an ox, a pig or more often a calf, while pickled tongue is usually that of a young OX, a VITELLONE.

Tongue is more often bought and served fresh than pickled. There are several recipes from Piedmont and Lombardy, mostly for ox tongue.

In one of the few recipes for pig's tongue from northern Italy, the tongue, boiled and peeled, is served with a sauce made with onion, celery, parsley, thyme, tomatoes, capers, vinegar and stock which is thickened with flour and flavoured with a small piece of chilli. In some places in Piedmont one can still find sliced sheep's tongues coated in batter and fried. This dish is based on an 18th-century recipe which must be of French origin.

It is the tongue of a calf or an ox, however, that is most frequently cooked at home. An excellent recipe from Umbria, *lingua in agrodolce*, is quoted by Guglielma Corsi in her book *Un Secolo di Cucina Umbra*. The calf's tongue is boiled and peeled, then sliced and lightly sautéed in butter and meat juice. The accompanying sauce is made with vinegar, sugar, sultanas, cinnamon, cocoa, candied citron, pine nuts and orange rind cut into tiny pieces. The mixture is boiled until the sugar has dissolved, and then poured over the tongue. It is left to cool and served cold the next day.

In an old Milanese recipe, an ox tongue is boiled and peeled and then sliced and finished in a SOFFRITTO of butter, onion, parsley and carrot, to which stock and green olives are added. Some of the olives are cut into strips and others pounded.

Tongue used always to be cured at home and this is still sometimes done. Pickled tongue is cured with saltpetre and spices, boiled, curled and pressed; this is the tongue sold in many delicatessens, and in grocers and supermarkets in vacuum packs. However, the best delicatessens sell tongues that are not curled and pressed but left in their original shape, though with all the root removed.

Pickled tongue can also be bought raw and boiled at home. The tongue is cooked in water flavoured with onion, celery, carrots and other herbs and spices. After simmering for between 2 hours (for calf's tongue) and 4½ hours (for ox tongue), it is ready. Halfway through the tongue is peeled and then put back into the liquid to finish cooking. Tongue is not spoiled by being cooked for a long time, so it is always safer to err on the side of longer cooking. The root is removed and used by the thrifty cook to make stuffings and rissoles. The peeled tongue is served hot with SALSA VERDE or other sauces, or it is left to cool in its original shape and served with salad.

In Tuscany, Emilia and Umbria you can sometimes find wild boar's tongues which have been smoked. These are a great delicacy.

linguine
a pasta

Long flat pasta, about 3–4mm/⅛in wide. Linguine, which are also called *bavette* by some manufacturers, can be used instead of spaghetti when the sauce does not necessarily call for homemade pasta. Traditionally, linguine are dressed with an oil-based sauce – such as garlic, oil and chilli – or with octopus or cuttlefish.

[see recipe below]

Lombardia
Lombardy

The large region of northern Italy has always known wealth. The land is rich and the people are hard-working and rich. However, until the 20th century, the Lombard labourer, obedient and servile, lived a very oppressed life, which was reflected in what he ate. This, particularly in the northern areas, was polenta every day, often with nothing else. This polenta was not only made from maize, as it is today, but also from spelt, millet and buckwheat, or from a mixture of different flours. Meat was so rarely eaten that in some localities Christmas was called *el dí de mangiá la carna* – the day on which meat is eaten.

Soups were also part of the regular diet, and we owe the now famous MINESTRONE to the resourcefulness of the region's housewives, who added pork rind and rice to the usual beans and seasonal vegetables. Soups, still traditionally eaten most days in winter, are made with everything from chestnuts to leeks, cauliflower, parsley, chicken livers, eggs and bread, all cooked in a nourishing stock. In my childhood home in Milan, my very Lombard father demanded soup every night as a first course – something that I hated, but had to eat, even if only two spoonfuls.

The use of rice to make risotto was a later development. It originated in the households of rich gourmets who were devising new and better rice dishes, just as today they are inventing new recipes around the more fashionable pasta.

linguine all'aglio, olio e peperoncino
pasta with garlic, oil and chilli

Serves 4
350g/12oz dried linguine or spaghetti
salt
5 tbsp extra virgin olive oil
3 garlic cloves, sliced
½–1 tsp crushed dried chillies

One of the best possible ways to serve LINGUINE is with this simplest of all dressings, which takes just a few minutes to prepare.

Cook the pasta in plenty of boiling salted water until al dente.

Meanwhile, heat the oil, garlic and chillies in a large heavy frying pan and sauté for 1 minute.

Drain the pasta, then immediately turn it into the frying pan. Stir-fry for about 1 minute, then serve immediately.

Pasta was rarely eaten in Lombardy until the 1950s, and there are only two traditional recipes. These are *ravioli di zucca* (pumpkin ravioli) from Mantua, and PIZZOCCHERI from Valtellina. The contrast between these two dishes, the first rich and opulent like the Renaissance that created it, the other as poor and humble as the forgotten northern valleys where it originated, typifies the complexity of the Lombard cuisine.

In fact there are almost as many cuisines as there are provinces in the region — of which there are 12. Certain common elements, however, link these cuisines together. Meat is braised or stewed rather than grilled or roasted: this reflects the Austrian influence on Lombard cooking. Green vegetables are not traditional food. And, most importantly, butter is the traditional cooking fat (although it has now been partly or mostly replaced by the 'healthier' olive oil). Other dairy products are eaten throughout Lombardy and milk is used in soups and puddings. Cream appears in many Milanese dishes, more so than in the food of any other region.

This use of cream is partly the result of a strong link between Milanese and French cooking. Over the centuries, France dominated Lombardy for long periods. French dishes were so popular in the 19th century that the Milanese aristocrats and wealthy bourgeois, who often found their social pleasures in Paris, took their cooks with them so that they could learn the finer points of the French cuisine from French chefs. The result, in modern-day Milan, is an exact and sophisticated cuisine. It is often only in private houses that you will eat a proper OSSOBUCO or a crisp and juicy COSTOLETTA. Only there, also, will you find a VITELLO TONNATO made without mayonnaise so that the sauce is not too rich and heavy.

The other pillar of Milanese cooking is *el stuvaa* – STUFATO in standard Italian – the traditional meat course of a Sunday lunch, a piece of beef stewed at length with spices, vegetables and wine.

The cooking of Milan stretches out towards the foothills of the Alps to embrace Brianza, famous for its sausages, SALAME and guinea fowl cooked in clay. Further east towards Veneto, polenta reigns supreme, not by itself as in the past, but as the accompaniment to succulent meat and fish dishes made with sauces that the polenta absorbs, itself becoming part of the dish. Polenta is also served with an array of local cheeses. Along Lake Garda the climate changes, as does the gastronomic scene. The cooking becomes lighter and fresher and the countryside is dotted with the sparkling green of the lemon and citron groves, as well as the silvery grey of the olive trees.

Of all Lombard towns, it is Mantua that best fulfils the expectations of its visitors. Standing apart from the usual tourist route, set in a romantic and misty valley, Mantua is rich both in art and in local dishes. Both have the same origin – the court of the Gonzagas. It was at their lavish banquets that ANOLINI stuffed with capon meat, spices and herbs were served, and where the local black and white truffles made the rich TIMBALLI even more luxurious. The white truffles, found along the River Po, once made a peasant dish – risotto with wild duck – worthy of a pope.

Another peasant dish linked to a famous historical personage is found in Pavia, where Francis I of France was served the now famous ZUPPA ALLA PAVESE. And Pavia's most famous risotto is linked to the monks of its Carthusian monastery: the RISOTTO ALLA CERTOSINA uses freshwater shrimps from the nearby rivers. The marshy plains around Pavia breed the best frogs, and these are served 'in GUAZZETTO' in the local trattorie.

I have left to the end this region's most important contribution to the gastronomy of Italy: i formaggi – the cheeses. The cattle that feed on the rich pastures of Lombardy provide a great number of excellent cheeses. Besides the world-famous GORGONZOLA and BEL PAESE, there are CRESCENZA,

QUARTIROLO, GRANA lodigiano, BITTO, TALEGGIO, BAGOSS and CAPRINI – which, although caprini means goat cheese, are here made with cow's milk, many of them still produced only on farms and only found locally – and the now world-famous MASCARPONE.

Last, but not least, I must mention the SALUMI of Lombardy, of which the salame di Varzi and the salame Milano are the most popular, along with the LUGANEGA sausage. BRESAOLA, air-cured fillet of beef, is one of the great products of Valtellina, as are violini, which are air-dried and salted thighs or shoulders of goat, an outstanding and quite rare product, poetically called violins because of their shape.

 [see recipe below]

lombata
a large cut of meat

The back of a calf or an ox from its shoulders to its haunch, with or without the bone. It is a term that

costolette alla milanese
milanese veal chops

Serves 6

6 veal chops

2 large eggs, lightly beaten

150–200g/5½–7oz/about 2 cups dried white breadcrumbs

150g/5½oz/generous ½ cup unsalted butter

salt

lemon wedges, to garnish

This is my translation of Ada BONI's classic recipe published in her book Cucina Regionale Italiana.

To prepare the chops, trim them at the point where the rib meets the backbone. Flatten them down a little and make small cuts all around them so that they will not shrink in cooking. Coat the chops in the beaten egg, then in the breadcrumbs, pressing the crumbs firmly into the meat with your hands.

Heat the butter in a frying pan that is large enough to hold the chops in a single layer. When the butter begins to colour, add the chops and cook over a lively heat until a crust is formed on the underside – about 3 minutes. Turn them over, turn the heat down and cook for 5 minutes. Season with salt and transfer the chops to a warmed serving dish. Garnish with lemon wedges to serve.

includes many different cuts. Fillet, cutlets, sirloin are all part of a lombata, and recipes are written for the individual cuts. That said, because of the various regional names of dishes, there are often references to lombata as a dish cooked in a special way, rather than meaning a butcher's cut.

lombatine
boneless veal or pork steaks

Taken from the loin, these are prepared in many ways – for example the veal lombatine in a buttery sauce and the pork in a tomato sauce. In Naples, pork steaks are cooked with peppers that have been previously grilled and peeled. I like to cook them as I cook my OSSOBUCO, without a tomato sauce.

lombo or lonza
loin of pork

This is the part of a pig's back from its shoulders to its haunch. Lombo is usually sold without the skin, which is a pity since, when properly scored, the skin is one of the tastiest parts.

Boned pork loin is usually roasted in the oven, in a little oil, with herbs. In Tuscany this dish is called ARISTA. The loin is also used for pot roasts and for *maiale al latte* (see recipe on page 198).

lonza
a salame

A regional name for an air-cured SALAME made from the leg muscle of a pig. This salame is found only in Le Marche and Umbria, where it is made in a small artisan way for family consumption.

luccio
pike

A freshwater fish but one that can sometimes be found in the sea at river mouths. The pike is large and savage. It is an excellent fish, although the big specimens are full of bones. For this reason, pike is used to make quenelles.

The best pike are found in the rivers and lakes of Umbria, Lazio and Lombardy. The recipes from Lombardy are straightforward, and less original than those from central Italy, the pike being served boiled with a hot piquant sauce based on capers and anchovies.

There is an interesting recipe in *La Buona Vera Cucina Italiana* by CARNACINA and Veronelli. In their *luccio alla perugina*, from Umbria, the pike is placed on a bed of wild mushrooms and onions and covered with equal quantities of wine and water. Then nearly half a litre of milk and some butter are added. When cooked, the fish is sprinkled generously with lemon juice.

Another recipe from central Italy calls for the pike to be cut in chunks, marinated in white wine and then poached in wine with vegetables, herbs and spices. When the fish is ready the cooking juices are pureed and spooned over the fish.

luganega
a sausage

This mild sausage with a delicate flavour is also called SALSICCIA *a metro* (sausage by the yard) because it used to be sold by length rather than weight. Lean and fat pork meat, flavoured with salt and pepper and other spices, is coarsely ground and then encased in a very long, narrow casing made out of pig's gut.

Luganega, an ancient food, is so called because the Romans first came across it in Basilicata, which at that time was known as Lucania. It is mentioned by Varro, Cicero and APICIUS.

211

The luganega of Lombardy is reputedly the best, especially that of Monza, the suburb of Milan more famous for its car race than for its sausage. In Monza, and other neighbouring towns, luganega can still be made to order, when grated Parmesan is added, and the mixture moistened with dry white wine instead of water.

Luganega, skinned and crumbled, is an essential ingredient in quite a few RAGÙS and stuffings. RISO E LUGANEGHIN is a classic dish from Lombardy. The luganega is cut into chunks and fried in butter and oil, rice is added and then meat stock.

Luganega is also eaten by itself: split open lengthways and grilled or fried and then gently stewed in white wine flavoured with sage. Or it is sautéed with mushrooms, preferably wild, and splashed with a little wine. Another classic dish is *luganega con le patate*. Potato cubes are stewed with the SOFFRITTO in stock and, when half cooked, the same amount of luganega cut into chunks is added.

lumaca
snail

One of the Christmas-time events of my childhood was the *gara delle lumache* – snail race – which my older brother and I organized on the long veranda outside the kitchen. The snails were taken from a covered bucket in which they were kept for several days prior to being cooked for Christmas Eve, as tradition demands in Lombardy.

The bucket from which our snails were taken was the first step in their preparation for one of my mother's great dishes. The bucket contained bran, to purge them, with a few sprigs of thyme for flavour. Cooking the snails was a lengthy process, but I would not recommend cutting any corners. The snails are rinsed in many changes of water, put in a large pot and covered with cold water and vinegar. This is heated until the snails come halfway out of their shells, at which point

the water is drained and the snails are removed from their shells with a small pointed tool. They are then washed again in heavily salted water, and rinsed until all the slime has gone. The spiral of viscera is then removed (some cooks leave it in, but it may be bitter) and finally the snails are cooked slowly in an earthenware pot in oil, garlic and plenty of chopped parsley. After about 20 minutes a glassful of white wine is added, and salt and pepper to taste. The snails are cooked very slowly for about 3 hours and just before serving a good squeeze of lemon juice is added. Served with slices of fried bread, they were utterly delicious. It is one of the few dishes I dream about and which I have only once made in this country – but it was in the summer, and the snails were rather small.

In Rome, for the feast day of St John, 24 June, the traditional dish is *lumache di San Giovanni* – snails in their shells cooked in oil with garlic, onion, chilli, mint and tomatoes. These snails are usually the very small ones known as *grigette di vigna*. The Venetian *bovoletti* are also very small and are cooked in a similar way but without the mint and tomatoes.

Lumache alla meranese is an interesting recipe from Alto Adige. The cleaned and shelled snails are cut in pieces and sautéed in butter and lard with onion, celery and garlic. Splashed with some good local white wine, they are cooked slowly in stock. Halfway through the cooking, a puree of peas is mixed into the pot. The Piedmontese recipe is somewhat similar, except that the local wine used is the red Barbera and walnut kernels are added at the end instead of peas. But it is in Pavia that snails become the main ingredients in a gourmet dish: they are cooked, shelled, in oil, garlic and parsley, and then, at the end of the cooking, boned frogs' legs, dry white wine and slivered truffle are added.

There are also lumache or *chiocciole di mare*, sea snails, with which the Venice lagoon abounds.

luppoli
hops

Also called *bruscandoli* in Veneto. The part that is eaten is the young shoot, before it flowers. It has the most delicious taste, similar to wild asparagus. It is prepared in the same way as asparagus, the spears being boiled until al dente and dressed with olive oil and lemon juice. Hops are also popular in central Italy and in Rome there is a marvellous soup, *zuppa di lupari*, as they are called in Roman dialect. To make this soup, the hop shoots are first stewed in olive oil flavoured with garlic and a little water. Prosciutto cut into strips is added, and then two beaten eggs. Covered with water, seasoned with salt and pepper, the soup is gently simmered until ready, and then ladled over toasted bread.

Sadly, hops are now rarely found, even in Rome or Venice, which was where Elizabeth David ate them, at the Locanda Cipriani on Torcello, in what she describes as 'a most remarkable risotto' in her book *An Omelette and a Glass of Wine*. I have often been to Venice in the spring, but always missed the hops, although I have enjoyed them in salad in the country near Spoleto in Umbria.

Luraschi, Giovanni Felice
19th-century chef

A Milanese chef of the first half of the 19th century, known today for his wide-ranging book *Nuovo Cuoco Milanese*, published in 1829. It was the first book to describe meals according to the customs of England, Russia, France and Italy. In the event, by far the best recipes are those that are obviously Milanese, even if they are not mentioned as such.

The book begins with a section on which provisions to buy, what is required from a good cook and what tools are needed in a kitchen. There follow instructions on how to lay the table and how to serve four different dinners: *all'italiana*, *alla francese*, *alla russa* and *all'inglese*, all of which are really quite similar. The recipes come next, grouped in 26 chapters, each covering a single type of food or method of cooking. There are many French methods, French-sounding recipes and Italianized French words, plus some rather odd methods invented by the writer.

Although the instructions are not very clear, the quantities approximate and the language pompous and wordy, the recipes are good and still valid and much of Luraschi's advice is sound and practical.

213

m

maccheroncini
a pasta

Also called *maccheroncelli* or *mezzi ziti*. A shape of
dried pasta similar to MACCHERONI but narrower
and shorter.

maccheroni
a pasta

A shape of pasta, both dried and homemade,
in the form of a hollow tube. Maccheroni are
usually about 4–5cm/1½–2in long and 1cm/½in in
diameter, although they vary from brand to brand.
There are also longer maccheroni which are broken
into about 10cm/4in pieces before they are cooked.

In some parts of southern Italy maccheroni
means pasta in general, from SPAGHETTI to DITALI to
any other durum wheat pasta. There are *maccheroni
alla* CHITARRA which are 'square' (ie in cross-section)
spaghetti, *maccheroncini* of Campofilone in Le
Marche which are similar to thin fettuccine and
always made with egg pasta, while the *maccheroni
con le noci* (walnuts) of Umbria are just square bits
of pasta.

In many regions of southern Italy maccheroni
are still also made at home. The thinned-out
dough is rolled around thick knitting needles, and
the maccheroni are dressed with a rich RAGÙ of
meat and tomatoes. Maccheroni are hand-made
in the same way in Sicily and Emilia-Romagna –
where *maccheroni di Bobbio* are served with a wild
mushroom sauce.

The earliest surviving reference to maccheroni
dates from 1279. It occurs in a document,
preserved in the Genoa city archives, which is a
notary's list of the items left on his death by one
Ponzio Bastone. Among these items is a basket
full of macharonis (*sic*). Here the meaning of
maccheroni is simply dried pasta; it does not refer
to its shape.

In the 16th century MESSISBUGO and SCAPPI
wrote recipes for maccheroni shaped like GNOCCHI.
Messisbugo describes them as being 'as large as
a chestnut and dragged on the back of a grater'.
This was done, as it still is today, to make ridges
on their surface. Scappi describes how to make
maccheroni a la romanesca with an iron tool similar to
a ridged rolling pin, which is shown in one of the
plates in his book. Maccheroni in those days was
dressed with sugar, cinnamon and cheese. There is
still a traditional dish from Rome, *maccheroni con la
ricotta*, in which the maccheroni are dressed with
the local ewe's milk RICOTTA, sugar and cinnamon
and eaten as a first course.

macchina per la pasta
pasta machine

There are now on the market many different
types of pasta machine, which roughly can be
divided in two groups: hand-cranked and electric.
The hand-cranked machine kneads the dough
after it has been roughly put together and then
stretches it and cuts it. The electric machine does
everything, from the mixing of the flour and eggs
to the drying. I had a hand-cranked machine all
my working life and find it invaluable for a family.

macco
broad bean soup

A soup made in Sardinia, Calabria and Sicily. It is traditionally eaten on St Joseph's Day, 19 March, to finish the dried pulses of the previous year before the new ones are harvested. It varies from region to region, but basically it consists of a thick soup of broad beans, mixed with wild plants (wild fennel in Sicily) or tomatoes, to which other pulses or pasta may be added. The whole thing is dressed with plenty of the local olive oil, black pepper and PECORINO cheese.

macedonia di frutta
fruit salad

Macedonia is so called by analogy with the country of the same name, which is inhabited by a mixture of different people – or that is one of the theories to explain this odd name. Macedonia is a favourite summer dessert both in restaurants and in homes. It usually contains bananas, apples and pears, in addition to which it should include a good variety of seasonal fruits, plus some tropical fruit such as pineapple or mango. The fruit, cut into small cubes, sprinkled with sugar and dressed with orange and lemon juice, is steeped for at least 2 hours and served chilled, without cream.

There is also a winter macedonia which is made with all sorts of dried fruits. These are first soaked in sweet white wine and water and then poached in the liquid, to which sugar and spices have been added.

macelleria
butcher's shop

In most parts of Italy, even in big cities, I find the butcher's shop fascinating – and possibly the cleanest shop you will come across. In the city, the window will have the meat beautifully displayed and arranged from palest pink to deepest crimson. The country butcher's shop sometimes has no window display. You walk in and there, on a higher level and behind a high counter, stands the butcher in all his glory, deftly slicing the meat and at the same time preaching, chatting, advising the throng of women waiting to be served.

Buying meat in an Italian town is a lesson in butchery and cooking, as long as you're not in a hurry. The piece of meat is cut, cleaned, chopped or minced according to the most detailed specification. Italian housewives, always demanding, are particularly fussy when buying meat, a purchase that is expensive and over which time and care must be spent.

Today most macellerie also sell all sorts of SALAMI and many packaged ingredients, or some prepared dishes.

mafalde

see LASAGNETTE

maggiorana
marjoram

A perennial herb that grows along the Mediterranean coast. It has a sweet flavour and is used in many regional cuisines. Above all, however, marjoram is the hallmark of the cooking of Liguria, a region famous for its herbs. In Liguria it is added to vegetable TORTE, to stuffed vegetables and to the stuffing of PANSÔTI, Ligurian ravioli.

magro
lean

In culinary terms the word is applied to any lean meat, or food made from it.

Magro also means 'meatless', when applied to a dish for fast days, or indeed to the day itself, as with Ash Wednesday, Good Friday or Christmas

215

Eve. RAVIOLI di magro are ravioli stuffed with spinach and ricotta rather than meat, and BRODO di magro is stock made only with vegetables. Although there are a great many recipes for dishes 'di magro' in old cookery books, the expression is now little used because religious traditions are rarely observed.

maiale
pig or pork

The word means both pig, the animal, and pork, its meat. Maiale is the most popular provider of food throughout the peninsula. Thanks to the pig the larder is replenished with all sorts of food for the rest of the year. All bits of the animal are eaten, and they really are enjoyed. '*Il maiale è come la musica di Verdi; tutto buono, niente da buttar via,*' or so goes an Italian saying: 'The pig is like Verdi's music; it's all good, there is nothing to throw away.'

When I was young we lived for a few years on a farm in Emilia, and I can still remember being woken up by the terrified screams of the poor pig, who seemed to know what was going to happen. All through that day, the farm was buzzing with frenetic activity. The NORCINO (the butcher who specialized in making pork products) came to the farm to kill and bleed the pig, to sort out the different cuts, to salt, mince, flavour, smoke them and cook them to make PROSCIUTTI, SALAMI, COTECHINI and SALSICCIE. The leftover meat was chopped up and put into a large earthenware pot for a RAGÙ.

By the evening the screams were forgotten as we dived into dishes of hot CICCIOLI. Huge copper pans, full of fat, were spluttering on the heat for hours, until all the fat was rendered to make STRUTTO. The crackling ciccioli were then retrieved and eaten with FOCACCIA. And on the next day, any bits and pieces left over were stewed in wine and tomatoes and served with a golden mound of steaming POLENTA.

Most country families still keep or share a pig, and the *maialatura* (slaughtering of the maiale) is something of a feast day. In some remote villages in southern Italy the maialatura has ritualistic overtones that go far back into history.

Nowadays pigs are big business, supplying the important SALUMI industry with its raw material. Many piggeries are situated near dairy farms, and the pigs are fed with whey, a by-product of cheesemaking. These pigs produce the sweetest and fattest prosciutti. They are, however, considered rather too large and fat by the purists, who prefer the lean meat of the mountain pigs, such as those of Umbria or Abruzzo, whose meat tastes of the berries and herbs on which they feed. Many local products are made on a small scale with this type of pig, and their taste is much stronger and more earthy.

Recipes for pork meat are very similar throughout the country, although every region claims to have its own special one. The great recipe claimed by both Le Marche and Emilia is *maiale al latte* (see recipe on page 198). Another winner is ARISTA *alla fiorentina* and, also from Tuscany, SCOTTIGLIA. Milan has its famous CASSOEULA, Italy's homeliest and most nourishing feast of pork meats, and *rostisciada* or ROSTICIANA, a dish with as many variations as there are cooks, but basically a simple dish of pork chops cooked with LUGANEGA sausage and lots of onion. Some recipes also include sage and/or tomatoes. Rosticciada is always served with polenta. In Tuscany, *maiale ubriaco* ('drunken pork') is a dish of pork chops fried in oil and then covered with red wine — traditionally Chianti — with garlic and parsley. The INVOLTINI of Naples are pork escalopes stuffed with prosciutto, capers, pine nuts, sultanas and breadcrumbs. The meat is rolled up, sautéed in strutto (pork fat) or oil and then gently stewed in a light tomato sauce.

When very young, *maialino da latte* (suckling pig) is roasted on the spit as PORCHETTA.

malfatti
green gnocchi

Malfatti means 'badly made' and refers to the
homely shape of these gnocchi; it certainly has
nothing to do with their delicious taste. The malfatti
of Lombardy are made with spinach, MASCARPONE,
egg, flour, breadcrumbs and Parmesan, while those
of Emilia-Romagna are made with Swiss chard,
RICOTTA, egg, flour and Parmesan. Both are cooked
in simmering salted water until they rise to the top,
and they are simply dressed with melted butter and
Parmesan or with a light and creamy tomato sauce.

[see recipe below]

malloreddus
gnocchi

A Sardinian type of very small gnocchi made
with durum wheat SEMOLINO and water, and
flavoured with saffron. They are usually served
with a RAGÙ made from local sausage and fresh
tomatoes. There is now a dried pasta called
gnocchetti sardi on the market, which is the
commercial version of malloreddus.

malfatti
spinach and ricotta gnocchi

Serves 4
1kg/2¼lb fresh spinach, or 500g/
  1lb 2oz frozen leaf spinach, thawed
salt and freshly ground black pepper
2 large eggs
200g/7oz/scant 1 cup ricotta
200g/7oz/generous 1½ cups Italian 00
  flour, plus extra for dusting
½ tsp grated nutmeg
100g/3½oz Parmesan cheese, grated
100g/3½oz/7 tbsp unsalted butter

**The original recipe from Emilia uses the green leaves of Swiss chard
instead of spinach in these rustic gnocchi. You can use either vegetable.**

Cook the fresh spinach with 1 teaspoon salt in a covered pan for
5 minutes. Drain and leave until cool enough to handle, then use your
hands to squeeze out all the water. Chop the spinach very finely or pass
it through the coarsest setting of a food mill.

In a bowl, beat the eggs, mix in the ricotta and beat again. Mix in the flour,
nutmeg, spinach and half the Parmesan. Taste and adjust the seasoning.

Dust your hands with flour and form the mixture into balls the size of
large marbles. Place them on a tray and chill for about 30 minutes.

To cook the gnocchi, bring 5 litres/9 pints/5 quarts salted water to the boil
in a very large saucepan. Add the gnocchi, a dozen at a time, and cook
them for 3–4 minutes after the water returns to the boil. Lift them out
with a slotted spoon and transfer them to a dish. Dot with a little butter,
sprinkle over a little Parmesan and keep them warm while cooking the
remaining mixture.

Meanwhile, melt the remaining butter in a small saucepan. Just before
serving, spoon the butter over the cooked gnocchi, sprinkle with the
remaining Parmesan and serve at once.

maltagliati
a pasta

The name means 'badly cut', and refers to rolled-out pasta dough: in Mantua, in south-eastern Lombardy, it is cut into long narrow triangles, while in Veneto and Emilia it is cut into small diamond shapes. Maltagliati are mostly used in soup.

mandarino
mandarin

This is one of the three citrus fruit that have grown in Calabria and Sicily for many centuries, the other two being the lemon and the orange. They are gathered from November until January and they are a traditional Christmas fruit. The most common varieties are the Palermitana and Paternó, both from Sicily. The now-popular *mandarancio*, which is bigger and has a tougher skin, is a more recent cross between a mandarin and an orange.

Mandarins are used to make sorbets, and to decorate fruit tarts. A recipe from *Il Talismano della Felicità* by Ada BONI suggests filling the emptied mandarin shells with a jelly made from the juice of mandarins and lemons. Mandarins are excellent crystallized. Segments of mandarin preserved in alcohol are prepared according to an old recipe from Naples, where special jars were made for the purpose.

mandorla
almond

There are two varieties of almond tree and they look identical, but one produces sweet almonds and the other bitter almonds. Sweet almonds are used to make PASTA DI MANDORLE, or *pasta reale* ('royal paste', as it was known in the past), and MARZAPANE — and all over Italy they are a favourite ingredient in sweets, cakes and puddings. Among the best-known preparations made with almonds are AMARETTI, RICCIARELLI and TORRONE. Almonds are also eaten toasted and salted or coated with sugar (CONFETTI) or with caramelized sugar (*mandorle pralinate*) or made into CROCCANTE. In southern Italy almonds also go into pasta sauces, with fried breadcrumbs, sultanas, basil or other herbs, and/or tomatoes.

Bitter almonds are called *ermelline* and are toxic. However, the prussic acid they contain is volatile, and evaporates on being heated. Often a few bitter almonds are added to sweet almonds to give the dish a stronger flavour, as in AMARETTI, where three or four bitter almonds are mixed with 200g/7oz of sweet almonds.

Almonds were often used in the past. APICIUS included them in stuffings for fowl and in soups, but it was the Arabs who exploited the almond's vast range of culinary possibilities, and launched it into the European repertoire, the launching pad — as with so many other foods and dishes — being Sicily. There, almonds were mainly used in cakes and sweets, as indeed they still are. But a few centuries later almonds began to figure prominently in many savoury dishes.

MARTINO da Como used almonds to thicken chicken stock for soups, and also mixed them with chicken breast, egg whites, rose water and a little sugar to make fritters. PLATINA has a long passage on almonds, including information on their medicinal properties. He writes that almonds are effective against drunkenness, but they must be eaten before drinking — and the number of almonds must be five! Vincenzo CORRADO has an interesting recipe called *mandorle alla moda* in which the toasted almonds are mixed with fish roe, fungi, truffles (optional), spices, sweet wine and stock. The pureed sauce is used to accompany fish pies. Many of ARTUSI's recipes use almonds, either by themselves or in combination with other flavourings.

218

mandorlato
nougat

A kind of nougat originating in Veneto. Whipped egg whites are folded into melted honey, and then almonds and a good measure of cinnamon are added. The mixture is cooled between sheets of rice paper. Nowadays mandorlato is made commercially, when it also contains candied citron.

manina
bread roll

A bread roll from Ferrara, where manina is the most popular local shape. Its name means 'little hand', because its shape bears a (rather faint) resemblance to crossed hands, with the first and fourth fingers of both hands pointing outwards. The bread is made of a compact dough, but is beautifully light. Ferrarese bread is some of the most delicious in Italy.

mantecato
cooking term

The past participle of *mantecare*, which means to pound into a paste, usually with butter. RISOTTO is mantecato at the end of its cooking, when butter and Parmesan are added to make it thick and creamy. In Piedmont and Valle d'Aosta rhere is a risotto that is mantecato with shredded FONTINA. The other dish that is mantecato is BACCALÀ – a speciality of Venice. The cooked baccalà is pounded in the mortar and then as much olive oil as can be absorbed is beaten into it. It becomes, in consistency and colour, like double cream. The dish is seasoned at the end and flavoured with parsley and garlic.

manzo
beef

In the past manzo meant a young ox. Nowadays it usually means the meat of a young ox or that of a heifer. Manzo is eaten more in northern Italy than in the central and southern parts of the country. This is because the fertile pastures of the Po Valley and the foothills of the Alps are excellent breeding grounds for cattle.

Manzo is often bought already sliced (when it is known as FETTINE), minced to make POLPETTE, or in a piece for pot roasting or braising. The shin is used for stews, often cooked in a tomato sauce, and the offal is prepared in many ways. Fillet is the most popular cut for steaks and even for roasting, although this is not a traditional way to cook beef in Italy.

Manzo in a single piece is used for the many BRASATI, STRACOTTI and STUFATI, such as the Lombard *manzo alla California* – this California used to be a suburb of Milan. The beef is braised at length, with onion, carrot and celery, in wine vinegar and milk, or cream for a richer dish. At the end of the cooking, the rich juice is pureed and then spooned over the sliced meat. One of my stand-by recipes is a joint braised long and slow in the oven with the same weight of sliced onions and salt. Nothing else.

Manzo alle acciughe or *alla certosina* is another version of this method of slow cooking. In this recipe, salted anchovies are added to the casserole after the beef has been browned in oil flavoured with garlic and nutmeg.

Manzo is also boiled, either as part of a BOLLITO MISTO or by itself, when it is known as LESSO or *manzo lesso*.

marasca

see AMARENA

Marche, Le

An aura of the pleasant life of days gone by seems to pervade the cooking of Le Marche, still unspoilt by modern whims of international fantasy, still based on the produce of the sea, the hills and the mountains.

The variety of fish caught along the region's Adriatic coastline is unequalled in any part of Italy. It includes crustaceans of all kinds, cuttlefish, octopus, squid and many varieties of molluscs, many of which are found only on this coast. Several species of blue fish are caught, as well as white fish: hake, sea bream, skate, sea bass, grey and red mullet, sole, turbot and monkfish.

It is small wonder that, with so many varieties of fish available, one of the best fish soups in Italy is the one made in this region. Called BRODETTO, the recipes for it are as numerous as the towns along the coast. A *brodetto marchigiano* should contain about eight varieties of fish and seafood. The brodetto from Ancona, when made by the fishermen on their boat, contains as many as 13 varieties and is flavoured with white wine, vinegar and saffron.

Another speciality, prepared by fishermen on the beach over a wood fire, is *muscioli alla* MARINARA. The mussels are spread out in a large iron pan, covered with olive oil and lemon juice and put over the fire. When they have opened, they are dressed with more lemon juice and eaten just as they are, with bread.

Few of the recipes for fish are elaborate. The fish is boiled, grilled or fried and the simple addition of highly scented herbs and the excellent local olive oil serves only to enhance its taste. To this feast of fresh fish, the marchigiani add a few of the best recipes for dried cod, or STOCCAFISSO: *stoccafisso in* UMIDO (with tomato, onion, carrots and celery); in POTACCHIO (strongly flavoured with rosemary and garlic); and in *teglia* (baked in layers with sliced potatoes).

Le Marche has also some excellent recipes for meat and vegetables. Among meats, the pig reigns supreme. It appears in its most popular form as a PORCHETTA at any country feast, or on market day. Porchetta is the centrepiece at any outdoor meal throughout central Italy, but it is the marchigiani who claim to be the creators of this succulent dish. The boned piglet, flavoured with fennel seeds and garlic, is roasted on the spit and served with thick chunks of homely bread.

The most renowed SALUMI are the COPPA *marchigiana*, the COTECHINO di San Leo, the *soppressata*, the SALAME di Fabriano and the CIAUSCOLO, a kind of soft salame flavoured with nutmeg, garlic, orange and lemon rind made only in Le Marche. And I must mention my favourite PROSCIUTTO – the prosciutto di Carpegna, which has a stronger flavour and a redder colour than Parma or San Daniele. It is sliced thicker than the other two and it is the perfect prosciutto for a PANINO.

Rabbits, always farmed, are popular, as is chicken; both are cooked *in potacchio* – first

MARCHE

ADRIATIC
SEA

•Pesaro

•Urbino

•Ancona

Apennines

Macerata•

Fermo•

Ascoli Piceno•

sautéed, then cooked slowly with a small amount of liquid, and flavoured with rosemary, lemon rind and garlic. Rabbit is also roasted with wild fennel and garlic, like a porchetta, and it is called *coniglio in porchetta*.

The beef of Le Marche has the same characteristics of being lean yet full of flavour as the more famous Chianina breed of Tuscany. With this beef, a chef in Pesaro created *medaglioni alla Rossini* – tournedos cooked in wine – in honour of the greatest gourmet among composers, and the greatest composer among gourmets. These are different from the more famous *tournedos Rossini* created for the composer by a Parisian chef. The medaglioni are cooked with prosciutto, wild mushrooms and cheese in the local VIN SANTO. When in season, a grating of white truffles is sprinkled on before serving.

White truffles found in Le Marche compete in excellence with those of Alba in Piedmont, which have a worldwide reputation. A well-known baked pasta dish with the peculiar name of VINCISGRASSI has grated truffle added to the stuffing. Truffle is also added to the *lasagne incassate*, which has a filling made with a RAGÙ of minced veal, chicken giblets, chicken breast, grated Parmesan and Gruyère. Besides the truffles, the fungi on the Apennines are just as abundant and varied as the fish in the sea. During the autumn they make a most artistic and appetizing sight on the market stalls of small towns.

The preparation of vegetables can be quite elaborate. Courgettes are baked, stuffed with chopped ham, breadcrumbs, garlic and parsley. Or, in a very old recipe, they are sautéed with GUANCIALE (cured pig's jowl), onion and garlic and then stewed with tomatoes. Cauliflowers are fried, coated in a light batter of egg, flour and dry white wine, to which some housewives add a spoonful of *mistra* – a local liqueur made with aniseed. A recipe I was given is for cauliflower florets stewed in oil, garlic, chilli, parsley and a little water for some 5 minutes and then finished off with a glass of white wine. Peas are cooked in the same way, but without the chilli.

Cheese always appears on the table at the end of the meal, the main cheese, as in the other regions of central Italy, being PECORINO, made from sheep's milk, to which cow's milk is sometimes added. In the town of San Leo, the pecorino is wrapped in walnut leaves and kept in earthenware jars until it is well aged. Another local cheese is *giuncata*, a fresh cheese, which is sold only where it is made.

Sweets are homely and simple. The best known is *frustingolo*, a sort of PANFORTE made with dried figs and sultanas plus nuts and spices, all kept together by honey and breadcrumbs. When good, it is certainly as good as the Tuscan panforte, and like panforte, frustingolo is the Christmas DOLCE.

The fruit in Le Marche is splendid: apples, peaches, figs and cherries all testify to the richness and fertility of this idyllic land. And fruit is the best way to round off a marchigiano meal, although the repertoire of sweets, however small, is tempting.

But it is *olive ascolane* (see OLIVA), named after the town of Ascoli Piceno, that nowadays have become the region's most popular food, served as an ANTIPASTO or a snack all over the peninsula.

marinara, alla
in the sailor's style

This does not refer to any particular combination of ingredients or method of cooking. Thus there is SPAGHETTI or vermicelli alla marinara, with oil, garlic and, sometimes, chilli, or with a tomato sauce. The only recipe that is literally 'alla marinara' is a PIZZA topped with tomatoes, garlic and oregano.

marinata
marinade

A mixture of ingredients, mostly liquid, in which meat or fish is steeped for a length of time. This can achieve several results, such as tenderizing or adding flavour, according to the marinade and the food in question.

A joint of beef is marinated to tenderize it, but also to add flavour. The marinade is usually red wine, to which onion, celery, herbs and other flavourings are added, the beef afterwards being braised or stewed. Boar, venison and hare are always marinated in wine to which some olive oil has been added. The same is done with kid and mutton. A joint of pork is placed in a marinade of white wine or wine vinegar, plus the usual herbs and flavourings, to make it less dry, before cooking it in some special way, such as for *maiale al latte* (see recipe on page 198). When making COSTOLETTA *alla Milanese*, some Milanese cooks marinate the veal cutlets in milk, so as to make the veal whiter and more delicate.

An interesting Tuscan recipe for guinea fowl calls for the jointed bird to be first fried in oil and then marinated in white wine, herbs and lemon juice for a few hours. Finally, the guinea fowl cooks slowly in the marinade. Prepared in this way, a guinea fowl or chicken, which can otherwise be dry, remains moist and juicy.

Fresh fillets of anchovies are marinated in olive oil, lemon juice or wine vinegar for at least one day before being eaten raw.

Marinetti, Filippo
1876–1944

Marinetti was one of the founders of the Futurist art movement, which soon included gastronomy. In 1930 *la cucina futurista* was officially inaugurated at a dinner at the restaurant Penna d'Oca in Milan. The manifesto published two years later gave directions for a different type of cooking, which would reshape the Italians as a master race. Among these suggestions was the abolition of pasta in the diet. 'Pasta,' Marinetti wrote, 'is a chain binding their feet or an ancient ruin in their stomach as if they were convicts or archeologists.' He then published a book, *La Cucina Futurista*, containing lists of menus, programmes for special dinners and recipes. It ends with a short dictionary of futuristic cooking, in which all foreign terms are banned. The recipes were written to shock and this they did by combining unsuitable foods, with the dishes often being served in the most exotic manner.

In my book *Entertaining all'Italiana* I created a dinner totally based on Marinetti's recipes. It comprised: *aereovivanda atlantica* – a legume puree, puff pastry and other ingredients in the shape of a plane; *trote immortali* – trout stuffed with almonds and calf's liver; and *fragolamammella*, two balls of ricotta flavoured with Campari and shaped like breasts. The recipes worked and were not too bad, but I wonder if I enjoyed adapting them far more than my guests did in eating the dishes. After a few years of interest, *la cucina futurista* was buried for ever.

maritozzi
bread rolls

A speciality of Rome, these are bread rolls studded with pine nuts, sultanas and orange and citron peel, thickly covered with icing sugar; they are sometimes cut in half and filled with whipped cream. It used to be the sweet bread given by a girl to her fiancé during Lent, hence its name, which derives from *marito* – husband.

marmellata
jam or marmalade

After years of confusion between the usage of the two terms, marmellata and *confettura*, it has been officially declared that marmellata is marmalade, meaning jam made from citrus fruit, while confettura is all other jams. This is the European declaration, but in everyday parlance the confusion often still exists.

Marmellata is made with sweet oranges – bitter oranges are not used in Italy – lemons, mandarins, citrons and also bergamots, which make a rare but delicious marmalade.

marrone
see CASTAGNA

Marsala
wine

Marsala was created by the Woodhouse brothers from Liverpool in 1773 and is named after the port in western Sicily in which they established their cellars and warehouse. By 1800 they were supplying Nelson's fleet with what was to become a great naval drink and later a fashionable one in England. It is now a DOC wine, produced and aged around Trapani.

Marsala is served cold as an aperitif or at room temperature as a dessert wine, depending on its sweetness. It is used in quite a few recipes, from the sweet ZABAIONE to meat dishes such as escalopes of veal.

Martino da Como
15th-century chef

Chef to the Patriarch of Aquilea, Martino, also referred to as Maestro Martino, wrote a book of great importance: *Libro de Arte Coquinaria*. Martino was active between 1450 and 1475, but very little is known about the man himself. His manuscript, written in an odd Italianized Venetian, was only discovered at the beginning of the 20th century by the food historian J D Vehling who, in 1941, gave the manuscript to the Library of Congress in Washington, DC. Long before that, however, Martino's work was already known, since much of it was incorporated by PLATINA in his *De Honesta Voluptate et Valetudine*, published in 1475. Maestro

Martino's book has now been printed in its entirety in the remarkable anthology *L'Arte della Cucina*, edited by Professor E Faccioli.

Martino was Platina's mentor, as he acknowledges: 'Which cook, immortal gods, could be compared to my Martino from Como? From him comes most of what I write.' Professor Faccioli points out how well Martino's work compares with two other surviving cookery manuscripts from around the same time, one by an anonymous Tuscan writer and the other by a Venetian writer. Subjects are clearly divided and when dealing with ingredients Martino is specific about quantities and proportions. He discusses how food is prepared and is concerned about its appearance when served. Martino knew about the raw materials: that the best rice came from Lombardy, the best langoustines from Venice and the best sausages from Bologna. He is particularly strong on vegetable dishes, soups and the various *sapori*, which were the precursors of our sauces. Both soups and sauces are thickened with almonds and breadcrumbs.

The chapter on fish gives the best method of cooking every sort of fish, from the prized sturgeon and sea bass to the bony rascasse. The recipes for meat, poultry and game are interesting, yet they are simple enough for everyday food for a 21st-century family. The recipe for stuffed veal breast, for example, is a simplified version of *cima alla genovese*, a traditional dish from Genoa, for which I give a recipe on page 340. Martino was also clear and precise about cooking times. For partridge cooked with salt, sweet spices, pomegranate or lemon juice or verjuice, he recommends cooking not too long 'until very hot, but still rare, and turn it quickly and not slowly.'

Some historians believe this chef was the first to explore and draw from the wealth of Saracen cooking, from which he took the most suitable methods and ingredients. The *Libro de Arte Coquinaria* formed the basis on which European cooking was built.

marubini
stuffed pasta

Very similar to the stuffed pasta described in
the 15th century by PLATINA, marubini are little
scalloped rounds of dough which may be filled
either with braised beef, roast pork or veal, beef
marrow and Parmesan, or with breadcrumbs
mixed with melted beef marrow, lots of Parmesan
and eggs. Marubini are a speciality of Cremona
in south-east Lombardy, and are seldom found
anywhere else. They are traditionally cooked in a
rich meat stock, drained and dressed with melted
butter and Parmesan.

marzapane
marzipan

A mixture of sugar, ground almonds and eggs,
with which almond biscuits such as petits fours
are made. It is the same mixture as the English
and American marzipan. It is often flavoured with
cinnamon or lemon rind.

marzolino
a cheese

A cylinder-shaped PECORINO of about 500g/1lb,
made only from ewe's milk, in the provinces
of Siena and Arezzo in Tuscany. It is prepared
in March (Marzo), hence its name, and either
eaten fresh (after 2 weeks) or left to age, when
it becomes hard and slightly piquant. The best
marzolino comes from the Chianti area. It was
Michelangelo's favourite cheese. Every year, he
had the cheese made in his estate in the province
of Arezzo and sent to him in Rome.

mascarpone
a cream cheese

This creamy cheese, originally from Lombardy, is
now produced industrially all over northern Italy.
It is made with the cream of very fresh milk from
cows that have been fed on fresh or naturally dried
fodder, rather than fodder dried in silos, so the
aroma of the flowers and herbs is preserved.

Mascarpone is now exported in tubs bearing
an expiry date. This mascarpone is certainly not
as good as the farm product wrapped in muslin, as
sold in some cheese shops in northern Italy, but
it is good enough for making some puddings and
sauces. Of these the best-known is the relatively
modern TIRAMISÙ, originally from Treviso. An older
type of pudding is the crema mascarpone, which is
mascarpone beaten with sugar, egg yolks and rum.

Mascarpone can also be used to make a
savoury cream, by combining it with caviar,
truffles or smoked trout, and for a delicious pasta
sauce when mixed with egg yolks. Another use of
mascarpone in a savoury preparation is a layered
cheese made with mascarpone and Gorgonzola, a
modern creation very popular outside Italy.

mattarello or matterello
rolling pin

There are two kinds of this wooden tool in Italy:
one is the short thick one similar to that found in
kitchens in Britain and the United States, which
is used for pastry and biscuits. The other is a
typical Italian tool. It is a stick made of smooth,
well-sanded wood, about 80cm/32in long and
3cm/1¼in thick. It does not have handles but it
sometimes has a knob at one end which is used for
carrying it, with dough rolled round it, to a place
where the dough is unrolled to dry out.

The longer rolling pin must have been in use
in pre-Roman kitchens, as it is depicted in a bas-
relief in a tomb of an Etruscan necropolis north of

Rome, together with other tools for making pasta. In the 16th century it appears in an illustration in *Opera*, by Bartolomeo SCAPPI, in which two men are working on thinning the pasta dough. One man is rolling out the circle of dough, which the other is pressing down so as to stretch it out as thinly as possible.

mazzafegati
liver sausages

Pig's liver sausages made in Umbria and Le Marche. The Umbrian mazzafegati are quite sweet, as they are made with a mixture of pig's liver, sugar, sultanas and pine nuts. The mazzafegati from Le Marche are a mixture of the liver and lights of the pig, flavoured with spices and pushed into pig casing. These sausages are smoked for a few days and then air-cured and they are then eaten as a SALAME.

mazzancolla
king prawn

Also known by the grander name of *gambero imperiale*. The best mazzancolle, which can be up to 22cm/9in long, are found during the summer in the Tyrrhenian Sea along the coast of Lazio, where they are traditionally served fried. The prawns, with the shell removed but the head left on, are floured and fried in olive oil and then served sprinkled with parsley and garnished with lemon wedges. They are also grilled with the same flavourings plus a touch of chilli. They are eaten with the fingers, and all the delicious juice is sucked from the head.

Another traditional recipe from Lazio is *mazzancolle al coccio*, the coccio being the earthenware pot used. They are first sautéed in olive oil, garlic and chilli. When they are golden, they are splashed with dry white wine and, after 2 minutes, lemon juice and chopped parsley are

added. Unlike the GAMBERONI of other regions, mazzancolle are seldom used in fish soups, because their delicate flavour would be lost among other fish.

mazzetto odoroso or aromatico
bouquet garni

This is a bouquet garni consisting of parsley, rosemary, sage, thyme, bay leaf and, sometimes, marjoram. Celery leaves can also be part of the mazzetto. The herbs are always fresh. It is sold already prepared in some greengrocers' shops.

meascia
a pudding

This is the Lombard bread and butter pudding from Lake Como, which unfortunately is very little known outside Lombardy. The bread, cut into cubes, is soaked in milk and then mixed with eggs, lemon rind, slices of apple and pear, sultanas, sugar, white flour and POLENTA flour. After baking, the cake is sprinkled lavishly with chopped fresh rosemary, which gives meascia its characteristic and unusual flavour.

mela
apple

Italian cuisine would not be greatly affected by the absence of apples, whether as fresh fruit or the basis for puddings. The many varieties are nearly all foreign, apart from the Mantovana, from Mantua, and the Limoncella. The Mantovana is a red apple with a tasty and juicy pulp, while the Limoncella has a lemon-coloured skin and a tart taste.

Apples are often part of a FRITTO MISTO, when they are sliced, coated in batter and deep-fried.

225

Apart from this, however, they are not used in savoury dishes in traditional Italian cooking. They are used to make apple juice or jam, candied and used for puddings and in fruit salads. They are poached in wine and used in a few puddings and cakes such as a Lombard charlotte and a cake made in southern Italy, for which the recipe is given here.

[see recipe below]

melagrana
pomegranate

This beautiful small tree with shiny bright green foliage and vermilion flowers adorns many gardens in central and southern Italy. The pomegranate is known more for its associations with legends and history than for its culinary value. It was first cultivated principally as a decorative plant, but then – during the Middle Ages and the Renaissance – it became very popular as a flavouring.

Today, pomegranates are mainly eaten as a fresh fruit or used to make a drink called *granatina*.

CONTINUES OVERLEAF

torta di mele all'olio
apple cake made with oil

Serves 8–10

115g/4oz/generous ½ cup sultanas
 (golden raisins)
unsalted butter for the tin
150ml/5fl oz/²⁄₃ cup olive oil
200g/7oz/1 cup golden caster
 (superfine) sugar
2 large eggs
350g/12oz/scant 3 cups Italian
 00 flour, plus extra for the tin
1 tsp ground cinnamon
1½ tsp bicarbonate of soda (baking
 soda)
½ tsp cream of tartar
½ tsp salt
500g/1lb 2oz dessert apples, peeled and
 diced small
grated rind of 1 organic or unwaxed
 lemon

Of all the cakes made with apples (MELE), this is my favourite. It is a moist cake, particularly good at the end of a meal with a dollop of cream. It is also one of the very few cakes made with oil instead of butter. Use a mild Ligurian extra virgin olive oil if you can, but ordinary olive oil will do just as well.

Soak the sultanas in warm water for 20 minutes.

Meanwhile, preheat the oven to 180°C/350°F/Gas Mark 4. Butter and flour a 20cm/8in diameter springform cake tin.

Pour the olive oil into a bowl, add the sugar and beat until the sugar and oil become homogenized. Add the eggs one at a time and beat until the mixture has increased in volume and looks like thin mayonnaise.

Sift together the flour, cinnamon, bicarbonate of soda, cream of tartar and salt. Add the dry ingredients gradually to the oil and sugar mixture, folding them in with a metal spoon. Mix thoroughly and then add the diced apples and lemon rind.

Drain and dry the sultanas and add to the mixture. Mix very thoroughly. The mixture will be quite stiff at this stage.

Spoon the mixture into the prepared tin and bake for at least 1 hour, until a thin skewer inserted in the middle of the cake comes out dry. Remove the cake from the tin and cool on a wire rack.

RIGHT: Torta di mele all'olio

Equal parts of pomegranate juice and sugar are made into a syrup and diluted with water when cold. Pomegranate is not used much in cooking apart from in Venice, where the food has been influenced by the Middle East. One of the best-known dishes is, in the Venetian dialect, *paeta al malgaragno* – roast turkey with pomegranate sauce.

melanzana
aubergine

Italian cooking would be much poorer without this versatile vegetable. Although aubergines established themselves very successfully in Sicily and southern Italy in the 11th century, they did not become popular until fairly recent times. They were considered unhealthy and one 14th-century writer regarded them as 'causing males to swerve from decent behaviour'. In the 17th century they were connected with madness. ARTUSI wrote that up to 40 years before the publication of his cookery book *La Scienza in Cucina e l'Arte di Mangiar Bene* in 1891, 'aubergines and fennels were hardly seen on the market in Florence; they were considered vile food suitable for the Jews.'

Now the aubergine has become very popular all over the peninsula. Several different varieties grow well everywhere; they vary in size and shape, from round and the size of a tennis ball (these are the ones used for stuffing in Genoa) to large and plump or long and thin. They also vary in colour: some are deep purple, others are pale purple, some are ivory, some are streaky. But as long as they are firm and have a beautiful shiny skin, they all taste the same. Aubergines used to be salted to remove some of their bitterness, but the new varieties are much sweeter. Salting is, however, desirable when making dishes in which the aubergine is going to be fried, because the salt draws liquid out of the aubergines.

The many recipes for aubergines are from southern Italy and Sicily, where they have been eaten for much longer than in the north. The two most famous are CAPONATA and PARMIGIANA DI MELANZANE. Aubergines mix very well with pasta, as in PASTA ALLA NORMA or the elaborate PASTA 'NCASCIATA. At the other extreme, few dishes are as simple and delicious as *melanzane alla griglia*, which is ideal for a barbecue. The aubergines are cut lengthways in fairly thick slices, brushed with a mixture of olive oil, garlic, oregano, salt and pepper, and grilled. Whole aubergines can also be charred over charcoal, skinned and then cut in half and dressed with the same sauce. Sliced aubergines are coated with batter and fried.

Aubergines are ideal for stuffing. In the commonest filling the sautéed aubergine pulp is mixed with oregano, garlic, capers and anchovy fillets; another mixture combines mushrooms, bread and egg. A richer recipe from the Gargano peninsula in Puglia adds local sausage to the sautéed pulp, together with capers and black olives. In Calabria, tomatoes and CACIOCAVALLO are the main ingredients of the stuffing.

Aubergines lend themselves very well to being preserved. In the right climate, aubergines can be air-dried, instead of blanched, before being covered with oil and sealed in sterilized jars. The simplest method of preserving is described by Marcella Hazan in *Marcella's Italian Kitchen*. The aubergines, cut into strips, are soaked in salted water for 12–16 hours. They are then drained, wrung dry and dressed with 1 tablespoon of vinegar, mint, garlic and oregano. Placed in a pickling jar in layers, with a couple of fresh chillies and another tablespoon of vinegar, they are covered with olive oil. They can be kept in the refrigerator for up to 4 months and – Marcella Hazan writes – they have a taste 'remarkably like wild porcini'.

melone
melon

Also called *popone* in southern Italy, it was in Italy that this fruit was first cultivated on a large scale, and today melon is surely one of the foods that is most redolent of Italy. According to some botanists melon came originally from Persia, according to others, from Sudan. Melons were known to the Egyptians, and later to the Romans. The Emperor Tiberius was particularly fond of melon and made special studies of their cultivation under glass so that he could eat them all year round. Then, during the Dark Ages, they seem to have disappeared and were probably reintroduced by the crusaders on their return from the Middle East. What is certain is that by the 15th century, melon was a popular fruit.

PLATINA has a long entry in which he praises the tastiness of the fruit, but warns against it being 'cold and damp' and therefore indigestible. For this reason he suggests that it should be eaten at the beginning of the meal and followed by a drink of good wine, this being 'an antidote to its rawness and frigidity'. In the 17th century, Bartolomeo STEFANI suggests a version of ZABAIONE for convalescents, made with melon seeds pounded in the mortar and mixed with wine and egg yolks. From Vincenzo CORRADO we learn that 'melon is good in soup, or cooked in syrup to make cakes. It is also served fried with and without batter, and mixed with milk is made into a cream.'

In our times melon is mainly served with PROSCIUTTO and in a fruit salad.

Of the many varieties of melon, two are particularly connected with Italy. These are the *napoletano*, with its oval shape, bright orange flesh and green or yellow skin, and the cantaloupe. This variety reached Italy from Armenia in the 15th century, and was first cultivated in the garden of the papal residence at Cantalupo near Rome. At that time, the cantaloupe melons were so highly esteemed that they were used by the popes as gifts.

Finally, a tip: when buying a melon remember that the best ones are those that are the most scented and also the heaviest. Take two equal-sized melons, one in each hand, and buy the heavier. I have also read that the male fruit,

distinguishable by a black spot on the opposite end to the stalk, is best. Still, I quite agree with Francesco Sforza, Duke of Milan, who, in the 15th century, said, 'Three things in life are difficult: picking a good wife, choosing a good horse and buying a good melon.'

menta
mint

This herb does not feature prominently in Italian cooking. There are three main varieties: *Menta piperita* – peppermint – is used in the production of liqueurs and confectionery; *Menta romana* – spearmint – is the characteristic flavouring in a dish of Roman tripe, its pronounced piquancy beautifully counteracting the richness of the tripe; *mentuccia* (also called *nepitella*) – Corsican mint – is sweeter and more aromatic than other mint. It is used in quite a few dishes from central and southern Italy, and also in custards and ice cream.

menù
menu

This word has two different meanings. One is the actual list of the dishes offered in a restaurant or at a banquet, sometimes called the *lista delle vivande*. The other meaning covers the culinary organization for the creation of the whole meal. As such, it is indispensable for the provisions and it can cover the whole day or much longer. A chef will discuss the menu with the owner of the restaurant and/or with his sous chefs, just as the cook or housekeeper in a private house will discuss it with the mistress of the house. A menu is the strategy in the kitchen.

A new usage of the word is now evident in the restaurant world: the word menu is used by many restaurants to differentiate the types of meals. Thus there is a *menu turistico* – for the tourists – which is the cheapest, and, at the other end of the scale, a menu gastronomico or menu degustazione, where the chef offers the most personal and creative dishes, both very highly priced.

merenda
snack

'The tray was piled high – TARTINE with anchovy butter, smoked salmon, caviar, pâté de foie gras, prosciutto, small vol-au-vents filled with minced chicken and béchamel. On the trolley, jugs, pots, glasses and mugs. And inside the china and pewter pots there was tea, milk, coffee; in the jugs, lemonade and fruit juice.' This sumptuous spread was the pre-war teatime merenda that the privileged Finzi-Contini children enjoyed on a summer afternoon, as described in *The Garden of the Finzi-Contini* by Giorgio Bassani.

Merenda is eaten by all children, and by grown-ups too, but nowadays a spread such as that described above would only appear at a grand party, such as a First Communion, a confirmation or a baptism. The everyday contemporary merenda for children might be a PANINO with SALAME or with a piece of chocolate, a biscuit or two, a packet of crisps, a piece of FOCACCIA or a selection of other snacks.

Country labourers refer to any sort of snack, taken at any time of day, as merenda. It usually consists of bread with some sort of SALUME or cheese, and this merenda is frequently taken mid-morning, washed down by red wine. No particular drink, however, is connected with merenda.

meringa
meringue

Both Swiss and Italian meringue are made with the same ingredients: sugar and whipped egg whites, but in the Italian meringue the sugar is used in the form of a hot syrup, which lightly cooks the egg whites, resulting in a more resilient texture which is suitable for SPUMONI, CASSATA and all sorts of little pastries.

The most common use of meringue today is in the form of shells, which are filled with whipped cream. These are not usually made at home; they come into the category of PASTE and are bought in cake shops, PASTICCERIE.

merluzzo
cod

This is not a Mediterranean fish and is found only dried as STOCCAFISSO, salted as BACCALÀ or frozen. The Mediterranean equivalent is hake (NASELLO).

mesciua
a bean soup

In the Ligurian dialect mesciua means 'a mixture'. This soup, which used to be the staple of the poorest people, is now served in chic restaurants. It originated in the province of La Spezia and it consists of a mixture of cannellini beans, chickpeas and FARRO, cooked until soft and then simply dressed with Ligurian olive oil and pepper.

messicani
stuffed veal

Veal or pork bundles, with an odd name that means 'Mexicans'. It is not so odd when you see them, because they look like small Mexican tacos. Here, however, the resemblance ends, since messicani consist of thin slices of meat wrapped round a mixture of sausage, meat, Parmesan, eggs and nutmeg. They are threaded in pairs onto wooden sticks, and sautéed in butter flavoured with sage. A splash of MARSALA is the final addition to this delicate and tasty dish from Milan, which, like OSSOBUCO, is traditionally served with RISOTTO ALLA MILANESE.

Messisbugo
Renaissance writer

Christoforo di Messisbugo, born in Ferrara, was the author of *Banchetti, compositioni di vivande et apparecchio generale*, covering everything there is to know about organizing and cooking for lavish banquets. The book is dedicated to 'The Most Illustrious and Most Reverend Signor Don Ippolito d'Este, Cardinal of Ferrara', and was published posthumously in 1549 and reprinted 17 times. Ippolito d'Este was Messisbugo's master, who in 1510 died of indigestion, an end that can readily be understood when reading the menus created for him.

Messisbugo is considered the founder of the great tradition of the Italian haute cuisine. Dishes are still made today that are derived from his recipes, with very few alterations. One example is this soup of chickpeas and pork rind: 'Take your clean chickpeas and wash them in the water of the Po river and cook them in this water. And while they are cooking add some good rich stock and then add a good lump of chopped lard. And then take the pork rind, boiled separately, and cut it in small squares, and put them in the pot with some well chopped scented herbs; and put some mint, fresh or dried, and pepper and ginger. And then serve it.' Although the Po was no doubt cleaner then than now, it is hard to understand why the chickpeas are to be cooked in river water. Nevertheless, this is one of my favourite recipes for a chickpea soup, although I use olive oil or pancetta rather than lard.

The sections on bread and wine are equally informative, from the *pani da famiglia* (family bread) to be eaten with the *vino da famiglia*, up the social scale to the most delicate bread, FOCACCIA and CRESCENTINE to be served at a banquet, with 28 different wines.

Messisbugo's book also makes an important contribution to social history, since his writing extends beyond the kitchen and the table to include the customs and habits, ceremonies, hierarchy and pomp that surrounded the Italian courts. Much can be learned from Messisbugo's accounts of dinners and banquets, which are described in detail through their various stages and for which full menus are given.

mezzaluna
chopping knife

A knife with a curved blade and a handle at each end, used for chopping. The crescent shape (mezzaluna means half-moon) makes it possible to chop by rolling the blade from left to right and back, without lifting it off the surface. This makes it easy to control the fineness or otherwise of the chopping. The mezzaluna is found in every kitchen in northern and central Italy, while in the south a large knife is more commonly used. Personally, it is one of the very few tools I couldn't do without. I am using it in the photograph on page 49.

michetta
bread roll

The classic Milanese bread roll, made with grade 0 or even 00 flour. A michetta, also called *rosetta*, 'little rose', because it looks like a small rose, is a very crusty round roll and the bread inside is so highly leavened that the roll is almost hollow. Michette are very light and one of the most fragrant rolls there are. Their only disadvantage is that they do not keep: to be at their very best, they should come out of the oven at noon and be eaten by one o'clock.

midollo
bone marrow

There is enough marrow in one bone for a RISOTTO ALLA MILANESE, for which it was the traditional fat, or for a sauce. Marrow is also used in PASSATELLI and in various stuffings, such as that for sweet fried RAVIOLI, when it is mixed with candied fruits and pine nuts. In OSSOBUCHI the marrow is the tastiest part.

miele
honey

Until early in the 19th century, honey was the most frequently used sweetener. The Romans loved honey and put it in very many dishes, both sweet and savoury. It was also used as a preservative, as shown in a recipe by APICIUS: 'Cover fresh meat with honey, suspend it in a vessel; in winter it will keep but in summer it will last only a few days. Cooked meat may be treated likewise.'

In the Renaissance, honey was used to coat meat and poultry because 'it can penetrate the flesh and make it sweet and tender'. Some recipes for sweets and cakes, whose origins can be traced back to the Middle Ages and the Renaissance, such as PANFORTE and CERTOSINO, are still made with a high proportion of honey instead of sugar. So too are some Sicilian puddings.

Nowadays honey is mainly eaten by itself, or used in food for babies. But in Piedmont a delicious sauce, *salsa d'api*, or *saussa d'avie* in the local dialect, made with honey, walnuts and mustard, accompanies the BOLLITO MISTO.

Honey is produced in all the regions of Italy, from most flowers, ranging from acacia and chestnut to white clover and rosemary. Among those that merit a special mention are the honey of Vesuvius, which comes from the volcano flora, and the honeys of Calabria and Sicily, made from orange blossom. Tuscan and Sardinian honey from the strawberry tree (*miele amaro* or *miele di corbezzolo*) has a bitter flavour and a light golden colour tinged with green, while the honey from lavender, from Liguria, is very delicate and has the characteristic aroma of the lavender flowers. But, as so often, it is Sicily that offers the most highly prized varieties: among the best are the honey from *zagara* (the flower of the lemon tree), from thyme, and from thyme and mint from Trapani.

migliaccio
a cake

A cake made with FARINA GIALLA (maize flour). In Emilia-Romagna the flour is mixed with pig's blood and sugar. In Tuscany migliaccio is a polenta FOCACCIA containing sultanas.

milanese, alla
in the milanese style

The expression does not apply to a particular method of cooking or to the use of special ingredients, but rather to food that is cooked according to an original Milanese recipe. That said, the one common element in all cooking alla Milanese is the use of butter as the cooking fat. There is RISOTTO ALLA MILANESE, which is made with saffron, MINESTRONE ALLA MILANESE, made with rice and pork rind or PANCETTA, and *costolette alla milanese* (see recipe on page 210), where the cutlet is coated with egg and breadcrumbs and fried in butter. Asparagus or leeks alla milanese (see recipe on page 333) are served with butter and fried eggs.

millecosedde
a soup

A soup from Calabria whose name means 'a thousand little things'. It is made with all the dried beans available, plus cabbage, onion, celery and wild fungi, cooked together for hours in an earthenware pot. Some short tubular pasta is boiled separately and then mixed with the vegetables and dressed with olive oil and grated PECORINO cheese.

milza

spleen

The spleen of oxen, calves and pigs is sometimes used in traditional Italian cooking. It tastes like liver and has the same slippery texture. In Tuscany, calf's spleen is sometimes used with chicken liver to make CROSTINI. In Alto Adige the cooked and pounded spleen is mixed with egg, marjoram and garlic and the mixture is spread between two thin slices of bread. These sandwiches are cut into fingers, fried in butter and served in meat stock. This soup, called *milzschnittensuppe*, is traditional all over the Italian Tyrol. In a recipe from Rome, *milza in padella*, ox spleen is blanched and then cut into thin slices. Sautéed in olive oil and lard with garlic and sage for a few minutes, it is then flavoured with pounded salted anchovies.

minestra

a soup

A soup in which the various elements, whether cubes of vegetables, grains of rice or shapes of pasta, are quite separate and distinct, and are distinguishable from the stock in which they cook. This is what differentiates it from a ZUPPA, which is a thicker mixture that is often ladled onto bread.

Some minestre are light and delicate, such as STRACCIATELLA, minestra di PASSATELLI and MINESTRA PARADISO. These are made with good stock, traditionally a light meat stock, in which other ingredients (such as cheese, minced white meat and/or breadcrumbs), bound with egg, have been cooked. There are also thicker minestre, of peasant origin, based on one or more vegetables cut into cubes and cooked in water or stock, usually with pasta or rice added at the end. This category is vast and includes such classics as *minestra di pasta e fagioli* (pasta and bean soup), minestre of other legumes, of Savoy cabbage and rice, and of milk and rice.

Northern Italy has a large repertoire of nourishing soups, which is what the climate demands, while in central and southern Italy they are fresher and lighter. This can be seen when you compare how a bean and pasta soup is made in the different regions. In Veneto, which boasts the original recipe (see page 139), a SOFFRITTO is made with pancetta, and a ham bone is added to it, while the Neapolitan version is made with water, tomatoes and herbs, and dressed with olive oil at the end. The recipe on page 72 is for a tomato soup that is simplicity itself, *minestra di pomodori*.

Minestra is still served at the evening meal as a first course in many homes. Recently, however, it has lost ground to the more popular pasta or risotto dishes.

minestra mariconda

a soup

This delicate soup from Lombardy includes small dumplings made from soft breadcrumbs soaked in milk, bound with eggs and flavoured with Parmesan and nutmeg. The mixture is dropped, a teaspoonful at a time, into a good simmering homemade stock.

minestra maritata

a soup

There are three versions of minestra maritata, one from Naples, one from Calabria and one from Puglia, and they all contain different vegetables that go well together. The versions from Calabria and Puglia are very similar. They both contain chicory, wild fennel, bulb fennel, celery and batavia. The vegetables are blanched and then layered with olive oil and PECORINO, covered with soft breadcrumbs and baked in the oven. The resulting dish is more like a vegetable pie than a soup. In the Neapolitan version pork rind and sausage are also added.

minestra paradiso
a soup

A typical soup from Emilia, light and delicate, ideal to have in the evening after the large, heavy lunch that used to be characteristic of the region. The first recipe we have comes from Bartolomeo STEFANI, in the 17th century. In Stefani's version, the eggs are beaten with cream and sugar before being whisked into capon stock, while in the modern recipe the eggs are mixed with Parmesan and breadcrumbs and then whisked into stock, which is rarely – alas – made from capon.

minestrina
a soup

A thin soup made with best chicken stock or a light meat stock, containing either PASTINA (small pasta shapes), barley or semolina which have been cooked in the stock. Minestrina is rather out of fashion, and now tends to be regarded as food for invalids or for babies.

minestrone
a soup

A thick vegetable soup, the many different versions of which have one thing in common: the cut-up vegetables simmer for a long time in water and/or stock. The remarkable thing about this very slow cooking is that each piece of vegetable retains its shape and does not become mushy, while the soup acquires the taste of all the vegetables that have been cooked in it. This is the traditional old-fashioned minestrone; nowadays minestroni are often cooked for a shorter time.

Minestroni are soups of northern Italy, and can be divided into two broad categories according to the method of cooking: minestrone col SOFFRITTO and minestrone a CRUDO. In minestrone col soffritto the chopped vegetables are sautéed in butter, pork

fat, oil or lard, or in a mixture of these, together with PANCETTA and/or pork rind. The vegetables go into the pot in order according to how long they take to cook. They are then covered with water or stock and cooked for a long time. At the end rice, or sometimes small tubular pasta such as DITALINI, is added. The minestrone alla milanese overleaf is an example of this style.

In minestroni a crudo the raw vegetables are put into the water or stock together, without being first sautéed. Best olive oil is added towards the end of the slow cooking. Sometimes the olive oil is heated with garlic and other herbs before being added to the soup. This type of minestrone is usually made with pasta rather than rice. The Tuscan version is the classic example of this type of soup.

Any vegetable can go into a minestrone, but some are essential. These are onion, celery, carrots, potatoes, beans and tomatoes. The other frequently used vegetables are courgettes, cabbage, peas, green beans and leeks. In winter canned tomatoes are used instead of fresh, and dried beans replace fresh beans, which are only in season for a short period in the spring.

Minestrone is nicer when it is made a day in advance and reheated. It can also be served cold in the summer, but should never be served straight out of the refrigerator.

 [see recipe on page 236]

misticanza
wild salad

Originally this was a mixture of wild salads which were picked in the fields and along the banks of the ditches in the area of Lazio called Castelli-Romani. According to Roman gastronomes, misticanza should contain 21 different kinds of wild salad. Even if this is a little excessive, a good misticanza must contain rocket, chicory, sorrel, mint, *radichella* – a kind of dandelion – lamb's lettuce, purslane and other local edible leaves. Misticanza is now widely cultivated throughout the peninsula.

mitili
see COZZE

mocetta
cured goat ham

The boned and cured thigh of a chamois, wild goat or domestic goat – a speciality of the Valle d'Aosta. The boned meat, flavoured with garlic, herbs, juniper berries and pepper, is first salted like a PROSCIUTTO, and then hung in a dry cellar for 3–4 months. It is eaten with brown bread spread with butter and sometimes also with honey.

moleca
soft crab

A speciality of the Venetian lagoon, where it has been caught for over two centuries. In their natural habitat, moleche lose their shells in the spring and autumn, when they are ready to mate. However, this development can be induced in hatcheries called *vieri*, which are kept under strange-looking platforms in the lagoon between Chioggia and Pellestrina. After leaving the crabs in the baskets for 48 hours, the fishermen inspect them once a day and begin to take out the crabs that are near the moulting stage. These are put in other baskets, where they eventually become moleche. They are then quickly removed and sent directly to the market, since if they were left they would grow their shell again.

The Venetians love moleche and sometimes, to achieve gastronomic perfection, inflict a sadistic death on the poor creatures. The moleche are put into a bowl containing beaten egg, in which – having partaken of the egg – they drown. They

are then coated in flour and fried in olive oil, and the Venetians have their treasured *moleche col pien* – 'moleche with a stuffing', the stuffing being the egg. I did try once, when I was in Venice, to make moleche col pien, but halfway through the operation I took pity on the poor souls and threw them into a canal.

Molise

This little-known region was, until recently, part of the combined Abruzzo-Molise region. Its basic food is based on the cooking of the shepherds and of the *contadino* (the small farmer). In the autumn the shepherds take their flocks down to the lowlands of Puglia in an annual migration known as the *transumanza*, returning to the mountains in the spring in a journey whose origins date from pre-Roman times. Their food is whatever is to be found by the roadside, simply cooked on a wood fire.

CONTINUES ON PAGE 238

235

minestrone alla milanese
Milanese vegetable soup

Serves 6–8

150g/5½oz/¾ cup dried borlotti beans,
soaked for about 12 hours in
cold water

50g/1¾oz/4 tbsp unsalted butter

50g/1¾oz pancetta, chopped

3 onions, sliced

4 carrots, diced

2 celery stalks, diced

2 courgettes, diced

100g/3½oz green beans, diced

100g/3½oz/⅔ cup shelled fresh peas

200g/7oz Savoy cabbage, shredded

1.5–2 litres/3–4 pints/1½–2 quarts
meat stock (page 61) or chicken
stock or 3 good-quality bouillon
cubes dissolved in the same quantity
of water

350g/12oz floury (starchy) potatoes,
cut in half

225g/8oz ripe fresh tomatoes, blanched
and peeled, or canned plum
tomatoes, drained

salt and freshly ground black pepper

175g/6oz/scant 1 cup Italian rice,
preferably Vialone Nano

75g/2¾oz Parmesan cheese, grated

You can add small tubular pasta to this soup instead of rice, although the classic Milanese MINESTRONE is always made with rice.

Drain and rinse the beans.

Melt the butter in a large heavy pot, preferably earthenware, and add the pancetta and onions. Sauté gently for 5 minutes or so and then add the carrots and celery. After 2 or 3 minutes, add the borlotti beans. Sauté for a further 5 minutes, stirring frequently, then add the courgettes, green beans and peas. After 5 minutes or so, mix in the cabbage. Stir everything together for about 5 minutes to coat in the fat.

Add the stock, potatoes, tomatoes and salt and pepper to taste. Bring to the boil, cover the pan and simmer over a very low heat for about 3 hours.

Using a slotted spoon, lift out the potatoes, mash them with a fork, then return them to the soup. Taste and adjust the seasoning.

Add the rice and cook for about 10 minutes, until al dente. Stir in 4 tablespoons of the Parmesan and serve the remaining cheese separately.

The contadino owns small plots of land in which he manages to grow excellent vegetables in often unyielding soil. His basic diet consists of these home-grown vegetables, among which tomatoes, either fresh or preserved, are the most popular, plus bread and oil, SALAMI and SALSICCIE, the legacy of the beloved pig, which even today is owned by nearly every family.

Pasta is a staple, and is produced in many different shapes, some shared with Abruzzo to the north – *taccozze*, *sagne*, LAGANELLE and FUSILLI – others with Puglia to the south – *recchiettelle* and CAVATIEDDI. The staple of northern Italy, POLENTA, is also eaten in Molise more than in other southern regions: it is combined with fried vegetables in a dish called *polenta a tordiglioni*, and, in another dish, with sausage, just as it is in the north.

Soups reflect the poverty of the locals in mixtures of dried beans, pasta, pig's trotters and nettles. A thick broth of celery and potatoes, layered in earthenware dishes, is similar to the TIELLE of Puglia but without the fish.

Fish is prepared along the short coastline, either grilled or fried, and in soups usually containing tomatoes and chilli, here given the delightful name of *diavolillo* (little devil).

Meat is rarely eaten, with the exception of offal. Molise has the largest repertoire of tripe dishes in Italy, the tripe being mostly of lamb and kid. A delicious tripe dish which is especially good in this region is *trippa alla combusciana* – boiled ox tripe dressed with a vinaigrette and served with celery.

In a society dedicated to stock-breeding, cheeses – CACIOCAVALLO, SCAMORZA, PECORINO – are important products. They are mostly made locally. Worth mentioning is a cheese called BURRINO, originally from Campania, which can be eaten fresh and creamy when just made, or at 4–5 weeks old when slightly tangy.

Desserts often contain lovely ewe's milk RICOTTA, such as *calciuni* (fried ravioli stuffed with chestnuts, almonds and spices, and traditionally eaten at Christmas) and FRITTELLE *di ricotta*. As in the rest of southern Italy, most puddings are small nuggets of delight, more often fried than baked, since in the old days few households had an oven, while they all had a frying pan and plenty of good-quality olive oil – the superb condiment of Molisano food.

mollica
breadcrumbs

Soft breadcrumbs: the inside of a loaf or roll, as distinct from the crust. Mollica is used principally as a binder in POLPETTE and POLPETTONI, in fillings for RAVIOLI and other pasta shapes and in stuffings for vegetables, fish etc. In Calabria and Sicily fried breadcrumbs are the main ingredient in many pasta sauces as a substitute for the more expensive Parmesan. The taste is, of course, different, though not necessarily less good, but the appearance is similar. A classic recipe for *pasta con la mollica* is given here.

[see recipe on page 240]

molluschi
molluscs

These include three categories of sea creatures: single-shell creatures, such as limpets; bivalves (creatures in double shells), such as mussels and clams; and cephalopods – calamari, octopus and the like. All are extremely popular around the coast of Italy and are cooked in many ways, and are eaten raw wherever the sea is clean.

mondeghili
meatballs

This is the Milanese dialect word for meat patties; POLPETTE in standard Italian. It is a 'poor man's' dish made in Lombardy from the leftover meat of a boiled, braised or roast joint. The meat is minced and mixed with eggs, bread soaked in milk, a little MORTADELLA or SALAME, chopped parsley, grated lemon rind and grated nutmeg. The mixture is shaped into little balls, coated in dried breadcrumbs and fried in butter. Mondeghili are essentially family fare, although there are still some old-established trattorie in Milan that serve this traditional dish.

Montasio
a cheese

A DOP cheese from Friuli-Venezia Giulia and eastern Veneto, made from the rich and fragrant milk of the cows that feed on the mountain slopes, which is at its best in the summer, when the animals are free to graze where they want.

Montasio is a semi-fat, semi-soft cheese with a hard and compact texture, tiny eyes and a buff-yellow colour. It is eaten as a table cheese after 2 months' ageing, when its flavour is fresh and milky sweet. After about 5 months it has a stronger flavour, similar to PECORINO, and it becomes suitable for cooking, as in the delicious FRICO, a fried cheese pancake.

montebianco
chestnut dessert

This pudding from Piedmont and Valle d'Aosta is a sweet concoction of pureed chestnuts, previously cooked in milk flavoured with vanilla, rum and cocoa or grated chocolate, and covered with crème Chantilly (sweetened whipped cream) to resemble the snow-covered peak of Mont Blanc.

montone
mutton

A ram and its meat. The meat comes usually from a castrated animal killed when it is about 1½ years old. Mutton is nowadays rarely eaten, except occasionally in Molise, Abruzzo, Sicily and Sardinia. The recipe from Abruzzo is for a mutton RAGÙ which is slowly stewed with PANCETTA, onion, rosemary, wine, tomato and chilli. The juice is used to dress pasta and the meat is eaten as a second course. In a traditional recipe from Sicily, a leg of mutton is first marinated for a few hours in wine vinegar and olive oil flavoured with mint, oregano and garlic, then roasted.

mormora
striped bream

This bream, which can measure up to 50cm/20in but is usually about 15cm/6in long, is a very fine fish. Bream is more common in the Adriatic than in the other seas around Italy. It has a round, flat body, silver in colour, with characteristic dark grey vertical stripes. It is often part of a GRIGLIATA, mixed grilled fish, or it is roasted in the oven stuffed with herbs, garlic and dried breadcrumbs moistened with olive oil. Mormora is also cooked *al forno* – roasted, stuffed with fresh herbs (parsley and rosemary are always present) and cooked with oil, unpeeled garlic and dry white wine.

morseddu
pork dish

Traditionally this is a breakfast dish – the only dish in the whole of Italy that used to be cooked for breakfast – actually it was made for the mid-morning MERENDA of the labourers. It is made in Calabria using scraps from the ribs and offal (tripe should be there) of a pig, all cut into morsels, sautéed in a SOFFRITTO of LARDO and garlic and then cooked in red wine, herbs and lots of chilli. Morseddu is still served in country trattorie to stuff *pitta* (a traditional bread similar to the Greek pitta), PANINI or country bread. It is always washed down by a glass of red wine.

pasta con la mollica
pasta with breadcrumbs, tomatoes and anchovies

Serves 3—4
250g/9oz ripe fresh tomatoes, peeled
2 garlic cloves, finely sliced
1 tsp crushed dried chillies
1 tbsp chopped fresh flat-leaf parsley
6 tbsp extra virgin olive oil
350g/12oz spaghetti or linguine
salt
4 salted anchovies, boned and rinsed, or
*   8 canned or bottled anchovy fillets,*
*   drained*
1 tsp dried oregano
6 tbsp dried breadcrumbs

This used to be the traditional dish eaten in Calabria and Sicily on Fridays, when Fridays were fast days and no meat was eaten. **In the poor regions of southern Italy, breadcrumbs were, and often still are, used instead of expensive Parmesan or PECORINO cheese. The result is different, but I find it more harmonious and certainly just as good. The pasta must be long: spaghetti or LINGUINE. The recipe from Catania in Sicily contains fresh anchovies; that from Calabria uses the more easily available preserved anchovies.**

Halve the tomatoes, squeeze out some of their seeds and chop the flesh. Put the garlic, chillies, parsley and half the olive oil in a large frying pan and sauté for 1 minute. Throw in the tomatoes and cook over a moderate heat for 5 minutes, stirring frequently.

Meanwhile, cook the pasta in plenty of boiling salted water.

Chop the anchovy fillets. Pour the rest of the oil into a small frying pan and add the anchovies. Cook, mashing them against the bottom of the pan, for about a minute and then scoop them with their juices into the tomato sauce. Add the oregano and cook for 1 minute. Taste and check the salt. Take the pan off the heat until the pasta is ready.

Drain the pasta and slide it into the frying pan. Give it a good stir, sprinkle with the breadcrumbs and stir-fry for a minute before serving.

mortadella
smooth pork sausage

Mortadella is made from pork meat (cheaper products may contain a small percentage of beef or horse), plus egg whites and spices. It may also contain pistachios, wine and sugar. Of the meat, 70% is lean – shoulder, bits of leg, end of loin – while the rest is fat, which should be from the jowl. The best mortadelle have a lovely pink colour and are very large – they can weigh up to 50kg/110lb, although they usually weigh around 14kg/30lb. Once made, the sausage is subject to 'stufatura', slow steaming in special cookers, a difficult process undertaken by specialists called *stufini*.

Mortadella keeps well but, once sliced, it should be eaten as quickly as possible. It should not be cut as thin as PROSCIUTTO – a mistake that is often made outside Italy.

Mortadella is chiefly made in Emilia-Romagna in the provinces of Bologna, Reggio-Emilia and Modena, although some mortadelle are also produced in Lombardy, Veneto and Le Marche. The reputation of the mortadella from Bologna is so high, and its association with that city so strong, that in Milan mortadella used to be known as bologna, while in the United States it is often called boloney.

Apart from being sliced and served as part of an AFFETTATO, mortadella is often cut into cubes, to be served with drinks before a meal or mixed in rice salads. Mortadella also goes into a number of stuffings for pasta and into the mixture for POLPETTE and POLPETTONI.

mortadella di fegato
liver sausage

This type of mortadella is made in the province of Novara in Piedmont and contains the liver of the pig mixed with lean and fat pork meat, pork rind and PANCETTA, all moistened with local red wine. Nowadays, like the MORTADELLA of Bologna, this sausage is usually served as part of the ANTIPASTO; in the past it used to be served hot with POLENTA.

mortaio e pestello
mortar and pestle

The mortaio e pestello are found in any respectable Italian kitchen. The best mortai are made of marble while the pestello is made of wood. Mortai are used for pounding herbs, anchovies, garlic, walnuts, pine nuts, peppercorns, juniper berries, etc, in fact small quantities of any food that would be spoilt by using a food processor. In a mortar the food is bruised rather than chopped, thus squeezing out the juices and releasing more of the flavour. They are essential for making the best basil PESTO.

moscardino
small octopus

Small octopus with curled tentacles, also called *mughetto* and, in Venice, *polpetto*. The smaller they are, the more highly prized. The *moscardino bianco* is less highly regarded because its meat is tougher and it does not have the smell of musk that is characteristic of the regular specimen. Moscardini are fried and eaten in a FRITTO MISTO DI MARE.

mosciame
dried dolphin or tuna

This is a speciality of Liguria and Sicily. The Ligurian mosciame consists of the fillet of a dolphin, cut into strips, salted and dried in the sun. The word is also applied to the fillet of a tuna fish or swordfish, similarly treated. It should always be added to CAPPON MAGRO. In Sicily, in the province of Trapani on the western coast, mosciame is a by-product of the tuna fishing industry. It is sliced very thin and dressed with olive oil and lemon juice and served as an ANTIPASTO.

mostaccioli
cakes

Small cakes made in most regions of central and southern Italy. They differ not only in their shape, but also in the ingredients. The *mostaccioli abruzzesi* and *calabresi* use similar ingredients and are prepared in much the same way. The dough is a mixture of honey, chopped almonds, flour, orange peel, sugar and spices, moistened in Abruzzo with cooked must and in Calabria with white wine. In Lazio mostaccioli also contain pepper, and in Puglia there are more ground almonds than flour. There is also a Sicilian version, in which the mostaccioli are served with a thin honey syrup containing chopped almonds.

Mostaccioli are also made in Lombardy, in the province of Varese, north of Milan. These were a part of my childhood, and were always known by their dialect name of *mostazit*. They were created by the nuns of the Convent of Sacro Monte near Varese, who still make them for special religious festivals. Honey is used for sweetening, with cloves, cinnamon and nutmeg – characteristic ingredients of northern Italian medieval dishes. Mostaccioli in ancient Rome were biscuits made for wedding feasts. They were described by Cato, a Roman senator in the 1st century AD; they were also allegedly the last food St Francis of Assisi ate when he was dying.

mostarda
a preserve

There are three different kinds of mostarda. The best known is the *mostarda di Cremona*, or *mostarda di frutta*, which in Lombardy is the classic accompaniment to boiled meats. It consists of various candied fruits, whole or cut into pieces, which are covered with a thick honey and white wine syrup, highly flavoured with spices and mustard. Its taste is a combination of sweet and hot, rather than sweet and sour. *Mostarda di Venezia* is made with minced quince, powdered mustard and sugar, and it can be made at home.

Mostarda, *tout court*, is a very old Sicilian sweet made with grape must, sultanas, almonds and pine nuts. The mixture is poured into small shapes representing various objects, and dried in the sun.

mosto
must

The juice of the grapes from which wine is produced after fermentation. In Puglia, mosto is a common drink, and in other southern regions it is used to make sweets in combination with other ingredients.

mozzarella
a cheese

In theory this name should apply only to buffalo mozzarella, *mozzarella di bufala*; the correct name for mozzarella made with cow's milk being *fior di latte*. However, nowadays the name mozzarella covers both types of cheese. Buffalo mozzarella should be eaten within 24 hours, dripping with its own buttermilk. It is pure white with a taste all of its own – delicate, fresh and fragrant, and it squeaks when you cut it. It is far tastier and has more body than mozzarella made from cow's milk.

Mozzarella is the best-known example of a *pasta filata* ('spun paste') cheese, also known as a 'plastic curd' cheese. To make it, the curd is broken up and heated until it becomes elastic; it can then be stretched and kneaded into the familiar ball shape.

Mozzarella is a low-fat cheese and is very digestible. The best way to eat a buffalo mozzarella is uncooked and on its own, or with tomatoes and olives, and maybe with basil, as in insalata CAPRESE. Mozzarella is often used in cooking, when it is better to use a day-old cheese cut in slices and left to drain for a few hours. Cow's milk mozzarella is an acceptable alternative in cooked dishes. Mozzarella is used in many pizza toppings, in some pasta dishes in combination with tomatoes, and in some meat dishes. A well-known dish made with mozzarella is *mozzarella in carrozza*. Mozzarella can also be smoked (*affumicata*) over straw and wood chips.

[see recipe below]

muggine
see CEFALO

muscioli or muscoli
see COZZE

musetto
a sausage

A sausage made in Friuli and Venezia Giulia. The mixture is pork meat from the snout (*muso* means 'snout' or 'muzzle') and rind, spiced with pepper, cloves, nutmeg, cinnamon and chilli, plus occasionally coriander (a rarity in Italian cooking). Local white wine is added, and the mixture is pushed into a casing made of ox gut. It is boiled like a COTECHINO and served hot with *broade* (pickled turnips), which, with their sweet and sour flavour, temper the fattiness of the sausage. The best musetti are made from the black pigs of San Daniele, the same animals from which the renowned PROSCIUTTO di San Daniele is made.

mozzarella in carrozza
fried mozzarella sandwich

Serves 4
400g/14oz mozzarella cheese, cut into
  5mm/¼in slices
8 large slices of good white bread
salt and freshly ground black pepper
225ml/8fl oz/scant 1 cup full-fat
  (whole) milk
2 large eggs
75g/2¾oz/generous ½ cup Italian
  00 flour
vegetable oil, for frying

A classic snack from Campania. Its name literally means 'mozzarella in a carriage', the bread being the carriage. In Campania, buffalo mozzarella is used. You could use cow's milk mozzarella, although the result will not be quite as good.

Divide the mozzarella into 8 portions. Don't worry if it crumbles a little. Cut each slice of bread in half and lay a portion of mozzarella on 8 of the half slices. Sprinkle with salt and pepper and cover with another piece of bread.

Pour the milk into a soup plate. In another soup plate, beat the eggs together with a little salt and pepper. Spread the flour on a board or a plate.

Pour enough oil into a frying pan to come 1cm/½in up the side of the pan. Heat the oil quickly until it is very hot but not smoking.

While the oil is heating, dip one of the sandwiches very quickly into the milk, coat lightly with flour and then dip into the egg, letting any excess egg flow back into the soup plate.

Carefully slip the sandwich into the hot oil, using a spatula if necessary. Repeat with the remaining sandwiches, keeping them in a single layer. Cook the sandwiches, turning once or twice, until they are a deep golden brown on each side. Drain on kitchen paper and serve.

n

napoletana, alla
in the style of Naples

An expression that brings to mind gutsy tomato sauces, mozzarella, garlic and oil. But alla napoletana is not a method that can be applied to different dishes, rather it describes the way a particular dish is made in Naples. Thus *lasagne alla napoletana* is a rich LASAGNE dish made by Neapolitans for Carnival. The lasagne are layered with mozzarella, RICOTTA, tiny fried meatballs and local sausages. Another example is *minestrone alla napoletana*. This is similar to other MINESTRONI, but it contains local pumpkin. The most famous dish alla napoletana is the PIZZA, which was indeed created in Naples and whose topping is always made of tomatoes plus other ingredients.

nasello
hake

This fish, which belongs to the same family as the cod, is very plentiful in the Mediterranean. It has a greenish-grey skin, with almost black fins and a lovely tapered shape. The best specimens are between 20 and 40cm/8–16in in length. The taste of the flesh is very delicate.

Hake lends itself to many different ways of cooking. Of all the recipes, *nasello alla marchigiana* and *nasello alla palermitana* are the best known. For nasello alla marchigiana (from the region of Le Marche) the fish should be small enough to serve one per person. They are marinated for up to 2 hours in olive oil flavoured with onion, garlic, salt and pepper. Then they are coated with breadcrumbs, grilled and served with anchovy sauce. The recipe given here is for the more interesting nasello alla palermitana, originating in Palermo in Sicily.

Hake is excellent simply baked and served with an oil and lemon sauce (mayonnaise would be overpowering), or baked in white wine flavoured with onion and served with its reduced cooking juices to which some lemon juice and a grating of lemon rind are added. A large fish can also be cooked 'in UMIDO', as is done in the south. The fish is cut in steaks and stewed in a covered earthenware pot with chopped fresh tomatoes, capers, parsley, oil and white wine for about 15 minutes. Garlic and chilli are optional, but only a touch of both should be used or they will kill the delicate flavour of the fish.

[see recipe on page 246]

necci
chestnut flour crêpes

Necci are a speciality of the mountainous parts of the provinces of Lucca and Pistoia in Tuscany. They are a kind of crêpe made with chestnut flour, olive oil, water and salt. Necci are cooked in hot embers, using a special, and ancient, tool called *testi*, which are long-handled tongs with iron discs at the end. Necci are eaten warm, stuffed with RICOTTA or fresh PECORINO, and they are so popular that there is even an annual festival, the *sagra dei necci*, on 15–16 August in the pretty town of Bagni di Lucca.

nepitella

see MENTA

nero di seppia
cuttlefish, octopus or squid ink

The ink of cephalopods, used to colour and to impart a stronger flavour to the dishes to which it is added, mostly RISOTTO or SPAGHETTI sauces. In Venice it is the ink of the cuttlefish that goes into the famous *risotto nero* and into *seppie alla veneziana*, as it also does in Sicily's pasta sauces, while the ink of the octopus is commonly used in Le Marche, with spaghetti.

There is now on the market black spaghetti, where cuttlefish ink has been added to the semolina and water. Pesonally, I find it rather a gimmick. I prefer the normal white spaghetti which I then dress with a good cuttlefish sauce.

nervetti
boiled calf's trotters

One of the great traditional dishes from Milan. Nervetti is similar in texture to brawn, but whereas brawn is made with pork meat and pork jelly, nervetti is made with the shin and foot of a calf. And unlike brawn, nervetti contains no fat. The pieces of veal are added to boiling salted water containing the usual flavouring of vegetables and are cooked until the meat can be easily removed from the bone. It is then cut into strips and, when cold, dressed with olive oil, vinegar, sliced sweet onion, salt and pepper. It is one of the traditional dishes on show in all the best *salumerie* (delicatessens) of Milan and Lombardy. In the old days nervetti used to be served in country inns, always accompanied by a glass of wine.

nasello alla palermitana
breaded hake with anchovies

Serves 4
1.25kg/2¾lb hake, cleaned but with
head and tail left on
5 tbsp olive oil, plus extra for greasing
salt and freshly ground black pepper
3 or 4 sprigs of fresh rosemary
1 garlic clove, finely chopped
3 salted anchovies, boned and rinsed, or
6 canned or bottled anchovy fillets,
drained
4–6 tbsp dried breadcrumbs
juice of ½ organic or unwaxed lemon

Ideally you should use a whole fish, which looks more attractive. If you cannot find it you can use a piece of hake.

Heat the oven to 180°C/350°F/Gas Mark 4.

Brush the inside of the fish with a little of the olive oil and season with salt and pepper. Put the rosemary sprigs in the cavity and secure with one or more wooden toothpicks.

Heat the remaining oil in a small frying pan and sauté the garlic for half a minute or so over a low heat. Take off the heat and mash in the anchovies. Rub the fish all over with the anchovy mixture and then coat with the breadcrumbs, patting them firmly into the fish.

Place the fish in an oiled ovenproof dish, preferably metal, and bake for about 30 minutes, or until the fish is cooked right through. Five minutes before the fish is ready, sprinkle with the lemon juice.

A golden crust should form all round the fish, but if it appears to be too dry, baste with the cooking juices and a little extra oil.

nespola
loquat and medlar

Two different trees share this name, the nespola – medlar, and the nespola del Giappone – Japanese medlar or loquat.

The nespola del Giappone is an evergreen plant with beautiful lanceolate leaves and is grown as an ornamental tree in many gardens. The fruit, which ripens in early spring, has a sharp yet very pleasant taste, but it is not really satisfying to eat as it contains five large stones, leaving little room for the pulp. It is eaten as it is, unpeeled, as its skin is very thin.

The other kind of nespola, the medlar, is a native of Europe. It has an odd fruit, formed by a cup and a calyx, which turns red when fully ripe after the first autumn frost. The fruit is inedible until it has fermented, after a period of natural decay. Nespole are therefore laid on straw for a few weeks, or can be left on the tree and picked when soft and brown. A third alternative, to which I subscribe, is to forget them altogether: they are certainly not the most delectable of fruits.

nocciola
hazelnut

The best varieties of this nut come from the Langhe area in southern Piedmont, followed by those of Benevento in Campania. The shape of the nuts varies, from round, which are supposed to be the best, to slightly oval. Hazelnuts, usually dried, are eaten by themselves at the end of the meal, with walnuts and dried fruit. They are also widely used in confectionery, of which TORRONE and the GIANDUIOTTI of Turin are the best known. Turin's cake called torta GIANDUIA also contains a fair amount of hazelnuts.

While nowadays hazelnuts are used mainly in sweet preparations, in the past they were used in sauces to serve with meat and fish. An anonymous 14th-century Venetian writer gives a recipe for Extra Strong and Perfect Sauce: 'If you want to make an extra strong sauce, take cloves, cinnamon, ginger and hazelnuts skinned over hot embers and a little soft breadcrumb and sugar. Pound all these things together and moisten with vinegar; and this is a good sauce with any roast.'

noce
walnut

The walnut is the fruit of a beautiful tree which grows everywhere in the mildest areas of Italy. The main cultivation is in Campania, around Naples, where the best variety, 'Sorrento', grows. The nuts are best from October until the spring, and they should be eaten before the summer because they become rancid.

Walnuts are generally eaten with fresh and dried fruit at the end of a meal and they are also used to make sauces and stuffings. The best known of the sauces is the *salsa di noci* from Liguria (see recipe overleaf), which is served with PANSÓTI or TAGLIATELLE. This sauce is the direct descendant of sauces that have been made with walnuts since the Renaissance. One of these is described by Vincenzo CORRADO: 'With walnuts peeled and pounded with garlic and marjoram, a sauce for boiled meats is made.' In Piedmont, a very interesting stuffing for roast pheasant contains walnuts, soft local cheese, lemon and grape juice, a glass of port, butter and spices. Another stuffing combines walnuts, cream, minced veal, Parmesan, egg and nutmeg and is used to stuff chicken thighs which are then cooked in the oven.

Walnuts are also used extensively in cakes and sweets. An early example, from a 14th-century manuscript by an anonymous Venetian, is for walnut nougat, made with chopped nuts, honey and spices, all cooked together and then flattened and left to cool. Walnut cakes are made

247

CONTINUES ON PAGE 250

salsa di noci
walnut sauce

Enough for 4 helpings of pasta
25g/1oz crustless white country bread
100g/3½oz/scant 1 cup shelled
  walnuts, preferably blanched and
  skinned
1 garlic clove, peeled
3 tbsp freshly grated Parmesan cheese
3 tbsp extra virgin olive oil
3 tbsp crème fraîche
1 tbsp Greek-style yogurt
salt

This is an adaptation of the traditional Ligurian dressing for PANSÒTI (the local ravioli) and other local pasta. Be careful when you buy shelled walnuts (NOCI): they must be eaten soon after they are harvested or they will be rancid and ruin any dish you add them to. I buy a lot in their shells at Christmas, shell them and freeze them.

Soak the bread in warm water for about 5 minutes and then squeeze dry. Pound the bread, walnuts and garlic in a mortar (or blend in a food processor) and then add the Parmesan, olive oil, cream, yogurt and salt to taste; stir until evenly combined.

Traditionally, pepper is not added to this sauce.

nodini
veal noisettes

Serves 4
4 noisettes of veal, at least 3cm/1¼in
  thick
3 tbsp flour
salt
50g/1¾oz/4 tbsp unsalted butter
1 sprig of fresh sage
75ml/2½fl oz/5 tbsp dry white wine

NODINI is a classic dish from Milan, where veal is the most popular meat. In my home in Milan, nodini were always accompanied by very buttery potato puree. Another traditional accompaniment, when in season, is fresh peas gently sautéed in butter and prosciutto and, maybe, a few sliced onions.

Tie the noisettes into a round shape with thread and coat them lightly with flour, lightly seasoned with salt.

Heat the butter in a large pan, sauté the sage and then add the noisettes. Cook over a medium-high heat until just golden on both sides, being careful not to pierce the noisettes when you turn them.

Add the wine and sprinkle with salt. Cover and cook over a medium-low heat for about 20 minutes, until the wine has evaporated and the meat is beautifully glazed. If necessary add a tablespoon or two of hot water if the liquid has all disappeared.

RIGHT: Nodini

in most regions of northern Italy. The most
famous of them all is the aptly named *bonissima*
– 'very good' – from Emilia-Romagna. It consists
of a sweet pastry shell filled with a mixture of
chopped walnuts, honey and rum.

 [see recipe on page 248]

noce moscata
nutmeg

A grating of nutmeg appears in the list of
ingredients of many recipes. It brings out the
taste in spinach, it makes a béchamel sauce or a
vegetable SFORMATO more lively, it enhances the
flavour of fungi and it is a must in the stuffing
for RAVIOLI and TORTELLI. Nutmeg is often added
to RAGÙ, stews and fish soups, as well as to fruit
poached in wine and many traditional fruit cakes.
No good kitchen is without a little jar containing a
few nutmegs and the small grater for grating them.

Nutmeg was described by Pliny, although it
was not popular in Roman times. Its use spread
with the growing power of Venice, which brought
oriental spices to Europe, and with the great
eastward travels of the Genovese navigators. Its
heyday was during the late Middle Ages and early
Renaissance, when it figures in most recipes. By
the 16th century, however, nutmeg, like all other
spices, began to be used with more discrimination.

nodini
veal noisettes

Nodini are always of veal, and it is only in
Lombardy that they are a traditional dish. They
are cut from the lower part of the loin and have a
short bone; they are 2–3cm/about 1in thick, with
hardly any fat.

 [see recipe on page 248]

norcino
pork butcher

In central Italy a norcino is the man who
slaughters the pig and oversees the making of the
various pork products. The origin of this word is
Norcia, a town in southern Umbria, from where
the best pork butchers came. From there the
norcini went everywhere, as far as Rome and
Florence, each year in November to practise their
trade, returning home in April.

The importance of the norcini was
recognized in 1615, when Pope Paul V founded
the Confraternita Norcina. A few years later,
Pope Gregory XV raised it to the rank of
Arciconfraternita, with a seat in the church of San
Benedetto all'Arco in Rome.

The norcini carried on their migratory life
until World War II. They went by cart, or on foot,
following identical paths each year, and stopping
at the same farms. Nowadays some butchers
practise their profession locally, but as pig raising
is big business, most norcini are employed on
large farms from which SALAMI, PROSCIUTTI, COPPE
and CAPOCOLLI are sent for sale to shops – which in
central Italy are often called *norcinerie*.

O

oca
goose

Geese were already domesticated in Homer's time and a few centuries later the early Romans declared them sacred. In 390BC these sacred palmipeds showed their gratitude to the Romans, who had retreated to the Capitol, leaving the rest of Rome in the hands of the invading Gauls. The geese heard the Gauls, at night, trying to take the Romans' only remaining stronghold. Proving that watch-geese are better than watch-dogs, they set up such a quacking that they woke Manlius, the Roman general, and his soldiers. The Gauls were thrown back and Rome reconquered, thanks to the sacred geese.

The Romans' gratitude, however, was not to last forever, since some 250 years later they learnt from the same Gauls that geese were better cooked in pots than wandering around the streets. The Romans became very fond of roast or boiled goose and, according to Pliny, it was a Roman who first made capital out of the delicacy of an enlarged goose liver by fattening the birds in the cruel way that is still practised today.

During the Middle Ages and the Renaissance, goose remained popular. Even PLATINA, always ready to point out a food's ill effects, had nothing but praise for this bird. Vincenzo CORRADO has eight recipes for goose; I particularly like the one for *oca farcita alli spinaci*, goose stuffed with spinach, Parmesan, eggs, sorrel, parsley and spices. Cooked in beef stock, it is served with creamed spinach.

The traditional way to cook goose is to roast it with a stuffing of roast chestnuts, minced pork, fresh fruit, such as apples, oranges or pears, and a few crumbled AMARETTI. Goose is also preserved,

oca in pignatta being a speciality of Veneto. It is cooked slowly with herbs and other flavourings for quite a long time, to allow the fat to run out. Skinned and boned, it is then cut into chunks and preserved in a glazed earthenware pot – PIGNATTA – in layers with its own fat. The goose is ready after 3 months and is either eaten with beans or POLENTA or used to dress TAGLIATELLE.

Another method of preserving goose is found in a Jewish-Venetian recipe, in which chunks of goose meat are kept under salt for up to 8 days, then hung up to dry in a warm, ventilated place. They are then put into sealed earthenware pots and covered with melted goose fat. The Italian Jews have always made SALAMI with the goose neck and PROSCIUTTI with its legs.

offelle
sweet pastries

A speciality of Lombardy and Emilia. The Lombard offelle are made with PASTA FROLLA: in Pavia they are plain biscuits, oval-shaped with pointed ends, while those of Mantua are more like half-moon shaped RAVIOLI, stuffed with apricot jam, egg and butter. In Emilia the offelle are made with PASTA SFOGLIA stuffed with SAVOIARDI and marzipan. In Friuli offelle are a totally different thing: they are a kind of savoury ravioli stuffed with spinach and sausage.

Offelle have a long history and they appear in the menus of banquets described by Bartolomeo SCAPPI in the 16th century. The offelle he refers to were two scalloped discs of pastry sandwiched together with marzipan. In another menu, Scappi mentions *offelle alla milanese* filled with apricot jam.

olii varii
various oils

The consumption of oils other than olive oil is small, although it has increased in recent years. This is partly because of the high cost of olive oil and partly because of the emphasis on lighter ingredients. The most common of these oils are groundnut and sunflower, both used for frying.

Walnut oil, which used to be quite popular in Lombardy before World War II, is now very seldom made.

olio d'oliva
olive oil

The gentle and generous olive tree gives us its ancestral beauty, its marvellous wood and the most highly prized produce – its oil.

Through the centuries kings and priests of many countries and denominations have been anointed with olive oil, and olive oil is still used in the Roman Catholic Church to anoint children who are being confirmed and people who are dying. The ancient Romans had many uses for olive oil. Athletes oiled themselves to make their muscles supple, while noble and rich ladies maintained the freshness of their complexion and the softness of their bodies with it. The Romans also lit their lamps with olive oil and applied it to the blades of their ploughs to invoke a rich harvest, but most of all they liked it in their food. Even their breakfast, a kind of porridge, was doused with olive oil. Rich patricians dined on fish from the Black Sea preserved in olive oil, on roast cranes flavoured with herbs and spices and dressed with olive oil and on sweet dumplings of ricotta fried in olive oil. It was so essential that most patrician houses had their own FRANTOIO – olive press.

Olive oil kept this prominent position through the Middle Ages, being also used for health and beauty treatments. Much Renaissance food was fried, and olive oil was the fat used. It is very unlikely, however, that the poor people in the northern regions would have used olive oil, as it was not a local product. They most probably never heard of it.

The use of olive oil only became widespread in northern Italy after World War II; prior to that it was used only in salads and never in cooking. After the war, thanks mainly to Tuscan restaurateurs opening trattorie in the north, olive oil became the prime ingredient of Italian cuisine as a whole.

Italy is the world's second-largest producer (after Spain) of olive oil, and it is also one of the biggest consumers. Domestic production is not sufficient for the Italian market and some olive oil is imported and mixed with Italian oil.

The olives for the oil are harvested between October and January, always when they are just slightly underripe. The best method of picking is by hand, but this is also the most costly. The olives are collected by pickers with large wicker baskets, or by spreading large nets around the base of each tree and shaking it. As soon as they have been harvested, the olives are taken to the *frantoio* – olive press – where the oil must be extracted within a week, the best oil being produced within one or two days. The whole process takes place without using any heat or chemicals, so that the end result is the pure juice of the olive with all the nutritional value of the fruit still in it.

The fruit is cleaned and washed in cold water and then crushed in stone mortars or under granite millstones. The pulp is placed in pressing bags, which are then crushed between oil press plates.

The oil that is extracted is the *olio di prima spremitura* – first pressing. Most of this is marketed under the name of extra virgin olive oil. The remainder, which may not comply with regulations because of an over-pronounced taste or smell, too dark a colour or too high acidity, will be refined and is usually blended with virgin oil and sold as pure olive oil. Colour varies from oil to oil, but is not a determining factor as to quality.

Olive oil is best after 6 months but it should always be consumed within the year; it does not keep for more than 18 months even in the best, cool, dark, conditions.

Olive oil is produced in 19 of the 20 regions of Italy (it is not produced in Valle d'Aosta), Puglia being the biggest producer and Piedmont the smallest. Which oil to choose is a matter of personal taste. Liguria produces a pale golden oil which is sweet and delicate, suitable for most dishes and palates. The oil from Chianti is peppery and full-bodied, while the other famous Tuscan oil, the one from the province of Lucca, is fruitier and less peppery. From the south, there is the oil from Puglia, which has a detectable almond flavour, a taste that can also be savoured in oils from Calabria. There, almond trees often grow among the majestic olives, lending a particular beauty to the olive groves. Both Sicily and Sardinia produce excellent olive oils.

Olive oil 'buffs' insist on the right oil for the right dish: PESTO must be made with oil from the Riviera, a single-estate oil from Chianti will dress a bowl of cannellini beans or a RIBOLLITA, while a dish of ORECCHIETTE with broccoli must have the almondy flavour of an oil from Puglia. But in the end, most people choose according to their taste and purse. Extra virgin olive oil is used for salads and any dish that requires the addition of uncooked oil, while olive oil is often used for cooking. The simpler the dish, the greater the need to use the best oil. Olive oil is also used for deep-frying because it has a high smoking point.

olio di semi
vegetable oil

A mixture of various seed oils, such as sunflower, maize and peanut, vegetable oil is used for frying and cooking when the dish does not require the real flavour of olive oil.

oliva
olive

This is the small unassuming fruit of the olive tree, the tree that makes some of the countryside in Italy so unforgettably Italian. It is the *Olea europaea*, of which there are many varieties and cultivars, different varieties being grown in different areas.

In Italy more than 50 varieties are grown, divided into trees that produce olives for oil and trees that produce olives for the table. Among the more common varieties of olives for oil are the Coratina of Puglia, the Frantoio of Tuscany, Umbria and Puglia, the Leccino of Tuscany and the small, exquisite Taggiasca of Liguria.

By the end of May the modest flower of the olive tree becomes a tiny berry, which by September has grown into a full-size olive. Olives do not become fully ripe until winter, but different varieties are picked at different degrees of ripeness and this determines the taste. Green olives are picked before they are ripe, purple olives are picked when they are ripe and black olives when they are over-ripe. Once harvested, the olives are selected, graded and sized. Most of the olives are used to make oil (see OLIO D'OLIVA); a minority are preserved.

The newly harvested olives are very bitter and the green ones, which have to go through a process of de-acidification, are inedible. When the olives are treated industrially they are first immersed in a soda solution and then washed thoroughly in several changes of water, after which they are ready to be pickled. Methods of preserving olives, of which there are a great many, vary according to the region, the variety of the olive and the way they are to be used. Some growers still preserve their own olives, the ancestral method being a closely guarded secret. Various flavourings may be added to the brine, such as wild fennel, oregano, chilli or garlic. One of the most unusual, and most delicious, is a flavouring for black olives that is a speciality of Umbria, the ingredients being orange rind, garlic and bay leaves.

253

There is a traditional recipe for stuffed olives – *olive ascolane* – from Ascoli Piceno, in Le Marche, which are the only stuffed olives I really like. The local green olives are so large that, once stoned, they can be stuffed with minced pork, prosciutto, Parmesan and other flavourings, all bound with egg. They are then coated with egg and breadcrumbs and fried. Another traditional recipe for stuffed olives is from Sicily, the stuffing being a mixture of anchovy fillets and capers.

From Sicily comes an *insalata di olive schiacciate* in which black olives are stoned, squashed and dressed with olive oil, garlic, vinegar, chilli and oregano. Yet another Sicilian recipe is a salad of oranges, black olives and batavia endive or fennel.

As there is a distinct difference between the taste of green and black olives, particular dishes call for the use of one or the other. The olives that are added to pasta sauces such as PUTTANESCA and to fish dishes are usually black, while green olives are used in rabbit and chicken dishes. However, either green or black olives are served as a snack with an aperitif or used to decorate cold dishes.

The earliest recipe we have for preserving olives was written by Columella, a botanist who lived in the 1st century AD: 'Scald and drain olives and then place them in a layer in an amphora, covered with a layer of dry salt and a final layer of herbs.' A recipe for preserving olives written by Domenico Romoli, a steward in Florence in the 16th century, gives detailed instructions. He suggests using river water to which wine vinegar, orange, citron and lemon juice as well as the leaves of bay, elder and olive and sprigs of wild fennel should be added 'all to give the olives a gentle taste and scent'.

ombrina
a fish

This is a good fish, so sought-after that the catch around the peninsula is not enough to satisfy the hunger of the Italians. Many ombrine on the market are now imported from Africa. A variety of ombrina, the highly prized *ombrina boccadoro*, also called *ricciola* in southern Italy, can reach 2m/6½ft in length. Ombrina is an excellent fish with few bones and delicate white meat. It is cooked in the same ways as sea bass (BRANZINO) or in BRODETTO, highly flavoured with saffron.

onda, all'
creamy

All'onda, literally 'wavy', is an expression used in northern Italy to describe the ideal consistency of RISOTTO. It means creamily bound together; neither too liquid nor too dry.

orata
gilt-head bream

This is the French *daurade*, the most highly regarded member of the family *Sparidae*. It is a fish that looks beautiful and tastes delicious. It has a rather flat, yet full, body with a maximum length of about 60cm/2ft. There is no better description of an orata than that given by Giulio Cesare Tirelli, a great Venetian chef of the 16th century: 'The fish that carry the crown are indeed the queen of all the others because they are delicate beyond belief. It should not appear odd to somebody who is ignorant to hear that they have a crown, since this is very true and it is called a golden crown, placed by Mother Nature on the right spot, that is to say the head.'

The first recipe that Tirelli gives is, to my mind, the best, the orata being simply roasted with wild fennel, salt and olive oil and served with lemon juice. Another of his recipes for orata is to cook it 'between two plates', which means steamed, with grated nutmeg and lemon juice. Orata is never cooked in a complicated way since it only needs a few flavourings to bring out its superb flavour. In the recipe on page 339 it is paired with garlic and parsley, the flavours sealed between two layers of potatoes, and then baked.

orecchiette
a pasta

The traditional pasta of Puglia, literally 'little ears', still often made at home, a rather laborious and difficult job, since the dough for orecchiette is hard and unyielding, and every orecchietta has to be shaped by hand. The dough mixture is durum wheat SEMOLINO and water. After it has been kneaded to the right consistency, tiny bits of dough are plucked out and quickly pressed down with the thumb so that they resemble a smooth limpet-shell. The orecchiette are then left to dry for a few hours. Industrial orecchiette are now a popular pasta shape, perfect for most vegetable sauces.

The traditional way to prepare orecchiette is to boil them together with a special variety of turnip tops – CIME DI RAPA – also called *friarielli* in Naples. Once drained the orecchiette and the turnip tops are served together, dressed with salted anchovies pounded with garlic and chilli and gently heated in olive oil. Broccoli can be cooked with orecchiette in the same way, or they can be dressed with sultanas and pine nuts (see recipe on page 60). In another recipe rocket and orecchiette are added to half-cooked potatoes. This dish is usually served as a thick soup, dressed with a SOFFRITTO of the local olive oil, garlic and chilli.

orecchio
ear

The ear of a pig or of a calf is a tasty morsel to which chefs have dedicated a number of recipes. The ear is first thoroughly cleaned, then boiled and cut into strips. It is either served cold with a piquant sauce, or coated in egg and breadcrumbs and fried. A pig's ear must be included in a Lombard CASSOEULA.

origano
oregano

A herb that grows wild in dry and sunny parts of central and southern Italy. It is a perennial bush with white or pale pink flowers which are used, with the leaves, in flavourings. Oregano is mostly sold already dried, in bunches. It is the only herb that is better dried than fresh, since it has a strong yet sweet aroma.

Of all herbs, oregano is the one most closely associated with southern Italian food. It is used in pizzas and tomato sauces, with vegetables, both raw and cooked, and with fish and in many other recipes. In Sicily oregano is added to jars in which anchovy fillets or olives are preserved.

ortaggi
see VERDURE

ortica
nettle

Nettles have been an ingredient of peasant cooking for centuries. They are mostly eaten in soups with rice, the nettles being first sautéed in butter with onion and then covered with stock. The rice is added after about half an hour. Nettles are also used to make RISOTTO. In a recipe from Valle d'Aosta, nettles are chopped and cooked with two or three potatoes in goat's milk. When they are soft the potatoes are mashed and rice is added. At the very end, small pieces of TOMA, a local cheese, are added. In Calabria, where almost everything is cooked with pasta, the nettles are cooked in boiling salted water and when nearly done some spaghetti, broken up into 4cm/1½in lengths, is

CONTINUES ON PAGE 258

255

ossobuco alla milanese
Milanese ossobuco

Serves 4

4 ossobuchi, about 250g/9oz each
flour, for dusting
salt and freshly ground black pepper
2 tbsp olive oil
40g/1 ½oz/3 tbsp unsalted butter
1 small onion, finely chopped
½ celery stalk, finely chopped
150ml/5fl oz/⅔ cup dry white wine
300ml/10fl oz/1 ¼ cups meat stock
*   (page 61) or chicken stock*

Gremolada

1 tsp grated rind from an organic or
*   unwaxed lemon*
½ garlic clove, very finely chopped
2 tbsp chopped fresh flat-leaf parsley

The classic ossobuco from Milan is known throughout the world. Buy ossobuchi all the same size, so they take the same amount of time to cook.

Tie the ossobuchi around and across with string as you would a parcel and then lightly coat them in flour mixed with 1 teaspoon of salt.

Heat the olive oil in a heavy sauté pan which has a tight-fitting lid and is large enough to hold the ossobuchi in a single layer. Add the ossobuchi and brown them on both sides in the hot oil. Remove them to a side dish.

Add 25g/1oz/2 tbsp of the butter to the sauté pan together with the onion and celery. Sprinkle with a little salt, which will help the onion release its liquid and soften without browning. After about 10 minutes, when the vegetables are soft, return the meat to the pan along with the juice that has accumulated.

Heat the wine in a saucepan and pour it over the meat. Turn up the heat and boil to reduce by half, scraping the bottom of the pan with a spoon.

Heat the stock in the saucepan used for heating the wine and pour about half over the ossobuchi. Turn the heat down to very low and cover the pan. Cook the ossobuchi for 1½–2 hours, until the meat has begun to come away from the bone. Carefully turn the ossobuchi over every 20 minutes or so, taking care not to damage the marrow in the bone. If necessary, add more stock during cooking, but very gradually – no more than 3 or 4 tablespoons at a time. If by the time the meat is cooked the sauce is too thin, remove the meat from the pan and reduce the liquid by boiling briskly.

Transfer the ossobuchi to a warmed dish and remove the string. Keep warm in a cool oven.

Cut the remaining butter into 3 or 4 pieces and gradually add them to the sauce. As soon as the butter has melted, remove the pan from the heat. The sauce should not boil. The addition of the butter will give the sauce a glossy shine and a delicate taste.

Mix the ingredients for the gremolada together, stir into the sauce and leave for a minute or two. After that, just spoon the sauce over the ossobuchi and serve immediately.

added. The spaghetti and nettles are drained and dressed with a few tablespoons of best olive oil and lots of pepper. Only the tops of young nettles are used. In the early spring I make nettle PESTO with pistachio nuts, olive oil, garlic and Parmesan, which I use to dress pasta or rice.

orzo
barley

Barley is grown in northern Italy. The barley on the market today is always pearl barley, in which the husked grain has been polished. It is made into soups in Valle d'Aosta, Alto Adige and Friuli. These regions have many dishes originating in Germany and Austria, where barley is more popular than in Italy.

A tiny pasta shape, made from wheat flour and resembling little grains, is known either as orzo, or as *risoni* ('big rice').

Barley can be roasted and ground to make a caffeine-free alternative to coffee, often called simply 'orzo'. All through the war my mother, who adored coffee, had to make do with this awful drink, to which some ground dandelion root was added for bitterness.

orzotto
barley risotto

In recent years this dish has regularly appeared on the culinary scene. It is a RISOTTO made with pearl barley, which has the following great advantages over risotto: it does not overcook; it can be made adding the stock all in one go, as for a pilaf; and it can be made in advance. The most popular orzotto is with mushrooms, but it can be made with almost any other ingredients, as for a risotto.

ossobuco
shin of veal

Literally 'bone with a hole', ossobuco is obtained by cutting slices about 4cm/1½in thick across the hind shin of a milk-fed calf. Inside the circle of meat is the bone and inside the bone is the marrow, this being the essence and the *bonne bouche* of the dish.

The marrow is scooped out of the bone using a special tool called an *estrattore*, a long thin piece of metal with a narrow pointed spoon at one end; at the other end is a two-pronged fork, which is used to pick out meat from the shells of crustaceans – a very elegant tool for very sophisticated food.

The traditional recipe for *ossobuco alla milanese* with gremolada does not include tomatoes, since it probably precedes the use of tomatoes in local Lombard dishes. It is traditionally accompanied by risotto. Some chefs serve RISOTTO ALLA MILANESE – saffron risotto – while others prefer RISOTTO IN BIANCO – plain risotto. I opt for the latter because I find that the flavour of saffron interferes with the flavour of the lemony gremolada.

Ossobuco cooked with tomatoes is a traditional dish of Emilia-Romagna; it is not served with gremolada and is accompanied by boiled rice, generously dressed with melted butter flavoured with saffron.

[see recipe on page 256]

osteria
inn

Traditionally the osteria is a place where wine and simple food are served. It is a place where men gather and women are not welcome. During the day the customers consist mainly of old men who meet to play *scopa* – a card game. Recently some osterie, especially in cities, have been transformed into elegant, albeit rustic, restaurants, where good local food and local wines are served.

ovolo
fungus

The botanical name for ovolo is *Amanita caesarea*. The name amanita arouses fear in many people, since they know of the deadly toxicity of most of the *Amanita* family, the Death Cap among them. However, the *Amanita caesarea* is one of the best edible fungi.

Ovoli appear in late summer and autumn in oak and chestnut woods. They are easily spotted because of their beautiful orange caps, but they are very rare.

When young, ovoli are eaten raw. There is nothing better than a salad of ovoli except a salad of ovoli and white truffles, a speciality of Alba, a town in Piedmont, which offers another great dish, *ovoli all'albese*. This is ovoli mixed with very thinly sliced raw fillet of beef, which is sometimes mistakenly called CARPACCIO. The beef is dressed with olive oil and lemon juice and then covered with ovoli, which should be sliced with a truffle shaver, and flakes of very young Parmesan. When not so young, ovoli are delicious in a simple soup made with garlic and oil and served with croutons.

p

padella
frying pan

Frying pans, in at least three different sizes, are vital in every Italian kitchen. A large cast-iron pan is kept solely for fried food. The padella for frying has a long handle, which should be as long as the diameter of the pan, and sloped sides, while the padella for sautéing has two handles and slightly curved sides.

'In padella' or *spadellato* is a method of cooking where the food is first sautéed and then finished off at a lower temperature, with the optional addition of some liquid. In many recipes for pasta, the drained pasta is finished off in the padella in which the sauce has been cooked. It is a traditional method for cooking many southern pasta dishes which have now become popular all over Italy.

paesana, alla
cooking method

Alla paesana means cooked the peasant way. This has no precise meaning, but implies that the dish is made with plain, locally grown – or reared – ingredients. One well-known dish that uses this epithet is RISOTTO *alla paesana*, a risotto with vegetables, for which the recipe is given here.

[see recipe on facing page]

pagello
sea bream

Pagello is a good fish with lovely firm white flesh. It lends itself to being cooked in the simplest way, such as grilling or roasting, brushed with olive oil. In Campania, pagello fillets are cooked either in the oven or in a pan, covered with peeled plum tomatoes, plus olive oil, garlic and oregano.

paglia e fieno
a pasta

Fresh egg pasta consisting of yellow and green TAGLIOLINI, the green being made with spinach pasta. Paglia e fieno (meaning 'straw and hay') has only become popular in recent decades, when the appearance of food has become more important.

Paglia e fieno takes a long time to make at home, and thus is more often bought – fresh or dried. Pasta e fieno tends to stick together when you drain it. To partly avoid this, rather than draining it through a colander, lift it out of the pan with tongs, a special spaghetti drainer or a long wooden fork, and always remember to keep some pasta water to add to the sauce.

pagliata
offal

Pajata or *paiata* in Roman dialect, this is a part of the intestine of a young calf, lamb or kid, which contains a creamy substance. Pagliata is a traditional peasant dish of the Roman countryside and is prepared in many ways, the best known being as an accompaniment to RIGATONI. The pagliata is cooked in a tomato and wine sauce flavoured with cloves, rosemary and chilli, and spooned over the cooked rigatoni. Calf's pagliata is also grilled after being moistened, traditionally, with lard.

pagnotta
a bread

A large round loaf, of which the Tuscan pagnotta is the prime example. It is the oldest shape of bread. A pagnotta weighs from 500g to 1kg/ about 1–2½lb. It is traditionally sliced by the man of the household, who cuts it in a special way. Holding the pagnotta in the crook of his elbow, he slices it very thickly, moving the knife towards his chest.

pagro
sea bream

A member of the sea bream family, this fish is similar to the ORATA and the DENTICE but less delicate. A pagro can be as long as 75cm/2½ft but it usually averages about 30cm/12in. The best way to cook a pagro is to bake it, stuffed with herbs, garlic and breadcrumbs. In Liguria it is often cooked on a bed of sautéed dried porcini, garlic and parsley.

risotto alla paesana
risotto with vegetables

Serves 4

*1 litre/1¾ pints/4 cups homemade
     chicken or vegetable stock*
75g/2¾oz/5 tbsp unsalted butter
1 tbsp olive oil
1 onion, finely sliced
*250g/9oz/1¼ cups risotto rice,
     preferably Arborio or Vialone Nano*
1 carrot, diced small
2 celery stalks, cut into thin slices
100g/3½oz/¾ cup shelled fresh peas
*2 ripe fresh tomatoes, peeled, deseeded
     and coarsely chopped*
1 courgette (zucchini), diced small
75g/2¾oz Parmesan cheese, grated
salt and freshly ground black pepper

Seasonal vegetables are used in this RISOTTO, which is also known as *risotto primavera*. You can add asparagus spears or green beans, depending on the season.

Bring the stock to simmering point and keep it simmering.

Put 50g/1¾oz/4 tbsp of the butter, the oil and the onion into a heavy-bottomed saucepan and sauté gently until the onion is soft and translucent. Add the rice and cook for 1 minute, stirring constantly to coat the rice in the fat. Pour over about 200ml/7fl oz/generous ¾ cup of the stock and cook, stirring all the time, until nearly all the stock has been absorbed. Then add another 150ml/5fl oz/⅔ cup of the simmering stock and continue stirring. Regulate the heat so that the rice cooks steadily at a lively simmer.

When the rice has been cooking for about 10 minutes, add the carrot, celery, peas and tomatoes. Mix, and keep adding small amounts of stock whenever the rice begins to look dry.

After 5 minutes, add the courgette. Cook, stirring and adding more simmering stock as necessary. Do not add too much stock in one go – when the rice is nearly done, add no more than 4 tablespoons at a time. The risotto should be ready in about 20 minutes.

When the rice is tender but al dente, take the pan off the heat and mix in the remaining butter and half the Parmesan. Taste and add salt if necessary, and pepper. Stir thoroughly and turn the risotto into a warmed dish. Serve at once, with the rest of the Parmesan handed round separately.

paiolo
copper pot

The unlined copper pot in which POLENTA is made. It is shaped like a large, round-bottomed bucket and has a bucket handle. A paiolo is still a fixture in most kitchens in Italy, especially in the north. In the country it might still hang over the open fire in winter, full of water, and is used every day.

A paiolo is a beautiful object, so beautiful, in fact, that in the late 15th century a group of artists took it as their emblem and founded La Compagnia del Paiolo. The members of the compagnia, of whom the painter Andrea del Sarto was one, gathered to celebrate their mutual interests, chief among which, it seems, were the pleasures of the table.

There are now electric paioli for making polenta, which do all the boring stirring, but are certainly not beautiful objects. You plug the pot in, add the maize flour and after some 40 minutes the polenta is ready.

palombaccio, palomba or colombaccio
wood pigeon

Wood pigeon used to be very popular in Umbria, where the best recipes come from, and they were also found in Tuscany, Lazio and Le Marche. They are now rare in the wild but are bred in captivity and are often roasted, wrapped in prosciutto or cooked on the spit.

The best-known recipe, *palombacci alla ghiotta*, is from Umbria. A special roasting pan, called *leccarda*, is placed under the spit. The leccarda is filled with a sauce called *salsa* GHIOTTA, made with wine, herbs and seasoning, and the rotating pigeon is brushed regularly with the sauce. Halfway through the cooking, the giblets of the bird are removed, chopped and added to the sauce. When the pigeon is cooked it is jointed

and placed in the leccarda with one or two anchovy fillets.

Older wood pigeons are cooked in SALMÌ, often with the addition of anchovy fillets.

palombo
dog fish

Palombo can reach a length of 1.5m/5ft. This is the fish one can see cut into huge steaks on the stalls of the Rialto, the fish market in Venice, where it is called *vitello di mare* ('sea veal').

The most popular recipes are the Roman *palombo coi piselli* – with peas, tomatoes, parsley and garlic – and the Milanese 'palombo a COTOLETTA', in which the fish steaks are coated first in flour and then in egg and breadcrumbs, and then fried in butter and oil. This is traditionally served topped with a slice of lemon and a fillet of anchovy rolled around a caper.

pampepato or pan pepato
a sweet bread

A very peppery sweet bread dating from the Middle Ages. There are two kinds of pampepato, one made in Ferrara in Romagna and the other in central Italy. The Ferrarese pampepato is ring-shaped; it contains almonds and pine nuts and is often coated with chocolate icing. It is the local Christmas cake and before World War II bakers used to give pampepato to their customers at Christmas-time. This tradition stemmed from the Renaissance, when bakers gave pampepato (not chocolate-coated, of course) to the landlords for whom they worked. According to Waverley Root in *The Food of Italy*, the tradition was revived in 1945 when the city's bakers gave General Eisenhower a 5kg/11lb pampepato.

The pampepato from central Italy is shaped into small rolls, studded with almonds, walnuts, pieces of chocolate, sultanas and candied fruit.

pan di miglio
millet bread

On St George's Day, 23 April, the Milanese pan di miglio is traditionally eaten with cream, of which St George is the patron saint. Pan di miglio is a flat, round brioche, about 10cm/4in across, and I can still see it on my plate, a yellow island in a white sea, as I slowly poured more and more cream all round it. Pan di miglio used to be made with millet flour, but is now made with maize and wheat flour, plus butter, egg yolks, sugar, yeast and vanilla. Each round is covered with a sprinkling of sugar mixed with elderflowers, which are just coming into bloom at that time of the year. When I was a child, it was my favourite MERENDA ever.

pan di ramerino
rosemary bread

A sweet bread made in Tuscany, rosemary being the Tuscan herb par excellence; it goes with all their roasts and beans, and their FOCACCE, and it gives this bread a delicious pungent flavour. Pan di ramerino is a very old kind of bread: it is mentioned in Iris Origo's book, *The Merchant of Prato*, based on the correspondence conducted by a 14th-century merchant.

pan sciocco
unsalted bread

The Tuscans eat bread with everything and find that bread containing salt, however little, would interfere with the taste of the food it is eaten with. That is why their bread is saltless. You might not find pan sciocco to your taste when you first try it, but after a few mouthfuls with FINOCCHIONA or PECORINO you will see that the Tuscans, who are purists when it comes to food, have a point.

pan di Spagna
a sponge cake

A fatless sponge, similar to Madeira cake, used for layered sweet preparations such as TIRAMISÙ and ZUPPA INGLESE.

pan speziale

see CERTOSINO

pan con l'uva
raisin bread

This sweet bread from Milan was one of my favourite snacks, bought at the baker's shop on my way to school. I would queue, surrounded by other children all sniffing the freshly baked bread, and ask for '*un etto di pan con l'uva*' – 100 grams of raisin bread. I was handed a piece that was cut from a stick of crusty bread, lavishly studded with fat, juicy raisins. It was still hot, wrapped in buff-coloured absorbent paper, and I kept it to eat for my elevenses. It is still popular in Lombardy.

pancetta
cured pork

Exactly the same cut of meat as streaky bacon, namely the belly of a pig, but cured differently. Like streaky bacon, pancetta has layers of white fat and of pink meat. There are two kinds of pancetta: *pancetta tesa*, which is left in its natural state, like bacon, and cured for about 20 days, and *pancetta arrotolata* (rolled pancetta). Pancetta arrotolata is made from very fatty pancetta, and only shows two or three streaks of lean meat. It is flavoured with cloves and pepper, rolled up, sewn and tied up. Pancetta tesa can also be smoked and is a speciality of Alto Adige, Friuli and Valle d'Aosta.

Pancetta tesa is one of the most important elements in a SOFFRITTO, the starting point for so

263

many dishes. It is the main ingredient of some pasta sauces, such as CARBONARA, and a component in all kinds of SPIEDINI (kebabs), whether of meat, liver or fish. Pancetta arrotolata is eaten by itself, very thinly sliced, or with other SALUMI.

pancotto
bread soup

Literally, 'cooked bread', this is the most widespread of all peasant soups. It is made with good country bread, plus a combination of local ingredients. In a typical northern Italian version these added ingredients are butter and onion, plus sweet spices, and the soup, made with meat stock, is sprinkled with Parmesan cheese. In Liguria, herbs and grated PECORINO are the flavourings, while in the south tomatoes are a classic addition. The PAPPA COL POMODORO of Tuscany is pancotto by another name. In a version from Puglia the pancotto is made with rocket and potatoes, and the bread is added to the soup at the end.

[see recipe below]

pandolce
Christmas cake from Genoa

Also known as *panettone genovese*, it is shaped like a very shallow dome and has a triangle of cuts at the top. The dough is compact and stuffed with sultanas, *zibibbo* (dried Muscat grapes), pine nuts, candied pumpkin and citron, and it is flavoured with orange flower water, fennel seeds and various spices. When the cake is brought to the table a sprig of bay is placed on top and the youngest member of the party cuts the cake.

pandoro
Christmas cake from Verona

This cake has the delightful name of 'golden bread' because of its colour. The cake mixture consists of flour, eggs, butter and yeast. Pandoro is baked in a star-shaped mould with eight points, and lavishly covered with icing sugar. It has a very light texture and a buttery taste. Pandoro is hardly ever made at home. It is now widely available outside Italy.

pancotto
bread soup

Serves 4

175g/6oz stale crustless white bread
5 tbsp extra virgin olive oil
½–1 tsp crushed dried chillies
3 garlic cloves, chopped
2 tbsp chopped fresh flat-leaf parsley
1.5 litres/3 pints/6 ½ cups hot light meat stock (page 61) or chicken stock, or good-quality bouillon cubes dissolved in the same quantity of water
salt and freshly ground black pepper
freshly grated pecorino cheese, to serve

Use good, rustic-style bread such as Pugliese or pain rustique, not a sliced loaf, which will make a gluey, thick and unpleasant PANCOTTO.

Cut the bread into very small pieces and process for a few seconds, or chop coarsely.

Put the olive oil, chillies, garlic and parsley in a pan and sauté for 30 seconds. Add the bread and cook, stirring frequently, for 3 or 4 minutes, until the bread begins to turn pale brown. Add the hot stock, cover the pan and simmer for 30 minutes.

Taste and adjust the seasoning. Serve the soup with grated pecorino cheese on the side.

pane
bread

Bread, in Italy, has always been the staff of life. There are a number of sayings in which bread stands for food, or nourishment. One such is *'Senza il pane tutto diventa orfano'*, which could be translated as 'without bread one is deprived of everything'. The saying that expresses most clearly the place of bread in everyone's affections is *'é buono come il pane'*, used to describe a kind, generous, warm-hearted person. As children, we were not allowed to throw away even the smallest piece of bread. If we did, our fate in the next life would be to go around with a bottomless basket picking up all those crumbs of bread that had been thrown away by us and by other wicked children like us.

Many loaves have the sign of the Cross impressed into the dough before they go into the oven. In the country, some old people still make the sign of the Cross before cutting into a new loaf. Regional loaves have symbolic shapes for special occasions such as christenings or weddings, especially in the south, where traditions have not been totally swept away by progress.

The ancient Greeks were excellent bakers and the first to use the large wood oven for bread-making, something which has remained virtually unchanged ever since. The Romans, so good at making most things, never mastered the craft of bread-making; it was a job they left to the Greek slaves whom they brought back to Rome.

There are no recipes for bread in the cookery books of the Renaissance because the recipes that were written down were for grand dishes, whereas bread was a basic food made by bakers, who did not need any instruction. Domenico Romoli – a 16th-century Tuscan writer who was known as Panunto ('oiled bread') – made various comments on bread with which present-day dietitians and health-food addicts would not agree. He wrote that *'pane nero* [brown bread] is less nutritious and is difficult to digest and it generates wind and

pains, since the hull of the grain is of a dry and hot nature and produces melancholy and descends quickly into the stomach but nourishes little.' The predilection that Romoli shows for white bread probably stems from the belief that luxury food was good for you and that simple food was harmful. White bread came into the category of luxury food and was sold only in special shops that supplied grand households.

While up to World War II bread was often the main sustenance of many poor people, in subsequent years it started to become also the accompaniment to richer foods. In the 1960s the bread produced was highly industrialized and the quality suffered. But in the 1970s artisanal bread had a tremendous revival, thanks to a handful of people who kept the tradition alive. In 1971 a few food writers founded the Confraternita Amanti del Pane – the Brotherhood of Bread Lovers – with the object of bringing bread back to its former excellence. In 1983 the Museo del Pane was opened in Lombardy, near Pavia, in the Castello di Sant'Angelo Lodigiano, a splendid 13th-century building. In the Museo there are over 100 varieties of grain that were cultivated in the last century, and a display of every kind and shape of bread.

Today, some of the best PANETTERIE are in themselves like small bread museums, selling loaves of every kind and shape. Every region has its own traditional shapes of bread and it is reckoned that there are over a thousand different shapes. I have spoken to some bakers who reckon this to be a very conservative figure. Of these, some are still made only locally, while others are now produced all over Italy. The latter are mainly small white bread rolls, of which the MICHETTA and BIOVETTA, originally from the north, are the most common. In central Italy bread becomes larger and in the south larger still. There, bread is made with durum wheat SEMOLINO in loaves large enough to last for a week, such as the famous golden *pane di Altamura* in Puglia, the only bread to have been granted a DOP. In Sicily and Sardinia the bread

265

is also golden because of the use of local durum wheat semolina.

Bread is invariably put on the table, and eaten, at every meal or as a snack with cheese or SALAME, or even by itself when one is hungry.

Stale bread is seldom wasted but is used in many dishes, from soups and stuffings to meat loaf and puddings, and for PANGRATTATO.

pane integrale
wholewheat bread

Made with the whole grain of wheat, pane integrale is usually shaped 'a cassetta' – like a sandwich loaf – or made into PANINI.

panelle
fritters

Small fried FOCACCE made in Sicily with chickpea flour. Chopped parsley is often added to the mixture. Panelle are one of the many delicious street foods of the island.

panetteria
baker's shop

Panetterie have changed radically in recent times. While previously a panetteria was just a shop selling bread, FOCACCIA and some pasta, the new image of a panetteria in most towns is that of a 'designer' shop, with shelf upon shelf filled with the most appetizing and appealing bread, as well as focaccia, brioches, tarts, PIZZE, RAVIOLI, TAGLIATELLE etc. The windows of the smartest panetterie have elaborate and delightful displays of castles, farms and palaces – all made of bread.

When you enter the shop the all-pervading smell is so exquisite that it is impossible to buy only the bread you went in to buy. The choice is bewildering: there is specialized bread from different regions, bread in every shape, colour and size, bread sprinkled with cumin or caraway seeds or studded with sultanas or olives, all freshly baked at the back of the shop and quite irresistible.

panettone
Christmas cake from Milan

Although the *panettone genovese* (see PANDOLCE) claims an earlier birth date, it is the panettone di Milano that is now the panettone par excellence. This dome-shaped cake has conquered the world with its light texture and buttery flavour, enlivened by the fruity juiciness of sultanas and orange and citron peel. In recent years the tall cylindrical shape, created by the firm of Motta in the 1920s, has partly been giving way to the original shape of a squat dome, much to the delight of all true Milanese.

Panettone has now become the Christmas cake not only of Lombardy but of all the peninsula. And it is available all the year round. There is no doubt that a slice of panettone, taken with a cup of tea or coffee, a glass of sparkling wine or VIN SANTO, is a delicious treat, be it at breakfast, mid-morning, at tea-time or whenever one is peckish.

Nowadays there are many kinds of panettone on the market, some more successful than others. Panettone can be stuffed with or coated with chocolate, filled with ZABAIONE or MASCARPONE cream and many other fancy treatments. I prefer to buy plain panettone and eat it as it is or make my own pudding with it, as in the recipe below.

The origins of panettone go back to the Middle Ages, when a large sweet loaf was made in every home, on the top of which the master of the house would mark a cross. One story tells how, in the 15th century, there lived in Milan a poor baker called Toni who had a beautiful daughter. A young aristocrat fell in love with the daughter and, well aware of the difficulties that would arise from their different social status, he offered his services to the baker as an apprentice. He did well in his new trade, and soon he had created a better sweet bread, with more butter and more eggs, adding sultanas and candied peel. Before long, the more prosperous housewives of Milan flocked to buy this new sweet bread, which came to be known as *pan di Toni*, later corrupted to panettone.

Panettone is never made at home, because it would be too difficult a task, particularly as far as the rising is concerned.

[see recipe below]

budino di panettone
panettone pudding

Serves 4–6

unsalted butter, for greasing

200g/7oz panettone

2 tbsp rum

1 tbsp Marsala

300ml/10fl oz/1¼ cups single (light) cream

300ml/10fl oz/1¼ cups full-fat (whole) milk

¼ tsp ground cinnamon

grated rind of 1 small organic or unwaxed lemon

100g/3½oz/½ cup caster (superfine) sugar

3 large eggs

There are a number of recipes to use up leftover PANETTONE. This is one of the traditional Lombard panettone puddings as it was made years ago in my home, usually on St Biagio's Day (3 February), when all the panettone should be eaten. Another simpler way to serve any leftover panettone is to toast it and spread it with mascarpone.

Preheat the oven to 160°C/325°F/Gas Mark 3. Butter a pudding bowl (or other dome-shaped mould) that will hold about 1 litre/1¾ pints/4 cups.

Cut the panettone into thin slices. It doesn't matter if it crumbles. Sprinkle with the rum and Marsala.

Bring the cream and milk slowly to the boil with the cinnamon, lemon rind and sugar. Turn off the heat and set aside to cool.

Beat the eggs together very lightly and then pour in the milk mixture, beating constantly.

Put the panettone into the prepared bowl and pour over the egg mixture, then put the bowl in a roasting pan and pour in enough boiling water to come about two-thirds of the way up the sides of the bowl. Place in the oven and bake for 1–1¼ hours, until set.

Remove the bowl from the roasting pan, leave the pudding to cool and then chill until you are ready to serve.

Ease the pudding away from the inside of the bowl with a spatula and then invert the bowl onto a round dish. Tap the bowl and give the dish a shake or two: the pudding should gently unmould.

NOTE: For a finishing touch you can decorate the pudding with a sprinkling of grated chocolate or chopped almonds and serve it with pouring cream. Or you can spread whipped cream over the top.

panforte
Christmas cake from Siena

The best-known speciality of Siena, panforte is a highly spiced, rich, flat cake which, with the first bite, reveals its ancient origins. Historians differ as to whether panforte was first made in the 12th or 13th century. Some historians suggest that panforte was one of the *'pani mielati e pepati'* – honeyed and peppered breads – that Nicolò Salimbeni, mentioned in Dante's *Divine Comedy*, brought back to Siena from the Far East. Nowadays there is on the market also a *'panforte nero'* (black panforte), which contains chocolate.

Panforte is commercially produced and sold all over the western world, all year round. It can be made at home successfully if you follow this recipe.

[see recipe below]

panforte
fruit and spice cake

Serves 8–10
225g/8oz/1½ cups blanched almonds
100g/3½oz/scant 1 cup walnuts
50g/1¾oz/⅓ cup hazelnuts
100g/3½oz/generous ½ cup candied
    orange and lemon peel, cut into
    small pieces
1 tsp ground cinnamon
a generous pinch of ground coriander
a generous pinch of freshly ground white
    pepper
a generous pinch of freshly ground mace
100g/3½oz/generous ¾ cup Italian
    00 flour
175g/6oz/½ cup honey
75g/2¾oz/⅓ cup granulated sugar
rice paper, to line the tin

To serve
2 tbsp icing (confectioners') sugar
1 tsp ground cinnamon

PANFORTE is better eaten at least 1 week after it has been made. Wrapped in foil, it keeps well for 2–3 months.

Using a mezzaluna, finely chop the almonds, walnuts and hazelnuts. You can use a food processor, but be careful not to reduce the mixture to a paste. It must be very grainy. Put these ingredients into a large bowl. Add the orange and lemon peel, half the cinnamon, the coriander, pepper and mace. Mix with a wooden spoon until all the ingredients are well blended and then add 75g/2¾oz/9 tbsp of the flour.

Pour the honey into a lined copper or stainless steel saucepan and place it over a medium heat. Add the sugar and stir until the honey is completely melted and the sugar incorporated. Do not let the mixture boil. Remove the pan from the heat and tip the contents into the bowl with the nuts and spices. Using a wooden spoon, mix well but gently, until all the ingredients are well blended.

Preheat the oven to 180°C/350°F/Gas Mark 4.

Line the bottom and sides of a loose-bottomed 20cm/8in diameter tart tin (or shallow cake tin) with rice paper. Spoon in the mixture, smoothing the surface. Mix the remaining flour and cinnamon together and sift this mixture evenly over the top. Bake for about 35 minutes.

Remove from the oven and cool in the tin for about 10 minutes. Remove the sides and bottom of the tin and transfer the panforte to a wire rack to cool completely – about 8 hours. Wrap tightly in foil to store.

To serve, transfer the panforte to a serving dish and sprinkle over the icing sugar mixed with the cinnamon.

pangrattato
dried breadcrumbs

Breadcrumbs are made with crustless dried white bread. Brown bread is not usually used because its flavour might clash with the taste of other ingredients. Dried breadcrumbs play an important role in Italian cooking, from the Alps to Sicily. They are essential in most stuffings, they are used for coating POLPETTE, COSTOLETTE and other fried foods, they are used to thicken sauces, and they are sprinkled on gratin dishes as well as into buttered baking tins to prevent food from sticking. Dried breadcrumbs go into some country soups from central Italy and are also – as MOLLICA – an ingredient in many pasta sauces from southern Italy, where they are often added instead of grated cheese.

panino
bread roll

Panino is both a bread roll and a filled roll – correctly a panino IMBOTTITO. It all depends on the context. A panino is round or oval and is made with white or brown flour; the latter often has seeds scattered on the top. A panino imbottito of the sort offered in a bar is usually white bread of a soft and compact texture and may have various fillings, although the most common is some sort of SALUMI.

paniscia
bean soup

This traditional dish from Novara in north-east Piedmont consists of a thick bean and vegetable mixture which is added to a RISOTTO. Paniscia contains a small SALAME *della duja*, a duja being the earthenware container in which the salami are preserved. It is a salame only found locally, so in the recipe here, LUGANEGA is used.

 [see recipe on page 270]

panissa
chickpea polenta

A Ligurian POLENTA made with chickpea flour and water. It is eaten doused with olive oil, which should be the delicate local oil of the western Riviera.

panna
cream

Up to World War II, cream was little used in traditional dishes except in a few from northern Italy, most of them of French origin. Nowadays cream is added to some pasta sauces to make them more liquid. The best-known sauce based entirely on cream is used for dressing FETTUCCINE: *fettucine alla panna*, also called *fettuccine all'Alfredo* after its creator, the late owner of the restaurant Alla Scrofa in Rome.

Cream, whipped or liquid, is used in sweet preparations, although egg custard is often preferred, as it is in most ice creams.

269

panna cotta
a dessert

Literally, 'cooked cream', the traditional panna cotta from Piedmont and Valle d'Aosta is flavoured with peach eau-de-vie. Now the alcohol is usually white rum and the pudding is sometimes flavoured with different ingredients, such as coffee, chocolate or fruit syrup. Panna cotta is served chilled and unmoulded and, traditionally, by itself, although there is now a trend to serve fruit puree with it or to surround it with fresh fruit.

[see recipe on page 272]

paniscia
Piedmontese bean and vegetable soup

Serves 4–6

200g/7oz/1 cup dried borlotti beans, soaked for about 12 hours in cold water

1 knuckle (hock) of unsmoked bacon or ham

1 bay leaf

1½ onions (1 sliced, ½ finely chopped)

1 carrot, diced

1 celery stalk, diced

2 or 3 cabbage leaves, shredded

75g/2¾oz unsmoked pancetta, cut into cubes

40g/1½oz/3 tbsp unsalted butter

2 garlic cloves, finely chopped

2 sprigs of fresh rosemary, chopped

100g/3½oz luganega or other mild pure pork sausage, cut into chunks

225g/8oz/1¼ cups risotto rice

1 tbsp tomato puree

125ml/4fl oz/½ cup red wine

salt and freshly ground black pepper

PANISCIA **is a very nourishing risotto-style soup, a perfect all-in-one meal.**

Drain and rinse the beans, then put them in a large, heavy pan. Add the bacon knuckle, bay leaf, sliced onion, carrot, celery and cabbage. Cover with about 2 litres/4 pints/2 quarts cold water and bring slowly to the boil. Simmer, covered, for about 2 hours.

Leaving the soup to simmer gently, lift out the knuckle and remove the meat from the bone. Cut the meat into small pieces and set aside. Remove the bay leaf from the soup and discard.

Put the pancetta, butter, garlic, rosemary, luganega and the finely chopped onion into a clean saucepan and cook gently for 10 minutes, stirring frequently. Add the rice and stir well to coat all the grains. Mix in the reserved meat from the knuckle and the tomato puree, then cook, stirring, for 1 minute. Pour in the wine and boil briskly for a couple of minutes.

Add 200ml/7fl oz/generous ¾ cup of the simmering soup and stir. When the rice has absorbed nearly all the liquid, add another 150ml/5fl oz/ ⅔ cup of the soup. Keep stirring and adding more soup as the rice dries out, but do not add too much soup at one time. The rice should cook over a moderate heat.

When the rice is cooked, strain the remaining soup. Add any beans and pieces of vegetable to the rice, but do not add any more liquid. Give the rice a good stir and then taste and season with salt and pepper.

panna cotta
cooked cream dessert

Serves 6

10g/¹/₃oz gelatine leaves

*450ml/15fl oz/scant 2 cups double
(heavy) cream*

*150ml/5fl oz/²/₃ cup full-fat (whole)
milk*

*150g/5½oz/¾ cup caster (superfine)
sugar*

4 tbsp white rum

1 tsp pure vanilla extract

*neutral-flavoured oil, such as sunflower,
for greasing*

This is the classic recipe for the famous Piedmontese dessert.

Put the gelatine leaves in a bowl and fill it with cold water. As soon as the leaves soften, bend them so that they are all submerged in water. Leave for 10 minutes or so. Squeeze the leaves to remove excess water and put them in a small saucepan with 4 tablespoons water. Place over a low heat and stir until the gelatine has dissolved.

Mix the cream and milk together in a saucepan, add the sugar and bring very slowly to the simmer, stirring constantly. Stir in the rum and vanilla and then take the pan off the heat and stir in the gelatine. Mix very thoroughly.

Brush six 150ml/5fl oz/²/₃ cup ramekins with a little oil and pour the cream mixture into them. Leave to cool, cover with clingfilm and chill for at least 4 hours.

To unmould, place the ramekins in a sink of hot water for about 20 seconds. Run a palette knife around the sides of each ramekin, place a dessert plate over the top and turn the plate and the ramekin upside down. Give a knock or two to the bottom of the ramekin and then lift it away. It should come away easily, but if the dessert is still stuck, put the ramekin back into the hot water for a few seconds. Put the unmoulded desserts back into the refrigerator until ready to serve.

pansôti
ravioli

Large Ligurian triangular or square ravioli. The pasta dough is made in the traditional Ligurian way, with 1 egg to each 200g/7oz of wheat flour, and water, which is sometimes partly replaced by dry white wine. The stuffing consists of chopped wild herbs, soft local cheese, Parmesan, egg and a touch of garlic. Traditionally pansôti are dressed with walnut sauce, for which the recipe is given on page 248.

panzanella
a salad

A rustic, simple salad made all over central Italy, although it has gained popularity in other regions as well. Panzanella is essentially bread to which some very fresh vegetables are added. The bread should be the Tuscan unsalted white bread, preferably slightly stale. The essential vegetables are tomatoes and red onions and a few leaves of basil or marjoram and/or sage, but cucumber, peppers, celery, parsley, capers and anchovy fillets can be thrown in too. The salad is dressed with the best local olive oil, vinegar, salt and pepper.

[see recipe below]

panzanella
bread and vegetable salad

Serves 6

½ red onion, sliced into very thin rings
salt and freshly ground black pepper
6 tbsp extra virgin olive oil, preferably Tuscan
2 garlic cloves, bruised
2 fresh red chillies, split and deseeded
2 large ripe, firm tomatoes
2 handfuls of fresh basil leaves, torn
1 tbsp capers, preferably in salt, rinsed
about 2 tbsp red wine vinegar
200g/7oz best country bread, crust removed

This is one of the many traditional recipes given to me by my neighbour in Chianti. It is better made at least half an hour before eating.

Put the onion rings in a bowl with 1 teaspoon salt and cover with cold water. Leave to soak for up to 2 hours. This is not necessary if the onion is really mild or you don't mind the strong flavour of raw onion.

Put the olive oil, garlic and chillies in a bowl and leave to infuse for up to 2 hours.

Cut the tomatoes in half and squeeze out the seeds. Cut the tomato flesh into small cubes. Do this on a plate to collect the juice. Put the tomatoes in a serving bowl, and add the tomato juice, the basil and capers.

Drain and dry the onion and add it to the bowl. Remove and discard the garlic and chillies from the oil. Beat 2 tablespoons vinegar into the oil to form an emulsion and pour over the vegetables. Season with salt.

Thickly slice the bread and cut it into 2cm/¾in pieces. Sprinkle 3–4 tablespoons of water over the bread, mix lightly and add to the vegetables. Mix again until everything is thoroughly combined. Season with pepper, taste and adjust the salt and vinegar. Serve cold, but not chilled.

panzarotti or panzerotti
pasties

Small square or half-moon shaped pasties made in central and southern Italy with bread dough and stuffed with various ingredients, usually some combination of tomatoes, mozzarella, ricotta, eggs and anchovy fillets, flavoured with basil or oregano. Panzarotti are fried in olive oil. When they come into contact with the hot fat they swell up so that they look like a small *pancia*, 'belly', hence their name.

In Basilicata panzarotti have a very different stuffing based on a sweetened chickpea puree flavoured with chocolate and cinnamon. They are eaten at the end of a meal with sweet white wine.

paparot
spinach soup

This is one of the best-known soups of Friuli-Venezia Giulia. It is a spinach soup thickened with maize flour; traditionally the spinach is cooked in water, but some cooks – myself included – use a light stock. Once cooked, the spinach is very coarsely chopped, sautéed with a little garlic in LARDO and then cooked for a further half hour or so with some coarse-ground maize flour. This thickens the soup and gives it a most pleasing contrast of texture.

pappa
babies' food

This word not only means pappy food for babies, but it can also mean food like pasta or rice that has been cooked far too long.

pappa col pomodoro
bread and tomato soup

A classic Tuscan soup, of which there are as many versions as there are cooks. It is good hot, warm or cold. It combines two favourite Tuscan ingredients, bread and tomatoes. The bread is Tuscan unsalted bread, one day old and lightly toasted.

pappardelle
a pasta

Large TAGLIATELLE, now made commercially. They are one of the very few traditional pasta shapes from Tuscany, where they always accompany a rich hare stew, *pappardelle con la* LEPRE.

parmigiana, alla
cooking style

'The way it is made in Parma' suggests a dish that contains Parmesan cheese and possibly PROSCIUTTO. *Costolette alla parmigiana*, for instance, are breaded veal chops that are fried in butter and then simmered, with Parmesan flakes, in a little stock.

parmigiana di melanzane
baked aubergine

This classic dish, so called because it contains a good deal of Parmesan cheese, is so good that many regions, from north to south, claim its origin. The ingredients are so typically Neapolitan, however, that it seems certain that Naples must have been its birthplace. In some recipes grated chocolate is added, an ingredient that, used with aubergine, is another indication of its southern origin. Now that fried food is less popular, the aubergine is sometimes grilled, but I find this to the detriment of the dish. It is also made with courgettes.

[see recipe on facing page]

parmigiana di melanzane
baked aubergine

Serves 4–5

1.5kg/3¼lb aubergines (eggplants)

salt and freshly ground black pepper

5 tbsp olive oil

400g/14oz canned plum tomatoes,
    drained

1 garlic clove, bruised

a few fresh basil leaves, torn

vegetable oil, for frying

300g/10½oz mozzarella cheese, sliced

50g/1¾oz Parmesan cheese, grated

2 large eggs, hard-boiled and sliced

The recipe given here is my adaptation of a recipe from *Il Libro d'Oro della Cucina e dei Vini di Calabria e Basilicata (The Golden Book of the Cooking and Wines of Calabria and Basilicata)* by Ottavio Cavalcanti.

Cut the aubergines lengthways into slices about 5mm/¼in thick. Sprinkle generously with salt, put in a colander and leave to drain for about 1 hour.

Rinse the aubergine slices under cold water and pat thoroughly dry with kitchen paper.

Preheat the oven to 200°C/400°F/Gas Mark 6.

Put 2 tablespoons of the olive oil in a small saucepan with the tomatoes, garlic and basil. Season and simmer for 10 minutes. Puree the mixture in a food processor or food mill.

Put enough vegetable oil into a deep frying pan to come 2.5cm/1in up the side of the pan, and heat until very hot. Test the temperature by immersing the corner of an aubergine slice in the oil – it should sizzle. Put in as many aubergine slices as will fit in a single layer. Fry until golden brown on both sides, then lift them out and drain on kitchen paper. Repeat until all the slices are fried.

Grease a shallow ovenproof dish with 1 tablespoon of the remaining olive oil. Cover with a layer of aubergine slices, then spread over a little of the tomato sauce and some mozzarella slices. Sprinkle with a little salt, a lot of pepper and some Parmesan. Spread over a few slices of hard-boiled egg and cover with another layer of aubergines. Repeat the layers until all the ingredients are used up, finishing with a layer of aubergines and a sprinkling of Parmesan. Pour over the remaining olive oil and bake for about 30 minutes.

Leave to stand for at least 10 minutes before serving.

277

parmigiano reggiano
Parmesan cheese

Locals will tell you that parmigiano reggiano has been made there for over 2,000 years. That may or may not be so, but the cheese was already well known in the 14th century, when Boccaccio referred to it in the *Decameron*. Describing the *Paese di Bengodi* – the Village of Good Cheer – he wrote, '...and on a mountain all of grated Parmesan cheese dwelt folk that did nought else but make macaroni and ravioli.'

In 1545 MESSISBUGO served six dishes with Parmesan at the end of a dinner given by his lord Don Ercole d'Este. The cheese, cut into chunks, was served with truffles, fresh grapes and pears, fruits marinated in vinegar, fennel, pine nuts, pistachios and cardoons. This Renaissance custom of serving Parmesan with fruits and vegetables has lately been revived by many restaurants.

Parmesan, the most famous grating cheese in the world, had its origins in the province of Reggio Emilia, in the area that formed the Duchy of Parma, between Parma and Reggio Emilia. Thus it used to be called, simply, parmigiano until the cheese started to be made also in the province of Reggio. Nowadays parmigiano reggiano, one of the first cheeses to be granted a DOP mark, is made in well-defined areas in the provinces of Parma, Reggio Emilia, Modena, Bologna and Mantova.

Parmesan is made in small cheese factories, and the method has remained unchanged through the centuries, so that the cheese is still made as it was in Boccaccio's time.

The milk used comes from local cows fed on fresh forage, the best cheese being made between April and November. The milk is from both the morning and evening milkings and is partially skimmed; whey from the previous batch is added to help the fermentation. The cheese is curdled with calf's rennet, shaped and then salted in brine for 20–25 days.

The shapes are large, weighing between 30 and 35kg/66–77lb. An impressive statistic is the fact that it takes 16 litres/28 pints of milk to make each kilogram/2¼lb of cheese. The cheeses are matured in vast storerooms for different periods of time and are named by their age. Thus *parmigiano nuovo* is less than 1 year old, *parmigiano vecchio* is 1½–2 years old, and *parmigiano stravecchio* is 2 years old or more. No other Italian cheese is as large as a *forma di parmigiano* – a whole Parmesan – and no other cheese in the world is aged for so long.

Good Parmesan is of a lovely straw colour, crumbly in texture and with a mellow, rich and slightly salty taste. There is a special knife for cutting Parmesan. It has a short wooden handle and a small lanceolate blade that is wedge-shaped in cross-section, i.e. one edge is sharp and the other is thick. It therefore causes the cheese to break apart according to its natural structure, rather than slicing through it.

Everyone knows that Parmesan is widely used in Italian cooking. What is not always recognized, however, is that it is always used with discretion: it is used only when considered a vital ingredient in the finished dish, and never indiscriminately. It is a very common flavouring for risotti and pasta, but it is not used with most of the traditional fish and seafood risotti or sauces. Few meat dishes call for Parmesan, those that do being mostly recipes from Emilia, where Parmesan is the local cheese. It is never added to a Tuscan RIBOLLITA but is always on the table with MINESTRONE ALLA MILANESE. Similarly, it is often added to vegetables that have been sautéed in butter, but not to vegetables cooked in oil. Parmesan is used in stuffings, where it also acts as a binding agent; and it makes risotto thicker and more creamy.

One final, but important, point: Parmesan should not be bought already grated. Also, no more than the amount immediately needed is grated, since once grated, Parmesan loses some of its flavour.

278

parrozzo
a cake

The name of this cake, made in Abruzzo, is a corruption of *pan rozzo*, rustic bread. But there is nothing rustic about the contemporary parrozzo, which, based on an ancient cake, was created in 1911 by a patissier in Pescara. The patissier sent a parrozzo to the poet Gabriele d'Annunzio, who loved it so much that he wrote a poem about it in local dialect. Parrozzo is made with white flour, potato flour, ground almonds, eggs, sugar, and a touch of cinnamon and vanilla. When cold the cake is covered in chocolate icing. It is the traditional Christmas cake of the region, but it is now found all the year round.

passata
tomato puree

Tomatoes 'passed' through a sieve or strainer; now sold in bottles and cartons. It is a staple in most Italian kitchens.

passatelli
soup strands

This was originally a country soup, but the great ARTUSI upgraded it by including it in his book, a rare honour for a peasant recipe. Passatelli is made in two ways. The first version, from Romagna, is a mixture of dry breadcrumbs, bone marrow, Parmesan, nutmeg and eggs. The other recipe is from Pesaro in Le Marche and contains finely minced beef fillet in addition to the ingredients listed above. Both mixtures are pushed through the holes of a food mill or a potato ricer directly into simmering stock and cooked for a few minutes.

Local families have a special tool for making passatelli. This consists of a perforated concave metal disc with two wooden handles.

pasta

This is the generic word for any kind of dough, such as bread and pastry. 'Pasta' is also a paste, such as pasta di ACCIUGHE (anchovies), PASTA DI MANDORLE (almonds). When used by itself the word usually means pasta in its best-known sense, which, to be correct, in Italian is called *pasta alimentare*. And what is this food that in the last half a century has conquered the Western world? It is simply a mixture of flour or SEMOLA and water and/or eggs.

Having read and reread many accounts of the origins of pasta, I decided that they are far too nebulous. Pasta, as a mixture of some sort of ground cereal and liquid, was obviously made in ancient times. If the first pasta-makers were the Greeks or the Etruscans it does not matter. What is sure is that pasta was not brought back to Venice by Marco Polo in 1295, because there are references to it before that date. Personally I think that pasta was yet another Arab import into Sicily. In the past the Sicilians were recognized as the authority on pasta and Sicilian food was greatly influenced by the Arabs.

By the Renaissance, pasta – at that time called *vermicelli* – was enjoyed only by wealthy people. It became popular at the end of the 18th century, but only in southern Italy. Naples was the scene of the eruption of pasta as the food of the people; along with Vesuvius it became the symbol of Naples. In 1700 there were 60 shops selling pasta in Naples; by 1785 there were 280. On most street corners there was a *maccheronaro* selling MACCHERONI from his stall – maccheroni being the general local name for pasta. The first pasta factories were established around the Gulf of Naples and it is from there that pasta, and spaghetti in particular, reached the United States when the Italians began to emigrate there at the beginning of the 20th century.

But there was an American who fell in love with pasta much earlier. It was Thomas Jefferson, third president of the US, who, having no doubt enjoyed eating pasta on one of his visits to Italy, ordered a pasta-making machine to be sent to Monticello, his house in Virginia.

Up until World War II it was only in southern Italy that pasta was eaten daily, usually as a first course at lunch. But in the second half of the 20th century pasta has become the most popular starter to a meal also in northern Italy, where it has ousted the local RISOTTO. A dish of pasta is now often served as a PIATTO UNICO (one-course meal) but never with salad. It is the typical meal of southern Italians, and it provides a healthy and well-balanced diet based on pasta plus a sauce consisting either of a small amount of meat, or some vegetables, pulses, cheese or eggs.

In Italy, pasta usually means dried pasta. Fresh pasta is eaten far less frequently and is by no means considered superior, but rather a different kind of food which can be better or worse, depending on its quality.

Fresh pasta: In Emilia-Romagna fresh pasta is made using only eggs and 00 flour. The classic recipe is given here. In other regions one or two of the eggs may be replaced by water, which produces a softer and less tasty pasta. In the south the mixture is of durum wheat SEMOLINO, flour and water, a type of dough that is hard to knead and shape. All these mixtures, once the dough is rolled out, are called SFOGLIA. Rolling pasta totally by hand is a difficult job, but there are many machines for making fresh pasta at home. The MACCHINA PER LA PASTA will roll and cut the pasta, too.

Dried pasta: This is commercially made pasta, the composition of which is tightly controlled by law. It is made only with durum wheat SEMOLA and water. For *pasta integrale* (wholewheat pasta) the durum wheat is less refined. Equally important is the drying process, which must be gradual and lengthy. The best pasta is dried over 48 hours, as opposed to 32 for the more mass-produced type. The dies through which the mixture is extruded also play an important part: for the best pasta bronze dies are used, giving a rough surface that is ideal for retaining the dressing.

Dried pasta comes in many shapes and sizes, most of which are best suited to a particular type of sauce. Generally speaking, long pasta, such as spaghetti, is best with a sauce based on olive oil, as this keeps the strands slippery and separate. Thicker long shapes are dressed with sauces that may also be based on butter, cream and cheese, which also go well with medium-sized tubular pasta. These shapes are also perfect dressed with vegetables or pulses, while the large RIGATONI and PENNE are used for baked dishes.

Cooking pasta: Pasta may be everyday food, but it should be cooked with great care. It must be cooked in a large saucepan in plenty of salted water: there should be 1 litre of water to every 100g of pasta, to which 10g of salt is added when the water begins to boil. When the water comes to a rolling boil the pasta should be added and immediately stirred. The cooking time varies according to the shape and quality of pasta, and whether it is fresh or dried.

When the pasta is al dente it is drained through a colander or, for long pasta, by lifting it out with a long wooden fork or a spaghetti server. Some of the cooking water is sometimes reserved to add at the end, should the finished dish seem too dry. This is always done when cooking fresh pasta, since it absorbs more liquid.

Once drained, the pasta is transferred to the frying pan containing the sauce or to a warmed bowl and immediately dressed; it should never be left to sit in the colander or bowl without any dressing. Pasta shouldn't be dressed with too much sauce, nor should the sauce be watery.

Pasta can also be cooked using a totally different method, which I call 'the Agnesi method', since I learnt it from the late Vincenzo Agnesi, the founder of the Pasta Agnesi company. And here it is: bring a large saucepan of water to the boil, add the usual amount of salt and then add the pasta and stir vigorously. When the water has come back to the boil, cook, uncovered, for 2 minutes and then turn the heat off, put a clean towel over the pot and cover with a tight-fitting lid. Leave for the length of time suggested on the packet instructions. When the time is up, drain the pasta and dress as usual. Pasta cooked in this way will retain more of the characteristic flavour of the semolina. The other advantage is that it does not overcook if left a minute longer.

Pastasciutta is a term meaning pasta that, once cooked, has been drained and served with a sauce. *Pasta in brodo* ('pasta in soup') on the other hand, is pasta served in the liquid in which it has cooked, which is the brodo, or stock.

Pasta colorata or *aromatizzata* (coloured or flavoured pasta) – pasta that is yellow (saffron), brown (fungi), red (tomato) or black (cuttlefish ink) – has now become as widely available as the traditional green (spinach) pasta from Emilia.

Pasta ripiena (stuffed pasta) includes the large range of different types of RAVIOLI. The wrapping is made of egg pasta and the stuffing is different for each type of raviolo.

[see recipe on page 282]

pasta frolla
sweet pastry

Made with eggs or egg yolks, flour, butter and sugar, pasta frolla is most commonly prepared for fruit or jam tarts, when it is usually flavoured with grated lemon rind. It is also used for some TIMBALLI and PASTICCI containing pasta, meat, chicken, mushrooms and other savoury ingredients. For some preparations some of the egg is replaced by white wine, MARSALA or VIN SANTO.

ARTUSI gives three recipes for sweet pastry, two containing lard as well as butter. I have chosen the one without lard, because lard is not popular nowadays and good-quality lard is not easy to find.

[see recipe below]

pasta frolla dell'Artusi
Artusi's sweet pastry

Makes enough for 1 pie, about
20–25cm/8–10in in diameter
140g/5oz/generous ½ cup unsalted
butter
100g/3½oz/¾ cup icing (confectioners')
sugar, sifted
250g/9oz/2 cups Italian 00 flour
1 large egg
1 large egg yolk

This is my adaptation from Pellegrino ARTUSI's ever-popular book *La Scienza in Cucina e l'Arte di Mangiar Bene*, first published in 1891. To roll out the dough relatively easily, sprinkle icing sugar over the work surface. If more convenient, prepare this pastry a day in advance — this will make it more crumbly when cooked.

If the butter is too firm, then knead it with a wet hand on the work surface until it becomes malleable.

Mix the sugar with the flour. Add the butter, egg and yolk and knead very lightly to make a dough. At first, use a knife blade to blend the ingredients, in order to knead the dough as little as possible.

NOTE: To knead it more easily, mix the last crumbs with a drop of white wine or MARSALA, which makes the pastry more friable.

pasta all'uovo
fresh egg pasta

Makes enough for 4 as a first course,
3 as a main course
300g/10½oz/scant 2½ cups Italian 00
flour, plus extra for dusting
a pinch of salt
3 large eggs

Pasta is made in different ways in many regions, but the most popular fresh pasta is the pasta all'uovo made in Emilia, for which this is the traditional recipe.

Put the flour on the work surface and make a well in the middle. Add the salt and the eggs. Using a fork or your fingers, mix the eggs and draw in the flour gradually. Work quickly until it forms a mass. Scrape the work surface clean and wash your hands.

Alternatively, you can use a food processor. Put in the flour and salt, switch on the machine and drop in the eggs through the funnel. Process until a ball of dough is formed. Transfer the dough to a lightly floured work surface.

Knead the dough for about 5–7 minutes, until smooth and elastic. Wrap in clingfilm and leave to rest for at least 30 minutes – or up to 3 or 4 hours.

Unwrap the dough and knead on a lightly floured surface for 2–3 minutes, then divide into 4 equal parts. Take one piece of dough and keep the remainder wrapped in clingfilm. Roll out the dough using a rolling pin, or by machine following the manufacturer's instructions.

If you are making lasagne, or any type of stuffed pasta, proceed immediately to the cutting and stuffing. If you are making long pasta, before you cut it, leave the dough to dry until it is no longer sticky. Then feed each strip of dough through the broad cutters of the machine for TAGLIATELLE or FETTUCCINE, or through the narrow cutters for TAGLIOLINI. For TONNARELLI, roll the dough out only to the fourth setting of the machine. When dry, feed the sheet through the narrow cutter to achieve a sort of square spaghetti.

pasta di mandorle
marzipan

This is made with ground almonds, sugar and lemon juice – and often glucose. Another version calls for ground almonds and sugar, pounded together, to which egg white is added very gradually until the texture of the paste comes together. Pasta di mandorle can be flavoured with orange water or the grated rind of lemon, orange or mandarin.

At grand Renaissance banquets, elaborate sculptures were modelled in pasta di mandorle, the leading sculptors of the day sometimes being commissioned to create these *trionfi della tavola* ('triumphs of the table'), as they were called. They represented coats-of-arms, pagan deities, religious subjects or licentious figures, some of these sculptures even being covered with gold leaf.

Pasta di mandorle originated in Sicily and through the centuries nobody has surpassed the craftsmen of Palermo in modelling and colouring marzipan to make lifelike facsimiles of fruit, salame, cheese and all sorts of food.

pasta Margherita
a sponge cake

Similar to PAN DI SPAGNA but made with potato flour, pasta Margherita is used as a cake in its own right, *torta Margherita*, or as a base for puddings layered with cream, custard, jam, ZABAIONE and other such preparations. It was named in honour of the Queen of Italy, the same queen to whom the PIZZA Margherita was dedicated.

ARTUSI gives a recipe for this very light sponge cake, which he writes is so good that, when his friend who was a baker in Prato started to make it, no dinner party was given in the town without a torta Margherita being ordered from his shop.

pasta 'ncasciata
pasta pie

One of many sumptuous Sicilian dishes based on pasta, the recipes for it vary in the number of different ingredients included. Some have tiny meatballs, others suggest very small pieces of sautéed PANCETTA, sliced CACIOCAVALLO, sautéed chicken livers, spring peas, etc. It is a typical example of the local cuisine, where more and more ingredients are added to make a richer dish. The recipe given here is a basic one which you can enrich as you like.

'Ncasciata is the Sicilian word for *incassata* ('encased'), as the pasta is in this dish.

[see recipe on page 286]

pasta alla Norma
a Sicilian dish

The pasta, usually spaghetti, is dressed with a fruity tomato sauce, slices of fried aubergine and grated salted RICOTTA. The dish is so called because it is good enough to stand comparison with Bellini's masterpiece of the same name, the opera *Norma*, which in Catania – the composer's birthplace – is synonymous with perfection.

pasta rasa
soup dumplings

Pasta rasa is a speciality of Reggio Emilia, similar to PASSATELLI, although it never contains meat or beef marrow. It is made with dried breadcrumbs and Parmesan in equal quantities, bound with egg and flavoured with nutmeg. The mixture is pushed through a grater with large holes, spread out to dry on tea towels and, when dried, dropped into boiling stock.

pasta con le sarde
pasta with fresh sardines

This dish originated in the province of Palermo. It is like the history of Sicily on a plate: part Greek, part Saracen, part Norman. Sardines and wild fennel were Greek food, lightened and made more interesting by the inclusion of pine nuts and sultanas – a Saracen influence – all used to dress the Sicilian pasta, which is finished off in the oven, a method brought to the island by the Normans.

[see recipe on page 288]

pasta sfoglia
puff pastry

Pasta sfoglia, also called *sfogliata*, is the natural successor to the filo pastry of the Middle East; a similar type of pastry was also used by the Etruscans and the Romans.

pasta soffiata
choux pastry

The Tuscans say they taught the French how to make choux pastry at the time that their chefs were the leaders in haute cuisine. Paolo Petroni, in *Il Libro della Vera Cucina Fiorentina*, gives the honour for this export to the cook Pantanelli, who was one of Caterina de'Medici's retinue. Choux pastry is used to make BIGNÈ and GNOCCHI *alla parigina*.

paste
cupcakes and small cakes

These are the attractive and tempting little cakes that you see in every PASTICCERIA. Paste are very rarely made at home. The most common types are BIGNÈ, CANNOLI, CANNONCINI, AFRICANI and tartlets filled with fruit, almond cream, etc. They are mostly based on PASTA MARGHERITA, PASTA SFOGLIA and PASTA FROLLA.

pasta al tonno
pasta with tuna

Serves 4

2 garlic cloves, chopped

6 tbsp olive oil

a bunch of fresh flat-leaf parsley, chopped

a small piece of dried chilli

2 salted anchovies, boned, rinsed and chopped, or 4 canned or bottled anchovy fillets, drained and chopped

200g/7oz best canned tuna in olive oil, drained and flaked

salt and freshly ground black pepper

350g/12oz spaghetti

12 black olives

This simple pasta dish exists in many different forms – here is one of the most popular recipes. Use best-quality canned tuna, yellowfin if possible, not skipjack tuna.

Put the garlic, olive oil, parsley and chilli in a large frying pan and sauté gently for 1 minute. Add the anchovies and tuna, stir gently and cook for 10 minutes. Taste and add salt if necessary, and plenty of pepper.

Meanwhile, cook the spaghetti in boiling salted water until very al dente. Drain and turn it quickly into the frying pan. Stir-fry for a minute or so, mixing to coat the pasta with the sauce. Scatter with the olives and serve at once.

pasta 'ncasciata
pasta pie

Serves 6

2 aubergines (eggplants), about
   700g/1lb 9oz in total
salt and freshly ground black pepper
1 ½ quantities salsa di pomodoro 2
   (page 331)
vegetable oil, for frying
400g/14oz penne or rigatoni
50g/1 ¾oz Parmesan cheese, grated
1 tbsp dried oregano
2 large eggs, hard–boiled and sliced
150g/5½oz Italian salami, thickly
   sliced and cut into strips
200g/7oz mozzarella cheese, sliced
50g/1 ¾oz caciocavallo cheese, sliced
2 tbsp dried breadcrumbs
2 tbsp extra virgin olive oil

The pasta is encased ('ncasciata) in the fried aubergines. A stunning dish, full of different flavours.

Cut the aubergines lengthways into thin slices about 5mm/¼in thick. Place the slices in a colander, sprinkling salt between the layers. Leave to drain for about 1 hour.

While the aubergines are draining, make the tomato sauce.

Rinse the aubergines under cold water and pat each slice dry with kitchen paper, then fry them in plenty of hot vegetable oil. Do not fry too many at a time. When they are golden brown on both sides, remove the slices and drain on kitchen paper.

Preheat the oven to 190°C/375°F/Gas Mark 5.

Cook the pasta in boiling water until very al dente. Drain and immediately dress with the tomato sauce. Add the Parmesan and oregano, mix well and then taste and adjust the seasoning.

Use the aubergine slices to line the bottom and sides of a 20cm/8in diameter springform cake tin. Cover the bottom with a layer of pasta and then with sliced eggs, salami strips, aubergine slices, mozzarella and caciocavallo slices. Repeat these layers until all the ingredients are used, finishing with a layer of pasta. Sprinkle with the dried breadcrumbs and drizzle with the olive oil.

Bake for about 20 minutes or until the dish is heated right through.

Run a spatula round between the pie and the inside of the tin. Place a round serving dish upside down over the tin and invert the tin onto it. Leave to stand for a few minutes, then unclip the side of the tin and carefully remove it. Remove the bottom of the tin and serve immediately.

RIGHT: Pasta 'ncasciata

pasta con le sarde
pasta with fresh sardines

50g/1¾oz/⅓ cup sultanas (golden raisins)

50g/1¾oz/⅓ cup pine nuts

5 tbsp olive oil

1 onion, very finely sliced

salt and freshly ground black pepper

75g/2¾oz fennel leaf tops (the feathery fronds)

2 salted anchovies, boned and rinsed, or 4 canned or bottled anchovy fillets, drained

500g/1lb 2oz fresh sardines, filleted

1 tsp fennel seeds

350g/12oz penne or rigatoni

There are many versions of this typically Sicilian dish; this recipe is a good example.

Soak the sultanas in warm water for 10 minutes. Drain and dry well with kitchen paper. Dry-fry the pine nuts in a cast-iron frying pan for 3–4 minutes to release the aroma.

Heat 3 tablespoons of the olive oil in a frying pan, add the onion and a little salt and sauté gently, stirring frequently, for 10 minutes, until soft. Mix in the sultanas and pine nuts and continue cooking for 2 minutes.

Meanwhile, blanch the fennel in a large saucepan of boiling salted water for 1 minute. Using a slotted spoon, lift the fennel out of the water, drain and dry on kitchen paper. Reserve the cooking water. Chop the fennel and add to the onion mixture. Cook over a low heat for 10–15 minutes, adding a couple of tablespoons of the fennel water whenever the mixture appears dry.

Preheat the oven to 200°C/400°F/Gas Mark 6.

Chop the anchovies and about half the sardines and add to the onion mixture, together with the fennel seeds and a generous grinding of pepper. Cook for 10 minutes, stirring frequently and adding more fennel water whenever necessary. Taste and adjust the seasoning.

While the sauce is cooking, cook the pasta in the remaining fennel water until very al dente. Add more boiling water if necessary. Drain, return the pasta to the pan and dress immediately with the sardine sauce.

Grease a deep ovenproof dish with a little oil and turn the pasta into it. Lay the remaining sardines over the pasta, drizzle with the remaining oil and cover with foil. Bake for 15 minutes.

NOTE: In Italy this recipe is made with wild fennel, which is slightly different from the cultivated bulb fennel and has thick and plentiful fronds. If you can't get enough of the feathery leaf tops, make up the weight with finely chopped fennel bulb and flat-leaf parsley.

pastella
batter

The mixture for batter varies according to the region, the chef, and the type of food it is going to coat. Batter can be a mixture of egg, water and flour, of water and flour only, or of milk, egg and flour. Whipped egg white is a common addition, as are yeast and MARSALA or VIN SANTO.

pasticceria
cakes and cake shop

Both the collective word for pastries and cakes, and also the word for the shop where they are sold. Pasticcerie in every city and town and village are always open on Sundays and it is after church on Sunday that, traditionally, an Italian family buys its PASTE or TORTA for the midday meal.

pasticciata
a polenta dish

A word used to describe POLENTA. *Polenta pasticciata* is a baked dish (see recipe on page 322), usually made with leftover polenta cut into slices and layered either with a meat RAGÙ and/or with béchamel and cheeses or mushroom and ham. It is a very common dish in northern Italy.

pasticcini
biscuits

Petits fours, BACI DI DAMA and all kinds of rich biscuits, small cupcakes and the like. Pasticcini are always bought at the PASTICCERIA and, typically, served at tea parties or after-dinner gatherings.

pasticcio
a pie

A baked pie consisting of various ingredients – pasta, rice, vegetables, meat, fish – bound together by béchamel sauce and/or eggs. It is often contained in a pastry shell.

Pasticci were created by the grand chefs of the Renaissance; they were similar to the pies made in contemporary Elizabethan England. Meat, from capon to hare or partridge, or sometimes sea bass or other fish, was sealed in a case of sweetened pastry, usually enriched by wine. Bartolomeo SCAPPI gives recipes for pasticci of artichokes, fungi and truffles, of MORTADELLA and various SALUMI.

In the 19th century ARTUSI wrote a recipe for a *pasticcio di cacciagione* – game – which he serves cold. This pasticcio has a case of sweet pastry flavoured with wine and lemon juice, and it contains a partridge braised with MARSALA and other flavourings. The breast is cut into neat strips and the rest of the meat is pounded with soft breadcrumbs, an egg and the juices of the partridge. This mixture is then layered in the pastry shell with the partridge strips, strips of PROSCIUTTO and tongue and sliced black truffles.

Traditional pasticci still made today include the *pasticcio di tortellini* from Bologna, in which a sweet pastry case contains meat TORTELLINI dressed with roast juices. The *pasticcio*, or TIMBALLO, *alla napoletana* is made with small MACCHERONI, dressed with the juice from a beef joint and Parmesan, and a RAGÙ of mushrooms, sweetbreads, chicken livers and cockscombs, all contained in a sweet pastry case. Many pasticci today are not baked in a pastry case, so that the word has come to mean any baked dish made with pasta and other ingredients. The most popular of these modern pasticci is *pasticcio di pesce*, a dish of lasagne layered with seafood and fish, tomato sauce and béchamel.

[see recipe on page 290]

289

pastiera
Neapolitan tart

An elaborate tart which, although first made in Amalfi, has become particularly associated with Naples. It consists of a sweet pastry base over which is spread a mixture of RICOTTA, chopped candied fruits, sugar, eggs and grains of wheat that have been boiled in milk, all flavoured with lemon rind, orange water and spices. Strips of PASTA FROLLA are laid in lozenge patterns over the filling and the tart is baked.

Pastiera used to be made during the period between Twelfth Night and Easter, when the ricotta is at its best. The grains of wheat used were those left over from the previous harvest. Nowadays pastiera is made and sold all the year round.

pastina
small pasta shapes

Pastina is only used in stock, to make a MINESTRINA. There are all sorts of pastina: *stelline* (little stars), *ave-Marie* ('hail Marys' – tiny ridged tubes), *risi* (like grains of rice), *farfalline* (little butterflies), *alfabeto* (letters of the alphabet), *anellini* (little rings), ORZO and other tiny shapes.

pasticcio di penne con formaggi e funghi
baked penne with cheese and mushrooms

Serves 4–5
50g/1¾oz/4 tbsp unsalted butter, plus
*   extra for greasing*
20g/¾oz dried porcini, soaked, drained
*   and chopped*
500g/1lb 2oz fresh cultivated
*   mushrooms, thinly sliced*
1 garlic clove
salt and freshly ground black pepper
300g/10½oz penne
150g/5½oz Bel Paese cheese, thinly
*   sliced*
150g/5½oz fontina cheese, thinly sliced
75g/2¾oz Parmesan cheese, grated
200ml/7fl oz/generous ¾ cup double
*   (heavy) cream*

This recipe is from northern Italy. Use fresh porcini when they are in season instead of the cultivated mushrooms, and omit the dried porcini.

Preheat the oven to 200°C/400°F/Gas Mark 6.

Heat 25g/1oz/2 tbsp of the butter over a high heat and sauté the porcini and fresh mushrooms with the whole garlic clove. Add salt and pepper, reduce the heat and cook for 3 minutes. Discard the garlic.

Cook the pasta in boiling salted water until al dente. Drain and dress with the remaining butter.

Butter an ovenproof dish and cover the bottom with a layer of pasta. Distribute about a quarter of the mushrooms and sliced cheeses evenly over the pasta and sprinkle with 1 tablespoon of the Parmesan. Add another layer of pasta and cover with mushrooms and cheese as before. Repeat until you have used all the ingredients, finishing with a layer of sliced cheeses. Pour over the cream and sprinkle with salt and pepper.

Cover the dish with foil and bake for 10 minutes. Remove the foil and bake, uncovered, for a further 10 minutes, or until a light crust has formed. Remove from the oven and leave to stand for 5 minutes before serving.

RIGHT: Pasticcio di penne con formaggi e funghi

pasto
meal

There are only two meals in Italy, lunch and dinner, and at these meals many – although by no means any longer all – families, usually sit around the table together. Breakfast is not considered as a meal, most of the time consisting of a cup of coffee and a biscuit or two taken in solitary silence, or perhaps at a bar on the way to work. Children have CAFFÈ *e latte* (coffee and milk) with bread, FOCACCIA or other bread-based snacks. Working people (except in large cities) and schoolchildren go home for their lunch to enjoy together a plate of pasta, still the most common dish at midday.

The evening meal, often the lighter of the two, more often than any other meal finds the family round the table. The young are usually there too, often rushing out afterwards to meet friends for the cinema and then to eat a *burghi* (hamburger) or a pizza. Meals are not often taken in restaurants even by the young, who soon realize that it is far cheaper, and often far better, to eat mamma's food.

The time of these two meals varies. In the north lunch is between 12 and 1pm, and dinner is between 7.30 and 8, while in the south, and especially in Rome, nobody sits down to lunch before 2pm, or to dinner before 9–9.30pm.

patata
potato

Potatoes never conquered Italy as they did other European countries. They never became an everyday food, and perhaps for this reason they are treated as a dish in their own right and not just as an accompaniment to meat and fish.

TORTINI (pies) of potatoes are made with other vegetables – with onions in Lombardy, with green beans in Liguria, where they are called *polpettoni* (see recipe on page 137) – or with other ingredients as in the Neapolitan GATTÒ (see recipe

on page 174). Potatoes and fish and/or shellfish form the TIELLA from Puglia. Potatoes are also used to make GNOCCHI. They are roasted, stewed (often with tomato), fried, sautéed and pureed, but seldom served boiled and never without any dressing. The best Italian potatoes are from Campania, because of its volcanic soils.

[see recipe on facing page]

pecora
ewe

Ewe is eaten in remote parts of Abruzzo, Molise, Basilicata and Sardinia, mainly by shepherds. The tastiest meat comes from a sterile ewe. Before being cooked, the meat has to be marinated for at least one day, sometimes for three, to get rid of its rather unpleasant smell. The oldest known recipe is *coatto*, from Abruzzo, in which the cut-up leg is first blanched and then stewed in an earthenware pot with onion, garlic, herbs, oil, tomato, white wine and chilli.

pecorino
a cheese

Ewe's milk cheese is produced in every region of central and southern Italy. The best-known pecorini, each with their own DOP mark, are *romano*, *sardo* (from Sardinia), *siciliano* and *toscano*, all of which, although similar, have particular characteristics. The shapes vary in size and the length of ageing differs, the romano, at 8 months, being the longest.

Pecorino romano, which is hard after long ageing, is the best for grating and is essential to the preparation of many local dishes; it is the most popular of all pecorini. The best romano is produced in November, when some of the lambs go to the slaughterhouses and there is therefore more and richer milk available. Pecorino romano is

292

made in Lazio but, in spite of its name, far more is made in Sardinia.

Pecorino sardo can be eaten 2 weeks after being made and, used as a table cheese, should not age longer than 3 months. It is a very tasty cheese, slightly salty and piquant, the piquancy increasing with age. Some of the pecorini made in Sardinia are smoked.

Pecorino siciliano is the only one that can be eaten the day after it is made, when still unsalted; in this state it is called *tuma*. It has a very delicate flavour and is soft and creamy. After a month it becomes stronger and has a more distinctive flavour, which remains much the same for up to 3 months. After about the fourth month it becomes *formaggio da grattugia* – grating cheese. A special Sicilian pecorino is made in some villages near Enna, in the mountainous centre of the island; it is called *piacintinu ennese* and is coloured with saffron, thus acquiring a slightly metallic flavour. There are also some Sicilian pecorini that contain peppercorns, which are added to the curd.

Pecorino toscano is ripe after 2 weeks, when the inside part of the cheese is very creamy; it is then the sweetest of all pecorini. If aged it becomes hard and piquant but it is never considered a *formaggio da grattugia*. Goat's milk is sometimes added to the ewe's milk, especially in southern Tuscany; this makes the pecorino whiter and lower in fat. The *pecorino delle crete senesi*, from a district south of Siena named after its clay soil, is the favourite of the real connoisseurs of pecorino. It has a very particular taste given to it partly by the wormwood that grows in the clay soil and

patate in umido
stewed potatoes

Serves 4
700g/1lb 9oz waxy potatoes
salt and freshly ground black pepper
25g/1oz/2 tbsp unsalted butter
2 tbsp olive oil
50g/1¾oz pancetta, cut into cubes
1 onion, finely chopped
1 garlic clove, finely chopped
1 tbsp fresh marjoram or ½ tbsp dried
marjoram
1 tbsp tomato puree diluted with 7 tbsp
hot stock

These potatoes are an ideal accompaniment to grilled sausages, chops, sautéed chicken or an omelette. They are also good (without the PANCETTA) for a vegetarian supper.

Peel the potatoes and cut them into 2.5cm/1in cubes. Boil in lightly salted water for 5 minutes.

While the potatoes are cooking, put the butter, olive oil and pancetta in a large, heavy saucepan and cook for 1 minute. Add the onion and garlic and sauté gently for 5 minutes.

Drain the parboiled potatoes and add them to the pan, turning them over very gently to coat them thoroughly in the fat. Cook for 3–4 minutes.

Add the marjoram, diluted tomato puree and some salt and pepper. Stir well and cook, covered, until the potatoes are tender, turning them over often. Use a fork to turn the potatoes, as this breaks them up less than a spoon. If some pieces do break off, you can console yourself with the thought that this dish is also known as *patate alla contadina* – potatoes cooked the peasant's way.

Taste, adjust the seasoning and serve.

imparts its flavour to the ewe's milk. Another excellent pecorino toscano is that of Pienza.

Nowadays there is a considerable amount of pecorino in which cow's milk is added to the ewe's milk.

penne
a pasta

Penne are dried tubular pasta, a very popular shape, particularly suited for rich sauces. They are either ridged or smooth and the ends are cut at an angle so that they look like quill pens (penne means 'feather' or 'quill'). They are usually about 4cm/1½ in long, smaller ones being called *pennette*. Penne are one of the best shapes to use in baked dishes.

pentola
cylindrical saucepan

A cylindrical pan used mainly for boiling, for some kinds of stewing and for making soups, in other words for cooking food in liquid. Italians are, rightly, fussy about their pots and pans and know how important it is for the success of a dish to use the right size pan made from the right material. For instance, the pot for a RISOTTO must be large and deep with a round bottom, so that the mixing spoon can easily reach everywhere. The best metal for it is stainless steel with a copper bottom or heavy aluminium.

A pentola's diameter is generally the same as its height. But a pentola for pasta is taller, and does not need to be heavy. A respectable family would have at least two of these, one for cooking pasta for up to four people and a large one in which 1kg/2¼lb pasta can be properly cooked.

All pentole have two handles or, more rarely, a bucket-type handle as in a PAIOLO. This is a legacy of the past when the pot was hung on a hook over the fire.

peoci
mussels

The Venetian name for COZZE, with which the locals make the most delicious of all fish soups, *sopa de peoci*.

pepe
pepper

This spice was first used by the ancient Romans, who brought it back from North Africa at the time of the Punic Wars, as a preservative for meat and fish, as well as a seasoning for both savoury and sweet preparations.

The Byzantines brought pepper within reach of the shrewd Venetians, who immediately saw in this spice the future wealth that it was indeed to

LEFT: Penne

yield. Venice, and later Genoa, traded pepper all over Europe at extremely high prices, and pepper became a favourite condiment of northern cuisines, while Venice and Genoa got richer and richer. Their inhabitants, however, preferred scented herbs from the Apennines and the local vegetables from the vegetable gardens around the lagoon. Pepper, usually black, is the most common spice in contemporary Italian cooking.

peperonata
pepper and tomato stew

The Italian ratatouille. Although made only with peppers, onions and tomatoes, it shares with its French cousin the Mediterranean flavours and a similar method of cooking. Originally from southern Italy, peperonata is now a popular way to cook peppers everywhere, and nearly every cook has his or her own recipe.

Peperonata is usually served with roast or boiled meat or chicken, or with steaks. It can be served with any meat that does not have a sauce of its own, but not with a stew, for example, where the sauce would interfere with the taste of the peperonata. It is also excellent with a plain FRITTATA. In Basilicata peperonata, flavoured with chilli, is eaten with COTECHINO.

If any is left over, peperonata makes a delicious sauce for spaghetti.

[see recipe below]

peperoncino
chilli

Peperoncino has two meanings: chilli and small sweet peppers, red or green. To be precise, chilli should be called *peperoncino piccante*. In many regions of Italy, especially in the north, chilli, up to no more than 20 years ago, was hardly used; I would even say it was hardly known. In ARTUSI's book, first published in 1891, it appears in only two or three recipes, and it is called *zenzero*, as it is still known in Tuscany. Ada BONI, a Roman, in *Il Talismano della Felicità* does not add chilli to her *spaghetti olio e aglio*, nor to *bucatini all'amatriciana*, nor to any of her fish soups, apart from CACCIUCCO. But peperoncino piccante has always been a primary spice in the cooking of southern Italy, especially in

peperonata
pepper, onion and tomato stew

Serves 4
300g/10½oz mild onions, finely sliced
5 tbsp extra virgin olive oil
2 garlic cloves, sliced
1kg/2¼lb mixed red, yellow and green
  peppers, deseeded and cut into strips
salt and freshly ground black pepper
500g/1lb 2oz ripe fresh tomatoes, peeled
  and chopped
2 tbsp red wine vinegar
2 tbsp chopped fresh flat-leaf parsley

This is the classic PEPERONATA. In some recipes a pinch or two of dried chilli is added.

Sauté the onions in the olive oil in a heavy pan over a medium heat until soft. Add the garlic, peppers and salt. Cook for a further 10 minutes, stirring frequently.

Mix in the tomatoes and bring to a simmer. Add the vinegar, turn the heat down and cook for about 25 minutes, stirring occasionally. Add pepper to taste and sprinkle with parsley. Cook for a further minute or two before serving.

Basilicata and Calabria and to a lesser degree also in Campania and Puglia (oddly enough it hardly appears in original Sicilian or Sardinian food). It is added to RAGÙ and stews, fish and seafood, SALAMI and sausages. In Abruzzo and in Molise too, peperoncino is added to many dishes, from BRODETTO to the AMATRICIANA sauce – Amatrice is a town in the Apennines on the border between Lazio and Abruzzo. Farther north it is only used in a few dishes from the province of Siena where, as elsewhere in Tuscany, it is called ZENZERO (Italian for ginger), thus causing great confusion among foreigners. Nowadays peperoncino always means the hot variety and it is used in many dishes throughout the peninsula: in many tomato sauces for pasta, in grilled fish and seafood, with peppers, aubergines and broccoli, although never, at least I hope, in traditional dishes. Many restaurants (and many people) keep on the table some flaked or powdered peperoncino or a little bottle of *olio santo* ('holy oil'), which is extra virgin olive oil containing chilli, to be poured on whatever one likes, sometimes to the detriment of the original flavour of the dish.

The sweet pepper preserved in vinegar is also sometimes called peperoncino; this is usually the cigarette-shaped green pepper.

peperone
pepper

The peppers mostly associated with Italy are the sweet ones, sometimes known as capsicums, and in North America as bell peppers. Peppers grow everywhere in Italy, but the most highly prized ones come from around Cuneo and Asti in Piedmont, where they are served with the BAGNA CAÔDA, and around Nocera in Umbria. The best of the small pointed kind are the sweet green peppers from Lombardy.

While in other regions peppers are often eaten raw in salad, the Calabresi and Siciliani have always prepared them in many different ways. However, the simplest traditional recipe is from Piedmont: *peperoni arrostiti* is a classic ANTIPASTO in which the grilled peppers are peeled and dressed with olive oil, salt, and possibly a few anchovies, garlic, dried chilli and/or chopped parsley. There are recipes for sautéed peppers, for peppers cooked with eggs, mixed with a sweet and sour sauce (see recipe on page 46) or with sautéed potatoes (see recipe on page 73), for peppers with many different stuffings and for the well-loved PEPERONATA.

Peppers are now popular all over Italy, and most of today's leading chefs have created recipes for them, many matching peppers with pasta. This is a perfect combination, and one that has been popular in southern Italy for centuries.

There are no recipes for peppers in old cookery books, as they were once considered to be strictly peasant food. Only LURASCHI, in the 19th century, has a rather strange recipe for preserving them. ARTUSI ignored them altogether. But in the 1920s Ada BONI saw the enormous possibilities of this vegetable. In her *Il Talismano della Felicità* she wrote eleven recipes for peppers, some original, others adapted from traditional southern recipes.

In Calabria, small peppers are dried in the sun and made into strings which decorate windows and doors in the summer, and kitchens in the winter. Peppers of this kind are also preserved under oil or vinegar, *peperoni sott'olio* or *sott'aceto*, and served with boiled or roast meat. Anchovy fillets, basil leaves, pepper and cloves are sometimes added to the jars. I preserve peppers by grilling and peeling them and then putting them under oil with a few garlic cloves and some chilli.

[see recipe on page 298]

pepolino or serpillo
thyme

The Tuscan names for a variety of thyme that grows wild in Tuscany.

pera
pear

The popular Italian varieties are Abate, Coscia, Decana and Passacrassana, some ripening in July and August in central Italy, while the autumn or winter fruit are the varieties of northern Italy.

The best recipe for a pear dessert is *pere al Barolo*, from Piedmont. The pears are stewed, unpeeled, in Barolo wine with sugar and a flavouring of cinnamon and cloves.

A highly regarded pear GRAPPA is bottled with a pear in the bottle.

perciatelli
a pasta

Dried pasta, like thick spaghetti but hollow; it is more commonly called BUCATINI. Perciatelli is the name often used by pasta manufacturers in southern Italy.

pernice
partridge

There are three kinds of partridge in Italy: the grey partridge, also called *starna*; the red-legged partridge; and the Sardinian partridge, which is a North African species related to the red-legged partridge and which has very tasty, herby meat. The grey partridge is the least interesting, nowadays being mainly a farmed bird, but the most easily available. Partridges are good cooked in a casserole, stuffed with a few Muscat grapes and a little MASCARPONE. The juices are then deglazed with red wine and brandy and a little more mascarpone to add volume and sweetness.

pesca
peach

The peach tree was brought to Europe from Persia by Alexander the Great and it found in Italy the ideal growing conditions. However, large-scale cultivation of peaches, as of most other fruits, only began during the 19th century, the best being those grown in Romagna, Le Marche and Campania. There are four main groups of peaches: common yellow or white peaches, nectarines (*nettarina*, *pesca noce* or *nocepesca*), percocche and Saturnia or Tabacchiera, all of which include many different varieties. Among the best white peaches, my favourite are the small *pesche da vigna* ('vine peaches'), which grow in vineyards, the peach trees being used to support the vines (or so it was before the days of concrete posts). The pesche da vigna ripen late, at the same time as the vines. The *percocche* are used mostly in industry. The Saturnia or Tabacchiera, a squashed white peach, was developed in Le Marche in the 1980s and it has become very popular.

The earliest recipes for peaches date from Roman times, such as this one from APICIUS: 'Clean hard-skinned peaches and slice them and stew them. Arrange in a dish, sprinkle a little oil and serve with cumin-flavoured wine.' *Pesche al vino* is still a common way to serve peaches, although the wine will not be flavoured with cumin. The peaches are peeled and sliced, and then – just before eating them – red or dry white wine is poured over. Some people sprinkle a little sugar on top. Another traditional way to eat peaches is stuffed, for which the original Piedmontese recipe is given here. Peaches are delicious mixed with strawberries, dressed with lemon and orange juice. They are also used in tarts, in ice creams, jams and jellies, and are preserved in alcohol. White peaches are also used to make *persicata*, a stiff paste, which is cut into different shapes.

[see recipe on page 300]

peperoni ripieni di pasta
peppers stuffed with pasta

Serves 4

4 large yellow peppers

100g/3½oz black olives, pitted and
    chopped

2 tbsp chopped fresh flat-leaf parsley

1 salted anchovy, boned, rinsed and
    chopped, or 2 canned or bottled
    anchovy fillets, drained and chopped

1 garlic clove, chopped

1 tbsp capers, preferably in salt, rinsed

½–1 tsp crushed dried chillies

salt and freshly ground black pepper

5 tbsp extra virgin olive oil

300g/10½oz spaghetti

2 tbsp dried breadcrumbs

This is a modern dish, as attractive as it is delicious. You can use *ditalini* (small DITALI) or *pennette* (small PENNE) instead of spaghetti.

Grill the peppers until the skin is charred all over. Leave until they are cool enough to handle. Remove the pepper skins with a small sharp knife. Cut in half, remove the cores, seeds and ribs and pat dry.

In a large bowl, combine the olives, parsley, anchovies and garlic with the capers, chillies, salt and pepper and half the olive oil.

Cook the spaghetti in boiling water until slightly undercooked and then drain. Transfer to the bowl with the chopped ingredients and mix thoroughly. Taste and adjust the seasoning.

Preheat the oven to 220°C/425°F/Gas Mark 7.

Brush a roasting pan with some of the remaining oil. Place the pepper halves in the tin and fill with the spaghetti mixture, rolling it around a fork as you do when you eat it. Sprinkle with breadcrumbs and the remaining oil. Bake for about 10 minutes, until a light crust has formed. Serve hot or at room temperature.

298

RIGHT: Peperoni ripieni di pasta

peperone

pesche ripiene alla piemontese
stuffed peaches

Serves 4

4 large peaches, halved and stoned

40g/1½oz (about 12) amaretti biscuits

15g/½oz blanched almonds

40g/1½oz/3 tbsp caster (superfine)
* sugar*

2 tsp unsweetened cocoa powder, sifted

150ml/5fl oz/⅔ cup Moscato wine

25g/1oz/2 tbsp unsalted butter, plus
* extra for greasing*

Peaches are enhanced here by the flavour of almonds from the AMARETTI.

Preheat the oven to 200°C/400°F/Gas Mark 6.

Scoop out some of the flesh from the peaches to make large cavities. Chop and mash the flesh and place in a bowl. Crumble the amaretti and add to the bowl. Coarsely grind the almonds and then add to the bowl with most of the sugar, the cocoa and just enough wine to moisten the mixture. Mix well to combine.

Place the peaches in a buttered ovenproof dish and fill them with the mixture. Dot with butter. Pour the remaining wine around the peaches and sprinkle with the rest of the sugar. Bake for 20–25 minutes. Serve at room temperature.

pescatrice

see CODA DI ROSPO

pesce
fish

Only five out of the 20 regions of Italy do not have coastline and four of those have lakes and rivers, so they can make up for the lack of sea fish with freshwater fish. Just to make sure that they always have their fish, Italians are also great importers of salt cod and stockfish.

In Italy a fish, unless it is a very large specimen, is usually cooked and brought to the table with the head on. This is not only because the head imparts flavour during the cooking, but also because a decapitated creature is considered unattractive. In respectable restaurants the fish is filleted at the table by the waiter.

The Romans were so fond of fish that they had special tanks and inland pools built, some filled with seawater, so that they could have BRANZINI,

ORATE or DENTICI all the year round. Fish have seasons, just like vegetables and fruits.

The traditions of farming fish were carried on during the Dark Ages by monks, who had ponds in their monasteries filled with carp, tench, eel and trout.

The Renaissance chefs wrote chapter upon chapter on fish. Apart from being well liked, it was also the main food that could be eaten during Lent and on the many fast days throughout the year. The 16th-century chef Bartolomeo SCAPPI devoted a great part of his book to fish. There are recipes for every fish: sea and freshwater, stockfish, salted cod and preserved fish. Special emphasis was given to the cooking and presentation of the head of a large fish, considered one of the best parts. Scappi boils the head of a tuna fish in wine and vinegar and serves it with a highly flavoured sauce of ginger, cinnamon, coriander and mustard. The head of an OMBRINA is cooked in a white *court bouillon* and served with SALSA VERDE or *sapor bianco* – a sauce made with pounded almonds and soft breadcrumbs moistened with verjuice, ginger,

CONTINUES OVERLEAF

lemon or pomegranate juice and sugar to taste. At banquets the head was always presented by the head steward to the master.

Nowadays most Italians eat fish when they go out to a restaurant. Most contemporary restaurants and trattorie offer the same number of fish dishes as meat and chicken dishes.

pesce persico
perch

Perch is one of the best freshwater fish. It is caught principally in Lake Como, but it is also found in Lake Maggiore and Lake Garda. It has very white flesh and a non-fishy flavour suited to being cooked like veal. In Milan, in fact, the usual way to cook fillets of perch is 'a COTOLETTA' – coated in egg and breadcrumbs and fried in butter. It is traditional to use butter when cooking freshwater fish. The most traditional recipe is to serve pan-fried fillets of perch on a RISOTTO made with fish stock.

pesce San Pietro
John Dory

A fish with a rather flat, oval-shaped body and a large head, John Dory has a dark spot on each side; these spots, according to one of the legends that gave the fish its name, are St Peter's fingerprints. When the fishermen caught one of these fish, it began to wail so loudly that St Peter took pity on it, took it between his thumb and forefinger and tossed it back into the water, thus marking it with his fingerprints.

John Dory has a very tough skin but excellent white flesh. It is very good simply baked for 10 minutes in the oven, lightly coated with seasoned flour, in plenty of butter and oil. Before serving it is sprinkled with lemon juice. In a classic Venetian recipe the lightly floured fillets are sautéed in butter and then finished off in the oven covered with capers, tomatoes and butter.

pesce spada
swordfish

In the old days anyone who went to Sicily in the spring or summer would have noticed some strange boats, each with a very tall mast. At the top of the mast stood a man looking out to sea, trying to spot the shoals of swordfish on their way back from the eastern Mediterranean. Swordfish travel in an anti-clockwise direction, along the northern coasts of Africa to Asia Minor and back along the coast of Sicily. Once sighted, they are harpooned, just as they were in ancient Greek and Roman times. Alan Davidson, in *Mediterranean Seafood*, tells a story recorded by a traveller to Sicily in the 18th century: 'The Sicilian fishermen used a Greek sentence as a charm to lure the swordfish to their boats: if the fish overheard a word of Italian he would plunge under water and make off.'

It is a very large fish, usually around 3m/10ft in length, and is usually sold as steaks. There are many recipes for this fish, which has a consistency similar to meat. The best recipes are from Calabria and Sicily. In Bagnara, a town in Calabria where the swordfish fishing fleet is harboured, steaks are steamed with olive oil, lemon, capers and salt; oregano and parsley are added at the end. A good Sicilian recipe is for *involtini di pesce spada*: thinly sliced, the swordfish is spread with a mixture of prosciutto, mozzarella, Parmesan and herbs, rolled up and grilled. Having a firm flesh, swordfish is also excellent threaded on a skewer with bay leaves and grilled. Another way to serve the fish is grilled, with SALMORIGLIO.

Smoked swordfish is also very good. The belly of the fish, first lightly salted, is smoked over a fire of wood that must not contain any resin. It is eaten thinly sliced, dressed with a little olive oil and lemon juice and maybe a few capers; in Sicily it is also added, thinly sliced, to a tomato sauce for dressing FUSILLI or other pasta.

[see recipe on facing page]

pesce spada alla trapanese
swordfish in a tomato, olive and cornichon sauce

Serves 4

1 onion, chopped

2 tbsp extra virgin olive oil

4 cornichons

6 black olives, pitted

2 tbsp capers, preferably in salt, rinsed

1 celery stalk

salt and freshly ground black pepper

2 tbsp tomato puree diluted with
*   200ml/7fl oz/generous ¾ cup boiling*
*   water*

600g/1lb 5oz swordfish, thinly sliced

about 1 tbsp lemon juice

This is my adaptation of a recipe from *Il Gastronomo Educato* by Alberto Denti di Pirajno, a 20th-century Sicilian writer and a great gastronome. Try to buy steaks from the belly of the fish, which has a delicate flavour.

Put the onion in a large sauté pan and cover with 100ml/3½fl oz/scant ½ cup water. Bring to the boil and simmer, covered, for a couple of minutes. Turn up the heat, add the olive oil and continue cooking until the water has evaporated and the onion is golden. You must stir frequently as the water evaporates, so that all the bits of onion are golden without sticking to the bottom of the pan.

Meanwhile, chop the cornichons, olives, capers and celery and mix them all together. When the onion is golden, add the chopped mixture and season with salt and plenty of pepper. Cook over a gentle heat for 5–6 minutes.

Pour the diluted tomato puree into the pan and cook, stirring frequently, until the sauce begins to thicken, which will take a further 5–7 minutes.

Now add the fish and cook for about 5 minutes, turning it over once. The cooking time depends on the thickness of the steaks. It is better to undercook swordfish rather than overcook it.

Put the fish and its sauce on a warmed serving dish, pour over the lemon juice and serve at once.

303

pesto
basil sauce

This famous sauce has its origins in Liguria, where the basil is sweeter yet more aromatic than anywhere else, thanks to the perfect balance between humidity and hot sun. It is indeed odd that the only speciality from Liguria that genuinely needs a local ingredient should be the one that has travelled all over the world.

There are two fundamental types of pesto: the pesto of the western Riviera and the pesto of the eastern Riviera. The former, which includes the classic pesto genovese, is stronger and simpler, the latter is more delicate, containing less garlic, some pine nuts, grated PECORINO and/or Parmesan and other ingredients which make it less fierce. But, after that, there are as many recipes as cooks, and no Ligurian cook would actually know how much of this or that goes into it: it's all a question of judgement and personal taste. The basil is pounded in a mortar with some garlic, salt and, if

added, pine nuts or walnuts, the best local extra virgin olive oil being added drop by drop. This, at least, is the old-fashioned method; nowadays it is often made in the blender or food processor. Connoisseurs say this is to the detriment of its flavour, since the basil is being chopped by a metal blade, which might also warm the mixture, rather than pounded by a wooden pestle. There is a more delicate version of pesto, in which some butter or cream is added, and the garlic reduced.

Pesto is traditionally used to dress TRENETTE, TROFIE and PICAGGE; to a Genoese it would be inconceivable that it should be used with any other shape of pasta. The pasta is often cooked with sliced potatoes and green beans and all three ingredients are dressed with pesto and eaten together. Pesto is used also to dress potato GNOCCHI or to give a local touch – one spoonful is enough – to a MINESTRONE alla genovese.

[see recipe below]

pesto

Enough for 4 helpings of pasta
or gnocchi
20g/³⁄₄oz/2¹⁄₂ tbsp pine nuts
50g/1³⁄₄oz fresh basil leaves
1 garlic clove, peeled
a pinch of coarse sea salt
4 tbsp freshly grated Parmesan cheese
2 tbsp freshly grated mature pecorino
cheese
125ml/4fl oz/¹⁄₂ cup extra virgin olive
oil, preferably Ligurian

This is my recipe for pesto. You can vary it, but whatever you do, use a mild extra virgin olive oil, not a peppery one.

Preheat the oven to 180°C/350°F/Gas Mark 4.

Spread the pine nuts on a baking sheet and place in the oven for 3–4 minutes, to release the aroma of the nuts.

Put the basil, garlic, pine nuts and salt in a mortar. Grind with the pestle, crushing all the ingredients against the side of the mortar until the mixture has become a paste. You can use a food processor or a blender.

Mix in the grated cheeses and pour over the oil very gradually, beating with a wooden spoon.

pettine

see CONCHIGLIA DI SAN GIACOMO

petto
breast

Petto di POLLO, di TACCHINO, di ANATRA are breast of chicken, turkey and duck. Petto di VITELLO (breast of veal) is either boned – when it is known as PUNTA DI PETTO – and stuffed and made into a roll, or roasted with the bones in place. When used for roasting, breast of veal is larded with PANCETTA, brushed with STRUTTO or oil and cooked in a low oven. Breasts of chicken or turkey are boned and used for INVOLTINI, or cooked with delicate sauces in place of the more expensive veal.

[see recipe on facing page]

peverada
pepper sauce

Also called *peará*, this is a well-known sauce from Treviso, now made all over northern Italy. Recipes vary, but the one essential ingredient is a lot of pepper, as its name implies. Known since the 14th century, it was at that time a sauce for the wealthy, as it was rich in spices, particularly pepper, the most costly spice of all.

[see recipe on facing page]

piadina
a bread

The 19th-century poet Giovanni Pascoli, a native of Romagna, called piadina 'the national dish of the Romagnoli', because it used to be the daily bread of the local peasants. Like many other peasant dishes, it has now become fashionable as an accompaniment to cheese, SALAME and PROSCIUTTO served with drinks or as an ANTIPASTO.

Piadina used to be cooked on a *testo* – an earthenware disc that can be brought to a high temperature – but today it is more commonly cooked in a piping hot cast-iron pan. Piadina is made with wheat flour, lard and bicarbonate of soda or yeast. The kneaded dough is divided into small balls. Each ball is rolled out thinly and cooked until slightly charred. While it is still hot, ham, salami, sausages or a local cheese are laid on top and the piadina is folded over. The result is the most satisfying snack imaginable. There are now industrially made piadine on the market.

piatto
plate, dish or course

This word may mean plate, dish (in both senses) or course. Piatto, as a course, can be a *primo piatto*, such as a dish of PASTA, a soup or a RISOTTO, or a *secondo piatto*. The *terzo piatto* is usually no more than cheese and fruit. If vegetables are served separately after the meat, this is regarded as another piatto, since it comes on a different dish. Nowadays a meal might consist of a PIATTO UNICO – a one-course meal, plus cheese and fruit, of course.

Each course is served on a large dish which is handed around or placed on the table so that everyone can have a second helping. The practice of placing food on individual plates is only considered suitable for restaurants.

piatto unico
single course

A new term applied to a single-course meal. Some piatti unici used to be *entremets* (side dishes) at grand dinners, some are simple peasant dishes and others are vegetable dishes which can accompany meat or fish, but which are interesting enough to be a course on their own. SFORMATI, TORTE *di verdure*, various pizzas, thick soups, pasta or risotto are at times served as a piatto unico.

petti di pollo al ragù di porcini
chicken breasts in a mushroom sauce

Serves 4

5 tbsp olive oil

4 skinless, boneless chicken breasts

*75ml/2½fl oz/5 tbsp meat stock (page
    61) or chicken stock*

salt and freshly ground black pepper

1 onion, finely chopped

*200g/7oz fresh porcini mushrooms,
    cleaned and sliced*

75ml/2½fl oz/5 tbsp dry white wine

*300g/10½oz ripe fresh tomatoes,
    peeled, dseeded and diced*

This is a very unpretentious recipe, typical of Liguria, where fresh porcini are used whenever possible.

Heat 3 tablespoons of the olive oil in a sauté pan. Add the chicken breasts and cook on both sides until brown. Reduce the heat, add the stock and salt and pepper, and cook for 7–8 minutes or until the chicken is cooked through. Test by piercing with a thin skewer: the juice that runs out should be clear.

Meanwhile, heat the rest of the oil in a saucepan and sauté the onion until softened. Add the porcini and sauté for 1 minute, then pour the wine over them and cook until it has evaporated. Add the tomatoes and simmer until the sauce begins to thicken. Taste and adjust the seasoning.

Cut the chicken breasts in half lengthways and place them on a warmed serving dish. Spoon the porcini sauce over them and serve.

la peverada
pepper sauce

Enough for 4 servings

50g/1¾oz/4 tbsp unsalted butter

1 tbsp olive oil

2 garlic cloves, bruised

1 clove

3 tbsp dried breadcrumbs

*300ml/10fl oz/1¼ cups meat stock
    (page 61) or chicken stock*

salt and freshly ground black pepper

PEVERADA is a classic accompaniment to roast or boiled meats in northern Italy.

Put the butter, oil, garlic and clove in a small saucepan, preferably earthenware. Sauté until the garlic begins to colour, then remove and discard the garlic and clove.

Add the breadcrumbs and sauté for a minute or two, turning them over and over in the fat. Add about 100ml/3½fl oz/scant ½ cup of the stock and cook over a low heat until the sauce thickens. Add salt to taste and a very generous quantity of pepper.

Continue cooking for about 30 minutes, stirring frequently and adding a little more stock whenever necessary. The sauce should have a thickish consistency. Taste and adjust the seasoning.

picagge
a pasta

'Ribbons' in Genoese dialect, picagge are the local TAGLIATELLE. They are made in Genoa, and elsewhere in Liguria, with a PASTA dough that is less rich than the more common *pasta all'uovo* from Emilia-Romagna since it contains water as well as eggs. As a result it is softer, less elastic and less tasty. Picagge are traditionally dressed with PESTO, or with mushroom sauce.

piccata
escalopes

A Milanese dish consisting of veal escalopes, which are floured and fried in butter and then finished with various flavourings. Different versions include FRITTURA PICCATA with lemon juice and parsley, piccata with Marsala, and piccata with wild mushrooms, which are sautéed separately and added to the meat.

piccione
pigeon or squab

Piccione refers to a domestic bird, the wild bird being called PALOMBACCIO. There are two traditional recipes for pigeon: *piccione coi piselli* (stewed with peas) and *piccione alla ghiotta* or *alla leccarda* (roasted and basted with wine, with a sauce made from the liver of the bird).

pici or pinci
a pasta

These are a kind of thick spaghetti from the province of Siena, made with a dough that does not contain eggs, only flour, water and a little olive oil. The result is a soft pasta which is extremely pleasant, particularly when dressed with a rich RAGÙ of meat and fresh PORCINI or meat and local sausage, the traditional Sienese dressings.

piedino, zampetto
trotter or foot

Except for the feet of the ox, the trotters of all other animals are popular in Italy, especially pig trotters. All trotters are boiled for a long time and then boned. Pig and calf trotters, when cold, are sliced and dressed with extra virgin olive oil, lemon juice, a touch of French mustard and salt. A recipe from Sardinia is for boiled and boned lamb trotters finished in a tomato sauce flavoured with onion, garlic and parsley, while ARTUSI finishes the cooked and boned calf trotters in one of his signature ways, gently fried in plenty of butter, Parmesan and meat juice – and they are delicious.

Piemonte
Piedmont

Due to its proximity and history, France and its cooking is a very strong influence on the cuisine of this northern region. It is an elegant cuisine, and yet still tied to the land, thanks to the pride the locals have in their produce. As a result of this dichotomy the local cooking is best described as *cucina borghese* (the cuisine of the bourgeoisie).

Garlic is an important seasoning, which is not the case in the other northern regions. Vegetables are eaten in abundance and are among the best in the peninsula, such as the asparagus of Santena, the onions of Ivrea, the cardoons of Chieri and the peppers of Asti. Those vegetables, and others, come into their own in the best known of all Piedmontese antipasti, BAGNA CAÔDA. ANTIPASTI are certainly a highlight of the Piedmontese cuisine; perhaps only in Puglia is the array so formidable.

Then, of course, there are the white truffles of Alba, the jewel in Piedmont's crown. A salad of OVOLI fungi and white truffles, a BRUSCHETTA

PIEDMONT

Alps

L. Maggiore

•Biella
Novara•
Vercelli•

Turin•

Po

Asti• Tanaro

•Alba

•Alessandria

Cuneo•

of truffle cream and anchovy fillets layered with truffle, a plate of TAGLIATELLE dressed with butter and slivers of white truffle, a RISOTTO or two fried eggs covered with a sprinkling of truffles are musts during the truffle season.

Piedmont is one of the most important rice-growing regions. The quality of its rice was already appreciated in the 18th century when the future American president Thomas Jefferson smuggled two bags of rice out of Piedmont so that he could plant it on his estate in Virginia. There are many recipes for risotto – with cardoons, with artichokes, with Barolo wine, to mention but a few – and two traditional rice dishes, the rustic PANISCIA and the delicate riso con la FONDUTA.

Pasta is not of great importance in Piedmontese cuisine. The two original pasta dishes are AGNOLOTTI (a kind of ravioli) and TAJARIN (narrow tagliatelle) – both are dressed with butter and truffles during the season (see recipe on page 419).

Meat and game dishes abound. BOLLITO MISTO – called *gran bui* in the local dialect – is the classic boiled meat dish, which should contain at least five different cuts. SANATO is the most prized Italian veal: it is used raw, thinly cut, in *carne all'albese*, with a sprinkling, or a shower, of truffles on top; or for VITELLO TONNATO. The highly regarded beef from the local Fassone breed of cattle is braised in wine – BRASATO *al Barolo* or *al Dolcetto* – and also forms part of the bollito misto.

Cheeses are excellent and still mostly produced artisanally. These include the tangy-flavoured BRA, a cow's milk cheese to which ewe's milk is sometimes added, CASTELMAGNO, a powerful-tasting cow's milk cheese, a favourite of many kings from Charlemagne to Vittorio Emanuele II, and the soft, ubiquitous, yet outstanding TOMA.

Puddings, sweets, cakes and chocolates play an important part in the cuisine and the life of the locals. ZABAIONE, PESCHE RIPIENE, PANNA COTTA, the nutty, chocolate-flavoured torta GIANDUIA, the pretty BACI DI DAMA and, by way of contrast, the BRUTTI MA BUONI biscuits are just a few. These, and many others, are what the Piedmontese love to eat at the many cafés that are so much part of their social life.

pietanza
course

A somewhat old-fashioned word for any dish that is not a first course nor a pudding. It is more or less a synonym of second course.

pignatta
cooking pot

A cooking pot in the shape of a pine cone. A pignatta has two small ear-shaped handles and, sometimes, a flat lid. It is made of copper or, in the south where it is used for cooking legumes, of earthenware.

pignolata
Christmas sweet

The traditional Christmas sweet of Messina
in Sicily; its name stems from the fact that it
is shaped like a *pigna* (pine cone). Pignolata is
made up of many little balls, or stubby ovals, of
sweetened yeast pastry. These are baked or fried
and coated with white and/or chocolate icing.
They are then put together to form a cone. Some
cooks cover the pignolata with Italian meringue.

pinoccate
sweets

Traditional sweets from Umbria that used to be
sold around Christmas-time. Now they are made
industrially and are in the shops for most of the
year. They are made with pine nuts and sugar and
flavoured with citron peel.

pinolo
pine nut

The seeds of the stone pine or *Pinus pinea*, which
is the beautiful umbrella pine so characteristic
of many stretches of the Italian coast. If you
find yourself in Versiglia or along the Pineta di
Ravenna in late summer, collect all the large
cones you can find. It may take a long time to
crack the pinoli (children love doing it) but the
reward is worth the time spent. The pine nuts are
soft and creamy, and have an unmistakable and
delicious resinous flavour that seems to be lacking
from shop-bought pinoli.

Pine nuts are an important ingredient in many
dishes, the best known of these being PESTO. They
are part of many sweet and sour dishes of Arab
origin, for example in some versions of the Sicilian
CAPONATA, as well as in some excellent Sicilian
sardine dishes. Pine nuts are also used in biscuits
and various cakes and sweet preparations.

pinzimonio
a sauce

A traditional Roman ANTIPASTO, this is a 'dip' for
raw vegetables, consisting simply of olive oil, salt
and pepper. Pinzimonio was born in Rome where,
the Romans say, it must be made only with the
finest olive oil of the Roman countryside. The
vegetables are seasonal, from wedges of fennel and
paper-thin slices of artichokes to crunchy celery,
meaty peppers and sun-drenched tomatoes. Every
diner is given a small cup full of the dressing while
the vegetables are placed all together on a large
dish for everybody to help themselves.

pisello
pea

One of the oldest Mediterranean vegetables,
peas were mentioned by Homer in the *Iliad*.
From Greece, they came to Rome. The Romans
cultivated them on a large scale and prepared them
in many ways, as shown in APICIUS's recipes.

Garden peas, more or less as we know them
now, were developed in Italy in the 16th century.
They were a favourite of Caterina de' Medici,
which made them famous in France, where she
was Queen and then Queen Mother for more than
40 years. At that time they were often cooked in
their pods, with PROSCIUTTO, a recipe first written
by MARTINO da Como and which reappeared some
500 years later in *Il Talismano della Felicità* by the
Roman Ada BONI (in the recipe given here, the
peas are podded). Ada Boni writes 21 recipes for
peas, from *piselli all'inglese* ('the English way') to
piselli con le vongole – with clams, in which the peas,
cooked in a light tomato sauce, are mixed with the
cooked clams. Peas are hardly ever simply boiled,
except in piselli all'inglese, in which the peas,
cooked in water sometimes flavoured with fennel
fronds, are dressed with fresh unsalted butter. Peas
are gently stewed in a little stock, they are braised

with onion and, sometimes, tomatoes, or they are used with rice as in the delicious RISI E BISI of Veneto.

Peas are also used to make SFORMATI and in pasta sauces. The best known of these is made from peas gently cooked in butter with prosciutto and finished off with cream.

[see recipe below]

pissaladeira
a pizza

Also called *pizza all'Andrea* or *sardinaira*, this is a PIZZA from Liguria. It is in fact more akin to its French neighbour and namesake *pissaladière* than to its compatriot from Naples, which it pre-dates. It was originally called pizza all'Andrea because it was based on a favourite food of the admiral Andrea Doria (1466–1560). He used to eat a slice of bread doused with olive oil and rubbed with garlic, with a salted anchovy on top (tomatoes, of course, were not yet known in Europe). Some recipes now include tomatoes in the topping, but to me, that's wrong.

[see recipe on page 312]

pistacchio
pistachio nut

The fruit of a small deciduous tree, *Pistacia vera*, that has purple flowers and velvety leaves, widely cultivated on the slopes of Etna in Sicily.

Pistachio nuts link the Italian cuisine with that of the Middle East. They are used in both savoury and sweet dishes, many of them originating in Sicily and showing Arab influence, such as CASSATA and CANNOLI. And, of course, ice cream.

They are also used in the stuffing for *cima alla genovese* (see recipe on page 340), in galantines and MORTADELLA, and are eaten salted and in their shells – a popular snack. There is now on the market a PESTO made with pistachio nuts, which makes a delicious pasta sauce. Pistachios are also used in making sweets, such as TORRONE.

piselli al prosciutto
peas with Parma ham

Serves 4

1.5–1.6kg/3¼–3½lb fresh peas, in
*   their pods*
50g/1¾oz/4 tbsp unsalted butter
1 small onion, finely chopped
salt and freshly ground black pepper
150ml/5fl oz/²/₃ cup hot meat stock
*   (page 61) or chicken stock or water*
a pinch of sugar (optional)
70–100g/2½–3½oz prosciutto, cut
*   into strips*
triangles of bread fried in butter, to serve
*   (optional)*

I have translated the recipe for this traditional Roman dish from Ada BONI's *Cucina Regionale Italiana*. 'The dish,' she writes, 'which can be a gastronomic experience, is a true Roman creation. Roman peas are deliciously sweet and tender.'

Shell the peas. Melt the butter in a saucepan over a low heat and sauté the onion until it begins to change colour. Add the peas, season with salt and pepper, and moisten with stock. Cook over a brisk heat for 10 minutes if cooking fresh young peas, or until tender with older ones. No sugar is required with Roman peas – but some peas may require a little sugar to sweeten them. Two minutes before the peas are ready, add the prosciutto and stir gently.

The dish can be served accompanied with triangles of crisply fried bread, if desired.

pissaladeira

Serves 6

1 quantity pizza dough (page 314)

1kg/2¼lb Spanish or white onions,
*   finely sliced*

6 tbsp olive oil, plus extra for greasing

1 tsp sugar

salt and freshly ground black pepper

6 salted anchovies, boned, rinsed and
*   chopped, or 12 canned or bottled*
*   anchovy fillets, drained and chopped*

1 garlic clove, very finely sliced

2 tsp dried oregano

12 small black olives, pitted

PISSALADEIRA is a pizza from Liguria, which is softer and thicker than the usual Neapolitan PIZZA.

Make the pizza dough and leave it to rise, in one piece. While the dough is rising, prepare the topping.

Put the onions, olive oil, sugar and a little salt in a large sauté pan or frying pan. Cover and cook over a very low heat for about 45 minutes, or until the onions are soft and golden. Stir occasionally and add 2 tablespoons water if the onions begin to burn.

Add the anchovies and garlic to the onions and cook, uncovered, over a very low heat for a further 5 minutes, pounding the anchovies to a paste with a fork. Add pepper, then taste the mixture and add salt if necessary.

Preheat the oven to 220°C/425°F/Gas Mark 7. Brush a 25cm/10in diameter tart tin with olive oil.

Roll out the pizza dough to a thickness of about 5mm/¼in and large enough to line the tin. Press the dough into the tin and slightly up the sides. Spoon the onion and anchovy topping over the dough, spreading it out evenly. Sprinkle with the oregano and dot with the olives.

Bake for 15 minutes, then reduce the oven temperature to 190°C/375°F/ Gas Mark 5 and bake for a further 5 minutes. Remove from the oven and leave to stand until warm. Serve at room temperature.

pitta
a pizza

The Calabrese version of the Neapolitan PIZZA, pitta is the traditional accompaniment to MORSEDDU. It is made with bread dough, to which a tablespoon of melted pork fat is sometimes added. The many toppings are usually different from those of a Neapolitan pizza. Two unusual pitte deserve a mention: one is with CIMA DI RAPE (a favourite vegetable of the region) and spicy sausage, and the other is with elderflowers scattered in the dough and covered with ewe's milk RICOTTA. A rolled pitta is made with potato dough and filled with CACIOCAVALLO cheese and PANCETTA.

pizza
pizza

Pizza, though not the Neapolitan pizza, is ancient food. Cato, in the 1st century BC, describes flat rounds of bread dough dressed with olive oil, herbs and honey and baked on stones. Virgil wrote about *moretum*, a flat round of unleavened bread, while Horace referred to what must have been pizza dough cut into strips and baked. But the pizza we know now, the *pizza napoletana*, to give it its correct name, was the brainchild of the ingenious Neapolitans, who gave new life to the plain old-style pizza when they added the tomato. This happened at the end of the 18th century, when they had developed a red, large and sweet variety of tomato. The new vegetable soon became popular, and the tomato found its place as the favourite topping for pizza.

Pizza acquired such fame among writers and artists, as well as among the common folk, that the French writer Alexandre Dumas thought it worthy of an entry in his *Dictionnaire*, published in 1873. He wrote: 'Pizza is a sort of flat bun like the one made in St Denis; it is round in shape and made with bread dough. At first glance it seems simple, but on closer inspection it is seen to be really complicated.'

Pizza was sold from stalls and eaten in the streets, as indeed it still is. Soon *pizzerie* began to appear in Naples, and the popularity of pizza spread even to the aristocracy. When Queen Margherita went to Naples in 1889 with King Umberto I, she immediately wanted to sample the dish she had heard so much about. The owner of the famous pizzeria Pietro il Pizzaiolo prepared three different pizzas for the Queen. One was made with pork fat, cheese and basil, one with tomatoes and garlic and the third was made with tomatoes, mozzarella and basil – red, white and green, the colours of the Italian flag. This was the Queen's favourite and it took her name.

Pizza went to the USA with spaghetti, taken there by the immigrants in the early decades of the 20th century, and from there came to Britain, having unfortunately lost most of its authenticity on the way.

As Dumas pointed out, good pizzas are not easy to make. They need the hands of the Neapolitan *pizzaioli*, who have learnt the secret of stretching the dough from their fathers, and they need the heat of wood burning in brick-lined ovens. For this reason pizza is seldom made at home, nor is it usually eaten there.

Apart from Margherita, the other traditional pizze are: *alla romana* – with tomato, mozzarella, anchovies and oregano; *alla marinara* – with tomatoes, garlic and oregano; and *aglio e olio* – garlic, oil and oregano.

313

[see recipes on pages 314 and 316]

pasta per pizza
pizza dough

Makes two 30cm/12in pizzas
500g/1lb 2oz/4 cups strong white
*   (bread) flour*
1 sachet (7g) easy-blend (active) dried
*   yeast*
1 tbsp salt
1 tbsp olive oil
a little extra virgin olive oil, to finish

Neapolitan PIZZA is cooked to perfection in the fierce heat of a wood-burning oven; at home, use your oven's hottest setting.

Place the flour on the work surface, mix in the yeast and salt and make a well in the middle (in Italy we start all bread doughs on the work surface, not in a bowl). Pour the olive oil into the well, together with 200ml/7fl oz/generous ¾ cup warm water (it should be blood temperature). Begin to knead by gathering flour from the side of the inner wall of the well. Add more water (about 350–400ml/12–14fl oz /1½ cups in all) until you have a thick dough.

Knead for about 10 minutes and then divide the dough into two balls. Place them in two oiled bowls, cover with a damp cloth and then leave them to rise in a warm place (out of any draughts) until they have doubled in size, about 2½ hours.

Lightly flour two square baking sheets and preheat the oven to its hottest temperature.

Punch down one of the balls and stretch and roll it into a circle about 5mm/¼in thick. The dough will want to spring back at first, but eventually it will do what you want. Leave a thicker rim all round the disc. Do the same with the other ball of dough. Place the discs on the prepared baking sheets and add your chosen topping (see below and page 316).

Bake in the hot oven for about 12–15 minutes, until the pizzas are brown at the edges. While still hot, brush the rims with a little extra virgin olive oil.

pizza alla marinara

700g/1lb 9oz ripe fresh tomatoes, peeled
4 tbsp extra virgin olive oil
2 garlic cloves, very finely sliced
2 tsp dried oregano
salt and freshly ground black pepper

This is the original PIZZA and it is also the simplest.

Cut the tomatoes in half, squeeze out some of the juice and coarsely chop the flesh. Spread the tomatoes over the pizza dough bases, drizzle with the olive oil and sprinkle with the garlic, oregano, some salt and plenty of pepper. Cook as above.

pizza Margherita

200g/7oz buffalo mozzarella
4 tbsp extra virgin olive oil
salt and freshly ground black pepper
500g/1lb 2oz ripe fresh tomatoes,
    deseeded and chopped
12 fresh basil leaves
1 tbsp freshly grated Parmesan cheese

This PIZZA topping was created to honour the visit of Queen Margherita to Naples in the 19th century.

Grate the mozzarella coarsely into a bowl and add 2 tablespoons of the olive oil and plenty of pepper. Leave to stand for 1 hour or so.

Spread the mozzarella and the tomatoes over the pizza dough bases, sprinkle with the basil and Parmesan and drizzle with the remaining oil. Cook as on page 314.

pizza dolce
a cake

This is a traditional cake prepared for village feasts or saints' days: it does not refer to any particular cake. It is made with a basic bread dough, to which sugar, eggs, olive oil and spices are added.

In Rome at Easter the tradition is to enrich pizza dolce with RICOTTA flavoured with cinnamon and grated lemon rind kneaded into the dough. Another Roman speciality is *pizza dolce di polenta*. The dough is made with finely ground FARINA GIALLA (maize flour) mixed with ricotta, water, sultanas, pine nuts, cinnamon, sugar and STRUTTO (pork fat).

pizzaiola
a sauce

Pizzaiola, a sauce for meat or fish, owes its name to the fact that it tastes like a PIZZA topping. The main ingredients are olive oil, tomatoes, garlic and oregano, to which capers or black olives are often added.

 [see recipe on page 318]

pizzella
a type of pizza

This classic Neapolitan preparation is made with PIZZA dough, which is rolled out into small rounds, fried in olive oil and then covered with the usual tomato toppings. The pizzelle are finished off in the oven for 4–5 minutes. Pizzelle can also incorporate pieces of SALAMI, cheese or vegetables in the uncooked dough.

pizzeria

see PIZZA

pizzicheria
delicatessen

Known as *salumeria* in northern Italy, a pizzicheria could best be described as an Italian delicatessen, although this description does scant justice to the immense range of food on display. A 19th-century Roman pizzicheria, dressed for Easter, is vividly described by William Wetmore Story in *Roba di Roma*: 'Great sides of bacon and lard are ranged endwise in regular bars all round the interior, and adorned with stripes of various colours, mixed with golden spangles and flashing tinsel; while

CONTINUES ON PAGE 318

pizza rustica
sausage, prosciutto and cheese pie

Serves 6

150g/5½oz luganega or mild pure pork
*   sausage, skinned and crumbled*
1 tbsp olive oil
140g/5oz mozzarella cheese
250g/9oz fresh ricotta
50g/1¾oz smoked provola cheese, diced
50g/1¾oz Parmesan cheese, grated
½ garlic clove, chopped
2 tbsp chopped fresh flat-leaf parsley
2 pinches of chilli powder or crushed
*   dried chillies*
100g/3½oz prosciutto, cut into small
*   pieces*
100g/3½oz mortadella, cut into small
*   pieces*
2 large eggs, lightly beaten
freshly ground black pepper
1½ tbsp dried breadcrumbs
a little butter for the tin

Pastry

140g/5oz/generous ½ cup unsalted
*   butter*
1 tbsp caster (superfine) sugar
250g/9oz/2 cups Italian 00 flour
2 large egg yolks
1½ tsp salt

To glaze

2 tbsp cold water
1 large egg yolk
2 tbsp milk
a pinch of salt

A pie that shares nothing with *pizza napoletana* except the name. Pizza rustica, a speciality of Abruzzo, is a quintessential example of medieval cooking, when a savoury filling is contained in a sweet pastry case.

First make the pastry (see page 281), either by hand or in a food processor. Divide it into two balls, one larger than the other. Wrap them in clingfilm and chill.

Meanwhile, put the sausage and olive oil in a small frying pan over a medium-high heat and sauté for 5 minutes, turning it over and over. Transfer to a bowl and leave to cool.

Crumble the mozzarella and add it to the bowl, together with all the other ingredients except the breadcrumbs, and mix very thoroughly – hands are best for this. Chill.

Preheat the oven to 200°C/400°F/Gas Mark 6. Grease a 20cm/8in diameter springform cake tin with butter.

Take the pastry out of the refrigerator. As soon as it is malleable, roll out the larger ball and line the bottom and sides of the tin. Sprinkle the pastry in the tin with breadcrumbs and then spoon in the filling. Roll out the smaller ball of pastry to make a lid and place it over the filling. Turn the edges over to form a border and press together with the prongs of a fork.

Just before you bake the pie, mix the ingredients for the glaze together and brush over the pastry lid. Make some holes here and there with a fork. Bake for 10 minutes and then turn the oven temperature down to 180°C/350°F/Gas Mark 4 and bake for a further 45 minutes.

Do not serve the pie straight from the oven: let it cool for at least 10 minutes. It is also excellent served at room temperature.

over and under them in reticulated work, are piled scores upon scores of brown cheeses in the form of pyramids, columns, towers, with eggs set into their interstices. From the ceiling, and around the doorway, hang wreaths and necklaces of sausages – or groups of long gourd-like cheeses, twined about with box – or netted wire baskets filled with Easter eggs.'

The modern pizzicheria has every kind of SALUME, cheeses, canned goods, oils and vinegars and in addition a wide variety of prepared dishes.

pizzoccheri
buckwheat pasta

This is a kind of thick, large TAGLIATELLE made with buckwheat flour. It is the traditional pasta of Valtellina, an Alpine valley in Lombardy. Pizzoccheri is usually prepared as in the recipe given here, the recipe itself being simply called pizzoccheri.

[see recipe on facing page]

braciole di maiale alla pizzaiola
pork steaks with mozzarella and oregano

Serves 4
500g/1lb 2oz pork steaks, thinly cut
salt and freshly ground black pepper
2–3 sprigs of fresh marjoram
150ml/5fl oz/²/₃ cup red wine
225g/8oz canned plum tomatoes, drained
3 tbsp olive oil
1 garlic clove, crushed
4 tbsp flour
25g/1oz/2 tbsp unsalted butter
4 tbsp meat stock (page 61) or chicken stock
100g/3¹/₂oz mozzarella cheese, cut into very thin slices
1 tbsp dried oregano

The word PIZZAIOLA indicates that a dish contains ingredients that are used in the topping of a Neapolitan pizza.

Put the pork steaks in a dish and sprinkle with salt, pepper and the sprigs of marjoram. Pour over the wine and leave to marinate for about 1 hour.

Preheat the oven to 200°C/400°F/Gas Mark 6.

Puree the tomatoes through a food mill or sieve directly into a saucepan. Add 1 tablespoon of the olive oil, the garlic and salt and pepper to taste. Cook over a lively heat, without the lid, for 5 minutes. Set aside.

Lift the steaks out of the marinade (reserve the liquid) and pat dry with kitchen paper. Turn the steaks over in the flour, coating both sides thoroughly. Shake off any excess flour.

Heat the remaining oil and the butter in a large frying pan over a high heat. When the foam has nearly disappeared, slide in the steaks and cook briskly to sear both sides. Pour over the strained liquid from the marinade and let it bubble for about 30 seconds, then add the stock and salt and pepper and bring to the boil. Reduce the heat, cover the pan and cook for 5–7 minutes. When the meat is cooked, transfer it to an ovenproof dish.

Deglaze the frying pan with a little water and reduce it to only 3 or 4 tablespoons. Spoon it over the steaks. Cover each steak with a layer of mozzarella and place a spoonful of the tomato sauce in the middle. Sprinkle with oregano, salt and black pepper. Pop the dish into the oven for about 5 minutes, until the cheese has melted.

pizzoccheri
buckwheat pasta with potato and cabbage

Serves 6

Pasta

*200g/7oz/generous 1½ cups buckwheat
    flour*

*100g/3½oz/generous ¾ cup Italian
    00 flour*

1 tsp salt

1 large egg

*about 125ml/4fl oz/½ cup full-fat
    (whole) milk, warmed*

Dressing

225g/8oz potatoes, cut into cubes

salt and freshly ground black pepper

*300g/10½oz Savoy cabbage, cut into
    1cm/½in strips*

*75g/2¾oz/5 tbsp unsalted butter, plus
    extra for the dish*

1 small onion, very finely chopped

1 garlic clove, very finely chopped

6 fresh sage leaves, torn into pieces

*150g/5½oz fontina cheese, cut into
    slivers*

75g/2¾oz Parmesan cheese, grated

If you are not inclined to make pizzoccheri, use wholewheat spaghetti instead.

First make the pasta dough. Mix together the two flours and the salt on the work surface. Make a well in the middle and break the egg into it. Using a fork, begin to bring in the flour from the edge, while gradually adding the milk – you may not need all of the milk. Alternatively, you may need to add a little warm water or a couple of tablespoons of white flour. The dough should be soft and elastic, although it is much stickier and wetter than dough made with only white flour and eggs. Knead for 5 minutes, and then wrap the dough in a cloth or clingfilm and let it rest for a minimum of 1 hour.

On a lightly floured surface, roll out the dough to a thickness of about 3mm/⅛in. Cut the dough into noodles, about 2 x 10cm/¾ x 4in. Lay them out on clean cloths, not touching each other.

Preheat the oven to 180°C/350°F/Gas Mark 4.

Put a large saucepan containing about 4 litres/7 pints/4 quarts water on the heat. Add 1½ tablespoons salt and the potatoes and bring to the boil. After about 10 minutes, when the potato cubes begin to soften at the edges, add the cabbage and cook for about 5 minutes, until the cabbage has lost its crunchiness.

Slide in the pasta, mix well and cook for 5 minutes after the water has come back to the boil.

Meanwhile, put the butter, onion, garlic and sage in a small heavy-bottomed pan and cook gently, stirring very often, until the onion becomes pale gold. Remove the sage.

Butter a shallow ovenproof dish. When the pizzoccheri are cooked, drain the whole mixture in a colander. Spoon a ladleful or two of the pasta mixture over the bottom of the dish and add a little of the two cheeses, a little of the onion mixture and plenty of pepper. Add more pasta and repeat until the whole lot is dressed. Toss thoroughly.

Cover with foil and bake for 5 minutes, so that the cheese melts. Serve immediately.

Platina
1421–81

Bartolomeo Sacchi was born in Piadena, near Cremona, and it is from the name of his birthplace (Platina in Latin) that his sobriquet Platina was coined. Platina was the first humanist who also concerned himself with gastronomy. He was a classicist by training and wrote many treatises on art, literature and nature. He was made librarian to the Biblioteca Vaticana by Pope Sixtus IV in 1475.

Platina divided his great work, *De Honesta Voluptate et Valetudine* (*On Honest Pleasure and Health*), written in Latin, into 10 books, with a total of 417 chapters. Far from being primarily about cookery, the work is a comprehensive treatise on the relationship between man and nature. It begins by telling us where we should choose to live in summer and winter and what exercise is good for us, going on to such matters as how to lay a table indoors and out of doors. It then has chapters on various foodstuffs, such as salt, bread, all the fruits, which Platina recommends eating before the meal. All these chapters, with their moralizing and pedagogic instructions on health and well-being, are typical of the style of writing of a man of the Renaissance.

The section devoted to recipes is a transcription of the *Libro de Arte Coquinaria* by MARTINO da Como, whom Platina acknowledged to be his great master and with whom he shared culinary experiments. But it is a transcription in which Platina played an important part, as can be seen now that Maestro Martino's manuscript has been found.

De Honesta Voluptate was translated into most European languages and the first French edition in 1505 became a bestseller.

polenta
a cereal dish

To be precise, polenta describes not only the well-known yellow mixture of ground maize and water, but any other mixture of ground cereal or pulses mixed with water. Polenta, as we now know it, started to be made soon after maize arrived from the New World. Maize – given the name GRANOTURCO – grew very well everywhere in the northern regions and polenta, by the beginning of the 18th century, was the staple of the local people. It was often the only food eaten, which led to a lack of vitamins in the diet, with the result that pellagra, a potentially fatal disease, developed. Polenta was thought to be the cause of it, and the link with vitamin deficiency was discovered only in the 20th century. Polenta was reinstated and its consumption spread southwards to central Italy. Nowadays polenta, certainly no longer just a poor man's dish, is always the de rigueur accompaniment to stewed salt cod and stockfish, to a rich SPEZZATINO (stew), Milanese CASSOEULA (a pork and cabbage dish), or a joint of slow-cooked braised meat.

The maize can be coarsely ground, as in the *bramata* of the Alpine valleys, or finely ground as in the polenta of central Italy. The proportion of water to flour can always be different, giving a thinner or thicker mixture. In Veneto and in Friuli there is also a delicate *polenta bianca* made with white maize flour, while in the Alpine valleys of Lombardy a polenta is made with a mixture of maize and buckwheat; known as *polenta taragna* it is a favourite of the real polenta connoisseur.

Polenta should be made in a PAIOLO, the copper pan that is just right for the purpose. With one hand a thin stream of ground maize is poured into boiling salted water (the proportion of salt is 1½ teaspoons per litre of water), while with the other hand the maize is stirred rapidly into the water

CONTINUES ON PAGE 324

polenta

Serves 6

2 tsp salt

*300g/10½oz/2½ cups coarse-ground
polenta flour (wholegrain cornmeal)*

This is the traditional method for making POLENTA. It is made with traditional polenta flour, not instant polenta.

Choose a large, deep, heavy saucepan and fill it with 1.8 litres/3¼ pints/7½ cups water. When the water comes to the boil, add the salt. Remove the pan from the heat and add the polenta flour in a very thin stream, letting it fall through the nearly closed fist of one hand while the other hand stirs constantly with a long-handled wooden spoon. Return the pan to the heat and cook for at least 40 minutes over a medium heat, stirring constantly for the first 10 minutes and then every minute or so.

When thick and smooth, transfer the polenta to a bowl, previously moistened with cold water. Leave it to rest for a few minutes and then turn the bowl upside down onto a large round platter or a wooden board covered with a white napkin. The polenta will fall out and look, as it should, like a golden mound.

baked polenta

321

Serves 6

2 tsp salt

*350g/12oz/scant 3 cups coarse-ground
polenta flour (wholegrain cornmeal)
unsalted butter, for greasing*

I was given this recipe by the late Massimo ALBERINI, a great gastronome and writer. I make this with coarse-ground polenta, but finely ground polenta would cook more quickly.

Preheat the oven to 190°C/375°F/Gas Mark 5.

Bring 1.8 litres/3¼ pints/7½ cups water to simmering point in a large saucepan. Remove from the heat and add the salt, then gradually add the polenta flour in a very thin stream, letting it fall through the nearly closed fist of one hand while the other hand stirs constantly with a long-handled wooden spoon. Return the pan to the heat and bring slowly to the boil, stirring constantly in the same direction. Boil for 5 minutes, still stirring. Now transfer the polenta to a buttered ovenproof dish and cover with buttered foil. Bake in the oven for 1 hour.

polenta pasticciata
baked polenta with meat and porcini

Serves 4–6

300g/10½oz/scant 2½ cups coarse-ground polenta flour (wholegrain cornmeal)

2 tsp salt

Sauce

25g/1oz dried porcini

3 tbsp olive oil

25g/1oz/2 tbsp unsalted butter, plus extra for greasing

1 small onion, finely chopped

1 small carrot, finely chopped

½ celery stalk, finely chopped

350g/12oz lean minced (ground) beef

1 bay leaf

salt and freshly ground black pepper

2 tbsp tomato puree diluted with 100ml/3½fl oz/scant ½ cup meat stock (page 61) or chicken stock

6 tbsp freshly grated Parmesan cheese

There are many versions of POLENTA pasticciata: with meat, with mushrooms, with cheeses. This is one of the most popular.

First make the polenta following one or other of the instructions on page 321. Pour the hot polenta onto a wet surface – marble, plastic or similar, but not wood – and spread it out to a thickness of about 2.5cm/1in. Leave to cool.

Soak the porcini in 100ml/3½fl oz/scant ½ cup warm water for 30 minutes. Lift them out gently, wash under cold water, squeeze and dry. Chop them coarsely. Strain the soaking liquid through a sieve lined with muslin and set aside.

Preheat the oven to 200°C/400°F/Gas Mark 6.

Put the oil, butter and onion in an earthenware pot over a medium-high heat and sauté until the onion is soft. Mix in the porcini, carrot and celery and sauté for a few minutes. Add the minced beef and cook, stirring, until it has lost its raw colour, then add the bay leaf and salt and pepper to taste. Pour in the diluted tomato puree and the liquid in which the mushrooms have soaked. When the sauce comes to the boil, turn the heat down as low as possible and cook, uncovered, for about 2 hours. Taste and adjust the seasoning and remove the bay leaf.

Grease a shallow 20 x 15cm/8 x 6in ovenproof dish generously with butter. Cut the polenta into 1cm/½in slices and cover the bottom of the dish with a layer of polenta. Spoon over about one-third of the sauce and sprinkle with 2 tablespoons of the Parmesan. Repeat the layers of polenta, sauce and Parmesan until all the ingredients are used, then bake in the oven for about 30 minutes.

Leave to stand for a good 5 minutes before serving.

NOTE: This recipe is made with traditional polenta flour, not instant polenta. You can use instant polenta instead – it only takes 5 minutes to cook – it's not as good, but it does save time and effort.

RIGHT: Polenta pasticciata

with a long wooden stick or spoon to prevent lumps from forming. When all the maize has been added, the mixture must be stirred constantly for at least 45 minutes. The coarser the flour, the longer the cooking. But there is a quicker method, for which the recipe is given below the traditional method, on page 321.

There is on the market now a product known as *polenta istantanea*. It is part-cooked polenta, and needs only 5 minutes cooking time. The result, surprisingly enough, is good, even if not as good as traditionally prepared polenta.

Polenta is extremely versatile, as it complements the flavour of the dish it accompanies. Aficionados like polenta dressed only with butter and GORGONZOLA, CRESCENZA or other STRACCHINO cheeses. Those less keen on the basic flavour of polenta prefer it as an accompaniment to rich stews of meat or fish. Polenta is excellent with stewed cuttlefish, for instance, or with jugged hare or stewed venison. Polenta can be made in advance and, when cold, sliced and baked in layers with meat sauce and cheeses, when it is known as *polenta pasticciata*, for which the recipe is given here. Sliced polenta is also grilled or fried and served as an accompaniment to meat and game, or used as a base for BRUSCHETTA.

[see recipes on pages 321 and 322]

pollo or pollastro
chicken

Throughout the centuries, and indeed right up to the time when chickens began to be reared in batteries in the 1960s and 70s, chickens were food for the wealthy. The majority of the birds were kept for laying eggs and were eaten only when they were very old.

In Roman times cockerels were castrated, thus becoming capons, and raised in cages, a method which, according to Pliny, was first devised by a certain Lelius Strabo, who made a fortune out of Roman 'battery' poultry. The hens were kept for laying. However, chicken was not food for the tables of the patricians.

Chicken was not highly regarded also during the Renaissance, when the creativity of the great chefs was dedicated to more luxurious birds, such as peacocks and guinea fowl. Chicken was food for the sick and for children. There are only a few recipes in which the boned chicken is stuffed with meat, pistachios, prunes and other fruit and served either hot or cold in aspic. In the 18th century, Vincenzo CORRADO, whom I always find an inspired cook, wrote a recipe entitled *pollo alla beccaccino* – chicken in the manner of a snipe: 'The chickens are half cooked on the spit, then they are quartered and cooked in a sauce made with a generous wine, anchovies, the chicken livers fried and pounded, small capers, garlic, lemon zest and spices.' And in the 19th century ARTUSI was the first to use chicken instead of veal in VITELLO TONNATO (veal in tuna sauce).

In contemporary cooking chicken appears on the table in many different guises, but is not often roasted. There are many types of chicken on the market: farmed, industrially reared and free-range, the best of which is the *pollo ruspante*, a scraggy bird with meat full of flavour, which you have to tear off the bones, preferably with your teeth.

Tuscany has always had the reputation for producing the best chickens, and because their chickens are so tasty, the traditional Tuscan recipes are very simple. The best known of these are POLLO ALLA DIAVOLA, *pollo alla fiorentina* (jointed chicken coated in a light batter and fried) and *pollo alla toscana* (jointed and cooked in wine with wild mushrooms and fresh tomatoes). Other ways of cooking chicken, such as in FRICASSEA and alla CACCIATORA, are similar all over central Italy. The *pollo in* POTACCHIO from Le Marche is a local version of the cacciatora, which in Calabria and Sicily becomes *pollo con le melanzane* by the addition of some cubed aubergines, previously fried or grilled. In Lazio, fried peppers replace the aubergines.

One of the best recipes from the north comes from Valle d'Aosta: for *pollo alla valdostana* the chicken breast is coated in breadcrumbs and fried in butter and then topped with melting FONTINA cheese. In the northern regions, chicken is often boiled as part of a BOLLITO MISTO, or by itself for making chicken stock. These should be GALLINA, an old hen that has stopped laying, but has a stronger taste.

Most of the recipes mentioned above are made with the bird cut into portions, which is certainly the most popular way to cook chicken. When cooked whole it is roasted on the spit, *pollo allo spiedo*, or pot-roasted with a little white wine (see recipe on page 39); herbs and garlic, and sometimes a whole lemon pricked all over, are pushed into the bird's cavity. This latter is an excellent preparation, the flavour of the lemon gently pervading the whole chicken.

pollo alla cacciatora
chicken the hunter's way

This is a popular recipe from central Italy, made slightly differently wherever one goes. The chicken is always jointed and then sautéed in oil and/or STRUTTO (pork fat) with the usual SOFFRITTO. It is then flavoured with mushrooms and/or tomatoes and herbs, to which red wine or vinegar or both are added. The recipe on page 68 is one of the many versions.

pollo alla diavola
chicken the devil's way

A classic of Tuscan cuisine. The young chicken is cut in half down the back, opened up like a book and gently flattened with a meat pounder. Brushed with best olive oil, salt, pepper and chilli, it is cooked on a grill over a wood fire.

pollo alla Marengo
chicken marengo

This dish is one of the very few to which a precise date of birth can be ascribed. It was created by Napoleon's chef on 14 June 1800, and eaten by the General after he had won a bloody battle against the Austrian army on the fields of Marengo, a village in southern Piedmont. The traditional pollo alla Marengo is jointed chicken, sautéed in butter, then splashed with white wine and cooked with the usual flavouring vegetables. It is served sprinkled with parsley, surrounded by fried bread and river crayfish poached in wine.

pollo ripieno alla lunigianese
chicken stuffed with ricotta and greens

Stuffed chicken cooked in the way of the Lunigiana, the valley of the River Magra, which flows between Liguria and Tuscany. The chicken is stuffed with Swiss chard and wild greens, RICOTTA and GRANA, bound with egg, a typical Ligurian stuffing. The bird is then boiled and served with the Tuscan *salsa d'*AGRESTO, which is made with unripe grapes, walnuts, soft breadcrumbs, a little onion, parsley, sugar and garlic, all pounded together in the mortar.

polpa
meat or pulp

A general term for a piece of boned beef or veal, not necessarily a particular cut, but one that can be used for slicing thinly, for braising or stewing. So there *is polpa di petto* (of breast), *di stinco* (of shin), *di spalla* (of shoulder). The word polpa would never refer to a top-quality cut such as fillet.

Polpa also means pulp, whether of tomatoes, aubergines or peaches.

polpette
meatballs

Meatballs have a long and interesting history. MARTINO da Como has two recipes: in one they are similar to modern meatballs, made with chopped veal mixed with herbs, egg yolks, spices and grated cheese. The mixture is shaped like 'big mouthfuls', which are wrapped in caul fat and cooked on the spit. Martino's other meatballs are more like a veal roll than a meatball, the veal being stuffed with herbs and spices and pounded LARDO.

Writing in the 16th century, MESSISBUGO also makes his polpette with thin slices of veal stuffed with LARDO, minced herbs, garlic, salt, pepper, sultanas, fennel seeds and egg yolk. They are then wrapped in pig's or calf's caul fat before being cooked on the spit.

In the 19th century, LURASCHI is still describing polpette as veal rolls, while a few decades later, ARTUSI's meatballs are made with minced meat, either raw or previously cooked. From this we can deduce that the southern Italian polpette – always made with mince – became the Italian polpette supremo after the unification of Italy in 1860.

Made with minced raw or leftover roast or boiled meat, polpette can also be made of fish or

CONTINUES OVERLEAF

polpette alla casalinga
homemade meatballs

Serves 5–6

50g/1¾oz crustless white bread
4–6 tbsp full-fat (whole) milk
500g/1lb 2oz very lean minced (ground) beef
1 garlic clove, finely chopped
a small bunch of fresh flat-leaf parsley, finely chopped
50g/1¾oz mortadella, chopped
4 tbsp freshly grated Parmesan cheese
a grating of nutmeg
salt and freshly ground black pepper
3 large eggs
2 tbsp plain (all-purpose) flour
50g/1¾oz/½ cup dried breadcrumbs
25g/1oz/2 tbsp unsalted butter
2 tbsp olive oil

To finish
150ml/5fl oz/⅔ cup meat stock (page 61) or chicken stock or 600ml/20fl oz/2½ cups Tomato Sauce (page 331)

This is one of the many ways I make POLPETTE, for which I buy chuck steak and have it minced after the fat has been removed.

Soak the bread in enough milk to cover it. After about 5 minutes, squeeze it dry and place in a large bowl with the beef. Add the garlic, parsley, mortadella, Parmesan, nutmeg and salt and pepper to taste.

Lightly beat the eggs with a pinch of salt and mix half into the meat mixture. Mix very thoroughly with your hands, then shape the mixture into squashed balls the size of mandarin oranges.

Lightly coat with flour and then with the remaining egg. Dredge each meatball in breadcrumbs, patting the crumbs into the meat with the palm of your hand. Put in the refrigerator for at least 1 hour. If you have time, you can leave them for much longer to chill.

Fry the polpette gently on each side in butter and oil. When they are brown all over, add the meat stock or tomato sauce and cook, covered, for about 10 minutes. Serve hot.

NOTE: Instead of the meat stock or tomato sauce, I sometimes finish these polpette with a lemon sauce. For this, I mix 2 large egg yolks with the juice of 1 organic lemon and 250ml/9fl oz/1 cup hot meat stock. I add this just before I turn the heat off.

RIGHT: Polpette alla casalinga

polpette

of vegetables. Such basic food is obviously made in different ways in every region, town, village and family up and down the peninsula.

Other ingredients go into meatballs, some for binding – egg and/or béchamel, or bread soaked in milk – and some for flavouring – grated cheese, salami, spices, pine nuts, sultanas, garlic, onion and herbs. The mixture is pressed into shape, being 'squashed at the poles like the terrestrial globe', as ARTUSI so aptly puts it. The meatballs are coated in flour and/or egg and breadcrumbs, and then fried in fat: butter, oil, a mixture of the two or, alas rather rarely nowadays, STRUTTO. When nicely brown all over, they are sometimes finished in a tomato sauce or with a splash of lemon juice, or in a light mushroom sauce. The lemon juice dressing is particularly good with meatballs made with raw beef flavoured with parsley and garlic. The recipe given here is one of my favourites.

[see recipe on page 326]

polpettone
meat loaf

A meat loaf made with minced meat (which can be raw or cooked), SALAME or MORTADELLA, bound with egg and flavoured with Parmesan and herbs. The most modest and humble polpettone is made with leftover boiled meat, to which egg, Parmesan and soaked bread are added. The polpettone is shaped like a fat sausage, coated with flour or dried breadcrumbs and fried in butter and oil. When cooked, the cooking juices are thickened with eggs and lemon juice, and the sauce is spooned over the sliced polpettone. Or the sliced polpettone is finished off in a tomato sauce or served with a mushroom sauce.

In Liguria the word polpettone refers mainly to vegetable TORTE. The best-known is the polpettone of green beans, in which the cooked chopped beans are mixed with mashed potatoes, eggs and cheese, flavoured with herbs and baked in

the oven (see recipe on page 137). There is also a polpettone of preserved tuna, where the fish is mixed with potatoes and/or with eggs and Parmesan and then poached in white wine, vinegar and water, as in the recipe on page 431.

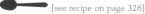 [see recipe on facing page]

polpo
octopus

Hardly the most attractive of sea creatures, polpo is certainly one of the best to eat. The true octopus, *polpo verace*, can measure up to 3m/10ft and has two rows of suckers on each of its eight tentacles. If large, octopus need to be bashed on a hard surface or with a meat pounder before cooking. There are many recipes for octopus, all based on boiling or on stewing, always with tomatoes and often with wine. Boiled octopus is usually served tepid, often with boiled potatoes cut into small pieces, everything dressed with capers, chopped parsley, lemon juice and oil and a touch of garlic.

Many frightening sailors' stories are woven around this creature, and indeed to see a large octopus clinging to a rock under water, as one may do in the summer when they stay close to the shore, is a terrifying experience. There is one story, though, that is rather different. It relates to the charming village of Tellaro, on the coast near La Spezia in Liguria, where there is an old church at the end of a rocky promontory. One night, a long time ago, the bell ringer accidentally left the bell rope dangling in the sea. That night a curious octopus got his tentacles entangled in the rope and the church bell began ringing furiously. Unknowingly, the octopus was giving the signal that pirates were about to attack, and the terrified inhabitants of Tellaro took to the hills, leaving only the bell ringer to unravel the mystery and the rope.

[see recipe on facing page]

polpettone freddo
cold meat loaf

Serves 6

50g/1¾oz crustless white bread
4–6 tbsp full-fat (whole) milk
500g/1lb 2oz lean minced (ground) beef
50g/1¾oz Italian salami, minced
1 large egg
2 tbsp freshly grated Parmesan cheese
3 tbsp chopped mixed fresh herbs, such
  as parsley, rosemary, sage and basil
1 tbsp very finely chopped onion
1 garlic clove, very finely chopped
grated rind of 1 organic or unwaxed
  lemon
salt and freshly ground black pepper
2 tbsp extra virgin olive oil

This is my favourite way of making a POLPETTONE: cooking it in a loaf tin in the oven avoids the nuisance of having to turn it over in the frying pan. This polpettone is also good hot, but I prefer it cold, lightly moistened with extra virgin olive oil and served with SALSA VERDE on the side.

Preheat the oven to 200°C/400°F/Gas Mark 6.

Put the bread in a bowl, cover with the milk and soak for 10–15 minutes.

Meanwhile, put the beef, salami, egg, Parmesan, herbs, onion, garlic and lemon rind in a large bowl and mix thoroughly.

Squeeze the bread to remove most of the milk and then add it to the meat mixture. Add salt and pepper and mix again. Grease a 500g/1lb 2oz loaf tin with oil and fill it with the mixture. Press down well and bang the tin on the work surface to release any air pockets. Brush the top with a little oil. Place in the oven and cook for about 35–40 minutes. The polpettone is cooked when it has shrunk from the sides of the tin.

Remove from the oven and carefully pour away the fat from around the meat. Leave the polpettone to cool in the tin and then turn out onto a carving board. Carve when completely cold and lay the slices, slightly overlapping, on a dish. Brush lightly with oil to serve.

329

polpo alla luciana
stewed octopus

Serves 4

1kg/2¼lb octopus
3 ripe fresh tomatoes, peeled and
  chopped, or 3 canned tomatoes,
  drained and chopped
100ml/3½fl oz/7 tbsp olive oil
2 garlic cloves, chopped
½–1 tsp crushed dried chillies
2 tbsp chopped fresh flat-leaf parsley
salt and freshly ground black pepper
chilli flakes
lemon juice

A traditional Neapolitan dish, named after the district of Santa Lucia in Naples, where it originated, and one of the best ways to cook an octopus, polpo alla luciana is traditionally eaten only with bread.

Prepare the octopus by cleaning and beating it, or ask your fishmonger to do this. Wash it and place it in a deep pot, preferably earthenware.

Add the tomatoes, olive oil, garlic, chillies, parsley, salt and pepper, tie a double sheet of foil around the pot and cover with a tight lid. Cook at the lowest possible simmer for 2 hours, without ever removing the lid.

Leave the octopus in the covered pot to cool for half an hour. Serve it straight from the pot, cutting out a piece of this monster for each person. Season with a touch of chilli and a few drops of lemon juice.

pomodoro
tomato

Tomatoes reached Italy at the end of the 16th century, but came to be used in cooking only in the late 17th century. It was in Naples that tomatoes found their new homeland and the Neapolitans soon saw the great potential of this new produce. The first cookery writers to grant them the status they deserve were Antonio LATINI and Vincenzo CORRADO. Latini wrote a recipe for a salsa combining the tomato with chilli, a sauce of undoubted South American origin. A century later Corrado has 12 recipes, most for stuffed tomatoes, many just as they are made now. The recipe for *pomodori alla napolitana* is identical to a modern one, the tomatoes being stuffed with anchovies, parsley, oregano and garlic 'all nicely chopped and seasoned with salt and pepper and covered with breadcrumbs; they are cooked in the oven and they are served.'

In the early 19th century Ippolito CAVALCANTI wrote more than 30 recipes for tomatoes, while ARTUSI has only two recipes, one in which they are stuffed with dried PORCINI and soft breadcrumbs and then baked, and the other in which the tomatoes are simply baked in butter. He also gives a recipe for a tomato sauce which he suggests to serve with pasta, rice or boiled meat. It is interesting to note that Artusi does not recommend peeling the tomatoes. Nor, in fact, does Ada BONI or any other writer until those of very recent times. This is most certainly due to the fact that the newer varieties of tomatoes have much tougher skins, to protect them when they travel.

Italians eat more tomatoes than any other vegetables, although they eat them mainly in the summer, when they are at their best: raw in salad, filled with various stuffings and sometimes baked, but mostly they are eaten in various sauces, two of which are given here.

The classic *salsa di pomodoro*, always referred to simply as SALSA, is made according to a ritual that takes place on a hot August day in every village from Liguria to Sicily. A large blue machine is brought out from its winter place of rest. Into the large funnel at the top go bowlful after bowlful of the villagers' tomatoes and out at the bottom flows a thick seedless and skinless liquid of the most vivid red. This smooth liquid is then boiled with a little salt in huge cauldrons and the next day the sauce is bottled. The bottles are sealed and boiled, the machine goes back to its resting place, and the villagers have their salsa for all the year. Urban dwellers also make their sauce, using fresh tomatoes when in season or from *pelati* (canned peeled tomatoes) or PASSATA.

Another way to preserve tomatoes is to dry them. There are two kinds of dried tomatoes: the first are tomatoes simply strung up and hung in the sun to dry; the second kind are fully desiccated tomatoes, for which the fruit is cut in half and left to dry completely in the sun or industrially in ovens. These dried tomatoes are reconstituted in water, usually mixed with vinegar, before they are used, while the first kind keep some of their natural juice.

Tomatoes are also preserved in CONCENTRATO form in tubes or cans. But the most popular way to preserve tomatoes is by canning. The best tomatoes for canning are plum tomatoes, of which the San Marzano is the best variety, because it has more flesh and fewer seeds than other varieties.

Like most Italian cooks I make my tomato sauces with canned tomatoes, except during the summer in Italy.

[see recipes on facing page]

salsa di pomodoro 1
tomato sauce 1

Makes 600ml/20fl oz/2½ cups
800g/1¾lb canned plum tomatoes
2 tsp tomato puree
1 tsp sugar
2 onions, chopped
2 celery stalks, chopped
5 tbsp extra virgin olive oil
salt and freshly ground black pepper
4 tbsp good red wine
25g/1oz/2 tbsp unsalted butter

A rich tomato sauce, which I like to use for dressing a bowl of PENNE, or to add to POLPETTE, leftover boiled meat or poached chicken.

Chop the tomatoes coarsely. This is best done by cutting the tomatoes with kitchen scissors while they are still in the can, having first poured a little of the liquid into a heavy-bottomed saucepan.

Put the tomatoes into the pan, together with the rest of their liquid, the tomato puree, sugar, onions, celery, olive oil, salt and pepper. Cook over a low heat for 15 minutes or so, and then puree the sauce through a food mill or in a food processor or blender.

Return the sauce to the pan and add the wine. Cook for a further 40 minutes. Stir in the butter, taste and adjust the seasoning.

salsa di pomodoro 2
tomato sauce 2

Makes 600ml/20fl oz/2½ cups
1 garlic clove
1 small onion or 2 shallots
1 tsp sugar
about 2 tbsp vegetable stock
750g/1lb 10oz ripe fresh tomatoes,
*   peeled and chopped*
salt and freshly ground black pepper
6 fresh basil leaves, torn
4 tbsp extra virgin olive oil

A quicker and more southern-tasting sauce than the above, and suitable for SPAGHETTI, GNOCCHI or fish.

Chop the garlic and onion together. Put them in a pan with the sugar and 2 tablespoons stock. Cover and cook very gently for 15–20 minutes, stirring every now and then and adding a little more stock or water if necessary. At the end of cooking the onion will be soft and the stock will have more or less evaporated.

Add the tomatoes to the pan, season with salt and pepper and cook for no longer than 5 minutes after the sauce has come to the boil. Add the basil and the oil just before serving.

porchetta
a roasted piglet

A young pig is boned and stuffed with garlic, rosemary, fennel or fennel seeds and other herbs and then roasted on the spit or in the oven. It is a speciality of central and southern Italy, usually sold as street food during festivals and country fairs and served between two thick slices of country bread or in a PANINO.

Of all the *porchette*, the Sardinian *porceddu* is one of the best. It used to be cooked in a hole in the ground, surrounded by myrtle, lentisk and strawberry tree twigs, then covered with red-hot stones and earth. Now it is roasted on a spit over a wood fire, the traditional woods being juniper, olive, lentisk and myrtle. While turning on the spit and absorbing the scent of all the woods, the piglet is doused with hot STRUTTO. It is either eaten hot immediately after cooking or bundled up in myrtle branches, left for at least 24 hours to absorb the scent, and eaten cold.

porcino
cep

This is the king of fungi, only equalled in quality by the OVOLO. Porcini appear in the spring, sometimes as early as the end of March, and they can be found up to the end of July. In the autumn there is another larger crop, from September to November.

The most common way to cook porcini is to sauté them in oil with garlic and parsley – TRIFOLATI. They are also used for sauces for POLENTA, pasta and rice, often mixed with chicken livers. The caps are often grilled or stuffed and then baked.

When porcini are used to dress pasta I like to make the plainest of all sauces, which I learnt from a friend in the Dolomites, an area rich in porcini. The fungi are diced and sautéed in plenty of butter – not oil – seasoned with grated nutmeg, salt and pepper and cooked for 15 minutes. The pasta should be of medium size and short, such as *pennette* (small PENNE). Having said this, a sauce made with sliced porcini, parsley and garlic sautéed in olive oil is also perfect for spaghetti or egg TAGLIATELLE.

Porcini are the best wild mushrooms for drying and there is now a sizeable industry which gives the Italians one of their most cherished foods all the year round. They can also be frozen raw, although they lose their flavour after about 2 months.

[see recipe on facing page]

porro
leek

The Romans were fond of leeks, which they ate in many ways. The emperor Nero had leek soup every day to make his voice project further, or so it is said, and the poet Horace liked leeks with pasta and chickpeas so much that he refers to them in one of his *Satires*. Leeks remained a favourite vegetable through the Middle Ages and the Renaissance, as an accompaniment to meat, in soups and as a flavouring. The 16th-century chef Bartolomeo SCAPPI has a simple recipe for a leek and onion soup. The leeks and onions, previously blanched, are chopped, sautéed in LARDO and then cooked in meat stock. At the end, beaten eggs, grated cheese and the 'usual spices' are added.

Nowadays leeks are mainly eaten in northern Italy, which is where they grow and where the best recipes come from. Leeks are also served simply with melted butter and cheese, used in MINESTRONE and ZUPPA *di verdura*, in FRITTATE and as a flavouring in some stews, braised meats, meat and fish stocks. They also make delicious pasta sauces.

When they are very young and thin, leeks are served raw. They are first soaked for an hour in cold water to get rid of their strong taste and the grit; they are then cut into thin rounds and dressed with olive oil, vinegar, a little mustard, salt and pepper.

[see recipe on facing page]

cappelle di porcini alla graticola
grilled cep caps

Serves 4

700g/1lb 9oz fresh porcini
salt and freshly ground black pepper
6 tbsp extra virgin olive oil
1 garlic clove, chopped
4 tbsp chopped fresh flat-leaf parsley

You can also prepare large brown mushroom caps this way but, of course, they will never taste quite as good as PORCINI.

Detach the stalks from the porcini caps and keep the stalks for a sauce or soup. Wipe the caps clean with kitchen paper and put them on a board. Sprinkle with salt and leave for half an hour or so to rid them of some of the liquid.

Gently pat the caps dry and put them, gill side down, on a grill pan. Drizzle them with half the olive oil, season with pepper and cook under a hot grill for 2 minutes.

Turn the caps over gently. Sprinkle the garlic and parsley all over the gill side and drizzle with the remaining oil. Grill for about 2 minutes.

They are delicious served hot, warm or cold.

porri alla milanese
leeks and eggs with butter and Parmesan

Serves 4

8–12 thin leeks
salt and freshly ground black pepper
50–75g/1¾–2¾oz/4–5 tbsp unsalted butter
4 tbsp freshly grated Parmesan cheese
4–8 large eggs

A favourite recipe for leeks from northern Italy is porri alla milanese, the poor man's version of asparagus alla milanese.

Preheat the oven to 160°C/325°F/Gas Mark 3.

Trim and thoroughly wash the leeks, leaving some of the best green tops attached. Cook in plenty of boiling salted water for about 5–7 minutes, until they are cooked through but still firm and compact. Drain thoroughly and gently squeeze out all the water with your hands. Pat dry with kitchen paper.

Butter an oval ovenproof dish and lay the leeks in it. Sprinkle with some of the Parmesan and dot with a little of the butter. Place the dish in the oven while you cook the eggs.

Heat the remaining butter in a large frying pan and break as many eggs into it as you wish – but no more than eight. Sprinkle the whites, but not the yolks, with salt. (Salt hardens the surface of egg yolks.) When the eggs are cooked, slide them gently over the leeks. Pour over all the butter from the pan, then sprinkle with the remaining Parmesan and a generous grinding of pepper.

portata
course

This used to refer to each course of a meal, meaning the food that was carried (*portato* in Italian), by a servant, from the kitchen to the dining room. Nowadays the use of the word portata is dying out, and it is more usual to speak of a PIATTO. Portata is still used, however, in connection with formal dinner parties, when it refers to a dish that comes from the kitchen, as opposed to the cheese and fruit, and some sweet preparations, which are laid out in advance.

portulaca
purslane

Also called *porcellanetta*, this is an annual that grows wild along the coast. It has typically Mediterranean, thick, fleshy leaves and a pleasantly acid taste. Portulaca was more widely eaten in the past, as it was in Elizabethan England. A salad of chopped onion, purslane and cucumber beats any other pleasure in life, or so wrote the 16th-century painter Bronzino.

potacchio
cooking style

'In potacchio' is a type of dish from Le Marche. A chicken, rabbit, piece of lamb or even a fish can all be 'in potacchio'. The jointed bird or rabbit, the cut-up lamb, a fish steak or fillet are sautéed in olive oil with onion and garlic. When just golden a couple of tablespoons of thick tomato sauce are added, and a little wine and water, and the dish is cooked slowly untll the main ingredient is tender. The characteristic of a potacchio is the final addition of a good quantity of chopped fresh rosemary, grated lemon rind and a little chilli.

pranzo
a meal

Nowadays pranzo means lunch, although some elderly northerners might still call pranzo the evening meal, as was done in the past. It is often the most important meal of the day and usually the whole family, schoolchildren included, gathers around the table. But customs are changing fast and more and more people, especially in big cities, take their pranzo in restaurants near their office or in the canteen.

The pranzi of the past, or at least the ones we know of because they are described in books, were eaten in the late afternoon and were grandiose affairs similar to banquets, consisting of many courses. Among the many menus that have caught my attention is one created and written down in the 16th century by Bartolomeo SCAPPI, chef to Cardinal Campeggio, for the dinner in honour of the Emperor Charles V. The dinner consisted of 789 dishes, divided into 13 courses, none containing meat since the dinner took place during Lent. The tablecloth and the napkins, as well as the gold spoons and forks, were changed three times during the meal. In the last change of linen, live birds were wrapped into the napkins, so that when the napkins were unfolded, a flock of twittering birds flew around the room to the surprise and delight of the guests.

Pranzi continued to consist of many dishes, which were set on the table all at once – *service à la française* – until the early 19th century, when the *service à la russe* was introduced in Paris. In this, the sequence of courses – the menu – was arranged in advance and each course was served to the guests separately, as is still done today. These pranzi, however, were still marathons of eating (I have seen many menus of dinners given by the kings of Italy) in comparison to the abstemious pranzi given now by the President of the Republic.

prataiolo
field mushroom

The field mushroom is not regarded very highly in Italy, since it does not grow in woods, where the best fungi are found. However, the taste of the field mushroom is sweet and rather delicate. It grows in fields in both the spring and autumn.

When very young prataioli are often served raw, thinly sliced and dressed with a light sauce of olive oil and lemon juice. A few slivers of Parmesan or Gruyère cheese are often added. Another popular way of preparing them is to marinate them for about 2 hours in olive oil, lemon juice, garlic, basil, salt and pepper.

Prataioli are the mushrooms used for cultivation. These are mainly used with RISOTTI and POLENTA, to accompany roast or braised meat or vegetable SFORMATI. For a more pronounced taste, a handful of dried PORCINI, previously soaked in warm water, is added to the cultivated mushrooms.

preboggion
herb mixture

A mixture of wild herbs and plants – including beet, borage, dandelion and mint – used to make a stuffing. Like many Ligurian preparations, preboggion is not found elsewhere in Italy. Preboggion is the main ingredient of the stuffing for the local ravioli, called PANSÒTI, for FRITTATE and soups.

prescinsena
a cheese

A curd cheese made in Liguria. The curd of full-fat cow's milk is strained through a cloth. Prescinsena, which is used as soon as it is made, is a main ingredient in many traditional dishes. It goes into the dough for FOCACCIA and bread, into the stuffing of RAVIOLI and PANSÒTI, vegetables and pies, and into local versions of *salsa di noci* (see recipe on page 248).

presnitz
a cake

A cake in the shape of a snail made in Venezia Giulia for Easter and Christmas. A very light and thin puff pastry is stuffed with dried fruit, nuts, honey, crumbled biscuits and grated chocolate, moistened with rum and bound with eggs.

prezzemolo
parsley

The parsley used in every household, almost every day, is the flat-leaf variety. The curly variety is occasionally used for decoration, being prettier, but it lacks aroma and flavour. Chopped fine, usually with a MEZZALUNA, parsley is a flavouring that goes into many sauces, RISOTTI, fish, seafood, soups, mushrooms and vegetable dishes, and it is always an ingredient of the MAZZETTO ODOROSO — bouquet garni. Oil, garlic and parsley is one of the most perfect combinations of flavours.

Parsley has been used since ancient times. PLATINA attributed a wide range of therapeutic properties to this herb, from being a remedy for the stings of scorpions and the bites of dogs, to relieving menstrual pains and giving protection against kidney stones.

primizia
early crops

A word used to describe the early crop of fruit and vegetables when, at the beginning of their respective seasons, they first appear on the market. Primizie were more in evidence, and much more of a real treat, in the past when the produce in the shops was all locally grown, and thus only to be found when in season. I still remember the delight of eating the first cherries in May, the first peas in April, the first peaches in June, and making a wish, which, we were told, will come true.

primo
first course

Short for *primo piatto*, the first course of a meal.
The primi are the strength of Italian cooking, to
the extent that many have been adopted by foreign
cuisines and made into main courses. Traditionally
speaking, primi consist of all the different types of
soups, pasta and RISOTTI. These days this primo is
sometimes also a SECONDO.

primo sale
a cheese

This is the name given in Sicily and Sardinia to
a PECORINO cheese put on the market after only
1 week of ageing, which must be eaten straight
away. Like pecorino it is also made with a mixture
of ewe's and cow's milk. Primo sale is a milky-
tasting cheese with a slight cheesy tang.

prosciutto cotto
ham

The boned thigh of a pig is cured with salt, saltpetre,
sugar, juniper berries, pepper and other spices, and
then cooked by steam and pressed into an oblong
mould. It is ready to be eaten a few days after being
cooked. Prosciutto cotto is no longer as popular
as it used to be, having lost ground to the more
fashionable PROSCIUTTO CRUDO. It is only produced
commercially, in Lombardy and Emilia-Romagna,
although it is sold all over northern and central Italy.
In southern Italy it is almost unknown.

prosciutto crudo
prosciutto

This cured ham, outside Italy, is known simply
as prosciutto – or, often inaccurately, as Parma
ham. It is the thigh (the ham) of a pig aged

about 11 months. There are various kinds of
prosciutto, Parma and San Daniele being the most
famous. All are cured in a similar way, although
the ageing time varies from 9 to 18 months, the
average nowadays being 14 months. Prosciutti
are still produced by traditional methods, and a
considerable porportion are made domestically
rather than commercially.

After slaughtering the pig, the ham is kept in
cold storerooms to firm up the meat. It is then
cleaned and stripped of excess fat, before being
gently pressed into its characteristic shape. The
salting, which takes about 2 months, is the trickiest
process to get right, since one of the essentials of a
first-class prosciutto is sweetness, but at the same
time the more it is salted the better the keeping
properties. After regular brushing, cleaning and
resting, the prosciutti are ready for their long
ageing. Finally, each prosciutto is stamped with
the mark of the Consorzio, which guarantees its
quality and denotes its origin.

Prosciutto di Parma accounts for half the total
consumption of prosciutto in Italy. *Prosciutto di
San Daniele*, which is made in Friuli, is considered
by many connoisseurs to be equal to, if not better
than, prosciutto di Parma. It has a characteristic
sweetish side to its flavour, an orangey tinge to its
colour and a guitar-like shape. Other prosciutti
that can be compared, but are only found locally,
are *prosciutto di Norcia* in Umbria and *prosciutto di
Carpegna* in Le Marche. Among many others are
the *prosciutto toscano*, tasty and on the salty side,
prosciutto dei colli di Mantova and the *prosciutto di
Sauris* in Friuli. In central Italy many households
keep pigs and make their own prosciutto, which
is nowadays usually boned before it is cured, for
easier keeping.

Prosciutto is still served at the beginning of
a meal with melon or figs, or with other SALUMI.
It also goes into delicate fillings for stuffed pasta,
it covers slices of veal to impart flavour, it is
chopped in various sauces and it is used in elegant
preparations such as mousselines and mousses.

provola
a cheese

A semi-soft cheese made with buffalo and cow's milk or sometimes only with cow's milk. It is a plastic curd cheese, similar to MOZZARELLA in shape and taste, but it is rather more solid, and it can be kept for a few days. Provola is often smoked.

provolone
a cheese

A plastic curd cheese made with full-fat cow's milk. The heated curd, once kneaded, is made into shapes, which can vary greatly in size and in shape: they may be large or small, round, oval, pear-shaped or tubular. The small ones are called *provolette*, the middle-sized ones *provole* and the large ones *provoloni*. Provolone has a smooth, shiny crust that comes away easily. The cheese itself is buff-coloured and is firm, yet malleable.

There are two main types of provolone. *Provolone dolce*, made with calf's rennet and aged for about a month, is a mild but very tasty table cheese, and is softer than the more mature cheese. *Provolone piccante*, made with kid's and lamb's rennet, is aged for up to 1 year, and the longer it is aged the more pungent it becomes. It is a table as well as a grating cheese. There is also smoked provolone, the small provolette being the shapes that are most commonly smoked.

Provolone was originally made in Campania, but the cheese became so popular after World War II that the main production is now in Lombardy, where there is far more cow's milk available.

prugna
plum or prune

Plums, also called *susine*, are eaten mostly as fresh fruit. They are sometimes poached in a cinnamon-flavoured wine syrup or used for making jam, which in its turn is a popular topping for a tart. The poached plums are called *prugne giubellate* or *sciroppate* and are kept for a year in sealed jars. Prunes – dried plums (*prugne secche*) – are usually poached in red wine.

Puglia

Puglia has short, mild winters, long sun-drenched summers and a rich fertile soil where everything grows in abundance. The vegetables are eaten raw, stewed, steamed, in pies and in tarts, and as the base for soups and pasta sauces. The variety of aubergine, broad bean and chickpea dishes speak of a strong connection with the cooking of Greece and the Middle East. Since antiquity,

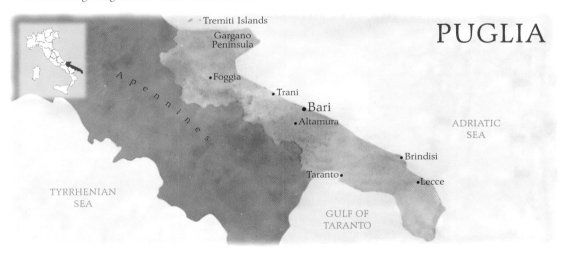

the heel of the Italian boot has had close ties with the countries of the eastern Mediterranean, particularly Greece. It is the region where the influence of Greece is strongest, and where the people seem almost to be more similar to their neighbours across the sea than to their compatriots on the other side of the Apennines. This influence is particularly evident in the way fish is cooked, especially in the many fish soups.

The sea along the long coastline is comparatively clean, since the coast is fairly free of large towns. Around the Tremiti Islands, sea turtles are still caught. The oysters from farms in the Gulf of Taranto are reared in the same way as they were when they were destined for the tables of the Roman senators. In Bari, fishermen are still to be seen carrying out a time-honoured procedure: they put small octopuses, newly caught, in a flat basket which they then twirl with a rhythmic movement so as to make the tentacles of the octopus curl. These octopuses are eaten raw with lemon juice and olive oil, as are the popular sea urchins and most other seafood. Fish pies (TIELLE) are peasant food now as they were in Greek times. But they are extremely rich peasant food, with layers of fish and/or mussels, potatoes and/or rice, onions, courgettes, all soaked in the local olive oil.

Pugliese olive oil competes with the Tuscan and Ligurian oils for top place in quality, but there is certainly no question of its being challenged in terms of the quantity produced. The extra virgin olive oil is exported everywhere, while much of it is mixed with less good grades to produce pure olive oil. The oil from Bitonto is of great repute, being considered by some gastronomes to be preferable to any other.

The other important product is cheese. Whether fresh or aged, dried or smoked, it is mostly farm-made from ewe's and cow's milk. There are SCAMORZE, MOZZARELLE, BURRINI, PROVOLONE and the creamy dreamy BURRATA, a speciality of this region.

But it is bread and pasta, the two keystones of Italian cooking, which find in Puglia their apogee. This is partly due to the fact that the best durum wheat, with which both pasta and bread are made, grows in the Pugliese plateau, and partly because of the strong local tradition of good-quality food. The best bread is made in the town of Altamura, in large shapes varying in weight from 1 to 10kg/2–22lb, a bread so excellent that it has been granted a DOP. The housewives are proud of their bread and the tradition of making it at home is still alive. Once a week, huge round loaves are prepared, using dough from the previous batch in place of fresh yeast. The leavened loaves are taken to the local oven and must be marked so that they can be recognized once baked. To do this, most households have their own mark, which is stamped into the loaf before baking. Some of these *marchi di pane*, which used to be made of wood, are very old and beautiful; they are carved with coats-of-arms, initials or some other design and they are now collectors' pieces.

Pasta-making is equally important and the shapes are more numerous in Puglia than anywhere else. The most popular of these are CAVATIEDDI, in the shape of shells, LAGANELLE (small lasagne), *minuicchi* (tiny gnocchi) and ORECCHIETTE ('little ears'). Pasta is combined with vegetables – *orecchiette con i broccoli* (see recipe on page 60) is one example – with fish, with meat and sausage.

The meat used for making a RAGÙ is often horse meat, which some locals prefer because of its slight sweetness. The ragù is made by cooking small rolled-up bundles of beef or horse meat, containing PANCETTA and PECORINO, in a rich tomato sauce. When the rolls are cooked, the sauce is used to dress orecchiette and the meat rolls are eaten afterwards with vegetables. Or at least this is the traditional way: I have been told that nowadays pasta and meat are sometimes served together.

Apart from horse, the Pugliesi eat a considerable amount of lamb and kid. Beef is rare because the pastures are not suited to feeding

338

cattle, but sheep and goats feed on dwarf bushes and herbs and the meat is permeated with the aroma of these local plants. The most usual, and the oldest, way of cooking the lamb or kid is by grilling it, larded and flavoured with rosemary and sage, or in FRICASSEA.

As for fruit, they all grow here, table grapes being probably the most widely produced. Finally, I must mention the almonds, which have been cultivated in Puglia since ancient times, having probably been brought to Puglia by the Phoenicians – thus pre-dating the Romans. The nuts have an intense yet delicate flavour, which sings loud and strong in the many sweet preparations in which they feature, like the CROCCANTE bars and the *rosata di mandorle*, almond cake, made without any flour. Unfortunately, Puglia's special cultivars yield scarcely enough even to satisfy the local hunger.

 [see recipe below]

punta di petto
boned calf's breast

The boned breast of a calf or a young ox is often served stuffed with minced pork and veal, prosciutto, Parmesan, breadcrumbs, seasonings, herbs and spices. In the *punta di vitello alla parmigiana* the meat is first sautéed in butter flavoured with parsley, rosemary, sage, cinnamon and onion and then cooked in the oven, basted with white wine, for about 2 hours. But the best known recipe for this cut is *cima alla genovese*.

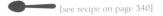 [see recipe on page 340]

puntarelle
chicory spears

This famous Roman vegetable is a type of chicory with long green leaves, eaten as a winter salad,

orata alla pugliese
baked gilt-head bream and potatoes

Serves 6
6–8 waxy potatoes
1 gilt-head bream, weighing
    1.5–1.8kg/3¼–4lb
salt and freshly ground black pepper
a bunch of fresh flat-leaf parsley
1 garlic clove
150ml/5fl oz/²/₃ cup extra virgin olive oil
100g/3½oz mature pecorino cheese,
    grated

A traditional way to cook fish in Puglia is to bake it with potatoes. I prefer to parboil the potatoes first, so that they will be ready at the same time as the fish. If you can't find gilt-head bream, you can use any other member of the bream family instead.

Boil the potatoes for 8–10 minutes, then drain, peel and set aside. When cold, slice them thinly. Season the fish inside and out with a little salt.

Preheat the oven to 200°C/400°F/Gas Mark 6.

Chop the parsley and garlic together. Pour 4 tablespoons of the olive oil into an ovenproof dish (I use a metal lasagne dish) and cover the bottom with half the potatoes, half the parsley and garlic mixture and half the cheese. Season with a little salt and plenty of pepper. Drizzle with a little of the oil and lay the fish on top. Spread over the remaining parsley and garlic, potatoes and cheese, season as before, and drizzle with the rest of the oil. Bake for 25 minutes. Leave to rest for about 5 minutes before serving.

which is prepared according to a special method. The outside leaves are removed (and used for a soup), while the central globe is cut into thin strips, which are placed in cold water where they become slightly curly. Drained, they are eaten raw, dressed with a sauce of olive oil, lemon juice or vinegar, garlic and chopped anchovy fillets. In Rome, where they are very popular, puntarelle are sold already prepared.

puttanesca
pasta sauce

Not the most elegant of names – *puttana* is a prostitute – but surely one of the most delicious of pasta sauces. The sauce is allegedly from the slums of Rome; it is quick to make, piquant and gutsy like the locals themselves, and is now made all over Italy. This recipe is a classic version.

[see recipe on facing page]

cima alla genovese
Genoese stuffed breast of veal

Serves 8

1kg/2¼lb boned breast of veal
1 onion, roughly chopped
1 celery stalk, roughly chopped
1 carrot, roughly chopped
1 bay leaf
4 black peppercorns
2 litres/3½ pints/2 quarts meat stock
  (page 61) or chicken stock

Stuffing

50g/1¾oz crustless good white bread
4–6 tbsp full-fat (whole) milk
1 small onion, finely chopped
25g/1oz/2 tbsp unsalted butter
100g/3½oz stewing veal, cubed
100g/3½oz calf's or lamb's sweetbreads,
  cleaned, blanched and diced
salt and freshly ground black pepper
25g/1oz/3 tbsp pistachio nuts, skinned
1 tsp chopped fresh marjoram
1 large egg
75g/2¾oz/½ cup cooked peas
3 tbsp freshly grated Parmesan cheese

A splendid recipe for PUNTA DI PETTO **(boned breast of veal), from Liguria. Cima alla genovese is always served cold, doused with olive oil.**

First prepare the stuffing. Soak the bread in the milk for 10 minutes or so. Sauté the onion in the butter until soft and then add the veal and cook for 10 minutes, stirring frequently. Mix in the sweetbreads and cook for a further 5 minutes. Season with salt and pepper and remove from the heat.

Remove the veal and sweetbreads from the pan and chop finely. Add 1 tablespoon hot water to the pan and boil for 1 minute, scraping the bottom of the pan with a metal spoon. Pour the pan juices into a bowl and add the remaining stuffing ingredients. Squeeze the milk out of the bread and add the bread to the bowl. Mix thoroughly and season to taste.

Make a horizontal cut in the breast of veal along one of the long sides. Put the stuffing into this pocket, not too tightly because it will swell as it cooks. Sew up the cut, shaping the meat into a neat roll.

Place the onion, celery and carrot in an oval casserole with the bay leaf and peppercorns. Add the stock and bring to the boil. When the stock is boiling, gently lower the meat into it. Turn the heat down to low and cook for 2 hours.

Lift out the meat and put it between two plates with a weight on top. Leave to cool completely. To serve, carve it into 1cm/½in slices.

spaghetti alla puttanesca
spaghetti in a chilli and anchovy sauce

Serves 4

350g/12oz spaghetti

6 tbsp olive oil

2.5cm/1in piece of fresh red chilli, deseeded and finely chopped

3 salted anchovies, boned, rinsed and chopped, or 6 canned or bottled anchovy fillets, drained and chopped

2 garlic cloves, very finely sliced

500g/1lb 2oz ripe fresh tomatoes, peeled, deseeded and cut into strips

100g/3½oz large black olives, pitted and sliced

1 tbsp capers, preferably in salt, rinsed

1 tbsp chopped fresh flat-leaf parsley

Cook the spaghetti in boiling salted water until al dente.

While the pasta is cooking, put the olive oil, chilli, anchovies and garlic in a large frying pan and cook for 1 minute, mashing the anchovies to a paste with a fork. Add the tomatoes, olives and capers and cook for 5 minutes, stirring frequently.

Drain the spaghetti, turn into the frying pan and add the parsley. Fry for 1 minute, tossing the pasta all the time.

Serve the pasta at once, straight from the pan.

RIGHT: Spaghetti alla puttanesca

q

quaglia
quail

Writing in the mid-19th century, Alexandre Dumas said: 'This is the most delightful and lovable of game. The flavour, colour and shape of a fat quail all give equal pleasure. It is an act of culinary ignorance to prepare quails in any way other than roasted in buttered paper.' The 20th-century cookery writer Livio Cerini di Castegnate, an expert on game, writes of quail roasted on the spit, the breast covered with slices of PANCETTA or with a slice of very white LARDO. In a recipe from Veneto the quails are roasted in the oven for a short time. The cooking juices are then sharpened by a small glass of GRAPPA and are made delicate and shiny by some butter.

In Le Marche, quails are plentiful; as well as being shot, they are caught in nets, set along the coastline. They are sautéed in butter with chopped PROSCIUTTO and then gently braised in white wine. They are often served around a mound of boiled rice dressed with plenty of butter and Parmesan. The same method is used in Lombardy, where quails are served with a creamy RISOTTO ALLA MILANESE. Nowadays there are many quail farms, which produce smaller birds that lack the gamey flavour of the wild specimens. The only advantage is that they are on the market all the year round.

quartirolo
a cheese

Quartirolo, made in Lombardy, is one of the greatest Italian cheeses. It is soft, with a fresh, creamy taste and a slight pungency. The thin yellowish crust is as good as the cheese it protects. Quartirolo belongs to the STRACCHINO family and is similar to, but less fatty than, the better-known TALEGGIO. Quartirolo is a DOP cheese and the best is made in September and October from the milk of cows feeding on pasture and hay rich in wild herbs and plants. The milk produced at this time of year is rich but not heavy, and full of flavour without being too tangy. Quartirolo, a table cheese, is made in square shapes of about 2.5kg/5lb and is matured for 5 days for the very fresh cheese, or up to 30 days.

r

radicchio
red chicory

Radicchio is the generic name for the red varieties of chicory that are cultivated by a special method of forcing and blanching. The most popular varieties are the radicchio rosso di Treviso, di Verona, di Castelfranco and di Chioggia. This last variety is now extensively cultivated in greenhouses and is available all year round. It is pretty, and crunchy, but lacking the flavour of its cousins. The radicchio of Treviso, with its elongated leaves, and of Castelfranco with its rosebud shape and variegated pink colour, are mainly used in cooking, while the radicchio of Verona and Chioggia are best in salads. Here is the classic recipe for grilled radicchio, a perfect accompaniment to grilled meats.

[see recipe on page 344]

rafano
horseradish

Also known as *cren* or *kren*, a native of eastern Europe, horseradish is rarely used in Italy, although it appears in quite a few recipes from Venezia Giulia. Grated horseradish is always part of the traditional accompaniment to a platter of boiled pork meats.

[see recipe on page 344]

ragù
pasta sauce

A rich sauce, usually made with meat and used to dress pasta. There are two basic meat ragù: *alla bolognese* and *alla napoletana*.

The ragù alla bolognese, and most other ragùs of northern Italy, is based on minced or finely chopped meat. Ragù alla bolognese is a classic dish made by most Italian cooks. The ingredients vary according to the whim of the cook, but all cooks are in agreement on two points: ragù must be cooked very slowly for at least 2 hours, and it should be cooked in an earthenware pot. Ragù alla bolognese is the traditional dressing for TAGLIATELLE. The recipe given here is my own version of this classic sauce. A new ragù, born in the 21st century, is the *ragù bianco*, a beef, veal and sausage ragù made on the same lines as the bolognese, but without any tomatoes. It is used to dress tagliatelle.

Ragù alla napoletana, and those of southern Italy, is a quite different dish, although still used to dress pasta. It is a piece of meat cooked for a long time, to which sausages and other ingredients are sometimes added. Like its northern cousin it is cooked in an earthenware pot, and it is even more demanding as to the long cooking time needed. Ragù alla napoletana is used to dress MACCHERONI or ZITI as a first course, while the meat from the sauce is eaten by itself, or with a vegetable, as the second course. The recipe is on page 78.

There are ragùs from other regions, but they are all variations on these themes. The name ragù is now also applied to fish sauces containing more than one kind of fish, stewed with tomato and wine.

[see recipe on page 346]

343

radicchio rosso alla Trevisana
grilled red radicchio

Serves 4
4 radicchio heads, about 1kg/2¼lb
6 tbsp extra virgin olive oil
salt and freshly ground black pepper

Although this dish is better made with the more flavourful RADICCHIO rosso di Treviso, the more widely available round radicchio di Chioggia is an acceptable substitute.

Heat the grill. Discard the bruised outside leaves of the radicchio, then cut the heads into quarters and wash and dry them thoroughly.

Place the radicchio in the grill pan, spoon over the olive oil and season with salt and a generous amount of pepper. Cook under the hot grill for 10 minutes, turning the pieces of radicchio so that they do not burn. Transfer to a serving dish and spoon over the juice from the grill pan. Serve hot or cold.

agnello al rafano
lamb in horseradish sauce

Serves 4
75g/2¾oz/5 tbsp unsalted butter
2 tbsp vegetable oil
1 onion, finely sliced
½ tsp dried thyme
2 bay leaves
75ml/2½fl oz/5 tbsp wine vinegar
175ml/6fl oz/¾ cup meat stock (page
*   61) or chicken stock*
salt and freshly ground black pepper
1.5kg/3¼lb leg or shoulder of lamb,
*   boned and cut into small cubes*
3 tbsp horseradish sauce
2 tbsp chopped parsley

This recipe is from Friuli-Venezia Giulia, where the food shows strong Slav influence, hence the use of horseradish (RAFANO). I had the dish years ago in a private house in Trieste, where it was served with tagliatelle, another non-Italian custom, and it was perfect.

Put 25g/1oz/2 tbsp of the butter, the oil, onion, thyme, bay leaves, vinegar, stock, salt and pepper in a casserole and bring slowly to the boil. Add the meat and cook, covered, over a moderate heat, for about 1½ hours, until the meat is very tender. At the end of the cooking there should be very little liquid in the pan. If necessary, reduce over a high heat. Discard the bay leaves.

Melt the rest of the butter in a small saucepan, add the horseradish and the parsley and cook, stirring constantly, for 1 minute. Pour the sauce over the lamb, stir to mix it with the cooking liquid and taste to check the seasoning. Serve hot.

RIGHT: Radicchio rosso alla Trevisana

rana
frog

In Italy all kinds of frogs are edible, but the *Rana esculenta* is the best. In Pavia, in southern Lombardy, famous for its Abbey as well as its frogs, frogs' legs are cooked 'in GUAZZETTO', with onions and white wine, or sautéed in oil and butter and then stewed in a tomato and white wine sauce liberally flavoured with sage, rosemary, parsley and thyme. Another local speciality is FRITTATA *di rane*. The frogs' legs are fried in hot oil for no more than a minute and then mixed into beaten eggs together with garlic and parsley. A more complicated recipe is made with boned and minced frogs' legs mixed with the local river crayfish, egg, Parmesan and mascarpone. This mixture, coated in dried breadcrumbs, is fried by the spoonful in oil.

The other great dish is RISOTTO ALLA CERTOSINA, or *risotto con le rane*, the rice being cooked with the frogs' legs in a stock made with other parts of the frog.

All frogs must be cleaned and prepared before cooking, but nowadays *coscette di rane* – frogs' legs – are usually bought already prepared, fresh or frozen.

rana pescatrice

see CODA DI ROSPO

rapa
turnip

One of the earliest known recipes for this humble root vegetable was written in about 1450 by MARTINO da Como. Called *rapa armate* – meaning 'armed

CONTINUES OVERLEAF

346

ragù alla bolognese
Bolognese meat sauce

Enough for 4 helpings of pasta
50g/1 ¾oz/4 tbsp unsalted butter
2 tbsp olive oil
100g/3½oz unsmoked pancetta, finely chopped
1 small onion, very finely chopped
1 small carrot, very finely chopped
1 small celery stalk, very finely chopped
200g/7oz lean braising steak, minced (ground)
200g/7oz minced (ground) pork
75ml/2½fl oz/5 tbsp red wine
2 tbsp tomato puree diluted with 100ml/3½fl oz/scant ½ cup hot meat stock (page 61) or chicken stock
a grating of nutmeg
salt and freshly ground black pepper
75ml/2½fl oz/5 tbsp full-fat (whole)milk

Every Italian cook has a favourite version of RAGÙ alla bolognese. This is mine, which is my mother's recipe and maybe my grandmother's as well. It is served with TAGLIATELLE or used to make LASAGNE and other baked pasta dishes but is never served with spaghetti.

Heat the butter, oil and pancetta in a deep, heavy-bottomed saucepan and cook gently for 2–3 minutes. Add the onion, carrot and celery and cook over a medium heat until the vegetables are soft, stirring frequently.

Add the beef and pork and cook until the meat has lost its raw colour. Pour in the wine and boil briskly for 2–3 minutes, until the liquid has almost evaporated.

Add the diluted tomato puree, season with nutmeg, salt and pepper and cook for 5 minutes, stirring frequently.

Meanwhile, bring the milk to simmering point in a separate small pan. Pour the milk over the meat (the liquid should just come level with it) and stir thoroughly. Cook, uncovered, over the lowest heat for at least 2 hours. The ragù should not boil, but just break a few bubbles on the surface. Stir occasionally during cooking and taste and adjust the seasoning at the end.

RIGHT: Ragù alla bolognese

turnips' – it suggests cooking the turnips in the ashes of a fire or boiling them. They are then cut into slices 'as thick as the blade of a knife, and have some good cheese cut in slices as large as the turnips, but thinner; and have some sugar, some pepper and some sweet spices all mixed together; and put a layer of the cheese on the bottom of a cake-pan so that they make a crust underneath, and over them place a layer of turnips sprinkling them with the spices and plenty of good butter. And in this manner prepare all the turnips until the pan is full and cook them for a quarter of an hour or more, like a cake. And serve this dish after the others.' Although turnips are no longer served at the end of the meal as Maestro Martino suggests, they are still very often cooked in much the same way in northern Italy, in layers with plenty of butter and grated Parmesan.

Riso e rape is a classic Milanese soup. The diced turnips are cooked in a good meat stock flavoured with a BATTUTO of lard, parsley and a touch of garlic. Halfway through the cooking, rice is added and the soup is served with grated GRANA, which by tradition should be padano and not parmigiano.

The other traditional dish made with turnips is *broade* or *brovade*, found only in Friuli and eaten as an accompaniment to pork. The sliced turnips are macerated in the dregs of pressed grapes until they begin to ferment and become acid. It is the sort of dish I am happy to leave untouched.

rascasse

see SCORFANO

raschera
a cheese

This excellent table cheese is produced in the province of Cuneo, with Piedmontese cow's milk, to which a small quantity of ewe's or goat's milk is often added. It is at its best in the summer and autumn, from the milk of animals grazing in high pastures. It is a DOP cheese in the form of a flattened disc or square, each cheese weighing about 8kg/18lb, and is aged in caves or underground cellars for at least 1 month and up to 5 months. The semi-hard cheese is pale, with irregular small eyes, a reddish rind and a savoury, salty flavour that intensifies with age.

ravioli
stuffed pasta

For several hundred years, the word ravioli referred to little round dumplings, of various mixtures, which today would be called GNOCCHI. What we now call ravioli were then called TORTELLI.

It was not until the end of the 18th century that ravioli had come to be what they are today. The Roman chef Vincenzo Agnoletti wrote a recipe for *ravioli di ricotta* which could have been written yesterday. He suggests shaping the ravioli either as half moons or in little squares. And in the early 19th century LURASCHI gives a recipe for ravioli made with chicken, cows' udders (which were a popular ingredient until the early 20th century), soft breadcrumbs, egg and Parmesan.

Surprisingly, ARTUSI takes a step backwards. In his introduction to *ravioli alla genovese* he writes: 'These should not really be called ravioli, because true ravioli are not made with meat and are not wrapped in pasta dough.' Artusi's other two recipes for ravioli are in fact recipes for gnocchi.

By the early decades of the 20th century, ravioli, firmly established as stuffed pasta shapes, were made in most regions. In Genoa they are stuffed with batavia, borage, brains, sweetbreads, minced pork and the usual eggs, Parmesan and soft breadcrumbs. In Liguria *ravioli di* MAGRO are stuffed with white fish, ricotta, borage, beets and Parmesan and dressed with a mussel or clam sauce. In Alto Adige ravioli are made with a dough of rye flour and stuffed with spinach and ricotta, or with fried sauerkraut. More often than not, these and other ravioli from northern Italy are dressed with melted butter flavoured with sage leaves and, sometimes, a touch of garlic.

In Le Marche, traditional ricotta-filled ravioli are dressed with a sauce made with sole cooked in wine and tomato sauce. The ravioli of Basilicata, containing ricotta, prosciutto and parsley, are dressed with oil flavoured with chilli, garlic and pecorino.

Ravioli have recently become very fashionable and are stuffed with anything an imaginative cook thinks suitable: asparagus, smoked salmon, ricotta and basil, ricotta and tomatoes, chicken and mascarpone, red radicchio, or seafood. The two ingredients that are always present are egg for binding and Parmesan for flavouring. Yet in spite of the variety that ravioli offer, few Italians make them at home. They buy them already made, fresh in the local deli or dried in supermarkets. The most popular ravioli are those containing meat – usually braised – or spinach and ricotta.

There are also two traditional kinds of sweet ravioli. One is made in Emilia-Romagna for St Joseph's Day (19 March) and consists of ravioli made with sweet pastry, stuffed with jam and then baked. The other is a more interesting recipe from Liguria. A Carnival sweet, these are made with pasta dough and stuffed with bone marrow, candied pumpkin and candied citron, and then fried and lavishly showered with icing sugar.

reginette
see LASAGNETTE

resta
string of garlic or onions

These plaited strings are made in southern Italy in order to keep onions and garlic heads all through the year. The reste are hung outside until winter, when they are hung in the kitchen around the open fire.

resta
a cake

This sweet bread is a speciality of the province of Como, Lombardy, traditionally made for Palm Sunday. It is similar to a squat PANETTONE, but richer in candied fruits and currants and raisins. It is called resta, which in dialect means 'fish bone', because it contains a small stick of olive wood which is stuck into the dough before baking.

rete
caul fat

A fatty, lacy membrane lining the stomach of an animal, rete is used to protect and to impart fattiness to the food it is wrapping. The most commonly used rete is from pigs. It is sold dried and folded in butchers' shops and it has to be moistened in warm water before use. Its best known use is with pig's liver in FEGATELLI DI MAIALE, one of the great Tuscan specialities.

349

rhum
rum

Rum appears more than any other spirit in northern Italian dishes. It became known in Piedmont in the second half of the 16th century. Emanuele Filiberto, Duke of Savoy, had created a Piedmontese navy which was based in Villefranche, then part of his dukedom. His sailors, who had tasted the sugary spirit from the West Indies on their travels, brought rum back to Piedmont when they came home on leave. The Piedmontese loved it and put it in many of their sweet preparations.

ribollita
a soup

A thick soup made in Tuscany. It was traditionally made in large quantities on a Friday, the fast day, so that it could be reheated on the Saturday, hence its name, which means 'reboiled'. Ribollita is made with seasonal vegetables plus beans and CAVOLO NERO, the Tuscan cabbage. My recipe also contains Savoy cabbage, which is included in the version made in Siena.

[see recipe on facing page]

ricciarelli
almond biscuits

Soft biscuits from Siena, which date from the Middle Ages; some historians see a link between ricciarelli and Arab sweets that the Crusaders may have brought back from the Middle East. They are a mixture of ground almonds and sugar moistened with egg white and then shaped into lozenges. Placed on a piece of rice paper, they are baked in a very low oven until dry, like meringues.

riccio di mare
sea urchin

Sea urchins are eaten raw, slit open with scissors and sprinkled with lemon juice. The best time to eat them is at the beginning of spring, just before they breed, when the coral is full and ripe. You do not get much, but what you do get is memorable.

In Sicily sea urchins are used for a fresh and quick pasta sauce for SPAGHETTINI, made with a few ripe tomatoes, oil, garlic and a touch of chilli; after 10 minutes the sea urchins are added and quickly sautéed for no more than 1 minute.

ricotta
a cheese

Ricotta is made from the whey after it has separated from the curd as a result of being heated as part of the cheese-making process. The strained whey is then heated again, which accounts for its name (meaning 'recooked'). The two traditional ricotte are the *piemontese* and the *romana*. The Piedmontese, also called *seras* or *seirass*, is very creamy, looking a little like MASCARPONE, although it is less rich. It can only be found in Italy and is not exported. Ricotta romana is the kind sold abroad, although real Roman ricotta is made with ewe's milk and has a much deeper flavour and lighter texture. Outside Italy the most easily available ricotta is a UHT product made from cow's milk, which is only suitable for cooking, added to other ingredients.

Ricotta, when good, can be eaten as it is with honey or flavoured with coffee. It is also used in many cakes and puddings such as CASSATA *siciliana*, PASTIERA *napoletana*, SFOGLIATELLE and CANNOLI. Roman specialities include CROSTATA *di ricotta* and a light baked pudding, for which the recipe is on page 64.

Ricotta is also used in many savoury dishes, such as vegetable pies and tarts. Mixed with spinach or Swiss chard it is essential in TORTELLI *di magro* and other stuffed pasta, and in MALFATTI, the green gnocchi from Emilia-Romagna. In central Italy, ewe's milk ricotta is added, crumbled, to vegetable soups, such as fennel, celery or spinach soup, just before serving.

In Sicily and Sardinia a whole ricotta is lightly smoked with a little salt. It develops a dark crust but remains soft and creamy inside. Another type of ricotta is *ricotta salata*. It is salted and hung to drain until dry, to be grated over pasta, an essential ingredient in many Sicilian pasta dishes, such as *pasta al pomodoro* (with tomato sauce).

la ribollita
Tuscan bean soup

Serves 6–8

*225g/8oz/generous 1 cup dried
    cannellini beans, soaked for about
    12 hours in cold water*

5 tbsp extra virgin olive oil

1 Spanish onion, sliced

½–1 tsp crushed dried chillies

salt and freshly ground black pepper

*2 ripe fresh tomatoes, peeled, deseeded
    and coarsely chopped*

1 tbsp tomato puree

3 potatoes, cut into small cubes

2 carrots, cut into small cubes

*1 small leek, both white and green parts,
    cut into small pieces*

3 celery stalks, cut into small pieces

250g/9oz cavolo nero, shredded

200g/7oz Savoy cabbage, shredded

2 garlic cloves, sliced

3 or 4 sprigs of fresh thyme

For cooking the beans

1 onion, cut into quarters

1 small celery stalk, cut into pieces

3 garlic cloves, sliced

*sprigs of fresh sage, rosemary and
    parsley*

To serve

1 or 2 mild onions

6–8 slices of country-style bread

2 garlic cloves, cut in half

2 tbsp extra virgin olive oil

This is how I was taught to cook la RIBOLLITA by my neighbours in Chianti. The beans need to soak for 12 hours and the soup needs to be prepared a day in advance to allow the flavours to develop before it is reheated, hence its name, 'reboiled'.

Drain and rinse the beans, then put them in a large, heavy stockpot with all of the ingredients for cooking the beans. Pour in enough cold water to cover the beans by about 5cm/2in and bring slowly to the boil. Cover the pan and cook very gently until the beans are very tender, about 1½ hours.

Using a slotted spoon, lift all the beans out of the liquid (leave the herbs and vegetables in the stock). Puree three-quarters of the beans into a bowl through the large holes of a food mill, or puree them coarsely in a food processor, then turn them into a bowl. Leave the remaining beans whole and set aside. Strain the cooking liquid into another bowl, discarding the herbs and vegetables.

Put the olive oil into the pot in which the beans were cooked. Add the onion and chillies, sprinkle with a pinch of salt and sauté for about 10 minutes. Add the tomatoes and tomato puree and cook for 2–3 minutes, then mix in the bean puree. Stir it around for a couple of minutes to let it take up the flavour, then add all the other vegetables, the garlic and thyme.

Measure the bean cooking liquid and add enough water to make it up to about 1.5 litres/3 pints/6 cups. Add it to the pot, together with salt, and bring to the boil, then cook over the lowest possible heat for about 2 hours. Add pepper, taste and check the seasoning. Remove from the heat and leave overnight.

The next day, preheat the oven to 180°C/350°F/Gas Mark 4.

Mix the whole beans into the soup. Slice the onions very finely – and arrange in a thin layer all over the surface of the soup. Put the pot in the oven and cook until the onion is tender; this will take about 1 hour.

Rub the bread with the halved garlic cloves, then toast under the grill. Put the bread into individual soup bowls and ladle the soup over it. Drizzle a little oil over each bowl and serve.

rigaglie
giblets

A bird's liver, heart, gizzard, unlaid eggs, cock's testicles and cockscomb are all rigaglie. A light RAGÙ can be made with them to use as a sauce for SFORMATI or RISOTTI.

rigatoni
a pasta

Tubular dried pasta, always with ridges, sometimes curved, in various diameters and lengths but generally about 4–5cm/1½–2in long. Rigatoni are particularly suited to being dressed with RAGÙ, sausages and other meat sauces and are one of the best shapes to use for baked dishes.

ripieno
stuffing or filling

This word applies to the food that is stuffed, such as *peperoni ripieni* (stuffed peppers) and to the stuffing itself. Italians are masters of this art: suffice it to mention the endless varieties of stuffed pasta, from AGNOLOTTI to RAVIOLI. Any *cucina povera* excels in creating this type of dish because of the need to make use of leftovers.

Aubergines, courgettes, peppers, tomatoes and onions are often stuffed, as are courgette flowers, mushroom caps, leeks and cabbage leaves. The vegetables are filled with breadcrumbs (soft or dried) or rice, garlic and herbs (the stuffing may also include other vegetables, nuts, olives, capers, sultanas or anchovies), and then baked (see recipe on page 298), stewed or occasionally, as in the case of the courgette flowers, fried.

Fish comes stuffed, too. The grandest recipe is for sea bass stuffed with seafood, while the simplest recipe is for sardines with breadcrumbs, parsley and garlic – ingredients that work well in many fish. A more interesting recipe for sardines, stuffed with breadcrumbs, pine nuts, sultanas, capers, garlic, parsley and pecorino is on page 374. Seafood such as squid and mussels are also stuffed (see the recipes on pages 74 and 119).

Fruit such as peaches are stuffed and baked (see recipe on page 300), and the large dried figs of Calabria are stuffed with hazelnuts, candied orange peel and honey, or with candied peel, cinnamon, brandy and almonds, then baked (see recipe on page 149).

Stuffed food makes a most satisfying dish for the creative cook, who is able to successfully combine different tastes and textures.

risi e bisi
rice and peas

This well-known dish could be described as a very thick soup or a rather runny RISOTTO. Risi e bisi is the most aristocratic of all rice dishes, since it used to be served at the Doge's banquet every year on St Mark's Day (24 April), when the first young peas are just coming in from the vegetable gardens around the lagoon.

[see recipe on facing page]

riso
rice

The Romans used rice mainly as a medicine; they traded in rice, but did not grow it. It was formerly thought that the Saracens or Venetians introduced rice-growing to Italy, but historians now believe that it was the Aragonese who first started to grow rice in Campania, where they landed in the 15th century.

The first document concerning rice is a letter, dated 1475, from the Duke of Milan to the Duke of Ferrara's ambassador, in which he promises to send twelve sacks of rice to be planted in

Romagna. Three hundred years later, the future president of the United States, Thomas Jefferson, decided that the superior quality of Italian rice justified his contravening the law that prohibited its export: he smuggled two sacks out of Piedmont and planted it on his estate in Virginia. By the 19th century rice was the most important produce of the northern regions of Italy. This resulted in the division of the country into two areas: pasta in central and southern Italy and rice in the north. That lasted until the 1960s and 70s, when pasta became the national food. However, the *risaie* – paddy-fields – of northern Italy still produce enough rice to make Italy one of Europe's major rice producers.

Four different types of rice are grown in the Po Valley: *ordinario*, short round rice used for puddings; *semifino*, a round grain of medium length suitable for soups and salads; *fino*, long-grain rice such as Vialone Nano, which is good for many RISOTTI with vegetables; and *superfino*, a very long-grain rice that is ideal for most risotti. The best varieties of superfino are Arborio, Roma and Carnaroli.

The better the rice, the longer it takes to cook, thus superfino takes 18 to 20 minutes, while ordinario takes only about 12 minutes. The fino and superfino grades are the ones used for making risotto because they absorb a lot of liquid during the cooking and swell up without breaking.

The main use of rice is in risotti and soups but it is also used for croquettes, in TIMBALLI and in stuffings. Rice has certainly not conquered the

CONTINUES ON PAGE 356

risi e bisi
rice and peas

Serves 4
900g/2lb young fresh peas in their pods
salt and freshly ground black pepper
25g/1oz/2 tbsp unsalted butter
2 tbsp mild extra virgin olive oil
1 small onion, very finely chopped
3 tbsp chopped fresh flat-leaf parsley
225g/8oz/1¼ cups risotto rice,
*   preferably Vialone Nano*
½–1 tbsp fennel seeds, according to
*   taste, crushed*
50g/1¾oz Parmesan cheese, grated

This classic dish from Venice should be made with very young peas.

Top and tail and shell the peas, keeping the pods and peas separate. Discard any blemished pods and wash the others. Put the pods in a saucepan and add about 1.5 litres/3 pints/6 cups water and 2 teaspoons salt. Boil until the pods are very tender. Drain, reserving the liquid, and puree the pods in a food processor or blender until smooth. If the puree is stringy, rub it through a sieve. Put the puree in a saucepan, add 1 litre/1¾ pints/4 cups of the cooking liquid and bring slowly to the boil; keep this stock on a gentle simmer.

Meanwhile, put the butter, oil, onion and 1 tablespoon of the parsley in a stockpot. Sauté very gently for 5 minutes or so. Add the peas and cook, stirring all the time, for 2 minutes. Stir in the rice. When the rice grains are coated in the butter and oil, pour in the simmering pod stock. Mix well and bring to the boil.

Add the fennel seeds and a grinding of pepper and then boil, covered, for 15–20 minutes or until the rice is cooked. Remove from the heat and mix in the Parmesan and the remaining parsley. Ladle the risotto into individual soup bowls and serve immediately.

riso arrosto alla genovese
rice baked with pork and dried porcini

Serves 3–4

20g/³⁄₄oz dried porcini
50g/1³⁄₄oz/4 tbsp unsalted butter
1 small onion, finely chopped
a bunch of fresh flat-leaf parsley,
*   chopped*
salt and freshly ground black pepper
1 garlic clove, chopped
300g/10¹⁄₂oz lean minced (ground) pork
600ml/20fl oz/2¹⁄₂ cups meat stock
*   (page 61) or chicken stock*
300g/10¹⁄₂oz/1¹⁄₂ cups risotto rice,
*   preferably Arborio*
40g/1¹⁄₂oz Parmesan cheese, grated
6 tbsp red wine

This is my adaptation of a recipe in *Cuciniera Genovese*, a book that is still considered the bible of Genoese cooking, by the 19th-century writers GB and Giovanni Ratto. It is the only traditional Italian rice dish that is cooked in the oven. In the original recipe the meat is veal and cow's elder (udder), a great delicacy that has now, alas, mostly disappeared. It is suggested that sausage can be used instead, but it must not be spicy or herby. All things considered, I suggest using minced pork. I make *riso arrosto* in a flameproof baking dish.

Preheat the oven to 200°C/400°F/Gas Mark 6.

Soak the porcini in 100ml/3¹⁄₂fl oz/scant ¹⁄₂ cup hot water for about 30 minutes. Remove the porcini from the water and, if there is still some grit, rinse them under cold water. Pat dry and chop them. Strain the soaking liquid through a sieve lined with a piece of muslin. This may not be necessary if you pour the liquid very gently so that any grit is left at the bottom of the bowl.

Melt the butter in an ovenproof pan and gently sauté the onion and parsley with ¹⁄₂ teaspoon salt until soft. Add the garlic and cook for 2 minutes, stirring frequently. Add the porcini, sauté for a minute or two, then mix in the pork and brown well. Pour in 4–5 tablespoons of the stock and cook over a very gentle heat for 5 minutes, stirring frequently.

Meanwhile, bring the remaining stock and the porcini liquid to the boil in another pan.

Add the rice to the pan with the meat mixture, together with 1¹⁄₂ tablespoons of the Parmesan, and stir well. Add the wine and cook for about 2 minutes, stirring constantly. Pour in the boiling stock, add pepper to taste and mix well. Cover the pan, transfer to the oven and cook until the rice is done and a lovely crust has formed on top, about 10–15 minutes.

Serve with the rest of the Parmesan on the side.

Right: Riso arrosto alla genovese

south to anything like the extent that pasta, from its base in southern Italy, conquered the north. In Sicily, for instance, the only traditional preparation in which rice appears is ARANCINI. Rice is also used in Sicily's *riso nero* – black rice – a pudding in which the rice is cooked in sugared milk, and then drained and dressed with melted chocolate. In Abruzzo they make a good TIMBALLO *di riso e funghi*, in which boiled rice is layered with wild mushrooms cooked in a tomato sauce. Other traditional preparations are the Neapolitan SARTÙ and the Roman SUPPLÌ. Another southern dish, TIELLA *di riso e patate*, is one of those generous Puglian dishes of layered rice, potatoes, courgettes, tomatoes, onions, fish and seafood and eggs – or a variety of these – which are so representative of the cooking of that region. In Liguria rice is used in an excellent dish called *riso arrosto alla genovese*, for which the recipe is given here.

There are as many different soups made with rice as there are cooks to make them. The rice is usually matched with a particular vegetable, although of course several vegetables are used in MINESTRONI. There are such soups as rice and turnips, rice and potatoes, rice and parsley, rice and chestnuts and others. They are all homely soups, prepared and eaten for supper by every family in northern Italy.

Rice can be served simply boiled and dressed with butter and Parmesan – called *all'inglese* (in the English way) – or prepared *all'insalata* – in salad – not a traditional method but a popular one in the summer. My favourite riso all'insalata contains tuna, tomatoes, petits pois, anchovy fillets and grilled peppers. It is dressed with olive oil and lemon juice, a drop of Tabasco, a touch of garlic and a sprinkling of parsley.

[see recipe on page 354]

riso in cagnona
rice dish

This traditional rice dish from Milan was a regular first course at lunch in most Milanese families before rice gave way to pasta. The boiled rice is dressed with plenty of butter, unsalted of course, previously melted to a beautiful golden colour with sage leaves and a garlic clove. The sage and garlic are removed before pouring the butter over the rice, which is sprinkled with a generous amount of Parmesan. That's all.

riso e luganeghin
rice dish

The Milanese have always bestowed affectionate diminutives on their favourite foods. Thus LUGANEGA became *luganeghin* and, mixed with rice, makes this delicious dish. The sliced luganega is first sautéed with a little onion in oil and butter. It is then splashed with full-bodied red wine and covered with stock. The rice is mixed in and then the rest of the stock is added, little by little, in the usual risotto way. The risotto is MANTECATO at the end with butter and Parmesan, and sprinkled with chopped parsley.

risotto
rice dish

Until the 19th century rice was mainly eaten in soups. Giovanni VIALARDI, chef to the first king of Italy, wrote a recipe which he called *risotto alla piemontese* in which the rice is cooked in stock with equal quantities of butter, cheese and sliced white truffles. Risotto as we know it now must have become popular at just about that time (about 1850), because ARTUSI gives 13 recipes, most of which are now regarded as classics. It is

CONTINUES OVERLEAF

risotto in bianco
basic risotto

Serves 4–6

1.2 litres/2 pints/5 cups light meat stock (page 61) or vegetable stock

50g/1 ¾oz/4 tbsp unsalted butter

1 small onion, very finely chopped

300g/10½oz/1 ½ cups risotto rice, preferably Arborio or Carnaroli (see note)

salt and freshly ground black pepper (optional)

50g/1 ¾oz Parmesan cheese, grated, plus extra to serve

This is the RISOTTO on which slivers of white truffle are showered when they are in season, and the one that, with RISOTTO ALLA MILANESE, can accompany OSSOBUCO ALLA MILANESE (page 256) and *costolette alla milanese* (page 210).

Bring the stock to a gentle simmer.

Meanwhile, heat half the butter in a fairly large, heavy saucepan, add the onion and sauté for about 15 minutes, stirring very frequently and adding a little water so that the onion does not brown.

Add the rice to the pan and stir until well coated with the butter. Cook, stirring constantly with a wooden spoon, until the outside of the grains becomes translucent and the rice begins to stick to the bottom of the pan.

Now pour over about 150ml/5fl oz/²⁄₃ cup of the hot stock. Stirring constantly, let the rice absorb the stock and then add another ladleful. Continue to add stock gradually and in small quantities, so that the rice always cooks in liquid but is never drowned by it. Stir constantly at first; after that you need to stir frequently but not all the time. The heat should be moderate, so that the rice cooks steadily at a lively simmer. If you run out of stock before the rice is cooked, add boiling water.

When the rice is cooked (good rice takes at least 18 minutes), take the pan off the heat. Taste and add salt, and pepper if you like. Add the rest of the butter, cut into small pieces, and the Parmesan. Put the lid firmly on the pan and leave for 1–2 minutes until the butter and the Parmesan have melted.

Give the risotto a vigorous stir and serve at once, with more Parmesan handed separately.

NOTE: This is the most versatile of all risotti. It is excellent by itself, but it can also have vegetables, fish, sausage or roasted chicken added to it, thus changing its flavour and appearance. The variety of rice used should vary according to the recipe, and so should the stock. For a vegetable risotto use Vialone Nano rice and vegetable stock; if you want a fish risotto, use Carnaroli rice and fish stock; for a RISOTTO ALLA MILANESE or a risotto with sausage or chicken, you can use Arborio or Carnaroli.

357

in northern Italy that risotto holds sway, mainly in Piedmont, Lombardy and Veneto.

Risotto is made according to a well-defined method and is not just a rice dish containing many other ingredients. Risotto is always made with long-grain Italian rice of the *fino* or *superfino* type (see RISO), which absorbs the liquid in which it is cooked without breaking or becoming mushy.

The basic method of making a plain risotto, called *risotto in bianco*, or *risotto alla parmigiana*, is given here.

Many risotti became popular in the 1930s, such as *risotto agli asparagi* (with asparagus), *risotto coi carciofi* (with artichokes) and *risotto alla pescatora* (with seafood), while other risotti have been created comparatively recently, such as the risotto with fish (see recipe below), or have been given new popularity, such as the risotto alla PAESANA, 'country-style risotto', with seasonal vegetables (recipe on page 261).

[see recipes on pages 357, 358 and 359]

risotto al branzino
risotto with sea bass

Serves 3–4

2 tbsp extra virgin olive oil

1 garlic clove, bruised

100g/3½oz skinless sea bass fillet, cut into small pieces

salt and freshly ground black pepper

1 tsp sweet paprika

5 tbsp dry sherry

2 tbsp brandy

1 litre/1¾ pints/4 cups fish stock

4 tsp olive oil

50g/1¾oz/4 tbsp unsalted butter

½ onion, sliced

250g/9oz/generous 1¼ cups risotto rice, preferably Carnaroli

2 tbsp dry white wine

a few leaves of fresh flat-leaf parsley

Of all the modern RISOTTI, this is one of the most successful. The sea bass gives the risotto a very delicate but delicious fish flavour. This recipe is adapted from that by a great Italian chef, Angelo Paracucchi, who died in 2004, but whose restaurant in the hills behind La Spezia, on the Ligurian coast, is still a place of pilgrimage for many gourmets.

Heat the extra virgin olive oil with the garlic in a frying pan over a moderate heat and add the fish. Season with salt, pepper and paprika, splash with the sherry and brandy and add a couple of tablespoons of the fish stock. Stir, remove the garlic and set aside.

Put the fish stock in a saucepan, bring to the boil and keep it at a very gentle simmer.

Heat the olive oil, half the butter and the onion in a heavy saucepan. Sauté gently for a few minutes, until the onion is soft but not brown, then stir in the rice and cook over a lively heat for a minute or two.

Add the wine and let it evaporate. Now pour over about 150ml/5fl oz/ ⅔ cup of the hot stock. Stirring constantly, let the rice absorb the stock and then add another ladleful. Continue to add stock gradually and in small quantities, stirring constantly at first, and then stirring frequently. The risotto should cook at a steady, lively simmer.

After cooking the rice for 12 minutes, stir in the sea bass with its sauce.

When the rice is done (after about 18–20 minutes), take the pan off the heat and leave for a few moments, then mix in the remaining butter. Garnish with parsley and serve immediately.

risotto alla certosina
rice with shrimps and frogs

This delicious risotto is said to have been created by the monks of the famous Certosa di Pavia who were only permitted to eat meat on Sundays. To sustain themselves during the rest of the week they created nourishing dishes with the shrimps and frogs caught in nearby rivers. A stock is made with these and then the rice, sautéed in a light SOFFRITTO of butter, onion, carrot and celery leaves, is cooked with the peas in the stock. The shrimps and frogs are added 5 minutes before the rice is ready. Some cooks also add tomatoes, obviously a later addition, and others add mushrooms.

risotto alla milanese
risotto with saffron

The only risotto that claims a date of origin, by virtue of a legend. In 15th-century Milan it became very fashionable to give food the semblance of containing gold, as gold was believed to have health-giving properties. In 1574, the daughter of the craftsman in charge of making the stained glass for the windows of the Duomo was getting married. One of the apprentices, who had a passion for adding saffron to the molten glass, hit on the idea of making the plain risotto for the wedding dinner turn gold like his windows. He

CONTINUES OVERLEAF

risotto alla milanese
risotto with saffron

Serves 4
1 litre/1 ¾ pints/4 cups meat stock
*   (page 61) or chicken stock*
85g/3oz/6 tbsp unsalted butter
1 shallot or ½ small onion, finely
*   chopped*
350g/12oz/1 ¾ cups risotto rice,
*   preferably Carnaroli*
6 tbsp red wine
1 small sachet of saffron powder or
*   ½ tsp saffron strands, pounded*
salt and freshly ground black pepper
50g/1 ¾oz Parmesan cheese, grated

In the old days beef bone marrow was used to add flavour to risotto alla milanese; it has a delicate yet deeply rich flavour that is particularly well suited to this risotto. You can use white wine instead of red if you prefer; the colour will be less deep and the flavour lighter.

Bring the stock to simmering point and keep it at a very gentle simmer.

Heat 50g/1 ¾oz/4 tbsp of the butter in a heavy saucepan, add the shallot and sauté until soft and translucent. Add the rice and stir until well coated with fat. Pour in the wine, boil for 2 minutes, stirring constantly, and then pour in 200ml/7fl oz/generous ¾ cup of the hot stock. Stirring constantly, cook until nearly all the stock has been absorbed and then add another 150ml/5fl oz/⅔ cup of the stock. Continue to add stock gradually and in small quantities, stirring constantly at first, and then stirring frequently. The risotto should cook at a steady, lively simmer.

About halfway through cooking (risotto takes about 18–20 minutes to cook), add the saffron dissolved in a little hot stock. When the rice is ready – it should be soft and creamy, not mushy or runny – taste and adjust the seasoning.

Take the pan off the heat and mix in the rest of the butter and 2 tablespoons of the Parmesan. Leave to rest for a minute or two and then serve, with the rest of the Parmesan handed separately.

gave some saffron to the host of the inn where the dinner was to take place and asked him to mix it into the risotto. The result was a most beautiful golden risotto.

Legend aside, Massimo ALBERINI, in his book *Storia del pranzo all'Italiana*, suggests that its origins lie in the East, and that it reached northern Italy via Sicily. This would explain the description *'alla siciliana'* which MESSISBUGO uses for a risotto appearing on the menu of a dinner given in 1543; it is very similar to risotto alla milanese, since saffron is added at the end. A recipe for this risotto, just as it is made now, was written by LURASCHI, who uses veal bone marrow and adds CERVELLATA, a Milanese sausage, halfway through the cooking.

The saffron used nowadays is usually powdered saffron from crocuses cultivated in Abruzzo, which is of the highest quality. If saffron strands are used they should first be gently pounded in greaseproof paper. At the end the risotto must be *all'onda*, which means that the grains should be separate yet bound together in a creamy consistency.

Arguments over how to make a perfect risotto alla milanese are endless. I give here my family's recipe, which is as good as any – and better than most. You can make slight changes to the ingredients but not to the basic method. It is important to use good stock that contains the right amount of salt.

Risotto alla milanese or *risotto in bianco* are the only risotti that are sometimes served as an accompaniment. By tradition they are served with OSSOBUCHI, MESSICANI and *costolette alla milanese*.

 [see recipe on page 359]

risotto nero
black risotto

Venice has given us the best risotto recipes, especially those that include fish. Risotto nero, called *risotto de sepie* in Venetian dialect, is rice

and cuttlefish. If these are the small *seppioline* they are left whole, otherwise they are cut in strips. Either way, they are first sautéed in an oil SOFFRITTO flavoured with garlic, onion and parsley and then cooked slowly in wine and, if necessary, a little water. The ink from the cuttlefish is mixed in and cooked for a couple of minutes, followed by the rice, to which fish stock is added gradually in the usual way. Some cooks add a couple of tablespoons of tomato sauce after the rice, but this is not included in the original recipe, which certainly pre-dates tomatoes.

robiola
a cheese

A cheese produced in Piedmont and Lombardy in many different shapes and weights. It is one of the oldest cheeses and, oddly enough, it used to be made by women – cheesemaking in Italy is traditionally a man's work. Many, if not all, industrial robiole are made with cow's milk, while the artisanal cheeses made in Piedmont are made with goat's or ewe's milk or a mixture, sometimes with added cow's milk. When fresh, after 3–8 days' ageing, robiola is quite runny and has a delicate buttery taste; when aged, up to 50 days, it is dry with a pronounced tangy flavour, at times reminiscent of truffles.

The best-known robiole are those of Le Langhe in the province of Asti in Piedmont and those of the Valsassina, an Alpine valley in the province of Lecco, Lombardy. The latter is a cow's milk cheese and it is usually eaten aged, when its taste becomes similar to TALEGGIO.

But the really outstanding robiola is the Robiola di Roccaverano, from Piedmont, the only robiola with a DOP mark. This is made with the whole milk of the local goats, sometimes mixed with cow's or ewe's milk. It is said to be at its best in October and November, during the goats' mating season. It can be eaten after 2–3 days, when it has a complex flavour of different herbs mixed with a delicious tinge of goatiness; it becomes more complex with ageing – up to 20 days. There is a Slow Food Presidium to protect the production of this cheese, which is the only Italian goat cheese which can compete with the best French *chèvre*. The robiole are made in small shapes in neighbouring dairies and then taken to the Presidium, where they are salted and aged. Robiola di Roccaverano is one of the greatest Italian cheeses.

rognone
kidney

The most popuar kidneys are those of a calf. Lamb and pig kidneys are also eaten, usually after being covered with salt to disgorge the liquid.

Rome has more recipes for kidneys than any other region, as it does for all offal. The kidneys, calf's or lamb's, are peeled, cored and sliced, and then quickly cooked in oil and butter and splashed with Marsala. They are also, when cooked, combined with sliced mushrooms sautéed in butter and flavoured with lemon juice. In Emilia the kidneys are splashed with balsamic vinegar or cooked as in the recipe given here.

Kidneys were ignored by the great cooks of the past, many of whom wrote recipes for liver, sweetbreads, brains, ears and lights (lungs). Ada BONI wrote a few recipes for calf's kidneys, plus one for ox kidneys and one for pig's. She suggests putting these last two in cold acidulated water, heating the water until hot but not boiling and then draining them. This operation has to be repeated three times before cooking the kidneys. In both recipes they are cooked in wine and tomato sauce. Marcella Hazan also treats lamb's kidneys before cooking by soaking them for 30 minutes in acidulated water.

[see recipe below]

rognoncini trifolati all'acciuga e limone
lambs' kidneys with anchovies and lemon

Serves 4
500g/1lb 2oz lamb's kidneys
2 tbsp wine vinegar
40g/1½oz/3 tbsp unsalted butter,
  softened
1 tbsp flour
2 salted anchovies, boned, rinsed and
  chopped, or 4 canned or bottled
  anchovy fillets, drained and chopped
3 tbsp extra virgin olive oil
1 garlic clove, finely chopped
salt and freshly ground black pepper
1 tbsp chopped fresh flat-leaf parsley
2 tsp lemon juice

Rognoncini denote small ROGNONI – and indeed lamb's kidneys are much smaller than those of a calf.

Split the kidneys in half lengthways and remove and discard the cores. Rinse the kidneys briefly, then put them in a bowl and cover with cold water. Add the vinegar and leave to soak for at least 30 minutes. Drain.

Mash together the butter, flour and anchovies. Set aside.

Heat the olive oil with the garlic in a frying pan over a medium-high heat, add the kidneys and sauté until they begin to change colour, which will only take a few minutes. It is important not to overcook them or they will become tough.

Reduce the heat and add the anchovy mixture very gradually, stirring constantly. Taste and adjust the seasoning. Cook for 1 minute. Turn off the heat, add the parsley and lemon juice and serve.

rombo
turbot or brill

The best Mediterranean rombi – flat fish with a rhomboid shape – are the *rombola* or *rombo liscio* (brill), and the *rombo* or *rombo chiodato* (turbot).

PLATINA wrote that rombo appeared only on the tables of princes. He suggests boiling the turbot over a very low heat and 'in a basket', to prevent it from breaking. Bartolomeo SCAPPI declares turbot the best of the flat fish.

There is an interesting recipe by LEONARDI called *rombo alla lombarda*, in which the turbot is baked between two layers of a buttery SOFFRITTO of onion, parsley, shallot, garlic and salted anchovy moistened with meat gravy.

Turbot is usually cooked in the simplest ways, usually with butter, with which it seems to have a special affinity. As in France, where turbot is more popular, the fish is often seasoned with tarragon, a herb rarely used in Italian cooking. In the simplest and most popular recipe, the floured fillets of turbot are gently fried in butter for about 5 minutes. When cooked, a little sauce made with melted butter, anchovy fillets, capers and lemon juice is spooned over the fish, which is sprinkled with chopped parsley, sometimes mixed with a little tarragon.

rosetta

see MICHETTA

rosmarino
rosemary

A perennial bush that grows wild near the sea. Its name, in fact, means 'sea dew', *ros* being the Latin for dew.

In the Middle Ages rosemary was considered almost miraculous since it possessed no less than 26 health-giving properties. In addition: 'If you would keep your face beautiful and clear, take rosmarino and boil its leaves in pure white wine and wash it.' And 'if you put rosmarino leaves under your bed, it will keep you from evil dreams.' And finally 'if you plant rosmarino in your garden or vineyard or orchard, your vines and fruit will grow in great abundance and it will delight your eyes when they fall upon it.' These are passages from a French medical treatise, translated into Italian in 1310 by a Tuscan notary and quoted by Iris Origo in *The Merchant of Prato*.

The main use of rosemary is in roasting meat. When a piece of meat or a bird is roasted on the spit, it is brushed with a sprig of rosemary dipped in olive oil. In northern and central Italy, where it is more popular than in the south, it is always added to roast potatoes. It is also used for a SOFFRITTO with garlic, and sometimes chilli, to add to bean soups.

rosolare
cooking method

A common method of cooking. When the BATTUTO (chopped mixture) is put on the heat with butter and/or oil, it is *rosolato* (sautéed) to make a SOFFRITTO, the starting point for most Italian dishes. Meat and vegetables are sautéed to bring out the flavour. It is a process that requires patience and care. The cook has to give constant attention to what is in the pan, watching over it and stirring it until it is done.

rosticiana or rostisciada
pork and onion dish

A dish from Milan that used to be a Sunday dish or one with which to celebrate the three harvests: of the silk cocoons, wheat and grapes.

 [see recipe on facing page]

rosticiana
sausages, pork and onions

Serves 4
500g/1lb 2oz onions, finely sliced
40g/1½oz/3 tbsp unsalted butter
salt and freshly ground black pepper
500g/1lb 2oz luganega sausages
1 tbsp olive oil
200g/7oz pork steak from the shoulder
or leg, thickly sliced
100ml/3½fl oz/scant ½ cup red wine

This recipe is from *La Lombardia in Cucina* by Ottorina Perna Bozzi, who points to the fact that it contains no tomatoes as proof that this is a very old recipe. Nowadays it is always served with POLENTA.

Cook the onions in the butter with 1 teaspoon of salt over a gentle heat for about 30 minutes, until they soften and begin to turn gold. Stir very often and add a tablespoon of water if necessary, to prevent burning.

Meanwhile, in a cast-iron frying pan, cook the sausages quickly in the olive oil until well browned all over. Remove the sausages to a board. Add the pork to the pan, cook for 2 minutes on each side, then remove to the board. Cut the sausages and pork into chunks and then return them to the pan. Pour over the wine and let it bubble away for 1 or 2 minutes.

Add the sausages and pork to the onions. Pour about 6 tablespoons water into the frying pan in which the meat was cooked and boil to deglaze, stirring and scraping the bottom of the pan to release the bits. Spoon these cooking juices over the onion and sausage mixture, cover with a lid and cook over a very gentle heat for 10 minutes.

Add pepper to taste and check the salt before serving. Serve very hot.

rotolo
a roll

This usually refers to a pasta dish. A sheet of pasta is rolled out thinly and spread with Swiss chard or spinach, RICOTTA and Parmesan, to which prosciutto, mushrooms or other ingredients may be added. The pasta is rolled up, wrapped in cloth and cooked for 30 minutes in simmering salted water. Instead of pasta, the dough can be a potato dough, for which the recipe is given here.

Rotolo can also refer to a meat roll: a thin slice of meat (usually veal) is covered with ingredients such as prosciutto, thin FRITTATA, cheese and, when rolled and tied, is cooked in butter and wine.

 [see recipe on page 364]

ruchetta
wild rocket

This is quite common in central Italy, where it is used as part of the MISTICANZA salad. It has a pungent flavour similar to cultivated rocket but much stronger.

rucola
rocket

This has a delightfully pungent flavour which makes any salad far more pleasurable. Only one traditional recipe uses rocket, a pasta sauce from Puglia, in which parboiled rocket is sautéed in olive oil with garlic and anchovy fillets. The pasta, cooked in the rocket water, is then layered with the rocket with a generous splash of olive oil.

rotolo di patate e spinaci
potato and spinach roll

364

Serves 6

*500g/1lb 2oz old floury (starchy)
   potatoes, scrubbed*

salt and freshly ground black pepper

1 onion, very finely chopped

1 tbsp olive oil

*1kg/2¼lb spinach, cooked and chopped,
   or 500g/1lb 2oz frozen chopped
   spinach, thawed and well drained*

100g/3½oz ricotta

100g/3½oz Parmesan cheese, grated

a grating of nutmeg

1 large egg yolk

1 large egg

1 tsp baking powder

200g/7oz Italian 00 flour

200g/7oz best cooked ham, thinly sliced

75g/2¾oz/5 tbsp unsalted butter

I have always found that my mother's recipe for *rotolo di spinaci* made with potato dough is much nicer and easier than the traditional method, which uses homemade pasta. Instead of dressing it with butter and Parmesan before browning it in the oven, you may prefer to cover it with a béchamel sauce flavoured with plenty of Parmesan and a grating of nutmeg.

Boil the potatoes in their skins in plenty of lightly salted water for about 20 minutes, until tender.

While the potatoes are cooking, prepare the filling. Sauté the onion in the olive oil for 2–3 minutes until soft. Add the spinach and cook for a further 2 minutes, stirring frequently. Transfer the spinach to a bowl and add the ricotta, half the Parmesan, the nutmeg, egg yolk and salt and pepper. Mix very thoroughly.

Drain the potatoes, peel them as soon as they are cool enough to handle, then push them through a food mill or potato ricer directly onto the work surface. Make a well in the middle of the potatoes, break in the whole egg and add a little salt, the baking powder and most of the flour. Knead for about 5 minutes, adding more flour if necessary. You might not need to add all the flour; it depends on the potatoes. The dough should be soft, smooth and slightly sticky. Shape the mixture into a ball.

Roll out the potato dough into a 35 x 25cm/14 x 10in rectangle. Cover it with the ham and then spread the spinach filling over it, leaving a 1cm/½in border all round. Roll the potato dough into a large salami shape and then wrap the roll tightly in muslin or cheesecloth and tie both ends securely with string.

Fill a fish kettle, or another long deep pan that can hold the rotolo, with water. Add 1 tablespoon salt and bring to the boil, then gently lower the roll into the water. Bring the water back to the boil and then cook, partially covered, for 30 minutes.

Carefully lift the roll out of the water, place on a board, unwrap it and leave to cool.

Preheat the oven to 200°C/400°F/Gas Mark 6.

When cold, cut the roll into 2cm/¾in thick slices and place them, slightly overlapping, in a warmed, buttered ovenproof dish. Melt the butter, pour it over the slices and sprinkle with the remaining Parmesan. Bake for about 15 minutes, until golden.

S

sagne chine
stuffed lasagne

The Calabrese dialect name for *lasagne ripiene* –
stuffed lasagne. This is a dish for grand occasions.
The lasagne are layered with tiny balls of minced
veal, sliced hard-boiled eggs, sliced SCAMORZA,
MOZZARELLA and PECORINO, all dressed with a rich
tomato sauce. During the spring, young peas or
artichokes are added to the layers.

salama da sugo
a cured sausage

Salama is made from fat and lean minced pork,
minced calf's and pig's livers, and ox's or pig's
tongue cut into small pieces, all flavoured with
spices and a full-bodied red wine. The mixture is
pushed into a casing made from the bladder of a
pig, and shaped like a small melon. It is dried in
a hot room for 3–4 days and then cured for 6 or
7 months. Salama is hand-made and produced
on a small scale, rather than industrially. It is
sold uncooked, and has to be gently boiled for
at least 4 hours, in a way that prevents it from
touching the bottom of the pot. It is served with
mashed potatoes and mashed pumpkin. It is the
most famous dish of Ferrara, the symbol of the
gastronomy of the city.

salame
salami

A cured meat product, consisting of minced or
chopped pork, or pork and beef, flavoured with
spices and herbs, well seasoned and pushed into
natural or artificial casings, and aged. Salame
is made all over Italy in various sizes and
with different flavours, including garlic, wine,
peppercorns, fennel and chilli. There are also
excellent salami made from *cinghiale,* wild boar, or
meticcio, a boar/pig hybrid, a speciality of Tuscany
and Umbria.

The following is only a short list of the most
popular salami, but in every town, or even village,
you will find *salame nostrano* (local salame) usually
excellent and representative of the local food.

Salame felino is the most delicate of all salami.
It is made near Parma, using the same large pigs
from which PROSCIUTTO is made. It contains only
20% fat, and is flavoured only with a little garlic
and white wine.

Salame milano is a delicate-tasting salame, made
with finely minced lean pork meat with tiny specks
of fat and flavoured with a little garlic and white
wine. The other well-known Lombard salame
is that of Varzi, which has the same flavouring
as Milano, but red wine instead of white. It is a
delicious salame, made on a relatively small scale.

Salame toscano, Tuscan salami, also called
FINOCCHIONA, is a robust salame flavoured with
fennel seeds and plenty of garlic.

Salame di Fabriano, from Le Marche, is the best
salame of central Italy. The lean pork meat is
coarsely minced, surrounding white cubes of pure
pork back fat, richly flavoured with peppercorns
and garlic.

Salame di Napoli is the only well-known salame
of southern Italy. The coarsely minced meat is
flavoured with chilli, as indeed are all the locally
made salami in the south.

Salame d'oca (goose salame) is made in some
parts of Piedmont and in Friuli. It is made with

365

minced goose meat, plus the usual seasonings and, often, MARSALA and stuffed into the goose's neck. Salame d'oca and *prosciutto d'oca* are traditional foods of Italian Jews.

salatini
savoury biscuits

The generic word for small savoury biscuits of the kind that are served with an aperitif. They are mostly made with puff pastry and flavoured with cheese, cumin seeds, fennel or herbs. Salatini are usually bought loose in patisseries or bakers' shops.

sale
salt

Ninety per cent of Italian salt is sea salt, obtained by the evaporation of sea water. The biggest salt works are in Sicily, which has been the source of much of Italy's salt for a long time.

Two grades of salt are sold: *sale grosso* (coarse, or crystals) and *sale fino* (fine). Sale grosso is used in the water in which pasta, rice or vegetables are boiled and in the curing of meat. It is also used to create the same effect as wrapping food in clay: a fish or chicken is laid on sale grosso and totally covered in the salt before being baked at a high temperature. The salt forms a crust and seals in all the juices of the fish or bird. A recipe for a fish cooked this way is given here. Sale fino dissolves more quickly and is used at table or in the kitchen in sauces and other preparations.

Salt is always added during cooking because it is only when heated that it dissolves evenly, and thus brings out the flavour of the food more effectively. Pasta cooked without the right amount of salt will be very noticeably lacking in flavour, especially if dressed with a delicate sauce.

Salt is used for preserving anchovies, for preparing BOTTARGA and MOSCIAME, in the making of all SALUMI and for preserving many vegetables.

Capers, for instance, are much better preserved in salt than under vinegar, which slightly alters their flavour. Basil and other herbs can be preserved in layers of coarse salt.

Salt was so important in Roman times that a road was built for transporting it from the Adriatic coast to Rome, the Via Salaria. The Venetians were quick to realize that they could draw wealth from the sea and very early in their history built *'saline'* (salt works) in and around the lagoon. Indeed, salt was the foundation of their wealth, which was later augmented by pepper and other spices.

 [see recipe on facing page]

salmì
cooking method

'In salmì' is an ancient method of cooking game, particularly hare or rabbit, favoured in northern Italy. The meat is usually marinated in wine with vegetables and spices, and then the marinade is used for cooking the meat over a low heat for several hours. In Piedmont it is called *civet*, or *cive*. In Venezia Giulia it is most likely to be venison that is cooked in salmi, and in Umbria wood pigeons are cooked in salmi without being marinated. Hare or rabbit in salmì is always accompanied by POLENTA.

[see recipe on page 368]

salmoriglio
dressing for fish or meat

A Calabrese and Sicilian dressing for grilled fish or, more rarely, for meat. The fish is usually swordfish or tuna and the meat is often CASTRATO, lamb or kid.

Salmoriglio is a mixture of extra virgin olive oil, lemon juice, oregano, parsley, salt and garlic which is poured over the fish or meat. Some connoisseurs claim that one or two teaspoons of sea water added to the salmoriglio, when it is used to dress fish, transforms a fairly ordinary dressing into a superlative experience for the palate.

salsa
sauce

An Italian salsa is either a juice derived in part from the main ingredient being cooked, or a separate preparation, or relish, to enhance the flavour of a dish. On its own the word 'salsa' always refers to salsa di POMODORO (tomato sauce).

The greatest use of sauces in traditional cooking is for dressing pasta, rice or POLENTA. Apart from as a dressing to these three staples, sauces are not used a great deal in Italian cooking. A roast will be served with only the defatted and deglazed meat juices. Even pasta is coated by sauce, not drowned in it.

Sauces once played an important role in the cooking of grand households. Going back to Roman times, APICIUS includes recipes for sauces made with spices or herbs and/or nuts, and/ or fruits, diluted with verjuice and oil. In the Renaissance, sauces were thickened with pounded almonds, breadcrumbs and, sometimes, egg yolks.

salsa verde
green sauce

A sauce from northern Italy for BOLLITO MISTO, other LESSI, boiled fish and hard-boiled eggs. This is an ancient sauce, the development of which is particularly well documented.

Salsa verde first appears under this name in the 14th century, in *Libro per Cuoco* by an

CONTINUES ON PAGE 370

dentice al sale
dentex baked in a crust of salt

Serves 4
1 sea bream (with head and tail left on), about 1kg/2¼lb
3kg/6½lb coarse sea salt

DENTICE is an excellent fish from the sea bream family and this is an excellent way to cook it — the crust of salt (SALE) preserves the full flavour of the fish. Any fairly large white fish such a sea bass can be cooked in the same way. This is my translation of a recipe in *La Cucina d'Oro*, edited by Giovanni Nuvoletti in association with the ACCADEMIA ITALIANA DELLA CUCINA.

Preheat the oven to 200°C/400°F/Gas Mark 6. Pat the fish dry, inside and out.

Spread a 2cm/¾in thick layer of salt on the bottom of a roasting pan. Lay the fish on top and cover with the remaining salt, patting it into the fish.

Bake for at least 1 hour. To test if the fish is cooked, break a little bit of the salt crust along the spine of the fish and pull out a fin. If the fin comes away easily with its bones, then the fish is ready.

Serve the fish in its salt crust and break it open at the table. The scales will come away together with the salt. Serve with mild extra virgin olive oil and lemon juice as the only accompaniments.

lepre in salmì
jugged hare

Serves 6

1 hare (jack rabbit), about
2–2.5kg/4½–5½lb, cut into
smallish pieces

75g/2¾oz/5 tbsp unsalted butter

50g/1¾oz unsmoked pancetta, cubed

1 onion, very finely chopped

1 tbsp flour

the liver, heart, lungs and blood of the
hare, chopped, or 200g/7oz pig's
liver, chopped

25g/1oz dark chocolate, grated

salt and freshly ground black pepper

200ml/7fl oz/generous ¾ cup double
(heavy) cream

Marinade

1 bottle of Barbera or other strong red
Piedmontese wine

2 sprigs of fresh thyme

2 sprigs of fresh rosemary

1 large onion, cut into pieces

2 garlic cloves, cut into pieces

1 celery stalk, cut into pieces

4 bay leaves

6 fresh sage leaves

2 cloves

a grating of nutmeg

1 cinnamon stick

5 juniper berries, bruised

1 tsp coarse sea salt

6 black peppercorns, crushed

In my Milanese home, a little grated chocolate was always added to this quintessentially Lombard dish. To be truly authentic the SALMÌ should also contain the liver, heart, lungs and blood of the hare.

Wash the pieces of hare and dry them thoroughly. Put them in a large bowl and add the wine and all the other marinade ingredients. Cover and leave in a cold place, but not in the refrigerator, for about 24 hours.

Remove the hare from the marinade; reserve the marinade. Dry the pieces thoroughly. Heat the butter and pancetta in a heavy saucepan. Add the onion and sauté until golden. Add the hare and brown very well on all sides, then sprinkle the flour over it and cook for about 5 minutes, turning the pieces over and over.

Cover with the marinade and add the offal and the blood, the chocolate and some salt and pepper. Cover the pot and cook slowly, over a very low heat, until the meat is tender. This could take 2 hours for a young animal, or up to 4 hours for an older one.

Transfer the hare to a warmed serving dish and keep warm. Remove the cinnamon and woody bits of herbs from the sauce and then puree the sauce through a food mill or in a food processor. Return it to the pan and mix in the cream, then return the hare to the pan and cook gently for 5 minutes for a final blending of flavours. Taste and adjust the seasoning.

Serve with soft polenta, perfect for the rich, gamey juices.

NOTE: If you prefer, you can cook the hare in the oven, preheated to 160°C/325°F/Gas Mark 3, for the same amount of time.

salsa verde
green sauce

Enough for 4–6 servings

25g/1oz/½ cup fresh white breadcrumbs

2 tsp red wine vinegar

1 small garlic clove

40g/1½oz fresh flat-leaf parsley

2 tbsp capers, preferably in salt, rinsed

*6 cornichons (if unobtainable, use an
    extra 1 tbsp capers)*

1 large egg, hard-boiled

*3 salted anchovies, boned and rinsed, or
    6 canned or bottled anchovy fillets,
    drained*

1–2 tsp Dijon mustard (optional)

*150–200ml/5–7fl oz/⅔–¾ cup extra
    virgin olive oil*

salt and freshly ground black pepper

I make a different SALSA VERDE acccording to what it has to accompany and what is best in my herb border (rocket or mint, basil, dill or tarragon). Sometimes I substitute a boiled potato for the bread, or I may omit the hard-boiled egg and add a raw egg yolk instead. This recipe is a guide, beyond which you can discover your own favourite version, always bearing in mind that a salsa verde made with lemon is best for fish, while for meat – such as a BOLLITO – it should contain vinegar. Dijon mustard is not used in the old, traditional salsa verde, but I like a little bit of it.

Put the breadcrumbs in a bowl and pour the vinegar over them. Set aside.

Peel the garlic, cut it in half and remove the green central core if necessary. The core has a pungent, rather than sweet, flavour.

Put the parsley, capers, cornichons, hard-boiled egg, anchovies and garlic together on a board and chop them very finely. Put this mixture into another bowl. Add the bread to the parsley mixture, working it in with a fork. Add the mustard, if using, and then gradually add the olive oil, beating the whole time, until the sauce has reached the consistency you like. Season with pepper, taste and add salt if necessary: the anchovies and capers may have given enough salt to the sauce. You might like to add a little more vinegar – it depends on the strength of your vinegar and how you like the sauce.

NOTE: The sauce can be made in a food processor, but do not overprocess it – the parsley should be in small pieces.

369

anonymous Venetian writer. The title of the recipe is 'Green sauce for kid and other boiled food' and it reads: 'Take parsley and ginger and clove and cinnamon and a little salt and pound everything and dilute with good vinegar; make it all well diluted and do not leave too long or it will spoil.' MARTINO da Como introduces garlic 'if liked'. Bartolomeo SCAPPI's recipe is nearer to that of today, with fewer spices and the introduction of toasted bread. Scappi uses parsley, sorrel, spinach tops, a little mint and rocket, which sounds a very good mixture.

ARTUSI's salsa verde has been the model for all subsequent versions. He uses parsley and a few leaves of basil, salted anchovy, capers, a little onion and even less garlic, everything diluted with 'olio fine' – a delicate oil – and lemon juice. This is the basic salsa verde, to which some cooks add a small amount of boiled and mashed potatoes, one or two yolks of hard-boiled egg or some fresh breadcrumbs, previously soaked in water or light stock, and a little mustard.

[see recipe on page 369]

salsiccia
sausage

One of the staples of peasant food, sausages are made all over Italy, from the mild *corda de Monscia* (also known as LUGANEGA di Monza) in Lombardy to the highly prized *salsiccia calabrese*, generously spiced with chilli, from Calabria.

The classic salsiccia is made with coarsely minced pork meat, of which two-thirds is lean and one-third fat. The meat is usually from the poorest cuts of the animal, such as the throat and belly. Different flavourings are added to the meat mixture according to local practice, for instance GRANA in Lombardy, Parmesan in Emilia and chilli or fennel seeds in the south. Salsicce, in the north, are mostly sold fresh and then cooked in different ways, while in central and southern Italy

salsicce are also cured and eaten cold, without further cooking.

Although the classic salsiccia is made with pork, some are made with other meats. The best known of these are the *salsiccia di bufalo*, containing buffalo meat mixed with turkey and pork fat, and the *salsicce di Napoli*, also called *salamelle*, a combination of pork and beef, plus garlic and chilli. Very popular are the *salsicce di fegato* – liver sausages – which are usually highly spiced.

The regional array of salsicce and *salsicciotti* and the even longer list of names that indicates different or very similar products is endless. For instance the luganega of Monza in Lombardy is different from the luganega of Treviso in Veneto and from the luganega of Basilicata, where the sausage originated.

Salsicce are cooked in so many ways that it would be impossible to list even only the most popular ones. The salsiccia with broccoli of Lazio is a classic, the sausage being fried in a little oil flavoured with garlic, and the broccoli added 5–10 minutes later. The dish is finished over a gentle heat with the addition of a couple of tablespoons of dry white wine and water. In Calabria a similar dish is made with CIME DI RAPA and chilli, while in Veneto salsicce are sautéed with onion and garlic, then splashed with red wine vinegar and served with POLENTA.

When I cook salsicce I fry them first, splash them with red wine and then cook them in tomato sauce and serve them with polenta. Alternatively, I follow ARTUSI's excellent recipe for *salsiccia colle uova*. Fresh sausage is cut in half lengthways and cooked without any fat. As soon as it is ready, beaten eggs are added and the dish is served when the eggs are set. A delicious FRITTATA.

saltimbocca alla romana
veal rolls

Serves 4
150g/5½oz prosciutto, very thinly sliced
8 veal escalopes, 60–70g/about 2¼oz
  each
8 fresh sage leaves
flour, for dusting
salt and freshly ground black pepper
1 tbsp olive oil
50g/1¾oz/4 tbsp unsalted butter
100ml/3½fl oz/scant ½ cup dry white
  wine

So delicious is this dish that it 'leaps into the mouth', as its name declares. Saltimbocca is a traditional Roman dish, which can be prepared in two ways. The traditional method is to pin a slice of prosciutto and a sage leaf on a thin slice of veal. In the other method, as in *La Buona Vera Cucina Italiana* by CARNACINA and Veronelli, which I prefer because it doesn't dry the prosciutto too much, the veal is rolled.

Place a slice of prosciutto over each veal escalope – the prosciutto should be a little smaller than the veal. Put 1 or 2 sage leaves in the middle and roll the veal to form a neat sausage-like shape. Secure with a wooden toothpick, threading it along the length of the roll, not across. Dredge in the flour mixed with a little salt and pepper.

Heat the olive oil and half the butter in a large frying pan. As soon as the foam begins to subside, put in the meat rolls. Brown on all sides until quite golden, not pale beige.

Heat the wine in a separate saucepan and pour over the saltimbocca. Turn up the heat and bubble the wine away for 1 minute.

Transfer the saltimbocca to a warmed dish, remove the toothpicks and keep warm.

Add a couple of tablespoons of boiling water to the pan, then add the remaining butter a little at a time, swirling the pan around and stirring constantly. Taste and check the seasoning. Pour the sauce over the meat and serve at once.

salto, al
cooking method

A method of cooking, or more precisely of heating up, by shallow frying very quickly in butter or oil, thus making the food jump in the pan, *salto* meaning 'jump'. It is often used for leftover pasta, rice or vegetables.

Risotto al salto is a traditional Milanese dish that used to be served in inns. It was born of the Milanese love for risotto. Travellers, often in a hurry, were not prepared to wait the 25 minutes it takes to make risotto, so the innkeeper kept some *risotto alla milanese* at the ready, which, on request, was *saltato* in a cast-iron frying pan.

salumeria

see PIZZICHERIA

salumi
cured pork products

Salumi is the collective noun for SALAME, PROSCIUTTO, COPPA, COTECHINO and all other products made by curing different kinds of meat in salt. There are two types of salumi, those made from one cut of the animal, such as prosciutto, and those made with minced meat stuffed into a casing, of which salame is the prime example. Salumi of the first type are usually made with cuts of pork, or with pork meat, although a few are made with cuts of beef (such as BRESAOLA), roe deer, wild boar or goat. The other type of salumi are made with a mixture of minced pork, beef and/or wild boar.

salvia
sage

A herb that grows easily in Italy, and is often used in cooking, especially in the north and in Tuscany. It is used to flavour white meat, or for sauces in conjunction with butter, as in the dressing for RAVIOLI and other homemade pasta. Sage is essential to the *fagioli all'uccelletto* of Tuscany (recipe on page 138) and to SALTIMBOCCA, but the dish totally based on sage is SALVIATA.

salviata
sage pudding

A baked egg custard highly flavoured with sage. It is a speciality of Tuscany, where the sage, although not pungent, is full of flavour. It must be young and fresh.

sanato
Piedmontese calf

This is a very prized calf – and, by implication, its meat – that is fed only on its mother's milk and egg yolks for up to 12 months. The veal is almost white, totally lean and very delicate. Sanato is used in a piece for ARROSTO MORTO, in slices for PICCATA with lemon or MARSALA, or cut into very small slices in FINANZIERA, a rich sauce with giblets and truffles.

sanguinaccio
a 'pudding'

In northern Italy this is a black pudding; in the south it is a sweet preparation. Both dishes use the first gift of the slaughtered pig, its *sangue* (blood). This should be used when very fresh; if possible, still warm. Milk is added to the pig's blood plus many spices and – for the savoury pudding – onions, the mixture being cooked and pushed into a casing. The sweet sanguinaccio is rich, creamy and dark, with nuts and chocolate, as in the sanguinaccio from Naples, which contains crème patissière in equal proportions with blood.

sarago
a fish

This is the name given to a few species of sea bream, of which the best are the *sarago maggiore* and the *sarago fasciato* – two-banded bream. They are both excellent fish with firm and delicate white flesh, which is delicious grilled or roasted. Saraghi are also added to fish soups, including the Tuscan CACCIUCCO. But the most interesting recipe for saraghi is a sort of roast on the spit, a speciality of the Tuscan coast. Small saraghi, boned and stuffed with a piece of PROSCIUTTO, are threaded on to a skewer with slices of bread and sage leaves. Moistened with oil, the fish are roasted and basted with the cooking juices mixed with white wine.

sarda or sardina
sardine

In correct culinary terms the first word refers to the fresh fish and the second to the preserved one. Sardines are very popular everywhere. In Venice they are often prepared *'in saor'* – as in the recipe for sole on page 391 – and they are also fried together with tiny artichokes or fennel wedges. In the south, fried sardines are served with a vinaigrette containing mint and lemon rind.

In Puglia one of the best baked dishes is made with boned sardines layered with a mixture of breadcrumbs fried in olive oil, grated PECORINO, garlic and parsley, with beaten eggs poured over the top before baking. In Liguria, sardines are baked in similar layers in a TORTINO *di sarde*. Sicily offers a number of excellent recipes, among them *sarde a beccaficu*, for which the recipe is given here, and the *pasta con le sarde* (see recipe on page 288).

Larger sardines can be stuffed in many different ways. In a recipe from Liguria they are stuffed with lettuce leaves and cheese. In the south they are stuffed with fresh breadcrumbs, egg, pecorino, capers, parsley and other flavourings.

The majority of sardines, though, are preserved in oil, to which lemon juice or tomato are occasionally added. This is still an important industry in Sicily, although now Spain is Europe's main producer of canned sardines.

[see recipe on page 374]

Sardegna
Sardinia

'Lost between Europe and Africa and belonging to nowhere,' wrote D H Lawrence last century, and in my experience it still is. All through the centuries Sardinia has remained very much apart from the mainland, keeping its identity and its cooking untouched. The many invaders – Phoenicians, Romans, Arabs, Catalans and Piedmontese –

SARDINIA

Olbia
Sassari
Nuoro
Bergamo
Oristano
Arborea
Cagliari
Carbonia

influenced only the coastal cooking, teaching the locals different ways to prepare fish. So there is *cassola*, fish stew, of Catalan origin, BURRIDA and *capponata* from Liguria, roasted spiny lobster and BOTTARGA, originally from Sicily. But the locals have always ignored the bounty of their sea and have based their food on the products of the land: artichokes, olives, wild plants and herbs, cheese, pork and lamb or kid, all of them accompanied by bread, which is the fulcrum of family cooking. Two kinds of bread are made only in Sardinia: the *pane civraxiu* and the CARTA DA MUSICA, both of which keep for a long time. Special breads are made for celebrations: shaped like flowers and garlands for weddings, dolls and soldiers for christenings, doves and eggs for Easter and black bread, in the shape of a wreath, for funerals.

According to the ritual that surrounds local cooking, it is the women who are the breadmakers

CONTINUES ON PAGE 376

sarde a beccaficu
baked stuffed sardines

Serves 4
*25g/1oz/2 tbsp sultanas (golden
    raisins)*
1kg/2¼lb fresh sardines
5 tbsp olive oil
*100g/3½oz/2 cups soft white
    breadcrumbs*
25g/1oz/3 tbsp pine nuts
2 garlic cloves, chopped
*2 tbsp capers, preferably in salt, rinsed
    and chopped*
2 tbsp chopped fresh flat-leaf parsley
2 tbsp freshly grated pecorino cheese
salt and freshly ground black pepper
2 tbsp orange juice
4–5 bay leaves, torn

In this well-known Sicilian dish the boned sardines are opened out flat, then rolled up and set in the dish with their tails in the air, making them look like little *beccafichi* (warblers) pecking at the dish.

Preheat the oven to 200°C/400°F/Gas Mark 6. Soak the sultanas in a little hot water while you prepare the fish.

Cut off the heads of the sardines, split them open underneath and clean them. Lay them open side down on a wooden board and press the backbone down gently. Cut the backbone at the tail end and remove it. Wash and dry the sardines.

Heat 3 tablespoons of the olive oil in a frying pan and add the breadcrumbs. Fry them gently until golden and then add the pine nuts, garlic, capers, parsley and the drained sultanas. Mix well and cook for a minute or two. Transfer the mixture to a bowl and mix in the pecorino and salt and pepper to taste.

Sprinkle the sardines on both sides with a little salt and a generous grinding of pepper. Spread a little of the stuffing on the inside of each fish, roll it up from the head end and secure with a wooden toothpick. Place them in an oiled ovenproof dish with their tails sticking up.

Drizzle the rest of the oil over the sardines and sprinkle with the orange juice. Stick the bay leaves here and there, cover with foil and bake in the oven for 20 minutes. They are good warm, at room temperature or cold, but not piping hot or chilled.

(in Italy breadmaking is traditionally man's work, like cheesemaking), while men cook the meat, often, just as they have done for centuries, out-of-doors. The principal method of cooking meat is on the spit. Whether kid, lamb or succulent piglet – *porceddu*, the Sardinian PORCHETTA – the animal is usually roasted whole, in the oven or on the spit, but is sometimes cooked in a way found only in Sardinia – in CARAXIU, in a hole in the ground. This method is thought to have been started by bandits on the run, to avoid being discovered, because it does not produce any smoke. All these roasts are flavoured with local herbs, myrtle and mint being the most common, and of all of them *porceddu* is without any doubt the most celebrated. For special occasions, the most elaborate of all roasts is made. Called *pastu mistu*, it consists of a large animal stuffed with a smaller one, which in turn contains another, and so on.

The island is also rich in game. From wild boar and roebuck and from partridges down to quails, thrushes and blackbirds, they all finish on the spit with rosemary, myrtle and other herbs.

Pork is not only roasted, it is also used to make excellent SALUMI and SALSICCE. The most highly prized is the PROSCIUTTO made from wild boar, which is lean and full of flavour thanks to the animals' habitat. The local sausages are spiced with wild fennel and chilli and flavoured with the local strong vinegar and/or with garlic. Some are aged and eaten raw, while fresh sausages are cut up and used to make a succulent pasta sauce.

The Sardinians learnt the craft of pasta-making from the Genoese, but the dough they use, made with durum wheat SEMOLINO and water, is similar to that made in southern Italy. A particular touch of their own is that they often add a pinch of saffron to the dough. The local MALLOREDDUS are so popular that their shape has now been reproduced in commercial dried pasta, known as *gnocchetti sardi*. CULURZONES or *culingionis* are local ravioli, traditionally dressed with a rich RAGÙ, often made with lamb or kid meat, or tomato sauce. A third

Sardinian pasta speciality is *fregola*, tiny balls of pasta, lightly coloured with saffron, which are cooked in stock or directly in a fish or a meat ragù. Fregola is a cousin of couscous.

Local cheeses have a place of great importance in such a pastoral community. The PECORINO sardo is well known throughout Italy, as well as being exported. Most of the pecorino romano – the aged pecorino used for grating – is actually made here. RICOTTA is prepared either fresh, salted for grating, or smoked; goat's cheeses are also fresh or seasoned. A local cheese worth a mention is *fetta*, which is almost identical to the Greek cheese of the same name. Unfortunately, most of these Sardinian cheeses, pecorino aside, are only found on the island.

In western Sardinia, near Oristano (the centre of BOTTARGA production), some of the land was reclaimed during the 1920s and 30s under the Fascist regime, and there are now wonderful green pastures with herds of cows which produce excellent milk. The butter of Arborea is comparable to the best butters of Lombardy.

Sardinian DOLCI are small, and usually eaten at the end of the meal with a glass or two of sweet wine. Most of them contain ricotta or other cheeses, cooked grape must and the local honey, which is reputedly one of the best in Italy. Many dolci are connected to festivities: *zippulas*, fritters in the shape of long sausages, are for Carnival; *pardulas*, small basket-shaped bread filled with ricotta or FIORE SARDO cheese flavoured with saffron and then doused with honey are the Easter treat; SUSPIRUS are almond macaroons flavoured with lemon, as light as their name implies (suspirus means 'sigh'); *aranzadas* are a sort of soft small nougat made with ground almonds, honey and orange rind and, to finish a list that could go on far longer, *seadas* or *sebadas* are large fried ravioli filled with fresh pecorino and served hot, covered with honey. Like Sicily, Sardinia is a treasure trove of small sweet biscuits and all sorts of sweets.

sartù
rice dish

This is the most sumptuous of all Neapolitan dishes. It consists of a timbale of boiled rice dressed with butter, Parmesan and meat juices, spooned into a charlotte mould, and filled with sautéed tiny meatballs, chicken livers, peas, dried porcini and diced mozzarella. The timbale is cooked in the oven for 30 minutes. There are two versions of sartù, one without tomato (in BIANCO), and the other, more modern, with a tomato sauce. This lavish dish is served at Christmas.

savoiardi
biscuits

Similar to sponge fingers, although savoiardi are lighter and less sweet. They are served as an accompaniment to ice cream, sorbet, fruit salad and creamy puddings. They are also used for making layers in sweet preparations, such as TIRAMISÙ.

savore, sapore
a sauce

This is a traditional preparation made in Emilia from grape must, cooked for a long time with pieces of fruit, among which pumpkin is essential. It is used as an accompaniment to BOLLITO MISTO or soft POLENTA or as a filling for some kinds of RAVIOLI and TORTELLI, such as pumpkin tortelli from Mantua.

The Tuscan *savor* contains also mustard, walnuts, parsley and olive oil, and it is served with boiled or roast meats.

scalogno
shallot

Shallots are sometimes used in the preparation of a SOFFRITTO because they soften faster than onions, and because of their delicate garlicky taste. However, they are not so commonly used as they are in France.

scaloppine or scaloppe
escalopes

Thin slices of meat cut, against the grain, from the boned top round of a calf, a young pig, or a turkey. The slices are then pounded to a thickness of about 5mm/¼in. Scaloppine are used for many dishes, being quick and convenient to prepare. They can be finished in many ways: with MARSALA and/or cream, with lemon, in a tomato sauce, with mushrooms or breaded and fried in butter.

There are many modern dishes made with scaloppine, but only a few traditional ones. Among these are FRITTURA PICCATA and scaloppine alla PARMIGIANA, where the breaded and fried scaloppine are covered with PROSCIUTTO and Parmesan and then finished in the oven for the cheese to melt. The other traditional dish is *scaloppine alla perugina*, for which the recipe is given here.

 [see recipe on page 378]

scamorza
a cheese

A plastic curd cheese, similar to MOZZARELLA, made with cow's milk, scamorza is moulded to an attractive pear shape and a cord is tied round the narrow top, each cheese weighing about 200g/7oz. Scamorza is white and creamy, quite dry, yet soft with a delicate milky flavour. It is eaten fresh. There are some smoked scamorze, and these can be distinguished by their brown rind.

scaloppine alla perugina
veal escalopes with prosciutto and chicken livers

Serves 4

2 salted anchovies, boned and rinsed, or
    4 canned or bottled anchovy fillets,
    drained
1 garlic clove
100g/3½oz chicken livers, cleaned and
    rinsed
1 tbsp capers, preferably in salt, rinsed
75g/2¾oz prosciutto
rind of ½ lemon, organic or unwaxed
6 fresh sage leaves
4 tbsp extra virgin olive oil
500g/1lb 2oz veal escalopes
1 tbsp lemon juice
salt and freshly ground black pepper

Alla perugina means 'in the style of Perugia', but in fact this dish could be from any central Italian town. The escalopes should be thinly sliced and smallish in size.

Chop together the first 7 ingredients – I find this is best done in the food processor.

Heat the olive oil in a large frying pan over a medium-high heat, slide in the escalopes and brown well on both sides. Reduce the heat, sprinkle with the lemon juice, a little salt and a lot of pepper. Cook them until done – thin escalopes should take 2–3 minutes. Transfer them to a warmed dish, cover with foil and keep warm.

Spoon the chicken liver mixture into the pan and cook over a lively heat for about 3 minutes. Turn the mixture over frequently.

Place a little mound of the chicken liver mixture on top of each escalope. Deglaze the cooking juices in the pan with 2–3 tablespoons hot water. Boil it up, scraping the bottom of the pan to loosen any cooking residue. Pour the pan juices over the scaloppine and serve at once.

scampo
Dublin bay prawn, langoustine

When just caught, scampi are eaten raw, splitting the shell on the underside and simply dressing them with olive oil and lemon juice. However, since they are rarely on the market in this prime condition, scampi are usually cooked. The most popular method is to fry them, having removed the shells and coated them in flour and egg, or just in flour. Large specimens are also grilled, in which case they are split in half and grilled in their shells.

The best scampi are found in the northern Adriatic, from Venice to Trieste, and the best recipes are therefore from there, such as the popular *risotto di scampi*. Rice, sautéed with onion and garlic and splashed with a generous glass of white wine, is cooked with the stock made from the shells and heads of the scampi. Halfway through the cooking, a couple of tablespoons of homemade tomato sauce are mixed in with the scampi, cut into small chunks, and at the very end the risotto is sprinkled with parsley, and made creamy with some extra butter. Some cooks add grated cheese. Another famous recipe of the area is *scampi alla busara*, in which the scampi are thrown into hot oil highly flavoured with garlic. After 1 minute, white wine is added and left to evaporate over a high heat, before finishing the dish with sweet paprika (the Slav touch) and fried breadcrumbs and parsley.

[see recipe on page 380]

scapece
cooking style

'*A scapece*' refers to a method of preparing and preserving fish and vegetables. This sweet and sour preparation is found all round the Mediterranean, but with different names. It is called *saor* in Venice and CARPIONE in Lombardy, where freshwater fish was originally used. Scapece is the actual name of the dish in Sicily, southern Italy and along the Adriatic coast of central Italy.

The fish prepared 'a scapece' is usually small or, if large, it is filleted. The fish is first coated in flour and fried in oil. The scapece varies from region to region but it is always a vinegary type of sauce to which other ingredients, such as mint and lemon, are added. The vegetables prepared 'a scapece' are usually courgettes and pumpkins.

Scappi, Bartolomeo
16th-century writer

To give an idea of the importance of Bartolomeo Scappi in the history of Italian gastronomy, I can do no better than quote Anne Willan in *Great Cooks and their Recipes*: 'Bartolomeo Scappi is to cooking what Michelangelo is to the fine arts; in its beauty as a printed work, in its ordered presentation and comprehensiveness, his *Opera* exemplifies the practical elegance of the high Renaissance.'

Scappi was born in Lombardy and the first reference of his life is as cook to Cardinal Grimani in Venice. But the first exact date we have is the date of a *pranzo* – dinner – his employer Cardinal Campeggio gave in honour of the Emperor Charles V. It took place in Trastevere in April 1536 on a day of Lent. The dinner consisted of 789 dishes. He later became chef to Popes Pius IV and Pius V and he achieved wider fame when his book was published in 1570.

Scappi's masterpiece *Opera dell'Arte del Cucinare* is divided into six sections, called books. The first book covers such subjects as the duties and the rights of a cook, the layout and organization of a kitchen, the utensils, the choice of food, the techniques for preserving food and such things; the second book is about all kinds of meat, from beef to small birds, and about the making of sauces and relishes; the third book deals with fish, how to prepare it, which fish to buy at certain times of the year and which is the best, such as the perch from Lake Como. The book ends with a section on vegetables, the right season to eat them, how to cook them, etc. The fourth book is dedicated to menus – over 100 – and the presentation and organization of banquets. The subject of the fifth book is pastry, PASTICCI, tarts, and all those preparations; and the last book is devoted to food for the sick and the convalescent. The other fascinating feature of this mammoth work are the plates illustrating all the tools, pots and pans, machines and gadgets necessary in a grand kitchen of the Renaissance.

scarola
batavia endive

A variety of chicory, also called INDIVIA, scarola is eaten raw in salad or cooked in various ways. It is one of the best vegetables for vegetable pies – which are often made with a pizza dough – because of the slightly bitter taste it develops in cooking. The scarola, sautéed in olive oil flavoured with garlic and/or onions, and sometimes chilli, is mixed with other ingredients such as capers, anchovy fillets, black olives or sultanas and pine nuts. It can also be mixed with spicy LUGANEGA sausage, Parmesan and RICOTTA. In southern Italy scarole are also stuffed. A mixture of breadcrumbs, anchovy fillets, sultanas, pine nuts and capers is pushed between the leaves of the blanched scarola, and it is then braised in a little stock and olive oil.

scarpazzone

see ERBAZZONE

scampi all'abruzzese
langoustines in a hot tomato sauce

Serves 4

24 raw langoustines

6 tbsp extra virgin olive oil

a large bunch of fresh flat-leaf parsley,
stalks discarded, chopped

3 garlic cloves, chopped

1 or 2 dried red chillies, depending on
how strong they are, chopped

2 tsp anchovy paste (see introduction)

500g/1lb 2oz very ripe, fresh tomatoes,
peeled, deseeded and chopped

125ml/4fl oz/½ cup dry white wine

salt and freshly ground black pepper

You can use raw tiger prawns if you can't get langoustines (SCAMPI). All crustaceans must be eaten very fresh, so I prefer to buy frozen, uncooked ones. Unfortunately, they will have a softer texture and a less intense sea flavour, but at least they are safe to eat. I use Italian anchovy paste that comes in a tube; if you can't get it, use 4 anchovy fillets, chopped and mashed.

Rinse the langoustines thoroughly, remove the heads and then remove the shells by cutting the carapace along each side where the upper shell meets the undershell. (The heads and claws can be used to make a stock for a fish risotto.)

Heat the olive oil in a frying pan, add the parsley, garlic and chillies and sauté gently for about 1 minute. Mix in the anchovy paste and cook gently for a further 30 seconds or so, stirring the whole time.

Now throw in the langoustines and let them take up the flavours of the oil for a minute before adding the tomatoes. Turn everything over in the pan once or twice and then add the wine. Cook at a higher heat for no longer than 3 minutes. Season with salt and pepper to taste. Serve at once, preferably straight from the pan.

NOTE: If you have any leftovers, chop the langoustines and use them to dress a dish of pasta, adding a little more olive oil if necessary.

schiacciata
a flat bread

Schiacciata means 'squashed' and is the name given in Tuscany and central Italy to a flat bread. It is made with a salted dough brushed with olive oil and sprinkled with herbs. Schiacciata is rarely made at home; a piece is bought at the PANETTERIA and eaten, as often as not, in the street. Schiacciata, PIADINA, CRESCENTINA and GNOCCO, are all similar flat breads, sometimes baked and sometimes fried. In central Italy, rounds of pressed CICCIOLI – crackling – are also called schiacciate.

schienali or filoni
spinal cords

A calf is the only animal of which the spinal cord is eaten. It is similar in texture and taste to sweetbreads and is used in the same way. Schienali are cleaned and blanched and then cooked in various ways, mostly coated with flour and fried and then added to a delicate RAGÙ or simply dressed with olive oil and lemon juice. They are usually only obtainable from specialist butchers.

---

sciumette
poached meringues

Serves 6–8

1 litre/1 ¾ pints/4 cups full-fat (whole) milk

1 tbsp pistachio nuts, chopped

4 large eggs, separated

200g/7oz/1 cup caster (superfine) sugar

½ tsp ground cinnamon

1 tbsp flour

The Ligurian equivalent of the French *oeufs à la neige,* these are meringues poached in milk. Sciumette are served at Christmas and carnival time, more often in homes than in restaurants.

Put 100ml/3½fl oz/scant ½ cup of the milk in a small saucepan, add the pistachios and heat until warm. Draw off the heat and set aside to infuse.

Whisk the egg whites until stiff. Mix half the sugar with the cinnamon and fold gently into the egg whites.

Put the remaining milk in a large shallow pan and bring to a simmer. Scoop out 3 or 4 dessertspoons of the meringue and slide gently into the simmering milk. The meringue will swell and the mounds must be kept well apart. After 2 minutes, gently turn each mound over and cook until firm on the outside. Transfer to a large dish. Repeat with the remaining meringue.

Mix the flour with the remaining sugar in a large bowl. Add the milk with the pistachios to the milk in which you cooked the meringues and bring to the boil. Pour the milk over the flour and sugar mixture, beating hard with a wooden spoon. Transfer to a pan and add the egg yolks, beating the whole time. Bring the mixture to the merest simmer and whisk constantly for 2 minutes. Put the pan in the sink, surrounded with iced water, and leave to cool, whisking frequently.

Pour a spoonful of the creamy custard over each meringue and serve the rest of the custard separately.

scorfano
rascasse

There are two species of rascasse around the coast of Italy: the black scorfano of the shallow waters and the red scorfano of deeper waters – both are mainly used in fish soups. Scorfano thickens the soup and gives it a delicious taste but has too many bones to be prepared in any other way.

scorzetta candita
candied peel

Candied peel, whether of orange, citron or lemon, is used extensively in sweet preparations. It is usually bought in segments. In Sicily, candied orange peel is traditionally made at home and served at the end of a meal with sweet wine.

scorzone

The summer truffle. See TARTUFO

scorzonera
black salsify

This delicious black-skinned, carrot-shaped root is popular in Piedmont, Liguria and Lombardy. The black skin is peeled off to reveal a creamy-white interior. In Liguria, blanched scorzonera is coated in a light batter containing whipped egg whites and fried in oil, or cooked in FRICASSEA – sautéed in oil with garlic and parsley, and then finished off in stock thickened with an egg yolk and flavoured with lemon juice.

In my home in Milan, blanched scorzonera was sautéed in butter with a little chopped PROSCIUTTO and then covered with béchamel and Parmesan and baked.

scottadito
barbecued baby lamb chops

Serves 4

1 tbsp chopped fresh marjoram
½ tbsp chopped fresh mint
1 tbsp chopped fresh thyme
1 garlic clove, finely chopped
freshly ground black pepper
8 or 12 lamb chops, depending on their
    size
juice of 1 lemon, organic or unwaxed
½ tsp Dijon mustard
4 tbsp extra virgin olive oil, plus extra
    for greasing
salt

Chops from a young lamb, served so hot as to burn the fingers, which is what the name means in Italian. Originally from Rome and the central Apennines, these chops are now made everywhere.

Mix all the herbs, garlic and pepper together and coat the chops with this mixture, using your hands and pressing it firmly into both sides of the meat. Place the chops in an oiled dish and set aside for at least 1 hour.

Light the barbecue and let the charcoal get very hot.

Meanwhile, strain the lemon juice into a small bowl. Add the mustard, then gradually add the olive oil, beating constantly. The sauce will become quite thick when well beaten. Taste and season.

When the charcoal is very hot, place the chops on the grill and cook until done: the cooking time depends on the heat of the fire and the thickness of the meat. As a rough guide, allow 3 minutes each side if you like your lamb pink, longer if you want it more cooked. Transfer the chops to a warmed dish and sprinkle with salt. Serve the lemon sauce separately.

scottiglia
a stew

Also called *cacciucco di carne*, scottiglia is a large stew originally from southern Tuscany, made with different types of meat and game. As with the fish in CACCIUCCO, scottiglia should contain at least five different meats; which might include wild boar, lamb, venison, hare, rabbit, pheasant, squab, thrush and skylark. The meats are browned separately, and then put in a large cauldron with tomatoes, wine, herbs and spices. When all the meats are cooked the scottiglia is ladled over toasted bread to absorb the rich juices, a typical Tuscan habit.

scrippelle or crispelle 'mbusse
crêpes

These pancakes are an old speciality of Abruzzo. The batter contains chopped parsley. When done, they are rolled up and put in individual soup bowls, sprinkled with grated PECORINO and Parmesan and covered with boiling capon or chicken stock. Scrippelle are also piled up flat, one on top of the other, layered with slices of cheese and meat RAGÙ in a sort of cake.

secondo
second course

Short for *secondo piatto*, the second course of a meal. It usually consists of a dish of meat or fish and is often, but by no means always, accompanied by a vegetable. In a lighter meal the secondo may be FRITTATA or a vegetable dish. Nowadays meals often have only a single course, a PIATTO UNICO.

sedano
celery

The Romans valued celery more highly as an adornment for tombs or as part of a garland than as a food. When they did eat celery, they dressed it with honey. APICIUS describes celery cooked in water to which soda has been added, and then dressed with a sauce made with pepper, lovage, onion, oregano, oil and wine. The soda was used to keep the celery green.

In her *Vegetable Book*, Jane Grigson says that Italian gardeners in the late 15th and early 16th centuries developed modern celery from an earlier bitter plant. In the early 17th century CASTELVETRO recommends serving raw celery after a meal.

Some of the earliest recipes for celery appear in CORRADO's *Il Cuoco Galante*. Corrado always blanches the celery and then finishes it off in various ways, such as in a ham sauce, or in capon stock. In another recipe, the celery is cooked with cream: my adaptation of this recipe is given on page 116.

There are two varieties of celery: white and green. Green celery is used mostly as a flavouring in stock, stews or as a base for a SOFFRITTO. White celery, which has a more delicate flavour, is braised in meat juices or in stock, or first blanched and then sautéed in butter or covered with béchamel and Parmesan and baked. A more substantial dish is made by wrapping each piece of celery, cut in half lengthways, with PROSCIUTTO, before covering it with béchamel and Parmesan and baking it. Blanched celery is coated in batter and deep-fried. White celery is also served raw in salad, dressed only with olive oil, salt and, possibly, lemon juice.

Celery soups, made with either variety, are a standby in every northern Italian family. The soffritto is made with onion and sometimes a potato, and small tubular pasta or rice are added at the end. The soup is always served with grated Parmesan.

sedano rapa or sedano di Verona
celeriac

Traditional dishes are found mostly in Piedmont and Veneto, celeriac being hardly known in the south. An excellent recipe from Veneto is for a soup in which the celeriac is sautéed with chunks of sausage and borlotti beans in the usual SOFFRITTO. Meat stock is added and when the beans are tender – about 2 hours – a few TAGLIATELLE are added.

selvaggina
game

In Roman times all kinds of game, both feathered and furred, were commonplace on the tables of the wealthy and on a few festive occasions they no doubt appeared on the tables of the plebs.

The cookery books of the past have many recipes for game, the first recipe appearing in the 14th-century *Libro della Cucina* by an anonymous Tuscan writer. In the 15th century MARTINO da Como wrote a recipe for a civet of game, and one for a pie of roe deer. Cookery writers of recent decades are writing fewer recipes for game, which is mostly reared on farms and thus has lost the gaminess of its flavour. The most popular game is hare and wild boar. Game, whether roasted or stewed, is usually served with POLENTA: soft with stews or grilled with roasts.

sementare
see CIECHE

semifreddo
an ice cream

Semifreddo ('half-cold') is the Italian ice cream par excellence. Made with egg custard, flavouring, Italian meringue and whipped cream, it is softer than other ice cream due to the high sugar content of the meringue. The most popular semifreddi are ZABAIONE and coffee.

semola, semolino
semolina

Both words mean semolina, but the first refers to the product of the grinding of durum wheat for the industrial production of pasta, while semolino is the refined product of the same grain used when making pasta at home, in soups and in the Roman dish *gnocchi alla romana*, for which the recipe is given here.

In southern Italy, Sicily and Sardinia semola is used to make a delicious bread of a beautiful golden colour. The durum wheat flour is usually mixed with white bread flour.

[see recipe on page 388]

387

seppia
cuttlefish

Cuttlefish are very popular everywhere and their uses are vast and varied. In Liguria and Tuscany they are cooked '*in zimino*', for which the recipe is given here. A recipe called *seppie in potaggio*, written in the 16th century by Bartolomeo SCAPPI, is similar to this one. He suggests adding chopped beets to the cuttlefish, which are stewed with onion in oil, butter and wine flavoured with pepper, cinnamon and saffron.

A traditional dish from the island of Elba is *seppie coi carciofi* – cuttlefish with artichokes. The sliced cuttlefish are cooked in oil, garlic and white wine, to which 1–2 tablespoons of tomato sauce and the ink of the cuttlefish are added halfway through the cooking. Very thinly sliced artichokes (they should be the variety with thorns) are added for the last 15 minutes. In Abruzzo cuttlefish

CONTINUES ON PAGE 389

gnocchi alla romana
semolina gnocchi

Serves 4

1 litre/1¾ pints/4 cups full-fat (whole)
*   milk*
salt
225g/8oz/1¾ cups coarse-ground
*   semolina*
3 large egg yolks
75g/2¾oz Parmesan cheese, grated
¼ tsp grated nutmeg
75g/2¾oz/5 tbsp unsalted butter,
*   softened, plus extra for greasing*

Also called gnocchi di SEMOLINO, these are the easiest gnocchi to prepare. The semolina should be Italian semolina, which is more coarsely ground than the traditional English-style semolina. These gnocchi can be dressed with a thin béchamel sauce or with cream and Parmesan.

Heat the milk with a little salt in a heavy saucepan. When it begins to simmer, add the semolina in a very thin stream, beating quickly to prevent lumps from forming. Cook for about 15 minutes, beating constantly until the semolina has formed a thick paste and comes away from the side of the pan.

Take the pan off the heat. As soon as the semolina has cooled a little, beat in the egg yolks, one at a time. When all the eggs have been thoroughly mixed in, add all but 4 tablespoons of the Parmesan, then add the nutmeg, 25g/1oz/2 tbsp of the butter and salt to taste. Incorporate everything thoroughly and then turn the mixture out onto a slab of marble or the work surface, previously moistened with cold water. Spread the semolina mixture to a thickness of 1cm/½in and then leave to cool completely. This will take about 2 hours.

Preheat the oven to 230°C/450°F/Gas Mark 8.

Cut the semolina into 4cm/1½in rounds. Place a layer of the rounds in a buttered ovenproof dish, use the trimmings to make another layer, and then cover with another layer of the gnocchi rounds, slightly overlapping.

Melt the remaining butter and pour it over the gnocchi. Sprinkle with the remaining Parmesan and bake for about 15–20 minutes, until the gnocchi are heated through. Leave to cool for a few minutes before serving.

NOTE: The whole dish can be prepared in advance and baked just before serving.

are marinated in oil, chilli and garlic and then stewed in wine until tender, with a final addition of chopped parsley and lemon juice. In Venice cuttlefish are stewed in white wine to which a little tomato sauce and the ink of the fish is added. Cuttlefish are also fried, in which case the small young *seppioline*, fried whole, are the best.

Cuttlefish are ideal for stuffing. One of the best methods is to stuff them with their own cut-up tentacles, some mussels, grated PECORINO and breadcrumbs, all bound with egg. They are cooked slowly in olive oil in an earthenware pot. In Venezia Giulia there is a traditional recipe in which the cuttlefish are stuffed with the meat from a crab, mixed with the cut-up tentacles, egg, butter and a little Parmesan.

The best-known cuttlefish recipe is RISOTTO NERO, where the ink is used to flavour and colour the risotto.

 [see recipe below]

serpentaria
see DRAGONCELLO

serpillo
see PEPOLINO

seppie in zimino
cuttlefish with Swiss chard

Serves 4
700g/1lb 9oz cuttlefish
5 tbsp olive oil
1 onion, finely chopped
2 garlic cloves, finely chopped
1 tbsp finely chopped celery leaves
1½ tbsp tomato puree
salt and freshly ground black pepper
500g/1lb 2oz Swiss chard

This is a traditional way of cooking cuttlefish in eastern Liguria and Versilia in Tuscany. If you can't find cuttlefish, use squid. If you can't get Swiss chard you can use spinach, but not the young sort that lacks flavour and is only suitable for eating raw in salads.

Ask your fishmonger to clean the cuttlefish. Wash them, then cut the body into 1cm/½in strips and chop the tentacles. Dry with kitchen paper.

Put the olive oil, onion, garlic and celery leaves into a heavy pot, earthenware if possible, and sauté gently for 10 minutes or so. Stir in the cuttlefish and continue cooking for 5 minutes, turning it over and over. Add the tomato puree and sauté for a further minute.

Add 4–5 tablespoons of hot water and salt to taste. Mix well, cover the pan and cook until the cuttlefish are tender, about 45 minutes.

Meanwhile, remove the white stalks from the Swiss chard (you can keep them for another dish) and wash the leaves. Drain and dry the leaves as you would with salad leaves and throw them into the pot. Cover the pot and cook for 10 minutes. Season with plenty of pepper and salt to taste. Serve straight from the pot.

sfincioni
Sicilian focaccia

Sfincioni are the FOCACCIA of Palermo; they are some of the best street food of the city. There are two types: the open sfincioni has a thick base of pizza dough and is covered with CACIOCAVALLO, tomatoes, onions, anchovies, breadcrumbs and oil. The other type, *sfincioni di San Vito*, so called because it was created by the nuns of the convent of the same name, has a stuffing made with minced pork, local sausage, RICOTTA and breadcrumbs. The stuffing is first sautéed in oil and then placed between two thin sheets of pizza dough.

sfogi in saor
sweet and sour sole

A well-known Venetian dish, *sfogi* is the Venetian word for sole and *saor* is dialect for *sapore*, an old word for sauce. The dish is of eastern origin, traditionally eaten during the Festa del Redentore, the third Sunday in July, when Venice turns out to celebrate the Holy Redeemer with a spectacular firework display and an equally spectacular feast. The feast is partaken of on every kind of boat, from gondola to fishing boat, as well as on the quaysides of the Giudecca and the Zattere. Apart from sfogi in saor, the traditional fare is roast duck, stewed beans, baked peaches with amaretti and jam stuffing and iced watermelon. As the fireworks light up the sky, bowls of *bovoletti aglio e olio* – small snails dressed with garlic and oil – are handed round to set the seal of enjoyment on the occasion.

[see recipe on fscing page]

sfoglia
homemade pasta dough

A rolled-out sheet of homemade PASTA dough. The sfoglia of Emilia-Romagna, made with soft wheat flour and eggs, is nowadays the most popular (see recipe on page 282).

Sfoglia, more correctly called PASTA SFOGLIA, also means puff pastry.

sfogliatelle or sfogliatelle ricce
puff pastry cakes

Puff pastry cakes from Naples containing a filling made with cooked SEMOLINO, sieved RICOTTA, diced candied fruit and spices. Some recipes add CREMA PASTICCERA to the filling. The traditional Neapolitan puff pastry used to be made with STRUTTO rather than butter. Sfogliatelle are extremely friable and, being very difficult to make, are usually bought in a PASTICCERIA.

sformato
savoury pudding

A kind of pudding, or mould, made with a coarse puree of vegetables, or occasionally of chicken or fish. It is bound with eggs and béchamel sauce and cooked in the oven, usually in a bain-marie. It is similar to a soufflé but not as exacting to make. In the past a sformato was served as a side dish at dinner parties; it is now served as a light main course for supper or as a first course.

Sformato, which literally means 'unmoulded', is traditionally made in a ring mould, so that the hole in the centre can be filled with a sauce before the dish is taken to the table. This might be a mushroom and chicken liver sauce or a tomato sauce, according to the main ingredient used for the sformato. Restaurants often make sformati in ramekins and call them *timballini* – small TIMBALLI.

Sformati are traditional in the *cucina borghese* (bourgeois cooking) of northern Italy. ARTUSI, the prime exponent of this cuisine, wrote many recipes for them.

[see recipe on page 392]

sfogi in saor
sole fillets in a sweet and sour sauce

Serves 6–8

50g/1¾oz/⅓ cup sultanas (golden raisins)

flour, for dusting

salt

700g/1lb 9oz sole fillets

vegetable oil, for deep-frying

2 tbsp olive oil

225g/8oz mild onions, thinly sliced

2 tsp sugar

125ml/4fl oz/½ cup good wine vinegar

4 bay leaves

50g/1¾oz/6 tbsp pine nuts

2–3 pinches of ground cinnamon

2 cloves

12 black peppercorns, lightly crushed

This is often served as an ANTIPASTO in Venice, but it makes a good main course too. You can use plaice fillets instead of sole, or sardines, which must be filleted but left in one piece, not divided into two fillets.

Soak the sultanas in a little warm water to plump them up. Meanwhile, spread some flour on a board and season with salt, then coat the fish lightly in the flour.

Heat the oil for deep-frying in a wok or a deep frying pan. When the oil is very hot but not smoking, slide in the sole fillets, a few at a time. Fry gently for about 3 minutes on each side until a golden crust has formed. Using a fish slice, transfer the fish to a plate lined with kitchen paper, to drain.

Heat the olive oil and onions in a small frying pan. Add a pinch of salt and the sugar. Cook the onions gently, stirring frequently, until golden. Turn up the heat and pour in the vinegar, then boil briskly until the liquid has reduced by half.

Lay the fish neatly in a shallow dish. Pour over the onion sauce and put the bay leaves on top. Drain the sultanas and scatter them over the fish, together with the pine nuts, spices and peppercorns. Cover the dish with clingfilm and leave to marinate in the refrigerator for at least 24 hours or, even better, for 48 hours.

Remove from the refrigerator about 2 hours before serving to bring the dish back to room temperature.

391

sformato di finocchi
fennel mould

Serves 6

700g/1lb 9oz fennel bulbs

50g/1¾oz/4 tbsp unsalted butter, plus extra for greasing

salt and freshly ground pepper, preferably white

300ml/10fl oz/1¼ cups full-fat (whole) milk

3 tbsp dried breadcrumbs

3 tbsp flour

2 pinches of grated nutmeg

3 large eggs, lightly beaten

3 tbsp freshly grated Parmesan cheese

Of all the SFORMATI, this is one of the most tasty and 'one of the most gentle' writes the great ARTUSI. He suggests serving it as an accompaniment to boiled capon, or by itself with a garnish of chicken giblets and sweetbreads.

Cut away the green tops, stalks and any bruised or brown parts from the outside of the fennel. Reserve a handful of the green tops. Cut the fennel bulbs into vertical slices about 5mm/¼in thick. Wash the slices and the reserved fennel tops and dry them.

Melt half the butter in a frying pan. When the butter begins to foam, add the fennel and cook for 5 minutes. Add a pinch of salt and half the milk. Cover the pan and cook very gently until the fennel is tender: this will take about 20 minutes. Keep an eye on the fennel and add a little water if it becomes too dry.

Chop the fennel to a very coarse puree, either by hand or in a food processor. Transfer to a bowl.

Preheat the oven to 190°C/375°F/Gas Mark 5. Grease a 2 litre/3½ pint/ 2 quart ring mould very generously with butter. If you are worried about unmoulding the sformato, line the bottom of the ring with greaseproof paper and butter the paper. Sprinkle the mould with the breadcrumbs and then shake off the excess crumbs.

Make a fairly thick béchamel sauce with the remaining 25g/1oz/2 tbsp butter, the flour and the remaining milk. Flavour with the grated nutmeg and some pepper and then add to the fennel in the bowl. Add the eggs and Parmesan, mix very thoroughly, then taste and adjust the seasoning.

Spoon the mixture into the prepared mould. Place the mould in a large baking dish and fill the dish with very hot water to come two-thirds of the way up the side of the mould. Place in the oven and cook for about 45 minutes, until a thin skewer or a toothpick inserted into the middle of the sformato comes out dry.

Leave to stand for 5 minutes. Run a palette knife around the side of the sformato, place a serving plate over the top and turn the plate and the mould upside down. Shake the mould lightly and lift it off. Remove the greaseproof paper, if used, and serve.

sgombro
mackerel

A lovely looking fish with dark blue wavy lines on its smooth, shining body, mackerel is not a highly prized fish. That may be due to the fact that unless it is eaten very fresh, its flavour becomes unpleasant. Personally, I love it. Mackerel are usually about 20–25cm/8–10in long; the best mackerel are caught in the Tyrrhenian Sea.

The best recipes for mackerel are from Liguria, where the fish is called *lacerto*, and from northern Tuscany. A traditional recipe from Liguria, mackerel with peas, is usually made in the spring when the first peas appear on the market and the mackerel are still plentiful. The fish, brushed with oil, are laid on a bed of small peas, generously dressed with oil and seasoned with a little garlic, marjoram and salt. The dish is cooked, tightly covered, over a very gentle heat, for about 10–15 minutes. A little white wine or hot water are added during the cooking.

In a traditional recipe from northern Tuscany the fish – which should not be too big – is filleted and then butterflied (not cut into two fillets). It is placed on an oiled baking dish, covered with a BATTUTO of shallot, parsley and oregano and then with a layer of chopped peeled tomatoes, garlic and salt, a little more oil and then baked for about 10–12 minutes. Some cooks now add a little chilli.

A recipe from Le Marche is for mackerel cooked in a pot – in POTACCHIO – with a lot of rosemary, a little garlic, some lemon rind, and some chilli, a seasoning which is one of the trademarks of the region.

Mackerel, left whole, are also grilled or pan-fried and finished with lemon juice or balsamic vinegar.

[see recipe below, photographs overleaf]

sgombri con le cipolle
mackerel with onion

Serves 4

400–500g/14oz–1lb 2oz onions, preferably Spanish or white, very finely sliced
2 large mackerel, filleted
200ml/7fl oz/generous ¾ cup dry white wine
100ml/3½fl oz/scant ½ cup white wine vinegar
8–10 juniper berries, crushed
salt and freshly ground black pepper
3 sprigs of fresh thyme
2–3 bay leaves

In eastern Liguria, where this dish comes from, it is served cold or at room temperature, never chilled. It should be eaten a day or two after it has been made, so that the onion becomes sweeter by being marinated in wine and vinegar, and to allow the flavour of the sauce to penetrate the fish.

Preheat the oven to 180°C/350°F/Gas Mark 4.

Spread half the onion in an ovenproof dish large enough to contain the fish in a single layer (I use a metal lasagne pan). Lay the fish on top and then cover with the rest of the onion.

Put the wine, vinegar and juniper berries in a bowl and mix in salt and pepper to taste. Pour over the fish and onions and tuck the herbs here and there under the onion. Bake for about 15 minutes.

Leave to cool, then chill the dish for at least 24 hours.

Remove from the refrigerator about 2 hours before serving to bring the dish back to room temperature.

Sicilia
Sicily

This alluring and fascinating island has had a chequered history. From the time when it was colonized by the Greeks, it has had to live under the rule of many occupying powers. Yet from each of these – Greeks, Saracens and Normans – the Sicilians acquired new learning and new skills, often adapting and improving them, whether in architecture, philosophy or cooking. They learnt the ways of Greek cooking so well that the rich Athenians used to employ Sicilian cooks. In fact, the foundations of Sicilian cooking, which in its turn has greatly influenced all Italian cooking, are Greek. It is based on simple local food: fish, with innumerable fish soups, and vegetables.

Over a millennium later, another great civilization overtook the island. This was a period of Arab domination, during which many new foods and new methods of cooking were introduced. The Saracens brought aubergines, spinach, bitter oranges, almonds, rice, apricots, sugar and spices.

They taught the Sicilians how to dry fruits and how to make the delicious sweets for which Sicily is still famous. It is also from the Saracens that the Sicilians learnt the basic techniques of making sorbet. And last but not least, the Arabs introduced to Sicily the art of distillation, the very word alcohol being a corruption of the Arabic *al-kohl*.

Next came the Normans, who brought to Sicily their own recipes from the north, their northern methods of cooking, and of preserving fish and meat. It was in the 12th century, during the Norman domination, that the first reference to spaghetti appeared. King Roger II (1095–1154) commissioned an Arab geographer to explore Sicily, and in his writings there is a reference to people making flour and water into strings which they called *itryah*. In Sicily and southern Italy spaghetti is still called *trii* in some recipes.

To this day the Sicilians' favourite food is pasta. In *brodo* or *asciutta* (in stock or drained), pasta appears at least once a day on the Sicilian table. The dish of pasta is dressed with a rich sauce, to be finally showered with grated local PECORINO or

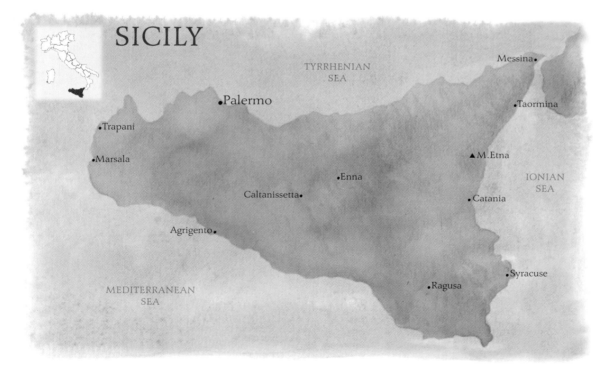

SICILY

TYRRHENIAN SEA

Messina

Palermo

Taormina

Trapani

Marsala

M.Etna

Enna

IONIAN SEA

Caltanissetta

Catania

Agrigento

Syracuse

Ragusa

MEDITERRANEAN SEA

with salted RICOTTA, a local speciality. Fish and pasta is a Sicilian culinary marriage, and from the many recipes I can only mention pasta with fresh sardines (see recipe on page 288), which is made all over the island in endless variations, the constants being the pasta, the sardines and the wild fennel. The other favourite way to serve pasta is with vegetables, especially with aubergines. A popular recipe is PASTA ALLA NORMA, with aubergine, tomato and salted ricotta.

Fish is still relatively plentiful, although local fish is nowadays often displayed next to fish from overseas. A visit to the Vucciria or the Ballarò market in Palermo or the fish market in Catania demonstrates the Sicilians' love for this food. The fierce swordfish, the torpedo-shaped tuna and the sinister-looking octopus lie next to the cheerful red mullet, and the creepy-crawly crustaceans, the hirsute sea urchin next to the sardines and anchovies in their silvery blue livery. The varieties of fish and seafood may be innumerable, but the manner of cooking is limited. This is because the Sicilians like to eat fish that is cooked simply, so as to enhance the taste of the fish itself, a rule written by the Syracusan Archestratus, whose 4th-century BC culinary notes are the earliest to be known in the Western world.

A characteristic of Sicilian cooking is that most dishes are based on simple ingredients, which are then embellished and enriched to make the end result a fantastic and almost baroque achievement. An example is the CAPONATA, which, starting with humble fried aubergine and onion, can end gloriously with a lobster on the top. Other vegetables are cooked as for caponata, the Sicilians relying more on vegetables than on meat for their nourishment. Fruit and nuts are plentiful, Sicilian oranges, almonds and pistachios being famous the world over.

But the food in which the Sicilians particularly excel are the DOLCI, an Arab legacy, and the sorbets. To this day Sicilian sorbets and ice creams are paragons of excellence, due as much to the Sicilian expertise as to the excellent fruit with which they are so often made.

smacafam
buckwheat polenta

One of the basic dishes of the peasant cooking of Trentino, this is polenta made with buckwheat, dating from the time when maize flour was not yet cultivated in Italy. The buckwheat polenta is mixed with sausage and onion, and then baked.

There is a smacafam prepared for Carnival which becomes a sweet by replacing the sausage and onion with sultanas, eggs, dried breadcrumbs, sugar and crumbled soft cheese.

soffritto
a cookery base

This word – which comes from *sotto friggere*, 'under-fry' – occurs in Italian recipes more often than any other, for the simple reason that a soffritto is the point of departure for innumerable Italian dishes. A soffritto normally consists of a little onion, a little celery, plus sometimes carrot and garlic, a handful of herbs – parsley, sage, rosemary or others – and maybe a little PANCETTA, all very finely chopped and gently sautéed in oil and/or butter until just beginning to colour. When the soffritto is ready, the main ingredient, be it meat, fish or vegetables, is mixed in.

sogliola
sole

Sole has several different names, according to the region in which it is caught, including SFOGI in Venice and *sfoglie* on the Adriatic coast, where it is more common than on the Tyrrhenian.

The sole of the northern Adriatic are small and excellent and they deserve the love and care the locals put into their preparation. Usually cleaned but not filleted, in Emilia sole are cooked *alla* PARMIGIANA – sprinkled with Parmesan after being sautéed in butter. In another recipe from Emilia, sole, coated in flour, are put in an ovenproof dish with sage, onion, white wine, a couple of tablespoons of strong meat juices, lemon juice and parsley. They are baked and served with small glazed onions. Further south, in Abruzzo, sole are roasted with olive oil, garlic, lemon juice and parsley. A few minutes before serving, a lot of chopped black olives (about two dozen for four people) and some lemon slices are added. One of the most interesting recipes for sole is this one from Caorle on the Venetian lagoon.

[see recipe below]

soncino

see VALERIANELLA

sopa coada
a soup

In the dialect of Veneto this is *zuppa covada*, 'broody soup'. A traditional dish from Treviso, sopa coada was devised to use up leftover roasted pigeons. These are put, with lots of Parmesan, in between slices of toasted bread in an earthenware pot. All the cooking juices and some meat stock are poured over and the dish placed in a very low oven to 'brood' for at least 4 hours, with a little stock added every now and then.

sogliole al basilico e ai pinoli
sole with basil and pine nuts

Serves 4
4 sole, about 300g/10½oz each
1 tbsp extra virgin olive oil
2 tbsp pine nuts, coarsely chopped
5–6 fresh basil leaves

Marinade
4 tbsp olive oil
3 tbsp lemon juice
1 tbsp chopped fresh basil
salt and freshly ground black pepper

An old recipe for SOGLIOLE, which comes from the town of Caorle, east of Venice, from a splendid book, *Antica Cucina Veneziana*, by the great food historian Massimo ALBERINI. The recipes have been adapted from the originals by Romana Bosco, a leading cookery teacher who runs the school Il Melograno in Turin. This is my translation.

Have the sole cleaned and skinned by your fishmonger. Wash the fish, dry thoroughly and lay them in a dish.

Prepare the marinade. Put the olive oil in a bowl, beat in the lemon juice until emulsified, then beat in the basil, salt and pepper. Spoon the marinade over the sole and leave to marinate for an hour or so.

Preheat the oven to 200°C/400°F/Gas Mark 6.

Lift the sole out of the marinade. Grease a shallow, large ovenproof dish with the olive oil and lay the fish in it. Place the dish in the oven and cook for about 10 minutes.

Meanwhile, heat the marinade and add the pine nuts. When the liquid gets to boiling point, pour it over the sole and leave to cook in the oven for a further 5 minutes or so. Sprinkle with basil leaves before serving.

RIGHT: Sogliole al basilico e ai pinoli

soppressa
a salame

A popular SALAME, now made in Veneto on an industrial scale. It is a large salame made from very coarsely ground pork. Both lean meat and fat are used, the fat accounting for a third of the volume. Soppresse are cured for about a year in dark, dry rooms. They are eaten as an ANTIPASTO or as an accompaniment to grilled POLENTA.

soppressata
a salame

Soppressata is made in central Italy. The most famous is the *soppressata di Fabriano* in Le Marche, still produced following an ancient recipe. It is made with lean pork from the shoulder mixed with fatty minced PANCETTA, packed into natural casing, which is washed in wine vinegar. It has a soft consistency and a delicate smoky flavour.

There is also a soppressata of Siena, a wonderful large sausage made with the pig's head and spiced with the same spices used for PANFORTE.

sorbetto
sorbet

Among the various frozen preparations, which include GELATI and SPUMONI, sorbets are the oldest. They were first made in Sicily about a thousand years ago, under Arab tutelage. The Sicilians soon became masters of the craft and have been helped in this by the fact that nowhere else in Italy is there such a variety of excellent fruit and nuts, including pomegranates, prickly pears and pistachio nuts.

Sorbets were, and occasionally still are, served during the meal, rather than at the end, to help the digestion and clean the palate in preparation for the next course. By the 19th century, they

CONTINUES OVERLEAF

400

sorbetto di limone al basilico
lemon sorbet with basil

Serves 4–6
8 lemons, organic or unwaxed
2 oranges, organic or unwaxed
350g/12oz/1¾ cups caster (superfine) sugar
24 large fresh basil leaves, chopped

The flavour of the lemon in this sorbet is immediately apparent, but the basil blends in so perfectly that it seems only to add a rather mysterious taste to the sorbet. It is extremely attractive to look at, its pale green colour speckled with the dark green spots of the basil. Use young, sweet basil, not an old pungent plant. You need to have an ice-cream machine to make a good sorbet.

Scrub and dry the fruit. Pare the rind in strips, without chipping into the white pith, and put it in a saucepan. Add 600ml/20fl oz/2½ cups water and the sugar. Bring slowly to the boil and simmer until the sugar has dissolved. Turn up the heat to moderate and boil rapidly for 3–4 minutes. Take off the heat and leave to cool completely.

Remove the rind from the cold syrup. Squeeze the lemons and oranges, strain the juice and add to the syrup with the basil leaves.

Freeze the mixture in an ice-cream machine.

RIGHT: Sorbetto di limone al basilico

were also served as dessert and the word sorbetto disappeared from cookery books, *gelati* being used to refer both to ice creams and to water ices. Recently, however, the word – and the sorbets – have experienced a revival, made not only with the usual fruits but also with herbs and flowers.

 [see recipe on page 400]

sottaceti
garnish

A garnish made with vegetables preserved under vinegar (*aceto*). Carrots, cauliflower, mushrooms, celery and tiny onions are blanched, dried carefully, cut into small pieces and put into jars with bay leaves, salt and peppercorns. They are then covered with white wine vinegar and the jars are hermetically sealed. Sottaceti are made both artisanally and industrially.

Sottaceti are used as part of an ANTIPASTO and to accompany cold dishes, mostly of meat, but not PROSCIUTTO and CULATELLO and other more delicate SALUMI, the flavour of which would be killed by the sottaceti.

sottobosco
wild berries

Sottobosco, which could be translated as 'from the woods', refers to wild strawberries, wild raspberries, blackberries, blueberries and possibly some redcurrants. As a dessert, sottobosco is dressed with lemon juice and/or sugar or even, for the purists, served as it is. Those less dedicated to purity ask for sugar and cream.

spaccatina
a bread

A round loaf of bread from Abruzzo with a deep cut in the centre. Spaccatina is a *pane condito*

('seasoned bread'), the dough being dressed with LARDO, STRUTTO or olive oil.

spaghetti
a pasta

The word means 'little strings' and its first use in reference to pasta was recorded in *Il Dizionario Domestico*, published in 1846. Before that this long pasta was called VERMICELLI and it had been made for centuries. The earliest questionable reference to it is in a 12th-century Sicilian document which refers to some Arabs near Palermo making long strings out of flour and water. But what is certain is that this shape of pasta was already made in Italy before Marco Polo returned from China to Venice in 1295.

Spaghetti as we know it became the pasta of Naples in the late 18th century and by the 19th century pasta began to be made in factories. Torre Annunziata and Gragnano, two towns south of Naples, became the centre of pasta manufacture, the manufacturing process being finished out of doors. In the hot sun, spaghetti was festooned over rows of long racks that lined the street. It was in Naples that spaghetti were first matched with tomato sauce, which still remains the best way to dress a plate of spaghetti.

Of all the shapes of pasta, spaghetti is the most versatile and the most popular. Made with durum wheat SEMOLA and water, it comes in two or three different thicknesses, depending on the manufacturer. Like all pasta it must be cooked in plenty of boiling salted water and it must not be over-drained. Experts never drain it through a colander, but lift it out of the water with tongs, a special wooden fork or a large wicker strainer. This allows the spaghetti to retain the *goccia* (drop'): spaghetti should be quite moist when the sauce is added. In southern Italy a small earthenware jug full of the pasta cooking water is brought to the table, the water to be added to the spaghetti after it has been dressed, such as with CARBONARA sauce or with *cacio e pepe*.

The best sauces for spaghetti are based on olive oil. They are numerous but certainly do not include Bolognese sauce, spaghetti Bolognaise being an American creation. Some of the most traditional spaghetti dishes include:

Spaghetti aglio, olio and peperoncino – the cooked spaghetti are stir-fried in plenty of olive oil flavoured with garlic and chilli.

Spaghetti cacio e pepe – a classic recipe from Rome in which the pasta is dressed with mountains of grated PECORINO cheese and plenty of black pepper.

Spaghetti alla nursina – in the autumn in Norcia in Umbria the spaghetti are stir-fried with olive oil and finely sliced local black truffles (see recipe on page 420).

Spaghetti alle punte di asparagi – a recipe from Umbria in which the tips of cooked wild asparagus (not al dente) are sautéed in oil with a few tomatoes and mixed into the cooked pasta.

Spaghettini alla siracusana – from Siracusa in Sicily, the pasta is stir-fried in a SOFFRITTO of anchovy fillets, olive oil, black olives and garlic.

Spagheti alle vongole in bianco, with fresh clams, olive oil, garlic and parsley, is the best recipe, from Naples. Spaghetti alle vongole are also made with tomato sauce.

spaghetti al nero
spaghetti with cuttlefish

This is the pasta lovers' answer to RISOTTO NERO. Originally from Sicily, it is a dish of spaghetti dressed with cuttlefish. The nero ('black') comes from the ink contained in the little bag in the body of the cuttlefish.

The cuttlefish, cleaned and cut into strips, are sautéed in olive oil, garlic, parsley and a touch of chilli. Splashed with wine, they continue cooking slowly until the juice is thick and full of flavour and the cuttlefish are tender. The sauce is then ready to be spooned over the spaghetti. As with risotto nero, some recipes suggest adding 2 tablespoons of tomato sauce after the wine.

spaghettini
thin spaghetti

These are particularly good with seafood or tomato sauces. In southern Italy spaghettini are often called VERMICELLI.

speck
smoked ham

An Austrian type of smoked PROSCIUTTO, speck is a traditional product of Alto Adige. Recently it has become popular throughout Italy. Speck now features very frequently in ANTIPASTI. It is kneaded into CANEDERLI and bread and is served with sauerkraut together with various cuts of pork, and it is also used for pasta sauces.

[see recipe on page 404]

403

spezie
spices

Spices were used in the past more than they are now. The Romans used spices to add flavour to many foods and also to disguise the unpleasant tastes often present when their meat or fish were not fresh, or so it is said.

During the Dark Ages, when spices were relatively cheap in the East, the Arabs monopolized the trade from China, India and the Middle East to Europe. Later the Venetians took over and built their wealth on this trade. However, in the 16th century, when Vasco da Gama opened the new route from the East via the Cape, Portugal began to share in the spice trade and Venice lost its monopoly.

CONTINUES ON PAGE 405

salsa allo speck
speck sauce

Enough for 4 helpings of pasta
40g/1 ½oz/3 tbsp unsalted butter
200g/7oz speck, cut into julienne strips
100ml/3½fl oz/scant ½ cup dry
*   white wine*
a generous pinch of powdered saffron or
*   ½ tsp saffron strands*
salt and freshly ground black pepper
150ml/5fl oz/²/₃ cup double (heavy)
*   cream*
6 tbsp freshly grated Parmesan cheese,
*   plus extra to serve*

Of all pasta shapes, I find TAGLIATELLE the best to be generously dressed with this creamy, smoky sauce, made with smoked ham (SPECK).

Heat the butter in a frying pan large enough to hold the pasta later. When the butter is sizzling, add the speck and sauté for 5 minutes. Add the wine and cook briskly until the wine has nearly all evaporated.

If you are using saffron strands, place them in a metal spoon and crush them with a teaspoon. Add the saffron and some pepper to the frying pan and stir well. After 1 minute or so, pour in the cream and bring to the boil, stirring constantly. Taste and add salt if necessary. Take off the heat.

When the pasta is cooked, drain it and transfer to the pan of sauce. Stir-fry for 1 minute and then add the cheese. Serve at once, handing round extra Parmesan in a bowl.

spezzatino di manzo alla bolzanese
beef stew with paprika and sage

Serves 4–6
25g/1oz/2 tbsp unsalted butter
2 tbsp olive oil
2 mild onions, sliced
about 20 fresh sage leaves
900g/2lb stewing steak, cut into cubes
1 tsp paprika
250ml/9fl oz/1 cup red wine
1½ tbsp flour
400g/14oz passata (strained tomatoes)
salt and freshly ground black pepper

I very much like this recipe from Alto Adige. It shows how to make a basic SPEZZATINO, which you can vary by changing the herbs, eliminating the paprika, or introducing other spices or vegetables. The recipe also works very well with stewing veal or pork.

Heat the butter and oil in a large saucepan, add the onions and sauté until soft, about 7–10 minutes. Add the sage and sauté for 1 minute, then add the meat and brown well on all sides. Mix in the paprika and add the wine. Turn up the heat and boil briskly to reduce, stirring constantly. Sprinkle with the flour and cook for 1 minute. Add the passata and salt and pepper to taste.

Bring to the boil, cover and cook very gently for about 2 hours, until the meat is tender. Turn the meat over occasionally and check that it isn't sticking to the bottom of the pan, adding a little hot water if necessary.

Bartolomeo SCAPPI was the first cook to moderate the use of spices and introduce more herbs, a trend taken up a century later by the great French chef François de La Varenne. It was then that the fashion for scents – rose, iris, lavender and orange flower – entered the kitchen. At about the same time coffee and chocolate became the rage and took over the role of luxury foods. Spices became cheaper and lost the allure given by a price that had placed them beyond many people's reach.

In the late 19th century, and in the 20th century up to World War II, spices were used with great discretion. Those mainly associated with traditional Italian cooking are nutmeg, cloves, pepper and cinnamon, which used to be called the four Lombard spices. Ada BONI clearly specifies that the amount used should be a *nonnulla* – a mere nothing. Chilli, which was not one of the original spices, is now extremely popular all over the peninsula. Saffron has always found a place in Italian cooking and more recently exotic spices, such as ginger, cumin or caraway, have also begun to be used.

spezzatino
a stew

The word comes from *spezzare* (to break), since the meat, usually a cheap cut, is cooked in chunks. Spezzatino is an everyday dish made at home, sometimes with potatoes, peas or peppers and usually containing tomatoes. Spezzatino is traditionally cooked in an earthenware pot. The meat is sometimes coated with flour before being sautéed in a SOFFRITTO, and it is then cooked over a gentle heat – or in the oven – with wine. In Tuscany wild boar is cooked in spezzatino, while in southern Italy spezzatino is also made with lamb's or kid's offal. The vegetables and flavouring vary, and there are various classic regional recipes.

 [see recipe on facing page]

spiedini
small skewers

Spiedini – which refers to both the skewers and the food – have been a peasant dish since ancient times. Meat, offal, fish or vegetables are cut into small pieces and threaded onto a skewer with PANCETTA, onion, other vegetables and herbs placed between them. Spiedini are usually marinated in olive oil, salt and pepper and then grilled, preferably over wood or charcoal. In a traditional Lombard dish called *spiedini all'uccelletto*, small bits of veal and LUGANEGA sausage are skewered interspaced by sage leaves. In present-day cooking, the favourite spiedini are made with seafood.

spigola
sea bass

Another word for BRANZINO, the name by which the fish is most commonly known in southern Italy, where it is usually grilled or baked. See recipes on pages 56 and 205.

spinaci
spinach

Spinach was not known to the ancient Romans; it reached Italy with the Arabs around the turn of the first millennium, as did so many other foods. It was improved through selected cultivation and by the middle of the 18th century it was so popular that Vincenzo CORRADO devoted ten recipes to it. One of these, a precursor of the SFORMATO, is called *spinaci in budin*, literally 'in pudding'. The spinach is blanched and lightly sautéed in butter, then chopped and pounded with bone marrow, candied citron, Parmesan and spices. Heated egg yolks, cream and milk, thickened with breadcrumbs, are added and the mixture is then cooked in the oven in a buttered large mould or individual moulds. The dish is served unmoulded and hot.

Spinach is widely used, not only as a vegetable but also in fillings. Among the many spinach-filled dishes are TORTELLI *di ricotta e spinaci*, AGNOLOTTI *piemontesi*, ROTOLO *di vitello* (veal roulade) and *pollo ripieno*, in which the minced chicken meat is mixed with spinach, wrapped in the chicken skin and roasted in plenty of butter. Spinach appears in a number of pies and tarts, of which TORTA PASQUALINA is the best known. Then there are GNOCCHI of spinach and potatoes or of spinach and ricotta, croquettes and endless other preparations using this most popular vegetable.

The recipe for *spinaci alla romana* is given here. This dish becomes *spinaci alla genovese* when a few anchovy fillets are pounded in the oil. *Spinaci alla fiorentina* is chopped spinach sautéed in butter and garlic into which a béchamel containing a good deal of Parmesan is mixed; the dish is baked in the oven. Very young spinach is eaten raw, dressed with a sauce of pounded anchovy fillets, garlic and pine nuts.

The classic Italian spinach grows in bunches, of which the Gigante d'Inverno ('winter giant') is the best. Spinach is cooked only in the water that clings to the leaves after it is washed. When served as a vegetable, it is dressed simply with olive oil and lemon juice, and perhaps a touch of garlic, or it is sautéed in oil and flavoured with a good squeeze of lemon juice – *spinaci all'agro* – while in northern Italy it is sautéed in plenty of butter and a tablespoon or two of grated Parmesan is added before serving. Spinach was always served like that in my home in Milan, as an accompaniment to roast veal, roast chicken or to COTOLETTE.

[see recipe below]

spongata or spongarda
a pie

Spongata is one of the oldest of all Christmas DOLCI. It dates from the 15th century and it originates from the town of Brescello in Emilia-Romagna. From there it travelled to nearby Busseto – it was allegedly a favourite of Giuseppe Verdi, who was born near Busseto – and from there to Liguria (*spongata di Sarzana*) and to Lombardy (*spongata di Crema*); the recipes are all slightly different.

---

spinaci alla romana
spinach sautéed with sultanas and pine nuts

Serves 4

1kg/2¼lb fresh spinach
salt and freshly ground black pepper
25g/1oz/2 tbsp sultanas (golden raisins)
½ garlic clove, finely chopped
4 tbsp olive oil
25g/1oz/2 tbsp unsalted butter
25g/1oz/3 tbsp pine nuts, toasted

A traditional recipe from Rome.

Trim the spinach and wash in a few changes of cold water until there is no sand at the bottom of the sink. Put the leaves in a large saucepan with 1 teaspoon salt and cook until tender, about 3 minutes. Drain the spinach and leave until cool enough to handle, then squeeze out all the moisture with your hands.

While the spinach is cooking and cooling, soak the sultanas in warm water for 10 minutes. Drain and dry.

Sauté the garlic in the olive oil and butter for 30 seconds and then add the spinach, sultanas and pine nuts. Fry gently for 5 minutes, turning frequently. Season well to taste.

Basically spongata consists of two thin layers of sweet pastry stuffed with a rich mixture of toasted bread, raisins, candied peel, walnuts, sultanas, MOSTARDA di frutta, cinnamon, nutmeg, coriander and mace, all bound in clear honey. The pie is lavishly sprinkled with icing sugar before it is served. It is now industrially made and is available in many PASTICCERIE.

spremuta
fruit juice

A spremuta is the pure juice of a citrus fruit, to which water and sugar are sometimes added.

spumone
an ice cream

A very soft ice-cream concoction, originally from Naples and Sicily. The outside consists of a layer of vanilla ice cream, while the inside is a differently flavoured parfait. However, the more modern version of spumone is simply a kind of parfait. An old Piedmontese pudding made with mascarpone, sugar and eggs and flavoured with rum and candied citron is also known as spumone. The name derives from *spuma*, 'foam'.

 [see recipe below]

---

spumone al caffè
coffee-flavoured iced mousse

Serves 6–8
2 tbsp very finely ground espresso coffee
4 large egg yolks
115g/4oz/generous ½ cup caster (superfine) sugar
¼ tsp ground cinnamon
300ml/10fl oz/1¼ cups single (light) cream
2 tbsp brandy
300ml/10fl oz/1¼ cups double (heavy) cream
2 egg whites

Sometimes this SPUMONE can separate, with the coffee cream falling to the bottom. This happens when the coffee is not very well pulverized, but it tastes just as good.

Line a 1 litre/1¾ pint/4 cup loaf tin with clingfilm.

Crush the coffee with a rolling pin until it is very powdery. Put the egg yolks, sugar, cinnamon and coffee in a bowl and beat until well blended.

Heat a saucepan half full of water and when little bubbles form on the bottom of the pan, place the bowl containing the egg mixture over it. Beat until the mixture has reached the consistency of a mousse and has more than doubled its volume. Keep the water just below simmering point.

Heat the single cream. When it is warm, pour it over the egg mixture, beating constantly. Take off the heat, add the brandy and continue beating until the mixture is cool.

Whip the double cream until soft peaks form and then fold it gently into the egg mixture. Whisk the egg whites until stiff peaks form and then fold them gently into the mixture.

Spoon the mixture into the prepared tin. Freeze for at least 3 hours, until firm, stirring the mixture twice during this time.

spuntino
a snack

This is the modern word for MERENDA, snack. Spuntino can be anything from a piece of FOCACCIA, a mini-pizza, a sandwich or even a fruit salad, or it can also mean a small meal.

starna

see PERNICE

stecchi
a type of snack

A speciality of Genoa and Bologna. Stecchi means sticks, and on these short sticks, traditionally made of olive wood, a selection of sautéed morsels are threaded. They could include veal, sweetbreads, brains, tongue, artichoke segments, porcini and even slivers of truffle. The Ligurian stecchi are coated in a mixture of breadcrumbs and eggs and fried in olive oil, while the Bolognesi stecchi are dipped in a thin béchamel sauce and then coated with egg and breadcrumbs and fried.

Stefani, Bartolomeo
17th-century chef

Stefani was chef to the Gonzaga family during the second half of the 17th century. In the preface to his book *L'Arte di Ben Cucinare*, published in 1662, he wrote that he learnt his art 'from that Giulio Cesare Tirelli that in these matters did not have any superior'; Tirelli was his uncle and master. Stefani was the last in the centuries-long line of great Italian chefs. By the late 17th century it was the new haute cuisine of Versailles and the culinary dogmas of the French chef La Varenne that had become all the rage with the European aristocracy.

The court of the Gonzagas at Mantua was among the richest and most civilized of all the great European courts. Yet it was the only one where the cuisine was never so extravagant as to become divorced from the cooking of the people, and it always made use of the superb local ingredients. For this reason many of the dishes created for the court, such as the TORTELLI di zucca (pumpkin ravioli) and the MALFATTI, still feature in the local cuisine. There is no doubt that Stefani was partly responsible for this union.

Stefani was the first great chef to write practical advice for ordinary people. In a chapter addressed to '*Signori lettori*' ('Dear Readers') he gives an account of where in Italy the best ingredients are to be found. In one section Stefani lists the cost of 'ordinary food for eight people' for one day. This includes 5kg/11lb of meat, pasta, cheese, STRUTTO, eggs, lard, salad, RICOTTA, oil, pepper, raisins and vinegar. The total cost comes to a little over six lire!

The recipes in the book are grouped under broad headings, such as meat and poultry, soups (the first recipe for MINESTRA PARADISO is included), and how to prepare various vegetable pies, preserves, tarts, etc. Stefani rejected the heavy use of spices in favour of a cleaner style of cooking based on herbs, fruit and flowers.

[see recipe on facing page]

stelline
a pasta

Stelline, or 'little stars', are one of the many tiny pasta shapes for clear soups. They are boiled in a good stock and the result is a bowl of gentle, comforting MINESTRINA.

stinco
shin or shank

Although it is the same cut of meat as OSSOBUCO, stinco is cooked in one piece and carved just

zuppa di taccole
pea soup

Serves 4
500g/1lb 2oz mangetout (snow peas),
  topped and tailed
1 onion, chopped
1 large garlic clove, chopped
1.2 litres/2 pints/5 cups good chicken stock
25g/1oz/3 tbsp toasted pine nuts
1 tbsp sugar
juice of 1 lemon, organic or unwaxed
salt and freshly ground black pepper
4 slices of good-quality white bread
4 tbsp olive oil
50g/1¾oz Parmesan cheese, grated,
  plus extra to serve

I have adapted this recipe from STEFANI's original, which suggests using the pods of tender young peas.

Cook the mangetout with the onion and garlic in the stock for 20 minutes and then puree in a blender.

Meanwhile, pound the pine nuts with the sugar and lemon juice in a mortar. Stir this mixture into the puree and season to taste with salt and pepper.

Fry the bread in the olive oil until crisp and brown.

To serve, put a slice of fried bread in the bottom of each warmed serving bowl and sprinkle it liberally with Parmesan. Reheat the soup and pour it over the bread in each bowl. Serve immediately, with more Parmesan handed separately.

before serving. It can be the shin of a young calf, a lamb or a pig. Calf shin is a speciality of Trieste, where it is generously brushed with olive oil or butter, flavoured with rosemary and lemon juice and roasted in a very low oven. Pig's shin can be cooked in the same way or it can be pot-roasted with onion, garlic and herbs, in white wine. In Alto Adige, pork shins are served with sauerkraut.

[see recipe on page 410]

stoccafisso
stockfish

Dried (not salted) cod. The cod (hake or ling is also occasionally dried) used is usually from Norway. The head is removed and the fish is air-dried – the result is a fish that is as hard as wood. The best stockfish is known as *Ragno*.

Before cooking stockfish it must be beaten, to break down the fibres, and soaked in several changes of water for at least 48 hours. In Italy stockfish is also sold already prepared for cooking. It is eaten in all regions of Italy, but especially in Liguria and Veneto, from where most of the traditional recipes come. In the south, BACCALÀ (cod that is salted before being dried) is more popular. However, confusion arises from the fact that in some places, and everywhere in Veneto, stoccafisso is called baccalà, and thus many of the recipes are wrongly named.

The two most popular recipes from Veneto are *baccalà* MANTECATO (beaten with plenty of olive oil, until it becomes very creamy) and *baccalà alla vicentina* (see recipe on page 456). In Liguria a dish is made in which the mashed stockfish is mixed with mashed potatoes. In another Ligurian recipe the stockfish is cooked with cubed potatoes in oil flavoured with mashed anchovy fillets. But in most regions stockfish is cooked in UMIDO (in a tomato sauce), flavoured with local herbs and/or spices and usually served with POLENTA.

stinco in umido con le patate
stewed shin of pork with potatoes

Serves 3–4

1 shin of pork, about 1kg/2¼lb

salt and freshly ground black pepper

1 mild onion, finely sliced

4 garlic cloves, chopped

4 tbsp olive oil

250ml/9fl oz/1 cup beer

*2 tbsp chopped fresh rosemary, sage
    and thyme*

400g/14oz canned chopped tomatoes

*about 150ml/5fl oz/²⁄₃ cup meat stock
    (page 61)*

*800g/1¾lb waxy potatoes, cut into
    chunks*

This recipe originally comes from Venezia Giulia, where beer is used, but STINCO is a classic cooked all over northern Italy, with slight variations, some of which use red wine.

Preheat the oven to 180°C/350°F/Gas Mark 4.

Singe any coarse hair from the shin of pork. Sprinkle it with 1 teaspoon salt and a good grinding of pepper and pat the seasoning into the rind.

Put the onion, garlic, 1 teaspoon salt and the olive oil in a flameproof casserole and sauté gently for 3–4 minutes. Add 3–4 tablespoons of water and continue cooking over a low heat until the onions are soft – this will take about 15 minutes.

Push the onion and garlic to one side of the pan, turn the heat up a little, add the pork and brown on all sides. Pour over the beer and boil for 2–3 minutes. Add the herbs, then mix in the tomatoes with their juice and half the stock. Cover the casserole with a tight-fitting lid and cook in the oven for 2 hours, until the meat falls easily from the bone. If necessary, add a little more stock during cooking and turn the shin over. Taste and adjust the seasoning of the cooking juices, which should be rich and savoury.

Meanwhile, parboil the potatoes. When nearly cooked, add them to the casserole, about 15 minutes before the cooking time of the meat is up, with a little more stock if the cooking juices are too dry. Turn the potatoes over in the sauce and put the casserole back in the oven.

Let the meat rest for about 5 minutes and then cut it into chunks. Serve the meat surrounded by the potatoes.

storione
sturgeon

In the past sturgeon were plentiful and swam up the River Po to spawn; the best were found in the Ticino where it flows into the Po. Wild sturgeons are now rare, but the fish is very successfully farmed, both for its flesh and its eggs (caviar).

Sturgeon is cooked in wine flavoured with garlic, anchovies and parsley. It is also good roasted, grilled, fried, 'a COTOLETTA', or poached and served with the tuna fish sauce used for VITELLO TONNATO. Sturgeon is often first marinated in vinegar, white wine or lemon juice.

The roe, unless preserved for caviar, is usually breaded and fried in butter.

stracchino
a group of cheeses

A group of cheeses made in northern Italy. They are nearly all made with full-fat cow's milk that is fresh and still warm, mixed with the milking of the previous evening. Stracchino cheeses used to be produced mainly in September and October, and their name comes from the fact that they were made from the milk of cows which arrived *stracche* – 'tired' in Milanese dialect – at the end of the summer, after being driven down to the valleys from their summer pastures in the Alps. Nowadays stracchino is made industrially and produced all the year round.

Fresh stracchino is the same as CRESCENZA. QUARTIROLO, ROBIOLA, TALEGGIO and GORGONZOLA are all matured stracchini, with particular characteristics of their own.

stracci
a pasta

This pasta, in the shape of large triangles or small LASAGNE, originally from Liguria, is made at home. It is often a green pasta, made with spinach, and it is dressed with PESTO, or, in central Italy, with lamb RAGÙ.

stracciatella
a soup

Because of its simplicity, stracciatella is made with only the best meat stock. It also needs excellent Parmesan and good fresh eggs. These two ingredients are beaten together, sometimes flavoured with a grating of nutmeg, and stirred into the hot stock. Stracciatella is a traditional soup of Lazio and of Le Marche, where the nutmeg is replaced by lemon rind.

411

stracotto
braised meat

This term, which means 'extra cooked', is a popular braised beef dish of northern and central Italy, which differs from the other similar dishes, STUFATO and BRASATO, in that the meat is not usually marinated in wine, the wine being added to the meat during the cooking. Unfortunately, as is so often the case with Italian gastronomy, all is not quite as organized as it should be, and cookery writers use each of the three names in a loose way.

In a traditional stracotto from Emilia, the larded piece of beef is spiced with cloves and nutmeg. In Tuscany these spices are replaced by rosemary and other fresh herbs, and the stracotto is cooked in oil, fresh tomatoes are preferred to the tomato puree of the north and garlic is used much more generously.

Stracotto also means over-cooked, and it is mainly used for pasta or rice.

strangolapreti or strozzapreti
dumplings or pasta

Literally, 'priest chokers'. The name points to the fondness of priests for good food: they used to eat so many of these little GNOCCHI that they choked on them. It is the name given to any type of gnocchi in southern Italy.

In Naples, strangolapreti are potato gnocchi and the dressing is a classic Neapolitan tomato sauce (see recipe on page 331) or a Neapolitan ragù (see recipe on page 78), while in Basilicata they are made with pasta dough and dressed with a very hot RAGÙ. In northern Italy the name strangolapreti makes an appearance in Trentino, where it is applied once again to little gnocchi, this time made with a mixture of BIETOLA, Swiss chard or spinach and bread soaked in milk or stock. They are served with melted butter and cheese.

In southern Italy there is also a homemade pasta called strangolapreti or strozzapreti made in the shape of CAVATIEDDI and another pasta flavoured with lemon and made in the shape of ORECCHIETTE, which is fried and eaten just as it is, without any dressing, with a glass of sweet wine.

strascinati or strascinari
a pasta

A shape of pasta made in Basilicata. The dough, made with durum wheat flour and melted STRUTTO, is rolled into sausages about 5cm/2in long. These are *strascinati* – dragged – over a special wooden tool called a *cavarola* that leaves a design on the pasta. In the past, families had their own cavarola with their special design. Traditionally, strascinati are dressed with tomato sauce highly spiced with chilli, and PECORINO.

strascinato
cooking method

A method of cooking used for green vegetables such as spinach, BIETOLA, chicory, CIME DI RAPA or broccoli. The vegetables, which have usually been steamed or blanched, are quickly sautéed in oil or STRUTTO, flavoured with garlic and sometimes chilli, and are *strascinato* – dragged – across the bottom of the pan to absorb the flavouring.

strucolo
rolled pastry

A type of strudel from Friuli-Venezia Giulia. There are two kinds of strucolo, one sweet, with pastry similar to Austrian strudel but stuffed with RICOTTA, breadcrumbs and sultanas. The other is a savoury roll, such as my mother's recipe for *rotolo* on page 364.

struffoli
sweets

Neapolitan DOLCI, these are little balls of dough made with flour, egg and butter, flavoured with orange and lemon. They are fried in oil and then coated in a hot syrup of honey, spices, candied peel and sugar. Once made, they are piled up to form a cone or made into a ring, and decorated. Struffoli are prepared at Christmas-time and during the last week of Carnival.

strutto
rendered pork fat

To make strutto, fresh pork fat is cut into small pieces and cooked very slowly for a long time in an earthenware pot. It is then strained through a fine sieve into a warmed jar or other container, which in the past used to be the pig's bladder.

Because of health considerations, strutto is used now very little. There is on the market a very refined industrial strutto which is used for fried food – but not for fish. Unfortunately, as it is so refined, this strutto has lost the flavour of the original, which made so many southern dishes so incredibly delicious.

stufato
cooking method

A dish as well as a method of cooking meat. The meat, which can be one large cut or small pieces, – usually called *stufatino* – is first marinated with various flavourings in red wine and is then cooked in a covered container in the marinade for several hours. It is usually cooked on the hob over a low heat, not in the oven, so that more wine can be added gradually when needed. The end result must be meat that is pervaded by the taste of its rich sauce, and tender and juicy enough to explain the Milanese saying *'El stua besogna mangiall conel cugiaa'* ('stew should be eaten with a spoon').

In northern Italy a stufato of beef in a single piece is often the Sunday dish in the winter, and in Brianza, an area north of Milan, it assumes a festive role when it is cooked for the wedding dinner. A good stufato bodes well for a marriage.

Stufato can also be a dish made with vegetables braised in stock, milk or tomato sauce. In Tuscany there is a *stufato di fave* (broad/fava beans), in which the beans are cooked slowly, on a bed of chopped PANCETTA, oil, garlic and onion moistened with meat stock, in an earthenware pot. But the archetype of a stufato of vegetables is that from Basilicata, which is halfway between a thick soup and a vegetable dish. Onion, wedges of artichoke, potatoes, broad beans and diced pancetta are stewed in stock in an earthenware pot for several hours. At the end the pot is placed uncovered over a high heat to evaporate the extra liquid.

succo
fruit juice

This is the pure juice of a fruit, with no water or sugar added.

sugna
pork fat

Fresh pork fat, taken mainly from the back of the pig. Sugna is either used fresh, shortly after the killing of the pig, or it is rendered in an earthenware pot to make STRUTTO.

sugo
juice

Juice, the liquid that is extracted from fruit (also called SUCCO), vegetables or meat during cooking. *Sugo di carne* – the cooking juice of a roast, a steak or an escalope – is used to dress pasta or rice, as well as to serve with the meat.

There is some confusion caused by an overlap between the words sugo and SALSA. For example, what some writers call a *sugo di pomodoro*, others call a *salsa di pomodoro*.

suino
pork

Another word for MAIALE. Suino is mainly used as an adjective, for instance *carni suine* – pork meats.

supplì
rice croquettes

Rice croquettes fried in olive oil, a speciality of Rome and central Italy. There are two versions of supplì. *Supplì al telefono* consist of little croquettes of risotto containing PROSCIUTTO into which MOZZARELLA cubes are pushed. When you bite into them the melted mozzarella stretches into long threads, like telephone wires (hence the name). The other version is made with risotto dressed with a rich ragù. Supplì are a popular snack found in most bars.

 [see recipe below]

susina

see PRUGNA

suspirus
Sardinian sweets

One of the most delicate yet tasty biscuits, whose name means 'sighs' in Sardinian dialect. They are little balls, the size of walnuts, made with ground almonds, sugar and egg white, which are coated with lemon icing.

supplì al telefono
rice croquettes

Serves 8–10
500g/1lb 2oz/2½ cups risotto rice
about 2 litres/3½ pints/2 quarts
*   light meat stock (page 61) or*
*   chicken stock*
100g/3½oz/7 tbsp unsalted butter
125g/4½oz Parmesan cheese, grated
salt
a grating of nutmeg
100g/3½oz mozzarella, diced
100g/3½oz lean prosciutto, chopped
2 large eggs, lightly beaten with a little
*   salt*
a little chopped parsley
flour, beaten eggs and dried breadcrumbs
plenty of oil, for frying

Following the method for risotto in bianco (page 357), prepare a good risotto with the rice, stock, butter, some of the Parmesan, salt and nutmeg. When it is done, pour it over a marble slab, spread it out and leave to cool.

Combine the mozzarella, prosciutto, eggs, parsley, the rest of the Parmesan and salt (and some pepper if you like it) and knead well with your hands.

Make some balls the size of an orange from the risotto and form into the characteristic oblong shapes; make a hole in the middle of each ball with your finger, fill the hole with the stuffing and cover firmly.

Coat the supplì in flour, then in the beaten eggs and then in breadcrumbs. Fry them, a few at a time, in hot oil. When they are crackling and golden, drain on kitchen paper and serve at once, piping hot.

RIGHT: Supplì al telefono

t

tacchino
turkey

This bird is popular in northern Italy, where it is the traditional Christmas fare. In Lombardy a young hen turkey is boiled with lots of vegetables and served with MOSTARDA di frutta, or it is roasted, often stuffed (as in the recipe given here). In Piedmont the young bird, stuffed with boiled rice, grilled peppers, calf's liver and the bird's giblets, is roasted, basted with wine, and at the end the sauce is made more delicate by the addition of a cupful of cream.

The most interesting recipes come from Venice (the Venetian dialect word for turkey is *paeta*). In *paeta al malgaragno* (with pomegranate) the bird is roasted, basted with pomegranate juice and served with a sauce of sautéed giblets sharpened by pomegranate seeds and lemon juice. For *paeta alla schiavona* the turkey, stuffed with celery, chestnuts and prunes, is roasted on the spit. Another recipe for a stuffed, roasted bird, *paeta col pien*, has a typically Italian stuffing of PROSCIUTTO, SALAME, garlic, parsley and Parmesan, plus the Venetian sweet touch of candied peel and crumbled *favarini* (local soft biscuits).

Turkey breasts and legs are very popular and are cooked in the same way as veal escalopes or veal joints.

[see recipe on facing page]

taccola
mangetout

A variety of pea, which is eaten pod and all when the peas are just beginning to develop. Mangetout are popular only in Lombardy and Piedmont, where they are boiled or steamed and then sautéed in butter and sprinkled with grated Parmesan. A recipe suggests dressing the cooked mangetout with a sauce of cream and melted butter, flavoured with garlic (removed before serving) and Parmesan. During the truffle season, the blanched and buttered mangetout are showered with flaked FONTINA cheese and baked; the truffle is shaved over the top just before serving. A recipe for a mangetout soup is on page 409.

tagliarini
see TAGLIOLINI

tagliata
a meat dish

One of the new dishes served mostly in restaurants, tagliata consists of a thick T-bone steak, grilled or quickly fried, and served already cut diagonally into slices about 5mm/¼in thick (*tagliare* means 'to cut'). The tagliata is served in its cooking juices to which oil or butter, herbs and pepper are added. Tagliata is also called Robespierre as a funny reference to the guillotine.

tagliatelle
a pasta

The classic egg noodles of Emilia-Romagna. Tagliatelle are made with the traditional Emilian rich pasta dough of flour and egg (for which the recipe is on page 282), which should be rolled out

CONTINUES OVERLEAF

tacchino ripieno alla Lombarda
turkey stuffed with meat, chestnuts and fresh fruits

Serves 12

1 bronze hen turkey, about 5–6kg/
11–13lb, with giblets

200g/7oz unsmoked pancetta

2 tbsp olive oil

150g/5½oz/generous ½ cup unsalted
butter

100g/3½oz luganega or other coarse-
grained, mild continental sausage,
skinned and crumbled

50g/1¾oz minced (ground) veal

½ tsp grated nutmeg

¼ tsp ground cinnamon

salt and freshly ground black pepper

100g/3½oz pitted prunes, soaked if
necessary

2 dessert apples, peeled, cored and diced

2 pears, peeled, cored and diced

300g/10½oz chestnuts, peeled

50g/1¾oz/½ cup shelled walnuts

100ml/3½fl oz/scant ½ cup dry
Marsala

1 onion, sliced

1 sprig of fresh rosemary

1 sprig of fresh sage

150ml/5fl oz/⅔ cup dry white wine

1 tbsp flour

Stock

1 small carrot

1 onion

1 celery stalk

1 bay leaf

4 or 5 parsley stalks

6 black peppercorns, crushed

1 tsp salt

150ml/5fl oz/⅔ cup red wine

It may be presumptuous of me to call this recipe 'alla Lombarda', as there is no traditional recipe with this name. However, this is how turkey (TACCHINO) was cooked in my home in Milan, from a recipe by my paternal grandmother who came from Voghera in south-west Lombardy. The original recipe did not use olive oil, but LARDO, cured pork fat, which is difficult to find outside Italy.

First make the stock. Put the neck, gizzard and heart (reserve the liver) from the turkey giblets into a saucepan and add all the other ingredients for the stock. Add cold water to cover the ingredients by 5cm/2in, bring to the boil and then simmer for about 2 hours. Strain and set aside.

Preheat the oven to 180°C/350°F/Gas Mark 4.

Chop half the pancetta and put it in a small pan with the olive oil and 50g/1¾oz/4 tbsp of the butter. Add the sausage and veal and the chopped liver from the turkey. Sauté for 5 minutes and then add the spices and salt and pepper. Transfer to a bowl and add all the fruits, nuts and Marsala. Mix very thoroughly, then taste and adjust the seasoning.

417

Rub the turkey with salt and pepper inside and out and push the stuffing into the body cavity and the neck. Sew up the openings with a needle and kitchen string. Put the bird in a roasting pan and cover its breast with the remaining pancetta. Tie it in place with string. Set aside about 25g/1oz/2 tbsp of the butter and add the rest, cut into pieces, to the roasting pan together with the onion, rosemary and sage.

Cook the turkey for 30 minutes and then add the wine and enough stock to come about 2–3cm/about 1in up the sides of the pan. Cook, basting very often, until the bird is done, which will take a further 3–3½ hours.

About 30 minutes before the end of cooking, remove the pancetta covering the breast, turn the oven temperature up to 200°C/400°F/Gas Mark 6 and let the turkey breast become brown and shiny. Test to see if the bird is done by piercing the thickest part of a thigh: the juices should run clear.

Transfer the bird to a warmed dish and cover with foil. To make the gravy, strain the cooking juices into a pan and add the remaining butter blended with the flour, bit by bit, stirring vigorously and swirling the pan. If you want more gravy, add some stock. Bring to a simmer and boil gently to cook the flour. Transfer to a warmed sauceboat and serve.

thinly. It is then cut into long strips. According to the ACCADEMIA ITALIANA DELLA CUCINA, raw tagliatelle should be 1mm thick and 6mm wide. The usual width, however, is 8mm.

One of the earliest recipes we have for tagliatelle, by SCAPPI, dates from the 16th century. The dough is the same as today's, although he replaces one or two eggs with some water. Then, as now, achieving the right thinness of the SFOGLIA was an essential part of the procedure. MESSISBUGO writes that the sfoglia for pasta should be stretched 'by you and your friend, so that it will become as thin as paper.'

Nowadays most cooks make tagliatelle by machine, electric or hand-cranked, or buy them ready made. Tagliatelle made with egg are also available dried, and if they are made by a good Italian manufacturer are often better than shop-bought 'fresh' tagliatelle.

The classic Emilian dressing for tagliatelle is RAGÙ ALLA BOLOGNESE. But tagliatelle are a marvellous vehicle for most meat or creamy sauces and they are also perfect for baked dishes.

tagliolini or tagliarini
a pasta

Long pasta, narrower than TAGLIATELLE (it should be 2mm wide), ideal for soups or for a soufflé of pasta. To make the soufflé, slightly undercooked tagliolini are dressed with a creamy cheese sauce and an egg yolk. Egg whites are folded in and the soufflé is baked in the usual way.

A recipe from Tuscany dresses the tagliolini with a RAGÙ made with kid offal braised in butter and wine – it is quite delicious. There is also an old recipe from Modena for a sweet TORTA DI TAGLIOLINI.

tajarin
a pasta

These are the narrow, homemade TAGLIATELLE of Piedmont. The usual dressing is the juice from a roast, melted butter and sage, or a sauce made with butter and white wine added off the heat. But the most famous Piedmontese way to serve tajarin is to dress them lavishly with melted butter and Parmesan and then to cover them with thinly sliced white truffles.

[see recipe on facing page]

Taleggio
a cheese

A DOP cheese originally made in an Alpine valley of the same name in Lombardy. Taleggio, made from cow's milk, has a high fat content. It is made in 20cm/8in square shapes that weigh about 2kg/4½lb. It is aged for 1–2 months, in special storerooms which have the same climatic conditions of the caves in which the cheese was originally aged. Taleggio is soft, pleasantly salted and has a reddish crust which connoisseurs reckon to be as good as the paste of the cheese. It is also used for cooking: on pizza, mixed into béchamel sauce for baked dishes, in RAVIOLI and in FRITTATA.

tarallo or taralluccio
biscuit

Every town in southern Italy offers travellers the delight of its taralli – biscuits shaped like rings, figures of eight or knots. Usually savoury, there are now also some sweet taralli, which I find rather uninteresting. Taralli are made with a yeast dough enriched with egg or sweet white wine, and are flavoured with fennel seeds, cumin or pepper. They are the most popular snack of the south, now industrially produced and enjoyed everywhere.

tajarin all'albese
tagliatelle with white truffles

Serves 4
75g/2¾oz/5 tbsp unsalted butter
4 tbsp dry white wine
a grating of nutmeg
salt and freshly ground black pepper
egg pasta tagliatelle (page 282) made
with 3 large eggs and 300g/10½oz/
scant 2½ cups Italian 00 flour or
500g/1lb 2oz fresh tagliatelle or
350g/12oz dried egg tagliatelle
50g/1¾oz Parmesan cheese, grated
1 white truffle, about 50g/1¾oz,
cleaned

TAJARIN are the Piedmontese fresh pasta, narrower than the classic TAGLIATELLE of Emilia-Romagna.

Melt the butter and then pour in the wine. Boil briskly to reduce by half, which will take 4 or 5 seconds. Season with nutmeg, salt and pepper.

Cook the tagliatelle in boiling salted water until al dente. Drain and transfer immediately to a warmed serving bowl. Pour the butter sauce over the pasta, mix in the Parmesan, then slice the truffle over the top with a truffle slicer or a small knife. Serve immediately

tarantello
tuna fish salame

A tuna fish SALAME made in Taranto, Puglia, hence the name. The salted and cured belly of tuna is minced and combined with spices, and then pushed into natural casing.

tartelletta
small sweet tart

Usually filled with jam or fresh fruit and sold in PASTICCERIE as part of the array of PASTE.

tartina
a snack

An elegant snack, often served with drinks, consisting of half a bridge roll or a small, thin slice of bread, covered with a slice of PROSCIUTTO – CRUDO or COTTO – or of smoked salmon, or a spread of butter and shrimp, butter and truffle, butter and sardine, and other combinations. It can be garnished with a shrimp, capers, olives, a slice of hard-boiled egg, a rolled-up anchovy.

tartufo
truffle

Both white and black truffles are found in Italy, but it is the white that is the Italian truffle par excellence. The white truffle (*Tuber magnatum*) is known either as *tartufo bianco* or *tartufo d'Alba*, because the best of these truffles are found near Alba, in southern Piedmont. They are also found in smaller quantities in Umbria, Tuscany, Emilia and Veneto.

The white truffle has an intense aroma that has been described as a perfect marriage between a clove of garlic and a piece of the best Parmesan. It has a smooth rind, a squashed globular shape, often multi-lobed, and a colour varying from yellowish-grey to yellow-ochre with greenish tinges – it is sometimes said to resemble a potato – and it varies in size from 2–15cm/¾–6in. It is found in woods, where it grows in symbiosis with poplars, willows, oaks and lime trees, between October and December. The white truffle is usually eaten uncooked.

The taste of the black truffle (*Tuber melanosporum*) is milder than that of its white cousin, and it is usually brought out by cooking. It is blackish-brown in colour, with an irregular globular shape, covered with 'warts'. It varies in size: larger specimens may be 7–8cm/about 3in in diameter. It is associated with hazel and oak trees, and is in season between October and March. The black truffle is known as *tartufo nero* or *tartufo di Norcia*. Norcia is in Umbria, but this truffle is also found in Le Marche, Veneto and Lombardy. Small dogs are trained to find these buried jewels, but pigs are also occasionally used in Umbria. Black truffles are now cultivated, although with limited success.

The other truffle found in Italy is the *scorzone*, or summer truffle (*Tuber aestivum*), which has a pleasant truffly flavour, but it is certainly not as good as the white or black truffle.

The Romans loved truffles. APICIUS suggests either grilling them, wrapped in caul fat, or stewing them in wine. Writing in the 15th century, PLATINA cooks truffles in hot embers, having washed them in wine, and serves them hot, sprinkled with pepper. MESSISBUGO includes truffles in many of his menus; they are served raw at the end of the meal with cardoons, Parmesan and fennel. In a recipe in *La Cuciniera Piemontese*, published in 1798, small truffles are wrapped in pastry and baked, while in another recipe they are gently cooked in oil with parsley, shallots and herbs and splashed with champagne.

The truffle is one of the most adaptable of all foods; it seems to keep its strong identity whatever food it is combined with. The white truffle is perfection on a delicate RISOTTO or on a dish of TAGLIATELLE (see recipe on page 419), yet it can also improve the aggressive pungency of a BAGNA CAÔDA or the velvety richness of a FONDUTA. A few shavings sprinkled over a CARPACCIO transform

---

spaghetti alla nursina
spaghetti with black truffles

Serves 4
75g/2¾oz black truffles
100ml/3½fl oz/7 tbsp olive oil
1 garlic clove, crushed
2 salted anchovies, boned, rinsed and chopped, or 4 canned or bottled anchovy fillets, drained and chopped
salt and freshly ground black pepper
350g/12oz thin spaghetti

The black truffle gives a majestic flavour to a dish of humble spaghetti.

Scrub the truffles gently under cold water and pat them dry with kitchen paper, then grate them through the smallest holes of a cheese grater.

Put the truffles with half the olive oil in a small saucepan and cook over a very low heat for 1 minute. Take off the heat, add the garlic and anchovies and mash the mixture with a fork. Return to the heat and cook very gently for 5 minutes, stirring the whole time. The heat must be very low – on no account should the sauce be allowed to boil. Taste and add salt if necessary, and a generous amount of pepper.

Cook the spaghetti in boiling salted water until al dente. Toss with the remaining olive oil in a warmed serving dish and spoon over the truffle sauce. Serve immediately.

it into a gourmet dish. The milder-tasting black truffle makes a most delectable pasta sauce, for which the recipe is given here. A shaving of either kind of truffle gives any filling a lift. It changes the flavour of the simplest meatball, makes a gourmet dish out of a cheese FRITTATA, a POLENTA PASTICCIATA or even fried eggs.

 [see recipe on facing page]

tartufo gelato
an ice cream

This is a very popular ice cream, originally created by a *gelateria* in Pizzo in Calabria and now industrially made. It is a large ball of chocolate and hazelnut ice cream, filled with melted chocolate fudge sauce and rolled in cocoa powder.

tartufo di mare
a mollusc

Provided you know where it has been caught, the tartufo di mare is best eaten raw with a squeeze of lemon juice. It is also used instead of the VONGOLA to make pasta sauces.

tegame
shallow saucepan

A shallow saucepan, made of copper or earthenware, with straight sides and two 'ear' handles. A tegame is a fixture of any Italian kitchen because of its versatility. It is used for frying, sautéing, for braising vegetables and for making FRITTATA. A small tegame is called *tegamino* and is used for the cooking and presentation of food directly to the table. A classic use of a tegamino is for frying two eggs.

tellina
a clam

Telline are small clams, mainly found on the sandy beaches of the Tyrrhenian Sea, which need a lot of cleaning to wash away the sand. A delicious soup is made in Rome with telline, oil, garlic, white wine and parsley, served ladled over toasted bread.

temolo
grayling

'Temolo is an excellent fish, especially that caught in the river Adda. It can be cooked in any way, but it is best fried.' Thus wrote PLATINA in the 15th century. Today temolo, though rare, is found not in the river Adda itself but in the lake it feeds, Lake Como. It is still regarded as an excellent fish, 'the sea bass of freshwater fish', and it is cooked in the same way as a trout.

testa or testina
head

Testa refers only to the head of a pig, while testina is the head of a calf, lamb or kid. A pig's head is always sold cut in half and charred to get rid of all the hairs. Some parts, such as ears or temples, are cooked in particular recipes such as the Milanese dish of *tempia e ceci* (temple and chickpeas), traditionally made on All Soul's Day.

Of all the pig's head recipes, my favourite is the *coppa di testa* made in Lazio and Umbria. The half head is soaked for a few hours in two or three changes of cold water; then it is boiled with onion, carrot, celery and bay leaf for about 4 hours, until the meat comes away easily from the bone. All the edible bits are cut up and mixed with chopped pine nuts, pistachios, garlic, grated orange and lemon rind, cinnamon, chilli, salt and pepper. Wrapped in cloth in a large sausage shape, it is pressed down and left to get cold. When cold it is served with SALSA VERDE. I find it easier to press the cut-up meat in a loaf tin lined with foil.

Lamb's and kid's head, also cut in half, is roasted, sprinkled with lemon juice and flavoured with garlic and herbs, or it is wrapped in sliced LARDO and then braised in wine. These testine are especially popular in central and southern Italy and in Sicily and Sardinia.

Calf's head is a favourite of northern Italy, where it is part of a BOLLITO MISTO or it is sliced thinly, after being boiled, and served dressed with oil, lemon juice, parsley, salt and pepper.

testaroli
Tuscan crêpes

Testaroli are, like NECCI, cooked in ancient tools called *testi*, which are long-handled tongs with iron discs at the end.

In Lunigiana, a poor and mountainous area of northern Tuscany, testaroli were in the past the most common fare. Made with brown wheat flour and water, the thin dough is baked in a *testo*, which is heated over the fire until red hot, and then cut into lozenge shapes. These shapes – a sort of brown lasagne – are then boiled and placed in layers with a rather liquid pesto. Testaroli are among the great dishes that are made only in situ, where there are a few trattorie that specialize in them.

tiella
baking dish

Tiella is the name in southern Italy for an oven dish – *teglia* in standard Italian – and also for the food baked in it. A tiella will usually contain potatoes, onions, tomatoes, garlic and olive oil, to which may be added fish, mussels, pork, rice, courgettes, mushrooms or celery, or some combination thereof. The two best-known tielle are the *tiella di patate e cozze* – potatoes and mussels

– from Puglia, and the *tiella di maiale e funghi* – pork and mushrooms – from Calabria.

timballo
a mould

A round mould, as high as it is wide. The word also applies to the dish made in such a mould, a savoury baked dish, sometimes in a pastry case. A timballo is made with pasta or rice, dressed with meaty sauces or layered with vegetables. In the past, some splendid timballi were made for banquets: the sensuous description of the timballo served at a 19th-century banquet in *Il Gattopardo* (*The Leopard*) by Giuseppe Tomasi di Lampedusa inspired me to try and recreate that fabulous dish: '...when the knife broke the crust [out came]... masses of glistening macaroni, to which the meat juice gave an exquisite hue of suede.' The recipe is given here.

The mixture of a timballo can be spooned into small moulds to make *timballini*. Restaurants often use the word timballini for other mixtures cooked or served in a small timbale mould or ramekin, such as the spinach recipe given here.

[see recipes on facing page and page 424]

timo
thyme

The best thyme is the wild variety native to the Ligurian mountains. The other common kind, called PEPOLINO or serpillo, which grows wild in Tuscany, is also good. Thyme, although not a very common herb, is used as a flavouring in many meat and fish dishes, in most marinades, and is one of the essential herbs in a bouquet garni.

timpano
The name given to a TIMBALLO in Naples.

timballo di maccheroni del Gattopardo
pasta pie in a sweet crust

423

Serves 6–8
Sweet pastry (page 281)

Filling
140g/5oz/generous ½ cup unsalted
  butter, plus extra for greasing
100g/3½oz luganega sausage, skinned
  and crumbled
150g/5½oz skinless, boneless chicken
  breast, cut into thin strips
100g/3½oz chicken livers, trimmed and
  cut into small pieces
100ml/3½fl oz/scant ½ cup dry
  white wine
4–5 tbsp passata (strained tomatoes)
salt and freshly ground black pepper
100–150ml/3½–5fl oz/½–⅔ cup
  strong meat stock (page 61) or
  chicken stock
100g/3½oz prosciutto, thickly sliced
  and then cut into thin strips
100g/3½oz black truffle, grated, or
  2 tsp truffle paste
250g/9oz maccheroncini or pennette, or
  small tubular pasta
75g/2¾oz Parmesan cheese, grated
2 tbsp dried breadcrumbs
2 large eggs, hard-boiled and cut into
  wedges

Glaze
1 large egg yolk
2 tbsp milk
2 pinches of salt

The excellence and the beauty of this dish is worth the time and effort involved. The use of sweet pastry to envelop savoury ingredients is characteristic of the cuisine of past centuries.

First prepare the pastry. Dust the dough lightly with flour, wrap it in clingfilm and chill.

Next make the filling. Heat 50g/1¾oz/4 tbsp of the butter in a small saucepan, add the sausage and cook for a minute or two, stirring frequently. Add the chicken breast and cook for 5 minutes, then add the chicken livers. As soon as they have lost their raw colour, splash with the wine and boil briskly until the wine has nearly all evaporated. Mix in the passata and season with salt and pepper to taste. Reduce the heat and cook very gently for a further 10 minutes or so, adding a couple of tablespoons of the stock when the mixture becomes dry. Transfer to a bowl and mix in the prosciutto and truffle.

Preheat the oven to 220°C/425°F/Gas Mark 7.

Cook the pasta in boiling salted water until very al dente. Drain well and add to the meat mixture. Add half the Parmesan and the remaining butter and mix very well. Add a little more stock if the mixture seems dry.

Butter a 20cm/8in diameter springform cake tin or raised pie mould. Roll about one-third of the pastry into a circle large enough to cover the bottom of the tin and press it into the tin. Roll out half the remaining pastry into a long strip and use it to line the sides of the tin. Seal the joins with cold water, pressing them together. Sprinkle the remaining Parmesan and the breadcrumbs over the bottom. Pile half the pasta mixture into the mould and then gently place the hard-boiled eggs here and there. Add the remaining pasta mixture and level the top.

Roll out the remaining pastry into a circle, place it on top of the pasta and seal the pastry lid to the side strip. Gently beat together the ingredients for the glaze and brush over the pie. Make a few decorations with the pastry trimmings and brush with glaze before fixing to the top of the pie.

Bake in the oven for about 10 minutes. Turn the heat down to 180°C/350°F/Gas Mark 4 and continue baking for a further 20 minutes, until the pastry is beautifully golden all over.

Leave the timballo to cool in the pan for about 10 minutes, then unmould it onto a round dish and serve.

timballini di spinaci
spinach timbales

Serves 4

600g/1lb 5oz cooked spinach or frozen leaf spinach, thawed

25g/1oz/2 tbsp unsalted butter, plus extra for greasing

1 tbsp finely chopped onion

2 large eggs

100g/3½oz Parmesan cheese, grated

200ml/7fl oz/generous ¾ cup double (heavy) cream

3 tbsp freshly squeezed orange juice, from an organic or unwaxed fruit

a grating of nutmeg

salt and freshly ground black pepper

2–3 tbsp dried breadcrumbs, for the moulds

Tomato sauce (see page 331), to serve

These are usually served with a tomato sauce, or with a mushroom or cheese sauce. Instead of small timbales, you can use an 850ml/1½ pint/3½ cup ring mould for this recipe and bake it for 40 minutes.

Preheat the oven to 190°C/375°F/Gas Mark 5.

Thoroughly squeeze the liquid out of the spinach. Heat the butter, add the onion and sauté gently until the onion is soft. Add the spinach and sauté for about 5 minutes to let it take up the flavour. Transfer to a food processor and blend to a very coarse puree, or chop well by hand. Put the mixture in a bowl.

In another bowl, lightly beat the eggs with the Parmesan. Add the cream and orange juice with nutmeg and salt and pepper to taste, then mix in the spinach very thoroughly.

Grease four 150ml/5fl oz/⅔ cup moulds or ramekins very generously with butter. Check that the bottoms are really well covered with butter and then sprinkle with dried breadcrumbs. Shake off the excess crumbs and then fill the moulds with the spinach mixture.

Put the moulds in a roasting pan and pour boiling water into the pan to come two-thirds of the way up the sides of the moulds. Bake until set, about 20 minutes.

When the timballini are ready, loosen round the side of each mould with a small spatula and turn the moulds over onto warmed plates. Serve at once, spooning some tomato sauce around them.

tinca
tench

A freshwater fish of the same family as the carp. It used to be found in plenty in the lakes of northern and central Italy; today, though less plentiful, it is caught mainly in rivers. Tench is a very good fish, but it is full of bones.

The most popular method of cooking tench is in the oven, stuffed with Parmesan, breadcrumbs, garlic, herbs and spices. In a recipe from Tuscany, fried small tenches and young peas are cooked in white wine and tomato sauce flavoured with garlic and basil. In Lombardy a popular risotto is *risotto di tinca*. The fish is cut into chunks, which are braised in white wine and tomato sauce. The heads of the

tiramisù
mascarpone pudding

Serves 6
150ml/5fl oz/²⁄₃ cup strong espresso
*   coffee*
3 tbsp brandy
50g/1¾oz dark chocolate (minimum
*   70% cocoa solids)*
3 large egg yolks and 2 large egg whites
4 tbsp caster (superfine) sugar
250g/9oz/generous 1 cup mascarpone
about 18 Savoiardi biscuits
chocolate-coated coffee beans,
*   to decorate*

This relatively modern pudding has endless variations. Every cook can add his or her touch. I like to sprinkle grated chocolate over the top, rather than cocoa powder, and to put pieces of chocolate inside too.

Mix the coffee and brandy together. Grate about a quarter of the chocolate and set aside. Cut the rest of the chocolate into small pieces.

Beat the egg yolks with the sugar until pale and foamy. Fold in the mascarpone a tablespoon at a time and then whisk thoroughly until the mixture is very smooth.

Whisk the egg whites until stiff and fold gradually into the mascarpone mixture. Mix thoroughly but lightly.

Dip the biscuits one at a time into the coffee and brandy mixture. Turn them over once or twice until they become pale brown, but do not let them soak up too much liquid. Lay about 6 or 7 biscuits on an oval dish, to make a base. Spread over about a quarter of the mascarpone cream and scatter with some chocolate pieces. Dip more biscuits into the coffee mixture and make another layer. Spread with another quarter of the cream and scatter with chocolate pieces. Cover with the last layer of moistened biscuits and spread with half the remaining cream. (I make the second layer one or two biscuits smaller than the base, and the top layer smaller still.)

Cover the pudding with clingfilm and put it, with the reserved cream, in the refrigerator for about 6 hours.

Before serving, remove the clingfilm and spread the reserved cream over the top, smoothing it down neatly with a spatula. Sprinkle the grated chocolate all over the top and decorate with the coffee beans.

fish are used to make the stock for cooking the risotto, to which the boned morsels of tench and all the cooking juices are added at the end.

tiramisù
a pudding

This needs no introduction. Oddly enough, in a country where the dishes are often centuries old, tiramisù is a relative newcomer. It was created in the second half of the 20th century, allegedly by the owner of the El Toulà restaurant in Treviso. Tiramisù means 'pick me up', which the pudding does, as it is generously laced with coffee and some kind of alcohol. There are several versions of tiramisù and here is mine.

 [see recipe on facing page]

tocco
a sauce

In Ligurian dialect tocco is a sauce used to dress pasta, gnocchi or rice. *Tocco di carne* is made with a piece of beef or veal that is slowly braised in butter and bone marrow with onion, carrot and celery. It is then splashed with white wine, and a little tomato puree, herbs, a few dried PORCINI and a grating of nutmeg are added. The meat is traditionally eaten as a second course or on a separate occasion.

Tocco di funghi is made with fresh porcini sautéed in oil and then finished in a puree of fresh tomatoes to which ground pine nuts and parsley are added at the end.

toma
a cheese

A semi-soft cheese from Piedmont and Valle d'Aosta, made from cow's milk and cream, in cylindrical shapes of between 15 and 35cm/6–14in

in diameter and weighing between 1.8 and 8kg/4–18lb. The methods of production are artisanal and the quality of the toma Piemontese DOP cheese is controlled by legislation. Toma can be fresh with a milky yet slightly salty flavour, or aged for a few months, when it becomes quite strong. Fresh toma is sometimes used as a dressing for POLENTA.

tomaxelle
stuffed veal rolls

Tomaxelle were created in Liguria to use up leftover cooked meat, and there are many versions of the dish, some of them now made with fresh veal escalopes, as in the recipe given here.

[see recipe on page 428]

tomino
a cheese

Small TOMA made in cylindrical shapes of about 200g/7oz. They are made from cow's milk or cow's and ewe's and/or goat's milk and are always eaten fresh. Tomini are eaten by themselves at the end of the meal, or flavoured with pepper and served with a light dressing of olive oil and chopped herbs, part of the unending list of a Piedmontese ANTIPASTO.

tonnarelli
a pasta

A shape of fresh pasta made in Rome and throughout Lazio, tonnarelli are like SPAGHETTI but square in cross-section. The most famous recipe is *maccheroni alla* CHITARRA, from Abruzzo.

Tonnarelli are traditionally made with durum wheat SEMOLINO, but they can also be made with egg and wheat flour pasta dough. They are easier to make than TAGLIATELLE, because the dough does not need to be rolled out thin. Tonnarelli are good with most sauces suitable for spaghetti.

tomaxelle
stuffed veal rolls

Serves 4
500g/1lb 2oz veal escalopes
flour, for dusting
50g/1¾oz/4 tbsp unsalted butter
1 tbsp olive oil
4 tbsp dry white wine
1 tbsp tomato puree
200ml/7fl oz/generous ¾ cup meat
*   stock (page 61) or chicken stock*

Stuffing
20g/¾oz dried porcini
100g/3½oz calf's or lamb's sweetbreads
1 tbsp white wine vinegar
100g/3½oz lean stewing veal
25g/1oz/½ cup fresh white
*   breadcrumbs*
3–4 tbsp meat stock (page 61)
*   or chicken stock*
1 tbsp pine nuts, chopped
1 tbsp chopped fresh marjoram
1 tbsp freshly grated pecorino or
*   Parmesan cheese*
a grating of nutmeg
a pinch of ground cloves
1 large egg
1 garlic clove, very finely chopped
salt and freshly ground black pepper

The Ligurians are masters of stuffed food, in fact every Ligurian dish seems to contain another dish that is equally good.

First prepare the stuffing. Soak the porcini in a cupful of warm water for at least 30 minutes. Lift out, rinse under cold water and dry very thoroughly.

Blanch the sweetbreads for 2 minutes in boiling water to which you have added the wine vinegar. Drain and pat dry with kitchen paper. Remove the blood and lumps of fat and as much of the covering thin membrane as you can.

Chop the sweetbreads together with the veal and porcini. Soak the breadcrumbs in the stock, squeeze out, and put the crumbs in a bowl with the remaining ingredients for the stuffing. Add the meat mixture and some salt and pepper and mix very thoroughly together.

Cut the escalopes into pieces about 10–12cm/4–5in long. Spread the stuffing evenly over each slice and then roll up the slices. Tie with kitchen string and coat the rolls lightly with flour.

Heat the butter and oil in a large sauté pan or frying pan. When the butter begins to colour, add the veal rolls and brown on all sides. Add the wine and reduce for 1 minute, then add the tomato puree. Cook, stirring, for half a minute, then mix in about 100ml/3½fl oz/scant ½ cup of the stock. Bring to the boil and cook gently for 15–20 minutes, turning the tomaxelle over from time to time. Whenever the liquid dries out, add a couple of tablespoons of stock. If the liquid appears too thin at the end of cooking, transfer the tomaxelle to a warmed serving dish and reduce the cooking juices until they are nice and thick. Serve hot.

tonno
tuna fish

A very large fish, which can be as long as 3m/10ft. It swims at amazing speed, its beautiful dark blue body looking like a torpedo flashing through the water. Tuna fish live in deep water but move near the shore in early summer to spawn. It is then that the Sicilian *mattanza del tonno* (slaughter of the tuna with harpoons) takes place.

Tuna has been compared to pork, both for its fatty meat and because it has no waste. It is popular in central and southern Italy, where it is mostly grilled, but it is in Sicilian cooking that it truly comes into its own, with an array of recipes, some of which originate from Roman times. The Sicilian writer Alberto Denti di Pirajno boils the fish in a vinegary *court bouillon* to which a thick paste of anchovy fillets is added, a flavouring similar to the ancient GARUM. Another southern recipe is *tonno alla marinara*: the tuna steaks are cooked in the oven in olive oil with black olives, tomatoes, capers, dried breadcrumbs and basil. The Calabrese add fresh chilli, their favourite spice.

Two recipes from Livorno are worth a special mention. The first, *tonno ubriaco* ('drunken tuna'), is made by frying the steak in oil with garlic and parsley and then cooking it in Chianti. In the other, tuna with peas, the fish is sautéed in olive oil with plenty of garlic and then braised with peas in a tomato sauce. In Veneto a similar recipe is prepared, the fish and the peas being cooked in red wine instead of tomato sauce.

Tuna is also preserved. In the old days, it was preserved in oil in barrels, *tonno sott'olio*, the best part being the VENTRESCA (belly). In the best delis tonno sott'olio is still sold by weight, and it is a much better product than canned tuna. Preserved tuna is used with beans and red onions in the popular Tuscan dish *tonno e fagioli*, for which I give the recipe here. It also makes an ideal filling for ripe tomatoes, or for hard-boiled eggs, mixed with the yolks and mayonnaise, or for peppers, mixed with mashed potatoes. Traditional pasta sauces made with canned tuna are numerous in the south (see recipes on pages 285 and 466), while in the north tuna is used in rice salads, often with peas, as well as in VITELLO TONNATO. Another excellent dish is *polpettone di tonno* (tuna roll), served cold, with a very light mayonnaise or a dressing of olive oil and lemon juice. The recipe is given here.

In Sicily BOTTARGA is made with the salted and pressed roe of tuna fish.

[see recipes on page 430–1]

topinambour
Jerusalem artichoke

These nutty-tasting little tubers are eaten only in northern Italy, where the most popular way to prepare them is TRIFOLATI: they are first blanched and then sautéed in olive oil and butter, with shallots, garlic and parsley, to which anchovies are sometimes added. They are also cooked alla PARMIGIANA: blanched, sautéed in butter and then showered with Parmesan and baked. They are also excellent cold, previously boiled and dressed with SALSA VERDE, or raw with BAGNA CAÓDA.

429

tordo
thrush

These attractive birds are considered a great delicacy in Italy. They have dark meat with a strong aromatic flavour, given by the berries they like to eat. Thrushes are usually roasted on the spit, basted with olive oil, with slices of LARDO and sage leaves in between each bird. In Veneto, braised thrushes flavoured with juniper berries are boned, cut into strips and added to a RISOTTO with the strained cooking juices. In Chianti the locals cook their prey in oil with garlic, sage and black olives. Halfway through the cooking they add a handful of black grapes.

trance di tonno in salsa rinascimentale
tuna steaks in a sweet and sour sauce

Serves 4

12 pitted prunes

100ml/3½fl oz/scant ½ cup dry
  white wine

4 tbsp olive oil

4 fresh tuna steaks, no more than
  2cm/¾in thick

1 shallot, very finely sliced

1½ tbsp balsamic vinegar

½ tsp grated nutmeg

¾ tsp ground cloves

¼ tsp ground cinnamon

salt and freshly ground black pepper

½ tsp powdered saffron or
  1 tsp saffron strands

100ml/3½fl oz/scant ½ cup meat stock
  (page 61) or chicken stock

Nowadays tuna steaks are usually simply grilled, and very good they are too. For a change, try this recipe, which is my adaptation of a 16th-century recipe by Bartolomeo SCAPPI. The sweet and sour sauce tempers the oiliness of the fish.

Soak the prunes in the wine for about an hour.

Preheat the oven to 200°C/400°F/Gas Mark 6. Grease a shallow roasting pan with 1 tablespoon of the olive oil and lay the tuna steaks in it.

Put the remaining oil, the shallot, balsamic vinegar, nutmeg, cloves, cinnamon, salt and pepper into a saucepan and bring to the boil.

Lift the prunes out of the wine and add the wine to the saucepan. If you are using saffron strands, put them in a metal tablespoon and squash them with a smaller spoon. Heat the stock, stir in the saffron then add the saffron liquid to the saucepan. Stir well and simmer for about 15 minutes.

Cut the prunes into strips and scatter over the fish.

Taste and adjust the seasoning of the sauce, then spoon over the fish. Bake for 15 minutes, until the fish is cooked through. Baste twice during cooking. Serve hot.

tonno e fagioli in insalata
tuna and bean salad

Serves 4

½–1 red onion, according to size

salt and freshly ground black pepper

2 x 400g/14oz cans cannellini beans

5 tbsp extra virgin olive oil

200g/7oz canned Italian or Spanish
  tuna in olive oil, drained

The onions must be very sweet, not pungent.

Slice the onion very thinly and put it in a small bowl. Cover with cold water, add 1 teaspoon salt and set aside for at least 1 hour. This will make the onion sweeter and more digestible.

Rinse the beans under cold water and drain well. Tip them into a bowl and dress them with half the oil and salt and pepper to taste. Toss gently but thoroughly and then pile the beans into a serving dish. Flake the tuna and put it on top of the beans.

Drain the onion slices and pat them dry with kitchen paper. Sprinkle on top of the tuna. Pour over the rest of the oil and season with salt and pepper to taste.

polpettone di tonno
tuna roll

Serves 3–4

*200g/7oz canned tuna in olive oil,
drained*

2 large eggs

*1 large egg, hard-boiled and coarsely
chopped*

*2 tbsp chopped fresh flat-leaf parsley,
plus 4–5 parsley stalks*

50g/1¾oz Parmesan cheese, grated

a grating of nutmeg

salt and freshly ground black pepper

*100ml/3½fl oz/scant ½ cup wine
vinegar*

*100ml/3½fl oz/scant ½ cup dry
white wine*

1 small onion, sliced

To serve

4–5 tbsp extra virgin olive oil

1 tsp lemon juice

capers, preferably in salt, rinsed

black olives

lemon slices

An easy dish to make, and a good one to eat as long as you use best-quality canned tuna in olive oil.

Using a fork, flake the tuna in a bowl. Add the raw and hard-boiled eggs, chopped parsley, Parmesan, nutmeg and plenty of pepper. Mix thoroughly. Moisten a piece of muslin, wring it out and lay it out flat. Place the tuna mixture on the cloth and roll it into a 7.5cm/3in diameter log shape. Wrap the cloth around it and tie both ends with string.

Place the roll in a shallow oval sauté pan or roasting pan into which it just fits. Add the vinegar, wine, parsley stalks, onion and a little salt, then pour in enough cold water to cover the roll by about 1cm/½in. Cover the pan with a lid or a double thickness of foil and bring to the boil, then cook over a very low heat for 45 minutes.

Lift the tuna roll out of the liquid and transfer it to a board. Place a plate over it and put a weight on top of the plate. Leave to cool for at least 2 hours.

When the roll is cold, unwrap it carefully and cut into 1cm/½in slices. Arrange the slices, very slightly overlapping, on a dish. Beat together the oil, lemon juice and a pinch of salt until emulsified, then spoon this dressing over the slices. Scatter the capers and olives here and there and garnish with lemon slices.

431

torrone
Italian nougat

A bar made with egg white, honey and toasted almonds, flavoured with different essences, spices or liqueurs, torrone is one of the classic sweets of Christmas everywhere in Italy. The best known torrone has its origins in Cremona. For centuries it was made on a small scale, until in 1881 Secondo Vergani started a firm dedicated to its production. Vergani, together with a few other manufacturers, still make the best traditional torrone di Cremona.

Other kinds of torrone are made in other parts of Italy, often using hazelnuts or pistachios instead of almonds. In Aquila, the capital of Abruzzo, a softer torrone is made, which contains chocolate. In Sicily there are two varieties, both with obvious Saracen origins, one containing candied fruit and the other sesame seeds. Naples offers a torrone consisting of an outer layer of Madeira cake filled with marzipan and candied fruit, while in nearby Benevento it is made with the excellent local hazelnuts and local honey.

The *torrone gelato* of Calabria is shaped like a little log. It is made of icing sugar which is heated and into which candied fruits and toasted almonds are incorporated; the chilled nougat is then covered with chocolate icing. Here is a recipe for a soft torrone, which can be made at home.

[see recipe below]

torrone molle
soft nougat

Serves 8

115g/4oz/generous ¾ cup blanched almonds

200g/7oz/generous ¾ cup unsalted butter, at room temperature

200g/7oz/1 cup granulated sugar

115g/4oz/1 cup unsweetened cocoa powder, sifted

1 large egg

1 large egg yolk

115g/4oz plain biscuits, such as digestives (graham crackers), crushed

2 tbsp dark rum

candied flowers and blanched or sugared almonds, to decorate

This is one of the traditional puddings of northern Italian families. This recipe is from my family home. It must be made with the best cocoa powder.

Preheat the oven to 180°C/350°F/Gas Mark 4.

Spread the almonds on a baking sheet and bake for 7–10 minutes, until they turn golden. Put them in a food processor and process until very coarsely ground – not reduced to a powder.

Cream together the butter and sugar until light and fluffy. Add the cocoa a spoonful at a time and beat hard until it has been completely incorporated. This takes a little time and some beating; it can be done in a food processor. Now mix in the almonds.

Lightly beat together the egg and the yolk and add to the butter mixture, stirring until well blended. Add the biscuits and rum and mix thoroughly.

Line a 600ml/20fl oz/2½cup loaf tin with clingfilm and spoon the mixture into it. Press it down well to eliminate any air pockets and level the top with a spatula. Cover with clingfilm and refrigerate for at least 4 hours.

To serve, turn out, remove the clingfilm and decorate with candied flowers, such as violets or rose petals, and blanched or sugared almonds.

torta
a cake or a pie

In the past the word almost always applied to a savoury pie. One of the earliest known recipes appears in the *Libro de Cucina del Secolo XIV* by an anonymous Tuscan writer. It is the prototype of the English nursery rhyme 'Sing a Song of Sixpence'. This pie contained an inner compartment made of pastry in which cooked thrushes were placed. The lid could be lifted after baking, and some live thrushes were put in next to the cooked ones. 'And when the pie was open, the birds began to sing…'

There are many recipes for elaborate, gargantuan pies in Renaissance cookery books, but by the 17th and 18th centuries torte began to be lighter and similar to those we eat now. Traditional regional cooking is rich in *torte di verdure* – vegetable pies with pastry. Two such are TORTA PASQUALINA, from Genoa, and *torta di zucchine* – with courgettes. Baked dishes without pastry are often called TORTINI.

The first recipe for a cake rather than a pie or tart, which is virtually the same as today's PAN DI SPAGNA, was written by LEONARDI. Called *gattò di Torino glassato*, the cake is flavoured with lemon rind and covered with royal icing. It was not until the 19th century that torte, in the sense of cakes, became popular; this followed their introduction into Italy by Marie Louise of Austria, Duchess of Parma, and her Viennese cooks. ARTUSI gives many excellent recipes for cakes; nonetheless, there are relatively few that are genuinely old, regional preparations. By and large, the Italians do not eat cakes except occasionally.

[see recipes on pages 434 amd 436]

torta gianduia
see GIANDUIA

torta di pane
bread pudding

A torta di pane is the traditional sweet preparation made to use up leftover bread, a frequent necessity in a country where so much bread is eaten. There are as many different bread puddings as there are households. Some are made with apples or pears, others are highly flavoured with spices and/or studded with pieces of bitter chocolate and/or enriched with candied peel and nuts. The only ingredients that are always included are eggs, milk, sugar and, of course, bread. One special pudding from Veneto is made by soaking the stale bread in wine and sugar instead of milk and sugar; it is called *torta di pane ubriaca* – drunken bread pudding – and it is very good.

torta paradiso
madeira cake

A kind of very light and delicate Madeira cake, created by the Pasticceria Vigoni in Pavia, southern Lombardy, in the second half of the 19th century. The recipe is a well-guarded secret, and although torta paradiso has been copied by other PASTICCERIE, the copies do not match up to the original.

torta pasqualina
Easter pie

This, the best known of all vegetable pies, is traditionally made in Liguria at Easter. Like many dishes from this region, it calls for much skill, devotion and time. The dough is made with flour and water to which a little olive oil is added, to produce a pastry very similar to filo pastry, and like filo it is stretched until transparent. It is filled with artichokes, Swiss chard or spinach, and is usually served at room temperature.

When I was at a friend's house in Santa Margherita one Easter, I watched Albina, locally born and bred, making a superb torta pasqualina. After preparing the dough, she divided it into 20 balls (traditionally there should be 33, one for each year of Christ's life) and left it to rest while she made the filling. This consisted of Swiss chard, cut into very thin strips, sautéed in butter and onion and flavoured with marjoram. She then returned to the pastry and, taking one ball at a time, thinned it out by rolling it round one hand before passing it at fantastic speed to the other hand, just like a Neapolitan pizza maker. Hard to describe but quite hypnotic to watch. Each of the resulting paper-thin sheets was brushed with oil and placed in an oiled copper pan.

Having laid the first ten sheets, Albina placed the filling on top, covered with some PRESCINSENA, the local soft cheese, mixed with cream. She then made six holes in the filling and into each one she put a knob of butter, an egg, a little grated Parmesan and salt and pepper. The remaining ten layers of pastry were then built up, all paper thin, all moistened with oil. The last layer was pricked with a fork, and the torta pasqualina was baked in a moderate oven for an hour. It was magnificent.

torta di riso
rice cake

Many different versions of this cake are made in Tuscany and Emilia-Romagna, and in most other regions. In some recipes the cooked rice is put in a sweet pastry shell; in others some cocoa is added to half the rice so that the cake is prettily divided into two colours. The recipe for my favourite torta di riso is on page 134.

torta di mandorle
almond cake

Serves 6–8
unsalted butter, for greasing
3 large eggs, separated
150g/5½oz/¾ cup caster (superfine) sugar
50g/1¾oz/6 tbsp potato flour
150g/5½oz/1½ cups ground almonds
2–3 drops pure almond extract
1½ oranges, organic or unwaxed
icing (confectioners') sugar, to decorate

Of the many Italian sweet TORTE, those made with almonds are among the most popular. This gluten-free cake is perfect served with soft fruit or fruit sorbets.

Preheat the oven to 180°C/350°F/Gas Mark 4. Grease a 20cm/8in diameter springform cake tin generously with butter.

Beat the egg yolks with the caster sugar until pale and thick. Add the potato flour and then the ground almonds and incorporate well. Add the almond extract, grated rind of one of the oranges and the strained juice of 1½ oranges. Whisk the egg whites until they form stiff peaks and fold gently into the almond mixture.

Spoon the mixture into the prepared tin and bake for 45 minutes, or until a skewer inserted in the middle of the cake comes out dry.

Leave to cool in the tin for 5 minutes and then turn out onto a wire rack to cool. When cold, wrap in foil. Sprinkle with icing sugar before serving.

torta di tagliolini
pasta cake

There are two kinds of torta di tagliolini, one made in Verona and the other in Modena. In both, tagliolini are placed uncooked in layers with chopped almonds, sugar, plenty of butter, lemon and orange juice and some liqueur, and then baked in the oven. In the torta of Modena the ingredients, which also include candied peel, are baked in a case of sweet pastry. These delicious cakes are best made with thin homemade TAGLIOLINI, because the bought kind is too thick.

tortelli
stuffed pasta

RAVIOLI stuffed with vegetables, made for festive occasions. They are mostly square-shaped and, like most stuffed pasta, they come from the Po Valley.

Many different stuffings are used, but tortelli stuffed with spinach and RICOTTA are the most popular of them all. The tortelli of Mantua, *tortelli di* ZUCCA, are stuffed with the local pumpkin, with AMARETTI and MOSTARDA di frutta, while the pumpkin tortelli of Reggio Emilia and Ferrara (where they are called CAPPELLACCI) omit the

torta sbrisolona
crumbly almond and polenta cake

Serves 6

115g/4oz/generous ¾ cup blanched almonds

115g/4oz/generous ½ cup granulated or caster (superfine) sugar

150g/5½oz/1¼ cups Italian 00 flour

115g/4oz/scant 1 cup coarse-ground polenta flour (coarse cornmeal)

grated rind of 1 organic or unwaxed lemon

a pinch of salt

2 large egg yolks

115g/4oz/½ cup unsalted butter, at room temperature, plus extra for greasing

icing (confectioners') sugar, to decorate

Mantua in southern Lombardy boasts many specialities, of which this sweet TORTA is one. Its name comes from *sbriciolare*, meaning 'to crumble', because the cake breaks into lots of delicious nutty crumbs when it is cut. In Mantua it is eaten with sweet wine.

Preheat the oven to 200°C/400°F/Gas Mark 6. Grease a shallow 20cm/8in diameter cake tin generously with butter and line the bottom with baking parchment.

Spread the almonds on a baking sheet and bake for 7 minutes or until golden brown. Remove from the oven and turn the oven down to 180°C/350°F/Gas Mark 4. Put the almonds in a food processor with 2 tablespoons of the caster sugar and process until they are reduced to a coarse powder.

In a bowl, mix both flours, the remaining sugar, the almonds, lemon rind and salt. Add the egg yolks and work with your hands until the mixture is crumbly. Add the butter and work again to incorporate it thoroughly, until the dough sticks together in a crumbly mass.

Spread the mixture evenly in the prepared tin, pressing it down with your hands. Bake for 40–45 minutes, or until the cake is golden brown and a skewer inserted in the middle comes out dry.

Turn the cake out onto a wire rack and peel off the baking paper. Leave to cool. Before serving, sift icing sugar over the cake.

amaretti and mostarda but are more lavish with Parmesan. All these tortelli are dressed only with butter and grated Parmesan. The traditional tortelli of Bologna contain a mixture of ricotta, Parmesan, parsley and eggs, and they are dressed with a buttery tomato sauce made with a touch of onion.

There is also a different kind of tortelli made in Lombardy and Emilia-Romagna. These are sweet tortelli, made from a dough similar to profiteroles without the filling but lavishly dusted with icing sugar. They are eaten hot at Carnival, on St Joseph's Day (19 March) and often halfway through Lent, when traditionally the pleasures of the flesh can be enjoyed for 24 hours.

tortellini
stuffed pasta

The small stuffed pasta are folded round and the ends pressed together to form a ring. The legend of why they are shaped like that is based on the story of an innkeeper in Bologna who peeped into the room of a beautiful girl sleeping naked on her bed. Thinking about her belly button, he went into the kitchen and produced tortellini.

They are stuffed with minced chicken, pork, PROSCIUTTO, MORTADELLA, Parmesan, eggs and flavourings. They are cooked and served in stock, as a soup. Homemade tortellini are for festive occasions only, since making them entails hours of dedicated labour.

tortelloni
stuffed pasta

A large version of TORTELLI and, as with tortelli, the filling is RICOTTA and spinach, or ricotta, parsley and Parmesan, although these days it can be anything the cook fancies.

tortiglioni
a pasta

Large tubular pasta with spiral ridges. They are ideally suited for dressing with a thick vegetable sauce or a meat RAGÙ, or for baked pasta dishes.

tortino
vegetable pie

Usually without pastry, tortini are baked vegetable dishes. Their motherland is Liguria, although there they are often called POLPETTONI (see recipe on page 137), a word which elsewhere in Italy means a meat loaf. Tortini are made with various vegetables: artichokes, green beans, spinach, aubergines, cardoons or courgettes. The vegetables are first blanched, then chopped and sautéed in olive oil and butter with garlic or onion. Bread soaked in milk or mashed potatoes are added, as well as eggs for binding, herbs and Parmesan for flavouring. The tortino is then baked. In the *tortino di carciofi*, a speciality of northern Tuscany, the artichokes are finely sliced into segments and stewed in oil and water.

Toscana
Tuscany

Tuscan cuisine reaches perfection through its simplicity. This simplicity was certainly not evident in the banquets given by the Medicis, especially during the High Renaissance. The extravagance and prodigality, and perhaps vulgarity, that characterized these banquets can be seen from the description of a banquet given by Ferdinand I for the wedding of his niece Maria to Henry IV, King of France, in 1600. The sculptor Giambologna was commissioned to model statues made of sugar, one of these being an equestrian statue of the King.

Among the countless dishes were turkeys made to resemble the mythical, many-headed

TUSCANY

Carrara
Pistoia
Lucca
Prato
Pisa
Florence
Arno
Livorno
Arezzo
Siena
VALDICHIANA

LIGURIAN
SEA

Elba
Grosseto

TYRRHENIAN
SEA

hydra, great domed concoctions of stuffed puff pastry, prosciutti shaped like cockerels, quails en croûte, chicken stuffed with ravioli, roasted piglets, thrushes and skylarks. The sweets included citron tarts, iced cakes, large wafers filled with cream and small almond biscuits filled with cream. At the end of the meal there were trays of MARZOLINO and *raviggiolo* – the two famous Tuscan cheeses; raw artichokes, celery and fennel; peaches in wine, quince cheese, candied apples and fresh strawberries.

These gastronomic excesses, however, were limited to the court and the nobility. Ordinary people went on eating pig's liver, FAGIOLI *al fiasco*, all the delicious local vegetables and pulses (legumes) and the beloved CASTAGNACCIO, chestnut cake, which is still the favourite sweet served in the poorest homes as well as in patrician palaces. Tuscan cooking is often described as '*una cucina povera*', which means a cuisine without elaboration or frills.

A meal begins with one of the soups for which the Tuscans are justly famous, such as RIBOLLITA or *zuppa di* FARRO. These are nourishing, thick and fragrant, full of vegetables, beans, herbs and olive oil. They are ladled over the local unsalted bread, often rubbed with garlic.

Pasta is not a forte of local cooking. There are only two traditional recipes, PAPPARDELLE *con la lepre* and the Sienese PICI. Both are more an accompaniment to rich sauces than dishes in their own right. It is only recently that pasta has been served in restaurants in Tuscany and this is more for the benefit of the tourists than for the locals, who usually prefer to choose a soup. In country trattorie you can still sometimes see old locals eating pasta with a spoon and fork, as some foreigners do.

While neither pasta nor RISOTTO are traditional in Tuscany, meat certainly is. The 20th-century writer Giuseppe Prezzolini says of Tuscan cooking: 'lean, tasty, full of spirit and of aroma, made for people who have a quick mind and do not want a pot belly. Tuscan cooking never thought of risotto nor created macaroni, keeps fats at a distance, while keeping the spit and grill close by, with the purifying flame of wood and charcoal. Tuscan cooking excels in fried food, and roasts without sauces.' The meats are roasted with rosemary or fennel, or grilled, the BISTECCA *alla fiorentina* being the prime example of the latter. The Tuscans know good meat, as indeed they should, having the best beef in Italy from the Chianina breed of cattle, the best pork from the Cinta Senese breed of pig and the best chickens, the Livornesi and those of the Valdarno. They cook the chickens in many ways, as they do rabbits, often quickly in PADELLA, in olive oil, garlic and herbs.

Olive oil is what makes Tuscan food so unmistakably Tuscan. Rather than a dressing, it is the main character in the gastronomic scenario. Food is sautéed and fried in it, soups are '*benedette*' by it – given a last-minute benediction by spooning oil into them – and every vegetable, raw or cooked, is made tastier with a couple of tablespoons of it. Olive oil is also used in the preparation of sweets, such as *castagnaccio* and all the fritters in which the local cooking is particularly rich.

The appeal of Tuscany's vegetables is unending: fennel, artichokes, asparagus, tomatoes and, above all, beans, particularly the small white cannellini bean. Beans are served with pork – ARISTA, grilled chops, or as FEGATELLI – with tuna, or simply by themselves with plenty of sage and garlic – *fagioli all'uccelletto* (see recipe on page 138).

Apart from a few pork SALUMI such as FINOCCHIONA and mountain PROSCIUTTO, the Tuscan specialities are the salumi made from wild boar. All kinds of game are popular, from venison and boar to thrushes and skylarks, not only for their gastronomic value but also because of the Tuscan passion for shooting almost anything that moves.

Along the Tuscan coast the fish soup CACCIUCCO and the red mullet of Livorno (see recipe on page 444) are the principal dishes in the northern area, while further south the catch is grey mullet, which is usually grilled, as well as cuttlefish and octopus, which are prepared in many ways. Another speciality found only in Tuscany are the elvers – CIECHE – caught at the mouth of the Arno near Pisa. They are thrown alive into a frying pan with very hot olive oil, flavoured with sage and garlic. They are served either as they are or with a couple of tablespoons of tomato sauce.

One of the main elements common to all Tuscan cooking, apart from its simplicity and the excellence of the primary ingredients, is the wide use of herbs. Thyme, sage, rosemary and tarragon are added to soup, meat and fish. Spices are also common, fennel seeds and chilli being quite popular. Chilli is called ZENZERO in Tuscany, a word that elsewhere in Italy means ginger. This gives rise to endless misunderstandings with foreigners, who cannot taste the 'ginger' that is supposed to be in the tripe or the sausages of Siena.

Tuscany offers the best PECORINI, mostly made with ewe's milk, of which those from the Crete Senesi and from Pienza are the most highly prized. Also famous is the MARZOLINO of Chianti. The usual way to end a meal is with pecorino which, in April, is accompanied by young raw broad beans.

Apart from the creamy and mouthwatering ZUCCOTTO of Florence and the richly medieval PANFORTE from Siena, all the DOLCI have a genuine country simplicity and a limited appeal.

totano
a type of squid

A cephalopod similar to a squid, but with a longer and tapered body, which allows it to leap out of the water and glide through the air for short distances. It is found off the coasts of Sardinia, Liguria and Tuscany, where it is sometimes wrongly called *calamaro*. Its flesh is tougher and less tasty than that of a squid, though it can be cooked in similar ways. Small totani (*totanetti*) are often part of a FRITTO MISTO DI MARE.

tramezzino
sandwich

Little sandwiches made of bread – usually white – and containing various fillings, often moistened with a little mayonnaise. Tramezzini are eaten in bars with aperitifs; they are very rarely prepared at home.

In Trentino, delicious tramezzini are made with grilled POLENTA containing a slice of PROSCIUTTO COTTO or SPECK.

trancia
fish steak

A steak cut from a large fish, be it tuna fish, swordfish or hake. The steaks are often grilled and dressed with a lemony sauce such as SALMORIGLIO.

They are also baked, or cooked in a large sauté pan in oil and white wine plus flavourings, or stewed, as in western Sicily, with tomato sauce, black olives, capers and cornichons (see recipe on page 303). Trance di tonno are excellent finished in a sweet and sour sauce (see recipe on page 430). Steaks of white fish are used in Puglia in their TIELLE, baked between two layers of potatoes.

treccia
a bread, a cheese

Treccia means 'plait', and in Milan the word is used for a plaited loaf of white bread. It is about 30cm/12in long, with a golden crust and a compact dough inside.

The same word is used for a cow's or buffalo's milk cheese of the MOZZARELLA type, twisted to form a thick plait.

trenette
a pasta

A long, thin Ligurian pasta, similar to LINGUINE. PESTO is the classic sauce for trenette, although a mushroom sauce could be contemplated by even the most stringent purist.

Trentino–Alto Adige

The cooking of these two northern areas, which are joined together for administrative reasons, is very different. In Trentino, to the south, the influence of the cooking of Veneto is total, while – in gastronomic terms – the Alpine region of Alto Adige (also known as Süd Tirol, South Tyrol) could be described as an Austrian province, albeit with an Italian influence.

In Trentino, as in Veneto, POLENTA is a staple. It is made with either maize flour (cornmeal) or buckwheat flour (known as *polenta nera*, 'black polenta', because of the dark colour of

the buckwheat) or a mixture of the two, and sometimes potato flour. It is eaten with pork of any kind, with cheeses or with STOCCAFISSO.

Polenta is also eaten with a stew of mixed mushrooms, in which the Dolomites are particularly rich. The harvest of wild mushrooms includes ceps, chanterelles, CHIODINI and *russole*, plus many other species that grow only in this area. The largest fungi market in Italy is in Trento, where on some days as many as 250 different species have been counted.

The traditional pasta dishes are STRANGOLAPRETI, which in Trentino are like big spinach gnocchi, and *tagliatelle smalzade*, tagliatelle dressed with the juice of roast meat and cream. The real peasant dish of Trentino is a thick soup of tripe, which is very thinly sliced and cooked with onion, leeks and potatoes, with breadcrumbs added at the end.

Cheeses, nearly all made from cow's milk, are an important product of Trentino, the best being

VEZZENA. Apples are grown in great quantity, and their quality is first class. Some local restaurants have created savoury recipes based on these fruits; one such is *risotto alla renetta* (with Reinette apples), in which you can detect the influence, however slight, of German cooking.

In Alto Adige the cooking is wholeheartedly and unashamedly Austrian. It is cooked by people who were originally Austrian for tourists who are mainly German. The food, in restaurants as much as in homes, is truly traditional. Oddly enough, while many dishes from Alto Adige have been incorporated into the cooking of Trentino, none from Trentino has made the slightest impression on the chauvinistic inhabitants of Alto Adige, even pasta having been almost entirely ignored. There are only three dishes that the two sub-regions have in common: one is the bread dumplings called KNOEDEL in Alto Adige and CANEDERLI in Trentino. The other two are soups: *mus*, a liquid polenta dressed with lots of melted butter and poppy seeds, and *la zuppa di vino*, a soup made with beef stock, white wine, egg yolk and cinnamon.

The pig is king of the table, and pork dishes are often accompanied by sauerkraut. It is boiled, roasted or made into SALUMI, usually smoked, of which SPECK is now famous all over the peninsula. In the Dolomites furred game is often eaten during the season, in particular CAPRIOLO, roe deer (see recipe on page 86). Another dish, originally from Bressanone but now also made in Trentino, is a favourite of tourists; it has the amusing name of '*piatto dell'elefante*' ('elephant's dish'). It consists of many meats – pork, beef, venison, veal, chicken, liver sausages, frankfurters – and seasonal vegetables boiled together and placed on a bed of boiled rice, dressed with melted butter.

The only traditional pasta dish of Alto Adige is *ravioli alla pusterese*, the pasta being made with rye and wheat flour. The stuffing is either spinach and RICOTTA or sauerkraut, in which case the ravioli are fried rather than boiled. Bread is brown, and also made with wheat and rye flours; the latter is grown in the local valleys.

The puddings and sweets are as Austrian as their names. *Kastanientorte* is made with chestnut puree mixed with butter, flour, sugar and eggs; the cake, when baked, is covered with whipped cream. The local strudel contains seasonal fruit and egg custard and is flavoured with poppy seeds. *Zelten*, made with a yeast dough of rye flour, is studded with dried figs, sultanas, dates, pine nuts and walnuts. Zelten is one of the many preparations to have been adopted by the Trentini who, like their neighbours to the north, make it for Christmas. But in its journey south, zelten has shed the rye flour for wheat flour and gained some eggs, and as a result has become white, and lighter, giving it the Italian flavour and appearance that is totally lacking in the cooking of Alto Adige. After all, this area only became part of Italy in 1919.

trifolare
cooking method

A method of cooking some vegetables, such as mushrooms, courgettes, aubergines and Jerusalem artichokes. The sliced vegetables are sautéed in olive oil, garlic and parsley; these are the basic elements, to which anchovies, capers and wine may be added. In Liguria this method of cooking is called *al funghetto*. Oddly enough, only one meat dish shares the name and method: ROGNONI (kidneys) trifolati, for which the recipe is on page 361.

[see recipe on page 442]

funghi trifolati
sautéed mushrooms with parsley and garlic

Serves 4
25g/1oz dried porcini
500g/1lb 2oz fresh mushrooms, wild
  and cultivated
4 tbsp extra virgin olive oil
15g/½oz/1 tbsp unsalted butter
2 shallots, finely chopped
1 garlic clove, finely chopped
4 tbsp chopped fresh flat-leaf parsley
salt and freshly ground black pepper

Fresh porcini are the best FUNGHI to prepare in this way, but the dish is also good as I have described it here, with a mixture of wild and cultivated mushrooms and a handful of dried porcini to boost the flavour.

Put the dried porcini in a bowl, cover with hot water and leave for about 30 minutes.

Meanwhile, clean the fresh mushrooms. Unless they are very dirty, wipe them with damp kitchen paper rather than washing them. Cut them into thick slices.

Lift the porcini out of the water. Wash them under cold running water if you find some grit still attached. Cut them into small pieces.

Heat the olive oil and butter in a large sauté pan and sauté the shallots until soft. Add the garlic, half the parsley, a little salt and plenty of pepper. Cook, stirring constantly, for 1 minute and then add the porcini. Cook for 5 minutes or so and then throw in the fresh mushrooms and another tablespoon or so of parsley. Cook over a lively heat for about 10 minutes, turning the mushrooms over very quickly so that they do not stick to the pan. There should be very little liquid left by the end of cooking.

Sprinkle with the rest of the parsley before serving.

RIGHT: Funghi trifolati

trifolare

triglia
red mullet

There are two varieties of red mullet: *triglia di fango* – mud – and *triglia di scoglio* – rock, which is better and is generally redder in colour.

This beautiful fish was highly valued by the Romans, who kept them in seawater pools to fatten them artificially. Large specimens fetched extremely high prices during the early Empire. The poet Juvenal mentions a very large specimen weighing over 2kg/4½lb that was bought for 6,000 sesterces, a sum that could have bought a large field at the time. Eventually, when three large red mullet were sold together for 30,000 sesterces, the emperor Tiberius imposed a sumptuary tax on the fish market.

Red mullet were also highly prized during the Renaissance. MARTINO da Como cooked them in the simplest way by grilling them, using a sprig of rosemary to baste them with oil, vinegar and salt.

In the 18th century the Neapolitan Vincenzo CORRADO cooks them in the oven covered by a little sauce consisting of chopped onion, garlic, marjoram, anchovy fillets, capers, rosemary, olive oil, lemon juice, salt and pepper. ARTUSI in the 19th century wrote five recipes for the fish, in one of which the red mullet are marinated for several hours in oil, lemon juice, salt and pepper and then, coated in breadcrumbs, are baked in the marinade, with slices of PROSCIUTTO in between them and a few sage leaves. Ada BONI in *Il Talismano della Felicità* has eight recipes for red mullet, of which my favourite is that for the fish baked in greaseproof paper with dried mushrooms, chopped prosciutto, oil, butter and a little meat juice 'without tomato', she specifies.

Red mullet is still one of the most popular fish. It should be cooked with the liver inside, which is considered the *'bonne bouche'*. It is excellent grilled, or baked 'al CARTOCCIO' (wrapped in greaseproof paper or foil) with herbs and wild fennel, as it is done in Sicily. In Abruzzo, red mullet is cooked in a pot in white wine and olive oil, with prosciutto and bay leaves.

 [see recipe below]

---

triglie alla livornese
red mullet in tomato sauce

Serves 4

*4 red mullet, weighing about 250g/
9oz each*

4 tbsp flour

6 tbsp extra virgin olive oil

1 garlic clove, very finely chopped

1 small onion, finely chopped

1 bay leaf

½ tbsp chopped fresh thyme

a small piece of dried chilli

salt and freshly ground black pepper

*400g/14oz canned chopped tomatoes,
drained*

2 tbsp chopped fresh flat-leaf parsley

This recipe is from Livorno, on the Tuscan coast. The head of the fish is left on because it gives flavour to the dish, and also because the fish looks better this way.

Ask your fishmonger to clean the fish, scale it well and remove the gills. The liver of red mullet should be left in the cavity. Wash the fish under cold running water and dry thoroughly. Coat the fish with flour.

Heat the olive oil in a large frying pan over a medium heat. Slide in the fish and sauté for about 2 minutes on each side.

Add all the other ingredients and turn down the heat. Cook gently for 10 minutes, basting the fish occasionally and turning it over once.

Taste and check the seasoning before serving.

RIGHT: Triglie alla livornese

trippa
tripe

Trippa means the four parts of the stomach of a ruminant; of the four kinds of tripe, the best is the honeycomb tripe. In Italy it is the tripe of a young ox or a heifer that is eaten. All tripe is sold cleaned and partially cooked.

In Italy, as in France, tripe is highly appreciated because of its delicate flavour and its property of making the juices in which it cooks rich and thick. It is also very nourishing and highly digestible. Tripe is not as easy to cook as one might think, since it can be spoilt by being cooked for too long or too short a time. It should remain al dente but not be so chewy as to be like rubber. The actual cooking time depends on how long it has been pre-boiled by the butcher.

There are many excellent recipes for tripe, the best being from northern Italy, with one or two from the central regions. However, all the recipes are basically similar, since the tripe, cut into 1cm/½in strips, is cooked with the usual flavouring vegetables, wine, stock and, sometimes, tomatoes. In Milan, boiled borlotti beans are often added 20 minutes before the end of the cooking time. *Trippa alla bolognese* is finished with beaten eggs and grated Parmesan. *Trippa alla romana* is flavoured with wild mint and a lot of grated PECORINO, while in Siena and Arezzo a delicious dish is made with the addition of a good amount of chilli.

One of my favourites is *trippa alla savonese*, also called *natalini con le trippe*, a dish that was traditionally eaten on Christmas Day in Savona, a city on the western Riviera of Liguria. The tripe, cut into strips, is cooked in rich beef stock with

trippa alla milanese
Milanese tripe

Serves 4

1kg/2¼lb calf's tripe, precooked,
*   preferably honeycomb tripe*
75g/2¾oz/5 tbsp unsalted butter
1 tbsp vegetable oil
1 large onion, sliced
1 celery stalk, cut into thin strips
5 fresh sage leaves
1 carrot, cut into small pieces
25g/1oz unsmoked pancetta, chopped
4 large ripe fresh tomatoes, peeled and
*   chopped, or 200g/7oz canned*
*   tomatoes, chopped*
salt and freshly ground black pepper
a pinch of ground cinnamon
a generous grating of nutmeg

In my home in Milan, where this recipe, also called *büsecca*, comes from, beans were not added. However, if you like them, add 200g/7oz of cooked borlotti (canned beans are all right for this dish) about 20 minutes before the tripe is properly done. The cooking time may vary from about 45 minutes to over 2 hours, depending on how long the tripe has been precooked; ask your butcher for advice. This dish is always served with POLENTA.

Wash the tripe and cut it into strips, 1cm/½in wide and 5cm/2in long. Put the butter and oil in a heavy stockpot over a low heat. Add the onion, celery, sage, carrot and pancetta and sauté gently, stirring constantly. When the vegetables are soft, add the tripe and cook for 10 minutes or so, stirring often. Add the tomatoes, a cupful of water or stock, the salt and pepper and the spices. Bring slowly to the boil.

Cover the pan and simmer gently until the tripe is tender but not overcooked. Begin to taste it after some 30 minutes, although some tripe needs cooking for up to 2 hours. If necessary, add half a cupful of boiling water during the cooking. The tripe should cook in enough liquid to nearly cover it.

cardoons, pine nuts, tomatoes and herbs. Some pasta, usually long MACCHERONI cut into pieces, is added at the end, and the soup is dressed with a generous amount of the superb local olive oil.

 [see recipe on facing page]

trito
chopped vegetables and herbs

A chopped-up mixture, usually consisting of herbs, garlic, onion, celery and carrot, or any combination of these. A BATTUTO is similar, except that it should contain PANCETTA or pork back fat, which a trito should not. A trito, or a battuto, is the basis of a SOFFRITTO, or it can be added 'a CRUDO' (raw) to dishes, soups or sauces.

trofie
a pasta

A kind of homemade pasta, a speciality of the eastern Riviera of Liguria. Pieces of dough are dragged over the work surface with the fingers, so that they take the shape of a spiral. Trofie are now also available dried. They are traditionally boiled with a potato and some green beans, and then dressed with PESTO.

trota
trout

When the trout is small and fresh, there is no method of cooking better than the Milanese *trotella al burro*. The trout, lightly coated in seasoned flour, and with a sprig of fresh sage in its cavity, is fried on both sides in plenty of nut-brown butter until a lovely golden crust forms. As it cooks, the fish retains its moisture inside this crust. In another good simple recipe, from

Piedmont, the fish is baked and finished with a red wine sauce flavoured with anchovy fillets. In Abruzzo, where the local trout from the Sangro river are said to be among the best, the fish is cooked in an earthenware pot, in a tomato sauce made with fresh tomatoes, olive oil and garlic. This is one of the very few recipes in which oil and tomatoes are used with trout.

In the past, trout were acclaimed as one of the best freshwater fish. The innumerable rivers and streams running down from the Alps and the Apennines were full of them. Bartolomeo SCAPPI commented on the deliciousness of the trout caught in the Tiber and on the size of the large trout of Lake Maggiore and Lake Como. Some of these, he reported (in true fisherman's style), weighed more than 40 Milanese pounds, in other words some 30kg, or 70lb! Many of the recipes from the past refer to large trout which hardly exist any longer; they were cut into pieces and stewed in vinegar, sugar and spices, or with prunes and spices.

 [see recipe on page 448]

447

tuttifrutti
ice cream

A modern ice cream made with various fruits, fresh, preserved or candied, or a mixture of fruit with vanilla ice cream.

trotelle al vino rosso
trout in red wine

Serves 4

4 trout, cleaned, but with heads and
tails on
salt and freshly ground black pepper
1 tbsp olive oil
1 tbsp chopped celery leaves
2 shallots or 1 small onion, very finely
chopped
300ml/10fl oz/1¼ cups red wine
1 bouquet garni
100ml/3½fl oz/scant ½ cup fish stock
50g/1¾oz/4 tbsp unsalted butter, plus
extra for greasing
1 tbsp flour
1 tsp anchovy paste

This recipe from Piedmont is a good way to serve trotelle, small trout (TROTA).

Preheat the oven to 200°C/400°F/Gas Mark 6.

Put the trout in a single layer in a buttered ovenproof dish. Sprinkle with salt and pepper and bake for 10 minutes, turning the fish over halfway through the cooking.

While the trout are cooking, put the oil, celery leaves and shallots in a small saucepan and sauté until the shallot is soft. Add the wine, bring to the boil and then add the bouquet garni and fish stock. When the mixture is boiling pour it over the fish. Return to the oven and cook for a further 10–15 minutes.

Carefully lift the trout onto a warmed oval dish and keep warm. Strain the liquid into a small saucepan and bring to simmering point. Blend together the butter, flour and anchovy paste and add, bit by bit, to the simmering sauce, swirling the pan around until the mixture has been completely incorporated into the liquid.

Coat the trout with some of the sauce and serve the rest separately.

u

uccellini scappati
a meat dish

The name of this dish from Lombardy means 'the little birds that have flown away'. In fact the birds were never there, but the dish looks as if it was made with little birds, and this makes it very popular with Italians. It is made with an assortment of pork or veal, little pieces of pig's or calf's liver rolled in PANCETTA slices and then skewered between sage leaves. The uccellini are sautéed in hot butter, and then cooked in white wine. They are always served with POLENTA.

Umbria

One of the smallest regions of Italy, Umbria is still unspoilt and peaceful, looking today just as it did when the Renaissance painters immortalized it. The cooking is based on family traditions with fresh and natural flavours.

Meat is important fare; it is here that the craft of butchering the pig and preparing the various cuts for SALAMI is at its best. The meat of the Umbrian pigs is particularly tasty because the animals live in the mountains and feed on wild plants, herbs and even truffles. Pork products – salami, sausages, cured and smoked meat and PROSCIUTTO – appear as the pièces de résistance on every restaurant's ANTIPASTO trolley. The selection is vast. Umbrian prosciutto is lean and full of flavour, CAPOCOLLO, made from the neck of the animal, is flavoured with wild fennel, fresh and dried sausages are made in many towns and even MORTADELLA is as excellent as the more famous one from Bologna. The splendid PORCHETTA – suckling pig – is roasted on the spit and flavoured with

wild fennel and lots of garlic. And, as in all other regions of central Italy, it is the main attraction in village markets.

Beef is equally good, especially when it comes from cattle bred near the border with Tuscany, where the Umbrian breed has been crossed with the famous Chianina breed. The sheep and goats bred on the hills, the variety of game in the mountains and the farm birds and rabbits all go to make Umbria a paradise for the meat lover. Umbrian squabs are famous all over Italy. Wild birds are very popular, especially *colombacci* – wood pigeons – which are cooked alla GHIOTTA. In Todi, the pigeon, cooked in red wine in a pot with the

usual flavourings, is boned, minced and mixed with its cooking juices and then spread onto the local bread.

The abundance of meat in Umbria should not overshadow the importance of the local fish. As it is one of the five regions without a coastline, freshwater fish reign supreme. Carp, pike and eels are caught in Lake Trasimeno and trout in the nearby streams. The noble roach, the LASCA, is still found in this lake. In the past this fish was considered such a delicacy that it was sent to Rome every year at Easter for the Pope's dinner.

Pasta manufacture is an important industry. The repertoire of local pasta dishes is similar to that of neighbouring regions, and there are two local specialities: *umbrici*, very long, thick spaghetti, traditionally dressed with a lamb RAGÙ; and *ceriole* (or *ciriole*) *ternane*, fairly thick, wide, short tagliatelle made with a dough that contains water as well as eggs, and dressed with oil, lots of garlic and sometimes a little chilli. The oddity about ceriole is that they are served halfway between a pasta in BRODO (in stock) and a *pastasciutta* (drained pasta).

In Umbria pasta is often served with a grating of the local black truffles, found around Norcia and Spoleto; a recipe using the truffles in a sauce is given on page 420. Truffles are added also to trout cooked in oil with garlic, anchovy fillets and SOTTACETI (preserved vegetables). The other great local produce is the lentils that grow on the spectacular high plain of Castelluccio. And last but certainly not least is the local olive oil, sweet and delicate, which is the base of all dishes. A dish that is found only in Umbria, called *impastoiata*, consists of polenta into which cannellini beans (cooked separately in plenty of rich tomato sauce) are mixed. It does not sound very attractive, but when well made it is excellent.

Another speciality of the region is chocolate, which has made Perugia, the region's capital, a famous name all over the world. The well-known company Perugina is based there, and makes the cleverly named chocolates, BACI ('kisses'). These are modern sweets, but there is a large number of traditional DOLCI that show the creativity of the locals in linking them to ancient rituals, traditions and superstitions. For instance, a cake called ATTORTA is made in the shape of a coiled snake, and eating it is supposed to protect you from snake bites. *Stinchetti* are almond paste sweets that look like miniature shin bones, and legend has it that if you eat them you will not break your leg.

umido
cooking method

To cook 'in umido' is to stew very slowly in a small amount of liquid. This liquid is usually a tomato sauce, often with the addition of wine, or concentrated meat juice. The food cooked in umido is generally meat which should 'stew in its own juice', with a little extra liquid being added if necessary. By the end of the long cooking the juice should be dark and thick. ARTUSI wrote: 'Umidi are the dishes which generally are more appetizing, therefore it is appropriate to give them special care, so that they will be more delicate, will taste good and be easy to digest.'

SPEZZATINI, BRASATI, STRACOTTI and STUFATI are all part of the family of umidi. Each is made slightly differently, but the principle of slow cooking in a small amount of liquid is the same.

The fish that are most usually cooked in umido are STOCCAFISSO and BACCALÀ, in other words fish that must be cooked at length. Steaks from a large fish such as grouper or swordfish are also prepared in this way, as are octopus, cuttlefish and squid. This method is also used for vegetables that are cooked in a tomato sauce, for example cauliflower (see recipe on page 98) or potatoes (page 293).

uovo

egg

Always a hen's egg if not otherwise specified. Although eggs are used in interesting ways in a number of Italian dishes, the only really Italian egg dish is FRITTATA. Hard-boiled eggs (*uova soda*) are popular everywhere, often filled with a mixture of tuna or anchovy fillets, parsley and egg yolks, or just dressed with SALSA VERDE, or covered with fried breadcrumbs, parsley and garlic. *Uova soda e* SALAME is the traditional ANTIPASTO for Easter Sunday lunch, when eggs are plentiful and salami are just ready to be eaten.

In the south eggs are often combined with peppers. An excellent dish is made with hard-boiled eggs, grilled peppers and anchovy fillets; a mixture of scrambled eggs and peppers is also made by mixing eggs into a PEPERONATA. In a dish from Calabria, aubergines, potatoes and peppers are stewed in oil and garlic, and at the end the eggs are added and cooked whole on the bed of vegetables. The same principle is used in a recipe called *uova in purgatorio*, in which the eggs are cooked in a tomato sauce flavoured with basil. *Finte trippe* (so called because the eggs look like TRIPPA, tripe) is a dish from Rome consisting of a frittata, cut into thin strips and mixed into a rich tomato sauce.

Eggs are used whole to enrich soups, such as ZUPPA ALLA PAVESE or ACQUACOTTA, or they are mixed with breadcrumbs and Parmesan and cooked in the stock, as in STRACCIATELLA.

Uova al tegamino or *al burro* (fried eggs) becomes a gourmet dish with the addition of a few slivers of white truffle, which is how they are often eaten in Piedmont during the truffle season, while in Umbria, black truffles and SCAMORZA cheese are sliced over the fried eggs.

Other eggs, such as duck's, quail's or gull's, are served occasionally, but are not connected with traditional Italian cooking.

uva

grapes

Uva is a bunch of grapes, *un acino d'uva* is a single grape. Those luscious bunches hanging from vines almost everywhere in Italy are eaten as they are — *uva da tavola* — or used to make wine, depending on their variety.

In cooking, grapes are sometimes added to quails, pheasants or other game, although the recipes are of French origin. Grapes are also used with custard on tarts and tartlets.

uvetta or uva passa

sultana

In the past, sultanas — dried white grapes — were mostly used in savoury dishes. Being very sweet, they were the perfect ingredient for Renaissance sauces, in which the emphasis was on the sweet and sour. Today some savoury dishes use uva passa, often with pine nuts, but mostly they are used in cakes and other sweet preparations, such as PANETTONE and PANFORTE. There are many different kinds of dried grapes, from the seedless golden *sultanina* to the large Malaga and the delicious *zibibbo*, from Muscat grapes.

451

V

valerianella
lamb's lettuce

Also called *soncino*. This early salad is the herald of spring. It is the traditional salad eaten on Easter Sunday, after the AGNELLO *pasquale* (Easter lamb).

Valerianella has a slightly lemony taste, most pleasing and delicate. It is dressed with olive oil, lemon juice and salt but no pepper, which is too spicy for such a delicate salad. Valerianella, widely cultivated, is also found wild in fields; the wild plant has a more pronounced flavour.

Valle d'Aosta

This small region is the north-western outpost of Italy, bordering France and Switzerland. It is mountainous, and its cooking is that of mountain folk. The two most important elements are bread, made traditionally from a mixture of rye flour and wheat flour, and soups, which often contain bread. The best-known of the soups are *soupe valpellinentze*, made with stale bread, cabbage and the local cheese, FONTINA, and *ueca*, made with all the vegetables that are in season, plus barley and fontina. POLENTA is also a staple, dressed with butter and cheese or with stewed meat of various kinds. And everything is lavishly dressed with the delicious local butter. Pasta is ignored, as are most RISOTTI, although there are two local risotti: *risotto alla Valdostana*, made with fontina, and a risotto with pumpkin.

All the soups are based on good stock. In country kitchens the stockpot is always on the fire. The Valdostani breed dairy cattle and in the old days, when they only killed the animals that were too old for milk or for work, the resulting meat

was perfect for stock. It was boiled for several hours with all the vegetables. Once the stock was made, the meat was salted and put in barrels, layered with herbs and garlic, and this preserved meat was used all the year round. CARBONADE, a classic local dish, used to be made with preserved meat, although now fresh beef is used more often (see recipe on page 87). The other meat dish of renown is the *costolette alla valdostana*, for which the recipe is given here. The same recipe is also used nowadays with chicken breast instead of veal.

Game, although now much rarer than in the past, is still an important part of the local cuisine. Roe deer, wild goat, partridge and occasionally grouse, as well as the more common hare and pheasant, can be enjoyed during the season. MOCETTA, a kind of smoked PROSCIUTTO, is made with the leg of a wild goat, a roe deer or even a farmyard goat. It is extremely tasty and a classic

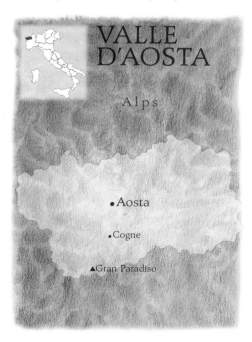

ANTIPASTO. Another SALUME is *boudin*, made with pork blood mixed with boiled potatoes, LARDO and spices pushed into natural casing. Boudin is boiled or fried, like black pudding. One of the best LARDI comes from this region: the *lardo di Arnad*, a DOP product, eaten raw, thinly sliced, as an antipasto.

The other main pillar of Valdostana cooking is cheese, the excellence of which is due to the rich and varied pastures at high altitudes where the cattle spend their summers. The valleys around Aosta, the region's capital, account for the main production of fontina, which is among the best cheeses to be found anywhere. It is also one of the oldest. A local legend tells the story of Pilato, a Roman consul, who, on his way to Gaul, stopped near Aosta and enjoyed a piece of fontina with a glass of the local white wine. Fontina is often used in local dishes, notably in the FONDUTA, and in the POLENTA *côncia*, polenta layered with fontina and butter and then baked. TOMINI, small fresh cow's milk cheeses, are dressed with olive oil and lemon juice and served as part of the ANTIPASTO.

I still remember a great meal I had years ago in a well-known restaurant near Aosta. My antipasto consisted of the following: mocetta, tomino cheese, sliced puffball fungi coated in egg and breadcrumbs and fried in butter, grilled skewers of fontina and local mountain prosciutto, tiny rissoles of meat and spinach, ramekins of *polenta côncia* and nettle mousse surrounded by BAGNA CAÓDA. After that the *ueca* soup arrived, and then we went on to lasagne with fontina, carbonade with polenta and PANNA COTTA. All local dishes and all delicious.

In this rustic cooking there are two traditional puddings that are worthy of the high table. One is panna cotta, the origins of which are also claimed by Piedmont. The other is *fiandolein*, which consists of an egg custard flavoured with rum and lemon rind, poured over thinly sliced rye bread.

Fruit is not particularly abundant in this mountainous region. There are good chestnuts, with which the modern pudding MONTEBIANCO is made, and excellent SOTTOBOSCO. And to finish, I must mention honey, the best from the Valle di Cogne, where the beehives are situated high on the slopes of the Gran Paradiso peak.

I read that the cooking of this region was the favourite of Englishmen visiting Italy in the 18th century. Maybe it was the butter and the cream, making everything taste rich and delicious.

[see recipe below]

453

costolette alla valdostana
veal chops with cheese

Serves 4

4 slices of brown bread
100g/3½oz/7 tbsp unsalted butter
1 large egg
salt and freshly ground black pepper
4 veal chops, trimmed
about 150g/5½oz/about 1½ cups dried
  white breadcrumbs
100g/3½oz fontina cheese, sliced

Preheat the oven to 200°C/400°F/Gas Mark 6.

Put the bread on a baking sheet. Melt a little of the butter and brush it over the bread. Place in the oven for about 6 minutes, until golden brown.

Beat the egg with a little salt and pepper. Dip the chops in the egg and then in the breadcrumbs. Pat the crumbs firmly into the meat, using your hands.

Heat the remaining butter in a large frying pan, and when the butter foam begins to subside, add the chops and cook on both sides until golden brown. Place the chops on the toasted bread and cover with some slices of fontina. Bake in the oven until the cheese has melted.

Veneto

Within this rich region there is considerable variety against a backdrop of common elements. This facet of the cuisine of Veneto results from the time when the Republic of Venice, La Serenissima, held sway over the entire region, and yet allowed the local communities to keep their separate customs and traditions.

The Venetians have a love of refinement. It was in Venice that the first fork was used in the 11th century, it was in Venice that the first napkins were set on the tables and it was in Murano, in the Venetian lagoon, that the most beautiful glasses were blown to embellish the tables. New food, and table manners, travelled from Venice to the rest of Italy and then to northern Europe.

It was one of these new foods, maize, that, in the 17th century, became 'the golden thread running through the cooking of the whole region'.

The locals began to cook maize flour in the same way as they had cooked other flours for centuries. They boiled it in water and soon realized that this new POLENTA was far superior to all others. Polenta, plain, grilled or fried, became the constant accompaniment to meat, fish and game. It was so popular that in 19th-century Venice it was sold from barrows in the streets by *polentari*, who dressed it there and then with butter and cheese, in the same way as the *maccheronari* of Naples were selling their spaghetti.

The Venetians also popularized rice. It was grown in Lombardy in the 15th century, but at first it was food for the wealthy. The Venetians, during their many voyages to the Middle East, had seen the tremendous possibilities of this foodstuff and when it became more common their womenfolk soon began to create a host of delicious RISOTTI. They matched rice with their other two favourite foods, fish and vegetables. The happiest child of these marriages is RISI E BISI. There are more than 40 local risotti in which rice is combined with as many different ingredients: scallops, cuttlefish, eel, tench, quails, tripe, asparagus, spinach, hops, artichokes or mushrooms.

There are very few traditional pasta dishes in Veneto. One of them is a soup, pasta and beans (see recipe on page 139), which is actually made everywhere in Italy, but which achieves perfection in Veneto, thanks partly to the local borlotti beans which are large, with a sweet yet earthy flavour and a very thin skin. The other pasta of Veneto is BIGOLI, thick spaghetti, the only pasta traditionally made with wholewheat flour.

Treviso is famous worldwide for its RADICCHIO; that of Castelfranco is less well known but both are equally good grilled with olive oil. The Rialto market is the place where the foundations of Venetian cooking can so easily be studied. In the spring, wild and cultivated salads are displayed in separate mounds in all the hues of green. On the next barrow the large white asparagus of Bassano are testimony to the excellent produce of the mainland. Peas represent the lands reclaimed by the islands on the lagoon, as do the little artichokes, including *canarini*, so called because of their yellow colour, and *castraure*, which are eaten raw, each leaf dipped in a pool of olive oil.

The same wealth of fruit and vegetables, straight from the orchards and vegetable gardens, is seen in the provincial markets: in the Piazza delle Erbe in Verona, in the vast piazza of the same name in Padua, in barrows along the river Sile in Treviso, in Vicenza and in Belluno.

The other basic food of Venice and the lagoon is fish, and this also is best understood and appreciated at the Rialto market. The array is vast: fish of every kind, colour and size, all marked with a little sticker that tells you if it is frozen, farmed or wild. Grey and pink shrimps, prawns, scampi, spider crabs, soft-shell crabs, all crawling over each other in a blind struggle to return to their habitat. Monstrous octopus sit next to cuttlefish and squid. There are shiny purple mussels, variegated and grey clams, small snails and big snails, and row after row of different fish, from large slabs of shark to small silvery anchovies and tiny white GIANCHETTI.

Away from the sea, STOCCAFISSO was adopted instead. (Dried cod, or stoccafisso, is called BACCALÀ in Veneto, whereas elsewhere in Italy baccalà is salted cod.) Many recipes were created for this dried fish, two of the best ones being *baccalà alla vicentina*, for which the recipe is given here, and *baccalà* MANTECATO. And around Lake Garda there are many restaurants offering freshwater fish – trout, salmon, carp and tench – often combined with rice in delicious risotti.

Inland, there are a few meat dishes which are all of the slow-cooking type, where the juices are more important than the actual meat. One such is called *pastissada*, which is sometimes made with horse meat. The meat the locals like best is poultry. Ducks, chickens, turkeys, geese and guinea fowl are cooked in many ways. Traditional recipes include turkey with pomegranates, and guinea fowl

with an ancient sauce called PEVERADA. Peverada is also served with game, enriched by local white truffles when in season.

There are three great cheeses made in the mountains: ASIAGO, MONTASIO and VEZZENA, plus delicious artisanal goat cheeses.

The DOLCI mostly take the form of simple biscuits, such as ZALETI and BAICOLI, and equally simple cakes, all enjoyed with a glass or two of sweet wine, the drink that unites all echelons of Venetian society. The best known of all the puddings of the region is the relatively new TIRAMISÙ.

[see recipe on page 456]

veneziana
a bun

A large sweet bun, originally made in Venice on New Year's Eve. The dough is similar to that of PANETTONE but it does not contain sultanas or candied fruit; it is flavoured with lemon and orange. Veneziane are covered with white sugar crystals, and with flaked almonds.

veneziana, alla
cooking style

Meaning cooked 'in the Venetian way', although no specific method is implied with this term. The best-known dish is FEGATO ALLA VENEZIANA (calf's liver with onions, for which the recipe is on page 148).

ventaglio

see CONCHIGLIA DI SAN GIACOMO

baccalà alla vicentina
salt cod cooked in milk

Serves 4
500g/1lb 2oz salt cod
150ml/5fl oz/²⁄₃ cup olive oil
1 large onion, very finely sliced
a small bunch of fresh flat-leaf parsley,
*   chopped*
2 garlic cloves, chopped
2 salted anchovies, boned, rinsed and
*   chopped, or 4 canned or bottled*
*   anchovy fillets, drained and chopped*
500ml/18fl oz/2¼ cups full-fat (whole)
*   milk*
2–3 tbsp flour
½ tsp ground cinnamon
salt and freshly ground black pepper
4 tbsp freshly grated Parmesan cheese

This dish, from the province of Vicenza in the Veneto region, traditionally uses dried (not salted) cod; here I use salt cod, which is easier to find.

Soak the cod in a large bowl of cold water for a minimum of 24 hours, changing the water four or five times. If you can, soak it for 48 hours.

Preheat the oven to 150°C/300°F/Gas Mark 2. Skin the salt cod and cut it into thick slices.

Heat the oil in a saucepan over a low heat and sauté the onion until soft. Add the parsley, garlic and anchovies and cook over a very low heat for no more than 1 minute, stirring constantly. Pour in the milk and bring to the boil. Stir well and boil for a couple of minutes, then take the pan off the heat.

Mix the flour with the cinnamon and a little salt and pepper and dip the fish pieces in it to coat them. Place the fish in a flameproof earthenware pot in which the slices will fit tightly in a single layer. Add the cheese and cover with the milk mixture. Bring slowly to the boil, cover the pot and then cook in the oven until all the liquid has been absorbed, which will take 2–2½ hours. The liquid should only occasionally bubble during cooking; it should never boil. This is traditionally served with polenta.

ventresca
tuna fish belly

The ventresca di TONNO, which is regarded as the best part of the fish, is often used for preserving. It is traditionally preserved in wooden barrels or, more often nowadays, in large cans, and is then sold by weight. The best manufacturers also pack ventresca in retail-size cans.

In Puglia, fresh ventresca is used to make one of the most appetizing local TIELLE, layered with sliced potatoes, chopped parsley, shreds of garlic, grated PECORINO and olive oil.

In central Italy the word ventresca is also used to refer to belly of pork.

verdure
vegetables

For centuries vegetables have been one of the glories of the Italian cuisine, never having been regarded solely as an accompaniment to meat. In the Renaissance, vegetables appeared either as a salad at the beginning of the meal or in the last course, in pies or in sweet and sour sauces. They were never on the table with the meat and fish dishes. One must remember, however, that the recipes we read in old cookery books were not for the everyday meals of ordinary people. Indeed, in the past vegetables were often the main part of any meal, as meat was too expensive.

In spite of being so popular, no more than one, or at the very most, two, vegetables are served as an accompaniment, CONTORNO, when they are usually cooked simply: lightly sautéed in butter or olive oil or simply dressed with a little olive oil. They are also braised in oil and/or butter and some water or stock plus some flavourings or herbs.

When served as a salad, vegetables are boiled and then dressed with olive oil, lemon juice or vinegar. Sometimes they are boiled before being sautéed in butter and/or oil. The times for boiling vegetables are usually far longer than British or American cooking times, especially when it comes to asparagus, green beans, Brussels sprouts and leeks. The point at which vegetables are considered al DENTE is very different. I recently read an article in the daily newspaper *Corriere della Sera* where the timings suggested are: 3–4 minutes for spinach and leaf beets; 6–8 minutes for broccoli florets; 10 minutes for asparagus, green beans, fennel, small potatoes, cut-up pumpkin and courgettes; 30–40 minutes for carrots, artichokes, onions, potatoes and celeriac; 30–60 for beetroot and cardoons. Contemporary English and American cookery writers suggest a maximum of 3 minutes for green beans and asparagus. Ultimately, my advice is: cook any vegetable as long as you like.

Vegetables come into their own when they are served as a separate dish. They may be prepared in SFORMATI or TORTINI, fried in a light batter, stewed in tomato sauce (in UMIDO) or meat juices, stuffed, wrapped or filled, pureed, combined in earthy vegetable stews, or with pasta, rice or pulses.

vermicelli
a pasta

Vermicelli is the name given to thin spaghetti in southern Italy; some manufacturers use this name instead of SPAGHETTINI. All sauces for spaghetti are suitable for vermicelli. There are also on the market some thin vermicelli, called *vermicellini*.

verzata
a cabbage dish

This typical dish of the Lombard cuisine consists of Savoy cabbage (*cavolo verza*) braised in a SOFFRITTO with PANCETTA and butter to which strips of pork rind and small local sausages, both cooked separately, are added for the last 5 minutes. The Savoy cabbage is traditionally a winter vegetable, dug out of the frozen earth, when it has the best flavour.

Vezzena
a cheese

A cow's milk cheese made on the plateau around Mount Vezzena, which divides the region of Trentino from that of Veneto, where the pasture is very mixed and the herds are free to roam. Made in discs about 10cm/4in deep and 30–40cm/12–16in in diameter, Vezzena is a hard DOP cheese similar to the better-known ASIAGO.Like Asiago it is a table cheese when young (4–8 months) and a grating cheese when aged for 18–24 months.

Vialardi, Giovanni
1804–72

Giovanni Vialardi was a chef and chef pâtissier to Carlo Alberto of Savoy and his son Vittorio Emanuele II, who became the first king of Italy in 1861. Vialardi wrote a book called *Trattato di Cucina*, published in 1854, in which there are 2,000 recipes of Piedmontese, Italian and foreign origin. There are recipes for BABÀ à la polonaise, pâté de foie gras and charlotte as well as for Piedmontese soups such as *zuppa alla canavesana* – cabbage soup – and *risotto alla piemontese*. But the best recipes are those for puddings and cakes, as the subtitle of the book implies – *Pasticceria Moderna, Credenza e Relativa Confettureria*.

vignarola
a vegetable dish

A vegetable dish from Rome, made with the new season's vegetables: broad beans, peas and wedges of globe artichoke added to gently fried onions. The dish is finished with lettuce leaves and sometimes is flavoured with a cupful of dry white wine.

vin santo
'holy wine'

Not a fortified wine but a wine made with grapes (usually white) that are left to dry for several weeks before fermentation; the resulting wine is aged in barrels for between 3 and 10 years. It is produced mainly in Tuscany, although excellent vin santo is made also in Veneto, Trentino and, in very small quantities, in Umbria and Le Marche. Usually sweet, vin santo has a deep golden amber colour, a nutty aroma reminiscent of wild berries and a pleasantly bitter aftertaste. It is sipped after dinner with CANTUCCI, which are dipped into it, or with RICCIARELLI or with cakes such as PANFORTE. In Tuscany vin santo is used to moisten the CROSTINI to be topped with chicken liver pâté.

vincisgrassi
lasagne

A dish from Le Marche with an odd name, this is one of the great lasagne dishes. Vincisgrassi is the Italianization of the name of the Austrian general, Prince Windischgrätz, who was commander of the Austrian forces stationed in the Marches during the Napoleonic Wars. The dish was allegedly created for the Prince by a local chef for a banquet in his honour. However, a similar sauce for pasta, called Pringsgras, was included in a book by Antonio Nebbia, *Il Cuoco Maceratese*, published in 1779.

 [see recipe on facing page]

vino cotto
'cooked wine'

This is a kind of syrup made with very fresh grape must in Puglia, in Sardinia (where it is called *sapa*) and in Emilia-Romagna (*saba*). It is used in biscuits and cakes. In Puglia 'vino cotto' is also prepared with fresh figs which are cooked for hours; this is even sweeter than the grape vino cotto and it is used mainly to moisten sweet preparations.

virtù
vegetable soup

This soup, 'le virtù' to give it its full name, is made in Abruzzo in May. It mixes seven of the previous year's dried pulses (the fact that there are seven virtues gives the soup its name) with young new vegetables. Other ingredients are a pig's trotter, a piece of snout and some rind. When the dried pulses and the pork are cooked, and the pork bones removed, a SOFFRITTO of onion, garlic, tomato puree and parsley is added and the soup is livened by the fresh flavour of wild chicory, spinach, Swiss chard and other green vegetables. It is thickened by a good handful of pasta, traditionally of seven different shapes.

vitello
calf or veal

The best meat comes from a calf slaughtered when still milk-fed yet fat enough. The meat is pale pink, with only a little white, hard fat. Veal is very popular in northern Italy, especially in Lombardy and Piedmont; Lombardy offers the best-known recipes, such as OSSOBUCHI, VITELLO TONNATO, FRICANDÒ and many others. The sophisticated cuisine of this region, based on butter, seems to highlight the delicacy of a piece of veal. But Piedmont rears the best calves – the SANATO.

CONTINUES OVERLEAF

458

vignarola

vincisgrassi
lasagne with prosciutto, mushrooms and sweetbreads

Serves 8

100g/3½oz/7 tbsp unsalted butter

50g/1¾oz prosciutto, chopped

1 onion, cut in half

1 carrot, cut in half

250g/9oz fresh chicken livers, trimmed,
*   cleaned and cut into small pieces*

4 tbsp dry white wine

1 tbsp tomato puree diluted with
*   100ml/3½fl oz/scant ½ cup warm*
*   meat stock (page 61) or chicken stock*

20g/¾oz dried porcini

100g/3½oz brown mushrooms, cleaned
*   and sliced*

1 garlic clove, bruised

2 tbsp olive oil

250g/9oz mixed calf's brains and
*   sweetbreads, cleaned and blanched*

100ml/3½fl oz/scant ½ cup single
*   (light) cream*

½ tsp freshly grated nutmeg

¼ tsp ground cinnamon

salt and freshly ground black pepper

béchamel sauce made with
*   100g/3½oz/7 tbsp unsalted butter,*
*   70g/2½oz/generous ½ cup flour and*
*   1 litre/1¾ pints/4 cups milk*

50g/1¾oz Parmesan cheese, grated

Lasagne

400g/14oz/3¼ cups Italian 00 flour

200g/7oz fine semolina

4 large eggs

40g/1½oz/3 tbsp unsalted butter, at
*   room temperature*

4 tbsp vin santo or Marsala

1 tsp salt

1 tbsp vegetable or olive oi

This is the original recipe for VINCISGRASSI; it is superb, though rather complicated. Nowadays the pasta is usually made only with flour and egg.

Put 75g/2¾oz/5 tbsp of the butter, the prosciutto, onion and carrot in a saucepan over a low heat and let the vegetables cook gently to flavour the butter. Lift out the vegetables and discard. Turn up the heat, add the chicken livers and sauté for about 1 minute. Pour in the wine and reduce briskly until it has evaporated. Add the diluted tomato puree, mix well and bring to the boil. Reduce the heat and simmer very gently for 30 minutes. Add a little water if the liquid dries out.

While the chicken livers are cooking, soak the porcini in 3 tablespoons warm water for 20 minutes. Drain, reserving the liquid. Sauté the brown mushrooms with the garlic in the olive oil for 5 minutes. Discard the garlic.

Strain the porcini liquid through a sieve lined with cheesecloth. Chop the porcini and put them into the chicken liver sauce with the fresh mushrooms and the porcini liquid. Finely chop the brains and sweetbreads and add to the sauce with the cream and spices. Taste and adjust the seasoning and simmer for 10 minutes.

Make the béchamel sauce and cover with clingfilm to prevent a skin forming.

To make the lasagne, mix the flour and semolina on a work surface, make a well in the centre and drop in the eggs, butter, vin santo and salt. Mix and knead, following the instructions on page 282.

Butter a 28 x 20cm/11 x 8in lasagne dish. Cut the pasta into 28cm/11in strips about 10cm/4in wide. Cook three or four lasagne at a time in plenty of boiling salted water to which you have added 1 tablespoon oil.

Mix three-quarters of the Parmesan into the béchamel sauce, spread 3 tablespoons over the bottom of the dish and cover with a layer of lasagne. Spoon over 3–4 tablespoons of the chicken liver sauce and the same amount of béchamel. Cover with a layer of lasagne, and repeat until all the ingredients are used up, finishing with a layer of lasagne and béchamel. Leave to stand for 4 hours for the flavours to combine.

Preheat the oven to 200°C/400°F/Gas Mark 6. Bake the vincisgrassi for about 25 minutes. Sprinkle with the remaining Parmesan. Melt the remaining butter, pour it over the top and leave to stand for about 5 minutes before serving.

A Piedmontese dish that takes pride of place is a pan-roasted breast of veal, a particularly moist cut full of flavour, which is stuffed with PROSCIUTTO, fungi, white truffles and tongue.

In Liguria the two traditional veal dishes are TOMAXELLE and *vitello all'uccelletto*, consisting of a piece of rump flavoured with sage and pan-roasted in white wine. Emilia-Romagna shares many of the Lombard recipes, giving them the robust character of the local cuisine. Two such dishes are ossobuchi and COTOLETTE, which, unlike the classic Lombard ones, are flavoured with tomatoes. *Vitello al latte* – cooked in milk in the same way as *maiale al latte* (see recipe on page 198) – is another speciality of Emilia-Romagna. Traditionally veal went no further south than Emilia-Romagna, with the exception of the Roman SALTIMBOCCA.

vitello tonnato
veal with tuna

This northern Italian dish certainly deserves its wide reputation. There are two basic recipes, the old Milanese one and a younger Piedmontese version. In the Milanese version, known as *vitel toné* in local dialect, the piece of veal is gently boiled with the usual flavourings in water and wine. When cooked, the meat is carved and coated with a sauce made with mashed preserved tuna, anchovy fillets and capers diluted with the pureed cooking juices, lemon juice and a couple of tablespoons of cream. The Piedmontese version, influenced by nearby France, is made with mayonnaise instead of cream. The other main difference is that while the Piedmontese dish is always served cold, the Milanese vitello tonnato is traditionally served hot.

vitellone
calf meat

A castrated calf or a heifer that has been allowed to graze before being slaughtered at up to

24 months. It is a favourite meat in northern Italy, used in place of beef for many dishes, such as ARROSTO MORTO, SPEZZATINI and even VITELLO TONNATO. In Tuscany the vitelloni of the Chianina breed are used for the famous BISTECCA *alla fiorentina*.

vongola
clam

There are several species of vongola, the most common being the *vongola gialla*, also called simply vongola. The most prized is the *vongola verace* (the carpet shell). The first is small with a yellow shell, and the other, much larger and much better, has a grey shell with a dark blue line in the middle.

All clams are cooked in the same way. It is in and around Naples that you will eat the best *zuppa di vongole*, ladled over toasted bread, and the best *spaghetti alle vongole*. Both these dishes come in two versions, with and without tomatoes. When vongole are used to dress pasta they are sometimes removed from the shell. A delicious spaghetti sauce is made by mixing clams with mussels. Clams make an excellent salad when dressed with extra virgin olive oil, a touch of vinegar, salt and black pepper and mixed with the diced heart of a celery.

In Venice vongole are used to make *risotto di caparozzoli* (the Venetian name for clams), in which the risotto is made with a fish stock and the strained cooking liquid of the clam, and the dish is finished with butter and chopped parsley.

In Liguria there is an odd, but delicious, recipe called *arselle all'uovo* – arsella being the Ligurian name for the carpet shell clam. The cleaned clams are thrown over sautéed onions and parsley, moistened with white wine, and cooked for 5 minutes or so; egg yolks and lemon juice are added and cooked for 1 minute.

W, X, Y

The letter W is used only in the parts of northern Italy where German is still spoken. The letters X and Y do not feature in the Italian language: the letter S is used for X in most cases and the letter I for Y.

würstel
a sausage

A small *würst* (sausage) or a small frankfurter. They are produced in Trentino-Alto Adige and also in Lombardy and Emilia. The meat used is beef, minced very fine and mixed with salted pork back fat flavoured with spices. Würstel are subjected to a special stewing process, after which they are ready to be eaten. They are traditionally served with sauerkraut and often with other pork products. A classic salad consists of boiled cubed potatoes and cut-up würstel, dressed with olive oil, vinegar and a teaspoon of French mustard.

461

Z

zabaione
zabaglione

Serves 4
5 large egg yolks
7 tbsp caster (superfine) sugar
a pinch of ground cinnamon
5 tbsp dry Marsala
5 tbsp sweet white wine

This famous dessert is said to have been created in the 17th century as a result of a mistake by the chef to Duke Carlo Emanuele I of Savoy. He accidentally poured some fortified wine into an egg custard. It soon became the pudding served by the Piedmontese aristocracy and has remained popular ever since.

In Italian homes zabaione is often served cold, the zabaione being mixed with whipped cream. Hot or cold, zabaione is served in glasses or glass cups.

Make sure there is plenty of room in the pan in which you whisk the yolks with the sugar: as you incorporate air they transform into a thick foam and greatly increase in volume.

Put the egg yolks with the sugar in a large double boiler or a round, heavy-based saucepan and beat with a wire whisk or a hand-held electric mixer until pale yellow and creamy. Beat in the cinnamon.

Place the top of the double boiler or the saucepan over a pot of simmering (not boiling) water. Add the Marsala and then the wine, whisking all the time. The zabaione will swell into a light frothy mass and then it will begin to form soft mounds. Remove from the heat immediately and spoon into wine glasses or small bowls. Serve hot. If you want to serve it cold, pipe some whipped cream over the top.

NOTE: VIN SANTO or Madeira can be used instead of MARSALA.

zafferano
saffron

This spice consists of the stigmas of the *Crocus sativus*. It is very expensive because of the labour involved in extracting it from the flowers: 150,000 stigmas are needed to produce 1kg/2¼lb of saffron. In Italy, saffron is mostly sold in powdered form.

Saffron was used a great deal in the Middle Ages and the Renaissance. It was added as automatically as pepper and salt to give taste and the fashionable golden colour. It was also considered to be very wholesome.

Saffron is no longer used with such liberality. Its marriage with rice in RISOTTO ALLA MILANESE is old-enduring, as is that with BRODETTO, the fish soup of the Adriatic, and with fish stews. Like

zaleti
polenta biscuits

Makes about 40
75g/2¾oz/½ cup sultanas (golden raisins)
4 tbsp dark rum
250g/9oz/2 cups finely ground polenta flour (fine cornmeal) or instant polenta
100g/3½oz/generous ¾ cup Italian 00 flour
1 tsp baking powder
a pinch of salt
115g/4oz/generous ½ cup caster (superfine) sugar
150–200ml/5–7fl oz/⅔–¾ cup full-fat (whole) milk
100g/3½oz/7 tbsp unsalted butter, plus extra for greasing
grated rind of ½ lemon, organic or unwaxed
icing (confectioners') sugar, to decorate

Traditional Venetian biscuits – zaleti means 'little yellow ones' – sold in every PANETTERIA and PASTICCERIA in Venice, Treviso and other cities in Veneto. They are often served with a glass of wine, into which they are dipped.

Put the sultanas in a bowl and add the rum. Leave them to soak for at least 30 minutes. Drain and pat them dry.

Preheat the oven to 180°C/350°F/Gas Mark 4. Generously butter two baking sheets.

Sift the two flours together into a bowl with the baking powder and salt, and then add the caster sugar.

Pour 150ml/5fl oz/⅔ cup of the milk into a small saucepan, add the butter and heat gently until it melts. Gradually, with one hand, pour this liquid into the bowl of flour while you work it into the mixture with the other hand. Mix in the sultanas and the lemon rind. The mixture should be soft, but not so soft that you cannot shape the biscuits. If necessary, gradually add a little of the remaining milk. If you have time, put the mixture in the refrigerator for 30 minutes or so; it is easier to shape when it is cold.

With floured hands, pinch off a piece of the mixture about the size of a walnut and then roll it between the palms of your hands to a shape similar to a tiny baguette. Place each piece on a baking sheet, leaving space between the zaleti as they will spread out during baking.

Bake for about 10–12 minutes, but check after 8 minutes. They are ready when they turn deep yellow and are browning at the edges. Leave to cool on a wire rack. To serve, sprinkle with icing sugar.

other spices, it has become more popular in recent decades. One of the newest and most fashionable recipes is *pasta allo zafferano*. The saffron is added to the dough, as indeed it was in the Renaissance, or, if used with dried pasta, it is put in the boiling water and a buttery sauce is made with a little saffron to add colour to the dish.

zampetto

see PIEDINO

zampone
a sausage

This INSACCATO sausage was created out of necessity in Modena in 1511. The town was under siege by the army of Pope Julius II and the townspeople found themselves without any casing for the sausage meat. The answer to the problem was to use a pig's trotter and push the meat into that.

Zamponi are made with rind and meat from the shoulder, head, neck and shin, and fat, all very finely minced together and flavoured with nutmeg, cinnamon, cloves, salt and pepper. The mixture is pushed into a boned trotter. Before cooking, zampone is soaked for a few hours; it is then wrapped in a cloth to prevent the skin from splitting and cooked at a bare simmer for at least 4 hours. The result will be a tender sausage with a delicate taste and a light, jelly-like, gluey texture. Nowadays, zamponi are very often sold pre-cooked, in which case they only need to simmer for about an hour.

Zampone is traditionally accompanied by LENTICCHIE IN UMIDO (see recipe on page 202), beans or potato puree; *zampone con le lenticchie* is the traditional meal on New Year's Day in northern Italy. In Modena it is often served with a special ZABAIONE made with very little sugar and with balsamic vinegar in place of Marsala. It is a delicious combination.

zenzero
ginger

Ginger, one of the first spices to reach Europe, was far more popular in the Middle Ages and the Rensaissance than it is now. The word zenzero is the cause of great misunderstanding in Tuscany, where it is used instead of PEPERONCINO (chilli).

zeppole
fritters

Small sweet fritters made with choux pastry, zeppole are a speciality of Campania, Puglia and Sardinia, where they are called *zippulas* and are served covered with honey. They are shaped into rings or buns. The bun-shaped zeppole are sometimes filled with CREMA PASTICCERA.

In Salerno and its province, zeppole are made with puff pastry and stuffed with a mixture of pureed chestnuts and chocolate.

465

ziti, zite
a pasta

A thick, long, hollow shape, traditional in Campania, usually dressed with RAGÙ *alla napoletana*, and in Sicily, where it is served with a sultana and breadcrumb sauce or with a tuna sauce, as in the recipe given here. The ziti are usually broken into 10–12cm/about 4in pieces before cooking.

[see recipe on page 466]

ziti alla palermitana
ziti in a tuna fish sauce

Serves 4

5 tbsp extra virgin olive oil
1 small onion, finely chopped
salt and freshly ground black pepper
2 garlic cloves, finely chopped
2 salted anchovies, boned, rinsed and
    chopped, or 4 canned or bottled
    anchovy fillets, drained and chopped
350g/12oz ripe fresh tomatoes, peeled,
    deseeded and coarsely chopped
2 tsp dried oregano
75g/2¾oz best yellowfin canned tuna in
    olive oil, drained and flaked
350g/12oz ziti
50g/1¾oz caciocavallo cheese, grated

If you cannot find ZITI, use BUCATINI or another tubular pasta.

Heat the oil in a large saucepan over a low heat, add the onion and two pinches of salt and sauté in the oil for about 7 minutes, stirring frequently.

Mix in the garlic and cook for a further 2 minutes. Mix in the anchovies, mashing them against the bottom of the pan with a spoon. After 1 minute or so, throw in the tomatoes and oregano and cook for about 30 minutes.

Add the tuna and cook for a further 10 minutes. Taste and add plenty of black pepper, and salt if necessary.

Break the ziti into pieces of about 12cm/5in and cook the pasta in plenty of boiling salted water until al dente. Drain well (tubular pasta has a tendency to retain some water). Dress the pasta with the sauce and cover with a shower of grated caciocavallo. Serve at once.

zucca
pumpkin

The two most popular varieties are the large round pumpkin of northern Italy, with its bright yellow pulp and thick green knobbly skin, and the long, pale green pumpkin of southern Italy, used to make a peculiar sort of jam and, with a few tomatoes, a deliciously sweet pasta sauce.

In Mantua pumpkin TORTELLI are made with the addition of AMARETTI and MOSTARDA di frutta. In Reggio Emilia those last two ingredients are replaced by a larger quantity of PARMIGIANO REGGIANO, a stuffing similar to the large CAPPELLACCI of Ferrara. In Lombardy pumpkin risotto is quite popular, the cubed pumpkin being added before the rice to the basic onion SOFFRITTO. My favourite pumpkin dish is GNOCCHI — for which the recipe is given here — which appeared weekly on our table in Milan during the autumn.

Some writers of the past do not seem to differentiate between zucche and ZUCCHINE — courgette. Only the ever-precise SCAPPI calls pumpkin zucca turchesca, an adjective which at the time meant foreign. He makes a soup of diced pumpkin mixed with egg and cheese. In other recipes, Scappi suggests filling smaller specimens with various ingredients, in much the same way that the green pumpkins of southern Italy are cooked now: the seeds are taken out, without splitting the pumpkin open, and it is stuffed with meat, PECORINO and herbs and braised in the oven. Most of Scappi's recipes can be traced back to those appearing in *De Honesta Voluptate et Valetudine*, written a century earlier by PLATINA, who in his turn had included all the recipes by MARTINO da Como. Plagiarism in cookery writing is a very old sin!

[see recipe on facing page]

gnocchi di zucca
pumpkin gnocchi

Serves 4–5

1 tbsp vegetable oil

*500g/1lb 2oz butternut or kabocha
    squash*

500g/1lb 2oz sweet potatoes

*200g/7oz/generous 1½ cups Italian
    00 flour*

2 tsp baking powder

a good pinch of salt

2 large eggs

4 tbsp freshly grated Parmesan cheese

a generous grating of nutmeg

Cinnamon dressing

75g/2¾oz/5 tbsp unsalted butter

25g/1oz Parmesan cheese, grated

1 tbsp sugar

1 tsp ground cinnamon

Sage dressing

75g/2¾oz/5 tbsp unsalted butter

6 fresh sage leaves, snipped

50g/1¾oz Parmesan cheese, grated

Butternut or kabocha squash mixed with sweet potatoes come close to the spicy sweetness and moist texture of a northern Italian pumpkin. These GNOCCHI are a speciality of Veneto and southern Lombardy. The cinnamon dressing is the classic dressing from Veneto, while the sage dressing from Lombardy is the one that is mostly used everywhere else.

I find it easiest to make the gnocchi with a piping bag and a plain large nozzle, but you may prefer to shape the gnocchi into small balls, using floured hands.

Heat the oven to 180°C/350°F/Gas Mark 4.

Line a baking sheet with foil and brush the foil with oil. Wipe the squash and cut it in half. Scoop out and discard the seeds and fibres and place the squash, cut side down, on the foil. Pierce the sweet potatoes with a skewer and place them on the foil with the squash. Bake for about 1 hour, until both vegetables can be pierced easily with a fork.

Peel the sweet potatoes and scoop the flesh out of the squash. Puree both vegetables through a food mill or a potato ricer into a bowl. Mix in the flour, baking powder and salt and then break in the eggs. Mix very well to incorporate, then add the Parmesan and season with nutmeg and salt to taste. If you have time, put the mixture in the refrigerator for 30 minutes or so; it is easier to shape when it is cold.

Bring a large saucepan of salted water to the boil. To pipe the gnocchi, fill the piping bag with the squash mixture and hold it over the saucepan, squeezing it with one hand and cutting the mixture with the other as it comes out of the nozzle. Cut short shapes about 2cm/¾in long, letting them drop straight into the simmering water. Don't cook all the gnocchi together, but do it in three batches. Cook them for 1 or 2 minutes after they have risen to the surface of the water. Lift out with a slotted spoon and place in a shallow, large ovenproof dish. Dress each batch separately and keep the dish warm in a low oven.

For the cinnamon dressing, melt the butter in a bain-marie or double boiler and then pour it over the gnocchi and sprinkle with Parmesan, sugar and cinnamon.

For the sage dressing, put the butter and sage leaves in a small saucepan and let the butter melt and begin to foam. Spoon over the gnocchi and sprinkle with the Parmesan.

467

zucchine
courgette

An extremely popular vegetable, grown everywhere. Really fresh young courgettes are excellent steamed, cut in half and dressed with olive oil and lemon juice, a touch of garlic and oregano, a herb that combines particularly well with this vegetable. In northern Italy, blanched courgettes are covered with a creamy béchamel sauce and a generous amount of Parmesan and then browned in the oven. They are also simply sautéed in butter and oil, usually cut into batons, cooked until quite tender and flavoured with oregano. In Liguria courgettes, sliced on the diagonal, are sautéed in oil and garlic and then cooked with tomatoes and basil.

Courgette batons coated in light batter are fried and served by themselves or as part of a FRITTO MISTO. Courgettes make excellent SFORMATI with lots of Parmesan and a little nutmeg, perfect with FONDUTA. A FRITTATA of courgettes is rightly very popular, and nowadays sauces for pasta are successfully created with this delicate vegetable. In Catania I had a delicious dish of tagliatelle dressed with a pistachio and basil PESTO and covered by courgettes sautéed in garlicky oil.

In a Sicilian dish, *zucchine all'*AGRODOLCE, fried courgettes are marinated in a sweet and sour sauce. In Naples *zucchine a* SCAPECE are similar to the Sicilian agrodolce, but while the Sicilian dish contains sultanas and pine nuts, the Neapolitan vinegary sauce is flavoured only with fresh mint and garlic.

Courgettes are particularly well suited to being stuffed. In Mantua the flesh of blanched courgettes is sautéed with onion in butter and then mixed with RICOTTA, Parmesan, eggs and a few crumbled AMARETTI. The mixture is piled into the halved courgettes and the dish is baked. Other popular stuffings are béchamel sauce, mushroom and ham, or a light RAGÙ of veal.

In LEONARDI's *L'Apicio Moderno,* first published in 1790, there is a recipe for '*zucchette alla milanese*', which is still a classic of northern Italy. The courgettes, cut in half and with the pulp removed, are blanched. They are then stuffed with the pulp – previously sautéed in butter with onion and parsley – mixed with cream, egg yolks, grated Parmesan and nutmeg. The stuffed courgettes, dotted with butter, are placed 'on a well-buttered silver dish' and baked. ARTUSI, a century later, stuffs his courgettes with canned tuna mixed with courgette pulp, egg, Parmesan and 'scent of spices' and cooks them in a buttery tomato sauce, another recipe that is still in the modern repertoire.

zuccotto
a Florentine pudding

Zuccotto is made from sliced sponge cake layered with custard and whipped cream and studded with chocolate pieces, hazelnuts and almonds, or with candied peel. It is always served very chilled. The top is decorated with alternate brown and white segments, made of cocoa powder and icing sugar, that converge in the centre, a pattern that reminds the Florentines of the dome of their cathedral.

zuppa
soup

Every cuisine is rich in soups, a dish that is more representative of local cooking than any other. In Italian cooking, soup competes with pasta and rice for sheer diversity.

The word zuppa, unlike soup in English, is not a generic term, since MINESTRA, MINESTRINA and MINESTRONE are also soups. When used by itself, zuppa refers to a thick vegetable soup that is not pureed or creamed, nor does it contain pasta or rice.

A zuppa is usually made with lots of vegetables, which are often not sautéed, but put directly in the stock or water – 'a CRUDO'. In soups made 'a crudo' a light SOFFRITTO of garlic and herbs – and sometimes chilli – is added at the end, or just a good glug of olive oil. There are a few soups made from only one or two vegetables, such as *zuppa di patate e broccoli* from Campania. In a well-known chicken soup – *zuppa di pollo* – from Treviso, the roasted chicken is boned, cut into small pieces and put into the bowl together with croutons. The stock, made with calf's head, is ladled over it. Parmesan is usually served with all zuppe.

zuppa alla pavese
stock with poached eggs

When Francis I of France was defeated by Charles V at the battle of Pavia in 1525 he took refuge in a nearby farmhouse. The embarrassed, yet deeply honoured, housewife was just preparing some soup. She had to think quickly how, with only humble ingredients to hand, she could turn a simple stock into a soup fit for a king. So she fried some stale bread, put it in the soup bowl, broke two new-laid eggs over it and slowly ladled the boiling stock over them. The whites curdled gently and the yolks remained soft. With a generous grating of GRANA PADANO, she set the bowl before the king. The soup met with royal approval, and the king insisted that the recipe be given to one of his servants. This is the story, but these kinds of soup are typical of all regions.

zuppa di pesce
fish soup

It is not surprising that fish soups play an important part in the cooking of a country that has well over 2,500km/1,500 miles of coastline. They are mostly local soups, sometimes with different names, made differently from one place to another, but all are ladled over bread, which is sometimes toasted.

On the Adriatic, from Trieste to Puglia, the zuppa di pesce is called BRODETTO, and is supposedly the oldest of all fish soups. Although the name is the same, the versions are many and varied. In southern Puglia, the zuppa di pesce of Bari is the richest, made with rascasse, cuttlefish, molluscs and seafood. Bari also offers a fish soup that is not found anywhere else, in which the different kinds of molluscs and seafood are placed in a SOFFRITTO of onion, garlic, celery, carrot and parsley into which a good quantity of salted anchovies have been pounded.

On rounding the Capo di Santa Maria di Leuca, the heel of the Italian boot, into the Gulf of Taranto, a large variety of its rich sea catch is combined in the *zuppa tarantina*, which contains a lot of celery. The fish is sautéed in a SOFFRITTO of lots of celery, garlic and parsley, to which tomatoes are added.

The infinite number of fish soups in Sicily are similar to those of the Tyrrhenian Sea to the north, with the exception of one from Messina called *zuppa di neonata*. Neonata means newborn, and here it applies to baby sardines and anchovies, known collectively as BIANCHETTI. The baby fish are cooked in water with olive oil and garlic.

The specialities of Naples and the neighbouring coastline are zuppa di VONGOLE and zuppa di COZZE, while further north the traditional shellfish soup of Lazio is the zuppa di TELLINE (a type of clam), which make the best of all seafood soups. In northern Tuscany we encounter one of the best known of Italian fish soups, the CACCIUCCO of Livorno, which contains chilli, locally known as ZENZERO, as does the brodetto of Abruzzo.

On entering Liguria we come to a realm of glorious fish soups which, although derived from Greek, Middle Eastern, Catalan and Provençal cuisines, have become characteristic of the local cooking. A speciality of Lerici, in the Gulf of La Spezia, is a soup of DATTERO DI MARE, a mollusc rarely found elsewhere. The soup is flavoured with onion and tomatoes, but without any garlic. The local mussel soup is made 'in BIANCO' – without tomatoes, but with more garlic. The soup of the eastern Riviera, from Genoa to Sestri Levante, is called *bagnun*. It is a humble soup, made only with boned fresh anchovies cooked in white wine and olive oil, tomatoes, garlic and parsley and more than the usual amount of black pepper. The bread here is brown, which distinguishes the bagnun from most other fish soups. Also from this coast is BURIDDA, of which there is a version made only with STOCCAFISSO. The last Ligurian soup to be mentioned is the CIUPPIN, which is usually pureed, but further to the west, near the French border, it also appears with the fish cut in pieces, similar to bouillabaisse.

In Sardinia there are fish soups similar to those found down the Tyrrhenian coast, plus the most chic of all, the *zuppa di aragosta* – spiny lobster. The lobster, cut in chunks, is cooked in an oil-based tomato sauce flavoured with garlic and parsley.

zuppa inglese
custard and cake dessert

Serves 6

3 large egg yolks

150g/5½oz/generous 1¼ cups icing (confectioners') sugar

50g/1¾oz/7 tbsp Italian 00 flour

450ml/16fl oz/2 cups full-fat (whole) milk

grated rind of ½ lemon

300g/10½oz sponge cake, cut into slices no more than 1cm/½in thick

4 tbsp cherry brandy

2 tbsp cognac

2 tbsp Drambuie

1 tbsp rum

55g/2oz dark chocolate, melted

25g/1oz/3 tbsp chopped toasted almonds (optional)

This pudding, whose name means 'English soup', is made in many parts of central and southern Italy. It is often translated as 'trifle', and it has as many variations as the English pudding. In the south it has a meringue topping, while in Emilia-Romagna it has layers of two different coloured custards: egg custard and chocolate custard. In Tuscany it is more liquid, which may account for the name 'zuppa'. If you can get hold of any, the Italian liqueur ALCHERMES should be used instead of cherry brandy.

First make the custard: put the egg yolks and the sugar in a heavy saucepan, beat well with a wooden spoon until smooth, and then beat in the flour. In another pan, heat the milk with the lemon rind until it just comes to the boil, then immediately pour the milk onto the egg mixture, beating constantly. When the milk has been incorporated, put the pan over a low heat and bring slowly to the boil, stirring all the time, then simmer for 5 minutes, to cook the flour.

Smear the bottom of a deep serving dish or bowl with 4 tablespoons of the hot custard. Line the bottom of the dish with a layer of sponge cake. Mix all the spirits together in a small bowl, dip a pastry brush into the mixture and brush over the cake until saturated.

Cover with one-third of the remaining custard. Place another layer of cake slices over the custard, and soak it with spirits.

Divide the remaining custard into two parts. Mix the melted chocolate into one of the parts and spread this over the cake in the bowl. Add another layer of sliced cake, soak it with the remaining spirits and cover with the last of the custard. Top with the almonds, if using. Chill for 2–3 hours before serving.

470

Bibliography

Accame, Franco; Torre, Silvio; Pronzati, Virgilio. *Il Grande Libro della Cucina Ligure* (De Ferrari Editore)

Adami, Pietro. *La Cucina Carnica* (Padova. Franco Muzzio Editore 1985)

Agnesi, Vincenzo. *Alcune Notizie sugli Spaghetti* (Imperia 1975)

Agnoletti, Vincenzo. *Manuale del Cuoco e del Pasticcere* 1852 (Reprint A. Forni 1983)

Alberini, Massimo, con ricette di Romana Bosco *Antica Cucina Veneziana* (Casale Monferrato. Piemme 1990)

Alberini, Massimo. *Storia del Pranzo all'Italiana* (Milano. Longanesi 1965)

Alberini, Massimo. *Liguria a Tavola* (Milano. Longanesi 1965)

Alberini, Massimo. *Piemontesi a Tavola* (Milano. Longanesi 1967)

Alberini, Massimo. *Emiliani e Romagnoli a Tavola* (Milano. Longanesi 1969)

Alberini, Massimo. *Mangiare con gli Occhi* (Modena. Edizione Panini)

Alberini, Massimo. *4000 Anni a Tavola* (Milano. Fabbri 1972)

Alberini, Massimo. *Cento Ricette Storiche* (Firenze. Sansoni 1974)

Alberini, Massimo & Giorgio Mistretta. *Guida all'Italia Gastronomica* (Touring Club Italiano 1984)

Alliata di Salaparuta, Enrico. *Cucina Vegetariana e Naturismo Crudo* (Palermo. Sellerio 1988)

Anderson, Burton. *Treasures of the Italian Table* (New York. William Morrow 1994)

Apicius. *Cookery and Dining in Imperial Rome* Edited and translated by Joseph Vehling (New York. Dover Publications 1977)

Archestratus. *The Life of Luxury* Translated by G. Wilkins & S. Hill (Totnes. Prospect Books 1994)

Artusi, Pellegrino. *La Scienza in Cucina e l'Arte di Mangiar Bene* with Introductory Note by Piero Camporesi (Torino. Giulio Einaudi Ed 1985)

Baldassari Montevecchi, B. *La Cucina di Emilia-Romagna* (Milano. Franco Angeli 1980)

Baldini, Filippo. *De' Sorbetti* 1784 (reprinted Firenze. Forni)

Bareham, Lindsay. *In Praise of the Potato* (London. Grafton Books 1991)

Benedetti, Benedetto. *L'Aceto Balsamico* (Consorteria dell'Aceto Balsamico 1986)

Benini, Zenone. *La Cucina di Casa Mia* (Firenze. Olimpia 1983)

Benporat, Claudio. *Storia della Gastronomia Italiana* (Milano. Mursia 1990)

Benporat, Claudio. *La Cucina Italiana del 400* (Firenze. Leo Olschki 1996)

Bergese, Nino. *Mangiare da Re* (Milano. Feltrinelli 1969)

Bevilacqua, Osvaldo & Mantovani, Giuseppe. *Laboratori del Gusto* (Milano. Sugar 1982)

Black, Maggie. *A Taste of History* (London. English Heritage 1993)

Boni, Ada. *Il Talismano della Felicità* (Roma. Carlo Colombo reprint 1984)

Boni, Ada. *Cucina Regionale Italiana* (Milano. Mondadori 1975)

Bonomo, Giuliana. *Il Grande Libro del Pesce* (Milano. Mondadori 1989)

Braudel, Fernand. *The Mediterranean & the Mediterranean World in the Age of Philip II Vol 1* (New York. Harper & Row 1976)

Brera, Giovanni & Veronelli, Luigi. *La Pacciada* (Milano. Mondadori 1973)

Brillat-Savarin, Jean Anthelme. *The Philosopher in the Kitchen* Translated by Anne Dayton (London. Penguin Books 1970)

Brydone, Patrick. *A Tour through Sicily and Malta* (Edinburgh 1840)

Bugialli, Giuliano. *Classic Techniques of Italian Cooking* (New York. Simon & Schuster 1982)

Campbell, Susan. *The Cook's Companion* (London. Macmillan 1980)

Camporesi, Piero. *Alimentazione, Folclore, Società* (Parma. Pratiche Editrice 1980)

Camporesi, Piero. *Il Paese della Fame* (Bologna. Il Mulino 1978)

Camporesi, Piero. *La Carne Impassibile* (Milano. Il Saggiatore 1983)

Capnist, Giovanni. *I Dolci del Veneto* (Padova. Franco Muzzio Ed. 1983)

Capnist, Giovanni. *La Cucina Veronese* (Padova. Franco Muzzio Ed. 1987)

Cardillo Violati, Leda & Majnardi, Carlo. *I Picchiarelli della Malanotte* (Foligno. Dell' Arquarto 1990)

Carnacina, Luigi & Veronelli, Luigi. *La Buona Vera Cucina Italiana* (Milano. Rizzoli 1966)

Carnacina, Luigi & Veronelli, Luigi. *La Cucina Rustica Regionale Italiana* (Milano. Rizzoli 1966)

Carnacina, Luigi & Buonassisi, Vincenzo. *Il Libro della Polenta* (Firenze. Giunti Martello 1974)

Carnacina, Luigi & Buonassisi, Vincenzo. *Roma in Cucina* (Firenze. Giunti Martello 1975)

Castelvetro, Giacomo. *The Fruit, Herbs & Vegetables of Italy* Translated by Gillian Riley (London. Viking 1989)

Castiglione, Baldassare. *Il Libro del Cortegiano* (repr. Milano. V. Mursia 1972)

Cavalcanti, Ippolito. *Cucina Teorico-Pratica* (Napoli. Tipografica dei Gemelli 1847)

Cavalcanti, Ottavio. *Il Libro d'Oro della Cucina e dei Vini di Calabria e Basilicata* (Milano. Mursia 1979)

Cato, Marcus Porcius. *On Agriculture* Translated by W.D. Hopper (London. Heinemann 1934)

Cerini di Castagnate, Livio. *Il Cuoco Gentiluomo* (Milano. Mondadori 1980)

Cervio, Vincenzo. *Il Trinciante* (1581) (reprinted Firenze. Il Portolano 1979)

Columella. *De Re Rustica* Translated by H.B. Ash (London. Heinemann 1934)

Conoscere I Salumi (Milano. Librex 1984)

Le Conserve della Nonna (Milano. Librex 1982)

Corrado, Vincenzo. *Il Cuoco Galante* (Napoli. Stamperia Raimondiana 1778)

Corsi, Guglielma. *Un Secolo di Cucina Umbra* (Assisi. Ed. Tipografica Porziuncola)

Couffignal, Huguette. *La Cucina Povera* (Milano. Rizzoli 1982)

Cunsolo, Felice. *Guida Gastronomica d'Italia* (Novara. Istituto Geografico de Agostini 1975)

Il Cuoco Milanese e la Cuciniera Piemontese (Milano. Francesco Pagnoni 1863)

David, Elizabeth. *A Book of Mediterranean Food* (London. John Lehmann 1950)

David, Elizabeth. *Italian Food* (London. Macdonald 1954)

David, Elizabeth. *An Omelette and a Glass of Wine* (London. Dorling Kindersley 1984)

Davidson, Alan. *Mediterranean Seafood* (London. Penguin Books 1972)

Davidson, Alan. *North Atlantic Seafood* (London. Macmillan 1979)

Davidson, Alan. *The Oxford Companion to Food* (Oxford University Press 1999)

Davidson, Alan & Knox, Charlotte. *Seafood* (London. Mitchell Beazley 1988)

Davidson, Alan & Knox, Charlotte. *Fruit* (London. Mitchell Beazley 1991)

Del Conte, Anna. *Portrait of Pasta* (London. Paddington Press 1976)

Del Conte, Anna. *Secrets from an Italian Kitchen* (London. Bantam Press 1989)

Del Conte, Anna. *Entertaining all'Italiana* (London. Bantam Press 1991)

Del Conte, Anna. *The Classic Food of Northern Italy* (London. Pavilion Books 1995)

Denti Di Parajno, Alberto. *Il Gastronomo Educato* (Neri Pozza Editore 1950)

Dettore, Mariapaola. *Il Pane dall'Antipasto al Dolce* (Milano. A Garzanti 1979)

Di Corato, Riccardo. *451 Formaggi d'Italia* (Milano. Sonzogno 1978)

473

Di Corato, Riccardo. *838 Frutti e Verdure d'Italia* (Milano. Sonzogno 1979)

Dowell, Philip & Bailey, Adrian. *The Book of Ingredients* (London. Dorling Kindersley 1980)

Dumas, Alexandre. *Dictionary of Cuisine* Translated by L. Colman (USA. Simon & Schuster 1958)

Eramo, Cia. *La Cucina Mantovana* (Padova. Franco Muzzio 1980)

The Faber Book of Food Edited by Colin Spencer & Claire Clifton (London. Faber & Faber 1993)

Faccioli, Emilio. *L'Eccellenza e il Trionfo del Porco* (Milano. G. Mazzotta 1982)

Faccioli, Emilio. *Arte della Cucina* Vols I & II (Milano. Il Polifilo 1966)

Falavigna, Ugo. *Arte della Pasticceria a Parma* (Parma. Luigi Battei 1987)

Fast, Mady. *Mangiare Triestino* (Padova. Franco Muzzio 1993)

Field, Carol. *The Italian Baker* (New York. Harper & Row 1985)

Field, Carol. *Celebrating Italy* (New York. William Morrow 1990)

Francesconi, Jeanne Carola. *La Cucina Napoletana* (Napoli. Delfino 1965)

Goethe, J.W. *Italian Journey 1786-1788* Translated by W.H. Auden & E. Mayer (San Francisco. North Point Press 1982)

Goria, Giovanni. *La Cucina del Piemonte* (Padova. Franco Muzzio 1990)

Gosetti della Salda, Anna. *Le Ricette Regionali Italiane* (Milano. Solaresi 1967)

Gozzini Giacosa, Ilaria. *Mense e Cibi della Roma Antica* (Casale Monferrato. Piemme 1995)

Grande Dizionario della Gastronomia (Milano. Readers' Digest Spa 1990)

Ill Grande Manuale della Cucina Regionale Edited by Stella Donati (Bergamo. Euroclub Italia 1979)

Gray, Patience. *Honey from a Weed* (London. Prospect Books 1986)

Grigson, Jane. *Fish Cookery* (London. David & Charles 1978)

Grigson, Jane. *The Mushroom Feast* (London. Michael Joseph 1975)

Grigson, Jane. *The Vegetable Book* (London. Michael Joseph 1978)

Grigson, Jane. *The Fruit Book* (London. Michael Joseph 1982)

Guarnaschelli Gotti, Marco. *La Cucina Milanese* (Padova. Franco Muzzio 1991)

Hazan, Marcella. *The Classic Italian Cookbook* (London. Macmillan 1980)

Hazan, Marcella. *The Second Classic Italian Cookbook* (London. Jill Norman & Hobhouse 1982)

La Cucina Piemontese 1798 (reprint Forni 1980)

Larousse Gastronomique

Lasøe, Thomas & Del Conte, Anna. *The Mushroom Book* (London. Dorling Kindersley 1996)

Liddell, Caroline & Weir, Robin. *Ices* (London. Hodder & Stoughton 1993)

Lombardi, Liliana. *Il Grande Libro della Pasta e dei Cereali* (Milano. Mondadori 1992)

Luard, Elisabeth. *European Peasant Cookery* (London. Bantam Press 1986)

Luraschi, Giovanni Felice. *Nuovo Cuoco Milanese* 1853 (reprint Forni 1980)

Maffioli, Giuseppe. *La Cucina Trevigiana* (Padova. Mursia 1981)

Maffioli, Giuseppe. *La Cucina Veneziana* (Padova. Mursia 1982)

Mantovani, Giuseppe. *La Cucina Italiana: origini, storie e segreti* (Roma. Newton Compton 1985)

Marinetti, Filippo. *La Cucina Futurista* (Milano. Stabilimento Grafico Matarelli 1932)

Mayer, Barbara. *Cakes* (London. Jill Norman & Hobhouse 1982)

McGee, Harold. *On Food & Cooking* (New York. Charles Scribner's 1984)

McGee, Harold. *The Curious Cook* (San Francisco. North Point Press 1990)

Medagliani, Eugenio & Gosetti della Salda, Fernanda. *Pastaio* (Cunsinallo. Alessi 1985)

de' Medici, Lorenza. *Florentines* (London. Pavilion Books 1992)

di Messisbugo, Christoforo. *Libro Novo* 1557 (reprint Forni 1982)

Metz, Vittorio. *La Cucina del Belli* (Milano. Sugar Co. 1984)

Il Mio Formaggio (Milano. Librex 1982)

Monelli, Paolo. *Il Ghiottone Errante* (Milano. Garzantti 1935)

Moretti, Maria Cecilia. *Sapori e Voci di Lago* (Foligno. Dell'Arquata 1985)

Naso, Irma. *Formaggi del Medievo* (Torino. Il Segnalibro 1990)

Norman, Jill. *The Classic Herb Book* (London. Dorling Kindersley 1990)

Novelli, Renato. *Le Marche a Tavola* (Ancona. Il Lavoro Editoriale 1987)

Olivero, Nello. *Storie e Curiosità del Mangiare Napoletano* (Napoli Ed. Scientifiche Italiane 1983)

Origo, Iris. *The Merchant of Prato* (Boston. David Godine 1986)

Owen, Sri. *The Rice Book* (London. Transworld 1993)

Pane, Rita & Mariano. *I Sapori del Sud* (Milano. Rizzoli 1991)

Perna Bozzi, Ottorina. *La Lombardia in Cucina* (Firenze. G. Martello 1982)

Perna Bozzi, Ottorina. *Vecchia Brianza in Cucina* (Firenze. G. Martello 1975)

Petroni, Paolo. *Il Libro della Vera Cucina Fiorentina* (Firenze. Bonecchi 1974)

Petroni, Paolo. *Il Libro della Vera Cucina Bolognese* (Firenze. Bonecchi 1978)

Piccinardi, Antonio. *Dizionario di Gastronomia* (Milano. Rizzoli 1993)

Pisanelli, Baldassare. *Trattato della Natura de' Cibi et del Bere* 1611 (reprint Forni)

Platina, Bartolomeo. *Il Piacere Onesto e la Buona Salute* 1475 Edited by Emilio Faccioli (Milano. Einaudi 1985)

Plotkin, Fred. *Italy for the Gourmet Traveller* (London. Kyle Cathie 1996)

Plotkin, Fred. *Recipes from Paradise* (New York. Little Brown 1997)

Porcaro, Giuseppe. *Sapore di Napoli* (Napoli. Gallina 1985)

Rattazzi, Ilaria. *Tutti gli Usi della Frutta* (Milano. Sperling & Kupfer Ed. 1985)

Ratto, G.B. & Giovanni. *La Cuciniera Genovese* (Genova. Fratelli Pagano)

Righi Parenti, Giovanni. *La Grande Cucina Toscana Vols I & II* (Milano. Sugar Co. 1982)

Righi Parenti, Giovanni. *La Cucina degli Etruschi* (Milano. Sugar 1972)

Riley, Gillian. *The Oxford Companion to Italian Food* (Oxford University Press 2007)

Il Riso nella Ristorazione (Ente Nazionale Risi)

Roden, Claudia. *A Book of Middle Eastern Food* (London. Nelson 1980)

Roden, Claudia. *The Book of Jewish Food* (New York. Kopf 1996)

Root, Waverley. *The Food of Italy* (USA. Random House 1971)

Roratro, Giampiero. *La Cucina di Carlo Goldoni* (Venezia. Stamperia di Venezia 1983)

Rossetto Kasper, Lynne. *The Splendid Table of Emilia-Romagna* (New York. William Morrow 1992)

Rumhor Von, Karl Friedrich. (1822) *The Essence of Cookery* Translated by B. Yeomans (Totnes. Prospect Books 1993)

Sala, Orietta. *La Frutta della Campagna* (Milano. Idealibri 1987)

Santich, Barbara. *The Original Mediterranean Cuisine* (Totnes. Prospect Books 1995)

Santini, Aldo. *La Cucina Maremmana* (Padova. Franco Muzzio 1991)

Sassu, Antonio. *La Vera Cucina di Sardegna* (Roma. Anthropos 1983)

Scappi, Bartolomeo. *Opera dell' Arte del Cucinare* 1570 (reprint Forni 1981)

Schneider, Elizabeth. *Uncommon Fruits and Vegetables* (New York. Harper & Row 1986)

Servi Machlin, Edda. *The Classic Cuisine of the Italian Jews* (New York. Dodd, Mead 1981)

Simeti, Mary Taylor. *Sicilian Food* (London. Random Century Group 1988)

Stefani, Bartolomeo. *L'Arte di Ben Cucinare et Instruire* 1662 (Reprinted Firenze. Forni 1983)

Steingarten, Jeffrey. *The Man Who Ate Everything* (USA. Knopf 1997)

Stobart, Tom. *Herbs, Spices and Flavourings* (The International Wine & Food Publishing Co. 1970)

Stobart, Tom. *The Cook's Encyclopedia* (London. Batsford 1980)

Tannahill, Reay. *Food in History* (USA. Stein & Day 1973)

Taruschio, Ann & Franco. *Leaves from the Walnut Tree* (London. Pavilion Books 1993)

Tasca Lanza, Anna. *The Heart of Sicily* (London. Cassell 1993)

Touring Club Italiano. *Guida Gastronomica d'Italia* (Milano. Touring Club 1931)

Vialardi, Giovanni. *Trattato di Cucina Pasticceria Moderna* 1854 (reprint Forni)

Westbury, Lord. *Handlist of Italian Cookery Books* (Firenze. Leo S. Olschki Editore 1963)

Wheaton, Barbara Ketcham. *Savouring the Past* (London. Chatto & Windus 1983)

Willan, Anne. *Great Cooks and their Recipes* (London. Elm Tree Books 1977)

Zaniloni Riveccio, Maria. *Polenta, Piatto da Re* (Milano. Idealibri 1986)

476

Index

Italian terms are cross-referenced to the English term if there is more detail to be found. Words such as 'with', *alla* and *di* are ignored for the purposes of alphabetization. Italian and Latin terms and book titles are listed in *italics*. Page numbers in *italics* indicate a map or photograph. Page numbers in **bold** denote a recipe.

480

481

488

493

494

495

Acknowledgements

For this edition my warmest thanks go to my editors, Rebecca Spry, who put me and kept me on the right path, and Maggie Ramsay, the most thorough editor I have ever come across. I valued tremendously her knowledge of all things Italian. Thank you also to Laura Edwards, the photographer, Lucy O'Reilly, the food stylist, and Cynthia Inions, who produced these glorious photographs which represent exactly my kind of dishes. Thank you to Georgina Hewitt for designing such a stunning-looking book. And last but certainly not least my warm thanks to my agent Vivien Green, for her constant support and enthusiasm for my work.

Anna Del Conte is widely recognised as the doyenne of Italian cooking. In 1987 she was awarded the prestigious *Duchessa Maria Luigia di Parma* prize for *Gastronomy of Italy*. Her books include *Italian Kitchen, Cooking with Coco* and *The Classic Food of Northern Italy*, which in 1996 won both the *Guild of Food Writers Book Award* and the *Orio Vergani* prize of the *Accademia Italiana della Cucina*.

In 1994 Anna received the *Premio Nazionale di Cultura Gastronomica Verdicchio d'Oro* prize for her contribution to the dissemination of knowledge concerning authentic Italian cooking. In 2010 she was awarded the honour of *Ufficiale dell'Ordine al Merito della Repubblica Italiana*; it was proposed to the President by the Italian Ambassador, Giancarlo Aragona, and the honour was given in recognition of the importance of her work in keeping alive Italy's good image in the UK. She was also awarded the *Guild of Food Writers Lifetime Achievement Award* in 2011.